D0609420

PLANTS of Western Oregon, Washington & British Columbia

PLANTS of Western Oregon, Washington & British Columbia

EUGENE N. KOZLOFF

TIMBER PRESS

Copyright © 2005 by Eugene N. Kozloff. All rights reserved.

Page 2, *Darlingtonia californica,* California pitcher plant (Sarraceniaceae).

All photographs by the author unless otherwise specified. Line drawings of plant structure by the author, and those of most plants from C. L. Hitchcock et al. (1959–1969), *Vascular Plants of the Pacific Northwest,* except for those of *Parnassia californica* from W. L. Jepson (1925), *A Manual of the Flowering Plants of California,* and the subspecies of *Festuca idahoensis* from L. E. Pavlick (1968), The taxonomy and distribution of *Festuca idahoensis* in British Columbia and northwestern Washington, *Canadian Journal of Botany* 61: 345–353. Map by Allan Cartography, Medford, Oregon.

Published in 2005 by

Timber Press, Inc.
The Haseltine Building
133 S.W. Second Avenue, Suite 450
Portland, Oregon 97204, U.S.A.
www.timberpress.com

For contact information for editorial, marketing, sales, and distribution in the United Kingdom, see www.timberpress.com/uk.

Designed by Susan Applegate
Printed through Colorcraft Ltd., Hong Kong

Library of Congress Cataloging-in-Publication Data
Kozloff, Eugene N.
    Plants of western Oregon, Washington & British Columbia/Eugene N. Kozloff.
        p.   cm.
    Includes bibliographical references and index.
    ISBN 0-88192-724-4 (hardback)
    1. Plants—Oregon—Identification. 2. Plants—Washington (State)—Identification. 3. Plants—British Columbia—Identification. I. Title. II. Title: Plants of western Oregon, Washington, and British Columbia.
    QK182.K69 2005
    581.9795—dc22   2005001585

A catalog record for this book is also available from the British Library.

Contents

Color plates follow page 272

Preface

A BOUT 1990, I decided that the flora of western Oregon, Washington, and southern British Columbia deserves a book of its own, one useful to amateur naturalists and students, and also to professional biologists who need to identify plants but who are intimidated by existing manuals. Most of the compendia that deal in detail with the higher plants of the Pacific Northwest cover the regions both east and west of the Cascade Range. Too often they oblige the user to work through complex keys and descriptions for genera and species that are not represented on the Pacific side. Furthermore, many do not adequately cover the interesting flora of southwestern Oregon.

This new book, using a relatively small vocabulary of scientific terms, is designed for the identification of vascular plants—ferns and their relatives, conifers, and flowering plants—that grow west of the crest of the Cascades, from southern Oregon north through southern British Columbia. It is also very useful on the higher portions of the slopes east of the crest of the Cascades. But below about 3000 ft. (910 m) on the eastern side, the flora really changes, and from then on east to Idaho it is very different. Every effort has been made to include all native plants that a diligent botanist has a reasonable chance of finding. A few rarities that have been reported in just one or two places may not be mentioned because records of their occurrence were not known to me; the chance of encountering any of them is very slim. Care has been taken to incorporate updates in classification and nomenclature, and to provide color photographs of a large number of the approximately 2500 species known to occur in the region.

It is difficult to have complete coverage of species that are not native. Well-established weeds are definitely in this book, but new introductions show up every year, and many cultivated species become established in places where they were not planted. Some aliens in the general category of garden plants are dealt with, but no attempt has been made to include those that have been found just once or twice in otherwise mostly natural areas. I have also drawn the line at daffodils, the fragrant English violet, and a few other plants that almost everyone will connect with flower beds.

The user of this guide will wonder if I have seen all the species that it covers. In many years of studying the flora of the Pacific states, I have found the majority of them in the wild or in gardens devoted to native plants. Most of the others, especially grasses, sedges, and rushes, had to be studied as dried specimens in herbaria. From herbarium material I have learned much about attributes easily overlooked or not apparent in plants or photographs of them in the flowering stage. The characteristics of mature fruits and seeds, for instance, are often as important as flower structure for distinguishing families, genera, and species. Herbarium specimens whose labels give accurate data on where plants were collected have also been helpful in planning field trips to places where they may still be found. In the case of a relatively few species—at most perhaps 50 that were not represented in the herbaria I have consulted—I have had to rely on information in monographs and other references, including original descriptions.

The herbarium of the University of Washington has been especially important for my work, and I express my gratitude to its director, Richard Olmstead, its previous director, the late Melinda Denton, and three successive permanent or temporary collections managers: Sarah Gage, Sharon Rodman, and David Giblin. All have generously helped me by providing space to work, allowing me to borrow specimens I could examine over and over again in the herbarium or at my home institution, Friday Harbor Laboratories, and giving me the benefit of their knowledge of the regional flora. It has been extremely valuable to be able to study the specimens used by C. L. Hitchcock and his colleagues during preparation of their monumental *Vascular Plants of the Pacific Northwest.* Peter Zika, who has worked regularly at the herbarium, has been of immense help with respect to several distinctly different categories of native and alien plants.

On visits to the herbarium at Oregon State University I have benefited from courtesies extended by its director, Aaron Liston, and its curator, Richard Halse. They also helped me solve specific problems in certain genera. Kenton Chambers, a former curator, and Henrietta Chambers promptly and pleasingly answered many questions, by letter, by telephone, or in person, about geographic distributions and key characteristics of various species. The herbarium includes the collections previously housed at Willamette University and the University of Oregon, and is therefore very complete for Oregon plants.

On field trips, especially valued help came from Susan Ley and Linda Beidleman. These cheerful, seemingly tireless colleagues were energetic and observant hunters of plants. They were also careful drivers and never complained when, after a long, hard day of exploring, I asked for just one more stop at a habitat that looked promising.

Susan and numerous students in workshops on plant identification sponsored by the San Juan Nature Institute, North Cascades Institute, Salal Chapter of the Washington Native Plant Society, and by me exposed problems in early versions of the keys that make up most of this book. Earlier work with Linda on *Plants of the San Francisco Bay Region* was a valuable experience that prepared me for this new project.

To the University of Washington Press I am indebted for permission to use drawings made by Jeanne Janish and John Rumely for the five-volume *Vascular Plants of the Pacific Northwest.* A few other illustrations are taken from Jepson's *A Manual of the Flowering Plants of California* and from *Canadian Journal of Botany.* Numerous color photographs were provided by Linda Beidleman, Wilbur Bluhm, and Michael Fahey.

Many professional and amateur botanists or horticulturists not already mentioned have been of great assistance in interpreting distinctions between species, proposing changes in keys, helping me locate specimens I needed, sending seeds, or leading me to plants in the field: Darren Borgias, Alison Colwell, Carol Goodwillie, Leslie Gottlieb, Dharmika Henshel, Arthur Kruckeberg, Rhoda Love, Vernon Marttala, Cathy Maxwell, Robert Meinke, Saundra Miles, John Roth, Steven Seavey, Robert Soreng, Paula Springhart, Veva Stansell, Scott Sundberg, and Maria Ulloa-Cruz. John Spady and Craig Staude came to my rescue many times when the computers I used begged for their magical skills. Much credit is due also to Patty Carey, Kathy Carr, and Maureen Nolan, who responded with efficiency when I needed a book or journal from the university library. On a number of field trips, my wife, Anne, assisted with photography when I needed it and helped in various other ways, like insisting I stay calm when there were so many plants and so little time. Timber Press was helpful throughout the process of publication.

Finally, my thanks go out to the plants I knew before starting work on this book, and to those I had not seen previously in the field but was able to find when I needed them. Hunting for them on rocky slopes and in bogs, salt marshes, and many other habitats has given me much satisfaction and plenty of healthful exercise.

If this book is helpful to you, I will be pleased. On the basis of what I know about guides to the flora, the variability of species, and the risks inherent in compiling information that may not be perfectly understood, I expect some will discover errors, ambiguities, inconsistencies, important omissions, or other problems in this volume. If you bring these to my attention, your courtesy and cooperation will be warmly appreciated!

Introduction

TO USE THIS BOOK EFFECTIVELY, one needs to become familiar with conventions according to which plants are named and classified. It is also important to appreciate that plant classification is not a static science. While many species have been described and named on the basis of poor specimens or insufficient comparative study, and names may sometimes seem to be changed unnecessarily, much of modern systematic botany focuses on understanding evolutionary relationships between species, and the connections between genera, families, and higher categories. The information provided here is for those who need an explanation of how and why plants are named, how to use keys correctly, and how to do this without getting too deeply involved with some firmly entrenched botanical jargon, much of which is badly conceived.

Scientific Names

Scientific names of animals, plants, fungi, and bacteria are Latinized words. The roots of which they are composed are usually based on Greek or Latin words, or on names of geographic regions or persons, mythical or real. For example, the genus name of the California poppy, *Eschscholzia californica,* proposed in 1820, commemorates Johann Friedrich Gustav von Eschscholtz, a naturalist on the Russian expedition to California in October 1816; the species name obviously refers to California, known as a region long before a portion of it became a state. *Trifolium* (three leaflets) is the genus to which clovers belong; *T. microcephalum* (small flower heads), *T. repens* (creeping), and *T. pratense* (of meadows, pl. 303) are species names of some clovers common in our region.

Most changes in scientific names are made when research leads to new interpretations of relationships within a group of related species or related genera. For instance, an expert who has carefully studied the range of variation within what had been thought to be a single species may decide to break it up into subspecies, or even divide it into two or more species. Another expert, after reevaluating the extent to which the plants in this complex intergrade, may argue for reverting to the original idea that there is just one species and that recognition of subspecies is unwarranted. Sometimes a well-established genus or species is shown to have previously been given a different name that has chronological priority; in that case the older name should be used, unless there is a problem of one kind or another with it. Revisions, and explanations of the rationale for changes, are usually published in scholarly journals, but they may also appear in books concerned with the flora of a region.

In monographs and research papers that deal with plant taxonomy, it is conventional to cite the authors of the names of species, subspecies, and varieties involved in the study, and also the year in which the names were proposed. Here is an example: *Berberis aquifolium* Pursh 1814, for the so-called Oregon grape (pl. 158), widespread in our region. A little later, the shrub was referred to another genus, *Mahonia.* The newer combination is sometimes still used and if cited correctly will be *Mahonia aquifolium* (Pursh 1814) Nuttall 1821. Note that the name of the author of the species name is now in parentheses and is followed by the name and date of the reviser. Similar treatments are accorded the names of subspecies and varieties. In most regional floras, the names of many authors are abbreviated. While it is likely that most of us will guess that L. refers to Carl Linnaeus, we may need to consult a list that tells us that T. & G. stands for John Torrey and Asa Gray, C. & R. for John Merle Coulter and Joseph Nelson Rose, and H.B.K. for the trio of Friedrich Wilhelm Heinrich Alexander von Humboldt, Aimé Jacques Bonpland, and Carl Sigismund Kunth. Furthermore, the dates are usually omitted; after all, users of a guide for identification are not likely to want to see an original description, and even if they did they would have trouble locating it unless they were also given an exact citation for the scientific treatise in which it was published, most likely long ago. In this book neither authors of plant names nor dates of publication are given. Anyone who really needs this information can find it in the comprehensive references listed in the last section of this chapter.

Subspecies, Varieties, and Related Matters

Many species of plants, especially those that are widely distributed, exhibit regional differences. A good example is *Clarkia amoena,* in the evening-primrose family (Onagraceae). Its range extends from British Columbia to central California, and several subspecies are currently recognized. *Clarkia amoena* subsp. *amoena* is found in the region just north of San Francisco Bay, and it soon gives way to subspecies *whitneyi* and then to subspecies *huntiana* (pl. 393), whose distribution extends to southwestern Oregon. In the Puget Trough of Washington, the Willamette Valley of Oregon, and a few other places, there is *C. amoena* subsp. *lindleyi* (pl. 394). The differences between most of these and other subspecies are slight, and there is intergradation and presumably hybridization wherever they are in contact. Nevertheless, typical specimens of each subspecies are sufficiently distinct to merit subspecific names.

There is a joker in the deck, however. This is *Clarkia amoena* subsp. *caurina* (pl. 392), found on Vancouver Island, British Columbia, on islands of the San Juan Archipelago of British Columbia and Washington, on the Olympic Peninsula, Washington, and in the Columbia River Gorge, separating Washington and Oregon. In general, its flowers are significantly smaller than those of other subspecies of *C. amoena,* and it seems not to intergrade with *C. amoena* subsp. *lindleyi,* which is close to it geographically but that starts to flower, on average, about 3 weeks to a month later. Subspecies *caurina* was originally described as a species but was demoted to subspecific rank in a carefully researched monograph. If it were returned to its original status as species, one could agree that this is logical, because the plant is a little out of the range of variation exhibited by the several subspecies with larger flowers; if left as a subspecies of *C. amoena,* it is at least easily identifiable. One cannot be faulted, considering the state of our knowledge, for choosing one solution or the other. Eventually, the matter may be settled definitively by further study.

For a long time, "variety" has been used more or less interchangeably with "subspecies" to designate plants that deviate in some minor way from those on which the original description was based. Sometimes, however, it is used to designate what are essentially "sub-subspecies." "Form" (or "forma") carries this concept further, so there can be species, subspecies, variety, and form, an array of categories likely to bewilder all but extremely well informed specialists concerned with a particular group of plants. Remain calm if you find that what is called a subspecies in one reference is given the status of variety in another. As a rule, when specialists publish their revisions of a genus or family, they use "subspecies" or "variety," not both, unless the latter designates a rank below that of subspecies. For instance, in *The Jepson Manual: Higher Plants of California* (1993), all authors concerned with the large family Onagraceae consistently broke species down into subspecies; in the pea family (Fabaceae), however, "variety" is employed in keys to most genera, "subspecies" is used in keys to others, and in at least one genus both terms are used. *Flora of North America* seems not to have restricted specialists to one term or the other; in most treatments of individual families, however, just "variety" or "subspecies" is used. Once a definitive study of a family or genus is published in the *Flora,* most derivative works, including regional floras such as this book, will probably tend to follow the same pattern, at least for a while.

This brings us to "lumping" and "splitting." Suppose that obviously related plants growing over a wide geographic range exhibit differences in size of petals, form of leaves, and habit of growth. If the variation in visible attributes is so gradual that there are no clear lines of separation between plants from one region to another, then lumping all specimens into one species may be best. If, however, specimens from certain areas are consistently different from those in other areas, and if they seem to be at least partly isolated reproductively, it would perhaps be best to split them into subspecies. Separation into species is justified when all available evidence suggests that plants from one region are very different from those of another region, and that they either do not hybridize or do so only infrequently. Nevertheless, in some groups of plants, including oaks (*Quercus*) and manzanitas (*Arctostaphylos*), two species commonly recognized as distinct may hybridize with one another. Sometimes the hybrids are so unlike either parent that they have been given species names. Intergeneric hybrids also exist; most of these have been produced by horticulturists.

When there are doubts about relationships in a species complex, splitting may be the best course to follow, at least temporarily, in scientific works. It will keep the controversy out in the open, whereas lumping may lead to the premature assumption that no problem in classification is perceived. An example that shows how keeping track of minor differences may eventually lead to a much better understanding of relationships is that of the *Leptosiphon bicolor–L. minimus* complex in the phlox family (Polemoniaceae). *Leptosiphon bicolor* (pl. 427), widespread in our region, was described in 1848. What appeared to be merely a regional variant, with smaller, less richly colored flowers, was named variety *minimus* (as a variety of *Linanthus bicolor,* a newer combination for *Leptosiphon bicolor*) in 1948. Studies at the molecular level show, however, that *bicolor* and *minimus* evolved from separate ancestral species; *Leptosiphon minimus* (pl. 428) therefore deserves the status of species.

Family names also sometimes change. This usually happens when specialists decide that certain of the genera in a particular family differ sufficiently from others that they should be removed and placed elsewhere. Families may also be combined, as was done, for instance, in *The Jepson Manual*, in which fumeworts and bleeding hearts (Fumariaceae) and poppies (Papaveraceae) are united because of strong evidence supporting this view. These two groups are, however, treated separately in *Flora of North America*. A more catastrophic change involves what has been the snapdragon family (Scrophulariaceae). Molecular research on this large assemblage indicates that it is not a unified group. Of the genera in our region, a few are now destined to become part of the broomrape family (Orobanchaceae; something that had been suggested many years ago), others to be placed in Plantaginaceae or Phrymaceae. Relatively few genera will probably remain in Scrophulariaceae, and to them *Buddleja,* previously in its own family (Buddlejaceae), is likely to be added. Studies of the primrose family (Primulaceae), all of which are herbaceous plants, have led to recommendations for placing certain of its genera in Myrsinaceae, a family that up to now has included only trees and shrubs, most of which are subtropical or tropical. For additional radical changes of this sort, stay tuned!

Are the names that appear in the most recently published flora for a particular region always the best? Not necessarily. A name that has just been rejected may, after an intensive study of more specimens and a thorough search of the pertinent botanical literature, be restored, or still another name may be proposed as a replacement. If a name you have used for many years has just been reduced to a synonym, do not despair. In a few years it may once again be in good standing.

From what has been written in the preceding paragraphs, it should be clear that the results of research on the flora of a region, or on the relationships of plants in a particular group, are likely to disagree with earlier studies. This does not mean, however, that the latest work is in every respect the best or most authoritative. One portion of it may definitely be outstanding; another part may be seriously flawed and under-researched. This is often true of large-scale compendia, whether produced by one or many authors. It is important to bear in mind that many species vary considerably, that they may intergrade with other species, and that they may hybridize. The author or authors of a systematic work are only part of the problem.

Common Names

While rules for botanical nomenclature standardize scientific names of plants, they do not apply to common names. "Carrot," an English word for *Daucus carota,* has enjoyed stability for more than two centuries. For the weedy form of this species, the wild carrot, "Saint Anne's lace" (Saint Anne was the patron saint of lace makers) and "Queen Anne's lace" are just as accurate for English-speaking people, and in other languages there are similarly reliable names for the plant. Unfortunately, relatively few of the many wild plants in our region have common names that are as well accepted as those given to the carrot and its roadside counterpart.

Most common names used in this book have been chosen from those published in Abrams et al.'s *Illustrated Flora of the Pacific States,* Hitchcock and Cronquist's *Flora of the Pacific Northwest,* Peck's *A Manual of the Higher Plants of Oregon,* Jepson's *A Manual of the Flowering Plants of California,* and the volumes of *Flora of North America* that have been published. Remember that these names are not official. If they help you, that's good, but most who use this book have probably reached the stage where they wish to know the scientific names of at least some of the genera and species they encounter.

Measurements

Throughout the keys, measurements are given in metric units: meters (m), centimeters (cm), millimeters (mm), and micrometers (μm). This is done partly because it is a more logical system, partly because other modern references needed for additional details also use the metric system, now obligatory in scientific work. For those not already well acquainted with linear metric units, a comparison of them with English units will probably be helpful.

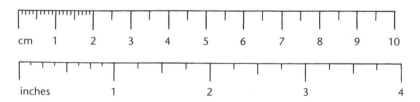

Centimeters (divided into millimeters) and inches

A meter, consisting of 100 cm, equals slightly more than 39 inches; 2.5 cm, or 25 mm, about 1 inch; 5 cm, or 50 mm, about 2 inches; and so on. In this book, meters are used for large measurements such as the approximate height of shrubs and trees; centimeters and millimeters for sizes of leaves, petals, and other relatively small structures; and micrometers (thousandths of a millimeter) only for very small structures such as spores.

Most who deal with plants and animals are thoroughly accustomed to the metric system and are getting used to the idea that 5 kilometers (5000 m) is equal to about 3 miles and that a liter (1000 milliliters) of milk or gasoline is slightly more than a quart. Our maps, however, generally record heights of mountains in feet, so in this book elevations are given in the English system as well as in the metric system. Also, inches are used in connection with annual rainfall, which in formal scientific works and in most other countries is given in centimeters or millimeters.

Using Keys for Identification

Keys for identification make use of pairs of contrasting characteristics: leaves that are directly opposite one another versus those that alternate along the stem, or petals that are pink versus those that are blue. These characteristics are presented in a series of couplets. In this book the two choices in the first couplet are always numbered 1. If the first 1 (leaves opposite) is a better choice than the second 1 (leaves alternate), proceed to the next couplet, numbered 2 under the first 1, and see where that takes you. Don't wander into the territory under the second 1, because if the key has been constructed correctly, all choices under that deal with plants that have alternate leaves, something you've already decided the plant in front of you does not have.

In many cases, the one or more basic characters stated in a particular choice are followed by additional features enclosed by parentheses. These can be helpful in confirming that the choice you are making is the correct one, but they may not be exclusively limited to that species or group of species. For example, if a characteristic such as "leaf blades with toothed margins" is followed, in parentheses, by "limited to coastal salt marshes," this does not mean that all plants whose blades have smooth margins do not grow in salt marshes. Geographic distributions may also be added and are often helpful in confirming identifications. Furthermore, they often tell you to start over, because the plant you thought was keyed correctly came from a vacant lot in Seattle, not from a pine forest in Josephine County in southwestern Oregon.

The more you use keys, the more quickly the language of plant classification will become part of your vocabulary. Experience will enable you to make judgments more rapidly and to skip extensive portions of keys that are obviously not pertinent to the specimens you are trying to identify. After a while you will be able almost automatically to place many species in families and genera without using preliminary keys. If you know, for instance, that the plant you are trying to identify is a manzanita of some sort, you can go directly to the genus *Arctostaphylos* instead of starting at the beginning of the key to the heath family (Ericaceae).

If you have never used a key before, try this little exercise with the "unknown" that is illustrated here. It belongs to the geranium family (Geraniaceae), and selected portions of the key to species of this family in our region are reproduced here, with successive correct choices **boldfaced**.

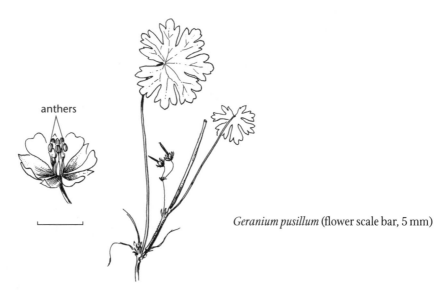

anthers

Geranium pusillum (flower scale bar, 5 mm)

1 Leaves pinnately lobed or pinnately compound
1 **Leaves palmately lobed** . . . . *Geranium*

Geranium

1 Perennial to more than 60 cm tall; petals deep reddish purple, about 20 mm long
1 Annual or biennial, rarely more than 50 cm tall, **petals not more than 15 mm long**
   2 Petals at least 7 mm long
   2 **Petals less than 7 mm long**
     3 Primary lobes of larger leaf blades separated for more than two-thirds of the distance
      to the point where the petiole is attached
     3 **Primary lobes of larger leaf blades not separated for more than two-thirds of the**
      distance to the point where the petiole is attached
       4 Flowers with 10 anther-bearing stamens
       4 **Flowers usually with 5 anther-bearing stamens** . . . . *G. pusillum*

Because the plant has palmately instead of pinnately lobed leaves, take the second choice in the key to genera and thus arrive at *Geranium* rather than *Erodium.* In the key to species of *Geranium,* it fits the second choice 1 better than the first, because the petals are only about 5 mm long. Then the second choice 2 is better than the first, again because of the size of the petals, and the second choice 3 is better than the first, because the primary lobes of the leaf blades are separated for only about half the distance to the petiole. Finally, because the flowers have five anther-bearing stamens, the second choice 4 is better. The plant you have in your hand is therefore *Geranium pusillum.*

The key, Herbaceous Flowering Plants, used to get the specimen to the geranium family, is considerably more complicated than most keys to the plants of individual families. This is because there is so much more diversity among all plant families than within an individual family. Nevertheless, geraniums fit easily into Group 4, All Other Herbaceous Flowering Plants, because they are not parasitic or saprophytic (Group 1), grasslike (Group 2), or aquatic (Group 3). By diligently considering the various choices under Group 4, you would eventually arrive at Geraniaceae.

In this book there is never more than one couplet with the same number in a key. Do not be alarmed if the second choice of couplet 1 leads you to an unexpectedly high number, such as 10, or even 18. This is because numbers 2 through 9 or 17, respectively, were used in construction of the part of the key under the first choice of couplet 1. Just remember to keep moving a little farther to the right each time you decide which choice is the correct one. In an especially long key, however, the indenting is sometimes adjusted back to the left-hand margin on a new page, to save space and prevent excessive indenting. The numbering of the choices continues in sequence, however, so there should be no confusion if you follow the numbering. As a general rule, when a genus is represented in our region by more than a single species, the key leads first to genus. Keys for the genera are listed in alphabetical order following the introductory key. This system enables those who have learned the characteristics of many genera to skip the introductory key and go directly to genus. In a few keys you may be led to a "complex" of two or more genera whose species can be more conveniently dealt with if they are grouped together. Usually, the genera involved are closely related, sometimes spin-offs from what had been a single genus.

Are keys always reliable? Even the best keys sometimes fail, because the variation of some species with respect to a particular character, such as leaf size, leaf form, petal length, or petal color, is greater than was realized by the biologist who constructed the key. On the other hand, the extremely wide ranges of variation expressed in some keys may be a hindrance. For example, suppose the petal length of one species is known to range from 11 to 30 mm, and in another, closely related species from 16 to 32 mm. A choice between "petals usually 15–20 mm long" versus "petals usually 23–28 mm long" will be much more useful if it works 99% of the time. If information about unrelated characters, such as the shape of the petals and the characteristics of the leaves, is combined with the measurements, this will of course be helpful.

Closely related species or subspecies, especially those that vary extensively and intergrade, are often difficult to distinguish. Do not feel bad if you cannot arrive at an unequivocal determination. It is better to remain undecided, or to say "probably," than to claim to be certain.

Comments on Standard Botanical Terminology

Some terminology routinely used in botanical descriptions and keys can discourage beginners, and sometimes bother even knowledgeable botanists. The terms are comparable to shorthand: "tetradynamous," applicable to the mustard family (Brassicaceae), means that the flowers have four longer stamens and two shorter ones; "gamopetalous" means that the petals are united at the base; "emarginate" refers to a leaf or a petal that has a notch at the tip; a structure that has a papery texture is said to be "chartaceous." Obviously, each of these terms can be replaced by words in plain English, and to a large extent that is done in this book. Relatively few terms not already in your vocabulary are used here. Most, such as "stamens" and "pistils," are important, used repeatedly, and so easy to learn that it is pointless to try to avoid them. A glossary is provided for easy reference.

Much botanical terminology was coined before the life cycles of plants were clearly understood. Some of it was poorly conceived and does not respect the evolutionary relationships of structures or stages that occur in the life cycles. In flowering plants and gymnosperms (conifers and their relatives), there is an alternation of sexual and asexual generations, just as there is in ferns, fern relatives, mosses, and liverworts. Most botanists, however, are satisfied with using terms such as "male," "female," and "ovary" for structures that are part of the asexual, spore-producing generation, not the sexual generation, which in flowering plants and gymnosperms is microscopic. There is a long list of other terms that arose as spin-offs from the idea that certain parts of a flower are male or female structures; "gynoecium," "epigynous," "hypogynous," "perigynium," "gynaecandrous," "androecium," and "androgynous" are some. Of these, "perigynium," for a specialized, somewhat flask-shaped bract that encloses the pistil of sedges, is the only one used in this book. It figures so prominently and so repeatedly in keys to *Carex* that it is easier to live with it than to invent a new term and try to make it popular.

Some Plain Talk

By now, it is clear that some unavoidable botanical terminology is necessary if plants are to be identified by keying. Nevertheless, some of the most important components of the vocabulary are very ordinary words and phrases: "usually," "sometimes," "about," "rarely," "nearly always," "close to," "typically." This is because plants vary, the result of genetic difference or differences in the environment in which they live, usually both. So if the petal length of a particular species, variety, or subspecies is stated to be "about 11 mm," this should be interpreted to mean that some individuals may have slightly longer or shorter petals. Try to be at least a little flexible in dealing with this sort of thing. It would be nice if the characteristics of a plant species could be stated as precisely as the contents of a vitamin pill or the amount of fat in an ounce of cereal, but so far no one has found a way to do this.

Picture Keying

The use of this manual requires a much smaller vocabulary than that found in most similar treatises, but even then not everyone will wish to identify plants by keying. Many will prefer simply to leaf through the pages of illustrations to arrive at determinations of species. Except for students who should learn how to use at least some basic botanical terminology, there is nothing wrong with this practice, jokingly called "picture keying." Some very well informed amateur naturalists, in fact, are conscientious picture keyers, and some professionals who are comfortable with keying lilies and orchids are known to slip into a picture-keying mode when confronted with a grass or sedge. Whatever your own propensities, please bear in mind that not all species included in this book are illustrated. Unless a plant is unmistakably the same as the one in a drawing or color photograph, it is prudent to find the part of the key in which that species is dealt with and look at the characteristics that separate it from look-alikes. An index of names, including synonyms and common names, is provided.

Distributions of Species

Two main types of plant distribution must be dealt with in books like this. One type may be called general geographic distribution: "W of crest of the Cascades, Brit. Col. to N Oreg." or "close to the Pacific coast, Curry Co., Oreg., to Calif." The other type is altitudinal distribution: "montane, generally above 4000 ft. (1220 m)" or "usually high montane but occasionally found as low as 2000 ft. (610 m)." In a single entry, of course, it is possible to combine geographic and altidudinal information.

It is best to be flexible in dealing with both types of distribution, because occasionally a species is found well outside its generally accepted range. This is especially likely to happen in an area where few or no collections have been made, and where the microclimate—in terms of temperature, moisture, and sunlight or shade—is decidedly different from that of the region as a whole. A commonly observed phenomenon along this line is the presence, at the top of an isolated peak that is only 3000–4000 ft. (910–1220 m) high, of a species that is otherwise not often below about 5000 ft. (1520 m). Furthermore, in the case of many montane species that are found both east and west of the crest of the Cascades, the altitudinal range often dips lower on the eastern side than on the western side.

Many plants covered in this book have a wide distribution west of the crest of the Cascades. If a species is found in suitable habitats from southern British Columbia to the Oregon-California border, no special comment is given before its name in the key. For a species whose geographic distribution is limited, the area in which it is known to occur is pointed out. Bear in mind, however, that there is a reasonable chance that a plant stated to occur in Josephine and Jackson Counties of Oregon may sooner or later be found farther west in Curry County or farther north in Douglas County and perhaps even in Lane County. Furthermore, it may be very rare in some portions of its documented range.

The distributions of weeds present special problems. The majority of those dealt with here occur almost throughout our region, at least where conditions are favorable for their growth. Many are species that settlers inadvertently brought in long ago with their clothing, shoes, mattress material, domestic animals, or plants for farms and gardens. Some plants cultivated for their flowers or crop value escape and gain a foothold, but they, in general, are less likely than most weeds to colonize large areas. So many weeds show up in places far from where they were reported 20–30 years earlier that it seems best not to state their present distribution positively. Just assume that at least a few may yet become common in another area in the next 20–30 years.

Seasons of Flowering

In a book whose coverage extends from the interior of British Columbia to the California border, it is slightly risky to give, in connection with each species, the time that it is going to be in flower. One reason for this is that along a north–south gradient, a particular species that blooms in the lowlands of southwestern Oregon in late March or early April may not bloom until late April in northwestern Washington and southern British Columbia. A gain of 2000 ft. (610 m) in elevation also makes a substantial difference at any latitude.

In general, most plants that we think of as wildflowers bloom in lowland areas between about April 1 and May 15. At elevations of about 4000 ft. (1220 m), flowering will be mostly from late May to early July. At higher elevations, above 5000–6000 ft. (1520–1830 m), most flowering will be from July to late August. Grasses, as most of those who suffer from hay fever know, generally flower most luxuriantly in very late May and early June at the latitudes of Portland, Oregon, and Seattle, Washington, whereas at comparably low elevations in extreme southern Oregon, many grasses other than those in or close to water have already withered by the middle of June. Most plants flowering in lowland areas in mid to late summer are members of the sunflower family (Asteraceae). Even in sunny, warm areas, some of them do not start to bloom until August. Many weeds, incidentally, are in this late-flowering category. Some others will bloom almost anytime if the soil is not dry and the weather not too cold. In this book, key characteristics of plants that flower very early, such as February, or that have extremely narrow or extremely wide seasons of flowering, are often accompanied by a note to this effect.

Conservation

Although the characters of underground parts, such as roots, bulbs, and tubers, are important in the identification of species in certain families or genera, they are only rarely mentioned in this book. To protect the native flora, it seems best to concentrate on habit of growth, stems, leaves, flowers, and fruit. With or without the help of a hand lens, many plants can be identified in the field without causing them any damage.

It must be mentioned that most states and other jurisdictions, such as national forests and state and county parks and preserves, have strict rules to minimize damage to the fauna and flora. We are indebted not only to public agencies for managing large tracts of land whose plant and animal life we can enjoy, but also to organizations such as The Nature Conservancy, which have done so much to acquire and manage areas whose plant and animal life deserve protection.

Important Comprehensive Works on the Flora

Abrams, L., and collaborators. 1923–1960. *Illustrated Flora of the Pacific States: Washington, Oregon, and California.* 4 volumes. Stanford, California: Stanford University Press. Fully illustrated with line drawings; difficult for most amateurs to use and some sections badly out of date, nevertheless a very important work.

Douglas, G. W., Straley, G. B., Meidinger, D., and Pojar, J. 1998–2002. *Illustrated Flora of British Columbia.* 8 volumes. Victoria: British Columbia, Ministry of Environment, Lands and Parks; Ministry of Forests.

Flora of North America: North of Mexico. 1999– . New York and Oxford: Oxford University Press. Detailed treatments, prepared by specialists, of families, genera, and species, with complete keys and small maps showing the approximate distribution of each species; some illustrations; nomenclature and synonymies brought up to date; appearing as volumes are completed.

Gilkey, H. M., and Dennis, L. R. J. 2001. *Handbook of Northwestern Plants.* Revised edition. Corvallis: Oregon State University Press. In general, easy to use for common plants of western Oregon and Washington but not pretending to be complete for this region and barely touching southwestern Oregon; has some helpful line drawings and a few photographs; grasses, rushes, and sedges omitted.

Hickman, J. C. (editor). 1993. *The Jepson Manual: Higher Plants of California.* Berkeley: University of California Press. A compilation of keys and terse descriptions contributed by more than a hundred specialists; uneven in accuracy and quality but valuable because the validity of most species names has been carefully checked; illustrations, which focus mostly on diagnostic characters, are numerous but small; useful in southern Oregon, especially the Siskiyou Mountain region, for species whose distribution extends into that region.

Hitchcock, C. L., and Cronquist, A. 1973. *Flora of the Pacific Northwest.* Seattle: University of Washington Press. A reduction, to one volume, of the five-volume *Vascular Plants of the Pacific Northwest;* the keys are similar, but the illustrations are necessarily small and the descriptions are shortened.

Hitchcock, C. L., Cronquist, A., Ownbey, M., and Thompson, J. W. 1955–1969. *Vascular Plants of the Pacific Northwest.* 5 volumes. Seattle: University of Washington Press. Fully illustrated with line drawings; covers not only British Columbia, Washington, and much of Oregon but also Idaho, Montana, and part of Canada east of British Columbia; does not, however, deal with the southwestern part of Oregon.

Peck, M. E. 1961. *A Manual of the Higher Plants of Oregon.* Second edition. Portland, Oregon: Binfords and Mort. Covers both the eastern and western parts of the state but contains no illustrations of individual species, and now considered to be out of date. The Flora of Oregon Project is eventually to lead to production of a new manual for the state.

The Geographic and Geologic Setting of the Flora

WITHIN THE REGION of western Oregon, Washington, and British Columbia, there are many common denominators in the flora. Among trees, for instance, Douglas' fir (*Pseudotsuga menziesii,* pl. 34), bigleaf maple (*Acer macrophyllum*), and madroño (*Arbutus menziesii,* pl. 242) are widespread. Salal (*Gaultheria shallon,* pl. 252), snowberry (*Symphoricarpos albus* subsp. *laevigatus,* pl. 202), and various other shrubs can be found in many places at least as far south as the San Francisco Bay region, and the sword fern (*Polystichum munitum,* pl. 8) is also nearly ubiquitous. There are, however, some geographic areas characterized by distinctive assemblages of plants, and there are particular habitats, such as salt marshes, backshores of sandy beaches, and sphagnum bogs, in which only a few species adapted for growth under such conditions will be found. Within the region, furthermore, there are some endemics—species whose distribution is limited at most to a few contiguous counties. The success of endemics usually depends on a particular soil type, other environmental features, or geologic history.

This chapter will help you understand how various portions of our region originated and why they are unique. The explanations of complex geologic events that took place long ago are necessarily brief and must not be considered definitive. They will nevertheless give you some idea of how the major areas west of the crest of the Cascades developed.

The Cascades

Until about 350 million years ago, the ocean shore of the Pacific Northwest was about where the western boundary of Idaho is today. All of the land mass west of that line was put in place since then, some of it by volcanic activity, but most of it by the addition of material from the ocean floor to the continent. As an oceanic plate collided with the continental plate and slid slowly under it, much of the lighter sedimentary

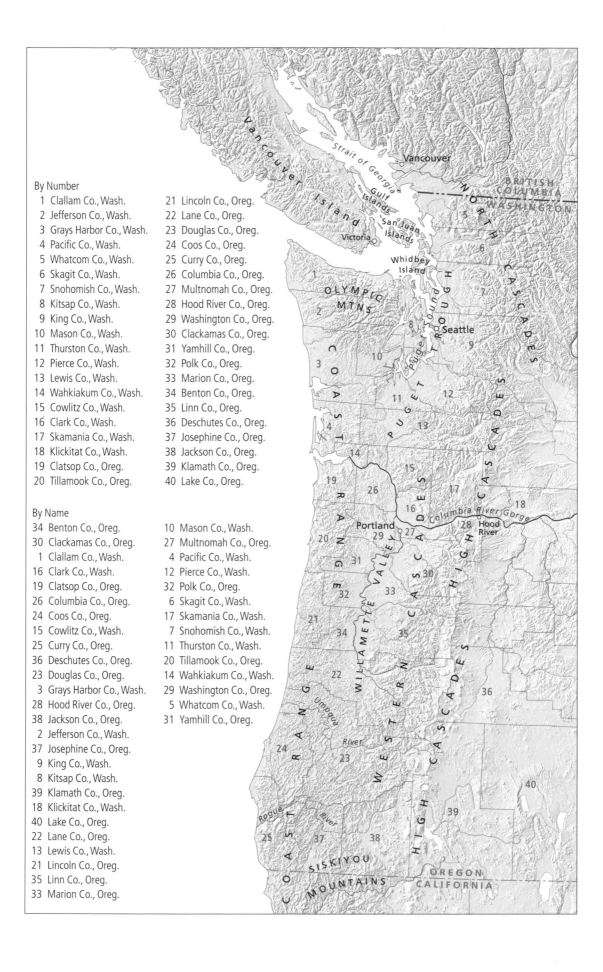

By Number

1 Clallam Co., Wash.
2 Jefferson Co., Wash.
3 Grays Harbor Co., Wash.
4 Pacific Co., Wash.
5 Whatcom Co., Wash.
6 Skagit Co., Wash.
7 Snohomish Co., Wash.
8 Kitsap Co., Wash.
9 King Co., Wash.
10 Mason Co., Wash.
11 Thurston Co., Wash.
12 Pierce Co., Wash.
13 Lewis Co., Wash.
14 Wahkiakum Co., Wash.
15 Cowlitz Co., Wash.
16 Clark Co., Wash.
17 Skamania Co., Wash.
18 Klickitat Co., Wash.
19 Clatsop Co., Oreg.
20 Tillamook Co., Oreg.

21 Lincoln Co., Oreg.
22 Lane Co., Oreg.
23 Douglas Co., Oreg.
24 Coos Co., Oreg.
25 Curry Co., Oreg.
26 Columbia Co., Oreg.
27 Multnomah Co., Oreg.
28 Hood River Co., Oreg.
29 Washington Co., Oreg.
30 Clackamas Co., Oreg.
31 Yamhill Co., Oreg.
32 Polk Co., Oreg.
33 Marion Co., Oreg.
34 Benton Co., Oreg.
35 Linn Co., Oreg.
36 Deschutes Co., Oreg.
37 Josephine Co., Oreg.
38 Jackson Co., Oreg.
39 Klamath Co., Oreg.
40 Lake Co., Oreg.

By Name

34 Benton Co., Oreg.
30 Clackamas Co., Oreg.
1 Clallam Co., Wash.
16 Clark Co., Wash.
19 Clatsop Co., Oreg.
26 Columbia Co., Oreg.
24 Coos Co., Oreg.
15 Cowlitz Co., Wash.
25 Curry Co., Oreg.
36 Deschutes Co., Oreg.
23 Douglas Co., Oreg.
3 Grays Harbor Co., Wash.
28 Hood River Co., Oreg.
38 Jackson Co., Oreg.
2 Jefferson Co., Wash.
37 Josephine Co., Oreg.
9 King Co., Wash.
8 Kitsap Co., Wash.
39 Klamath Co., Oreg.
18 Klickitat Co., Wash.
40 Lake Co., Oreg.
22 Lane Co., Oreg.
13 Lewis Co., Wash.
21 Lincoln Co., Oreg.
35 Linn Co., Oreg.
33 Marion Co., Oreg.

10 Mason Co., Wash.
27 Multnomah Co., Oreg.
4 Pacific Co., Wash.
12 Pierce Co., Wash.
32 Polk Co., Oreg.
6 Skagit Co., Wash.
17 Skamania Co., Wash.
7 Snohomish Co., Wash.
11 Thurston Co., Wash.
20 Tillamook Co., Oreg.
14 Wahkiakum Co., Wash.
29 Washington Co., Oreg.
5 Whatcom Co., Wash.
31 Yamhill Co., Oreg.

material in the uppermost stratum of the seafloor was scraped off onto the continental plate or tucked under its edges. Some deeper and heavier material below the sedimentary layer was also deposited on the continental plate. In this way, submarine mountain ranges were formed. As the process continued, and as folding, faulting, uplifting, changes in sea level, and glacial activity took place, exposed mountains such as the Coast Ranges and the North Cascades became what they are today.

The Cascades are dealt with first, partly because the crest of this range forms the eastern border of the entire area with which this book is concerned. Geologists divide the Cascades into three portions. The North Cascades extend from British Columbia to the area of Snoqualmie Pass, Washington; the relatively low Western Cascades and the High Cascades, which are tightly bound together, run southward from Snoqualmie Pass into northern California.

The North Cascades are the oldest and were founded by several masses of ancient submarine rocks carried eastward by the oceanic plate until they ended up on the continental plate. This happened perhaps 150 million years ago. The rock masses were squeezed together and sliced up by horizontal faults, then by vertical faults, processes that led to huge slabs stacked on top of one another. Long afterward, more vertical faults cut the mountains into several divisions that are roughly oriented in a north–south direction. Less than about 2 million years ago, there was considerable volcanic activity in the region.

The birth of the Western Cascades is believed to have taken place about 50 million years ago when undersea volcanoes developed not far south of what is now Eugene, Oregon. Eventually, a chain of volcanoes reaching deep into Washington completed the formation of the low mountains of the Western Cascades. About 5 million years ago, after volcanic activity shifted eastward, the majestic peaks of the High Cascades formed. One of them was Mount Saint Helens, which, after a long period of inactivity, erupted violently in 1980. The last gasps of this and other volcanoes of the High Cascades have not yet been heard.

Rainfall on the western slope of the Cascades, and even at the foot of the mountains, is plentiful. The annual average at Monroe and Sedro Woolley, Washington, and at Eugene, Oregon, is in the range of 48–50 inches (120–130 cm); in Portland and Seattle it is typically in the neighborhood of 35–40 inches (89–100 cm). In general, rainfall increases at higher elevations. At Newhalem, Washington (approximately 1500 ft., 460 m, above sea level), it is about 80 inches (200 cm), and at Snoqualmie Pass, Washington (approximately 3000 ft., 910 m), it is about 62 inches (160 cm). On a few high peaks it may exceed 140 inches (360 cm).

Before the arrival of settlers, forest-friendly portions of the western slope of the Cascades were almost completely covered by evergreen and deciduous species up to the tree line, which at most points is at about 7000 ft. (2130 m). At lower elevations, Douglas' fir (*Pseudotsuga menziesii,* pl. 34), grand fir (*Abies grandis,* pl. 28), western hemlock (*Tsuga heterophylla,* pl. 35), and western red cedar (*Thuja plicata,* pl. 27) are still the dominant conifers. Especially common deciduous trees are bigleaf maple (*Acer macrophyllum*), vine maple (*A. circinatum,* pl. 38), and red alder (*Alnus rubra*). At about 4000–5000 ft. (1220–1520 m), noble fir (*Abies procera*) becomes prominent, and just below tree line there are alpine fir (*A. lasiocarpa*) and mountain hemlock (*Tsuga mertensiana*). In open areas, comparable sets of shrubs and herbaceous plants succeed one another at successively higher levels. As one moves eastward through the mountain passes into the region not covered by this book, the climate becomes drier and the vegetation changes accordingly. Lodgepole pine (*Pinus contorta* subsp. *murrayana*), ponderosa pine (*P. ponderosa* var. *ponderosa*), Engelmann's spruce (*Picea engelmannii* var. *engelmannii*), western larch (*Larix occidentalis*), and western juniper (*Juniperus occidentalis* subsp. *occidentalis*) are the trees that predominate at elevations and on soils that favor their growth.

The Coast Ranges and Olympic Mountains

Like some components of the North Cascades, the Coast Ranges of Washington, Oregon, and California, and also Vancouver Island and the mountains closest to Vancouver, British Columbia, are derived from sand, rocks, and other sedimentary material that was scraped from the superficial layers of the seafloor and deposited on the continent or under its leading edge. Sometimes, heavier rocks from deeper strata of the seafloor also became incorporated into the scrapings. The formation of coastal mountains took place under water, so the present-day inland location of a coastal range is due to other events in the earth's history. Furthermore, some originally coastal mountains are now very far from the ocean shore. Outstanding examples are the Wallowa and Blue Mountains of northeastern Oregon. It may be hard to believe that the coastline was anywhere near these, but indeed it was; it ran along an almost diagonal line in a northeastern direction from what is now the southwestern corner of Oregon.

The emergence of the Coast Ranges of the Pacific region from their oceanic birthplace is believed to have begun first in California and to have continued gradually farther north. There is evidence, for instance, that Coos Bay, Oregon, was out of the water much earlier than Astoria, in the northwestern corner of the state, which was still under water until as recently as about 20 million years ago.

The Olympic Mountains, not quite continuous with more southern portions of the Coast Ranges, may nevertheless be considered, on the basis of geography, to be part of them. They started to develop about 50 million years ago. The mass of material scraped from the oceanic plate onto the continental plate consisted of many kinds of rock, including considerable lava that had been deposited on the ocean floor as a result of submarine volcanic activity. After glaciers reamed out Puget Sound and Hood Canal, the Strait of Georgia, and the Strait of Juan de Fuca, the Olympic Peninsula as we know it was formed. Vancouver Island and the westernmost strip of the mainland of British Columbia can be traced back to assemblages of rocks that the eastward movement of the oceanic plate pressed against and under what are now the North Cascades. Eventually, however, a subsidence separated the prospective Vancouver Island from the mainland. The area was for a time filled with sediment eroded from the mountains, but this was scraped out by glaciers that formed the Strait of Georgia.

Along the Olympic coast, as along the Pacific Northwest coast in general, the direction of moisture-laden winds is prevailingly from the west or southwest to the east or northeast. Much of the load of water these winds carry is dropped between the shore and the high peaks. At or close to the shore the average annual rainfall is generally at least 70–80 inches (180–200 cm), and in some spots it is considerably higher. On the peak of Mount Olympus, where the elevation is about 8000 ft. (2440 m), the annual average is over 150 inches (380 cm), much of it falling as snow, which accumulates to a depth of many feet. Portions of the eastern side of the peninsula may also be fairly wet, but on the northeastern side the rainfall slacks off. At Sequim, Washington, the average annual rainfall is only about 20 inches (50 cm), approximately the same as in coastal portions of central California. Victoria, located on the southeastern corner of Vancouver Island, and the islands of the archipelago formed by the Gulf Islands of British Columbia and the San Juan Islands of Washington, are also beneficiaries of the rain-shadow effect conferred upon them by the Olympic Mountains. Their average annual rainfall is usually about 25–30 inches (64–76 cm).

Rainfall along the western coast of Vancouver Island is similar to that on the western side of the Olympic Peninsula. On a few peaks in the mountains, it exceeds 120 inches (300 cm). Along the eastern shore there is a drier belt continuous with that of the area around Victoria. South of the Olympics is a coastal plain through which rivers draining the Olympics run to the coast, either directly or by joining the Chehalis River, which enters Grays Harbor. Below this are the Willapa Hills and Black Hills, which are the main components of the Coast Ranges in Washington; these are also drained by tributaries of the Chehalis River. Farther south is Willapa Bay, the eastern shore of which is close to the Willapa Hills. The rainfall in this general region is about the same or lower than that for comparable elevations west of the Olympics.

In Oregon, the Coast Ranges are nearly continuous, and the rivers draining them run westward to the coast or eastward to the Willamette Valley. The Umpqua and Rogue River valleys are the most impressive breaks in the chain of mountains. Some of the tributaries of these two rivers begin in the Cascades, at elevations much higher than that of Mary's Peak, west of Corvallis, whose summit is only about 3900 ft. (1190 m) above sea level. In northern California there is a comparable break in the Coast Ranges where the Klamath River pierces them, and in central California there is a wide gash in the mountains where the Sacramento and San Joaquin Rivers approach San Francisco Bay.

Rainfall on the western side of the Coast Ranges in Oregon is ample although not as high as on the Olympic Peninsula; it diminishes on the eastern side as a result of a rain-shadow effect comparable to that caused by the Cascades and Olympic Mountains. In the Coos Bay–North Bend area, for instance, the annual rainfall is about 60 inches (150 cm); on Mary's Peak it is more than 150 inches (380 cm); at Roseburg, east of the mountains and at nearly the same latitude as Coos Bay, it is only about 35 inches (89 cm).

The vegetation over much of the length of the western slope of the Coast Ranges in Washington and Oregon, and that at lower and moderate elevations in the Olympic Mountains, is similar. The predominant coniferous trees throughout are Douglas' fir, grand fir, western hemlock, and western red cedar, but close to the shore, Sitka spruce, an almost strictly coastal tree, is also abundant. Among deciduous trees, bigleaf maple (*Acer macrophyllum*), vine maple (*A. circinatum,* pl. 38), red alder (*Alnus rubra*), and western dogwood (*Cornus nuttallii,* pl. 228) stand out. Prominent shrubs forming the understory or growing along the edges of the forest or in the open are salal (*Gaultheria shallon,* pl. 252), red huckleberry (*Vaccinium parvifolium,* pl. 269), red-flowering currant (*Ribes sanguineum*), thimbleberry (*Rubus parviflorus,* pl. 526), salmonberry (*R. spectabilis,* pl. 527), dewberry (*R. ursinus*), ocean spray (*Holodiscus discolor,* pl. 512), osoberry (*Oemleria cerasiformis,* pl. 514), long-leaved Oregon grape (*Berberis nervosa,* pl. 159), snowberry (*Symphoricarpos albus* subsp. *laevigatus,* pl. 202), and western hazelnut (*Corylus cornuta* var. *californica*). *Rhododendron macrophyllum* (pl. 264) and evergreen huckleberry (*V. ovatum,* pl. 267) are abundant in some places, and where rainfall is high there is likely to be devil's club (*Oplopanax horridus,* pl. 59). Near the coast in southern Oregon, an outstanding addition to the complex is western azalea (*R. occidentale,* pl. 265). The preceding list of trees and shrubs is by no means complete, and a list of herbaceous plants would be very long.

The Coastal Strip

The narrow coastal strip, in our region, extends from the western side of southern Vancouver Island to the Oregon-California border. Here, summer temperatures are cooler than those in the Willamette Valley and much of the Puget Trough, and the average annual rainfall is much greater, as pointed out previously. The coastal strip includes many bays bordered by salt marshes. These usually develop in places where rivers and smaller streams deposit silt that mixes with marine sediments and organic matter to form a rather firm substratum for the growth of plants. The salinity in the substratum of a salt marsh is typically slightly less than that of seawater. When the marsh is inundated by high tides, however, plants growing in it are temporarily exposed to water of greater salinity. Some species, including seashore salt grass (*Distichlis spicata*), maintain a constant salinity in their tissues by excreting excess salt; others, such as pickleweed (*Salicornia virginica*), accumulate salt and can tolerate concentrations nearly double that of seawater.

There are also extensive beaches of sand along the coastal strip, and the backshores of these support plants specialized for living on a substratum that is freely drained, reflects sunlight back to the leaves and stems, and is often unstable in a windstorm. Within an area of about 50 north–south miles (80 km) just north of Coos Bay, sand dunes form a band that in places is about 3 miles (5 km) wide. Thousands of years ago, after much beach sand had collected along the shore of this region, the coastline shifted westward and the sand was left high and dry. It was blown farther and farther inland, creating a large area of somewhat mobile dunes. The vegetation on these is generally sparse. Among the native plants that can stabilize a low dune is dune grass (*Leymus mollis* subsp. *mollis*); a still more effective stabilizer is beach grass (*Ammophila arenaria* subsp. *arenaria*), brought to North America from Europe to reduce the extent to which loose sand moves in the direction of homes and highways. There are dunes in other areas along the coastal strip, but they are not so extensive as those mentioned here, which are within the Oregon Dunes National Recreation Area. Some portions of them are protected; others are freely and catastrophically exploited by people in dune buggies.

In the Oregon Dunes, there are places where old hillocks have been stabilized and where groves of shore pine are accompanied by a wide variety of shrubby plants, including evergreen huckleberry (*Vaccinium ovatum,* pl. 267) and bristly manzanita (*Arctostaphylos columbiana,* pl. 243). There are also many herbaceous species that thrive on the sandy soils of stabilized dunes.

Other special habitats on the open coast include cliffs and bluffs facing the ocean, where the flora includes some species limited to these situations. While bogs characterized by sphagnum mosses occur at various elevations in many portions of the region west of the Cascades, they are especially common in coastal areas. Sphagnum bogs are characterized by high acidity and low levels of nutrients, especially nitrogen. It is in them that we find the little carnivorous plant called round-leaved sundew (*Drosera rotundifolia*) and a complex of other species that can live where the nutritional resources of the substratum are rather slim. In Oregon, some coastal sphagnum bogs have the California pitcher plant (*Darlingtonia californica,* pl. 540). This remarkable member of our flora will be mentioned again in connection with the Siskiyou Mountain region.

The Rogue River Region

State boundaries were not established to separate one floristic province from another. Much of the flora of extreme northwestern California and that of southwestern Oregon is similar because these areas are related in proximity and geologic origin. It is considerably farther north, where the Rogue River flows, that the geographic distributions of many California species end and the ranges of characteristically northwestern species begin. Users of the valuable references by Hitchcock and his collaborators will have noted that these books do not deal with species of the Siskiyou Mountain region unless these are also found farther north; the more recently published *Jepson Manual* for California, on the other hand, includes many of the species found in southwestern Oregon.

Please do not imagine that the Rogue River is a sharp line crossed by only a few plants. Douglas' fir (*Pseudotsuga menziesii,* pl. 34), western hemlock (*Tsuga heterophylla,* pl. 35), madroño (*Arbutus menziesii,* pl. 242), salal (*Gaultheria shallon,* pl. 252), evergreen huckleberry (*Vaccinium ovatum,* pl. 267), and western sword fern (*Polystichum munitum,* pl. 8) are just some of the many species whose distribution extends from British Columbia deep into California. Nevertheless, to a botanist with a comprehensive knowledge of the flora of California and that of the Pacific Northwest, it is obvious that the Rogue River region is a rough dividing line. Incidentally, within California there is a comparably important change in the flora where the Klamath River, on its way to the ocean, interrupts the Coast Ranges.

The Siskiyou Mountain Region

In southwestern Oregon, occupying the counties of Douglas, Jackson, Josephine, and Curry, are the Siskiyou Mountains, also called the Klamath Mountains. The Siskiyous spread also into northwestern California, especially Del Norte, Humboldt, and Siskiyou Counties, where there are named subdivisions, such as the Trinity, Marble, and Salmon Mountains.

As might be expected in a region that extends from the coast to the Cascades, and where the mountains are interrupted by river valleys, the climate varies. At Brookings, on the Oregon coast close to the boundary with California, the average annual rainfall is about 75 inches (190 cm), but at Cave Junction, where the elevation is about 1500 ft. (460 m) and where the East and West Forks of the Illinois River unite, the annual rainfall is 45–50 inches (110–130 cm). At Ashland, farther inland and farther south, the elevation is close to 2000 ft. (610 m), and the rainfall only around 20 inches (50 cm). The highest peak in the Siskiyous of Oregon is Mount Ashland, 7533 ft. (2300 m), about 20 miles (30 km) southwest of Ashland. It is capped by snow during much of the year.

The Siskiyous and their sister ranges are much older than the Coast Ranges that they more or less interrupt. They began to originate undersea, probably more than 100 million years ago, after the oceanic plate and continental plate, which had been moving in about the same general direction, started to collide. As the oceanic plate slid under the continent, an immense amount of heavy rock from well below the superficial stratum of the seafloor was scraped onto the continent. As a result, the Siskiyous have large deposits of peridotite, an ancient rock consisting to a large extent of magnesium silicate. Much of the peridotite, as a result of its interaction with water, has been converted into serpentine, a greenish or blackish rock that feels slightly slippery. After serpentine has weathered, it becomes reddish, and soils derived from it also tend to be of this color.

While plants need magnesium for many processes, including the synthesis of chlorophyll, an excess of magnesium interferes with the uptake of calcium, which plants also need and which is scarce in serpentine soils. Furthermore, the relatively high concentrations of cobalt, chromium, and especially nickel in serpentine are toxic to many plants. In some plants, however, mechanisms have evolved either for preventing the uptake of nickel or for the ability to accumulate it without suffering toxic effects. A large part of the flora of the Siskiyous now consists of plants adapted for life on serpentine soils. Many of them—about 250 species—are endemics that grow nowhere but on the serpentine soils of the Siskiyou Mountain region. To a considerable extent, it is the rich variety of serpentine endemics that makes this part of North America botanically so unique.

In the region as a whole, many species of the flora of the Pacific Northwest and California are also present. Some mix with the serpentine-loving plants, others skirt the serpentine deposits. There is also an exceptional assortment of conifers. Another interesting attribute of the Siskiyou Mountain region is the presence there of some species that are otherwise primarily restricted to areas east of the crest of the Cascades.

As you use the keys in this book, you will encounter notations stating that certain plants are found in Douglas, Jackson, Josephine, or Curry County. Many of these, but not all, are serpentine endemics. Serpentine is by no means restricted to the Siskiyous; it is present here and there in other areas of Oregon, Washington, and British Columbia. One place of easy access is Washington Park of the city of Anacortes, Washington, where plenty of serpentine can be seen at the shore as well as in upland areas. Conspicuous among the serpentine-dependent or serpentine-tolerant plants found there are the Rocky Mountain juniper (*Juniperus scopulorum,* pl. 26) and the little fern called Indian's dream (*Aspidotis densa,* pl. 12).

One of the many especially interesting assemblages of plants found in the Siskiyous, and also in some of the sister ranges in California, are those in wetlands that have developed in areas where the soils are derived from serpentine rock. These are dominated by the carnivorous California pitcher plant. While this species occurs in many sphagnum bogs close to the Oregon coast, it is only in the Siskiyous that one finds it with the orchid *Cypripedium californicum* (pl. 691), the lilylike *Narthecium californicum* (pl. 672) and *Hastingsia bracteosa* (pl. 667), *Viola primulifolia* subsp. *occidentalis* (pl. 606), the daisylike *Rudbeckia californica,* and several other distinctive species. The wet places in which these plants grow usually slope enough to allow water to flow slowly and continuously through them. Such pitcher-plant fens have a substantially lower acidity than typical sphagnum bogs.

The Willamette Valley

The Willamette Valley of Oregon occupies a relatively flat area between the Cascades and the Coast Ranges. Its northern end is in the vicinity of Portland, where the Willamette River, unusual among large North American rivers in that it flows northward, joins the Columbia. Most of its important tributaries originate in the Cascades, but some drain into it from the Coast Ranges and the Calapooya Mountains; the latter, running from east to west south of Eugene, mark the southern end of the Willamette Valley.

Where the Willamette River flows through Eugene, the elevation is only about 400 ft. (120 m) above sea level, and at the edge of downtown Portland it is nearly at sea level. Thus most of the valley is relatively flat, except for a few hills, some of which are inactive volcanoes. The climate is relatively mild, with rainfall in most places averaging 35–45 inches (89–110 cm) a year. Summer weather is generally dry. Temperatures below 20° Fahrenheit (–7° Celsius) are not common and likely to occur only in December and January. The Willamette Valley itself, and the mountain ranges bordering it, once had extensive forests. Production of lumber was, from the early stages of settlement, an important part of commerce in the region. Much of the land that had been cleared was fertile and needed little modification. Well suited to agriculture, the valley became an important center for farming. As the population increased—the Portland area now has more than 500,000 people, Eugene and Salem about 100,000 each—the building of houses, roads, shopping malls, airports, dumps, and civic expansions have claimed much of the land. Only a few tracts of native vegetation resemble those present in the mid-19th century. Weeds rule in the cities and towns and in many areas that were opened up for agriculture.

In portions of the Willamette Valley that still have considerable natural vegetation, the complex of common trees, shrubs, and herbaceous plants is similar to that at lower elevations in the Coast Ranges and on the western slope of the Cascades.

The Puget Trough

The Puget Trough, extending from southwestern British Columbia through western Washington, is topographically similar to the Willamette Valley and is essentially a northward continuation of it. At its southern end is Vancouver, Washington, just across the Columbia River from Portland; its northern sector includes the Puget Sound region, Strait of Georgia, and the cities of Victoria, Nanaimo, and Vancouver, British Columbia. The annual rainfall in most of the trough is more or less the same as in the Willamette Valley, but within the rain shadow of the Olympics, as explained under The Coast Ranges and Olympic Mountains, there is a distinctly drier area.

So far as winter temperatures, summer temperatures, and summer dryness are concerned, the Puget Trough is much like the Willamette Valley. It is also similar to the valley in the extent to which its terrestrial habitats have been modified by development. Scot's broom, furthermore, is more noticeable in the Puget Trough than almost anywhere else in the Pacific Northwest, and its rapid proliferation has led to the destruction of native plants in many areas.

The shores of Puget Sound and its contiguous saltwater areas have many salt marshes, some of which are extensive. The vegetation of these is similar to that of salt marshes on the coast, but a detailed list of plants for coastal salt marshes and those in the greater Puget Sound region would be different. In fact, some of the salt-marsh plants found from about Coos Bay southward are not represented in salt marshes of any other part of the Pacific Northwest.

The San Juan Archipelago deserves special mention. Some of the many islands in this chain, including most of the larger ones, belong to the United States and are called the San Juan Islands; the rest belong to Canada, where they are called the Gulf Islands. They exhibit much geologic diversity, with several major components piled like slabs one on top of another. The presence of certain fossils in some of the older slabs, laid down between about 500 million and 200 million years ago, indicate that portions of these had been shifted by continental drift from Asia to North America. About 80 million years ago, as the submarine plate was colliding with the continental plate and sliding under it, the slabs that now make up much of the archipelago were deposited on top of it. Some of the islands have substantial deposits of limestone. There is also much exposed bedrock as well as many large erratic boulders and deposits of gravel. The erratics and gravel consist to a large extent of rocks that were dragged into the region by glaciers, whose scouring of the Puget Trough ended about 12,000 years ago.

Good drainage and relatively low rainfall are influences that discourage or slow the growth of some plants in many areas of the San Juan Islands. Although the flora in general is similar to that of much of western Washington and mainland British Columbia, several common species, such as western dogwood (*Cornus nuttallii,* pl. 228), vine maple (*Acer circinatum,* pl. 38), and poison oak (*Toxicodendron diversilobum,* pl. 42), are absent or rare. Conversely, some plants that are uncommon west of the Cascades are abundant; among these are Rocky Mountain juniper (*Juniperus scopulorum,* pl. 26), soapberry (*Shepherdia canadensis,* pl. 239), and Douglas' maple (*A. glabrum* var. *douglasii,* pl. 39). It should be said that at Anacortes, Sequim, and a few other places bordering the Puget Trough in Washington, and around Victoria on Vancouver Island, the flora is comparable to that of the San Juan Islands with respect to the presence or absence of the species just mentioned.

The Columbia River Gorge

The gorge of the Columbia River, extending for about 70 miles (110 km) eastward from Portland, Oregon, and Vancouver, Washington, was formed within the last 2 million years. The Cascades were already rather well developed when the river, backed up by huge amounts of water that had accumulated behind the mountains, broke through them and flowed to the coast. As the last ice age was ending, there were again enormous amounts of water flowing westward, and it was during this period that the gorge was sculpted further and became essentially what it is today: a region of cliffs and spectacular waterfalls.

The plant life of the gorge changes gradually as one moves from Portland and Vancouver to Bonneville Dam, then Hood River, then The Dalles. At first the flora is much like that in western Oregon and Washington except for the appearance of a few more eastern elements, some of which may extend even a little west of Portland. By the time a plant hunter has reached the area between Hood River and the Dalles, there has been a considerable change in the vegetation; most of the common species that prevail here are not often seen farther west. Conversely, of course, not many species found near Portland are still present. Much of the gradual and then more abrupt change at either end of the gorge is related to climate, especially rainfall. At Hood River, the average annual rainfall is near 30 inches (76 cm), but at The Dalles it usually does not quite reach 20 inches (50 cm).

Most plants found in the lowlands west of Hood River are dealt with in this book. For those in the eastern part of the gorge you will need another reference.

Major Plant Groups

THE PLANT KINGDOM, excluding fungi as well as seaweeds and other algae, can be divided into three main categories: mosses and liverworts, ferns and fern relatives, and seed plants. This book is concerned with the last two of these assemblages as they are represented in western Oregon, Washington, and British Columbia. Both are characterized by more complex tissues than are found in mosses and liverworts. In particular, it is the vascular tissues, consisting mostly of specialized living cells and tubular remnants of cells, that are well developed in these so-called higher plants. Vascular tissues transport water, inorganic nutrients, and the organic substances, such as sugars, manufactured by a plant. Without extensive development of such tissue, mosses and liverworts cannot grow to a large size and cannot be physiologically active when faced with a shortage of moisture.

Another important feature of vascular plants is this: while they still have alternating sexual, gamete-producing, and asexual, spore-producing generations in the life cycle, it is the asexual generation that is the more prominent and independent. In mosses and liverworts it is the sexual generation that is more prominent. In ferns and their relatives, the sexual stage is independent, but it is short-lived and can function only where there is some free water; in seed plants it is not only very temporary but also microscopic.

Ferns do not produce seeds. Seeds are characteristic of flowering plants and those called gymnosperms, which in our region are represented by conifers such as pines and firs. In flowering plants, however, the seeds develop within some sort of fruit, which at maturity may be dry like a peapod, or juicy like a cherry. In gymnosperms, the seeds are almost always exposed; even in the few species in which they are covered, the covering is not formed in the same way as a true fruit.

More attributes of the main groups of vascular plants found in our region will be found in the introductions to Ferns and Fern Relatives (p. 34), Needle-Leaved, Cone-Bearing Trees and Their Relatives (p. 53), and Flowering Plants (p. 60).

Ferns and Fern Relatives

I N OUR REGION, representatives of eight families of plants fit the image that most people would recognize as ferns. Six other families (including three that are technically ferns—Azollaceae, Equisetaceae, and Marsileaceae—but that are sufficiently different to deserve special treatment) consist of plants that do not look like ferns but are related to them because of their similar life cycles and certain structural attributes, such as the presence of tissues concerned with distribution of water and dissolved substances. It is convenient to deal with these diverse families as fern relatives.

Ferns

In a typical fern, some or all the leaves, or specialized portions of certain leaves, bear structures called sporangia. The sporangia are generally concentrated in masses called sori. Each sorus, more often than not, is protected for at least a time by a flap- or disklike structure called an indusium. The function of sporangia is to produce spores, which are eventually released and dispersed by wind. A spore that reaches a situation where there is sufficient moisture may develop into a small sexual plant called a prothallium. This produces a few egg cells or many sperm, sometimes both. If a film of water from rain or dew is present, sperm can swim to the egg cells, located singly in microscopic flask-shaped structures, and fertilize them. A fertilized egg cell develops into a new plant of the spore-producing generation. At first there is only a tiny leaf, a short stem, and a root. Soon, however, more leaves and roots are formed, and the young fern becomes independent of the prothallium, which disappears.

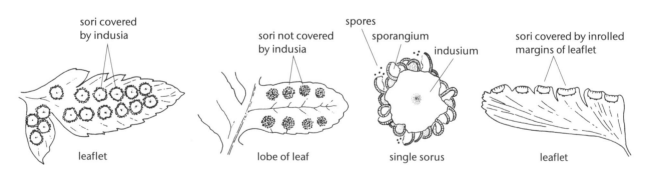

Reproductive portions of fern leaves

The key presented here takes advantage, as much as possible, of easily visible features, especially leaf form and the disposition of spore-bearing structures. It leads sometimes to a single species, sometimes to a genus. Keys to genera with two or more species are listed alphabetically after the general keys. Family names are given in parentheses, sometimes following the names of individual species, sometimes at the beginning of treatments of individual genera. For those who wish to have a key to families represented in our region, this follows the keys to species of the various genera.

In a few cases, species or subspecies are distinguished, at least in part, on the basis of measurements that can be made only with a compound microscope equipped with a micrometer scale. Most persons, professional or amateur, will be satisfied to stop short of involvement with such minute details, but it would be unfair not to provide the information.

1 Plants with a single leaf of the current season, this leaf divided into 2 parts: one part bearing beadlike sporangia 1–2 mm wide, the other part sterile and either a simple blade, pinnately lobed, or compound and with many ultimate lobes (in *Botrychium multifidum* the petiole and sterile portion of the leaf of the preceding year are usually also present; in casual fieldwork, ferns of this group, some restricted to sphagnum bogs, are less likely to be noted than most of those under the other choice 1)

  2 Sterile portion of leaf divided 1 or more times, the sporangium-bearing portion also distinctly branched . . . . *Botrychium*

  2 Sterile portion of leaf a simple, oval blade, the sporangium-bearing portion not branched (sporangia somewhat embedded in short, paired lobes on both sides of the upper part of the stalk; usually in sphagnum bogs and rarely seen) . . . . *Ophioglossum pusillum* (*O. vulgatum* var. *pseudopodum*)
                                                 ADDER'S-TONGUE FERN

1 Plants not as described in the other choice 1 (if the aboveground portion appears to consist of a single leaf, this is because the leaves arise at intervals from an underground rhizome; in some species there are separate fertile and sterile leaves, but the individual sporangia on fertile leaves are not so much as 1 mm in diameter)

  3 Leaves once-pinnately lobed or pinnately compound, the lobes or leaflets not deeply divided again (the margins may be toothed, however; if the leaves are clearly more than once pinnate, take the other choice 3)

    4 Leaves pinnately lobed, of 2 types: temporary sporangium-bearing leaves, produced each growing season, and sterile leaves that persist from year to year (the sporangium-bearing leaves have narrower lobes than the sterile leaves) . . . .
    . . . . *Blechnum spicant*, pl. 2
                                     DEER FERN

    4 Leaves, whether pinnately lobed or pinnately compound, all of 1 type

      5 Leaves pinnately lobed, the lobes broadly attached to the rachis
      . . . . *Polypodium*

      5 Leaves pinnately compound, the leaflets separated from the rachis by short stalks

        6 Leaf blades commonly more than 30 cm long; petioles not dark reddish brown, conspicuously scaly near the base; leaflets much longer than wide and pointed at the tip; sori circular, the indusium umbrellalike, with a central attachment stalk . . . . *Polystichum*

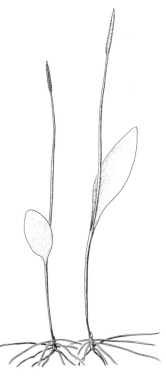

Ophioglossum pusillum,
adder's-tongue fern

6 Leaf blades rarely more than 15 cm long; petioles dark reddish brown, not conspicuously scaly near the base; leaflets not often more than 1 cm long, not much longer than wide and not pointed at the tip; sori elongated, the indusium attached along one of the longer edges (Brit. Col. to Calif., also with a wide distribution in central and E North America) . . . . *Asplenium trichomanes* subsp. *trichomanes*, pl. 1

MAIDENHAIR SPLEENWORT

Asplenium trichomanes subsp. *quadrivalens* has been found from S Brit. Col. to N Oreg. as well as in E North America. Its spores are larger than those of subsp. *trichomanes* (37–43 µm instead of 27–32 µm), and it is restricted to limestone deposits.

3 Leaves at least bipinnately lobed or bipinnately compound

7 Leaves commonly at least 75 cm long (often more than 1.5 m long), arising singly from an underground rhizome, the general outline of the blade triangular; sporangia, when present, in a continuous band at the edges of the ultimate lobes and partly covered by the margins, which are rolled under . . . . *Pteridium aquilinum* subsp. *pubescens*, pl. 15

BRACKEN

In some populations, sporangia may not be formed on all leaves; nevertheless, any large fern with a triangular blade in which the lobes have margins that are rolled under is *P. aquilinum* subsp. *pubescens*.

7 Leaves not as described in the other choice 7

8 Plants with 2 different kinds of leaves, the lobes of the sporangium-bearing ones more slender (usually about 6–8 times as long as wide) than those of the sterile leaves and also with smooth, inrolled margins (in some clumps of *Aspidotis densa* there may be only a few sterile leaves; nevertheless, the combination of dark brown petioles and proportionately slender sporangium-bearing lobes distinguish this species)

9 Petioles dark brown; most leaves of a clump usually of the sporangium-bearing type (commonly, but not exclusively, associated with serpentine rock) . . . . *Aspidotis densa* (*Cryptogramma densa, Onychium densum*), pl. 12

INDIAN'S DREAM

9 Petioles greenish or yellowish; sporangium-bearing leaves usually not outnumbering the sterile leaves of the same clump . . . . *Cryptogramma*

8 All leaves of 1 type (but not all may bear sporangia)

10 Sporangia confined to the edges of the leaflets, forming continuous or interrupted bands and covered at least partly by the inrolled margins of the leaflets

11 Inrolled, sporangium-bearing margins of each leaflet interrupted; leaflets somewhat fan-shaped; petiole and its divisions dark brown or nearly black, shiny . . . . *Adiantum*

11 Inrolled, sporangium-bearing margins of each leaflet continuous; leaflets not at all fan-shaped; petiole brown or blackish but not especially shiny

12 Undersides of divisions of leaf blades scaly and/or conspicuously hairy . . . . *Cheilanthes*

12 Undersides of divisions of leaf blades neither scaly nor conspicuously hairy . . . . *Pellaea*

10 Sporangia not confined to the edges of the leaflets, not forming bands and not covered by the inrolled margins

13 Underside of leaf blades covered with small waxy scales, these appearing to be powdery and yellowish; sporangia distributed along the veins rather than in well-defined sori (leaf blades approximately triangular; petioles dark brown, shiny) . . . . *Pentagramma triangularis* subsp. *triangularis* (*Pityrogramma triangularis*)

GOLDBACK FERN

13 Leaves not as described in the other choice 13

14 Sori elongated (about 4 times as long as wide when young), adjacent to and nearly parallel to the midribs of the ultimate leaf lobes (evergreen; leaves forming crowns, the blades sometimes more than 1 m long, the ultimate lobes widest at the base and tapering gradually to the tip; in our region mostly near the coast) . . . . *Woodwardia fimbriata*, pl. 3

GIANT CHAIN FERN

14 Sori neither conspicuously elongated nor adjacent to the midribs of the ultimate lobes

  15 Sori not covered by an indusium

    16 Leaves arising more or less singly from an underground rhizome, the blades broadly triangular in outline, nearly or fully as wide as long . . . . *Gymnocarpium*

    16 Leaves forming dense clusters, the blades narrowly triangular, much more than twice as long as wide (montane, not often found below about 5000 ft., 1520 m) . . . . *Athyrium alpestre* subsp. *americanum* (*A. distentifolium*)
ALPINE LADY FERN

  15 Sori covered by an indusium (look carefully, because the indusium of older sori may have shriveled, been shed, or been covered by the enlarging mass of sporangia)

    17 Indusium umbrellalike, with a central attachment stalk (leaflets pinnately lobed) . . . . *Polystichum*

    17 Indusium hoodlike or somewhat horseshoe-shaped, attached on one side of the sorus, not umbrellalike

      18 Leaves arising singly (but often close together) from an underground rhizome (leaves rather delicate, mostly 15–25 cm long; sori circular, the indusium hoodlike, arching over at least part of each one; mostly on rocky slopes) . . . . *Cystopteris fragilis*
BRITTLE FERN

      18 Leaves forming distinct crowns, although the crowns may develop at the tips of underground rhizomes

        19 Leaf blades either triangular (widest at the base) or nearly as wide at the base as near the middle . . . . *Dryopteris*

        19 Leaf blades usually widest near the middle, becoming conspicuously narrower (less than half as wide) at the base

          20 Indusium a small sac that soon ruptures, leaving radiating lobes that may be partly or wholly hidden by the sporangia (leaves generally 10–20 cm long; petioles usually dark reddish brown at the base; leaflets deeply lobed, the lobes with toothed margins) . . . . *Woodsia*

Pentagramma triangularis subsp. *triangularis,* goldback fern

Cystopteris fragilis, brittle fern

20 Indusium either somewhat horseshoe-shaped (attached deep in the cleft that separates the 2 arms of the horseshoe) or hoodlike, broadly attached at one side of the sorus (after the sporangia of a sorus are well developed, the remnant of the indusium may be obscured)

   21 Margins of ultimate leaf lobes smooth .... ***Thelypteris nevadensis*** (*Dryopteris oregana*)
                                                                         SIERRA WOOD FERN

   21 Margins of ultimate leaf lobes distinctly toothed

      22 Indusium somewhat horseshoe-shaped, attached deep in the narrow cleft that separates its 2 broad arms (the orientation of the axis of the cleft often nearly or fully coincides with that of a small vein); underside of larger leaf lobes with long, hairlike outgrowths (these often shed early, however) .... ***Dryopteris filix-mas***
                                                                            MALE FERN

      22 Indusium attached at one side of the sorus, the curved line of attachment nearly coinciding with the axis of a small vein; underside of leaf lobes without hairlike outgrowths (mature spores yellow; Alaska to Calif. and eastward) .... ***Athyrium filix-femina*** var. *cyclosorum*, pl. 4
                                                                      LADY FERN

        Athyrium filix-femina var. *californicum,* California lady fern, most easily distinguished from var. *cyclosorum* by its brown spores, is reported from N Oreg. to Calif. and eastward. Most plants from our region fit into var. *cyclosorum,* which is widespread and common throughout our region, as well as in Calif. and eastward.

Adiantum

1 Leaf blades about as wide as long, the first 2 divisions of the petiole branching dichotomously 2–3 times; most leaflets lopsided, about twice as long as wide .... ***A. aleuticum*** (*A. pedatum* var. *aleuticum*), pl. 11
                                                                              FIVE-FINGER FERN

1 Leaf blades usually longer than wide, the petiole continued as a single axis with alternate leaflets; leaflets not conspicuously lopsided, mostly slightly wider than long (lower Rogue River valley, Oreg., to Baja Calif.) .... ***A. jordanii***
                                                                        CALIFORNIA MAIDENHAIR

Botrychium

1 Sterile portion of leaf as wide or wider than long, the primary divisions again deeply lobed at least once

   2 Sterile portion of leaf with at least a short stalk (this only a few mm long in *B. pumicola*); ultimate lobes of sterile portion blunt

      3 Stalk of sterile portion at least 2 cm long; mature blade usually at least 10 cm long, pinnately divided as many as 4 times, not fleshy, typically persisting into the next growing season; usually in sphagnum bogs (the most common *Botrychium* at lower elevations in our region) .... ***B. multifidum***
                                                                          LEATHER GRAPE FERN

      3 Stalk of sterile portion only a few mm long; mature blade not often more than 5 cm long, not divided more than 3 times, somewhat fleshy, not persisting into the next growing season; high montane, growing in pumice (Cascades of Klamath and Deschutes Cos., Oreg.; not likely to be found W of the crest) .... ***B. pumicola***, pl. 9
                                                                        PUMICE GRAPE FERN

   2 Sterile portion of leaf without a stalk, the first divisions arising where it diverges from the sporangium-bearing portion; ultimate lobes of sterile portion usually pointed

      4 Sterile portion of leaf usually at least 10 cm long, sometimes more than 20 cm long (usually in damp woods and thickets; rare in our region) .... ***B. virginianum***
                                                                        VIRGINIA GRAPE FERN

      4 Sterile portion of leaf rarely more than 6 cm long (mostly above 4000 ft., 1220 m) .... ***B. lanceolatum*** subsp. *lanceolatum*
                                                                       TRIANGLE MOONWORT

1 Sterile portion of leaf usually decidedly longer than wide, the primary divisions not deeply lobed

  5 Primary lobes of sterile portion of leaf not well defined, most of them again shallowly lobed . . . . ***B. montanum***

                                      WESTERN GOBLIN

  5 Primary lobes of sterile portion of leaf well defined, most of them cleanly separated to the rachis

    6 Primary lobes of sterile portion of leaf again deeply lobed (sterile portion separated from the fertile portion at or above the midlevel of the leaf as a whole) . . . . ***B. pinnatum***

                              NORTHWESTERN MOONWORT

    6 Primary lobes (except perhaps the lowermost ones) of sterile portion of leaf not again deeply lobed

      7 Sterile portion of leaf generally separated from the fertile portion below the midlevel of the leaf as a whole, often separated just above ground level (some successive leaf lobes overlapping) . . . . ***B. simplex***

                                   LEAST MOONWORT

      7 Sterile portion of leaf usually separated from the fertile portion at or above the midlevel of the leaf as a whole

        8 Successive leaf lobes overlapping or nearly touching . . . . ***B. lunaria***

                                   MOONWORT

        8 Successive leaf lobes (at least the lower 3–4) well separated . . . . ***B. minganense***

                                MINGAN MOONWORT

Cheilanthes

1 Leaflets nearly or fully twice as long as wide; scales arising from the primary rachis and its branches slender, many times as long as wide and not conspicuously broadest at the base (mostly above 2500 ft., 760 m) . . . . ***C. gracillima***, pl. 13

                                    LACE FERN

1 Leaflets nearly circular, not so much as 1.5 times as long as wide; scales arising from the primary rachis and its branches usually not more than 5 times as long as wide and broadest at the base (not likely to be found below 3000 ft., 910 m; SW Oreg. to Calif.) . . . . ***C. intertexta***

                                  COASTAL LIP FERN

Thelypteris nevadensis,
Sierra wood fern

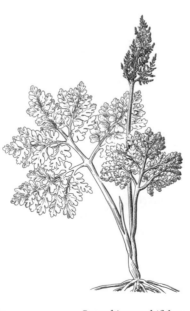

Botrychium multifidum,
leather grape fern

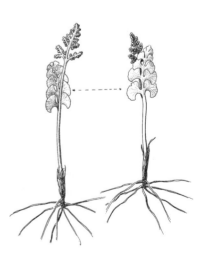

Botrychium lunaria,
moonwort

Cryptogramma

Cryptogramma acrostichoides is the only common species in our region. Try to identify specimens by using the aboveground characters, thus avoiding the necessity to expose the rhizome.

1 Leaves arising singly along a creeping rhizome not more than about 1.5 mm thick (leaves delicate; Alaska to Wash. but strictly high montane in our region) . . . . *C. stelleri*
STELLER'S PARSLEY FERN

1 Leaves crowded together on a short, stout rhizome
   2 Leaves firm, the vegetative ones remaining green through the winter; leaves with hairs on the upper surface along the veins and along the groove of the petiole (common lowland to montane species, typical of rocky slopes) . . . . *C. acrostichoides* (*C. crispa*)
AMERICAN PARSLEY FERN

   2 Leaves rather thin and delicate, withering before winter; leaves without hairs on the upper surface along the veins or along the groove of the petiole (high montane, Brit. Col. to Calif., Idaho, and Montana) . . . . *C. cascadensis*
CASCADES PARSLEY FERN

Dryopteris

1 Leaf blades mostly tripinnate, not more than twice as long as wide
   2 Leaf blades typically broadly triangular, distinctly widest at the base; rachis and midribs of primary divisions of blades with glandular hairs; on the lowest primary divisions of the blade, the secondary divisions nearest the rachis are alternate, and the ones pointing downward are much longer than the ones pointing upward (usually rooted in rotting wood) . . . . *D. expansa* (*D. austriaca, D. dilatata*), pl. 6
WOOD FERN

   2 Leaf blades, in general, triangular, but the width about equal at the level of the lowest 2–3 primary divisions; rachis and midribs of primary divisions of blades without glandular hairs; on the lowest primary divisions of the blade, the secondary divisions nearest the rachis are typically opposite, and the ones pointing downward are at most only slightly longer than the ones pointing upward (Brit. Col. to Wash. and eastward) . . . . *D. carthusiana*
TOOTHED WOOD FERN

1 Leaf blades bipinnate, generally more than twice as long as wide
   3 Leaf blades nearly as wide at the base as at the middle; underside of midribs of primary divisions of leaf blade with conspicuous scales, these mostly 2–3 times as long as wide; evergreen; plants of well-drained, often rocky habitats . . . . *D. arguta*, pl. 5
COASTAL WOOD FERN

   3 Leaf blades less than half as wide at the base as at the middle; underside of midribs of primary divisions of leaf blade with slender hairs, these at least several times as long as wide (the hairs may be shed early); deciduous; plants of moist habitats (widespread in our region but not often encountered) . . . . *D. filix-mas*
MALE FERN

Cryptogramma acrostichoides,
American parsley fern

Gymnocarpium

For separating the two species, the size of the spores is probably more reliable than the proportions of the leaflets.

1 Members of each pair of leaflets on the second primary division of the leaf blade mostly of decidedly unequal length, the upper ones smaller than the lower; blades to about 25 cm long; spores 27–31 μm in diameter (Alaska to Oreg.) . . . . *G. disjunctum*
WESTERN OAK FERN

1 Members of each pair of leaflets on the second primary division of the leaf blade of approximately equal length; blades not often more than 15 cm long; spores 34–39 μm in diameter (Alaska to Wash.) . . . .
. . . . *G. dryopteris*
COMMON OAK FERN

Pellaea

1 Leaf blades oval or nearly triangular in outline, pinnately divided 2–4 (generally 3) times (S Oreg. to Calif.) . . . . *P. andromedifolia*, pl. 14
COFFEE FERN

1 Leaf blades slender, pinnately divided only twice (SW Oreg. to Calif.; in our region, not common below 2000 ft., 610 m) . . . . *P. brachyptera*
SIERRA CLIFF BRAKE

Polypodium

1 Leaves firm, somewhat leathery; most lobes of larger leaves at least 12 mm wide at their bases; sori commonly more than 3 mm wide (leaves dark green; tips of leaf lobes rounded; strictly coastal) . . . . *P. scouleri*
LEATHERLEAF FERN

Dryopteris filix-mas,
male fern

Gymnocarpium dryopteris,
common oak fern

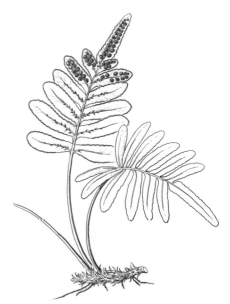

Polypodium scouleri,
leatherleaf fern

1 Leaves not so firm as to be leathery; lobes not often so much as 12 mm wide at their bases; sori rarely more than 3 mm wide

  2 Upper surface of midrib of leaf blade distinctly hairy; tips of some or most lateral lobes pointed

    3 Most lateral lobes tapering gradually to a point (the tapering may begin close to the base of the lobe); veins on lobes ending free, not uniting with others; outline of young sori circular (widespread) . . . . *P. glycyrrhiza*, pl. 10
LICORICE FERN

    3 Lateral lobes tapering rather abruptly to a point (the tapering does not begin before the middle of the lobe); some veins on lobes uniting with others; outline of young sori usually oval (mostly near the coast; Oreg. to Calif.) . . . . *P. calirhiza*
COMMON CALIFORNIA POLYPODY

  2 Upper surface of midrib of leaf blade not hairy; tips of lateral lobes usually rounded, occasionally somewhat pointed

    4 Sori with a large proportion of modified sporangia (these obviously different from the functional sporangia); outline of young sori circular (Brit. Col. to N Oreg.) . . . . *P. amorphum*
DIFFERENT POLYPODY

    4 Sori without modified sporangia (but a few sporangia of abnormal shape may be present); outline of young sori oval (not often found in coastal areas or below 2000 ft., 610 m) . . . . *P. hesperium*
WESTERN POLYPODY

Polystichum

1 Leaf blades once-pinnately compound

  2 Leaf blades becoming obviously narrower at the base (in other words, the lower leaflets are much shorter than those well above the base; they are also nearly triangular in outline and not much longer than wide); petioles of leaves not more than about one-sixth as long as the blades; spores with spinelike outgrowths (rare below 4000 ft., 1220 m) . . . . *P. lonchitis*
HOLLY FERN

  2 Leaf blades about as wide at the base as those well above the base (in other words, the lowest leaflets are generally at least three-fourths as long as those well above the base; furthermore, they are much longer than wide); petioles of leaves usually more than one-sixth as long as the blades; spores more or less smooth, without spinelike outgrowths

    3 Indusium with rough margins but without numerous hairlike outgrowths; leaves not often more than 50 cm long, the leaflets usually conspicuously overlapping; usually on exposed, rocky hillsides . . . . . .
. . . . *P. imbricans* subsp. *imbricans*
IMBRICATE SWORD FERN

    3 Indusium bordered by numerous nearly hairlike outgrowths; leaves sometimes more than 80 cm long, the leaflets usually not obviously overlapping; common in woods and sometimes on dry, rocky hillsides (in which case some plants may be small and have overlapping leaflets, thus resembling *P. imbricans*) . . . . *P. munitum*, pl. 8
WESTERN SWORD FERN

        Late in summer, after the indusia have shriveled, the hairlike outgrowths may no longer be evident; *P. munitum* is, however, by far the most common *Polystichum* in the region.

1 Leaves bipinnately divided, at least the lower primary leaflets with 1 or more distinct lobes or separate secondary leaflets

    4 At least the lower portion of the leaf blade bipinnately compound (the primary leaflets divided so deeply that there are at least some secondary leaflets; Alaska to Brit. Col.) . . . . *P. braunii*
BRAUN'S SHIELD FERN

    4 None of the leaf blade fully bipinnately compound (some or many of the primary leaflets may be deeply lobed, but these lobes are not pinched in enough at the base to be true secondary leaflets)

5 Most of each primary leaflet on the lower half of the frond so deeply divided that the lobes are nearly leaflets (leaves not often more than 30 cm long; petioles, especially on their lower portions, with membranous scales; montane, not likely to be found below about 5000 ft., 1520 m) . . . . *P. lemmonii* (*P. mohrioides* var. *lemmonii*)
LEMMON'S FERN, SHASTA FERN

5 None of the primary leaflets so deeply divided that the lobes are nearly leaflets

  6 Primary leaflets of much of the blade divided for most of their length into regularly spaced lobes; leaves commonly at least 40 cm long, sometimes more than 80 cm

    7 Petioles usually with membranous brown scales for all of their length; small bulblets produced at the bases of some leaflets near the tip of the blade . . . . *P. andersonii*
ANDERSON'S SHIELD FERN

    7 Petioles usually with membranous brown scales for not much more than half their length; bulblets not produced at the bases of leaflets. . . . . *P. californicum*, pl. 7
CALIFORNIA SHIELD FERN

  6 Leaflets rather irregularly divided into lobes and mostly only near their bases; leaves not often more than 30 cm long

    8 Lobes of primary leaflets with sharp, bristlelike tips (montane, not likely to be found below 4500 ft., 1370 m) . . . . *P. kruckebergii*
KRUCKEBERG'S SWORD FERN

    8 Lobes of primary leaflets without sharp, bristlelike tips (montane, mostly E of the crest of the Cascades and not likely to be found below 4500 ft., 1370 m) . . . . *P. scopulinum*
ROCK POLYSTICHUM

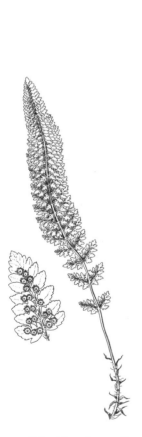
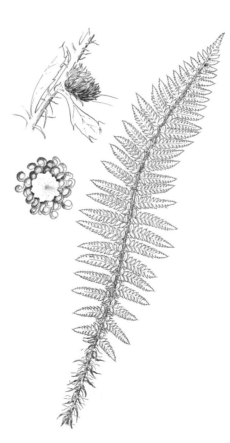
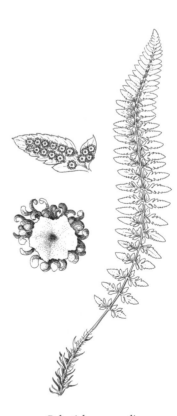

Polystichum lemmonii, Lemmon's fern

Polystichum andersonii, Anderson's shield fern

Polystichum scopulinum, rock polystichum

Woodsia

1 Underside of leaf blades and edges of the rachis not hairy; radiating lobes of the ruptured indusium usually 10 or more and mostly at least 5 times as long as wide .... *W. oregana* **subsp.** *oregana*
 OREGON WOODSIA

1 Underside of leaf blades and edges of the rachis decidedly hairy (the hairs partitioned into units); radiating lobes of the ruptured indusium few and usually not more than 3 times as long as wide (not often found below 3000 ft., 910 m) .... *W. scopulina*
ROCKY MOUNTAIN WOODSIA

Specimens whose spores are 42–50 μm or 50–57 μm in diameter have been assigned, respectively, to *W. scopulina* subspp. *scopulina* and *laurentiana*. Our region is within the known distribution of both.

Fern Families

The families of ferns are distinguished primarily on the basis of microscopic characters that are difficult for nonspecialists to deal with. This key is mostly artificial, making use, wherever possible, of obvious features such as the habit of growth and form of the leaves. Note that some families, because the genera within them are so diverse, appear more than once.

1 Sporangia restricted to 1 of the 2 divisions of the single leaf produced during the growing season (the vegetative portion of the leaf of the previous year may have persisted, however); sporangia without an annulus (a strip of thick-walled cells that straightens out in dry weather, tearing open the ripe sporangium, thus allowing spores to escape); young leaves not coiled .... **Ophioglossaceae**
ADDER'S-TONGUE FAMILY (*Botrychium, Ophioglossum*)

1 Sporangia either on vegetative leaves or on specialized leaves but not on a division of the only leaf produced during the growing season; sporangia with an annulus; young leaves coiling, unrolling as they enlarge
  2 Sori developing close to the edges of the ultimate leaflets or lobes (they are sometimes covered by inrolled margins of the leaflets or lobes but not by indusia)
    3 Leaves arising from a creeping rhizome and widely spaced; petioles green, not dark and shiny, with a prominent groove; leaves often more than 1 m tall .... **Dennstaedtiaceae**
BRACKEN FAMILY (*Pteridium*)

    3 Leaves produced in clusters, often in the form of a crown (there is a rhizome, but it is usually so short as to be unnoticeable, and the leaves are therefore crowded); petioles brown to black, shiny, not grooved; plants rarely so much as 50 cm tall .... **Pteridaceae**
BRAKE FAMILY (*Adiantum, Aspidotis, Cheilanthes, Cryptogramma, Pellaea*)
In *Cryptogramma* and also to a considerable extent in *Aspidotis,* leaves that produce spores are different from those that do not. Some botanists split this family more finely, placing *Adiantum* in Adiantaceae; *Aspidotis, Cheilanthes, Pellaea,* and *Pentagramma* (first choice 6) in Sinopteridaceae; and *Cryptogramma* in Cryptogrammaceae.

  2 Sori or individual sporangia not located close to the edges of leaflets or ultimate lobes
    4 Leaves of 2 types: those that are strictly vegetative and persist for more than 1 growing season and those that bear sporangia and wither after a few months .... **Blechnaceae**
DEER-FERN FAMILY (*Blechnum*)

    4 Leaves all of the same type (but some may not produce sporangia)
      5 Sori (or continuous lines of sporangia) not covered by indusia
        6 Sporangia densely crowded into continuous lines along the veins (in other words, the sporangia are not concentrated in distinct sori); leaf blades more or less triangular, compound, the primary leaflets then divided into lobes; undersides of leaf blades covered with a powdery, whitish or yellowish deposit .... **Pteridaceae**
BRAKE FAMILY (*Pentagramma*)
Some botanists would place *Pentagramma* in Sinopteridaceae.

6 Sporangia concentrated in distinct sori; leaf blades once deeply lobed, not compound; undersides of leaf blades not covered with a powdery deposit . . . . **Polypodiaceae**
POLYPODY FAMILY (*Polypodium*)

5 Sori covered, at least early in their development, by indusia (in some species, only traces of the indusia are likely to be found after the sori are fully developed)

7 Veins reaching the edges of the ultimate leaf lobes . . . . **Thelypteridaceae**
MARSH-FERN FAMILY (*Thelypteris*)

7 Veins not reaching the edges of the ultimate leaf lobes

8 Successive sori (these elongated) attached to one another in a row along the midribs of the leaf lobes (indusium tough, persisting after the sori have released their spores) . . . . **Blechnaceae**
DEER-FERN FAMILY (*Woodwardia*)

8 Successive sori not attached to one another in a row along the midribs of the leaf lobes (but they may be elongated)

9 Primary leaflets not deeply divided again; petiole and rachis of leaves mostly dark brown or purplish brown; sori more than twice as long as wide, the indusia attached along one of the longer margins . . . . **Aspleniaceae**
SPLEENWORT FAMILY (*Asplenium*)

9 Primary leaflets often divided 1 or more times; petiole and rachis not mostly dark brown or purplish brown; sori of various shapes (circular, oval, crescentic), but not so much as twice as long as wide (arrangements of indusia also various) . . . . **Dryopteridaceae**
WOOD-FERN FAMILY (*Athyrium, Cystopteris, Dryopteris, Gymnocarpium, Polystichum, Woodsia*)

Fern Relatives

This key and the ones that follow distinguish the families, genera, and species of what are usually called fern relatives. Three of the six families—Azollaceae, Equisetaceae, and Marsileaceae—are, however, technically ferns.

1 Largest plants, these usually only about 2–3 cm long, floating on quiet fresh water or stranded on mud above the waterline; leaves scalelike, with 2 unequal lobes, the lower ones serving as floats; stems obscured by overlapping leaves but branching above every third leaf; roots short, inconspicuous, and not branched . . . . **Azollaceae**, p. 46
MOSQUITO-FERN FAMILY (*Azolla*)

1 Plants not floating and not as otherwise described in the other choice 1

2 Leaves arranged in circles, their basal portions united and forming sheaths around the stems at the nodes, only the tips free and these sometimes shed early (main stems either unbranched or producing slender branch stems at the nodes; sporangia borne on conelike structures at the tips of the main stems; aerial stems of some species of 2 types, those with conelike sporangium-bearing structures not green) . . . . **Equisetaceae**, p. 46
HORSETAIL FAMILY (*Equisetum*)

2 Leaves not arranged in circles, and their basal portions not united in such a way as to form sheaths around the stems

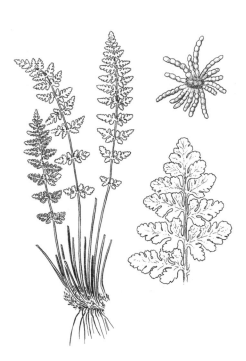

Woodsia oregana subsp. *oregana*, Oregon woodsia

3 Plants with branching stems and scalelike or slender leaves, therefore superficially resembling mosses in their general habit of growth

    4 Mats formed by plants, as a rule, not rising more than about 2–3 cm; leaves not so much as 4 mm long; sporangia on the upper part of the reproductive portion of a fertile stem producing smaller spores than those on the lower part . . . . **Selaginellaceae**, p. 52
                            SPIKE-MOSS FAMILY (*Selaginella*)

    4 Mats of plants, at least when reproductive, rising well above 5 cm; leaves of most species more than 4 mm long; all sporangia producing spores of the same size . . . . **Lycopodiaceae**, p. 49
                        CLUB-MOSS FAMILY (*Diphasiastrum, Huperzia, Lycopodium*)

3 Plants not at all resembling mosses in their general habit of growth

    5 Plants with several to many slender, tapering leaves, the bases of these attached to a short stem; most leaves with 2 sporangia at the base, one type producing spores much larger than those produced by the other (plants usually completely or partly submerged in fresh water but sometimes growing on moist soil) . . . . **Isoetaceae**, p. 48
                                QUILLWORT FAMILY (*Isoetes*)

    5 Leaves either substantial and bearing 4 leaflets at the tip or nearly hairlike, without a distinct blade; plants with a creeping rhizome from which the leaves originate; sporangia (producing 2 types of spores) saclike, borne on short stalks originating near the bases of the leaves (plants growing in shallow water, at least partly exposed) . . . . **Marsileaceae**, p. 51
                             MARSILEA FAMILY (*Marsilea, Pilularia*)

AZOLLACEAE Mosquito-Fern Family

Mosquito ferns are small floating plants that are often abundant in freshwater ponds. Their leaves are divided into two lobes; the upper lobes, about 1 mm long, cover the lower ones and also nearly obscure the stems. The pale bluish green color of the upper lobes is due, in part, to the presence in them of a symbiotic blue-green bacterium, *Anabaena azollae*. In summer, the plants often become reddish.

Azolla

1 Plants rarely so much as 2 cm long, the branching compact and almost regularly dichotomous; largest hairs on the upper leaf lobes usually consisting of 2 (sometimes 3) cells . . . . *A. mexicana*, pl. 16
                              MEXICAN MOSQUITO FERN

1 Plants commonly at least 2 cm wide, the branching often more nearly pinnate than dichotomous; all hairs on the upper leaf lobes consisting of only 1 cell . . . . *A. filiculoides*
                              MOSQUITO FERN

EQUISETACEAE Horsetail Family

The plants called horsetails and scouring rushes, all belonging to the genus *Equisetum*, have perennial underground stems from which the upright, aboveground stems develop. The stems are hollow, jointed, and ribbed lengthwise. The leaves are reduced to scalelike structures attached to each other in a way that they form a sheath at each joint. Spores are produced in structures that resemble the cones of coniferous trees.

The cell walls of horsetails and scouring rushes contain considerable amounts of silica. When the epidermis has small silicified projections, these make the surface of the stems gritty. Before commercial scouring powders were developed for cleaning pots and pans, pulverized stems of some species were used for this purpose.

Hybrids between various species of our region are occasionally encountered but appear not to be common. Their spores are atypical in being white instead of green, and also of irregular shape.

Equisetum

1 Aerial stems of 2 types, some green and extensively branched, others not green and not branched (the stems that are not green have conelike sporangium-bearing structures at their tips, but these stems do not live long and may have disappeared by the time the green stems are fully developed; nevertheless, if none of the green stems has conelike structures, it is probably safe to assume that this choice is the correct one)

2 Green stems commonly more than 50 cm tall (sometimes more than 1 m) and more than 8 mm thick, usually with 20–40 ridges; nongreen stems (those bearing conelike structures) usually at least 10 mm thick . . . . *E. telmateia* **subsp.** *braunii*, pls. 18
GIANT HORSETAIL

2 Green stems rarely so much as 40 cm tall or more than 5 mm thick, usually with 10–12 ridges; nongreen stems (those bearing conelike structures) rarely more than 5 mm thick . . . . *E. arvense*
FIELD HORSETAIL

1 All aerial stems green and usually at least some of them with conelike, sporangium-bearing structures at the tip

  3 At least some of the aerial stems in the colony with regular, successive whorls of branches

    4 Main stems usually with 15–25 ridges (rarely as few as 9), the internal cavity generally occupying at least half of the thickness; teeth of the sheaths 1.5–3 mm long, without obvious hyaline margins; upper branches of robust plants sometimes bearing small conelike structures . . . . *E. fluviatile*
WATER HORSETAIL

    4 Main stems with only 5–10 ridges, the internal cavity occupying less than one-third of the thickness; teeth of the sheaths 3–7 mm long, with narrow but distinct hyaline margins; conelike structures strictly limited to the main stems . . . . *E. palustre*
MARSH HORSETAIL

  3 Aerial stems either not branched or only sparingly and irregularly branched, the branches not in regular, successive whorls (in *E. fluviatile* and *E. palustre,* choice 4, some stems of a colony may fit this description, but others will have regular, successive whorls of branches)

    5 Teeth of the sheaths encircling the stems usually soon shed, only the basal portions persisting; conelike sporangium-bearing structures rounded at the tip (aerial stems to more than 1 m tall, usually living only 1 year; stems usually with 16–30 ridges) . . . . *E. laevigatum*
SMOOTH SCOURING RUSH

The upright stems of *E. laevigatum* are rarely branched, but the plants often have numerous, slender auxiliary stems arising from the base.

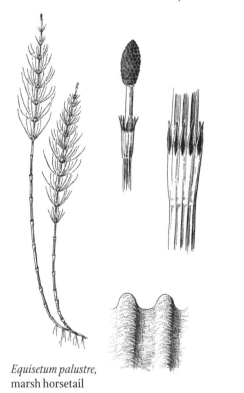

Equisetum palustre,
marsh horsetail

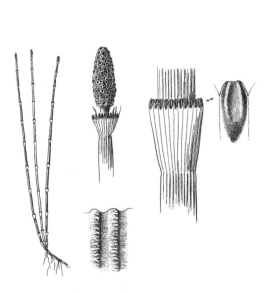

Equisetum laevigatum,
smooth scouring rush

5 Teeth of the sheaths encircling the stems generally persisting, at least at many nodes; conelike sporangium-bearing structures typically sharp-pointed

    6 Aerial stems commonly at least 80 cm tall and more than 5 mm thick, with more than 20 ridges and living several years; sheaths encircling the stems usually with a prominent dark ring well below the one that extends into the teeth . . . . *E. hyemale* subsp. *affine*, pl. 17

        COMMON SCOURING RUSH

    6 Aerial stems not often more than 30 cm tall or 2 mm thick, with only 5–12 ridges and living only 1 year; sheaths encircling the stems without a dark ring below the one that extends into the teeth

        7 Tips of teeth on leaf sheaths usually upright, with a broad membranous border around the darkly pigmented portion (Alaska to NW Oreg. and eastward across the continent) . . . . *E. variegatum* subsp. *variegatum*

            VARIEGATED SCOURING RUSH

        7 Tips of teeth on leaf sheaths usually curving inward, and with only a narrow and inconspicuous, early withering, membranous border around the darkly pigmented portion (mostly coastal, Alaska to Wash.) . . . . *E. variegatum* subsp. *alaskanum*

            ALASKAN SCOURING RUSH

ISOETACEAE Quillwort Family

Quillworts usually grow in shallow water or on wet mud, but a few species are found on soil that is only damp. The quill-like leaves, cylindrical or three-angled, arise in a tight cluster from a short, bulbous stem. A conspicuous sporangium is located on the inner surface of the swollen base of most of them. Identification of species often requires microscopic study of the spores. There are two types of these: megaspores, produced by some sporangia, and microspores, which are smaller and produced by other sporangia.

Isoetes

1 Plants usually either barely covered by water, partly exposed, or completely exposed on wet soil

    2 Sporangium completely or almost completely covered by a veil-like membrane; usually partly submerged in shallow water (Brit. Col. to Calif.) . . . . *I. nuttallii*

        NUTTALL'S QUILLWORT

    2 Only the upper part of sporangium covered by a veil-like membrane; on wet soil and essentially terrestrial (Brit. Col. to Calif.) . . . . *I. howellii*

        HOWELL'S QUILLWORT

1 Plants submerged (sometimes deeper than 50 cm) in permanent lakes or ponds

    3 Leaves tapering abruptly to a fine tip (larger spores 0.3–0.5 mm, 300–500 μm, in diameter; not likely to be found below 4000 ft., 1220 m) . . . .*I. bolanderi*

        BOLANDER'S QUILLWORT

    3 Leaves tapering gradually to the tip

        4 Leaves rather stiff; larger spores (0.5–0.7 mm, 500–700 μm, in diameter) with ridges or low bumps but without prickles or distinctly raised bumps (Alaska to Calif. and eastward) . . . . *I. occidentalis* (*I. lacustris* var. *paupercula*)

            WESTERN QUILLWORT

        4 Leaves flexible; larger spores (0.4–0.5 mm, 400–500 μm, in diameter) with little prickles or distinctly raised bumps

            5 Larger spores with sharp-tipped prickles; smaller spores usually less than 30 μm in diameter (Alaska to Calif. and across the continent) . . . . *I. echinospora*

                PRICKLY-SPORED QUILLWORT

            5 Larger spores with raised, blunt bumps; smaller spores usually more than 30 μm in diameter (Alaska to N Wash.) . . . . *I. maritima*

            MARITIME QUILLWORT

LYCOPODIACEAE Club-Moss Family

Club mosses slightly resemble some true mosses in their habit of growth, but they are generally much larger than mosses and are completely different in that the conspicuous, persistent stage is the spore-producing generation. (In mosses, the persistent generation is sexual; the asexual, spore-producing generation is temporary and represented by a stalk and capsule that develop from a fertilized egg and that remain attached to the sexual parent until the sporophyte, as it is called, has released its spores and withered.) The leaves of species in our region are slender or scalelike, and even the largest are not much more than 1 cm long. Sporangia are concentrated on club-shaped or conelike structures somewhat similar to those of horsetails and scouring rushes. These may be single or clustered at the tips of upright stems.

1 Some upright stems with short branchlets that produce 4-leaved buds (the buds, called gemmae, eventually fall off and may produce new plants) .... *Huperzia*
1 Upright stems without short branchlets that produce 4-leaved buds
    2 Leaves bearing sporangia green and similar to the sterile leaves in being slender; upright stems (not persisting through the winter) rarely so much as 10 cm tall, not branching (in wet places, especially sphagnum bogs) .... ***Lycopodiella inundata*** (*Lycopodium inundatum*)
                                                  BOG CLUB MOSS
    2 Leaves bearing sporangia not so green as the sterile leaves and also of a different form (they are not often more than about twice as long as wide)
        3 Most leaves in 6 or more lengthwise rows along the stems (main stems and branches, including leaves, cylindrical) .... *Lycopodium*
        3 Most leaves in 4–5 lengthwise rows along the stems (branches usually flattened or squarish but sometimes more or less cylindrical) .... *Diphasiastrum*

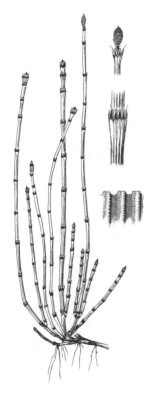

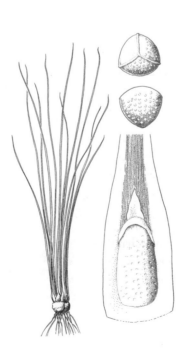

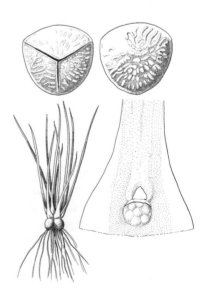

Equisetum variegatum
subsp. *variegatum*,
variegated scouring rush

Isoetes howellii,
Howell's quillwort

Isoetes occidentalis,
western quillwort

Diphasiastrum

1 Branches flattened, leaves pressed down much like the scale-leaves of some conifers, such as cypresses (in our region only in Brit. Col. and Wash. but widely distributed in N North America, Europe, and Asia) . . . . ***D. complanatum***
NORTHERN RUNNING PINE

1 Branches (including the leaves) squarish or more or less cylindrical, not flattened
  2 Branches squarish, the leaves, in 4 lengthwise rows, pressed down rather tightly (Alaska to Wash., also in extreme NE North America and Asia) . . . . ***D. alpinum***
ALPINE CLUB MOSS
  2 Branches more or less cylindrical, the leaves, in 5 lengthwise rows, not pressed down (Alaska to Oreg., across much of N North America, and also in Asia) . . . . ***D. sitchense***, pl. 19
SITKA CLUB MOSS

Huperzia

1 Largest leaves 6–10 mm long, typically widest above the middle of their length (upright stems to about 20 cm tall; usually along streams in forests; N Brit. Col. to N Oreg.) . . . . ***H. occidentalis*** (*Lycopodium selago* var. *occidentale*)
WESTERN FIR MOSS

1 Largest leaves not more than 7 mm long, narrowly oval, not widest above the middle of their length (in our region not likely to be found below about 1500 ft., 460 m)
  2 Upright stems commonly at least 12 cm tall (sometimes 20 cm); leafy buds produced by 2–3 circles of leaves at the tips of stems (Alaska to Wash., also E Asia) . . . . ***H. miyoshiana***
PACIFIC FIR MOSS
  2 Upright stems not often so much as 12 cm tall; leafy buds produced by leaves at various levels along the stems (Alaska to Wash., also E Asia) . . . . ***H. haleakalae***
ALPINE FIR MOSS

Lycopodium

1 Conelike sporangium-bearing structures 2 or more on upper branches of upright stems (the leaves on these branches and a portion of the main stem fewer and more widely separated than the leaves lower down; Alaska to Calif., also E of the crest of the Cascades and in E North America) . . . . ***L. clavatum***, pl. 20
GROUND PINE, RUNNING PINE

1 Conelike sporangium-bearing structures single at the tips of main stems or branches that are densely leafy throughout
  2 Conelike sporangium-bearing structures borne at the tips of unbranched main stems; horizontal stems exposed on the surface of the ground; most leaves 5–8 mm long, not prickly (Alaska to Wash. and across much of North America) . . . . ***L. annotinum***
STIFF CLUB MOSS

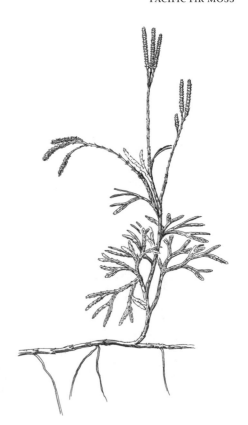

Diphasiastrum complanatum,
northern running pine

2 Conelike sporangium-bearing structures borne at the tips of branch stems; horizontal stems buried; leaves to about 5 mm long, those on main stems below the branches somewhat prickly (Alaska to Wash., also in Asia and across much of North America) . . . . **L. dendroideum** (*L. obscurum* var. *dendroideum*)
PRICKLY TREE CLUB MOSS

MARSILEACEAE Marsilea Family

Plants of the marsilea family grow partly submerged in shallow fresh water or in mud that has been exposed by a drop in the water level. The leaves, arising singly or in groups along creeping stems, are either substantial, with four palmately arranged, wedge-shaped leaflets at the top of a hairy petiole, or very slender and only about 2–5 cm long. Sporangia develop within short-stalked, egg-shaped or round capsules (sporocarps) attached to the stems.

1 Leaves about 0.5 mm wide, not more than 5 cm long, without leaflets; mostly restricted to shallow vernal pools and rarely seen . . . . **Pilularia americana**
AMERICAN PILLWORT

1 Leaves to about 15 cm long, with 4 leaflets (commonly 1–1.5 cm long and widest at the tip) diverging from the end of a hairy petiole; at the margins of lakes, ponds, and slow streams, and sometimes in marshlands . . . . **Marsilea vestita**, p. 52
CLOVER FERN

> *Marsilea oligospora* (*M. vestita* var. *oligospora*) found E of the crest of the Cascades in Oreg. and Wash., and also in Calif., Idaho, Montana, and Wyoming, differs from the more widespread *M. vestita* in that its petioles and leaflets are very hairy instead of just slightly hairy. Furthermore, of the 2 teeth on the basal portion of capsules within which sporangia develop, the upper one is typically low, blunt, and sometimes scarcely noticeable rather than slender and pointed, as it is in typical *M. vestita*.

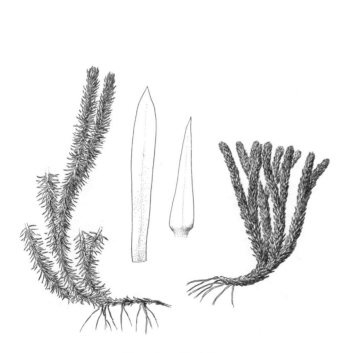

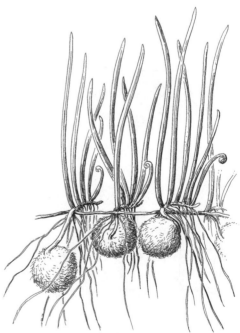

Huperzia occidentalis,
western fir moss

Pilularia americana,
American pillwort

SELAGINELLACEAE Spike-Moss Family

Species of *Selaginella*, like club mosses, superficially resemble some true mosses because of their habit of growth. Their sporangia, sometimes conspicuously orange, are produced on the inner faces of slightly modified leaves clustered on more or less quadrangular terminal portions of the stems. Selaginellas that grow in exposed situations are usually extremely drought resistant. They may appear to be lifeless after a long episode of dry weather but quickly recover after a few rainy days.

Selaginella

1 Sterile leaves oval, less than twice as long as wide, and of 2 sizes: the lower ones (directed outward) slightly larger and more broadly oval than the leaves of the 2 rows above them, and with short, pointed tips (in shady, damp places in the Columbia River Gorge and some similar situations in N Oreg., S Wash., and Idaho; easily found at Multnomah Falls, Multnomah Co., Oreg.) . . . . ***S. douglasii***
DOUGLAS' SELAGINELLA

1 Sterile leaves mostly 4–5 times as long as wide (and tapering gradually to a slender tip)
  2 Bristles at the tips of sterile leaves at least one-fourth as long as the blades and often more than 1 mm long, giving the tips of the sterile branches a fuzzy appearance; plants forming dense cushions, most of the branch stems upright (mid to high montane) . . . . ***S. scopulorum*** (*S. densa* var. *scopulorum*)
ROCKY MOUNTAIN SELAGINELLA

  2 Bristles at the tips of the sterile leaves much less than one-fourth as long as the blades; plants sprawling and often forming mats but not dense cushions in which most stems are upright
    3 Stems often more than 20 cm long, branching loosely and usually growing on tree trunks, especially of *Acer macrophyllum* and *Alnus rubra,* in damp forests near the coast, but sometimes found on damp rocks . . . . ***S. oregana***, pl. 21
OREGON SELAGINELLA

    3 Stems rarely more than 10 cm long, forming rather tight mats in rocky habitats (common in lowland areas) . . . . ***S. wallacei***, pl. 22
WALLACE'S SELAGINELLA

Marsilea vestita,
clover fern

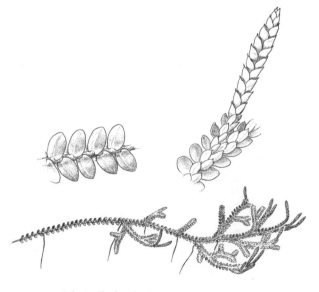

Selaginella douglasii,
Douglas' selaginella

Needle-Leaved, Cone-Bearing Trees and Their Relatives

C ONE-BEARING PLANTS do not have flowers, and their seeds are not enclosed by tissue comparable to that of a fruit. They are therefore assigned to a group called gymnosperms, whose name means "naked seeds." In nearly all species native to our region, the seeds are borne on the surface of overlapping scales that eventually become woody, like those of a cone of a pine, fir, or cypress. In junipers, however, the cone scales become fused together and remain fleshy; in a yew, each seed becomes loosely surrounded by a fleshy cup.

The formation of seeds is preceded by a sexual process. The cone scales first produce spores that develop in situ into microscopic female plants that contain egg cells. These can be fertilized by sperm nuclei developing in microscopic male plants derived from pollen grains that have landed on the cone scales. The pollen is produced on the underside of scales that make up small, short-lived conelike structures. In yews, the sexual process takes place on the structure where the single seed eventually develops.

In the cone-bearing plants in our region, the leaves are either needlelike, as in pines, firs, and redwood, or scalelike, as in cypresses and most junipers. Keys to genera with two or more species are listed alphabetically after this key. For those who wish to have a key to families represented in our region, this follows the keys to species of the various genera.

1 Low shrub with prostrate branches (leaves needlelike but rarely so much as 1.5 cm long, mostly in whorls of 3; seed cones fleshy, the scales fused, greenish at first, then bluish and coated with a waxy deposit; coastal, usually on bluffs and backshores of sandy beaches, but also montane) . . . . *Juniperus communis*, pl. 25
COMMON JUNIPER, GROUND JUNIPER
Variation in *J. communis* is discussed on p. 57.
1 Substantial tree or at least very large shrub
  2 Leaves scalelike on normal mature foliage (needlelike leaves are present on small seedlings and some-times on abnormal specimens)
    3 Seed cones somewhat fleshy, the scales fused together and not separating when ripe (cones greenish at first, becoming bluish, covered with a waxy coating) . . . . *Juniperus*
    3 Seed cones becoming woody, the scales separating at maturity . . . . *Calocedrus-Chamaecyparis-Cupressus-Thuja* **complex**
  2 Leaves needlelike
    4 Needles either in bundles of 2 or more, or numerous at the tips of short side branches

5 Needles in bundles of 2 or more; seed cones without exposed sterile bracts alternating with seed-bearing scales; evergreen trees .... *Pinus*

5 Needles numerous at the tips of short side branches; seed cones with conspicuously exposed sterile bracts alternating with seed-bearing scales; deciduous trees (montane, common E of the crest of the Cascades but rarely encountered on the W slope) .... *Larix occidentalis*
WESTERN LARCH

> In *L. lyallii,* Lyall's larch or alpine larch, which grows at high elevations on the E slope of the Cascades of S Brit. Col. and Wash., and also in E Brit. Col., Alberta, Idaho, and Montana, the young branches have a cobwebby hairiness, the needles are about as thick as wide, and the cones are generally at least 3.5 cm long; in *L. occidentalis* the cobwebby hairiness is lacking, the needles are obviously wider than thick, and the cones do not often exceed a length of 3.5 cm.

4 Needles neither in bundles nor clustered at the tips of short side branches

6 Bare portions of branches rough due to persistent stalks, to about 1 mm long, of needles that have been shed; needles usually from about half as thick as wide to fully as thick as wide, stiff and with prickly tips .... *Picea*

6 Bare portions of branches not especially rough, the stalks of needles that have been shed either no longer present or much less than 1 mm long; needles not so much as half as thick as wide and without prickly tips

7 Needles narrowing to pointed tips

8 Needles yellow-green on the underside; seeds borne singly in fleshy cups, these red at maturity and soon disappearing .... *Taxus brevifolia*, pl. 36
WESTERN YEW

8 Needles dark green on both surfaces; seeds produced in cones about 2.5 cm long, these persisting for at least several months (coastal, Curry Co., Oreg., to Calif.) .... *Sequoia sempervirens*, pl. 37
COAST REDWOOD

7 Needles narrowing to blunt or even notched tips

9 Seed cones pointing upward, generally restricted to the upper branches, usually at least 8 cm long, and falling apart or knocked apart after reaching maturity .... *Abies*

9 Seed cones hanging downward when mature and present on most parts of the tree, retaining their integrity long after seeds have been shed and even after falling

10 Cones without 3-pointed bracts alternating with seed-bearing scales (needles, in the common lowland species, of decidedly unequal lengths) .... *Tsuga*

10 Cones (mostly 5–8 cm long) with 3-pointed bracts alternating with seed-bearing scales .... *Pseudotsuga menziesii* var. *menziesii*, pl. 34
DOUGLAS' FIR, the state tree of Oregon

> In *P. menziesii* var. *menziesii,* the bracts that alternate with seed-bearing scales are pressed down instead of spreading slightly outward as they typically do in var. *glauca,* which has a wide distribution E of the crest of the Cascades and southward as far as Texas and extreme N Mexico. The needles of var. *menziesii,* moreover, are less inclined than those of var. *glauca* to have a grayish or bluish cast.

Abies

1 Needles nearly flat, considerably broader than thick, and without 2 faint lengthwise whitish lines on the upper surface

2 Needles dark green above, white beneath (except on the midrib), most of those on lower branches notched at the tip

3 Most needles on lower branches spreading outward; seed cones greenish (common in the lowlands down to nearly sea level but also found at considerably higher elevations) .... *A. grandis*, pl. 28
GRAND FIR

3 Many needles on lower branches, because of the way they twist at the base, directed upward and forward so that the stem is mostly hidden; seed cones purplish (mostly in Cascades and Olympic Mountains at 1000–4000 ft., 300–1220 m, but occasionally near sea level on the Olympic Peninsula and in the Puget Sound region) . . . . *A. amabilis*
AMABILIS FIR, LOVELY FIR, RED FIR

2 Needles grayish or bluish green on both surfaces, not notched at the tip

  4 Needles 4–7 cm long; scales of seed cones usually wider than long (in the Cascades and Siskiyou Mountains of SW Oreg. and NW Calif., also E of the Cascades; in our region mostly between about 3000 and 5000 ft., 910–1520 m, but occasionally found at lower or higher elevations) . . . . *A. concolor*
WHITE FIR

  4 Needles rarely if ever 4 cm long; scales of cones not wider than long (montane, Alaska to Calif. and eastward; in our region mostly well above 5000 ft., 1520 m) . . . . *A. lasiocarpa*
ALPINE FIR

1 Needles so thick that they may appear to be 4-sided, with 2 faint lengthwise whitish lines on the upper surface; seed cones with conspicuous bracts protruding beyond the seed-bearing scales

  5 Bracts of seed cones protruding to the extent that they are evident over most of the surface of the cones; cones usually 12–16 cm long (in the Cascades, Siskiyou Mountains of SW Oreg. and NW Calif., and in some places in the Coast Ranges of Oreg. and S Wash., mostly above 3000 ft., 910 m, but occasionally lower) . . . . *A. procera*
NOBLE FIR

  5 Bracts of seed cones not protruding to the extent that they are evident over more than one-fourth of the surface of the cones; cones to more than 20 cm long (Siskiyou Mountains of SW Oreg. and NW Calif., mostly above 4000 ft., 1220 m) . . . . *A. magnifica* subsp. *shastensis*
SHASTA RED FIR

Abies procera and A. magnifica subsp. shastensis intergrade to some extent; the latter is in fact considered by some specialists to be a hybrid, A. procera × magnifica.

Larix occidentalis,
western larch

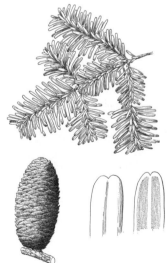

Abies amabilis,
lovely fir

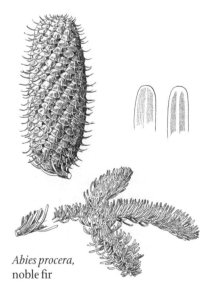

Abies procera,
noble fir

Calocedrus-Chamaecyparis-Cupressus-Thuja Complex

Some species of the *Calocedrus-Chamaecyparis-Cupressus-Thuja* complex are usually called cedars. True cedars (*Cedrus*), none of which is native to North America, are members of the pine family (Pinaceae) and thus closely related to pines, spruces, firs, and hemlocks.

1 Branchlets nearly cylindrical, the scalelike leaves all of 1 type (Curry, Josephine, and Jackson Cos., Oreg., to Calif., mostly above 3500 ft., 1070 m) . . . . *Cupressus bakeri*
BAKER'S CYPRESS

1 Branchlets flattened, the scalelike leaves of 2 types, pairs of one type alternating with those of the other type
   2 Seed cones nearly round
      3 Underside of branchlets with a whitish deposit forming a pattern of repeating x's; cones about 8 mm wide, usually with 4–6 scales (close to the coast; Coos Co., Oreg., to Calif. but also extending into the Siskiyou Mountains of SW Oreg.) . . . . *Chamaecyparis lawsoniana* (*Cupressus lawsoniana*), pl. 23
LAWSON'S CYPRESS, PORT ORFORD CEDAR
      3 Underside of branchlets without an obvious whitish deposit; cones 10–12 mm wide, usually with 7–10 scales, each with a pointed outgrowth (Siskiyou Mountains of SW Oreg. and NW Calif., otherwise mostly in the Cascades and Olympic Mountains) . . . . *Chamaecyparis nootkatensis* (*Cupressus nootkatensis*), pl. 24
YELLOW CEDAR, ALASKA CEDAR
   2 Seed cones elongated
      4 Tips of the scalelike leaves on the flat side of the branchlets reaching beyond the tips of those at the edges; leaves rarely so much as twice as long as wide; cones 1–1.5 cm long, usually with 5 pairs of obvious scales (the upper- and lowermost scales, however, not producing seeds) . . . . *T. plicata*, pl. 27
WESTERN RED CEDAR, the provincial tree of British Columbia
      4 Tips of the scalelike leaves on the flat side of the branchlets not reaching beyond the tips of those at the edges; leaves commonly at least twice as long as wide; cones 2–2.5 cm long, with 1 pair of seed-producing scales and 2 pairs of smaller scales at the base (Cascades and westward, from Marion Co., Oreg., to Baja Calif.) . . . . *Calocedrus decurrens*
INCENSE CEDAR, PENCIL CEDAR

Juniperus

1 Substantial tree or at least a very large shrub; leaves scalelike (unless the plant is abnormal, diseased, or only a small seedling); mostly in inland habitats (but *J. scopulorum* occurring near shore on S Vancouver Island, Gulf Islands, Brit. Col., and San Juan Islands, NE Olympic Peninsula, and Skagit and Island Cos., Wash.)
   2 Leaves mostly in whorls of 3 (making the branchlets nearly cylindrical), their margins very finely serrated and their upper surface usually with a resin-filled gland (use magnification of at least 15–20×) (Jackson Co., Oreg., to Calif.; also E of the Cascades) . . . . *J. occidentalis* subsp. *occidentalis*
WESTERN JUNIPER
   2 Leaves mostly opposite, their margins not finely serrated, and the shallow glands on their upper surface not conspicuously filled with resin (S Vancouver Island, Gulf Islands, Brit. Col., and San Juan Islands, Skagit and Island Cos., Wash., and a few adjacent areas; otherwise E of the Cascades) . . . . *J. scopulorum*, pl. 26
ROCKY MOUNTAIN JUNIPER

Calocedrus decurrens, incense cedar

1 Shrub with main stem and branches prostrate; leaves needlelike but not often more than 1.5 cm long, mostly in whorls of 3 . . . . *J. communis*, pl. 25

COMMON JUNIPER, GROUND JUNIPER

The trailing-stemmed, tightly matted form of *J. communis* growing in the Cascades and Olympic Mountains, mostly above 5000 ft. (1520 m), is sometimes given the varietal name *montana*. A similar plant found in the Siskiyou Mountains of SW Oreg. and NW Calif., and also on bluffs and backshores of sandy beaches along the coast, Wash. to Calif., has especially long, spreading branches and is less inclined to form tight mats; it is sometimes given the varietal name *jackii* but is perhaps just an ecotype of *montana*. The species as a whole is widely distributed in the N Hemisphere and varies extensively in habit of growth, and outside our region there are bushy or treelike forms that may reach heights of several meters.

Picea

1 Cone scales (rather thick for a spruce) with smooth margins; needles not sharp-tipped; branchlets slender, conspicuously drooping (tree to about 25 m tall; Josephine Co., Oreg., to Calif., mostly above 4000 ft., 1220 m) . . . . *P. breweriana*

WEEPING SPRUCE

1 Cone scales with decidedly irregular margins; needles sharp-tipped; branchlets stout, mostly spreading outward, not conspicuously drooping (trees to more than 40 m tall)

  2 Needles typically about twice as wide as thick, nearly flat on the upper surface; cones usually 6–9 cm long (mostly at or near the open coast, Alaska to Calif., but occasionally in the Puget Sound region, San Juan Islands, and Gulf Islands) . . . . *P. sitchensis*, pl. 29

SITKA SPRUCE

  2 Needles typically almost or fully as thick as wide, often somewhat 4-angled; cones not often so much as 6 cm long, generally 4–5 cm (mostly above 3000 ft., 910 m, E of the crest of the Cascades but known to occur in a few places on the W slope, in the Olympic Mountains, Wash., and in the Siskiyou Mountains of SW Oreg. and NW Calif.) . . . . *P. engelmannii* var. *engelmannii*

ENGELMANN'S SPRUCE

The range of *P. engelmannii* extends to Mexico, where the slightly different var. *mexicana* also occurs.

Pinus

1 Needles in bundles of 2 (when counting needles, look at several bundles because a few of these may not have the typical number)

  2 Needles dark green; bark usually with distinct lengthwise furrows as well as scaly, to more than 2 cm thick on old trees; seed cones usually conspicuously asymmetrical; height rarely exceeding 15 m; on coastal bluffs, dunes, bogs, Alaska to Calif.; also abundant in Puget Sound region, San Juan Islands, and Gulf Islands, but see the note following the other choice 2 . . . . . *P. contorta* subsp. *contorta*, pl. 31

SHORE PINE, COAST PINE

  2 Needles yellowish green; bark scaly but without lengthwise furrows, rarely more than 1 cm thick; seed cones only slightly asymmetrical; height commonly more than 20 m; trees characteristically forming dense montane forests, mostly in the Cascades and eastward . . . . *P. contorta* subsp. *murrayana*

LODGEPOLE PINE

Trees in the Puget Sound region, San Juan Islands, and Gulf Islands are often more than 15 m tall and have bark that is not markedly furrowed. In these respects they resemble *P. contorta* subsp. *murrayana*. Some authorities recognize another subspecies, *latifolia*, which is montane, grows tall, and has bark like that of *murrayana* but that tends to have asymmetrical cones that persist rather than falling off soon after shedding seeds. The range given for *latifolia* extends from the Cascades of Wash. and Oreg. northward, eastward, and southeastward; the range of *murrayana* would be from the southernmost portion of the Cascades of Wash. to Calif.

1 Needles in bundles of 3 or 5
  3 Needles in bundles of 3
    4 Seed cones 8–15 cm long, obviously asymmetrical, often remaining on the tree for many years and rarely opening except during fires (Josephine and Curry Cos., Oreg., to Calif.) . . . . ***P. attenuata***, pl. 30
           KNOBCONE PINE
    4 Seed cones not obviously asymmetrical, usually opening after reaching maturity
      5 Seed cones 15–25 cm long, the upper and lower surfaces of the scales about the same color (Douglas, Josephine, and Curry Cos., Oreg., to Calif.) . . . . ***P. jeffreyi***
           JEFFREY PINE
      5 Seed cones rarely more than 15 cm long, the lower surface of the scales usually darker than the upper surface (Siskiyou Mountain region of SW Oreg. and NW Calif., also at scattered localities in the Willamette Valley and Umpqua River valley, Oreg., and in a few places in W Wash.; otherwise mostly E of the crest of the Cascades, from Brit. Col. southward) . . . .
    . . . . ***P. ponderosa*** var. ***ponderosa***, pl. 33
           WESTERN YELLOW PINE, PONDEROSA PINE
  3 Needles in bundles of 5
    6 Seed cones not more than 8 cm long, without stalks, usually remaining at least partly closed and persisting on the tree for several years (montane, mostly above 5000 ft., 1520 m, often dwarfed at high elevations) . . . . ***P. albicaulis***
           WHITEBARK PINE
    6 Seed cones usually more than 15 cm long and with obvious stalks, typically opening freely
      7 Mature seed cones usually 25–40 cm long; needles usually 6–9 cm long, tapering gradually to a pointed tip (Cascades from Linn Co., Oreg., southward, and Siskiyou Mountains, to Calif. and Baja Calif.) . . . . ***P. lambertiana***
           SUGAR PINE
      7 Mature seed cones usually 15–25 cm long; needles usually 4–7 cm long, tapering rather abruptly to a blunt or pointed tip (lowlands of Puget Sound region, San Juan Islands, and adjacent areas; also in the Cascades, Olympic Mountains, Wash., Siskiyou Mountains, Oreg., to Calif.; also E of the Cascades) . . . . ***P. monticola***, pl. 32
           WESTERN WHITE PINE

Tsuga

1 Tip of tree usually drooping; needles on each branchlet of varying length, the shortest ones only about half as long as the longest ones; seed cones, after opening, not more than about 2.5 cm long; seed-bearing scales distinctly longer than wide (abundant in many coniferous forests up to about 5000 ft., 1520 m) . . . . .
  . . . . ***T. heterophylla***, pl. 35
           WESTERN HEMLOCK, the state tree of Washington
1 Tip of tree typically upright; needles on each branchlet mostly all about the same length; seed cones, after opening, mostly 4–6 cm long; seed-bearing scales as wide or slightly wider than long (montane, not common below about 5000 ft., 1520 m) . . . . ***T. mertensiana***
           MOUNTAIN HEMLOCK

Cone-Bearing Plant Families

1 Each seed borne singly within a fleshy cup, this red at maturity; pollen-producing cones with structures that resemble stamens of flowering plants because the pollen sacs are stalked (leaves alternate, needlelike, but considerably wider than thick, pointed at the tip) . . . . **Taxaceae**
           YEW FAMILY (*Taxus*)
1 Seeds borne in cones; pollen-producing cones without structures that resemble stamens of flowering plants (the pollen sacs are on the undersides of the scales)

2 Leaves (usually scalelike but sometimes in the form of needles to about 1.5 cm long) opposite or in whorls; mature seed cones either fleshy, with the scales fused, or woody and consisting of not more than 10 seed-bearing scales . . . . **Cupressaceae**
CYPRESS FAMILY (*Calocedrus, Chamaecyparis, Cupressus, Juniperus, Thuja*)

2 Leaves needlelike, alternate; mature seed cones woody and consisting of more than 12 seed-bearing scales

   3 Seed-bearing scales flattened, each bearing 2 seeds on the upper surface . . . . **Pinaceae**
PINE FAMILY (*Abies, Larix, Picea, Pinus, Pseudotsuga, Tsuga*)

   3 Seed-bearing scales not flattened, each usually bearing several seeds . . . . **Taxodiaceae**
BALD-CYPRESS FAMILY (*Sequoia*)

      Taxodiaceae and Cupressaceae have been combined into one family, called Cupressaceae, on the basis of morphological and DNA evidence.

Flowering Plants

A TYPICAL FLOWER consists of five major components that originate from the basal portion called the receptacle. The petals, whether separate or joined together, form what is called the corolla. The sepals, just below the petals, form the calyx. The parts concerned directly with reproduction are the stamens and the pistil or pistils. Stamens, in the anther sacs at their tips, produce pollen grains capable of developing into microscopic male plants. Pistils also produce spores, but these remain in the tissue, where they develop into microscopic female plants, each consisting of only a few cells, usually eight.

By the time a pollen grain, at first with only a single nucleus, has landed on the sticky stigma at the tip of pistil, it has two nuclei. One of these divides again, forming two sperm nuclei. After the tube produced by the pollen grain grows down into the pistil and its tip reaches a female sexual stage, one of its sperm can fertilize the egg. This develops into an embryo that becomes enclosed by tissue that forms a seed. Most of the pistil ripens into a fruit with as many seeds as have been produced within it.

Are you wondering what happened to the unlucky sperm nucleus that did not get to fertilize an egg? It generally unites with two nuclei of the female sexual stage, forming a tissue called endosperm. This is really a separate plant, just like the embryo, but it is programmed to grow, store up food, and live just long enough to nourish the embryo during its early development and eventual germination into a little plant. When you chew off kernels of corn from a cob, you are in fact eating many separate fruits, each one consisting mostly of a seed in which much of the space is occupied by endosperm tissue associated with an embryo.

The species of flowering plants are many times more numerous than those of gymnosperms. What you will see, as you key out families, genera, and species, is that the flowers of many of them deviate from the pattern described for a typical example. In some species, pistillate and staminate flowers may be separate, or even on separate plants. Many flowers have no corolla; some have no calyx. When a corolla is present, it may consist of many petals or be reduced to the point that there is only one or none. The number of stamens and pistils and the structure of these also varies extensively. Much of your keying experience will require careful study of fruits. Are they fleshy or dry when mature? Do they contain a single seed, a few seeds, or many? The more you learn as you look at flowers and fruits, as well as at leaves and stems, the faster your expertise will increase.

There are three main keys that deal with flowering plants. The first deals only with trees, shrubs, and vines whose stems become woody. The second, Herbaceous Flowering Plants (p. 70), is a key to families of plants that are either completely herbaceous or at least not so woody as to be noticeably so. The rest of the book consists of keys to families, which are arranged alphabetically in two groups: Dicotyledonous Families (p. 86) and Monocotyledonous Families (p. 365), with keys to genera and species. Dicotyledons may be distinguished from monocotyledons by the following comparison:

DICOTYLEDONS

Embryo plant within the seed has two cotyledons (first leaves) that will become evident at the time of germination (cotyledons often store most of the food that will be used for growth of the young plant during and for a time after germination; the two halves of a lima bean or green pea consist mostly of cotyledons in which food has been stored)

Sepals, petals, and stamens almost always in sets of five (but there are exceptions)

Leaf blades typically with a netlike arrangement of veins

Bundles of conducting cells, when seen in cross sections of stems, forming a ring or succession of rings

Stems, when seen in cross section, with a cambium (a ring of undifferentiated tissue that gives rise to conducting cells on both sides of it)

MONOCOTYLEDONS

Embryo plant within the seed has a single cotyledon that becomes evident at the time of germination

Sepals, petals, and stamens almost always in sets of three, rarely four, never five

Leaf blades typically with parallel arrangement of veins (but sometimes with a netlike arrangement)

Bundles of conducting cells, when seen in cross sections of stems, usually scattered and not forming a ring or succession of rings

Stems, when seen in cross section, without a cambium

Broad-Leaved Trees, Shrubs, and Woody Vines

This key, so far as possible, takes advantage of easily observed features such as growth form and characteristics of leaves and stems. In some cases, however, it is essential to examine inflorescences (including the catkins of willows, alders, oaks, and their relatives), flowers, and fruits. If, after you reach a particular couplet, the specimen you are keying lacks one or more structures necessary for making a firm decision, try both choices; one or the other may lead you in the right direction. Remember that the more you work with keys, the better you prepare yourself for dealing with uncertainties. Furthermore, you soon are able to leap over sections of the key that you know are irrelevant.

Sometimes this key leads you only to the name of a family. In that case, turn to the family and continue keying. Rather frequently, however, the key will lead you to a particular genus or even a single species within a family, so you should turn to the appropriate page in order to finish keying as well as look for illustrations that will help confirm your identification.

This key does not include all plants that botanists call subshrubs. These are woody only at the base, and their woodiness may not even be perceived unless they are uprooted. Species that fit into this category include, for instance, some members of *Castilleja* (paintbrushes), which most persons think of as herbaceous perennials and that can be reached by using the key, Herbaceous Flowering Plants. Common names of species are omitted from these keys, but they will be found in the complete keys to plants of the individual families.

1 Distinctly woody vines (such as blackberries, honeysuckles, or grapes) or low, creeping plants that are only slightly woody (these are not likely to rise more than 5 cm above the ground except when producing upright inflorescences)
    2 Leaves and stems opposite (look carefully, because one stem or leaf of a pair may fail to develop; in the case of deciduous plants that have dropped their leaves, the presence of opposite leaf scars will help)
        3 Leaves compound; flowers without a corolla but with petal-like white sepals (pistils numerous, each developing into a dry fruit with a persistent, feathery style; deciduous) . . . . *Clematis*, Ranunculaceae, p. 298
        3 Leaves not compound; flowers with a corolla

    4 Petals (5, about 2 mm long, white) separate (plant creeping, evergreen, sometimes forming dense mats; leaf blades oval, not often more than 2 cm long; flowers crowded in short, terminal inflorescences; fruit dry at maturity) .... ***Whipplea modesta***, pl. 338, Hydrangeaceae

    4 Petals united to the extent that there is a distinct tube and 5 lobes (the lobes may not all be the same size)

        5 Low, creeping evergreen plant, often on rotting wood; flowers hanging down, borne in pairs on upright leafless stems about 10 cm tall; corolla 1–1.5 cm long, approximately funnel-shaped, white to pink; fruit dry at maturity ..... ***Linnaea borealis*** **var.** ***longiflorus***, pl. 197, Caprifoliaceae

        5 Conspicuous vines, either evergreen or deciduous, generally climbing or clambering; flowers borne in clusters at the tips of the stems; corolla usually more than 1.5 cm long, orange or mostly pink; fruit fleshy .... ***Lonicera***, Caprifoliaceae, p. 180

2 Leaves and stems alternate (or mostly alternate, if some are in whorls, as they often are in *Empetrum nigrum*, pl. 240, Empetraceae, p. 204)

    6 Deciduous plants climbing with the aid of tendrils (modified leaves that appear near the tips of growing stems)

        7 Only the lower portions of stems likely to be woody, these portions sometimes with slender prickles; leaf blades not often more than 5 cm long, oval or nearly heart-shaped, neither lobed, toothed, nor hairy (staminate and pistillate flowers on separate plants; both types of flowers with 6 equal, greenish perianth segments; fruit fleshy, black when ripe; Rogue River valley, Oreg., to Calif.) .... ***Smilax***, Smilacaceae, p. 470

        7 Stems woody nearly throughout, without prickles; leaf blades roughly heart-shaped, also distinctly lobed and coarsely toothed, generally more than 10 cm long (flowers, borne in panicles, with 5 small greenish petals; fruits similar to those of a cultivated grape, to 1 cm wide, purplish and coated with a whitish bloom when ripe; Umpqua and Rogue River valleys, Oreg. to Calif.) .... ***Vitis californica***, Vitaceae, p. 364

            Cultivated species of grapes occasionally become established around abandoned homesteads and in other situations where they may appear to be wild. Certain of these are mentioned before the key to Vitaceae.

    6 Plants without tendrils

        8 Stems with prickles (leaf blades heart-shaped to variously lobed or compound, none modified as tendrils; petals and sepals 5; fruit a blackberry, consisting in reality of an aggregate of small, fleshy individual fruits, each enclosing a single seed; mostly large, coarse vines but sometimes forming a low ground cover; mostly deciduous) .... ***Rubus***, Rosaceae, p. 318

        8 Stems without prickles

            9 Vines climbing with the aid of aerial roots, and with palmately lobed leaf blades at least 4 cm long and wide (flowers, when produced, borne in umbel-like inflorescences, small, with 5 greenish petals; fruits about 5 mm wide, fleshy, black; escaping from gardens and undesirable in natural areas) .... ***Hedera helix***, Araliaceae

            9 Low, creeping plants with slender leaves about 1 cm long, grooved on the underside (staminate and pistillate flowers separate, barely 2 mm in diameter, with what may be interpreted as 3 bracts, 3 somewhat membranous sepals, and 3 greenish to purplish petals; fruit fleshy, about 5 mm in diameter, blackish (on coastal bluffs and also in some montane habitats) .... ***Empetrum nigrum***, pl. 240, Empetraceae, p. 204

1 Trees, shrubs, and also subshrubs that are woody only at the base

    10 Flowers crowded in heads like those of a dandelion, thistle, or daisy (corollas of individual flowers either all tubular and usually 5-lobed, or the marginal corollas drawn out into flat, raylike structures, as in a daisy; see the introduction to the family Asteraceae to confirm that you are in the right group, which in our region includes proportionately few shrubs and subshrubs—some species that are not obviously woody are not in the portion of this key because most persons are likely to think of them as strictly herbaceous plants; they are, however, in the complete key to genera and species of Asteraceae)

11 Ray flowers (yellow) present on some or all flower heads

  12 Leaf blades lobed and woolly-hairy; rays, when present, 2–5 mm long (flower heads in dense clusters; coastal, Coos Co., Oreg., to Calif.) . . . . *Eriophyllum staechadifolium*, pl. 114, Asteraceae

  12 Leaf blades neither lobed nor woolly-hairy; ray flowers consistently present, the rays usually at least 5 mm long

    13 Pappus consisting of slender awnlike structures, these noticeably broader at the base than at the tip and often shed early; phyllaries secreting a sticky gum . . . . *Grindelia*, Asteraceae, p. 136

    13 Pappus consisting of slender bristles; phyllaries not secreting a sticky gum

      14 Pappus with 2 series of bristles, those of the outer circle much shorter than those of the inner; stems extensively branched, the plants bushy (mostly in prairies, including some areas on Whidbey Island, Island Co., Wash.) . . . . *Heterotheca villosa* var. *villosa*, pl. 124, Asteraceae

      14 Pappus with 1 series of bristles . . . . *Ericameria-Pyrrocoma-Columbiadoria-Hazardia* complex, Asteraceae, p. 131

11 Flower heads without rays

  15 Staminate and pistillate flower heads on separate plants (leaves mostly 5–15 mm long; involucre 3–5 mm high; corollas white; pappus bristles in 2 series; Tillamook Co., Oreg., to Calif.) . . . . *Baccharis pilularis*, pl. 87, Asteraceae

  15 All or most flowers in each head with stamens and a pistil

    16 Phyllaries in only 1–2 series

      17 Stems white-woolly; leaf blades oval, nearly smooth-margined, white-woolly on the underside; corollas yellowish . . . . *Luina hypoleuca*, pl. 132, Asteraceae

      17 Leaf blades broadest near the base (sometimes nearly triangular), coarsely toothed, not white-woolly on the underside; corollas pink or purplish pink (Douglas Co., Oreg., to Calif.; also in the Cascades and E of the Cascades) . . . . *Ageratina occidentalis*, pl. 64, Asteraceae

    16 Phyllaries in 3 or more series

      18 Corollas white; phyllaries with prominent lengthwise ridges (leaf blades with glandular dots; SW Oreg. to Calif.) . . . . *Brickellia*, Asteraceae, p. 127

      18 Corollas yellow; phyllaries without several prominent lengthwise ridges (but there may be a prominent keel along the midline)

        19 Pappus bristles in 2 series, those of the outer series much shorter than those of the inner (plants not often more than 50 cm tall; leaf blades usually about 4–5 times as long as wide; most commonly found along dry streambeds or gravel bars of rivers, but occasionally in other habitats) . . . . *Heterotheca oregona*, pl. 123, Asteraceae

        19 Pappus bristles varying in length but all in 1 series and none much shorter than the others . . . . *Ericameria-Pyrrocoma-Columbiadoria-Hazardia* complex, Asteraceae, p. 131

10 Flowers not crowded into heads like those of a dandelion, thistle, or daisy

  20 Leaves mostly opposite or in whorls, sometimes both

    21 Low evergreen shrubs, not often so much as 25 cm tall, with at least 1–2 whorls of leaves below the inflorescences and with at least some opposite leaves below the whorls; margins of leaf blades toothed; petals white to pink or purplish; stamens 10; fruit 5-lobed, dry at maturity; growing in coniferous forests . . . . *Chimaphila*, Ericaceae, p. 208

    21 Plants not in all respects as described in the other choice 21

      22 Leaves compound

        23 Margins of leaflets smooth (leaflets usually 5–7; fruit dry, with a single seed and a broad, thin wing; deciduous tree) . . . . *Fraxinus latifolia*, pl. 386, Oleaceae, p. 263

        23 Margins of leaflets toothed

          24 Deciduous tree; leaves with 3 leaflets (some leaves merely deeply lobed); flowers (some purely staminate) in umbel-like corymbs; fruit dry, much of it consisting of 2 broad winglike structures, 1 joined to each seed . . . . *Acer negundo*, Aceraceae, p. 86

          24 Generally large deciduous shrubs but sometimes treelike; leaves usually with 5–9 leaflets,

sometimes only 3; flowers (all with a pistil and stamens) numerous in compound cymes; fruits fleshy, red or bluish at maturity . . . .***Sambucus***, Caprifoliaceae, p. 181

22 Leaves not compound (but they may be deeply lobed)

  25 Leaf blades palmately lobed

    26 Leaf blades with 3 lobes; corolla 5-lobed, white (flowers at the margin of the inflorescence sometimes larger than the others and sterile); fruit fleshy; deciduous shrubs . . .***Viburnum***, Caprifoliaceae, p. 181

    26 Leaf blades with more than 3 lobes (some may be much smaller than others); petals separate, greenish or nearly white; fruit dry, much of it consisting of 2 broad winglike structures, 1 joined to each seed; small or large deciduous trees . . . .***Acer***, Aceraceae, p. 86

  25 Leaves not palmately lobed

    27 Flowers in drooping, catkinlike inflorescences; pistillate and staminate flowers borne on separate plants; staminate flowers with 4 sepals, pistillate flowers with 2 sepals or none; petals absent; fruits on pistillate inflorescences at first pulpy, then hardening . . . .***Garrya***, Garryaceae, p. 235

    27 Plants not as described in the other choice 27

      28 Flowers obviously irregular, distinctly 2-lipped (anther-bearing stamens 4, sterile fifth stamen sometimes also present)

        29 Flowers with a sterile stamen as well as 4 anther-bearing stamens . . . . ***Penstemon***, ***Keckiella lemmonii***, or ***Nothochelone nemorosa***
see Scrophulariaceae choices 13–14 (p. 339)

        29 Flowers without a sterile stamen (coastal, Curry Co., Oreg., to Calif.) . . . . ***Mimulus aurantiacus***, pl. 567, Scrophulariaceae

      28 Flowers, as evident in the corolla (if present) and calyx, regular and not obviously 2-lipped (in some members of the Caprifoliaceae the corolla tube may show a slight bulge on one side, but the arrangement of corolla lobes is essentially regular)

        30 Stems, buds, and leaves covered with small scales, these easily scratched off with a fingernail (deciduous shrub; staminate and pistillate flowers on separate plants, both types without a corolla but with a calyx whose 4 lobes are at first greenish yellow; fruit fleshy, about 1 cm in diameter, red, and decorated with small yellowish pits) . . . ***Shepherdia canadensis***, pl. 239, Elaeagnaceae, p. 202

        30 Stems, buds, and leaves not covered with small scales

          31 Petals 4, separate, white, to about 1.5 cm long; stamens at least 20 (fruit dry, developing below the level at which the stamens and petals are attached; deciduous shrub) . . . . ***Philadelphus lewisii***, pl. 337, Hydrangeaceae

          31 Petals or corolla lobes not so much as 1 cm long; stamens fewer than 20

            32 Leaf blades to more than 20 cm long, with marginal teeth, conspicuously woolly-hairy on the underside; flowers numerous in elongated inflorescences; calyx with 4 short lobes; corolla mostly lilac or purplish, the tube about 7 mm long, about 4 times as long as wide, the 4 lobes shorter than the tube, spreading outward; occasionally escaping from cultivation . . . . ***Buddleja davidii***, Buddlejaceae, p. 176

            32 Plants not in all respects as described in the other choice 32

              33 Petals attached beneath the edge of a disklike structure within which the pistil is located

                34 Petals 4, less than 2 mm long, reddish brown; leaf blades to about 2 cm long . . . . ***Paxistima myrsinites***, pl. 222, Celastraceae

                34 Petals 5, 3–4 mm long, maroon or brownish purple, dotted with white or pale green; leaf blades commonly more than 5 cm long . . . . ***Euonymus occidentalis*** **var.** ***occidentalis***, pls. 220 & 221, Celastraceae

              33 Petals not attached beneath the edge of a disklike structure within which the pistil is located

35 Petals separate

   36 Leaf blades commonly more than 3 cm long, smooth-margined, not stiff; flowers sometimes in cymes, sometimes in dense hemispherical heads with 4–7 large, white or slightly yellowish bracts beneath them; petals 4, white; fruits fleshy, bright red, white, or bluish; trees or large shrubs ...... ***Cornus***, Cornaceae, p. 197

   36 Leaf blades rarely more than 2 cm long, the margins sometimes toothed, stiff; flowers in cymes; petals 5, white or blue; fruit 3-lobed, dry at maturity; upright or prostrate shrub .... ***Ceanothus***, Rhamnaceae, p. 305

35 Petals united, so that there is at least a short corolla tube

   37 Leaves without distinct petioles; corolla widely open, saucer-shaped (corolla pink or purplish pink; plants not often more than 25 cm tall; in sphagnum bogs) ......
.... ***Kalmia microphylla* subsp. *occidentalis***, pl. 254, Ericaceae

   37 Leaves with distinct petioles; corolla with a substantial tube, not at all saucer-shaped

      38 Leaf blades elongated, usually at least 5 cm long; flowers in pairs in the leaf axils, each pair with 2 large, partly united bracts below it; corolla yellow; fruits black when ripe, the bracts persisting .... ***Lonicera involucrata***, Caprifoliaceae, p. 180

      38 Leaf blades less than twice as long as wide; flowers not regularly paired in the leaf axils; corolla white or pink; fruits white or red when ripe

         39 Upright or sprawling shrubs; leaf blades not toothed but sometimes irregularly lobed, especially when larger than usual; flowers few in each terminal or axillary cluster; corolla usually pink; fruits round, white ....
.... ***Symphoricarpos***, Caprifoliaceae, p. 181

         39 Upright shrubs; leaf blades coarsely toothed; flowers in crowded inflorescences; corolla white; fruit slightly flattened, red when ripe ....
.... ***Viburnum ellipticum***, pl. 204, Caprifoliaceae

20 Leaves alternate

   40 Large tree (to more than 30 m tall); bark reddish, the outer layer peeling off and exposing a smooth surface; leaves evergreen, alternate, the blades usually 5–10 cm long, about twice as long as wide, smooth-margined (toothed on young seedlings); flowers in upright panicles; corolla 6–7 mm long, urn-shaped, 5-lobed, white; fruits (ripe in the fall) 8–10 mm in diameter, fleshy, red, covered with small bumps .... ***Arbutus menziesii***, pl. 242, Ericaceae

   40 Plant not as described in the other choice 40

      41 Flowers (at least the staminate ones) in catkins (plants in this category are oaks, willows, cottonwoods, alders, birches, hazelnuts, wax myrtles, and their relatives)

      42 Fruit a nut at least 1 cm in diameter

         43 Fruit an acorn (a nut partly enclosed by a scaly cup; staminate flowers in catkins)

            44 Staminate catkins upright; scales of cup enclosing the lower portion of the acorn drawn out into slender projections .... ***Lithocarpus***, Fagaceae, p. 232

            44 Staminate catkins drooping; scales of cup enclosing the lower portion of the acorn not drawn out into slender projections .... ***Quercus***, Fagaceae, p. 233

         43 Fruit a nut enclosed by a bur with spinelike outgrowths or by a pair of broad, leaflike bracts

            45 Fruit a nut enclosed by a bur with spinelike outgrowths (there are usually 2–3 nuts in each bur); nuts developing from pistillate flowers at the bases of upright staminate catkins; most leaf blades at least 4 times as long as wide, dark green, smooth-margined ... ***Chrysolepis***, Fagaceae, p. 232

            45 Fruit a nut enclosed by a pair of broad, leaflike bracts; nuts developing from pistillate flowers borne at the tips of young branches that also bear the completely separate staminate catkins; leaf blades not so much as twice as long as wide, light green, with toothed margins ....
.... ***Corylus cornuta* subsp. *californica***, Betulaceae, p. 149

42 Fruit not a nut

  46 Staminate and pistillate catkins on the same plant (but the staminate catkins may be very short-lived); leaf blades with easily visible marginal teeth

    47 Leaf blades with nearly microscopic black dots, these usually most easily seen on the underside near the margins; evergreen, large shrub or tree to about 10 m tall (pistillate catkins, when fruits are mature, slightly resembling blackberries and coated with a whitish, waxy deposit; leaves sometimes aromatic when bruised or rubbed; coastal, Grays Harbor Co., Wash., to Calif.; also near Tofino and Ucluelet, Vancouver Island, Brit. Col.) .... *Myrica californica*, pl. 381, Myricaceae

    47 Leaf blades without black dots; deciduous shrubs or trees

      48 Staminate and pistillate catkins superficially similar (but the staminate catkins about twice as long and drooping), the pistillate catkins not becoming woody and not persisting into the next winter .... *Betula*, Betulaceae, p. 150

      48 Staminate catkins and pistillate catkins distinctly dissimilar, the pistillate catkins more or less egg-shaped (much shorter than the fully developed staminate catkins) and becoming woody, resembling cones of coniferous trees and persisting into the following winter .... *Alnus*, Betulaceae, p. 150

  46 Staminate and pistillate catkins on separate plants; leaf blades of some species with smooth margins, those of other species distinctly toothed (deciduous trees and shrubs)

    49 Leaf blades (usually 3–5 cm long, about 3 times as long as wide) with yellow resin glands on the underside and with marginal teeth absent or only near the tips; fruits developing on pistillate catkins nearly round, 2–3 mm long, roughened by small glands that secrete wax .... *Myrica gale*, pl. 382, Myricaceae

    49 Leaf blades without resin glands on the underside, the margins either smooth or with teeth all around; fruits developing on pistillate catkins longer than wide, smooth or hairy, releasing seeds covered with long white hairs

      50 Leaf blades usually at least twice as long as wide, broadest well above the base .... *Salix*, Salicaceae, p. 324

      50 Leaf blades usually less than twice as long as wide, broadest near the base .... *Populus*, Salicaceae, p. 324

41 Flowers not in catkins

  51 Tree or large shrub; leaves (generally about 4 times as long as wide) with an aroma like that of *Laurus nobilis*, the European laurel or bay tree, used as a seasoning in preparation of food; flowers without petals but with 6 greenish sepals, 9 stamens, and a pistil that develops into an olive-shaped fruit to about 2 cm long, containing a single large seed (SW Oreg. to Calif.) .... *Umbellularia californica*, pl. 365, Lauraceae, p. 254

  51 Plant not as described in the other choice 51

    52 Corolla irregular, either resembling that of a pea (the uppermost petal largest; the 2 lowermost petals united by their lower edges to form a keel-like structure) or consisting of only 1 petal corresponding to the uppermost one of a pea flower; fruit resembling a peapod, dry when mature and with a single row of seeds

      53 Branches, including those bearing flowers, ending in sharp thorns, and mature leaves modified as spines (aggressive and undesirable) .... *Ulex europaea*, Fabaceae

      53 Branches not spine-tipped, and leaves not modified as spines

        54 Branches angled lengthwise; leaves very small, most of them with 3 leaflets (aggressive and undesirable) .... *Cytisus*, Fabaceae, p. 215

        54 Branches not angled lengthwise; leaves conspicuous, palmately or pinnately divided into 7 or more leaflets

55 Leaves palmately divided into 7 or more leaflets; corolla like that of a pea, consisting of 5 petals, the upper one largest, the 2 lowermost ones united by their lower edges to form a keel-like structure (coastal) . . . . ***Lupinus***, Fabaceae, p. 221

55 Leaves pinnately compound, the larger ones usually with at least 11 leaflets; corolla consisting of a single petal, this dark violet-purple, corresponding to the uppermost petal of a pea flower (introduced from E United States; established along the Columbia River, Wash. and Oreg.) . . . . . .
. . . . ***Amorpha fruticosa***, Fabaceae

52 Corolla regular, neither resembling that of a pea nor consisting of only 1 petal; fruit not resembling a peapod

56 Shrubs or small trees with branches or short side branches tapering to sharp tips and functioning as thorns (do not confuse thorns with prickles, which are characteristic of roses, blackberries, and gooseberries and which are outgrowths from the epidermis)

57 Leaf blades (about 2 cm long) with 3 more or less equally prominent veins diverging from the base; flowers small, with white petals, numerous in panicles or racemes; fruit 3-lobed and dry at maturity (in the Cascades and Siskiyou Mountains, Douglas Co., Oreg., to Calif.; not likely to be found below 3000 ft., 910 m) . . . . ***Ceanothus cordulatus***, Rhamnaceae

57 Leaf blades with a single prominent main vein (midrib)

58 Fruit like a cherry or plum, the sepals, for as long as they persist, beneath it (Willamette Valley, from Marion Co., Oreg., S to Calif.) . . . . ***Prunus subcordata***, Rosaceae, p. 317

58 Fruit like a small apple with the sepals, or remnants of these, at the free end

59 Petals not so much as 1 cm long; fruit red or nearly black when ripe; thorns very sharp . . . .
. . . . ***Crataegus***, Rosaceae, p. 312

59 Petals usually about 2 cm long; fruit yellowish, brownish orange, reddish, or purplish when ripe but not really red or blackish; thorns usually not very sharp (leaf blades often with 1–2 small, pointed lobes near the base) . . . . ***Malus fusca***, pl. 513, Rosaceae, p. 308

56 Plants without branches or side branches tapering to sharp tips (but they may have prickles, which are outgrowths of the epidermis and which are characteristic of roses, blackberries, and gooseberries)

60 Stems (and sometimes also the petioles and undersides of the leaf blades) with prickles (if the only sharp points are those of teeth at the margins of the leaf blades, take the other choice 60)

61 Leaf blades compound

62 Petals white or purplish red, not notched at the tip; fruit a raspberry (an aggregate of small, 1-seeded fruits), the sepals, if persisting, below it . . . . ***Rubus***, Rosaceae, p. 318

62 Petals usually pink, slightly notched at the tip; fruit not an aggregate of small fruits, the sepals, if persisting, above it . . . . ***Rosa***, Rosaceae, p. 317

61 Leaf blades palmately lobed but not compound

63 Leaf blades commonly more than 12 cm in diameter, with sharp prickles like those on the petioles and stems; fruits, when ripe, bright red, shiny, slightly flattened . . . .
. . . . ***Oplopanax horridus***, pl. 59, Araliaceae, p. 101

63 Leaf blades not so much as 10 cm in diameter, without prickles (prickles limited to the stems); fruits greenish to purplish when ripe, often with stiff, sometimes gland-tipped hairs, not flattened . . . . ***Ribes***, Grossulariaceae, p. 239

60 Stems without prickles (but if the leaf blades have marginal teeth, these may be sharp-tipped)

64 Leaves compound

65 Most leaves with 3 leaflets (sometimes with an additional pair of leaflets or lobes) . . . .
. . . . **Anacardiaceae**, p. 88

Caution: Of the 2 representatives of Anacardiaceae in our region, the more common one is *Toxicodendron diversilobum* (pl. 42), western poison oak. Contact with it should be avoided!

65 Most leaves with at least 5 leaflets

66 Marginal teeth of leaflets with stiff, sharp tips . . . . *Berberis*, Berberidaceae, p. 148

66 Marginal teeth of leaflets without stiff, sharp tips

  67 Tree or shrub; leaves once-pinnately divided into leaflets not often more than 6 cm long; inflorescence a flat-topped or rounded corymb, the flowers with white petals to about 6 mm long; fruit about 1 cm long, orange or some shade of red . . . . *Sorbus*, Rosaceae, p. 320

  67 Large shrublike plant but technically an herb because it is not woody and dies back each fall; leaves large, divided into 3 main divisions, each of these with 3 or 5 leaflets that may be more than 10 cm long; inflorescence 30–40 cm long, with many small flowers that lack petals; fruit about 4 mm long, dark when ripe (usually in shaded canyons, S Oreg. to Calif.) . . . . *Aralia californica*, pl. 58, Araliaceae, p. 101

64 Leaves not compound

  68 Corolla tubular, 10–15 mm long, with 5 lobes, white to pale purplish; evergreen shrub with evenly toothed leaves to more than 10 cm long; stems and upper surfaces of the leaves sticky, and often blackened by a fungus (Jackson and Josephine Cos., Oreg., to Calif.) . . . . *Eriodictyon californicum*, pl. 339, Hydrophyllaceae

  68 Plants not conforming in all respects to the description in the other choice 68

    69 Corolla about 15–18 mm wide, somewhat saucerlike, with 5 rather indistinct lobes, usually lavender; fruit a fleshy berry about 7–9 mm in diameter; leaf blades elongate-oval, to 5 cm long (SW Oreg. to Calif.) . . . . *Solanum parishii*, Solanaceae

    69 Plants not conforming to the description in the other choice 69

      70 At least some leaf blades lobed

        71 Corolla tubular, 5-lobed; stamens 5; pistil 1; fruit fleshy (deciduous shrubs) . . . . *Ribes*, Grossulariaceae, p. 239

        71 Petals separate; stamens at least 20; pistils several; fruits dry (deciduous shrubs)

          72 Leaf blades about as wide as long, the division into lobes more nearly palmate than pinnate; flowers in corymbs of about 20; petals 4 mm long; usually in situations not far from fresh water . . . . *Physocarpus capitatus*, pl. 515, Rosaceae

          72 Most leaf blades longer than wide, the division into lobes more nearly pinnate than palmate; petals only about 2 mm long . . . . *Holodiscus discolor*, pl. 512, Rosaceae, p. 308

      70 Leaf blades not lobed

        73 Flowers very numerous in each panicle, petals 5, white, pinkish, lavender, or blue, the lower part of each one slender and stalklike; calyx lobes 5, soon deciduous; stamens 5, alternating with the petals; fruit a capsule consisting of 3 divisions, these separating at maturity into nutlets; deciduous or evergreen shrubs, low and creeping to tall, sometimes with side branches forming sharp-tipped thorns . . . . *Ceanothus*, Rhamnaceae, p. 305

        73 Plants not as described in the other choice 73

          74 Leaf blades stiff, evergreen (not more than 3 cm long); flowers without petals; fruit a dry achene, retaining a feathery stigma usually at least 5 cm long . . . . . *Cercocarpus*, Rosaceae, p. 312

          74 Plants not as described in the other choice 74

            75 Clusters of flowers borne within cuplike or tubular involucres, these scattered along the branches or borne in umbel- or headlike inflorescences; flowers without corollas, but the calyces, with 6 lobes, white or colored; the involucres may also be colored; stamens 9; pistil with 3 styles; plants woody only near the base . . . . *Eriogonum*, Polygonaceae, p. 281

            75 Flowers not borne within cuplike or tubular involucres, and the plants not conforming to the rest of the description in the other choice 75

              76 Corolla absent (but the 4 sepals, united at the base, are sometimes yellowish enough to be mistaken for petals; most leaf blades shiny, at least 10 cm long; fruit egg-shaped, about 1 cm long, nearly black when ripe, poisonous; now abundant in Brit. Col., W Wash., and W Oreg.) . . . . *Daphne laureola*, pl. 593, Thymelaeaceae, p. 356

              76 Corolla present, but the flowers may be very small and inconspicuous

77 Staminate and pistillate flowers on separate plants (petals 5–6 mm long on staminate flowers, slightly smaller on pistillate flowers; pistillate flowers with several pistils; fruit fleshy, orange to bluish black; leaves usually at least 5 cm long, about 3 times as long as wide; usually in flower by early March) . . . . *Oemleria cerasiformis*, pl. 514, Rosaceae

77 All flowers with a stamens and a pistil

  78 Petals separate

    79 Stamens numerous (more than 10)

      80 Flowers numerous in elongated or nearly flat inflorescences at the tops of upright stems (several branches of flowers form the inflorescence as a whole); petals less than 3 mm long, white or pink; fruits dry . . . . *Spiraea*, Rosaceae, p. 321

      80 Flowers generally not more than 60 in the inflorescences, these on side branches; petals at least 4 mm long, white; fruits fleshy

        81 Most leaf blades either smooth-margined or toothed all around the margins; fruit like a cherry or plum, with a large seed; sepals, for as long as they persist, below the developing fruit . . . . *Prunus*, Rosaceae, p. 316

        81 Most leaf blades toothed on the upper two-thirds of the margins; fruit usually with 2 small seeds; sepals persisting at the free end of the fruit, as in an apple and most roses . . . . *Amelanchier*, Rosaceae, p. 312

    79 Stamens not more than 10

      82 Stamens 5, alternating with the petals (petals small, greenish; the inflorescences, with few flowers, therefore not showy; fruit fleshy when ripe; tree or large shrub) . . . . *Rhamnus*, Rhamnaceae, p. 307

      82 Stamens usually 10 (5–7 in 1 species of *Ledum*), not distinctly alternating with the petals (shrubs commonly more than 1 m tall; margins of leaf blades not toothed)

        83 Leaves deciduous (blades mostly 2–4 cm long); flowers borne singly in the axils of the leaves; petals about 1 cm long, with pinkish or coppery lengthwise streaks; stamens 10; not often found below 3000 ft. (910 m) . . . . *Elliottia pyroliflora*, pl. 250, Ericaceae

        83 Leaves evergreen; flowers borne in racemes originating at the bases of the current year's growth; petals usually about 8 mm long, white; stamens 10 in 1 species, 5–7 in the others . . . . *Ledum*, Ericaceae, p. 209

  78 Petals united for at least a short distance above the base

    84 Corolla opening widely, not urn-shaped (fruit dry when mature)

      85 Large shrubs, evergreen or deciduous, commonly more than 1 m tall; leaf blades usually more than 3 cm long, more than twice as long as wide, the undersides without glandular dots; corolla lobes mostly either white or pink; fruit at least 6 mm long and longer than wide . . . . *Rhododendron*, Ericaceae, p. 210

      85 Dwarf shrubs, evergreen; leaf blades to about 2 cm long and twice as long as wide; the undersides with small glandular dots; corolla lobes about 6 mm long; pinkish red; fruit 4–5 mm long and wide (Douglas, Josephine, and Curry Cos., Oreg.) . . . . *Kalmiopsis*, Ericaceae, p, 209

    84 Corolla urn-shaped (constricted slightly near the top), with 4–5 short lobes

      86 Corolla 4-lobed

        87 Upright deciduous shrub to more than 2 m tall; most leaves more than 3 cm long; corolla yellow, often tinged with red, or pale orange; fruit dry . . . . *Menziesia ferruginea*, pl. 258, Ericaceae

        87 Low evergreen shrubs rooting at the nodes; leaves usually less than 1.5 cm long; corolla pink; fruit fleshy, red, a cranberry (coastal, in sphagnum bogs) . . . . *Vaccinium*, Ericaceae, p. 211

      86 Corolla 5-lobed

        88 Flowers (and therefore also the fruits) 1 or a few in the leaf axils (in axillary racemes in the cultivated highbush blueberry, whose seeds are disseminated by fruit-eating birds) . . . . *Vaccinium*, Ericaceae, p. 211

        88 Flowers several to many in racemes or panicles

89 Inflorescences terminal racemes or panicles, these rarely so much as 5 cm long; leaf blades green in a few species but decidedly grayish in most (small to large evergreen shrubs) .... ***Arctostaphylos***, Ericaceae, p. 207

89 Inflorescences terminal or axillary panicles, these commonly more than 6 cm long; leaf blades dark green, the margins finely toothed

  90 Blades of most leaves not so much as twice as long as wide, slightly rough and leathery; fruit fleshy, blackish purple .... ***Gaultheria shallon***, pl. 252, Ericaceae

  90 Blades of most leaves more than twice as long as wide, smooth, not leathery; fruit dry (Josephine and Curry Cos., Oreg., to Calif.; not likely to be found below 3500 ft., 1070 m) .... ***Leucothoe davisiae***, pl. 257, Ericaceae

Herbaceous Flowering Plants

For any region that has a rich and diversified flora, it is almost impossible to construct a family key that is simple yet infallible. The main reason for this is that easily observed features, such as leaf arrangements, leaf shape, and the number of sepals, petals, stamens, and pistils, are neither sufficiently exclusive nor necessarily adhered to by all representatives of a particular family. For instance, in the buttercup family (Ranunculaceae), there are plants whose flowers have petals, others whose flowers do not. Sepals, furthermore, may look like petals. When true petals are present, they may all be alike, as they are in a buttercup, or they may be of different sizes, shapes, and colors, as in a larkspur. There is sometimes a single pistil that develops into a fleshy fruit, but more commonly there are a few to many pistils that become dry fruits.

The key to families (and also sometimes genera or particular species) of herbaceous plants is broken into four subdivisions, based partly on botanically important features, partly on superficial features and on habitats where the plants are found:

GROUP 1: Parasitic and Saprophytic Plants (p. 71). Terrestrial plants that are either attached to stems of other plants or that lack perceptible chlorophyll and are therefore not green. Parasitic or partly parasitic plants that have green leaves and are connected with their hosts underground are dealt with in Group 4.

GROUP 2: Grasslike Plants (p. 71). Terrestrial or aquatic plants that are grasslike. This category includes not only true grasses but also sedges, rushes, cattails, and a few other monocotyledonous plants. The leaves are usually narrow, with parallel veins, and the plants are often tufted. If a corolla or calyx, or both, are present, these are not showy. For irises and their relatives, whose leaves may be grasslike but whose flowers are conspicuous and usually colorful, go to Iridaceae, under Monocotyledonous Families.

GROUP 3: Aquatic Plants (p. 72). Aquatic, nongrasslike plants that float or are partly or wholly submerged. In some species, the floating leaves are very different from the submerged leaves. Some Group 4 plants grow in wet places but are not truly aquatic. If in doubt, try your plant in Group 3 first, because there are fewer choices to consider. If this does not lead you to a plausible identification, turn to Group 4. If the plant is obviously an iris, go to Iridaceae.

GROUP 4: All Other Herbaceous Flowering Plants (p. 75). Terrestrial, nongrasslike plants with distinct, green leaves. This group is the one with which you will probably deal most frequently, because it includes the majority of plants we think of as wildflowers, and also most weeds other than those in the grass family.

Try to learn the characteristics of the four groups so that you can quickly choose the one that probably includes the family of the plant you want to identify. After reaching what appears to be the correct family, find this family and continue keying to genus and species. When only one species, or only one or two genera of a family, meet the criteria of a particular choice, the names are given before the family name.

This system, using four groups, is by no means infallible. It should work most of the time, however, and even if you pick the wrong group because of not being sure whether a particular plant is parasitic, saprophytic, grasslike, or aquatic, you will soon find out. Furthermore, many of the families, including some of the larger ones, are very distinctive. After a little experience with them, you will probably be able to fit many plants into the right families without having to deal with the preliminary keys.

Following the keys to Groups 1–4, the families of flowering plants growing wild in our region are arranged alphabetically in two sections: Dicotyledonous Families (p. 86) and Monocotyledonous Families (p. 365).

GROUP 1 Parasitic and Saprophytic Plants

1 Plant attached to and parasitic on aboveground parts of another plant
    2 Plant with delicate, very slender, orange or yellow stems attached to herbs or shrubs; leaves reduced to scales; all flowers with a pistil and stamens; corolla white, 5-lobed; fruit developing above the level of attachment of the calyx and corolla; fruit dry when mature . . . . *Cuscuta*, Cuscutaceae, p. 201
    2 Plant usually stout, with green, yellow-green, or brownish stems attached to branches of trees or shrubs; leaves either scalelike or well developed; flowers either pistillate or staminate; corolla absent; fruit developing below the level of attachment of the calyx; fruit fleshy when mature, white, bluish, or purplish . . . . **Viscaceae**, p. 363
1 Plant not attached to aboveground parts of another plant (plant not green but it may be yellowish; leaves usually reduced to scalelike structures)
    3 Corolla regular; stamens at least 6, usually 10 (petals usually 5; sepals usually 4–5, sometimes none; fruit-forming portion of the pistil above the level at which the corolla and calyx are attached; parasites or saprophytes in forest soils) . . . . **Ericaceae**, p. 204
    3 Corolla irregular; stamens 4 or fewer
        4 Petals 3, separate, the lower one decidedly different from the upper ones; sepals 3, separate or united at the base; 1 functional stamen; fruit-forming portion of the pistil below the level at which the sepals are attached; saprophytes, usually in forest soils . . . . **Orchidaceae**, p. 419
        4 Corolla consisting of a long tube with 5 lobes, 3 forming a lower lip, 2 forming an upper lip; calyx 5-lobed; 4 functional stamens; fruit-forming portion of the pistil above the level at which the calyx is attached; parasites on roots of other plants . . . . **Orobanchaceae**, p. 268

GROUP 2 Grasses and Grasslike Plants

1 Plants aquatic (but if growing in salt water, they may be exposed at low tide), with proportionately long, narrow leaves, these with parallel margins for nearly their entire length
    2 Plants strictly marine; inflorescence (pistillate, staminate, or with flowers of both types) located within a boat-shaped bract . . . . **Zosteraceae**, p. 473
    2 Plants growing in fresh water; pistillate flowers, with 3 white petals, borne singly at the tips of long stems that reach the surface; staminate flowers, with 2 stamens, produced in clusters of many within a cuplike bract and soon becoming free-floating . . . . . *Vallisneria americana*, Hydrocharitaceae, p. 390
1 Plants terrestrial, aquatic (but not in salt water), or in wet habitats such as bogs, freshwater marshes, and salt marshes
    3 Flowers in a dense, cylindrical inflorescence at least 5 mm wide and several to many times as long as wide; plants rooted in mud or muck but only the lower part under water (the inflorescence may be abruptly separated into an upper staminate portion and lower pistillate portion)
        4 Inflorescence usually at least 1 cm thick, more than 15 cm long, abruptly separated into an upper staminate portion and lower pistillate portion, and without a leaflike bract originating at its base . . . .
        . . . . *Typha*, Typhaceae, p. 472
        4 Inflorescence to about 1 cm thick, not often more than about 8 cm long, all the small flowers with stamens and a pistil, with a long, leaflike bract (spathe) originating at its base . . . .
        . . . . *Acorus*, Acoraceae, p. 365

    3 Inflorescence not as described in the other choice 3

        5 Inflorescence with several globular heads of either all-staminate or all-pistillate flowers, the heads of pistillate flowers soon resembling burs (plants sometimes mostly submerged, but the inflorescence held above the water surface; leaves rather distinctly flattened) . . . . *Sparganium*, Sparganiaceae, p. 471

        5 Flowers of the inflorescence not in globular, all-staminate or all-pistillate heads

           6 Flowers or structures loosely comparable to flowers, whether with or without obvious perianth segments, usually in branched inflorescences; leaves, if with blades, flattened (and sometimes folded) or nearly cylindrical

              7 Flowers with 6 distinct perianth segments similar to sepals or petals of other plants . . . . **Juncaceae**, p. 393

              7 Flowers or structures loosely comparable to flowers without easily recognizable perianth segments (these are completely absent or evident only as bristlelike outgrowths)

                 8 Stems usually cylindrical; structures loosely comparable to flowers (florets) typically small, consisting of 3 stamens and a pistil enclosed by 2 bracts (lemma, palea); there are usually 2 or more successive florets in what is called a spikelet, at the base of which there are almost always 2 bracts called glumes; sheaths of leaves at least partly open and usually with a ligule, a semicircular membranous outgrowth or row of hairs where the blade joins the sheath . . . . . . **Poaceae**, p. 424

                 8 Stems usually 3-sided but sometimes cylindrical; perianth, if present, consisting of 1 to many bristlelike elements that do not look at all like sepals or petals; pistil 1, in the largest genus (*Carex*) enclosed within a flask-shaped structure (perigynium); sheaths of leaves closed, without a ligule where the blade joins the sheath . . . . **Cyperaceae**, p. 367

        6 Flowers (these usually with obvious perianth segments) on short pedicels in an upright, unbranched raceme; leaves, above their basal sheaths, nearly cylindrical, but the upper surface often flattened

           9 Plants spreading laterally by rhizomes; leaves scattered along the flowering stems as well as basal (lower flowers of the inflorescence with bracts that partly enclose their pedicels; perianth segments 6, in 2 whorls of 3, greenish white; stamens usually 6, pistil with 3 divisions, these united only at the base; plants typically found in bogs, marshes, and around lakes and ponds) . . . . *Scheuchzeria palustris* subsp. *americana*, Scheuchzeriaceae, p. 470

           9 Plants forming tufts, not spreading by rhizomes; leaves basal (the flowering stems lack leaves, but there may be bracts associated with the flowers)

              10 Plants mostly submerged in fresh or brackish water, the inflorescence a raceme raised above the water level; most flowers of the inflorescence with bracts beneath them and with 1 purplish perianth segment or none, 1 stamen, and sometimes 1 pistil; submerged flowers enclosed by sheaths of leaves near the bases of the plants without perianth segments or stamens, but the pistils with styles usually at least 5 cm long . . . . *Lilaea scilloides*, Juncaginaceae

              10 Plants usually growing in salt marshes or alkaline freshwater marshes, generally not submerged except perhaps temporarily; inflorescence a raceme without bracts; perianth segments (yellowish or greenish), in 1 or 2 whorls of 3; stamens 3 or 6; pistil with 3 or 6 divisions . . . . *Triglochin*, Juncaginaceae, p. 401

GROUP 3 Aquatic Plants

Aquatic plants that have proportionately long, grasslike leaves are in Group 2: Grasses and Grasslike Plants.

    1 Plants floating or submerged just below the surface; leaves absent, but the stems sometimes flattened so that they resemble leaves, sometimes egg-shaped, nearly round, or approximately boat-shaped, rarely more than 5 mm wide; roots, if present, not branched and sometimes only 1; flowers microscopic, when present restricted to the edges of the stems; plants reproducing vegetatively and often remaining attached to one another, thus forming small aggregations; occasionally found on wet soil after a drop in the water level . . . . **Lemnaceae**, p. 402

1 Plants with leaves or what appear to be leaves (they are sometimes divided into nearly hairlike lobes) and not in other respects as described in the other choice 1

  2 Leaves, or structures appearing to be leaves, divided into slender, sometimes nearly hairlike lobes

    3 Submerged leaves opposite, divided 1–4 times into slender lobes; floating leaves with nearly circular blades, the petiole attached near the center (stems with a slimy, somewhat gelatinous coating) . . . . *Cabomba caroliniana*, Cabombaceae, p. 176

    3 Submerged leaves, or structures appearing to be leaves, alternate or in whorls; floating or exposed leaves, if present, not with nearly circular blades to which the petiole is attached near the center

      4 Submerged structures appearing to be leaves (these are in fact modified stems, and alternate) with small bladders in which microscopic organisms are trapped (inflorescence raised above the water level; corolla 2-lipped, usually yellow) . . . . *Utricularia*, Lentibulariaceae, p. 254

      4 Leaves without bladders

        5 Leaves alternate; plants sometimes with floating leaves (these with 3-lobed blades) as well as submerged leaves; corolla regular, white . . . . *Ranunculus*, Ranunculaceae, p. 300

        5 Leaves in whorls (plants with long, weak stems)

          6 Leaves divided dichotomously, sometimes slightly rough to the touch because of small serrations on the lobes . . . . *Ceratophyllum*, Ceratophyllaceae, p. 192

          6 Leaves divided pinnately, the submerged leaves delicate, with nearly hairlike lobes (some species with terminal portions of stems emerging from the water and with leaves different from those on the submerged portions; corolla white or purplish) . . . . *Myriophyllum*, Haloragaceae, p. 241

  2 Leaves not divided into slender lobes

    7 Most leaves in whorls of at least 3 (but see the other choice 7 for a note concerning *Najas*, in which the leaves may superficially appear to be in whorls)

      8 Leaves to about 2 mm wide, with smooth margins and tapering rather evenly from the base to the tip, usually 8–10 in each whorl, extending stiffly outward at an angle of almost 90° to the stem; flowers and fruits inconspicuous, borne in the axils of the leaves; plants upright, typically not completely submerged, growing at the margins of streams, lakes, ponds, and in wet meadows . . . . *Hippuris*, Hippuridaceae, p. 242

      8 Leaves mostly at least 2 mm wide but sometimes slightly narrower, with finely toothed and nearly parallel margins, in whorls of 3–6, not extending stiffly outward at an angle of 90° to the stem; flowers, when produced, rising on long perianth tubes to the surface; plants otherwise completely submerged . . . . **Hydrocharitaceae**, p. 390

    7 Leaves not in whorls (but in *Najas* they may appear to be in whorls because each leaf of an opposite pair commonly has another leaf originating in its axil)

      9 Leaves opposite

      10 Leaves slender, not more than 1 mm wide, but usually at least 20 mm long; plants delicate, completely submerged

        11 Leaves with finely toothed margins, abruptly broadened at the base, clasping the stem, and without a stipule (each leaf of a pair commonly with another leaf originating in its axil) . . . . *Najas*, Najadaceae, p. 419

        11 Leaves with smooth margins, not abruptly broadened at the base, not clasping the stem, and with a prominent stipule . . . . *Zannichellia palustris*, Zannichelliaceae, p. 472

      10 Most leaves (at least the floating ones) more than 2 mm wide; plants typically only partly submerged

        12 Terminal portions of some stems (these bearing flowers) upright and extending above the surface; leaves with obvious petioles, the blades to about 2 cm long; flowers without petals but with 4 sepals and 4 stamens (these at the top of the fruit-forming portion of the pistil); fruit plump, about 4 mm long, slightly 4-angled . . . . *Ludwigia palustris*, Onagraceae

    12 Terminal portions of stems submerged or floating; leaves sessile, rarely so much as 1.5 cm long; flowers with neither petals nor sepals and with only 1 stamen; fruit flattened, breaking apart into 3 1-seeded units (in some species, staminate and pistillate flowers are separate) . . . . ***Callitriche***, Callitrichaceae, p. 177

9 Leaves either alternate, basal, or arising from stems buried in mud (or, in the case of *Lilaeopsis*, arising in clusters from a creeping stem and consisting entirely of hollow, cross-barred petioles—there are no blades)

    13 Leaves slender, not so much as 1 mm wide, but usually considerably more than 20 mm long, their basal portions bordered by prominent stipules; plants delicate, completely submerged . . . . ***Ruppia***, Ruppiaceae, p.469

    13 Plants not in all respects as described in the other choice 13

        14 Leaves without blades and consisting entirely of hollow, cross-barred petioles (leaves arising in clusters from a creeping stem; flowers in small umbels) . . . . ***Lilaeopsis occidentalis***, Apiaceae, p. 89

        14 Leaves with conspicuous blades

            15 Leaves with stout petioles arising from prostrate stems, the blades (simple or with 3 leaflets) normally held well above the water level; calyx and corolla 5-lobed, the corolla lobes with crowded scalelike hairs or with 3 wavy ridges on the upper surface; part of the fruit-forming portion of the pistil joined to the tube of the calyx; fruit thick-walled . . . . **Menyanthaceae**, p. 260

            15 Plant not as described in the other choice 15

                16 Mature leaf blades generally floating or raised slightly above the water level, either broadly heart-shaped, with the petiole inserted in the notch, or oval, with the petiole inserted near the center; flowers solitary, usually floating

                    17 Leaf blades broadly heart-shaped, with the petiole inserted in the notch; flowers at least 5 cm wide, with many petals or sepals (the color of the flowers, which may be yellow, white, or pink, resides in either the petals or sepals, depending on the genus) . . . . **Nymphaeaceae**, p. 262

                    17 Leaf blades oval, with the petiole (this with a slimy, somewhat gelatinous coating) inserted near the center; flowers about 2 cm wide, with 3–4 purplish petals and sepals . . . . ***Brasenia schreberi***, pl. 185, Cabombaceae, p. 176

                16 Leaf blades, if floating, not as described in the other choice 16

                    18 Leaf blades arrowhead-shaped and raised well above the water level (flowers, with 3 white petals and 3 sepals, arranged in whorls) . . . . ***Sagittaria***, Alismataceae, p. 366

                    18 Leaf blades not arrowhead-shaped

                        19 Leaf blades (to about 4 cm wide) either almost circular (in which case the petiole is attached near the center, as in a nasturtium) or approximately kidney-shaped and lobed . . . . *Hydrocotyle*, Apiaceae, p. 96

                        19 Leaf blades neither almost circular nor kidney-shaped and lobed

                            20 Obvious leaves basal, usually about 5 cm long, 2–3 mm wide; flowers few on a stem rising to or close to the surface; corolla white or very pale blue, about 15 mm long, with 5 lobes, the 2 upper ones much smaller than the 3 lower; corolla tube split lengthwise (starting between the 2 upper lobes) for much of its length; usually in water about 40–50 cm deep . . . . *Lobelia dortmanna*, pl. 196, Campanulaceae

                            20 Plant not in all respects as described in the other choice 20

                              21 Leaves narrow, usually at least 7 cm long but not more than 5 mm wide; flowers borne singly within a rolled-up bract, the perianth pale yellow, with a tubular portion at least 15 mm long and 6 lobes about 5 mm long (stems slender, weak, trailing or floating; flowers opening at the surface) . . . . ***Heteranthera dubia***, Pontederiaceae, p. 465

                            21 Plants, if with narrow leaves, not with flowers as described in the other choice 21

22 Petals (4–6) yellow (leaves oval or elongated, scattered rather evenly along the stems, whether these are submerged, upright and only partly submerged, or creeping over mud; sepals and petals originating above the fruit-forming part of the pistil; stamens 10) ...... ***Ludwigia hexapetala***, Onagraceae, p. 263

22 Petals, if present, not 5 and not yellow

  23 Leaves basal, usually raised well above the water level; petioles usually at least as long as the blades; flowers with 3 sepals, 3 white petals (often falling early), 6 to many stamens, and several to many pistils that develop into 1-seeded fruits (leaf blades narrowly oval) .... ***Alisma***, Alismataceae, p. 366

  23 Leaves scattered along the stems, sometimes floating; petioles, when present, not half as long as the blades; flowers not as described in the other choice 23

    24 Flowering stems upright, raised well above the water level; all leaves with similar broad blades, even if some float or are submerged; flowers small, in crowded inflorescences; calyx, with 5 lobes, white or pink to rose; corolla absent .... ***Polygonum***, Polygonaceae, p. 283

    24 All stems trailing through the water (but the inflorescences, if present, generally raised slightly above the water level); floating leaves, if present, with broad blades and decidedly different from the submerged leaves, which may be nearly threadlike or have substantial blades, sometimes with wavy margins (flowers, when produced, with 4 lobes resembling perianth segments) .... **Potamogetonaceae**, p. 466

GROUP 4 All Other Herbaceous Flowering Plants

This key does not include *Murdannia keisak* (Commelinaceae, a monocotyledonous family). This plant, introduced from East Asia and perhaps here to stay, has been found in essentially freshwater habitats at the edges of saltwater bays in northwestern Oregon and southwestern Washington. The elongated leaf blades are continuous with sheaths that encircle the nodes of the sprawling stems. The flowers have three sepals and three petals, the latter about 8 mm long and some shade of blue.

1 Plant obviously a cactus, with succulent, jointed stems bearing clusters of sharp spines (mostly on islands in N Puget Trough, Brit. Col. and Wash.) .... ***Opuntia fragilis***, pl. 186, Cactaceae, p. 176

1 Plant not a cactus

  2 Terrestrial plants growing along streams, with circular leaf blades to which the petioles attach near the center (leaf blades commonly at least 20 cm in diameter, sometimes more than 40 cm; Benton Co., Oreg., to Calif.) .... ***Darmera peltata***, Saxifragaceae, p. 331

     The flowers of *D. peltata* appear early in spring and wither before the leaves arise. For this reason, the plant is keyed here on the basis of leaf structure, and elsewhere on the basis of flower structure.

  2 Plants, if terrestrial, without large, circular leaf blades to which the petioles attach near the center

    3 Sunflowers, daisies, thistles, dandelions, and their relatives: flowers sessile and concentrated in composite heads, the bases of these surrounded by somewhat leaf- or scalelike bracts called phyllaries; corollas of individual flowers sometimes tubular, sometimes drawn out into a petal-like ray (ligule); style with 2 branches; fruit-forming part of the pistil below the level at which the corolla is attached; fruit an achene, this often bearing a pappus consisting of bristles or scales, which are probably modified calyx elements. Dry flower heads, with fully developed achenes, are often helpful in identification and may persist long after flowers have withered. This is the largest family of dicotyledonous plants in our region. Learn its characteristics right away so you can always turn directly to it .... **Asteraceae**, p. 103

    3 Flowers, if in dense heads, not as described in the other choice 3

      4 Plants with flowers densely packed on a fleshy stalk (spadix), this originating at the base of a large yellow or greenish white bract (spathe) that may be more than 20 cm long .... **Araceae**, p. 367

      4 Plants not as described in the other choice 4

5 Succulent plants growing in salt marshes and some inland alkaline habitats; branches opposite; stems jointed, with the flowers (very small and without petals) crowded into a short inflorescence; leaves reduced to scarcely noticeable scales .... *Salicornia*, Chenopodiaceae, p. 196

5 Plants, if succulent and growing in salt marshes, not as described in the other choice 5

  6 Leaves (all these arising from the base of the plant) to more than 50 cm long, consisting mostly of a tubular petiole, this with a hood bearing a proportionately small, bilobed blade; flowers, borne singly on long peduncles, hanging down, with 5 yellowish sepals and 5 purplish petals; in bogs and other wet places (mostly Lane Co., Oreg., to Calif. but also known from a few coastal localities farther N in Oreg.) .... *Darlingtonia californica*, pl. 540, Sarraceniaceae, p. 329

  6 Plants not as described in the other choice 6

    7 All leaves in a basal cluster and with conspicuous gland-tipped hairs (usually red) that trap insects (flowers small, produced at the top of a single stalk that is generally less than 20 cm tall; corolla white; mostly restricted to sphagnum bogs but occasionally in other wet places where there are mats of mosses) .... *Drosera*, Droseraceae, p. 202

    7 Leaves, if in a basal cluster, without conspicuous gland-tipped hairs that trap insects (*Pinguicula macroceras*, Lentibulariaceae, choice 64, has slimy, insect-trapping leaves but lacks the prominent gland-tipped hairs of *Drosera*)

      8 Leaves (some of them in whorls, others alternate) about 1 cm long, slender, with a lengthwise groove on the underside and with downturned margins; flowers, above 3 small bracts, about 3 mm long, with 3 sepals, 3 petals, 1 pistil, and/or 3 stamens; fruits nearly round, about 5 mm long, blackish .... *Empetrum nigrum*, pl. 240, Empetraceae, p. 204

      8 Plants not conforming in all respects to the description in the other choice 8

        9 Petals and sepals (or perianth segments, when the petals and sepals are similar) usually in cycles of 3 or 6; main veins of leaf blades usually nearly parallel to one another (there are some exceptions to both these criteria; in some saprophytic Orchidaceae, moreover, the leaves are reduced to scales)

          10 Flowers conspicuously irregular, the lowermost petal (lip petal) distinctly different from the 2 upper ones (fruit-forming portion of the pistil located below the level at which the sepals and petals are attached) .... **Orchidaceae**, p. 419

          10 Flowers regular, all the sepals and petals (or perianth segments, when the 3 petals and 3 sepals have the same form and color) alike

            11 Fruit-forming portion of the pistil located below the bases of the sepals and petals, or below the perianth tube formed by union of the petals and sepals .... **Iridaceae**, p. 391

            11 Fruit-forming portion of the pistil located above the bases of the sepals and petals .... **Liliaceae**, p. 403

> While Liliaceae has traditionally been dealt with as a unified group, more recent proposals place some genera into separate families. This matter is discussed under Liliaceae, under Monocotyledonous Families.

        9 Flower parts not often in cycles of 3 or 6; leaf blades, if not compound, usually with a single main vein that originates at the base, then branches, or with 3 or more main veins that diverge from the base

          12 Leaves, at least in the upper part of the plant, distinctly opposite or in whorls (a pair of opposite leaves may be united in such a way that they completely surround the stem)

            13 Leaves (at least some of the upper ones) in whorls

              14 Plant with a single whorl of leaves just below 1 or several flowers (there may also be scale-like leaves on the lower part of the stem, or a single basal leaf that usually disappears early)

                15 Whorl consisting of 3 leaves, each with 3 leaflets or lobes, the margins of these toothed; flower single, with 5 white, pink, or blue sepals, these not pointed at the tip (petals absent) .... *Anemone*, Ranunculaceae, p. 297

                15 Whorl consisting of more than 3 leaves, these neither lobed nor toothed; flowers (on ex-

tremely slender peduncles) several, with 5–7 white or pink petals, these with pointed tips . . . .
. . . . ***Trientalis***, Primulaceae, p. 295

14 Plant usually with at least 1–2 whorls of leaves on the upper portion of each stem, as well as well-developed alternate or opposite leaves at lower levels (in Rubiaceae, all or most leaves are in whorls)

    16 Corolla 2–3 cm long, white to reddish or purplish, consisting of 2 pairs of fused petals and 1 single upper petal; sepals 3, the lowermost one much enlarged, saclike, and with a prominent spur; stamens 5; upper leaves in whorls, lower leaves alternate or opposite; leaf blades to about 15 cm long, the margins rather evenly toothed; plants often more than 1 m tall (grown in gardens, sometimes escaping) . . . . ***Impatiens glandulifera***, pl. 156, Balsaminaceae

    16 Plant not as described in the other choice 16

      17 Stems cylindrical, smooth, usually with 1–2 whorls of leaves below the inflorescence; leaf blades usually more than 1 cm wide and with rather evenly toothed margins; flowers at least 1 cm wide, the 5 petals separate, white to deep pink; stamens 10; evergreen (somewhat shrubby but not often more than 25 cm tall; in coniferous forests) . . . . ***Chimaphila***, Ericaceae, p. 208

      17 Stems 4-angled, often with bristles that engage the skin or stick to clothing, and with almost all leaves in whorls; leaf blades not often so much as 1 cm wide and not toothed along the margins (sometimes they are short, slender, and bristle-tipped); flowers much less than 1 cm wide, the corolla consisting of a short tube and 3–4 lobes, these white, yellowish, greenish, pinkish, or bluish; stamens 3–4; annual or perennial . . . . **Rubiaceae**, p. 321

13 Leaves opposite (in certain species at least a few may be alternate and/or some may be in whorls, but if all are in whorls follow the other choice 13)

    18 Plants succulent, with 3-angled leaves more than 1 cm long (petals numerous, very slender, pink; stamens numerous; fruit-forming portion of the pistil united with the calyx cup, the fruit therefore developing below the 5 sepals; plants growing on backshores of sandy beaches; S Oreg. to South America) . . . . ***Carpobrotus chilensis***, pl. 40, Aizoaceae, p. 87

    18 Plants, if succulent, with leaves much less than 1 cm long

      19 Stems and leaves with stinging hairs; inflorescences in the axils of upper leaves; flowers small, greenish, pistillate or staminate (the 2 types may be in the same or separate inflorescences) . . . .
. . . . ***Urtica***, Urticaceae, p. 356

      19 Plant not as described in the other choice 19

        20 Flowers without a corolla and sometimes without a calyx (when a calyx is present, it may be brightly colored and thus resemble a corolla)

          21 Pistillate and staminate flowers separate (but both types may be in the same cluster); usually neither pistillate nor staminate flowers with a calyx, but staminate flowers sometimes with a calyx; most species with a milky sap . . . . **Euphorbiaceae**, p. 212

          21 All flowers with a pistil and stamens (calyx sometimes brightly colored)

            22 Calyx with a proportionately long tube, usually greenish yellow, pink, rose, purplish, or red, the lower portion of the tube persisting and adhering tightly to the fruit as this matures (stem nodes often swollen; flowers in umbel-like clusters; sometimes growing on backshores of sandy beaches) . . . . **Nyctaginaceae**, p. 261

            22 Calyx either a shallow, lobed cup or consisting of separate sepals, usually green (but sometimes white on the upper surface, or tinged with rose or a related color), none of it adhering to the fruit

              23 Stamens not necessarily the same number as the sepals; fruit partitioned lengthwise into 3 divisions; stem nodes not obviously swollen . . . ***Mollugo verticillata***, Molluginaceae, p. 261

              23 Stamens 5, the same number as the sepals; fruit not partitioned into divisions; stem nodes often obviously swollen . . . . **Caryophyllaceae**, p. 182

        20 Flowers with a corolla as well as a calyx (but the petals or corolla lobes may be inconspicuous)

24 Petals separate or nearly so, not united to the extent that there is an obvious corolla tube
  25 Flowers in small clusters, each cluster with numerous stiff, sharp-tipped bracts below it; petals 5, bluish or greenish white; sepals 5, persisting on the dry fruit, which is covered with scales; leaves irregularly toothed or lobed, sometimes prickly; usually in places that are wet, at least during part of the year . . . . *Eryngium*, Apiaceae, p. 95
  25 Plants not as described in the other choice 25
    26 Plants slightly woody at the base, forming a low ground cover in woods; leaves with 3 main veins; petals 5, white, soon becoming green and/or falling; calyx fused to the lower half of the fruit-forming portion of the pistil . . . . *Whipplea modesta*, pl. 338, Hydrangeaceae
    26 Plants either not woody at the base or not fitting all other criteria in the other choice 26
      27 Flowers with 2 petals (white, notched at the tip), 2 sepals, 2 stamens, on a distinct perianth tube that originates at the top of the fruit-forming part of the pistil; fruit covered with hooked hairs; in moist, shady woods . . . . *Circaea alpina* subsp. *pacifica*, pl. 391, Onagraceae
      27 Flowers with more than 2 petals, 2 sepals, and 2 stamens
        28 Flowers with 4 petals, 4 sepals, and 8 stamens (petals and sepals sometimes on a distinct perianth tube that originates at the top of the fruit-forming part of the pistil; petals notched at the tip) . . . . *Epilobium* or *Camissonia-Oenothera* complex (in part), Onagraceae, pp. 264, 266
        28 Flowers, if with 4 petals and 4 sepals (or 4 calyx lobes), not with 8 stamens (except perhaps in Lythraceae and Elatinaceae; see below)
          29 Calyx tubular, usually ribbed lengthwise, and with small teeth alternating with the lobes; stems angular (petals and calyx lobes 4–6, stamens 4–10, the number of these parts often varying on the same plant) . . . . **Lythraceae**, p. 257
          29 Calyx not tubular, not obviously ribbed lengthwise, and without small teeth alternating with the lobes or separate sepals; stems not angular
            30 Leaves with small stipules (look carefully); flowers borne in the leaf axils, singly or in small clusters; petals 2–5, the same number as the sepals; stamens either the same number as the petals and sepals or twice as many; fruit-forming portion of the pistil above the level at which the sepals and petals are attached; fruit a squat capsule with as many divisions as the number of sepals; plants usually growing in mud at the edges of lakes, ponds, or streams; not often encountered in our region . . . . **Elatinaceae**, p. 203
            30 Plants not in all respects as described in the other choice 30
              31 Stamens and petals 4 (annual, rarely so much as 7 cm tall; leaves small but succulent; flowers [each one with 4 pistils] about 2 mm wide, clustered at the ends of the stems or single in the leaf axils; usually on muddy, sandy, or gravelly soil) . . . . *Crassula*, Crassulaceae, p. 198
              31 Stamens more than 4 and not necessarily the same number as the petals
                32 Sepals 2 . . . . **Portulacaceae**, p. 289
                32 Sepals 5
                  33 Pistil deeply 5-lobed, the lobes eventually separating as 1-seeded divisions, each of which retains a style that becomes much longer than the portion containing the seed (fertile stamens usually 5 or 10; when 5, there are also 5 scalelike sterile stamens) . . . . **Geraniaceae**, p. 237
                  33 Pistil not deeply 5-lobed and not separating into 1-seeded divisions with long styles (fruit a capsule, dry at maturity, containing several to many seeds)
                    34 Stamens numerous, concentrated in a few clusters; stem nodes not swollen . . . . **Hypericaceae**, p. 247
                    34 Stamens not more than twice as many as the petals; stem nodes often obviously swollen . . . . **Caryophyllaceae**, p. 182

24 Petals united to the extent that there is an obvious corolla tube (this is sometimes as long as, or longer than, the corolla lobes)

 35 Corolla regular, the lobes equal; corolla tube without spurs or sacs and not at all 2-lipped

  36 Pistils 2 (but the stigmas or styles may be fused for a time); sap sometimes milky; seeds sometimes with tufts of hair (in Asclepiadaceae, one of the pistils may not develop into a mature fruit)

   37 Stamens united to form a tube around the pistils (flowers complicated!, corolla lobes turned back, and between them and the stamens is a crown with 5 concave, hoodlike lobes) . . . . *Asclepias*, Asclepiadaceae, p. 103

   37 Stamens not united to form a tube around the pistil . . . . **Apocynaceae**, p. 100

  36 Pistil 1; sap not milky; seeds without tufts of hair

   38 Stamens 4, in 2 pairs . . . . **Verbenaceae**, p. 359

   38 Stamens, if 4, not in 2 pairs

    39 Stamens in line with the corolla lobes . . . . **Primulaceae**, p. 292

    39 Stamens alternating with the corolla lobes

     40 Style with 3 lobes . . . . **Polemoniaceae**, p. 275

     40 Style either not lobed or with only 2 lobes

      41 Calyx consisting of 5 separate sepals; corolla 5-lobed; style usually 2-lobed (but sometimes not lobed); corolla not twisted in the bud stage; leaves often deeply lobed . . . . **Hydrophyllaceae**, p. 242

      41 Calyx 4- or 5-lobed; corolla 4- or 5-lobed; style not lobed; corolla usually twisted in the bud stage; leaves not lobed . . . . **Gentianaceae**, p. 235

 35 Corolla at least slightly irregular, the lobes sometimes of different shapes and sizes; corolla tube sometimes with a spur or sac arising from its lower side, sometimes 2-lipped

  42 Corolla tube with a spur or sac on its lower side

   43 Corolla mostly yellow or blue, markedly 2-lipped; fruit-forming part of the pistil free of the calyx; calyx lobes prominent, longer than the rest of the calyx; stems not 4-angled (upper leaves usually alternate) . . . . *Linaria*
        (see *Linaria-Antirrhinum-Cymbalaria-Kickxia* complex), Scrophulariaceae, p. 344

   43 Corolla white to pink or rose, sometimes 2-lipped; fruit-forming portion of the pistil fused to the calyx; calyx lobes sometimes so much reduced that they are not evident; stems sometimes 4-angled . . . . **Valerianaceae**, p. 357

  42 Corolla tube without a spur or sac on its lower side

   44 Stems prickly; bases of most large leaves with depressions that hold water; inflorescences dense, headlike, to more than 5 cm long, with long, stiff, sharp-tipped bracts beneath them; individual flowers also accompanied by sharp bracts; fruit-forming part of the pistil fused to the calyx (thus the fruit develops below the level of attachment of the calyx lobes) . . . . *Dipsacus*, Dipsacaceae, p. 202

   44 Plants not as described in the other choice 44 (fruit-forming part of the pistil free of the calyx)

    45 Stems not 4-angled (corolla markedly 2-lipped; style not divided) . . . . **Scrophulariaceae**, p. 337

    45 Stems 4-angled

     46 Corolla markedly 2-lipped; style divided near the tip into 2 lobes; plants usually with a strong aroma, this sometimes minty, sometimes unpleasant . . . . **Lamiaceae**, p. 248

     46 Corolla only slightly 2-lipped; style not divided; plants without a strong aroma . . . . **Verbenaceae**, p. 359

12 Leaves alternate or mostly basal
 47 Leaves generally more than 75 cm long, with 3 primary divisions, each with 3–5 leaflets, these usually at least 8 cm long (sometimes more than 20 cm); flowers in umbel-like clusters on the branches of the inflorescence, with 5 whitish petals and very small sepals; fruit blackish; often more than 2 m tall; usually growing along streams in shaded canyons (SW Oreg. to Calif.) . . . . *Aralia californica*, pl. 58, Araliaceae
 47 Plants not as described in the other choice 47
  48 All leaves basal, with petioles to about 40 cm long and with 3 diverging, fan-shaped, pale green leaflets to about 8 cm long (flowers, with neither petals nor sepals, in a short, dense inflorescence; foliage with an aroma slightly reminiscent of vanilla; growing in moist woodland habitats) . . . . *Achlys*, Berberidaceae, p. 148
  48 Leaves, if basal, with a petiole much shorter than 40 cm, and if with 3 diverging leaflets, these not fan-shaped and not so much as 5 cm long
   49 Flowers without a corolla but usually with a calyx (in some species that have separate staminate and pistillate flowers, the latter do not have a calyx; in other species the calyx may be colored in such a way that it resembles a corolla; furthermore, an involucre of bracts, located just below the flowers of some species, may resemble a calyx)
    50 Leaf blades compound, with at least 3 leaflets, sometimes many
     51 Flowers packed into dense, slightly elongate heads borne at the tips of the stems; sepals 4, often becoming reddish, the heads as a whole then reddish; stamens not more than about 12, and only 2 or 4 in some species (leaf blades pinnately or bipinnately compound) . . . . *Sanguisorba*, Rosaceae, p. 320
     51 Flowers in branching inflorescences, not packed into dense heads; sepals not becoming reddish; stamens commonly more than 12
      52 Pistillate and staminate flowers separate, the 2 types (in our region) on separate plants . . . . *Thalictrum*, Ranunculaceae, p. 304
      52 Most or all flowers with pistils and stamens . . . . *Cimicifuga elata*, pl. 480, or *Enemion*, Ranunculaceae, p. 300
    50 Leaf blades not compound, but they may be deeply lobed
     53 Leaf blades distinctly lobed
      54 Plants annual, rarely more than 10 cm tall; leaf blades less than 15 mm long, pale green, somewhat fan-shaped, usually with 3 primary lobes; flowers small, borne in clusters in the axils of the leaves; calyx tubular, with 4 lobes; pistil 1; stamen usually 1; in open or lightly shaded areas . . . . *Aphanes* (see *Alchemilla-Aphanes* complex), Rosaceae, p. 311
      54 Plants perennial, often more than 50 cm tall, the stems arising from rhizomes; most leaf blades more than 5 cm long and usually slightly wider than long, dark green, palmately lobed, coarsely toothed; flowers at least several in each branched inflorescence; sepals 4, separate, about 4 mm long, concave, whitish, often falling early; pistils several; stamens numerous; in shaded habitats, often near streams . . . *Trautvetteria carolinensis*, pl. 495, Ranunculaceae
     53 Leaf blades not distinctly lobed, but they may be toothed
      55 Leaf blades heart-shaped, to 10 cm wide, with the aroma of ginger when bruised; fruit-forming part of the pistil below the 3 sepals, which are drawn out into slender tails more than 2 cm long; low ground cover, usually in forested areas . . . . *Asarum*, Aristolochiaceae, p. 102
      55 Plants not as described in the other choice 55
       56 Flowers with numerous stamens (pistils at least 5) . . . . *Caltha* or *Enemion*, Ranunculaceae, pp. 298, 300
       56 Flowers with fewer than 10 stamens

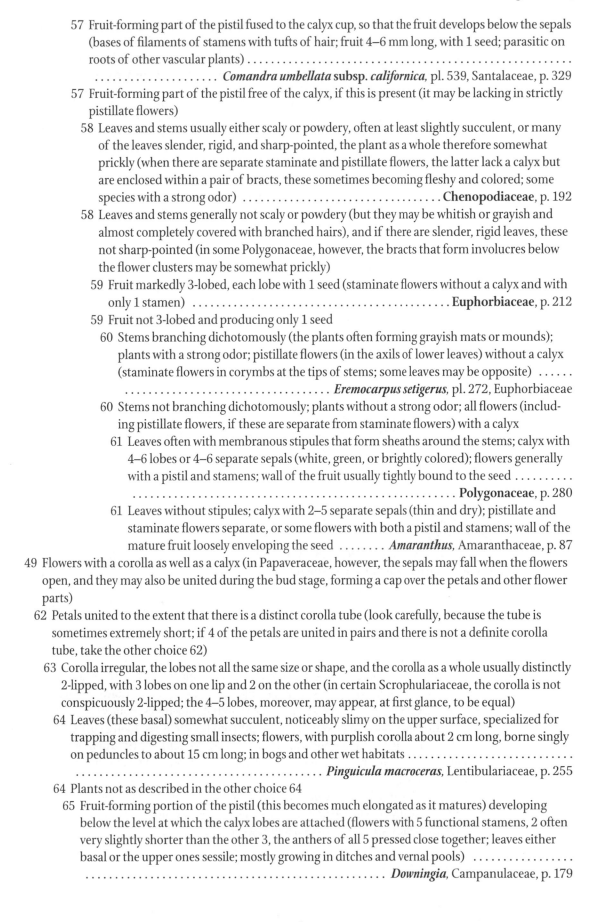

57 Fruit-forming part of the pistil fused to the calyx cup, so that the fruit develops below the sepals (bases of filaments of stamens with tufts of hair; fruit 4–6 mm long, with 1 seed; parasitic on roots of other vascular plants) . . . . ***Comandra umbellata* subsp. *californica***, pl. 539, Santalaceae, p. 329

57 Fruit-forming part of the pistil free of the calyx, if this is present (it may be lacking in strictly pistillate flowers)

58 Leaves and stems usually either scaly or powdery, often at least slightly succulent, or many of the leaves slender, rigid, and sharp-pointed, the plant as a whole therefore somewhat prickly (when there are separate staminate and pistillate flowers, the latter lack a calyx but are enclosed within a pair of bracts, these sometimes becoming fleshy and colored; some species with a strong odor) . . . . **Chenopodiaceae**, p. 192

58 Leaves and stems generally not scaly or powdery (but they may be whitish or grayish and almost completely covered with branched hairs), and if there are slender, rigid leaves, these not sharp-pointed (in some Polygonaceae, however, the bracts that form involucres below the flower clusters may be somewhat prickly)

59 Fruit markedly 3-lobed, each lobe with 1 seed (staminate flowers without a calyx and with only 1 stamen) . . . . **Euphorbiaceae**, p. 212

59 Fruit not 3-lobed and producing only 1 seed

60 Stems branching dichotomously (the plants often forming grayish mats or mounds); plants with a strong odor; pistillate flowers (in the axils of lower leaves) without a calyx (staminate flowers in corymbs at the tips of stems; some leaves may be opposite) . . . . ***Eremocarpus setigerus***, pl. 272, Euphorbiaceae

60 Stems not branching dichotomously; plants without a strong odor; all flowers (including pistillate flowers, if these are separate from staminate flowers) with a calyx

61 Leaves often with membranous stipules that form sheaths around the stems; calyx with 4–6 lobes or 4–6 separate sepals (white, green, or brightly colored); flowers generally with a pistil and stamens; wall of the fruit usually tightly bound to the seed . . . . **Polygonaceae**, p. 280

61 Leaves without stipules; calyx with 2–5 separate sepals (thin and dry); pistillate and staminate flowers separate, or some flowers with both a pistil and stamens; wall of the mature fruit loosely enveloping the seed . . . . ***Amaranthus***, Amaranthaceae, p. 87

49 Flowers with a corolla as well as a calyx (in Papaveraceae, however, the sepals may fall when the flowers open, and they may also be united during the bud stage, forming a cap over the petals and other flower parts)

62 Petals united to the extent that there is a distinct corolla tube (look carefully, because the tube is sometimes extremely short; if 4 of the petals are united in pairs and there is not a definite corolla tube, take the other choice 62)

63 Corolla irregular, the lobes not all the same size or shape, and the corolla as a whole usually distinctly 2-lipped, with 3 lobes on one lip and 2 on the other (in certain Scrophulariaceae, the corolla is not conspicuously 2-lipped; the 4–5 lobes, moreover, may appear, at first glance, to be equal)

64 Leaves (these basal) somewhat succulent, noticeably slimy on the upper surface, specialized for trapping and digesting small insects; flowers, with purplish corolla about 2 cm long, borne singly on peduncles to about 15 cm long; in bogs and other wet habitats . . . . ***Pinguicula macroceras***, Lentibulariaceae, p. 255

64 Plants not as described in the other choice 64

65 Fruit-forming portion of the pistil (this becomes much elongated as it matures) developing below the level at which the calyx lobes are attached (flowers with 5 functional stamens, 2 often very slightly shorter than the other 3, the anthers of all 5 pressed close together; leaves either basal or the upper ones sessile; mostly growing in ditches and vernal pools) . . . . ***Downingia***, Campanulaceae, p. 179

65 Fruit-forming portion of the pistil free of the calyx tube; flowers usually with 4 functional stamens, plus 1 sterile stamen (5 functional stamens in 1 genus, only 2 in some others) . . . .
. . . . **Scrophulariaceae**, p. 337
Research suggests that most genera that have been assigned to the large assemblage Scrophulariaceae should be withdrawn from it. Because all comprehensive treatises of the flora of the Pacific Northwest published before 2004 deal with Scrophulariaceae as a single family, the traditional arrangement is followed here. See the description of characters of Scrophulariaceae, under Dicotyledonous Families, for a more detailed discussion of the relationships of plants conventionally grouped together in this family, as well as for proposed redistribution of various genera into other families.

63 Corolla regular, all lobes almost exactly the same size and shape (if 2 upper lobes of a yellow corolla are slightly smaller than the 3 lower lobes, take the other choice 63, which will lead you to Scrophulariaceae)

66 Herbaceous vines with separate staminate and pistillate flowers, these with 5–7 corolla lobes (the pistillate flowers are solitary in the same leaf axils as those that give rise to racemes of staminate flowers; staminate flowers with 3 stamens; in pistillate flowers, the fruit-forming portion is united to the calyx and develops into a large fruit that often has a few to many soft or somewhat rigid prickles) . . . .*Marah oreganus*, pl. 236, Cucurbitaceae, p. 201

66 Plants, if vinelike, not in other respects as described in the other choice 66

67 Stamens in line with the corolla lobes (in other words, each stamen originates at or below the base of a corolla lobe)

68 Pistil with 5 styles; fruit a small, 1-seeded nut (plants mostly maritime, growing in salt marshes or on bluffs near the shore, but in the case of *Armeria* often far inland) . . . . **Plumbaginaceae**, p. 274

68 Pistil with a single style; fruit a capsule containing numerous seeds . . . . **Primulaceae**, p. 292
Research suggests that some genera of Primulaceae should be transferred to Myrsinaceae. Some information concerning this is given in connection with the characteristics of Primulaceae, under Dicotyledonous Families.

67 Stamens alternating with the corolla lobes (but sometimes absent between certain corolla lobes)

69 Corolla dry and membranous in texture, with 4 lobes (these either spreading outward, or upright and covering the fruit; stamens 4 or 2; sepals 4, usually with membranous margins; leaves basal in all but 1 species in our region) . . . . *Plantago*, Plantaginaceae, p. 273

69 Corolla not dry and membranous in texture, and with 5 lobes

70 Fruit-forming portion of the pistil united with much of the calyx, the fruit thus developing below the sepals (stigma divided into 2 or more lobes) . . . . **Campanulaceae**, p. 178

70 Fruit-forming portion of the pistil free of the calyx

71 Stigma 3-lobed (the separation sometimes begins lower, on the style) . . . .
. . . . **Polemoniaceae**, p. 275

71 Stigma either not divided, or divided into only 2 lobes

72 Sepals separate or nearly separate

73 Plants usually twining or trailing (but sometimes rather compact); flowers solitary; corolla generally more than 2 cm long, the lobes twisted together in the bud stage (and usually with distinct lengthwise pleats after opening) . . . . **Convolvulaceae**, p. 196

73 Plants usually upright; flowers usually in groups but sometimes solitary (when grouped, often in somewhat scroll-like inflorescences); corolla usually less than 2 cm long, the lobes not twisted together in the bud stage (but they may overlap) . . . **Hydrophyllaceae**, p. 242

72 Sepals united for much of their length, a substantial portion of the calyx therefore cup-shaped or tubular

74 Fruit-forming portion of the pistil deeply 4-lobed and typically separating into 1-seeded nutlets (usually roughened or bristly; in some species, not all the nutlets develop); flowers often in slightly scroll-like, 1-sided inflorescences . . . . **Boraginaceae**, p. 151

74 Fruit-forming portion of the pistil not deeply 4-lobed and not separating into 1-seeded nutlets; flowers solitary, or if in clusters, these not scroll-like, 1-sided inflorescences (corolla lobes often twisted together in the bud stage, each one sometimes with a pleat along the midline; fruit either a fleshy berry or a dry capsule) . . . . **Solanaceae**, p. 354

62 Petals separate or nearly so, not united to the extent that there is a distinct corolla tube (but in Fabaceae, first choice 76, 2 petals are joined by their lower edges; in *Impatiens*, Balsaminaceae, choice 90 under the second choice 76, 4 of the 5 petals are united in pairs; in *Limonium*, Plumbaginaceae, the petals are united only at the very base)

  75 Leaves compound, with at least 3 leaflets

    76 Corolla irregular (flowers with 5 petals, the 2 lower ones united by their edges to form a keel, and the uppermost one enlarged to form a banner; stamens usually 10, and the filaments of at least most of them usually united for at least part of their length; fruit like a peapod, with a single row of seeds) . . . . **Fabaceae**, p. 214

    76 Corolla regular, unless some of the petals do not develop normally (which is typical of some Ranunculaceae)

      77 Fruit separating early into 2 1-seeded halves (often bristly or ribbed lengthwise); inflorescence usually an umbel; flowers with 5 small petals; sepals, if obvious, reduced to small toothlike structures at the top of the fruit-forming part of the pistil; leaves, if bruised, usually aromatic . . . . **Apiaceae**, p. 88

      77 Fruit not separating into 2 1-seeded halves, and plants not as described in the other choice 77

        78 Flowers with a single pistil (the pistil may have more than 1 style, however)

          79 Stamens not more than 10; leaflets not toothed

            80 Leaflets 3; stamens 10; styles 5 (leaflets diverging at the end of the petiole, as in a clover, and 2-lobed; leaves with a very sour taste) . . . . *Oxalis*, Oxalidaceae, p. 270

            80 Leaflets more than 3; stamens 6; style 1 (flowers in a loose panicle, the buds nodding before opening; sepals and petals 6, the petals turned back and each one ending in a hoodlike structure) . . . . *Vancouveria*, Berberidaceae, p. 148

          79 Stamens more than 10

            81 Individual flowers not showy, borne in terminal racemes; fruits nearly spherical, about 1 cm long, fleshy, usually red, sometimes white (petals white, sometimes lacking) . . . . *Actaea rubra*, pl. 472, Ranunculaceae

            81 Individual flowers showy, borne singly or in loose inflorescences; pistil becoming a dry capsule consisting of 5 seed-producing chambers

              82 Petals red and yellow, not especially thick, with long spurs; sepals somewhat pointed, flat, red . . . . *Aquilegia formosa*, pl. 478, Ranunculaceae

              82 Petals mostly brownish red, thick, and without spurs; sepals bluntly rounded, markedly concave, green (SW Oreg. to Calif., also E slopes of the Cascades) . . . . *Paeonia brownii*, Paeoniaceae, p. 271

        78 Flowers with more than 1 pistil

          83 Flowers with numerous pistils, these developing into small, 1-seeded, dry fruits (the pistils may, however, be embedded in a fleshy receptacle, as they are in a strawberry; stamens usually numerous)

            84 Stipules present at the bases of the leaf petioles; small bracts usually present on the calyx, alternating with the lobes . . . . **Rosaceae**, p. 307

            84 Stipules absent at the bases of the leaf petioles; bracts not present between the sepals . . . . **Ranunculaceae**, p. 295

        83 Flowers with not more than 15 pistils

85 Plants not often more than 20 cm tall, evergreen; flowers few in inflorescences borne on leafless stems; petals similar to the sepals in being slender and greenish, but the petals with a conspicuous glandular depression near the base; leaves twice-compound in a more or less ternate fashion (the plants flower early; in late spring and summer they are characterized by the persistent pistils, which radiate outward) . . . . *Coptis*, Ranunculaceae, p. 298

85 Plants usually more than 1 m tall, dying down in winter; flowers small, numerous in inflorescences borne on leafy stems; petals white; leaves pinnately or bipinnately compound

86 Leaves bipinnately compound, the leaflets all approximately the same size, about twice as long as wide, tapering to slender tips; inflorescences consisting of numerous slender raceme-like branches; petals about 1 mm long; staminate flowers slightly larger than the pistillate flowers, the 2 types borne on separate plants; pistils usually 3, each producing 2–4 seeds . . . . *Aruncus dioicus*, pl. 506, Rosaceae

86 Leaves pinnately compound, the terminal leaflet about as wide as long, much larger than the others and palmately lobed; inflorescences somewhat flat-topped; petals about 5–6 mm long; all or most flowers with stamens and pistils; pistils 5 to about 15, each producing 1 seed (mostly along rivers in SW Wash. and NW Oreg.) . . . . *Filipendula occidentalis*, Rosaceae, p. 310

75 Leaves not compound, but they may be deeply lobed, and the divisions may be slender

87 Corolla irregular, the petals of different shapes and/or sizes

88 Flowers with at least 12 stamens

89 Corolla (mostly white) not more than 1 cm long; stamens (usually at least 10) all on one side of the flower; petals 6, usually deeply lobed, without spurs; calyx with 4–7 lobes, these without spurs (garden plants, sometimes escaping) . . . . *Reseda*, Resedaceae, p. 305

89 Flowers more than 1 cm long; stamens usually numerous, not all on one side of the flower; petals 4, in unequal pairs, those of the upper pair with spurs; calyx composed of 5 separate sepals, the uppermost one with a spur . . . . *Delphinium*, Ranunculaceae, p. 299

88 Flowers with not more than 10 stamens, these usually rather evenly (or at least symmetrically) arranged

90 Corolla consisting of 2 fused pairs of petals and 1 upper petal; sepals 3, the lower one much enlarged, saclike, sometimes with a prominent spur; stamens 5 . . . . *Impatiens*, Balsaminaceae, p. 146

90 Plant not as described in the other choice 90

91 Flowers with 2 sepals and 4 petals, 1–2 of which have a saclike spur at the base . . . . **Fumariaceae**, p. 234

91 Flowers with 5 sepals and 3 or 5 petals, which do not have spurs (in *Polygala*, 2 of the 5 sepals could be mistaken for petals because they are similarly colored)

92 Flowers with 3 petals, these united at the base, and the lowermost one boat-shaped; the 2 sepals at the sides of the flower pink like the petals; stamens 8 (SW Oreg. to Calif.) . . . . *Polygala californica*, pl. 437, Polygalaceae, p. 280

92 Flowers with 5 petals, these not united at the base, the lowermost one with a pouchlike spur; none of the sepals resembling the petals; stamens 5 . . . . *Viola*, Violaceae, p. 360

87 Corolla regular, the petals more or less equal in size and shape

93 Plants succulent with thick, fleshy leaves; sepals 5, united at the base; petals 5, united for some distance above the base (stamens 10; pistils 5) . . . . **Crassulaceae**, p. 198

93 Plants not succulent; sepals separate; petals separate

94 Each flower with many pistils

95 Leaves mostly about 5 cm long, less than 2 mm wide; each sepal with a spur near the base; pistils on an elongated receptacle commonly 2–3 cm long and more than 3 times as long as wide (petals greenish yellow or white, 2–3 mm long) . . . *Myosurus minimus*, pl. 485, Ranunculaceae

95 Most leaf blades broadening to more than 3 mm and commonly wider than 2 cm; sepals without spurs at their bases; pistils not on a receptacle that is so much as 3 times as long as wide . . . . **Ranunculaceae**, p. 295

94 Each flower with only 1 pistil

  96 Calyx fused, for at least part of the length of its cuplike or tubular portion, to the fruit-forming part of the pistil (thus the fruit develops, or begins to develop, below the bases of the calyx lobes; it may eventually, however, become greatly enlarged)

   97 Flowers, if with 5 petals, not also with 5 sepals or calyx lobes

     98 Flowers with 5 petals, 2 sepals, and 7–20 stamens (petals greenish yellow; plants succulent, prostrate; garden weed) . . . . *Portulaca oleracea*, Portulacaceae

     98 Flowers with 4 petals, 4 sepals, and 4 or 8 stamens (sepals sometimes turned to one side and adhering to one another after the flower opens) . . . . **Onagraceae**, p. 263

   97 Flowers with 5 petals and 5 sepals or calyx lobes

     99 Flowers (opening at night, remaining open the next morning) with many stamens; petals usually at least 4 cm long, bright yellow; about half the calyx cup fused to the squat, flat-topped, fruit-forming part of the pistil, the fruit eventually becoming a capsule about 2–3 cm long; plants usually more than 50 cm tall, sometimes 1 m (SW Oreg. to Calif., also E of the crest of the Cascades in Brit. Col., Wash., and Oreg.) . . . . *Mentzelia laevicaulis*, pl. 372, Loasaceae, p. 257

     99 Plants not in all respects as described in the other choice 99

       100 Flowers with 5 functional stamens alternating with 5 sterile stamens that are joined to the petals and divided into lobes, these sometimes slender and with a glandular swelling at the tip; petals white or becoming tinged with pink on aging, sometimes with numerous, almost hairlike filaments on both sides of the lower half; only a small part of the calyx cup joined to the fruit-forming part of the pistil . . . .*Parnassia*, Parnassiaceae, p. 272

       100 Flowers usually with 5 or 10 functional stamens, sometimes fewer than 5, not alternating with sterile stamens that are divided into lobes; petals generally white, greenish, brownish, pinkish, or reddening with age, rarely purple or yellow, and often divided into slender lobes, but these not all concentrated on the sides of the lower half as described in the other choice 100; about half to three-fourths of the calyx cup fused to the fruit-forming part of the pistil . . . . **Saxifragaceae**, p. 329

  96 Calyx not fused to the fruit-forming portion of the pistil (but if the calyx is tubular, it may closely envelop the pistil and, later on, the mature fruit)

   101 Much of the calyx tubular, this portion much longer than the lobes (the tube is also ribbed lengthwise)

     102 Stems 4-angled; leaves opposite, well developed all along the stems; calyx lobes 4–6, alternating with slender, toothlike outgrowths; petals 4–6, stamens 4–10; pistil with 1 style . . . . . . **Lythraceae**, p. 257

     102 Stems not 4-angled; most leaves (with blades to about 3 cm wide) basal, the extensively branched inflorescence with only small bractlike leaves; calyx lobes 5, not alternating with slender, tooth-like outgrowths; petals 5 (appearing to be separate but in reality joined together at the very base); stamens 5; pistil with 5 styles (near the high-tide line in coastal salt marshes, Coos Co., Oreg., to Calif.) . . . . *Limonium californicum*, pl. 422, Plumbaginaceae

   101 Calyx not tubular (the sepals are separate or joined only at the base)

     103 Flowers with 2 sepals and 5 petals . . . . **Portulacaceae**, p. 289

     103 Flowers, if with only 2 sepals, not with 5 petals

       104 Stamens more than 10

         105 Filaments of stamens joined to the pistil (calyx 5-lobed; petals 5) . . . . **Malvaceae**, p. 258

         105 Stamens not joined to the pistil (sepals 2–3, falling as the flowers open [in *Eschscholzia* the 2 sepals are united to form a cap that covers the other flower parts until the flower opens]; petals 4 or at least 6) . . . . **Papaveraceae**, p. 271

104 Stamens 10 or fewer

106 Flowers with 4 petals, 4 sepals, and usually 6 stamens, 2 of which are shorter than the other 4 . . . . . .
. . . . **Brassicaceae**, p. 159

106 Flowers with more than 4 petals and 4 sepals, and not with the arrangement of stamens described in the other choice 106

107 Pistil not deeply 4- or 5-lobed and not separating into 1-seeded divisions

108 Flowers with 5 petals (usually falling early), 5 sepals, and 5 stamens . . . . **Linaceae**, p. 256

108 Flowers with at least 6 petals (white to pink), 6–8 sepals, and numerous stamens (on rocky slopes, mostly at higher elevations) . . . . *Lewisia*, Portulacaceae, p. 291

107 Pistil deeply 4- or 5-lobed, the lobes eventually separating as 1-seeded divisions (flowers usually with 5 sepals, 5 petals, but 4 of each in 1 species of *Limnanthes*)

109 Petioles with thin stipules at the base; petals 5, usually pink or purplish; each division of the pistil retaining a style that becomes much longer than the portion containing the seed and that coils and uncoils in response to changes in humidity . . . . **Geraniaceae**, p. 237

109 Petioles without stipules; petals (5 in most species, 4 in 1 species) white or yellow and white; pistil with 1 style, this not persisting as the divisions of the pistil (5 in most species) ripen (usually in wet habitats) . . . . *Limnanthes*, Limnanthaceae, p. 255

Dicotyledonous Families

ACERACEAE Maple Family

The maple family consists of trees and shrubs with opposite branches and opposite, deciduous leaves. The flowers are usually in drooping racemes or dense clusters, and all species of our region are characterized by a five-lobed calyx. One species lacks petals; the others have five petals. The flowers may be strictly staminate, strictly pistillate, or have stamens as well as a pistil. The pistil, with two styles, develops into a distinctive dry fruit that consists of two broadly winged structures called samaras, each of which typically contains a single seed. The samaras, while still united or after separating, are scattered with the help of wind. Molecular evidence suggests that Aceraceae be merged into Sapindaceae, a family with more tropical representatives.

Acer

Besides the species in this key, there are two European maples that are occasionally encountered in situations where they might be assumed to be native. In *Acer platanoides*, Norway maple, the leaf blades are distinctive in that the tips of the teeth on the lobes taper to very slender points; in *A. pseudoplatanus*, sycamore maple, the undersides of the leaf blades are conspicuously white or grayish.

1 Leaves compound, with 3 or 5 leaflets; pistillate and staminate flowers on separate trees; petals absent (sometimes escaping from cultivation)

2 Most leaves with 3 or 5 leaflets, rarely with more than 5; leaflets usually only slightly hairy but sometimes rather densely hairy on the underside along the veins . . . . **A. negundo** var. **negundo**
BOX ELDER (central and E United States)

2 Most leaves with 3 leaflets, a few with 5; leaflets usually obviously hairy, especially on the underside and particularly when young . . . . **A. negundo** var. **californicum**
CALIFORNIA BOX ELDER (California)
The distinctions between *A. negundo* vars. *negundo* and *californicum* are not sharp. Most specimens cultivated or naturalized in our region seem to be var. *negundo*. Another variety occurs in Mexico and Guatemala.

1 Leaves palmately lobed but not compound; petals usually present

3 Leaf blades to more than 15 cm wide; fruits bristly-hairy (some flowers with stamens and a pistil, others with only stamens; both types on the same tree) . . . . **A. macrophyllum**
BIGLEAF MAPLE

3 Leaf blades rarely more than 9 cm wide

    4 Leaf blades with 7–9 lobes; sepals usually red; tree rarely more than 6 m tall, often somewhat shrub-like and with more than 1 trunk; 2 halves of fruit directed opposite one another (some flowers with stamens and a pistil, others with only stamens; both types on the same tree) . . . . *A. circinatum*, pl. 38
            VINE MAPLE

    4 Leaf blades with 3–5 lobes; sepals green; trees to about 10 m tall, with 1 trunk; 2 halves of fruit diverging at an angle of about 90° (staminate and pistillate flowers on separate trees, or staminate flowers and flowers with stamens and a pistil on the same tree; Alaska to Oreg., in the Cascades, Olympic Mountains, and Puget Trough; also E of the crest of the Cascades, where intergrading with var. *glabrum*) . . . . *A. glabrum* **var.** *douglasii*, pl. 39
            DOUGLAS' MAPLE

AIZOACEAE Sea-Fig Family

Only one of the many species of the Aizoaceae is likely to be encountered growing wild in our region. This is *Carpobrotus chilensis* (pl. 40; *Mesembryanthemum chilense*), called sea fig, described by a Spanish botanist from specimens found in Chile around 1800. Because all other species of *Carpobrotus* are indigenous to southern Africa, it is probable that this one somehow drifted to the Pacific coast so long ago that it now qualifies as a native. It grows on backshores of sandy beaches as far north as Coos County, Oregon.

The prostrate stems of *Carpobrotus chilensis* are sometimes more than 1 m long. The succulent leaves are as long as 5 cm, slightly curved, and three-angled. The flowers, 3–5 cm wide, have numerous narrow, magenta petals and many stamens. The calyx tube, more or less four-angled, is united with the pistil, which develops into a fleshy fruit that takes a long time to break apart and release its seeds.

AMARANTHACEAE Amaranth Family

All amaranths in our region are annuals. Some appear to be native; others were certainly introduced. The flowers, in dense inflorescences, lack petals, but have two to five sepals; below the sepals there are some bracts. In all species of our region, flowers with a pistil and those with stamens (usually five) are separate but on the same plant. The fruits are dry when mature, and each contains a disk-shaped, dark, shiny seed. Most of the species in our area behave as weeds. The family does, however, include a few attractive garden subjects, the most popular of which is *Celosia argentea*, cockscomb.

Amaranthus

1 Flowers in elongated, spikelike, axillary or terminal inflorescences

    2 Most stems and leaf petioles decidedly hairy, and leaf blades hairy on the underside, especially along the veins; sepals of pistillate flowers not tapering gradually to a slender bristle . . . .
    . . . . *A. retroflexus*
        ROUGH PIGWEED (South America)

    2 Stems and leaves scarcely if at all hairy; sepals of pistillate flowers tapering gradually to slender bristles . . . .*A. powellii*, p. 88
        POWELL'S AMARANTH

1 Flowers in clusters in the axils of the leaves, not in elongated, spikelike, axillary or terminal inflorescences

Acer macrophyllum, bigleaf maple

3 Flowers with 4–5 sepals; staminate flowers with 3–4 stamens; seed 1.3–1.7 mm long . . . .
. . . . *A. blitoides* (*A. graecizans* of some references)
PROSTRATE PIGWEED

3 Flowers usually with 3 sepals; staminate flowers with 1–3 stamens; seeds usually slightly less than
1 mm long

    4 Stems upright; sepals of pistillate flowers nearly equal and similar to those of the staminate
      flowers . . . . *A. albus*
TUMBLEWEED (South America)

    4 Stems prostrate; sepals of pistillate flowers decidedly unequal, only 1 of them well developed (widely
      distributed but in our region only from Josephine Co., Oreg., to Calif.) . . . . *A. californicus*
CALIFORNIA AMARANTH

ANACARDIACEAE Sumac Family

The sumac family has generously given us the mango (Southeast Asia), pistachio (probably Iran), and cashew (Central and South America) as well as some tropical and subtropical trees that are widely cultivated in warmer parts of the United States. The family also includes poison ivy and poison oak, the latter widespread in our region. Most persons who come in direct contact with poison oak are likely to develop at least a mild skin eruption in response to an oil in the leaves and stems. The severity of the case depends to a considerable extent on the degree of exposure. So learn the characteristics of the plant and try not to touch it or let your clothing touch it.

    Members of this family have alternate, simple or compound leaves, and small flowers. The flowers of our native species have a five-lobed calyx, five petals, one pistil, and five stamens. The fruit, containing a single seed, may look fleshy but is rather dry by the time the seeds have matured.

1 Leaflets somewhat triangular, the terminal one larger than the 2 lateral ones; flowers greenish, fruits red
   (mostly E of the Cascades but in our region from Josephine Co., Oreg., to Calif.) . . . . . *Rhus trilobata*, pl. 41
SKUNKBUSH

1 Leaflets rounded, more or less equal; flowers and fruits
  whitish (plants sometimes vinelike) . . . .
. . . . *Toxicodendron diversilobum*
(*Rhus diversiloba*), pl. 42
POISON OAK
Caution: Contact with *T. diver-silobum* should be avoided!

APIACEAE Carrot Family

Members of the carrot family have alternate leaves whose petioles are usually dilated, near their bases, into sheaths that clasp the stems. The stems, moreover, are often furrowed. The plants, or at least certain parts of them, usually have an aroma of some sort. The aromas and flavors of carrot, parsley, coriander, parsnip, celery, fennel, dill, and anise are due primarily to various oils.

    The flowers are nearly always concentrated in flat-topped inflorescences of the type called umbels (*Eryngium*, the first choice in this key, is an exception). The inflorescences may be compound, in which case the rays of a primary umbel give rise to secondary umbels, whose pedicels bear the flowers. The flowers have five petals (which may not be equal, especially in flowers that are located at the outer edge

Amaranthus powellii,
Powell's amaranth

of an umbel) and five stamens. The fruit-forming portion of the pistil is below the level at which the petals and stamens originate. If there are recognizable sepals, these will be just below the petals. The fruit consists of a pair of one-seeded divisions that are for a time joined tightly to a central partition. The fruit is often conspicuously ribbed or studded with bumps or bristles.

Some members of this family are poisonous, and others may irritate the skin. It is therefore wise to handle unfamiliar plants carefully.

Many species of Apiaceae grown in gardens, either as ornamentals, vegetables, or herbs, occasionally show up in places where they were not planted. Most of those found in our region as escapes, or simply as opportunists of no merit, are in the keys, but others should be expected.

1 Inflorescences vaguely resembling those of thistles because the bracts beneath each dense head of flowers are stiff and prickly (plants as a whole not often more than 30 cm tall; the blades of the basal leaves short in proportion to the petioles and sometimes poorly developed; usually found in places where shallow pools have dried out in late spring or early summer) . . . . ***Eryngium***
1 Inflorescences not at all resembling those of thistles; the bracts, if present beneath the primary or secondary umbels, not stiff or prickly
  2 Leaves reduced to hollow petioles, which are cross-barred and thus have a jointed appearance (small, creeping, aquatic perennials, most commonly found in saline maritime habitats) . . . .
. . . . ***Lilaeopsis occidentalis***
WESTERN LILAEOPSIS

  2 Leaves with well-developed blades (but these may be compound or at least divided into a few to many lobes or leaflets)
    3 Small, creeping, aquatic plants with nearly circular leaf blades, these either lobed or with rounded marginal teeth . . . . ***Hydrocotyle***
    3 Plants, if aquatic, not especially small, and not with nearly circular leaf blades

Amaranthus albus,
tumbleweed

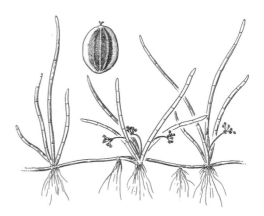

Lilaeopsis occidentalis,
western lilaeopsis

4 Ultimate divisions of leaf blades very slender, cylindrical or nearly so, sometimes hairlike (if distinctly wider than thick, not more than about 1.5 mm wide; all the species under this choice are introduced and most likely to be found in vacant lots and other disturbed areas—if the plant you are trying to identify is found in a habitat that is montane or otherwise mostly natural, it may be in *Perideridia,* some species of which have slender ultimate leaf divisions, but these are usually obviously wider than thick; furthermore, all perideridias have white corollas)

  5 Petals white; bracts present beneath primary and secondary umbels; fruit with a conspicuous notch at the base; plants not often more than 80 cm tall; foliage without the scent of anise, licorice, or dill
. . . . ***Ammi visnaga***
BISHOP'S WEED, BISNAGA (Eurasia)

  5 Petals yellow; bracts absent beneath primary and secondary umbels; fruit without a conspicuous notch at the base; plants to 2 m tall; foliage with a pleasing scent of anise, licorice, or dill

    6 Plants perennial, sprouting new stems from underground rootstocks; ribs of the fruit not distinctly winged . . . . ***Foeniculum vulgare***
SWEET FENNEL (Europe)

    6 Plants annual or biennial, not sprouting new stems from underground rootstocks; ribs of the fruit (especially the lateral ribs) distinctly winged . . . . ***Anethum graveolens***
DILL (Europe)

4 Ultimate divisions of leaf blades not cylindrical or hairlike (they may, however, be slender, but even then most of them are more than 1.5 mm wide)

  7 Leaves similar to those of a parsley or carrot, the divisions lobes rather than leaflets, usually less than 5 mm wide and 15 mm long (if the divisions are distinct leaflets, narrow and several to many times as long as wide, go to choice 18

    8 Plants often more than 2 m tall, the stems sometimes more than 2 cm thick; stems hollow, purple-spotted; leaves often more than 30 cm long; corollas white (widespread weed) . . . ***Conium maculatum***
POISON HEMLOCK

Conium maculatum is the deadly hemlock of ancient literature. The plant may cause a skin rash if handled.

    8 Plants rarely more than 1 m tall and not as described in the other choice 8

      9 Low, almost stemless plants on backshores of sandy beaches; leaves mostly prostrate, succulent, the lower leaflets usually with 3 broad lobes (fruits with prominent winglike ribs; Alaska to N Calif.) . . . .
. . . . ***Glehnia littoralis*** subsp. *leiocarpa,* pl. 43
BEACH SILVERTOP

      9 Plants mostly upright; leaves not especially succulent, the lower leaflets not with 3 broad lobes

        10 Fruit with a beak about 4 cm long (at least some long-beaked fruits will be found on plants that are still flowering; main body of fruit about 1 cm long; corollas white; weedy annual to 30 cm tall) . . . .
. . . . ***Scandix pecten-veneris,*** pl. 54
SHEPHERD'S NEEDLE

        10 Fruit either without a beak or the beak less than 1 cm long

          11 Fruit without stiff bristles or conspicuous bumps (but it is may be ribbed lengthwise and/or hairy)

            12 Fruit with a pronounced slender beak . . . ***Anthriscus***

            12 Fruit without a slender beak

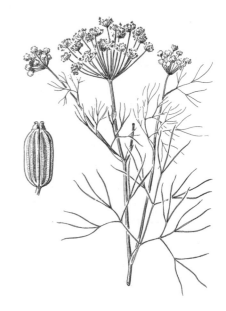

Foeniculum vulgare,
sweet fennel

13 Fruit with a short, cone-shaped projection at the tip (this develops just below the styles and is no longer than wide); plants to about 1 m tall (coastal, Japan and Aleutian Islands to N Calif.) . . . . *Conioselinum gmelinii* (*C. chinense, C. pacificum*)
PACIFIC HEMLOCK PARSLEY

13 Fruit without a conical projection at the tip; most species much less than 80 cm tall . . . . . *Lomatium*

11 Fruit with stiff bristles (sometimes hooked) or conspicuous bumps

  14 Bracts either absent beneath the primary umbels or small, slender, and not divided into lobes (flowers of secondary umbels with such short pedicels that they may seem to originate directly from the rays of the primary umbels) . . . . *Torilis*

  14 Bracts beneath primary umbels divided into lobes or leaflets (in *Yabea microcarpa* they resemble leaves on lower portions of the plant)

    15 Bracts beneath primary umbels so much divided that they resemble leaves on lower portions of the plant (secondary umbels with fewer than 10 flowers; corolla white; fruit with lengthwise ribs bearing distinctly hooked bristles; plants usually small and inconspicuous) . . . . *Yabea microcarpa* (*Caucalis microcarpa*)
CALIFORNIA HEDGE PARSLEY

    15 Bracts below primary umbels not so much divided that they resemble leaves on lower portions of the plant

      16 Spines on fruit arranged in distinct lengthwise rows . . . . *Daucus*

      16 Spines, bristles, or bumps on fruit scattered, not arranged in distinct lengthwise rows

        17 Both halves of fruit prolonged into a beak that is about one-third as long as the rest of the fruit; fruit with hooked bristles; corolla white . . . . *Anthriscus caucalis* (*A. scandicina*)
BUR CHERVIL (Eurasia)

        17 Neither half of the fruit prolonged into a beak (but the styles may persist); fruit with rounded bumps or stout hooked bristles; corolla yellow or purple . . . . *Sanicula*

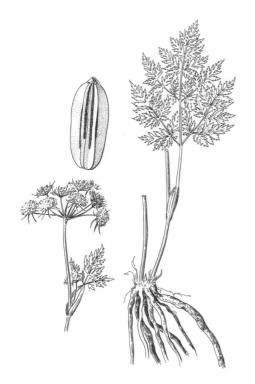

Conioselinum gmelinii,
Pacific hemlock parsley

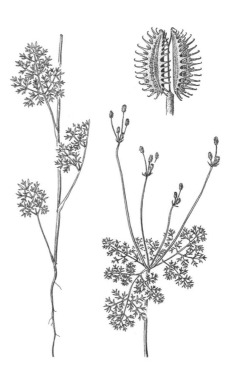

Yabea microcarpa,
California hedge parsley

7 Leaves not like those of a parsley or carrot, the primary divisions usually either fairly large (at least 1.5 cm long) or several to many times as long as wide, and sometimes slender

  18 Leaves deeply lobed in a palmate, pinnate, or bipinnate pattern but not truly compound (bracts present beneath primary and secondary umbels) ....*Sanicula*

  18 Leaves truly compound, at least the primary divisions clearly separate to the rachis and thus considered to be leaflets (species whose primary leaf divisions are very slender are also under this choice)

    19 Leaves with only 3 leaflets (each of these may be deeply lobed, however)

      20 Leaflets to about 8 cm long, elongate-oval and toothed but not lobed (plants spreading by underground rhizomes; upright stems commonly more than 50 cm tall and grooved lengthwise; umbels compound, to about 6 cm wide, usually without bracts; weed in gardens) . . . ***Aegopodium podagraria***
GOUTWEED (Europe)

      20 Leaflets usually more than 10 cm long and deeply lobed (leaf blades sometimes more than 40 cm wide; umbels to about 25 cm wide; corollas white; robust plants of moist habitats, especially near the coast; widespread) .... ***Heracleum maximum*** (*H. lanatum*), pl. 44
COW PARSNIP

Heracleum mantegazzianum, giant hogweed, often cultivated and sometimes escaping, grows to a height of more than 3 m. Its leaf blades are much larger than those of *H. maximum,* and its main stem, usually with red spots, may be more than 7 cm thick. Care should be taken to avoid getting sap from bruised leaves or stems of this plant on the skin. A certain component of the sap, if activated by sunlight, may cause a severe rash.

    19 Leaves with more than 3 primary leaflets, these arranged pinnately (the leaves may also be wholly or partly bipinnate or even tripinnate)

      21 Leaves only once-pinnate, but some of the leaflets may be conspicuously lobed

        22 Corollas yellow or reddish; largest leaves often more than 50 cm long, the largest leaflets sometimes more than 10 cm long and 5 cm wide; not aquatic or in very wet habitats . . . ***Pastinaca sativa***
PARSNIP (Europe)

        22 Corollas white; largest leaves not often so much as 50 cm long, the largest leaflets not often more than 7 cm long and 1.5 cm wide; in shallow water or in very wet habitats

          23 Most leaflets about 5 times as long as wide, with small, even-sized, sharp-pointed marginal teeth .... ***Sium suave***
HEMLOCK WATER PARSNIP

Submerged lower leaves of *S. suave* typically have much-divided blades that resemble those of parsley.

          23 Most leaflets not more than twice as long as wide and usually with rather large teeth of uneven size, or even with distinct lobes, especially above

            24 Fruit more than half as thick as wide, the lengthwise ribs slender, not especially prominent . ... ***Berula erecta***
WATER PARSNIP

            24 Fruit only about one-third as thick as wide, the broad lengthwise ribs very prominent (Lane Co., Oreg., to Calif.; mostly montane and not likely to be found below about 3500 ft., 1070 m) .... ***Oxypolis occidentalis***
COWBANE

      21 Leaves at least partly bipinnate, some of the primary leaflets divided into secondary leaflets or lobes (these in turn sometimes deeply divided)

        25 Bracts (at least 1) usually present beneath primary umbels (sometimes lacking in *Oenanthe sarmentosa* and *Perideridia erythrorhiza*) and regularly present beneath secondary umbels (corollas white—because of variation with respect to the presence and absence of bracts beneath the primary and secondary umbels, the species and genera under this choice and the other choice 25 are difficult to separate unequivocally, so you are therefore advised to try both; species with corollas that are other than white are definitely under the other choice 25)

26 Plants of relatively dry habitats (the stems arising from underground tubers or bunches of swollen underground roots); secondary leaflets usually slender, more than 10 times as long as wide (except in *P. howellii*); bases of the styles conspicuously enlarged; ribs of fruit not corky . . . . *Perideridia*

26 Plants growing in shallow water or in very wet habitats; most secondary leaflets only a few times as long as wide, with lobed or toothed margins; bases of styles not conspicuously enlarged; ribs of fruit corky

    27 Rays of primary umbels to 3 cm long; primary lateral veins of the leaves mostly directed into the marginal teeth; mature fruit more than 1.5 times as long as wide, nearly cylindrical; styles more than half as long as the fruit (sometimes fully as long); stems reclining, but the flowering shoots upright . . . . *Oenanthe sarmentosa*, pl. 47

        WATER PARSLEY, PACIFIC OENANTHE

    27 Rays of primary umbels to 6 cm long; primary lateral veins of leaflets mostly directed toward the clefts between the marginal teeth; mature fruit not much longer than wide; stems upright, not reclining . . . . *Cicuta douglasii*

        DOUGLAS' WATER HEMLOCK

        Cicuta douglasii is poisonous; handle it with care!

25 Bracts absent beneath primary umbels, present or absent beneath the secondary umbels

  28 Leaflets or lobes of leaves slender, at least several times as long as wide, and often with nearly parallel margins for much of their length

    29 Plants low, not often more than 15 cm tall, and usually with only 2–3 leaves; petals white; lateral wings of fruit incurved toward the midline (Linn Co., Oreg., to Calif. but not often below about 3000 ft., 910 m) . . . . *Orogenia fusiformis*

        TURKEY PEA

    29 Plants usually more than 15 cm tall and with more than just 2–3 leaves; petals usually yellow, white, or purple; lateral wings of fruit not incurved toward the midline . . . . *Lomatium*

  28 Ultimate divisions of the leaves (whether lobes or leaflets) not especially slender and not often more than 4 times as long as wide

Sium suave,
hemlock water parsnip

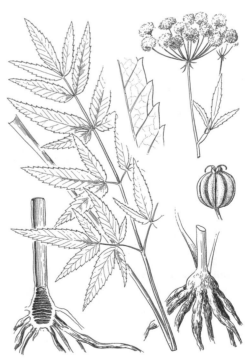

Cicuta douglasii,
Douglas' water hemlock

30 Corolla yellow or greenish yellow (bracts present beneath secondary umbels) . . . . *Tauschia*
30 Corolla white, greenish white, pinkish, or purplish but not yellow or greenish yellow
  31 Flowers or fruits not more than 10 in each secondary umbel; fruits more than 4 times as long as wide (bracts absent beneath secondary umbels) . . . . *Osmorhiza*
  31 Flowers or fruits usually more than 20 in each secondary umbel; fruits not more than 3 times as long as wide
    32 Secondary umbels nearly spherical, consisting of crowded, nearly sessile flowers (corollas white or pinkish; rays of primary umbels conspicuously hairy; in wet habitats almost entirely E of the Cascades, to Idaho, Nevada, and Calif.) . . . . *Sphenosciadium capitellatum*
      SWAMP WHITEHEADS
    32 Secondary umbels not nearly spherical, the flowers with obvious pedicels
      33 Primary umbels with 25–45 rays, these to 12 cm long . . . . *Angelica*
      33 Primary umbels with 7–20 rays, these not more than about 5 cm long
        34 Bracts absent beneath the secondary umbels; mature fruits about 1.5 mm long . . . . *Apium graveolens*
          CELERY (Eurasia)
        34 Bracts present beneath the secondary umbels; mature fruits at least 3.5 mm long . . . *Ligusticum*

Angelica
1 Bracts beneath secondary umbels at least 5 mm long; lower portions of rays of primary umbels and pedicels of secondary umbels without webbed hairs
  2 Primary leaflets usually bent sharply downward; fruit obviously flattened, 3–4 mm long, the ribs thin and not at all corky; not limited to coastal areas . . . . *A. genuflexa*
    KNEELING ANGELICA
  2 Primary leaflets not bent sharply downward; fruit only slightly flattened, 4–9 mm long, the ribs thick and corky; strictly coastal . . . . *A. lucida*
    SEA WATCH
1 Bracts beneath secondary umbels absent or inconspicuous; lower portions of rays of primary umbels and pedicels of secondary umbels with webbed hairs
  3 Leaflets thick and somewhat leathery, woolly-hairy on the underside (strictly coastal) . . . . *A. hendersonii*
    HENDERSON'S ANGELICA
  3 Leaflets not thick or leathery, and not woolly-hairy (but they may be hairy)
    4 Leaflets (and therefore the plant as a whole) somewhat grayish; inflorescence as a whole usually obviously hairy (in the Coast Ranges and near the coast, Coos Co., Oreg., to Calif.) . . . . *A. tomentosa*
      WOOLLY ANGELICA
    4 Leaflets not at all grayish, at least on their upper surfaces; inflorescence as a whole not obviously hairy . . . . *A. arguta*
      SHINING ANGELICA

Anthriscus
1 Fruit with hooked hairs, these with stout bases . . . . *A. caucalis* (*A. scandicina*)
    BUR CHERVIL (Europe)
1 Fruit without hooked hairs
  2 Bracts beneath secondary umbels oval, not more than 3 times as long as wide; beak of fruit only about 1 mm long . . . . *A. sylvestris*
    WOODLAND CHERVIL (Europe)
  2 Bracts beneath secondary umbels elongate, usually at least 4 times as long as wide; beak of fruit 2–3 mm long . . . . *A. cereifolium*
    CHERVIL (Europe)

Daucus

1 Bracts beneath the primary umbels shorter than the rays of the primary umbels and with slender lobes that only occasionally are lobed again; secondary umbels usually with more than 15 flowers; 1 flower near the center of the inflorescence usually with a purple corolla; biennial, to about 1 m tall (widespread weedy form of the carrot) . . . . *D. carota*, p. 96
SAINT ANNE'S LACE, QUEEN ANNE'S LACE, WILD CARROT (Europe)

1 Bracts beneath the primary umbels as long as the rays of the primary umbels and with lobes that are regularly divided again into 2–3 lobes; secondary umbels with not more than 12 flowers; none of the flowers distinguished by a purple corolla; annual, rarely so much as 50 cm tall . . . . *D. pusillus*
RATTLESNAKE WEED

Eryngium

The native species of *Eryngium* have rather restricted distributions. Eryngiums found anywhere else in our region, especially close to cities, are escapes from cultivation. One that has been reported is the European *E. planum*, smooth eryngo, grown for it attractive blue flower heads.

1 Flower heads usually purplish blue; small bracts beneath most individual flowers of a head 3-toothed (E Jackson Co., Oreg., E to Idaho and S to Calif.; in our region not likely to be found below 4000 ft., 1220 m)
. . . . *E. articulatum*
COYOTE THISTLE

1 Flower heads greenish

    2 Lowermost basal leaves consisting entirely of long petioles, the leaves originating at slightly higher nodes with distinct but proportionately short blades (middle Willamette Valley to Josephine Co., Oreg.) . . . . *E. petiolatum*, p. 96
OREGON COYOTE THISTLE

    2 Lowermost basal leaves with blades at least as long as the petioles (Josephine and Jackson Cos., Oreg., eastward and S to Calif.) . . . . *E. alismifolium*
ALISMA-LEAVED COYOTE THISTLE

Sphenosciadium capitellatum,
swamp whiteheads

Angelica arguta,
shining angelica

Hydrocotyle

1 Leaf blades lobed, the petiole attached at the point of separation of 2 of the lobes . . . . *H. ranunculoides*
WATER PENNYWORT

1 Leaf blades with shallow, rounded teeth, the petiole attached near the center
   2 Inflorescence consisting of a simple umbel . . . . *H. umbellata*
MARSH PENNYWORT
   2 Inflorescence consisting of several whorls of flowers (Curry Co., Oreg., to Calif.) . . . . *H. verticillata*
WHORLED MARSH PENNYWORT

Ligusticum

1 Fruit 3.5–5 mm long, each rib prominent but without a thin winglike edge (common, mostly lowland
   species, Wash. to Calif.) . . . . *L. apiifolium*
LOVAGE

1 Fruit 4–6 mm long, each rib with a distinct winglike edge
   2 Flowering stem usually with a single leaf, this much smaller than the basal leaves; umbels usually with
     fewer than 16 rays (in the Cascades, mostly above 4500 ft., 1370 m, but not often found W of the crest;
     also E of the Cascades and S to Calif.) . . . . *L. grayi*
GRAY'S LOVAGE
   2 Flowering stems usually with 2 leaves, these not much smaller than the basal leaves; umbels usually
     with more than 16 rays (SW Oreg. to Calif.) . . . . *L. californicum*
CALIFORNIA LOVAGE

Lomatium

1 Leaves not like those of a parsley or carrot, the ultimate divisions (lobes or leaflets) usually either fairly
   large (at least 15 mm long) and proportionately wide or several to many times as long as wide
   2 Ultimate divisions of leaves (these are considered to be lobes rather than distinct leaflets) narrow,
     generally at least 5 times as long as wide (corollas yellow or yellowish)

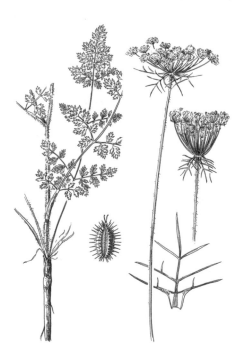

Daucus carota,
wild carrot

Eryngium petiolatum,
Oregon coyote thistle

3 Bracts beneath secondary umbels divided ternately once or twice; wings of fruit swollen and corky (Clark Co., Wash., to Lane Co., Oreg.) . . . . ***L. bradshawii***
BRADSHAW'S LOMATIUM

3 Bracts beneath secondary umbels not branched; wings of fruit thin, not at all swollen or corky
4 Ultimate divisions of leaves sometimes as much as 4 cm long, 3 mm wide; bracts beneath secondary umbels slender, much less than 1 mm wide (widespread) . . . .
. . . . ***L. triternatum*** **subsp.** ***triternatum,*** pl. 45
NARROW-LEAVED LOMATIUM
4 Ultimate divisions of leaves usually not more than 1 cm long or 1 mm wide; bracts beneath secondary umbels to about 1 mm wide (Jackson and Josephine Cos., Oreg.) . . . . ***L. cookii***
COOK'S LOMATIUM

2 Leaflets less than 4 times as long as wide
5 Leaflets smooth-margined or only faintly toothed, usually at least 2 cm long, sometimes 9 cm, and about twice as long as wide; corollas pale yellow . . . . ***L. nudicaule***
NAKED LOMATIUM
5 Leaflets conspicuously toothed and sometimes also shallowly lobed (corollas bright yellow)
6 Most leaflets with rather even-sized marginal teeth nearly all around (some leaflets may also be 3-lobed); fruit with a distinct notch at both ends; secondary umbels consisting partly or entirely of small sterile flowers (Josephine Co., Oreg., to Calif.) . . . . ***L. howellii***
HOWELL'S LOMATIUM
6 Leaflets with marginal teeth at their tips or, if the leaflets are lobed, at the tips of the lobes; fruit not notched at either end (Josephine Co., Oreg., to Calif.; also eastward to Lake Co., Oreg.) . . . .
. . . . ***L. californicum***
CALIFORNIA LOMATIUM

1 Leaves similar to those of a parsley or carrot, most of the ultimate divisions (lobes or leaflets) much less than 5 mm wide and 15 mm long (if the ultimate divisions are proportionately narrow and several to many times as long as wide, take the other choice 1)

Hydrocotyle ranunculoides,
water pennywort

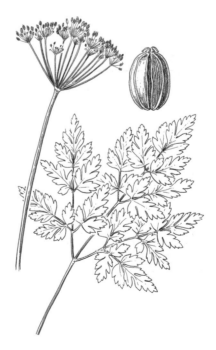

Ligusticum apiifolium,
lovage

7 Bracts beneath secondary umbels nearly or fully as wide as long, widest near the tip, and there divided into 3–5 teeth (corollas bright yellow; common and widespread) . . . . ***L. utriculatum***, pl. 46
SPRING GOLD

7 Bracts beneath secondary umbels either slender, considerably longer than wide, or absent
　8 Bracts beneath secondary umbels prominent, usually long enough to reach to or beyond the corollas (plants usually decidedly hairy; corollas white, purplish, or yellow; fruit 1–2 cm long, nearly 3 times as long as wide; mostly E of the Cascades, Brit. Col. to Calif. and eastward, but also in the Siskiyou Mountain region of SW Oreg. and NW Calif.) . . . . ***L. macrocarpum***
LARGE-FRUITED LOMATIUM

　8 Bracts beneath the secondary umbels, if present, not especially prominent or long enough to reach to the corollas
　　9 Ultimate lobes of each leaf crowded and many of them raised up to more than one plane, giving the leaf considerable depth (corollas yellow; foliage, if bruised, with an unpleasant odor; mostly E of the crest of the Cascades but known from the Gulf Islands of Brit. Col.) . . . . ***L. grayi***
GRAY'S LOMATIUM

　　9 Ultimate leaflets neither especially crowded nor disposed in more than one plane
　　　10 Bracts absent or inconspicuous beneath secondary umbels
　　　　11 Plant with an obvious aboveground stem from which the flower peduncles originate; corollas white, yellowish, or distinctly yellow (SW Brit. Col., including Vancouver Island, to Calif.) . . . . .
. . . . ***L. martindalei***
MARTINDALE'S LOMATIUM

　　　　11 Plant without an obvious aboveground stem other than the flower peduncles; corollas purplish (montane, mostly above 3000 ft., 910 m, and typically associated with serpentine soils; SW Oreg. to Calif.) . . . . ***L. engelmannii***
ENGELMANN'S LOMATIUM

　　　10 Slender bracts present and obvious beneath the secondary umbels
　　　　12 Secondary umbels without small sterile flowers; wings of the fruit about half as wide as the thickened central portion (corollas yellow; W slope of the Cascades from Marion Co., Oreg., to Calif.; also Rogue and Umpqua River canyons, Oreg.) . . . . . ***L. hallii*** (includes *L. nelsonianum*)
HALL'S LOMATIUM, CANYON LOMATIUM

　　　　12 Secondary umbels with small sterile flowers as well as fertile flowers; wings of the fruit much less than half as wide as the thickened central portion
　　　　　13 Plants sometimes more than 80 cm tall, with an obvious aboveground stem from which the flower peduncles originate; corollas maroon, purple, or yellow; wings of the fruit thickened and somewhat corky . . . . ***L. dissectum*** subsp. ***dissectum***
LACE-LEAVED LOMATIUM

　　　　　13 Plants not often more than 30 cm tall, without an obvious aboveground stem other than the flower peduncles; corollas yellow; wings of fruit thin, not at all corky (SW Oreg. to Calif.) . . . .
. . . . ***L. tracyi***
TRACY'S LOMATIUM

Osmorhiza

1 Fruits not becoming gradually more slender toward the base and without bristlelike outgrowths; corolla yellow; leaves bipinnately compound . . . . ***O. occidentalis***
WESTERN SWEET CICELY

1 Fruits becoming gradually more slender toward the base and with numerous bristlelike outgrowths; leaves bipinnately to tripinnately compound
　2 Fruits 12–25 mm long, the pair of styles at the top longer than wide; corolla greenish white . . . .
. . . . ***O. berteroi*** (*O. chilensis*), pl. 48
SWEET CICELY

2 Fruits 8–15 mm long, the pair of styles at the top wider than long; corolla typically pink or purplish but occasionally greenish . . . . *O. purpurea*
PURPLE SWEET CICELY

Perideridia

1 Ultimate lobes of leaves mostly 2–3 times as long as wide, conspicuously toothed; styles less than 1 mm long (Douglas and Josephine Cos., Oreg., to Calif.) . . . . *P. howellii*
HOWELL'S YAMPAH

1 Ultimate lobes of leaves slender, usually more than 10 times as long as wide, not conspicuously toothed (in *P. oregona* they may have an occasional lobe); styles at least 1 mm long

  2 Larger leaves only once-pinnately divided, with 3–5 pairs of leaflets, a few of these sometimes (in *P. oregana*) with 1 or more lobes

    3 Fruits fully twice as long as wide; bracts below primary umbels usually several but sometimes only 1–2 or absent (SW Wash. to Calif.) . . . . *P. oregana*
OREGON YAMPAH

    3 Fruits about as long as wide; bracts below primary umbels usually either absent or only 1–2 but sometimes several . . . . *P. gairdneri* **subsp.** *borealis*, pl. 49
GAIRDNER'S YAMPAH

  2 Larger leaves divided bipinnately or tripinnately

    4 Larger leaves, as a rule, divided tripinnately (on some leaves the divisions are all very slender, but on others they may be to about 4 mm wide); bracts below primary umbels usually several; rays of primary umbels generally at least 10 (montane, Douglas and Jackson Cos., Oreg., also E of the crest of the Cascades; to Calif.) . . . . *P. bolanderi* **subsp.** *bolanderi*
BOLANDER'S YAMPAH

    4 Larger leaves divided bipinnately; bracts below primary umbels 1 or none; rays of primary umbels 6–11 (in the Cascades and westward, Douglas, Josephine, and Klamath Cos., Oreg.) . . . *P. erythrorhiza*
RED-ROOT YAMPAH

        Perideridia erythrorhiza is the only yampah in our region that has rose-red or reddish brown roots; in other species the roots are tan or cinnamon brown.

Sanicula

1 Blades of lower leaves (at least the larger ones) ternately or pinnately compound, the primary divisions then pinnately lobed (corollas yellow)

  2 Fruit with numerous hooked bristles . . . .
       . . . . *S. graveolens* (includes *S. nevadensis*)
SIERRA SNAKEROOT

  2 Fruit with conspicuous, rounded or slightly pointed bumps (in *S. tracyi* a few near the top sometimes with bristles protruding from them)

    3 Plant growing from a rather slender taproot (SW Oreg. to Calif.) . . . . *S. tracyi*
TRACY'S SNAKEROOT

    3 Plant growing from a tuber, this generally irregular (SW Oreg. to Calif.) . . . .
      . . . .*S. tuberosa*
TUBEROUS SANICLE

Perideridia bolanderi subsp. *bolanderi*, Bolander's yampah

1 Blades of lower leaves lobed, not truly compound
  4 Leaves yellowish throughout the growing season (leaf lobes with coarse, sharply pointed marginal teeth; umbels compact, the bracts beneath them partly united at the base and conspicuously longer than the peduncles; strictly coastal) . . . .*S. arctopoides*, pl. 50
    FOOTSTEPS-OF-SPRING

  4 Leaves green throughout the growing season, and plants not as otherwise described in the other choice 4 (corollas yellow)
    5 Lower leaves pinnately lobed, usually noticeably longer than wide
      6 Corollas dark brownish purple . . . .*S. bipinnatifida*, pl. 51
        PURPLE SNAKEROOT

      6 Corollas yellow (Josephine and Curry Cos., Oreg., to Calif.) . . . .*S. peckiana*, pl. 53
        PECK'S SNAKEROOT

        In some references the fruits of *S. peckiana* are said to have hooked prickles only in the upper half, those of *S. bipinnatifida* to have such prickles all over. This may be true of some specimens of *S. peckiana,* but not all.

    5 Blades of lower leaves palmately or ternately lobed, not much longer than wide
      7 Leaf blades rarely more than 4 cm wide, the lobes separated for about two-thirds the distance to the petiole, rather sharply angled (Rogue River canyon, Oreg. to Calif.) . . . .*S. laciniata*
        COAST SNAKEROOT

      7 Leaf blades to more than 10 cm wide, the lobes separated nearly to the place where the petiole is attached, not sharply angled (widespread) . . . .*S. crassicaulis*, pl. 52
        SNAKEROOT

        In "var. *tripartita,*" believed to have genes of *S. crassicaulis* and *S. bipinnatifida,* the blades of the basal leaves are more nearly pinnately than palmately divided, and they may be distinctly longer than wide.

Tauschia

1 Stems smooth; primary umbels with 5–12 rays; pedicels of secondary umbels 1–3 mm long (Josephine and Curry Cos., Oreg., to Calif.) . . . .*T. glauca*
  GLAUCOUS TAUSCHIA

1 Stems perceptibly rough to the touch; primary umbels with 10–30 rays; pedicels of secondary umbels 3–15 mm long (Josephine and Jackson Cos., Oreg., to Calif.) . . . .*T. kelloggii*
  KELLOGG'S TAUSCHIA

Torilis

1 Peduncle of each primary umbel rarely more than 2 cm long, shorter than the leaf in whose axil it originates; bracts usually absent beneath primary umbels; half of each fruit with hooked bristles, the other half with rounded bumps or nearly smooth; plants often somewhat sprawling . . . .*T. nodosa*
  KNOTTED HEDGE PARSLEY (Eurasia)

1 Peduncle of each primary umbel usually at least 4 cm long, longer than the leaf in whose axil it originates; 1–2 bracts usually present beneath primary umbels; both halves of fruit with bristles, these curved or with hooks at their tips; plants usually upright
  2 Bristles on fruit with hooks at their tips; fruit 3–4 mm long . . . .*T. arvensis*
    HEDGE PARSLEY (Europe)

  2 Bristles on fruit curved but without hooks at their tips; fruit generally not more than 3 mm long . . . . . .
    . . . .*T. japonica*
    JAPANESE HEDGE PARSLEY (Eurasia)

APOCYNACEAE Dogbane Family

The dogbane family consists mostly of perennials with opposite, simple leaves. Both the calyx and corolla are five-lobed; the calyx lobes may be separate nearly to the base, but the corolla has a substantial tube. The pistil, with a single style, is usually free or almost free of the calyx. As the fruit ripens, the two halves of it separate, each half forming a pod that splits open after it has dried. In some genera, including *Apocynum*, the sap is milky.

Among the commonly cultivated plants of this family are two species of *Vinca*, called periwinkle. A large shrub popular in warmer portions of North America is oleander, *Nerium oleander*, native to the Mediterranean region.

1 Corolla not so much as 1 cm wide when open, greenish, whitish, or pink (sometimes streaked with pink or rose); corolla lobes not skewed in the same direction . . . . ***Apocynum***

1 Corolla 2–3 cm wide when open, usually purplish blue but white or pink in some cultivars; corolla lobes skewed slightly in the same direction (calyx lobes 2–3 mm long, the margins not hairy; fruits 2–2.5 mm long; stems trailing and rooting at the nodes or at the tips of the stems, thus spreading and forming large masses, especially on somewhat shaded banks; widely cultivated garden plant, occasionally becoming established in vacant lots, along roadsides, and even in places where it may appear to be native) . . . .
. . . . ***Vinca minor***, pl. 57
COMMON PERIWINKLE (Europe)

Vinca major, the greater periwinkle, another European species, is not common outside of gardens. Its corolla is 3.5–5 cm wide, and its calyx lobes (typically with hairy margins) and fruits are also much larger than those of *V. minor.* Furthermore, its stems tend to grow upright and may rise to a height of more than 1 m.

Apocynum

1 Corolla usually more than 5 mm long, more than 1.5 times as long as the calyx, white or pink (sometimes streaked with pink or rose); lower leaves with at least short petioles, not clasping the stems . . . .
. . . . ***A. androsaemifolium*** (includes *A. pumilum* and some named subspecies or varieties), pl. 55
BITTER DOGBANE

Hybrids, *A. androsaemifolium* × *cannabinum,* with pink corollas but otherwise more nearly similar to the latter than the former, fit the description of *A. floribundum* and several other so-called species. Perhaps the best name for all of them is *A. ×floribundum.*

1 Corolla less than 5 mm long, not more than 1.5 times as long as the calyx, greenish or whitish; lower leaves often clasping the stems . . . . ***A. cannabinum***, pl. 56
INDIAN HEMP

In some references, *A. sibiricum* and its subsp. *salignum,* whose leaves are typically sessile or nearly so and have a notch at the base, are treated as distinct from *A. cannabinum,* whose leaves typically have a petiole and are not notched. Other characteristics, such as the size of the fruits and the length of the hairs on the seeds, are also involved. Because of intergradation, however, it is difficult to place some specimens with confidence into one species or the other. Incidentally, the stems of *A. cannabinum* have long fibers that native Americans used for making ropes and cords.

ARALIACEAE Ginseng Family

The ginseng family, with about 50 genera, gives gardeners many species that are cultivated mostly for their leaves. English ivy, *Hedera helix*, a native of Eurasia, is known to almost everyone, but the family also includes the numerous houseplants called aralias. The several species of ginseng, native to Asia and eastern North America, belong to the genus *Panax;* they are harvested for the medicinal properties of their roots.

The flowers of most members of the family are borne in umbels. There are generally five petals and five stamens; sepals are usually small, sometimes absent. The fruits, which are at least slightly fleshy, develop below the level at which the petals and sepals (if present) originate.

There are only two species native to our region. Devil's club, *Oplopanax horridus*, is a large-leaved, painfully spiny shrub that is common in many areas west of the Cascades. Elk clover, *Aralia californica*, barely enters the southern part of our region. It is found mostly in moist, tree-shaded canyons, where it reaches a height of almost 3 m. In spite of its large size, however, it is an herb rather than a shrub, for its stems do not become woody and they die down late in fall.

1 Vine (lower portions of stems woody) climbing with the aid of aerial roots (leaves palmately lobed; flowers inconspicuous, in umbel-like inflorescences; fruits 5 mm wide, fleshy, black; common escape from gardens) . . . . *Hedera helix*
ENGLISH IVY (Europe)

1 Shrubs or large herbs

    2 Shrubs with spiny leaves and stems; leaves palmately lobed; flowers in small umbel-like clusters along a racemelike inflorescence; fruits red, shiny (along the W side of the Cascades and their foothills, on the Olympic Peninsula, and near the coast) . . . . *Oplopanax horridus*, pl. 59
DEVIL'S CLUB

    2 Large herbs (to about 3 m tall), not spiny; leaves compound, each of the 3 primary divisions pinnately divided into 3–5 leaflets, these often more than 10 cm long; flowers in umbel-like clusters on a cymelike inflorescence; fruits purplish black (S Oreg., in the Cascades, Coast Ranges, and Siskiyou Mountains, to Calif.) . . . . *Aralia californica*, pl. 58
ELK CLOVER

ARISTOLOCHIACEAE Pipe-Vine Family

The interesting pipe-vine family is poorly represented in our region. We have only three species of the genus *Asarum*, which are attractive ground covers with heart-shaped alternate leaves; when bruised, these give off an aroma similar to that of ginger. From above the fruit-forming part of the pistil there arise three gradually tapering sepals about 2 cm long; these usually have rather unorthodox colors. There is no corolla. The 12 stamens, attached to the style of the pistil, are of two different lengths. The fruit, a thick-walled capsule, has six seed-producing chambers.

Asarum

1 Leaves with whitish marbling along the larger veins; rhizomes deeply buried, the plants forming clumps more often than mats; sepals usually brownish green; sterile tips of the stamens longer than the pollen sacs (Siskiyou Mountains and the Cascades from Douglas Co., Oreg., to Calif.) . . . . *A. marmoratum*
MARBLED WILD GINGER

       Specimens from S Oreg. have in the past been identified as *A. hartwegii,* but this is believed to be restricted to Calif.

1 Leaves uniformly green; rhizomes close to the surface of the soil, sometimes partly exposed, the plants forming loose mats; sepals usually brownish red or maroon-red; sterile tips of the stamens shorter than the pollen sacs . . . . *A. caudatum*, pl. 60
WESTERN WILD GINGER

       Above 4500 ft. (1370 m) in the Cascades of Jackson and Klamath Cos., Oreg., there is a related species, *A. wagneri* (*A. caudatum* var. *viridiflorum*). It differs from the widespread *A. caudatum* in several respects: its leaves are deciduous, and the blades are much wider than long; the inner surfaces of the sepals are mostly white to light green, with red-maroon near the tips and margins and sometimes with a lengthwise red-maroon stripe; the flowers have a faint, unpleasant odor.

ASCLEPIADACEAE Milkweed Family

Milkweeds, so called because of their white sap, are perennial plants with opposite or whorled leaves. The flowers have a five-lobed calyx and corolla, and the five stamens are united in such a way that they form a tube around the pistil. Just outside this tube is a crownlike structure whose five lobes are called hoods. In the genus *Asclepias,* the only one in our region, there is a further complication: the inner face of each hood has an outgrowth called a horn. The two seed-producing halves of the pistil become somewhat distinct as the fruit ripens; after it has dried, the fruit cracks open and releases flattened seeds bearing tufts of long, silky hairs.

Asclepias

1 Leaves in whorls, most of the larger ones more than 10 times as long as wide, rarely more than 12 mm wide (leaves not hairy; corolla lobes to about 5 mm long, usually greenish white, tinged with purple; abundant in the Columbia River Gorge and E of the Cascades; occasionally found in the Willamette Valley and in Jackson, Josephine, and Curry Cos., Oreg.; to Mexico) . . . . *A. fascicularis* (*A. mexicana*), pl. 61
NARROWLEAF MILKWEED

1 Leaves opposite, most of the larger ones only about 3 times as long as wide and usually at least 20 mm wide
  2 Leaf blades woolly-hairy, not notched at the base, and with distinct petioles; corolla lobes rose-purple, about 10 mm long (widely distributed in W North America but in our region restricted to the Willamette Valley and to Douglas, Josephine, Jackson, and Curry Cos., Oreg.) . . . . *A. speciosa*, pl. 62
SHOWY MILKWEED

  2 Leaf blades not conspicuously hairy, notched at the base and therefore somewhat heart-shaped, sessile; corolla lobes dark reddish purple, about 5 mm long (Lane and Douglas Cos., Oreg., to Calif. and Nevada) . . . .*A. cordifolia*
PURPLE MILKWEED

ASTERACEAE Sunflower Family

In most temperate regions of the world, the Asteraceae has more species than any other family of flowering plants. Keying an unfamiliar member to genus and species is therefore likely to involve more choices and require more attention to microscopic details than would be necessary for keying plants of most other families. Recognition of the family itself is easy, however, because of the distinctive structure of the flower heads. Each head consists of several to many flowers attached to a disk-shaped, conical, or slightly convex or concave receptacle. Below and around this receptacle are leaflike bracts called phyllaries. When you are served a cooked artichoke, you pull off the phyllaries and nibble off the more nutritious portions, then scrape away the flowers and eat the receptacle. In only a few genera in our region are phyllaries absent or insignificant.

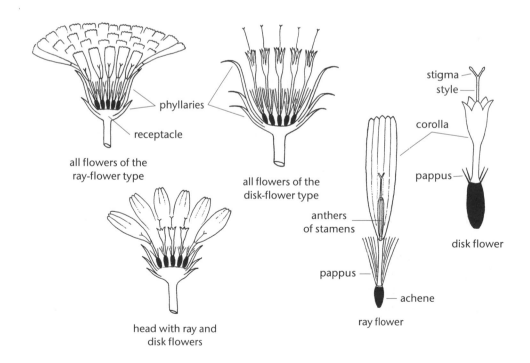

Asteraceae, structure of flowers and flower heads

There are two main types of flowers in Asteraceae: those in which the corolla is tubular and usually five-lobed, and those in which the corolla is drawn out into a petal-like structure. In a daisy, flowers with the tubular type of corolla occupy the central part of the head and are called disk flowers; those with a petal-like corolla are at the margin of the disk and are called ray flowers. In many members of the family there are only disk flowers or only flowers of the ray-flower type. It is therefore convenient to break up the family into three groups: those that have only disk flowers, those that have only flowers of the ray-flower type, and those that have both.

In flowers that have stamens and a pistil, the stamens are attached to the corolla, and their anthers are united into a tube that surrounds the style. Sepals, as we know them in other families, are absent or replaced by scales, toothlike structures, or bristles that form what is called a pappus. The fruit, called an achene, forms below the pappus and corolla, and is fused tightly to the single seed within it. When present, the pappus usually facilitates dispersal of the small dry fruit by wind, animals, or other means. Some or all flowers of the head may lack stamens or a pistil, and some may lack both. While strictly staminate flowers may have a pappus, it is the pappus attached to achenes that is especially important in classification of Asteraceae.

Of the numerous representatives of the family in our region, many are introduced, and some of these are among our most aggressive weeds. They establish themselves in lawns and gardens, colonize vacant lots and roadsides, and create problems for growers of commercial crops. But the family has given us many attractive garden flowers, food plants, and sources of valuable oils, dyes, and medicines.

Decide first to which of these three divisions the plant you are trying to identify belongs:

DIVISION 1. All flowers in each head of the ray-flower type (the size of the rays may vary considerably; when this is the case, the largest ones are closest to the margin); plants usually with milky sap. In a very few species in this division, the only flowers in the head originate at the margins.

DIVISION 2 (p. 107). All conspicuous flowers in each head of the disk-flower type, the corollas usually tubular and usually with five lobes. In a few species, the corollas of some flowers, especially those nearest the margins, are lopsided, with some lobes larger or at least longer than others; furthermore, the marginal corollas (especially in *Tanacetum*) sometimes form short, poorly developed rays, but these are not obviously longer than the corolla tubes.

DIVISION 3 (p. 113). At least some heads with both ray flowers and disk flowers. Some or all representatives of certain genera of Asteraceae have ray flowers that are small and easily overlooked; these species are keyed under Division 2 as well as under Division 3.

Now proceed with the key for that division. This will sometimes lead you directly to a species; just as likely, however, it will take you first to a genus name. In that case continue keying in that genus. The genera are listed in alphabetical order after the keys to all three divisions.

ASTERACEAE DIVISION 1

1 Leaves resembling those of grasses in being slender, smooth-margined, tapering to the tip, and scattered along the flowering stems (flowering stems, except in very robust plants, bearing only 1 head; corollas purple or yellow) . . . . *Tragopogon*
1 Leaves not resembling those of grasses
    2 Flowering stems not branched, each one bearing a single head
       3 Pappus consisting of flattened scales prolonged as bristles
          4 Each pappus scale ending in 2 prominent lobes, the bristle originating in the notch between them (SW Oreg. to Calif., also E of the Cascades as far as Idaho and New Mexico) . . . .
          . . . . *Uropappus lindleyi* (*U. linearifolius*), pl. 154
                                              NARROW-LEAVED UROPAPPUS
          4 Pappus scales tapering to the tip or bluntly rounded at the tip, where the bristle originates . . . .
          . . . . *Microseris borealis*
                                              NORTHERN MICROSERIS

3 Pappus consisting of slender bristles (these may be featherlike or barbed)
  5 Achenes without a beaklike prolongation (pappus bristles with very small barbs) . . . .
     . . . . *Microseris borealis* or *Nothocalais alpestris* (see *Microseris-Nothocalais* complex)
  5 Achenes with a beaklike prolongation (the pappus bristles originate from the tip of this)
    6 Pappus bristles with slender side branches, therefore somewhat featherlike
      7 Achene with a beak about 1 mm long; biennial or perennial . . . .
        . . . . *Leontodon taraxacoides* **subsp.** *taraxacoides*
                      HAWKBIT (Europe)
      7 Achene with a beak 2–3 mm long; annual or biennial . . . .
        . . . . *Leontodon taraxacoides* **subsp.** *longirostris*
                      LONG-BEAKED HAWKBIT (Europe)
    6 Pappus bristles not branched
      8 Achenes with short spines near the upper end, just below the slender beak . . . .
        . . . . *Taraxacum officinale* (includes *T. laevigatum*)
                      COMMON DANDELION (Europe)
      8 Achenes without spines . . . . *Agoseris*
2 Most flowering stems branched, with 2 or more heads
  9 Body of achene decidedly flattened (usually about half as thick as wide). In addition to the 2 species
    in choices 10, *Picris echioides*, bristly ox-tongue, from Europe, would key here. This weed, a nuisance
    in California, has been found in Douglas Co., Oreg., and is likely to spread quickly. Its achenes have a
    beak about as long as the body, but the feathery pappus bristles are in a single series. The plant as a
    whole is usually extensively branched and unpleasantly prickly, owing to abundant barbed hairs.
    10 Achene usually with a beak; outer pappus bristles not noticeably thicker than the inner ones;
      flower heads with as many as about 60 flowers (but in *M. muralis* with only 5 flowers) . . . .
      . . . . *Lactuca-Mycelis* complex
    10 Achene without a beak; some of the outer pappus bristles thicker than the inner ones; most flower
      heads with at least 80 flowers . . . . *Sonchus*
  9 Body of achene not decidedly flattened (it is about as thick as wide but may also be angular)
    11 Corollas white, pink, or blue
      12 Flower heads commonly at least 3 cm wide, the corollas at least 1.5 cm long; pappus consisting
        of small scales (flower heads sessile; corollas usually blue, sometimes pink or white; plants
        perennial, sometimes more than 1 m tall, extensively branched, leaves mostly small except at
        the base) . . . . *Cichorium intybus*, pl. 95
                      CHICORY (Europe)
      12 Flower heads less than 2 cm wide, the corollas not so much as 1 cm long; pappus consisting of
        slender bristles
        13 Corollas usually pink or at least with pink streaks but sometimes white; pappus bristles feathery
          (plants usually extensively branched; most of the leaves, except those near the base, small) . . . .
          . . . . *Stephanomeria*
        13 Corollas white; pappus bristles not featherlike
          14 Leaf blades arrowhead-shaped, not obviously hairy (but the inflorescence is hairy); flower
            heads usually with 10–14 flowers . . . . *Prenanthes alata* (*P. lessingii*), p. 106
                      WESTERN RATTLESNAKE ROOT
          14 Leaf blades elongated, not at all arrowhead-shaped, very hairy; flower heads usually with
            15–30 flowers . . . . *Hieracium albiflorum*, p. 137
                      WHITE-FLOWERED HAWKWEED
    11 Corollas (at least when fresh) yellow, orange, or reddish
      15 Pappus either absent or consisting of short, curved, spinelike structures
        16 Plants usually with 1 main stem, this upright; leaf blades more or less oval, not lobed; pappus
        absent . . . . *Lapsana communis*, pl. 128
                      NIPPLEWORT (Europe)

16 Plants with several main stems, these weak and falling down; larger leaf blades usually with a pair of lobes near the base; pappus, when present, inconspicuous, consisting of curved, spinelike structures (vicinity of Portland, Oreg., perhaps elsewhere) . . . . ***Lapsana apogonoides*** (China, Japan)

15 Pappus present in the form of slender bristles (sometimes branched and featherlike) and sometimes also of broad scales

  17 Pappus consisting of 5 bristles and 5 broad scales; leaves alternate but often appearing to be opposite when a branch stem produces a leaf at the same horizontal level as the one on the parent stem (achenes gradually widening from the base to the tip) . . . . ***Krigia virginica***
VIRGINIA DWARF DANDELION (E United States)

17 Pappus consisting only of bristles; leaves basal or alternate

  18 Pappus bristles branched, somewhat featherlike

    19 Achenes (at least the inner ones) with a beak as long as or longer than the main body . . . .
. . . . *Hypochaeris*

    19 Achenes with a beak shorter than the main body

      20 Beak about 1 mm long; biennial or perennial . . . . . ***Leontodon taraxacoides*** subsp. ***taraxacoides***
HAWKBIT (Europe)

      20 Beak about 2–3 mm long; annual or biennial . . . . . . ***Leontodon taraxacoides*** subsp. ***longirostris***
LONG-BEAKED HAWKBIT (Europe)

  18 Pappus bristles not branched

    21 Achenes not tapering to the tip and without a slender beak; pappus bristles dull brown or dirty white, but not white; leaf blades generally not lobed, but they may be toothed . . . .*Hieracium*

    21 Achenes tapering to the tip and often with a slender beak; pappus bristles white; leaf blades often conspicuously lobed

      22 Achenes with a crown of scales (these surround the base of the slender beak) . . . .
. . . . ***Chondrilla juncea***
RUSH SKELETONWEED (Europe)

Prenanthes alata,
western rattlesnake root

ASTERACEAE DIVISION 2

1 Blades of basal leaves deeply palmately lobed and about as wide as long (blades commonly more than 15 cm wide, at least slightly white-hairy on the underside; involucre usually with a few small, erratically placed phyllaries below a regular series of larger phyllaries; pappus consisting of slender bristles)

    2 All flowers in each head normally with stamens and a pistil; leaves on flowering stems similar to the basal leaves but smaller (in our region from the S portion of the Willamette Valley through Jackson and Josephine Cos., Oreg., to Calif.) . . . . ***Cacaliopsis nardosmia*** (*Luina nardosmia*)
                                                   SILVERCROWN

    2 Flower heads on some plants consisting entirely or mostly of pistillate flowers (staminate flowers, when present, usually concentrated in the center), those on other plants consisting entirely or mostly of staminate flowers; leaves along the flowering stems simple (flowers at the edges of pistillate heads sometimes with short rays; in wet habitats, especially stream borders and shaded lake margins; usually in flower by mid-February in lowland areas) . . . . ***Petasites frigidus*** subsp. ***palmatus***, pl. 139
                                                   COLTSFOOT

1 Blades of basal leaves not deeply palmately lobed (but the basal leaves or other leaves may be pinnately lobed)

    3 Involucre (individual phyllaries not always distinct) with spines that resemble fishhooks (in species of *Xanthium* only the pistillate heads have hooked spines; furthermore, each pistillate head has only 2 flowers—although these lack corollas, the styles of the pistils protrude out of the involucre)

        4 Flower heads all of 1 type, with distinct phyllaries characterized by spines that resemble fishhooks, and with flowers that have stamens as well as a pistil (corollas purple, the tips exposed) . . . . . ***Arctium***

        4 Flower heads of 2 types, staminate and pistillate, only the pistillate heads, which lack distinct phyllaries, with spines that resemble fishhooks (each pistillate head with only 2 flowers, these without corollas and with their styles projecting out of the involucre; staminate heads, with distinct phyllaries, above the pistillate heads and with numerous flowers that have corollas, these translucent, not colored)

           5 Stems with trios of sharp spines at the axils of the leaves; leaf blades much longer than wide, distinctly lobed, dark green on the upper surface, grayish on the underside . . . . . . ***Xanthium spinosum***
                                           SPINY COCKLEBUR

           5 Stems without spines at the axils of the leaves; leaf blades nearly as wide as long, toothed and indistinctly lobed, about the same color on both surfaces . . . . . ***Xanthium strumarium*** subsp. ***canadense***
                                           COCKLEBUR

Cacaliopsis nardosmia,
silvercrown

Xanthium strumarium
subsp. *canadense*,
Canadian cocklebur

3 Involucres without spines that resemble fishhooks (but straight or curved spines of other forms may be present; in species of *Filago, Hesperevax,* and *Psilocarphus* there are no phyllaries, therefore no distinct involucre; in *Micropus* the involucre consists of very small phyllaries; in all 4 genera the pistils of flowers at the edge of the disk are enveloped by small scales that could be mistaken for phyllaries)

  6 Phyllaries pearly white, completely membranous, not in the least obscured by woolly or cottony hairs (leaf blades conspicuously white-hairy on the underside; perennial with several to many upright stems to more than 60 cm tall; flowers on a particular plant staminate or pistillate, but some pistillate flowers often have stamens; achenes with a pappus of slender bristles) . . . . ***Anaphalis margaritacea,*** pl. 70
PEARLY EVERLASTING

  6 Phyllaries not pearly white, even if partly or wholly membranous

    7 Blades of lower leaves to more than 10 cm long, widest at the base and about as wide as long (thus nearly triangular), densely white-hairy on the underside; flowers at the center of the disk staminate, the few at the margin pistillate, forming cucumber-shaped achenes to about 8 mm long and with conspicuous stalked glands along the upper portion; pappus absent . . . . ***Adenocaulon bicolor***
TRAIL PLANT

    7 Plants not in all respects as described in the other choice 7

      8 Flower heads of 2 types, staminate and pistillate, the latter in the axils of leaves below the staminate portion of the inflorescence; pistillate flowers, without a corolla, single within each involucre; staminate flowers several within each involucre . . . . ***Ambrosia***

      8 Flower heads all much alike, even in species in which staminate and pistillate flowers are in separate heads (in any case, the plants do not meet all criteria in the other choice 8)

        9 Phyllaries of involucre with spines. Three uncommon, thistlelike weeds are not in the portion of the key under this choice. *Onopordum acanthium,* cotton thistle, from Eurasia, is distinctive because its stems, phyllaries, and undersides of the leaves are conspicuously woolly-hairy, and the stems have broad, long-spined wings that run the full length of the internodes, including the one below the single flower head; the corollas are purplish pink, and the slender pappus bristles are not featherlike. In the 2 species of *Carthamus,* from the Mediterranean region, the lowest 1–2 series of phyllaries resemble the upper leaves in being just as distinctly toothed or lobed; the corollas are yellow or orange, and the pappus bristles, present on some achenes, are scale- or daggerlike, serrated but not feathery; the leaves of *C. tinctorius,* safflower, are sharply toothed, whereas those of *C. lanatus,* distaff thistle, have spine-tipped lobes.

          10 Leaves with conspicuous white mottling (flower heads to 5 cm wide, with long spines; corollas purple; plants to more than 1 m tall) . . . . ***Silybum marianum***
MILK THISTLE (Mediterranean region)

          10 Leaves without white mottling (but the leaf veins may be white)

            11 Pappus bristles featherlike, the hairs conspicuous (leaves with spiny margins, and the phyllaries usually spine-tipped) . . . . ***Cirsium***

            11 Pappus bristles, if present, not distinctly featherlike (but they may have small barbs or very short hairs)

              12 Achenes attached by their bases to the receptacle; corollas of flowers at the edge of the disk not obviously larger than those near the center; pappus consisting of a single series of slender bristles, these roughened by the presence of small barbs . . . . ***Carduus***

              12 Achenes attached somewhat obliquely to the receptacle; flowers at the edge of the disk usually larger than those near the center; pappus consisting of 2 or more series of bristles

                13 Leaves prickly on the margins; pappus consisting of 10 smooth outer bristles and 10 shorter, barbed inner bristles (flower heads single at the ends of stems and surrounded by broad, prickly leaves; corollas yellow) . . . . ***Cnicus benedictus***
BLESSED THISTLE (Europe)

                13 Leaves not prickly on the margins; pappus, if present, consisting of several series of bristles with barbs or short hairs. . . . . ***Centaurea-Acroptilon* complex**

9 Phyllaries, if present (they are lacking in *Filago, Hesperevax,* and *Psilocarphus* and are rather insignificant in *Micropus*) without spines, but they may be divided in such a way that they have fringes of slender lobes

14 Phyllaries absent or insignificant

  15 True phyllaries present but inconspicuous, much smaller than the scales that envelop the pistillate flowers at the edge of the disk (phyllaries slightly hairy, their central portions greenish, their marginal portions membranous; bracts enveloping the pistillate flowers with beaklike tips; achenes without a pappus; plants as a whole white- or gray-woolly; Willamette Valley, Oreg., to Calif.) . . . . .
. . . . *Micropus californicus* **var.** *californicus*, pl. 136
SLENDER COTTONWEED

  15 True phyllaries absent (in other words, there is no involucre, but each pistillate flower at the edge of the disk is partly enclosed by a bract that could be mistaken for a phyllary)

    16 All or nearly all leaves opposite (plants conspicuously woolly-hairy; staminate flowers, each with an abortive pistil, located in the central portion of the head and surrounded by pistillate flowers; each pistillate flower enclosed within a lopsided, saclike scale from which only the style protrudes [the scale also has a slender outgrowth]; achenes without a pappus) . . . . *Psilocarphus*

    16 Leaves alternate (receptacle slightly conical, higher in the center than at the margin)

      17 Outer portion of the receptacle with several series of pistillate flowers, each one originating at the base of a thick, scalelike structure than soon hardens, becoming woody; stalklike inner portion of the receptacle with a group of staminate flowers surrounded by a ring of membranous scales; plants small but usually extensively branched, forming low, moundlike growths . . . .
. . . . *Hesperevax*

      17 Outer portion of the receptacle with 1 or more series of pistillate flowers, at least the outermost of these partly enclosed by boat-shaped, membranous scales; at least some flowers on the inner part of the receptacle with stamens and a pistil, and producing achenes that have pappus bristles; plants upright, slender, and not extensively branched. . . . . *Filago*
        Species of *Filago,* in general appearance, resemble those of *Micropus californicus,*
        which has only insignificant phyllaries. The presence of a pappus on the achenes of
        some flowers of *Filago,* however, distinguish this genus.

14 Phyllaries obvious

  18 Leaves (at least the lower ones) opposite or in whorls

    19 Lower leaves opposite, upper leaves alternate (small annual; corollas usually yellow, orange, or reddish; reddish ray flowers also present but the rays so short as to be easily overlooked; achene of each ray flower partly enveloped by a phyllary; achenes of ray flowers without a pappus but those of the disk flowers with a prominent pappus consisting of 10 silvery scales, those of the inner series about 1 cm long; Umpqua River valley, Oreg., to Calif.) . . . . *Achyrachaena mollis*
BLOW-WIVES

    19 All or nearly all leaves opposite or in whorls, and plants not as otherwise described in the other choice 19

      20 Phyllaries in a single series (leaves sessile; marginal flowers with yellow rays but these so small —less than 3 mm long—that they may be overlooked (pappus consisting of 3–5 slender scales and some shorter, broader scales that are fringed at the tip) . . . . *Lasthenia*

      20 Phyllaries in more than 1 series

        21 Most leaves in whorls of 3–4, some merely opposite (plants commonly at least 1 m tall; corollas purple; almost entirely E of the Cascades but known from SW Brit. Col.) . . . .
. . . . *Eupatorium maculatum* **var.** *bruneri*
JOE PYE WEED

        21 Leaves opposite, not in whorls

          22 Phyllaries in 2 series but all of them similar in size and shape; pappus consisting of numerous barbed bristles . . . . *Arnica*

22 Phyllaries in 2 series, those of one series very different in size and form from those of the other; pappus consisting of 2 or 4 stout, spinelike outgrowths, these with downward-pointing bristles or barbs (plants commonly more than 50 cm tall, sometimes more than 1 m tall, typically growing in wet habitats) . . . . *Bidens*

18 Leaves alternate (or occasionally a few opposite)

  23 Pistillate and staminate flower heads on separate plants

    24 Shrub to more than 1 m tall; young stems and leaves slightly sticky (involucres 5–6 mm high; corollas white; near the coast, Pacific Co., Wash., to Calif.). . . . . *Baccharis pilularis*, pl. 87
                                        CHAPARRAL BROOM, COYOTE BROOM

    24 Plants low, often mat-forming, our species mostly less than 20 cm tall when flowering; stems and leaves not sticky (they are commonly woolly-hairy) . . . . *Antennaria*
                Some populations of certain species of *Antennaria* consist entirely of pistillate plants.

  23 At least some flowers in each head with stamens and/or a pistil

    25 Style of the pistil of fertile flowers ringed by a distinct, often hairy swelling just below the level at which its 2 branches originate (without magnification this feature will not be evident; if you are not sure, read the two choices 26, which include plants that are distinctive in some other ways)

      26 Flowers at the edge of the disk usually sterile, their corollas larger than those of flowers nearer the center and often lopsided; phyllaries (except in *A. repens*) fringed by slender lobes; plants branched . . . . *Centaurea-Acroptilon* complex

      26 Flowers at the edge of the disk typically fertile, their corollas similar to those of flowers nearer the center and not lopsided; phyllaries not fringed by slender lobes; main stem (this sometimes more than 1 m tall) usually not branched except in the inflorescence (leaves widest near the base, tapering gradually to the tip, therefore nearly triangular, and with conspicuously and evenly toothed margins; montane, in the Olympic Mountains, Wash., Cascades, and Siskiyou Mountains, Oreg., to Calif. and eastward) . . . . *Saussurea americana*
                                          AMERICAN SAWWORT

    25 Style of the pistil not ringed by a distinct swelling at the level where its branches originate

      27 Achenes either without a pappus or the pappus consisting of flat scales or a circle of very small teeth

        28 Flower-bearing part of the head conical, usually as long as, or longer than, wide

          29 Coarse perennial; leaf blades to about 25 cm long, 15 cm wide, not lobed; phyllaries in 1 series, about 2 cm long, turning downward; flower-bearing receptacle dark, more than twice as long as wide, and commonly 3–5 cm long by the time achenes have formed; pappus absent . . . .
           . . . . *Rudbeckia occidentalis* var. *occidentalis*
                                         WESTERN CONEFLOWER

          29 Small plant, usually annual, not often more than about 25 cm tall; leaf blades to about 5 cm long, divided 2–3 times into numerous small lobes; phyllaries in 2 indistinct series, less than 5 mm long, not turning downward; receptacle about 1 cm long, not much longer than wide; pappus absent or consisting of a circle of small teeth (bruised foliage smelling like pineapple)
           . . . . *Matricaria discoidea*
                (*M. matricarioides* or *Chamomilla suaveolens* of some references), pl. 135
                                          PINEAPPLE WEED

        28 Flower-bearing part of the head not obviously conical

          30 Pappus consisting of long, flat scales of different lengths (blades of larger leaves deeply bipinnately lobed; inflorescences with several flower heads, the phyllaries all in 1 series but varying in length, green except for hairs and glands; corollas whitish or pale pink; Douglas Co., Oreg., to Calif.; also widespread E of the Cascades) . . . .
           . . . . *Chaenactis douglasii* var. *douglasii* (includes vars. *achilleifolia* and *rubricaulis*), pl. 94
                                          HOARY PINCUSHION

          30 Pappus either absent or consisting of a circle of small teeth

31 Achenes produced by marginal flowers not stalked but flattened and winged, the persistent style and each wing prolonged upward as a short spine (leaves pinnately lobed, the lobes then divided into pointed secondary lobes; flower heads sessile in the axils of the leaves; corollas of nonmarginal flowers greenish; Lincoln Co., Oreg., to Calif.) . . . . ***Soliva sessilis***
PRICKLY SOLIVA (South America)

31 None of the achenes flattened and winged, nor with spines as described in the other choice 31

  32 Blades of lower leaves to more than 10 cm long, widest at the base and about as wide as long, densely white-hairy on the underside (phyllaries uniformly green, without membranous margins and tips; flowers at the margin of the disk pistillate, those near the center staminate; upper portion of achenes with stalked glands; pappus absent) . . . . ***Adenocaulon bicolor***
TRAIL PLANT

  32 Leaf blades oval or elongated, not widest at the base

    33 Flower heads borne singly at the ends of stems (most larger leaves pinnately lobed; corollas of nonmarginal flowers yellow; achenes produced by marginal flowers distinctly stalked; in wet habitats, especially around salt marshes) . . . . ***Cotula coronopifolia***, pl. 102
BRASS BUTTONS (S Africa)

    33 Flower heads borne in inflorescences

      34 Flower heads in elongated inflorescences; corollas generally yellowish, sometimes clear yellow; marginal flowers without any traces of rays . . . . ***Artemisia***

      34 Flower heads in nearly flat-topped inflorescences; corollas bright yellow; marginal flowers sometimes with short, poorly developed rays, these not obviously longer than the corolla tube . . . . ***Tanacetum***

27 Achenes with a pappus consisting of slender bristles, these sometimes with branches (therefore feathery) or small barbs

  35 Phyllaries in a single series (but in species of *Erechtites* and *Senecio* there are often small, erratically placed bract- or phyllarylike outgrowths below or among the obvious, regularly spaced phyllaries)

Saussurea americana,
American sawwort

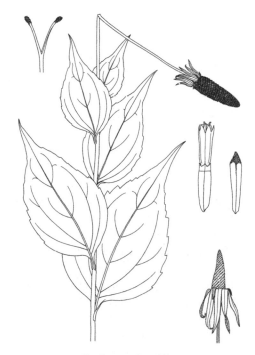

Rudbeckia occidentalis var.
occidentalis, western coneflower

36 Leaf blades distinctly toothed or lobed (annual, typically with a single stem from the base, but this may branch below the inflorescence)

  37 Flowers at the margin of the disk strictly pistillate (those nearer the center usually with stamens and a pistil); plants commonly at least 1 m tall . . . . ***Erechtites***

  37 Flowers at the margin of the disk with stamens and a pistil; plants usually less than 1 m tall . . . . ***Senecio***

36 Leaf blades not toothed or lobed (perennial)

  38 Leaf blades broadly oval, mostly 3–5 cm long, not more than about twice as long as wide, sessile, green on the upper surface and conspicuously white-hairy on the underside (plants slightly shrubby, not often more than 35 cm tall; stems white-hairy; corollas yellow, extending conspicuously out of the involucre) . . . . ***Luina hypoleuca***, pl. 132

                                                                       SILVERBACK

  38 Leaf blades more than 3 times as long as wide, tapering to rather distinct petioles

    39 Leaves scattered along the stems, most of the larger ones (including petioles) more than 10 cm long, sometimes more than 25 cm (smaller leaves on upper portions of the flowering stems sessile); flower heads usually numerous, borne in the axils of bracts of an elongate inflorescence; plants to about 1 m tall (high montane in the Cascades, mostly E of the crest, Oreg. to Calif.) . . . .

        . . . . ***Rainiera stricta*** (*Luina stricta*)

                                                          TONGUE-LEAF RAINIERA

    39 All leaves basal, the larger ones, including petioles, to about 5 cm long and concentrated near the base of the plant; flower heads borne singly at the tips of leafless stems; plants, when flowering, not more than about 15 cm tall (leaves silvery-hairy, the hairs mostly pressed down; high montane in the Siskiyou Mountains of SW Oreg. and NW Calif., and the Cascades, mostly E of the crest, Oreg. to Calif.) . . . . ***Raillardella argentea***

                                                         SILVERY RAILLARDELLA

35 Phyllaries, even when of similar size and form, in at least 2 series and sometimes overlapping like shingles on a roof

  40 Phyllaries (slender) in 2 series, those of the lower and upper series about the same length and width; plants perennial, woody at the base, usually with at least several main stems; leaf blades broadest near the base, coarsely toothed; flowers as many as about 12 in each head; corollas pink or purplish pink, sometimes white; in our region, from Lane Co., Oreg., to Calif. . . . . ***Ageratina occidentalis*** (*Eupatorium occidentale*), pl. 64

                                           WESTERN AGERATINA

  40 Plants not in all respects as described in the other choice 40

    41 Phyllaries, in several series, with membranous tips (the tips may be white, brownish, blackish, or some other color); plant as a whole usually woolly-hairy, but in some species the woolliness may not be pronounced . . . . ***Gnaphalium***

    41 Phyllaries without membranous tips; plants, as a whole, often hairy, but not conspicuously woolly-hairy

      42 Phyllaries with prominent alternating light and dark lengthwise lines (plants shrubby, woody at least near the base; flower heads longer than wide; corollas white or faintly yellowish, sometimes becoming tinged with pink or purplish; in our region limited to SW Oreg.) . . . . . ***Brickellia***

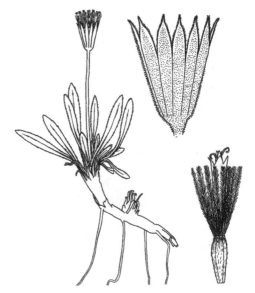

Raillardella argentea,
silvery raillardella

42 Phyllaries without alternating light and dark lengthwise lines

  43 Phyllaries (in 3–4 series, of increasing size upward) usually overlapping in such a way that they form distinct vertical rows (shrub to more than 1.5 m tall; younger stems with a feltlike covering of white hairs; leaf blades slender, most of them more than 10 times as long as wide; corollas bright yellow; plant with an unpleasant odor; mostly E of the Cascades except in SW Oreg.) . . . . **Ericameria nauseosa** (*Chrysothamnus nauseosus*), pl. 105

RABBIT BRUSH

> Several intergrading varieties of *E. nauseosa* have been named; the one in our region, if you cannot resist the temptation to push the identification beyond species, is *albicaulis*.

  43 Phyllaries not overlapping in such as way as to form distinct vertical rows, and plants not in all other respects as described in the other choice 43

    44 Tips of phyllaries typically pressed down tightly, not spreading outward (larger plants woody at the base; phyllaries in 4 series; generally found along dry streambeds or on gravel bars of rivers but occasionally in other habitats) . . . . **Heterotheca oregona** (*Chrysopsis oregona*), pl. 123

OREGON GOLDEN ASTER

    44 Tips of phyllaries not pressed down tightly, spreading outward to at least some extent

      45 Phyllaries, especially in their lower portions, with somewhat membranous or hardened, nongreen margins and often broadened above the middle; successive series of phyllaries often alternating and overlapping in such a way that their arrangement resembles that of shingles on a roof; pappus consisting of a single circle of bristles . . . . **Aster** (see *Aster-Machaeranthera* complex)

> Only 4 species of *Aster* in our region always or sometimes lack rays; these are dealt with at the beginning of the key to the genus.

      45 Phyllaries usually without decidedly membranous or hardened, nongreen margins and usually tapering evenly from near the base to the tip; successive series of phyllaries not clearly alternating and overlapping in such a way that their arrangement resembles that of shingles on a roof; pappus sometimes consisting of a single circle of bristles, sometimes of 2 circles, those of the outer circle very short . . . . **Erigeron**

> Only 3 species of *Erigeron* in our region always or sometimes lack rays; these are dealt with at the beginning of the key to the genus. Closely related to *Erigeron* is *Conyza*, whose small flower heads have such short white or pink rays that these are scarcely exposed and therefore easily overlooked.

ASTERACEAE DIVISION 3

1 Phyllaries of the involucre appearing to be in 1 series encircling the receptacle (even if they are in 2 series, as in *Arnica*, they are all alike and one series is not distinctly above the other; in species of *Senecio*, keyed under this choice, there are usually some small, erratically placed phyllaries on the lowermost part of the involucre)

  2 Phyllaries of the main series accompanied, on the lowermost part of the involucre, by a few small, erratically placed phyllaries (these sometimes absent in *S. bolanderi*) . . . . **Senecio**

  2 Lowermost portion of the involucre without any small, erratically placed phyllaries

    3 Phyllaries not even partly enveloping the achenes of the ray flowers

      4 Leaves opposite

        5 Pappus consisting of numerous bristles, these typically roughened by short barbs; plants perennial . . . . **Arnica**

        5 Pappus consisting of a few scalelike structures, each prolonged as a slender bristle; plants annual, typically growing in sunny areas that are wet in winter and early spring . . . . **Lasthenia**

      4 Leaves alternate

        6 Bushy perennials, sometimes slightly woody at the base; leaves typically woolly-hairy; pappus consisting of a few flat, membranous scales . . . . **Eriophyllum**

        6 Annuals; leaves not woolly-hairy (but sometimes there are woolly hairs in the axils of lower leaves); pappus consisting of slender bristles, these usually soon shed . . . . . **Crocidium multicaule**

GOLD STAR

3 Phyllaries plump, some or all of them partly or completely enveloping the achenes of the ray flowers

  7 Achene of each ray flower completely enveloped by a phyllary (the free edges of the phyllary touch or overlap; see *Madia exigua,* pp. 140, 141)

    8 Rays (yellow, orange, or reddish) reaching only slightly beyond the phyllaries, easily overlooked; pappus of disk flowers very conspicuous, consisting of 2 series of silvery scales that spread outward, some of the inner scales nearly or fully 1 cm long (Umpqua River valley, Oreg., to Calif.) . . . . *Achyrachaena mollis*
BLOW-WIVES

    8 Rays (usually yellow, yellow with a maroon blotch, or yellow with purple on the underside) conspicuous even if sometimes short; pappus of disk flowers either absent or consisting of small scales or short bristles, these featherlike

      9 Leaves and involucres somewhat silky-hairy; rays yellow, purplish on the underside . . . . *Lagophylla ramosissima*
COMMON HARELEAF

      9 Leaves and involucres not silky hairy; rays yellow, sometimes with a maroon blotch at the base (plants usually very glandular and aromatic) . . . . *Madia-Anisocarpus-Hemizonella-Kyhosia* **complex**

  7 Achene of each ray flower at most only partly enveloped by a phyllary (the edges of the phyllary do not touch or overlap)

    10 Bracts below the involucres, and sometimes also the phyllaries, tipped with tack-shaped glands . . . . *Calycadenia*

    10 Neither the bracts below the flower heads nor the phyllaries tipped with tack-shaped glands (but the plants may nevertheless be at least partly glandular)

      11 Rays 2–7, white, each usually with a purplish lengthwise line on the underside; leaves alternate (SW Oreg. to Calif.) . . . . *Blepharipappus scaber,* pl. 91

      11 Rays usually more than 7, yellow or white; at least the lower leaves opposite

        12 Leaf blades narrow, spine-tipped, those just below the flower heads extending beyond the heads; foliage unpleasantly aromatic; rays numerous, yellow, usually 2-lobed (Rogue River valley, Oreg., to Calif.) . . . . *Hemizonia fitchii,* pl. 122
FITCH'S SPIKEWEED

        12 Leaf blades not spine-tipped, those just below the flower heads not extending beyond the heads; foliage not unpleasantly aromatic; rays usually 6–10, white, often red- or purple-streaked near the base, usually 3-lobed (Jackson Co., Oreg., to Calif.) . . . . *Hemizonia congesta* **subsp.** *clevelandii* (*H. clevelandii*)
CLEVELAND'S HEMIZONIA

1 Phyllaries in at least 2 conspicuous series encircling the receptacle (if there are merely a few small, somewhat erratically placed phyllaries on the lowermost part of the involucre, take the other choice 1)

  13 Phyllaries in 2 series, those of the upper series conspicuously different in size and/or shape from those of the lower (all or most leaves opposite)

    14 Phyllaries of the lower series narrower than those of the upper series but longer; leaves not divided; plants to about 1 m tall . . . . *Bidens cernua*
STICKTIGHT

    14 Phyllaries of the lower series much smaller and shorter than those of the upper series; larger leaves pinnately or bipinnately divided into narrow lobes (plants not often more than 80 cm tall; along the Columbia River as far W as Sauvie Island, Multnomah Co., Oreg.) . . . . *Coreopsis tinctoria* **var.** *atkinsoniana,* pl. 101
COLUMBIA COREOPSIS

Coreopsis lanceolata, garden coreopsis, native to E United States, sometimes escapes. Its flower heads resemble those of *C. tinctoria* var. *atkinsoniana,* but its leaves are not lobed.

13 Phyllaries in 2 or more series and all of similar form, even if varying in size and the extent to which they are somewhat papery

  15 All or most leaves opposite

    16 Low, sprawling, succulent plants growing in salt marshes (usually found with *Salicornia*); leaves sessile, mostly at least 8 times as long as wide, not at all hairy (rays slender and often unequally developed, yellow) . . . . ***Jaumea carnosa***, pl. 127

                                                     JAUMEA

    16 Upright plants often more than 50 cm tall, not likely to be found in salt marshes; most leaves with distinct, even if short, petioles, the blades only about twice as long as wide

      17 Rays white, not more than about 2 mm long . . . . *Galinsoga*

      17 Rays yellow, more than 1 cm long . . . . ***Helianthus-Helianthella*** complex

  15 Leaves alternate

    18 Involucre with a gummy secretion . . . . *Grindelia*

    18 Involucre without a gummy secretion

      19 Shrubs (woody on at least the lower portions of the stems as well as at the base) or subshrubs (woody only at the base)

        20 Pappus on achenes of disk flowers double, the bristles of the outer series much shorter than those of the inner series . . . . ***Heterotheca villosa*** var. ***villosa*** (*Chrysopsis villosa*), pl. 124

                                        HAIRY GOLDEN ASTER

        20 Pappus on achenes of disk flowers in a single series, the bristles varying in length, but the shorter ones much more than half as long as the longer ones . . . .

         . . . . ***Ericameria-Pyrrocoma-Columbiadoria-Hazardia*** complex

      19 Plants not woody at the base or on the lower portions of the stems

        21 Margins of all phyllaries with membranous, often papery, brownish, or nearly transparent margins, only the central portion green (foliage usually aromatic even if not pleasantly so)

          22 Leaves compound or so deeply lobed that they are nearly compound

            23 Inflorescence usually almost flat-topped; flower heads about 6–7 mm high; rays usually 3–5, white, about 2 mm long; leaves finely divided . . . .

              . . . . ***Achillea millefolium*** (includes *A. borealis* and *A. lanulosa*), pl. 63

                                         YARROW

            23 Plants not conforming to all criteria in the other choice 23

              24 Rays white

                25 Disk not conspicuously convex; perennial, often more than 50 cm tall . . . .

                . . . . ***Tanacetum parthenium***, pl. 152

                                     FEVERFEW (Europe)

                25 Disk conspicuously convex (usually becoming more convex, sometimes conical, as achenes ripen); annual, not often more than 50 cm tall

                  26 At least the upper half of the disk with thin, scalelike structures between the disk flowers . . . . *Anthemis*

                  26 None of the disk with scalelike structures between the disk flowers . . . . *Matricaria*

              24 Rays yellow (perennial)

                27 Foliage aromatic; rays very short, sometimes barely evident; receptacles nearly flat . . . . .

                . . . . *Tanacetum*

                27 Foliage not aromatic; rays conspicuous; receptacles about as high as wide, sometimes a little higher than wide

                  28 Plants not often more than about 80 cm tall and not normally in wet habitats; leaves and stems obviously white-hairy; leaves pinnately divided, nearly compound, most of the divisions about the same size and with toothed margins; rays to about 13 mm long; occasionally escaping from cultivation . . . . ***Anthemis tinctoria***

                    GOLDEN MARGUERITE (Europe)

28 Plants commonly at least 1 m tall and growing in marshy habitats; leaves and stems not obviously white-hairy, but there are usually hairs on the undersides of the leaves; blades of larger leaves, in outline, somewhat triangular, divided into conspicuous, pointed leaflets, lobes, or teeth; rays at least 20 mm long, typically drooping (introduced in Fraser River valley, Brit. Col.) . . . .*Rudbeckia laciniata* var. *ampla*
TALL CONEFLOWER (Rocky Mountain region and central United States)

22 Leaves neither compound nor deeply lobed

  29 Plants not often more than 70 cm tall; leaf blades conspicuously toothed, lower ones nearly lobed; receptacle flat; rays white, usually 15–20 mm long; achenes without a pappus; widespread weed . . . . *Leucanthemum vulgare* (*Chrysanthemum leucanthemum*)
OX-EYE DAISY (Europe)

  29 Plants to more than 1 m tall; leaf blades smooth-margined; receptacle distinctly cone-shaped; rays white, pink, purple, or blue, usually 8–12 mm long; achenes of disk flowers with a pappus usually consisting of several short bristles and 2 longer bristles (the achenes of ray flowers generally lack the longer bristles); rare weed, occasionally found along Columbia River . . . .*Boltonia asteroides* (E United States)

21 Phyllaries (at least the outer ones) without membranous, papery, or transparent margins, most of them usually green or brownish throughout, but sometimes hardening, or the inner ones becoming slightly papery

  30 Receptacle nearly globular, about as high as wide, or conical and much taller than wide

    31 Receptacle nearly globular, about as wide as high . . . . *Helenium*

    31 Receptacle conical, much taller than wide (rays to more than 3 cm long; pappus a crown of teeth; Umpqua River valley, Oreg., to Calif.) . . . . *Rudbeckia californica* var. *glauca* (*R. glaucescens*), pl. 142
CALIFORNIA CONEFLOWER

  30 Receptacle not nearly globular or conical

    32 Rays bright yellow, usually more than 50, slender, mostly 1.5–2.5 cm long (plants commonly at least 1 m tall; blades of lower leaves to more than 40 cm long, rough on the upper surface; achenes with 4 lengthwise ridges, the pappus usually reddish) . . . . *Inula helenium*
ELECAMPANE (Europe)

    32 Rays, if bright yellow, neither more than 50 nor especially slender

      33 Pappus consisting of scalelike structures (the tips of these sometimes drawn out into slender awns), a crown of small teeth, or absent

        34 Disk rarely more than 1 cm wide; rays (about 8 mm long) white; small plants commonly found in lawns and along paths and roadsides . . . . *Bellis perennis*, pl. 90
ENGLISH DAISY (Europe)

        34 Disk of at least the larger flowers usually more than 1 cm wide; rays yellow; plants of natural habitats and, except for *Hulsea nana*, usually large

          35 Plants without a substantial concentration of basal leaves that are much larger than those on the flowering stems; annual or perennial, sometimes extensively branched; ray flowers not producing achenes . . . . *Helianthus-Helianthella* complex

          35 Basal leaves crowded and well developed (and usually much larger than any that might be on the flowering stems); perennial; each flowering stem bearing only 1 or a few flower heads (if there is more than 1 head, the one at the top of the stem is larger than those below it); ray flowers, as well as disk flowers, producing achenes

            36 High-montane plants to about 10 cm tall; basal leaves to about 6 cm long, the blades conspicuously lobed and sometimes woolly-hairy; flowering stems leafless, with single heads, the rays 8–10 mm long (in the Cascades, Oreg.; to Calif.) . . . .*Hulsea nana*, pl. 126
DWARF HULSEA

36 Large plants of low and moderate elevations, generally much more than 10 cm tall when flowering; leaves more than 10 cm long, either lobed or not lobed; flowering stems with at least a few
leaves and often with more than 1 head, the rays usually at least 15 mm long ....
.... ***Balsamorhiza-Wyethia* complex**

33 Pappus of achenes (of at least some flowers in the head) consisting of long, slender bristles, these
sometimes barbed or featherlike

37 Heads numerous in each inflorescence, the rays usually less than 6 mm long (and in species of *Conyza*
so small and inconspicuous as to be easily overlooked)

38 Rays yellow, generally at least 4 mm long; perennial .... ***Solidago-Euthamia* complex**

38 Rays white, either only about 1 mm long or so short as to be scarcely noticeable; annual .... ***Conyza***

37 Heads not often more than several in each inflorescence; rays usually (but not always) conspicuous

39 Rays yellow (plants to about 50 cm tall, slightly shrubby at the base; leaf blades usually about 4–5
times as long as wide; in our region mostly in prairies, including some areas on Whidbey Island,
Island Co., Wash.) .... ***Heterotheca villosa* var. *villosa*** (*Chrysopsis villosa*), pl. 124
HAIRY GOLDEN ASTER

39 Rays white, pink, blue, violet, or purplish

40 Ray flowers sterile, not producing achenes, the pistils small compared to those of disk flowers
(leaves grayish due to a fine, white wooliness; rays white, pink, or pale purple; low, somewhat
prostrate plants; coastal, on dunes and sandy bluffs, Coos Co., Oreg., to Calif.) ....
.... ***Lessingia filaginifolia* subsp. *californica***
(*Corethrogyne californica, C. filaginifolia* var. *californica*), pl. 131
BEACH LESSINGIA

40 Ray flowers usually fertile (sterile in *Machaeranthera canescens* var. *shastensis*), producing achenes,
the pistils similar to those of disk flowers

41 Apices of leaves, and also marginal teeth, which are usually present, with spinelike tips (leaves
grayish due to hairiness; rays about 10–20, to about 1 cm long, violet; mostly montane and
almost entirely E of the crest of the Cascades) ....
.... ***Machaeranthera*** (see *Aster-Machaeranthera* complex)

41 Marginal teeth, when present on leaf blades, without stiff, spinelike tips

42 Phyllaries, especially in their lower portions, with somewhat membranous, nongreen margins, and often broadened above the middle; successive series of phyllaries often alternating
and overlapping in such a way that their arrangement resembles that of shingles on a roof;
pappus consisting of 1 circle of bristles ....***Aster*** (see *Aster-Machaeranthera* complex)

42 Phyllaries without membranous margins, and usually tapering gradually from near the base
to the tip; successive series of phyllaries not clearly alternating and overlapping in such a way
that their arrangement resembles that of shingles on a roof; pappus sometimes consisting of
1 circle of bristles, sometimes of 2 circles, those of the outer circle very short ....***Erigeron***

Agoseris

1 Corollas, when fresh, orange to nearly red, usually becoming purplish as they dry (beak of achene as long
as or slightly longer than the body; mostly above 4000 ft., 1220 m; Lane Co., Oreg., to Calif.; also E of the
Cascades) .... ***A. aurantiaca* var. *aurantiaca*,** pl. 66
ORANGE AGOSERIS

1 Corollas, when fresh, yellow (but sometimes reddish on the back)

2 Beak of achene 2–3 times as long as the body

3 Perennial with a stout root-crown; hairs on phyllaries without purple cross-walls ...***A. grandiflora*,** pl. 67
LARGE-FLOWERED AGOSERIS

3 Annual with a slender root; some hairs on phyllaries usually with purple cross-walls ....
.... ***A. heterophylla* var. *heterophylla***
ANNUAL AGOSERIS

2 Beak of achene less than twice as long as the body

    4 Beak of achene fully as long as the body . . . . *A. elata*
                                        TALL AGOSERIS

    4 Beak of achene slightly shorter than the body

       5 Leaf blades narrow for their entire length and usually deeply lobed; in inland habitats . . . .
                . . . . *A. apargioides* var. *apargioides*
                                                      COMMON AGOSERIS
       5 Leaf blades widest near the tip, with only a few lobes or none; on backshores of sandy beaches . . . .
                . . . . *A. apargioides* var. *maritima*, pl. 65
                                                     SEASIDE AGOSERIS

Ambrosia

1 Stems sprawling, forming mats; leaves mostly alternate; involucre surrounding each pistillate flower with sharp spines, these soft at first but becoming hard and painfully sharp; limited to backshores of sandy beaches, sandy edges of salt marshes, and other maritime situations

    2 Leaf blades typically silvery and slightly toothed . . . . *A. chamissonis* var. *chamissonis*, pl. 69
                                             SILVERY BEACHWEED

    2 Leaf blades deeply bipinnately lobed and not conspicuously silvery . . . .
                . . . . *A. chamissonis* var. *bipinnatisecta*, pl. 68
                                                      BEACH BUR

        Ambrosia chamissonis var. *chamissonis* is more common in Calif. and Oreg. than farther N. Where it and var. *bipinnatisecta* occur together, they intergrade freely and some specimens are intermediate.

1 Stems upright; leaves mostly opposite; pinnately lobed; involucre surrounding each pistillate flower either not spiny or with only short, blunt spines; occasional weeds

    3 Primary leaf lobes with distinct, deeply separated secondary lobes; involucre of pistillate flowers, by the time achenes have ripened, with short, blunt spines; annual . . . . *A. artemisiifolia*
                                             COMMON RAGWEED (E North America)

    3 Primary leaf lobes with indistinct, shallowly separated secondary lobes; involucre of pistillate flowers not becoming spiny; perennial (usually found on hard-packed soils, including those behind backshores of sandy beaches and bays; introduced into our region and to the area E of the Cascades) . . . *A. psilostachya*
                                     WESTERN RAGWEED (California and Mexico)

Antennaria

Some of the species of *Ambrosia,* or at least certain populations, consist entirely of pistillate plants; others include staminate plants. There is, moreover, considerable intergradation, and keying to species with conviction is sometimes difficult.

1 Flower heads usually single at the tips of the stems; plants flat on the ground, the largest leaf blades only about 1 cm long, and the flower heads not often raised more than 10 cm above the vegetative portion (the leaves, after a period of dry weather, may appear to have white borders; Josephine Co., Oreg., to Calif.) . . . .
. . . .*A. suffrutescens*, pl. 73
                                             EVERGREEN EVERLASTING

1 Flower heads at least 3 in each inflorescence; plants mostly upright and more than 20 cm tall

    2 Peduncles of flower heads 1–3 cm long and rather widely separated, the heads thus not crowded together; upper portion of the flowering stem densely glandular (blades of basal leaves green on the upper surface and usually with 3 or more veins; mostly in coniferous forests above 3500 ft., 1070 m) . . .
. . . . *A. racemosa*
                                             SLENDER PUSSYTOES

    2 Peduncles of flower heads generally not more than 1 cm long and not widely separated, the heads thus crowded together; upper portion of the flowering stem not densely glandular (but it is usually hairy)

3 Stems typically upright, rarely spreading or taking root; blades of basal leaves commonly at least 3 cm long, sometimes more than 8 cm, several times as long as wide (plants densely woolly-hairy; montane and high montane) . . . . *A. lanata*
WOOLLY PUSSYTOES

3 Stems typically spreading and taking root, the plants thus forming low mats; leaf blades not often more than 3 cm long

  4 Leaves of the basal rosette with 1–3 main veins . . . . *A. howellii* (*A. neglecta* var. *howellii*)
HOWELL'S EVERLASTING

> Two varieties of *A. howellii* are sometimes recognized. In var. *howellii* the leaves of the basal rosette are green on the upper surface, definitely less hairy than on the underside; in var. *neodioica* the upper surface bears long hairs and is therefore somewhat whitish or grayish, at least for a time. Obviously, the separation into varieties is, at best, rather flimsy.

  4 Leaves of the basal rosette with a single main vein (leaves of the basal rosette usually about as hairy on the upper surface as on the underside, but sometimes the hairs on the upper surface disappear as the leaves age)

    5 Membranous tips of the middle and lower phyllaries typically light brown or otherwise discolored; portions of some stolons becoming woody and leafless . . . . *A. umbrinella*
UMBER PUSSYTOES

    5 Membranous tips of the middle and lower phyllaries typically white, pink, dark green, brown, or blackish); stolons not becoming woody

      6 Lower portion of membranous tips of the phyllaries dark green, brown, or blackish (mostly high montane) . . . . *A. media*
DARK PUSSYTOES

      6 Lower portion of membranous tips of the phyllaries not darkened . . . . *A. rosea*, pl. 72
ROSY PUSSYTOES, ROSY EVERLASTING

Anthemis

1 Rays bright yellow, to about 13 mm long (sometimes escaping from cultivation) . . . . *A. tinctoria*
YELLOW CHAMOMILE (Europe)

1 Rays white, not much more than 10 mm long

  2 Ray flowers with pistils, producing achenes; mature achenes with lengthwise ribs but without conspicuous bumps; only the upper half of the disk with scales separating the disk flowers; foliage without a strong, unpleasant odor . . . . *A. arvensis*
CORN CHAMOMILE (Europe)

  2 Ray flowers without pistils, not producing achenes; lengthwise ribs of mature achenes with prominent bumps; all of the disk with scales separating the disk flowers; foliage with a strong, unpleasant odor . . . . *A. cotula*
STINKWEED, DOG FENNEL (Europe)

Arctium

1 Petioles of larger leaves usually with angular ridges; flower heads usually 2.5–4 cm wide . . . . *A. lappa*
LARGE BURDOCK (Europe)

1 Petioles of larger leaves without angular ridges; flower heads usually 1.5–2.5 cm wide . . . . *A. minus*, pl. 74
SMALL BURDOCK (Europe)

Antennaria howellii,
Howell's everlasting

Arnica

1 Heads without well-developed rays (but some flowers may have short, inconspicuous rays)

  2 Leaf blades at most with only small, inconspicuous teeth (phyllaries sometimes more than 5 times as long as wide)

    3 Leaves, even the lowest ones, sessile; young flower heads not nodding (leaves, stems, and phyllaries sticky, glandular-hairy; high montane, Klamath Co., Oreg., to Calif.) . . . . *A. viscosa*
              SHASTA ARNICA

    3 Most larger leaves with well-developed petioles; young flower heads often nodding (see the second choice 12 for other characters of this species) . . . . *A. parryi*
              PARRY'S ARNICA

  2 Leaf blades typically with coarse teeth (young flower heads not nodding)

    4 Blades of lower leaves typically narrowing gradually to petioles that are broadly winged for much of their length (SW Oreg. to Calif.) . . . . *A. spathulata*, pl. 78
              KLAMATH ARNICA

    4 Blades of lower leaves typically narrowing rather abruptly to rather slender petioles, these at most only inconspicuously winged, but the petioles of leaves at higher levels on the stem may be conspicuously winged (mostly E of the crest of the Cascades but barely entering our region along the Columbia River Gorge; also in SW Oreg.) . . . . *A. discoidea*, pl. 77
              RAYLESS ARNICA

1 Heads with well-developed rays

  5 Leaves above those at the base usually in at least 5 pairs, sometimes as many as 12 pairs, and becoming only gradually smaller upward, the smallest usually more than half as long as the largest

    6 Margins of leaf blades distinctly toothed (mostly montane) . . . . *A. amplexicaulis*, pl. 75
              STREAMBANK ARNICA

    6 Margins of leaf blades almost completely smooth (mostly high montane) . . . . *A. longifolia*
              LONGLEAF ARNICA

  5 Leaves above the base usually in fewer than 5 pairs and usually becoming abruptly smaller upward

    7 Involucres slightly taller than wide

      8 Pappus white, not feathery, the barbs too short (montane) . . . . *A. latifolia*
        (includes vars. *latifolia* and *gracilis*, here not considered sufficiently distinct to be worth separating)
              BROAD-LEAVED ARNICA

      8 Pappus brownish or yellowish brown, nearly feathery because of the prominence of the barbs (montane) . . . . *A. diversifolia*
              LAWLESS ARNICA

        The common name apparently alludes to the variability of this plant, which is believed to have originated at various times and in various places as a hybrid, most likely *A. mollis* or *amplexicaulis* × *A. latifolia* or *cordifolia*.

    7 Involucres about as wide as tall

      9 Margins of leaf blades typically smooth, at most only with a few small teeth (leaf blades oval to widest near the base and sometimes somewhat heart-shaped; mid to high montane, Wash. to Calif.) . . . . *A. nevadensis*
              SIERRA NEVADA ARNICA

      9 Margins of most larger leaf blades coarsely toothed

        10 Blades of lower leaves broadest close to the base and often more or less heart-shaped (middle stem leaves with long petioles; mostly montane and high montane and mostly E of the crest of the Cascades) . . . . *A. cordifolia*, pl. 76
              HEART-LEAVED ARNICA

        10 Blades of lower leaves generally widest well above the base and not heart-shaped

          11 Lower leaves of flowering stems sessile or with short, inconspicuous petioles, rays 15–25 mm long; young flower heads not nodding (high montane) . . . . *A. mollis*
              CORDILLERAN ARNICA

11 Lower leaves of flowering stems with prominent petioles; rays rarely more than 15 mm long; flower heads sometimes nodding

    12 Each flowering stem with only 1 flower head; blades of lower leaves not so much as twice as long as wide and usually not more than 5–6 cm long; plants not especially hairy or glandular (Josephine Co., Oreg., to Calif.) . . . .*A. cernua*
          SERPENTINE ARNICA, NODDING ARNICA

    12 Each flowering stem usually with more than 1 flower head; blades of lower leaves sometimes more than 15 cm long; some portions of plants typically conspicuously hairy and/or glandular (mostly montane and mostly E of the crest of the Cascades but also in the Olympic Mountains) . . . . **A. parryi**
          PARRY'S ARNICA

Artemisia

1 Larger leaves so deeply lobed that they are nearly compound, and with numerous ultimate lobes

  2 Ultimate lobes of most larger leaves in threes of nearly equal length (leaves silky-hairy; mostly high montane in the Olympic Mountains, Wash., and Cascades of Brit. Col. and Wash.) . . . . . .**A. trifurcata**
      THREE-FORKED SAGEWORT

  2 Ultimate lobes of larger leaves not in threes of nearly equal length

    3 Ultimate leaf lobes slender, not more than 1 mm wide . . . .**A. campestris**, pl. 79
      NORTHERN WORMWOOD

      Artemisia campestris, with a wide distribution in North America and Asia, has been divided into several subspecies, some of which include named varieties. Low, sprawling plants found on backshores of sandy beaches (or at least near salt water) in the Puget Sound region, the San Juan Islands, and adjacent areas (pl. 79) appear to be closest to subsp. *caudata* in their habit of growth but differ in certain respects from specimens of subsp. *caudata* from the central and E United States. Plants from the open coast of Oreg., Wash., and Brit. Col. have been referred to subsp. *pacifica;* those from along the Columbia River have been called subsp. *wormskioldii;* those from the Cascades and mountains farther E perhaps fit best into subsp. *borealis.* While we may wish for a more nearly perfect solution to the taxonomy of the *A. campestris* complex, we must remember that this assemblage has already been intensively studied by more than one expert.

    3 Ultimate leaf lobes more than 1 mm wide

      4 Larger leaves with 1–2 pairs of deeply divided, stipulelike lobes at their bases (foliage aromatic; occasional weed) . . . . *A. vulgaris*
        COMMON MUGWORT (Europe)

      4 Leaves without stipulelike lobes at their bases

        5 Disk of flower head with numerous long hairs between the flowers (plants commonly more than 75 cm tall; occasional weed, more common E of the Cascades) . . . .*A. absinthium*
          WORMWOOD (Europe)

        5 Disk of flower head without long hairs between the flowers

          6 Most leaf lobes tapering gradually to the tips; inflorescence loose, the flower heads on conspicuous peduncles; plants often more than 50 cm tall (montane, Alaska to Calif. and eastward) . . . . *A. norvegica* var. *saxatilis*
           MOUNTAIN SAGEWORT

          6 Most leaf lobes tapering rather abruptly to the tips; inflorescence usually compact, the flower heads, with short peduncles, borne on the axis of the upper part and on short branches of the lower part; plants not often more than 50 cm tall (on backshores of sandy beaches, S Oreg. to Calif.) . . . . *A. pycnocephala*
          BEACH SAGEWORT

Artemisia vulgaris,
common mugwort

1 Leaves either smooth-margined, coarsely toothed, or shallowly lobed, with only a few ultimate lobes

  7 Shrubs; larger leaves (not often more than 4 cm long) more or less wedge-shaped, the broad tip typically divided into 3 short, nearly equal lobes or teeth (some leaves may have 4 or more such lobes or teeth); plants as a whole grayish

    8 Plants low and spreading, not often more than about 40 cm tall; leaves not often more than 2 cm long nor more than 3 times as long as wide; inflorescences slender, not conspicuously branched (mostly E of the crest of the Cascades but also found in the Siskiyou Mountains of SW Oreg. and NW Calif.) . . . . *A. arbuscula* subsp. *arbuscula*
DWARF SAGEBRUSH

    8 Plants sometimes more than 1 m tall; leaves commonly at least 2 cm long and more than 3 times as long as wide; inflorescence broad, with conspicuous branches (almost entirely E of the Cascades in Brit. Col., Wash., and Oreg. but occasionally found in the Siskiyou Mountains of SW Oreg. and NW Calif.) . . . . *A. tridentata*
SAGEBRUSH
Several subspecies or varieties of *A. tridentata* have been named.

  7 Plants mostly herbaceous; larger leaves not wedge-shaped and not divided at the tip into 3 or more lobes; plants as a whole not grayish (but the leaves are generally hairy and whitish or grayish on the underside)

    9 Larger leaf blades (not including lobes, when these are present) commonly more than 1.5 cm wide, sometimes more than 3 cm (plants sometimes more than 1 m tall; inflorescence with numerous and conspicuous branches)

      10 Involucres wider than long (and with as many as 35–40 flowers within the ring of marginal flowers; in our region montane, mostly at rather high elevations but occasionally lower, especially on isolated peaks; Alaska to N Oreg.) . . . . *A. tilesii* subsp. *unalaschcensis*
ALEUTIAN MUGWORT

      10 Involucres at least as long as wide

        11 Involucres not conspicuously longer than wide, the flower heads usually with 10–25 flowers within the ring of marginal flowers (NW Oreg. to Calif., mostly at lower elevations in our region; also present in the Columbia River Gorge and E of the Cascades) . . . . *A. douglasiana*
DOUGLAS' MUGWORT

        11 Involucres decidedly longer than wide; flower heads usually with only 2–8 flowers within the ring of marginal flowers (mostly, but not exclusively, found within a few km or miles of salt water) . . .
. . . . *A. suksdorfii*, pl. 80
COASTAL MUGWORT

    9 Larger leaf blades (not including lobes, when these are present) rarely so much as 1.5 cm wide

      12 Flower heads concentrated on short branches of the inflorescence; leaf blades usually green on the upper surface, white-hairy below, with at most only a few scattered lobes or teeth, most of these at or above the middle (generally growing below the high-water mark of rivers and lakes; found along the Columbia River as far W as Vancouver, Wash.) . . . . *A. lindleyana*
COLUMBIA RIVER MUGWORT

      12 Flower heads generally (but not always) well separated on branches of the inflorescence, which are sometimes at least 5 cm long; leaves usually white-hairy on both surfaces, extremely variable with respect to the extent to which they are lobed (mostly montane in our region) . . . . *A. ludoviciana*
WESTERN MUGWORT
The following key is an attempt briefly to characterize typical specimens of varieties that may be encountered in our region.

        13 Larger leaf blades mostly not lobed or with only a few short lobes . . . *A. ludoviciana* var. *ludoviciana*

        13 Larger leaf blades typically with 1 or more conspicuous lobes

          14 Primary lobes of larger leaf blades again toothed or lobed . . . . *A. ludoviciana* var. *incompta*

          14 Primary lobes of larger leaf blades not again toothed or lobed . . . .
. . . . *A. ludoviciana* subsp. *candicans* (*A. ludoviciana* var. *latifolia*)

Aster-Machaeranthera Complex

There are only two varieties of *Machaeranthera canescens* in this key; all others are in the genus *Aster*. Some species of *Aster* are keyed more than once to compensate for variability, especially of the width of leaf blades and degree to which the plants are glandular.

1 Flower heads usually without rays or with not more than 3 rays (rays, if present, white)
  2 Leaf blades ending in a short (less than 0.5 mm long), hyaline, and somewhat spinelike tip, this often curved back, hooklike (involucres consist of 3–5 series of phyllaries; ray flowers sterile; Josephine, Jackson, and Lake Cos., Oreg., to Calif.) . . . . . . *M. canescens* var. *shastensis* (*A. shastensis* var. *eradiatus*)
                MOUNT SHASTA MACHAERANTHERA
  2 Leaf blades not ending in a spinelike tip
    3 Underside of leaves rather densely covered with matted white hairs (Siskiyou Mountain region of SW Oreg. and NW Calif.) . . . . *A. brickellioides*
                BRICKELLBUSH ASTER
    3 Underside of leaves usually hairy but not densely covered with matted white hairs
      4 Plants usually 10–30 cm tall; flower heads clustered at the tops of the stems; leaf blades to 3 cm long, not more than 1 cm wide, usually widest above the middle (in prairies of the Puget Trough and N Willamette Valley) . . . .*A. curtus* (*A. rigidus* of some references), pl. 83
                SHORT WHITE-TOPPED ASTER
      4 Plants generally more than 30 cm tall; flower heads either on short peduncles and scattered along the upper portions of the stems or in a spreading, rather widely branched inflorescence; larger leaf blades usually at least 3 cm long, widest at or below the middle
        5 Inflorescence rather slender, the several flower heads on short peduncles scattered along the upper portions of the stems; peduncles hairy and also glandular; plants usually at least 60 cm tall (Lane and Douglas Cos., Oreg.) . . . . *A. vialis* (*Eucephalus vialis*)
                WAYSIDE ASTER

Artemisia tridentata,
sagebrush

Artemisia tilesii
subsp. *unalaschcensis,*
Aleutian mugwort

Artemisia ludoviciana,
western mugwort,
vars. *ludoviciana,* left,
and *incompta,* right

    5 Inflorescence spreading, with rather long branchlets; peduncles not hairy but sometimes glandular just below the involucres; plants mostly 30–60 cm tall (Josephine and Jackson Cos., Oreg., to Calif.) . . . . *A. siskiyouensis*
SISKIYOU ASTER

1 Flower heads usually with 5 or more rays (sometimes 4 in *A. oregonensis*)
  6 Blades of lower leaves with conspicuous marginal teeth, these with spinelike tips (involucres consist of 5–10 series of phyllaries; ray flowers produce achenes; stems and leaves characteristically gray-hairy; rays blue-purple; mostly montane and mostly E of the crest of the Cascades) . . . .
  . . . . *M. canescens* var. *canescens* (*A. shastensis* var. *latifolius*)
HOARY MACHAERANTHERA

  6 Marginal teeth, if present on leaf blades, without spinelike tips
    7 Flower heads with 4–7 white rays (usually 5), these to 7 mm long (plants generally more than 60 cm tall, usually with clusters of flowers on several branch stems; leaves to about 9 cm long, 3 cm wide, widest near the middle; Lane and Douglas Cos., Oreg.) . . . . *A. oregonensis*
OREGON WHITE-TOPPED ASTER

    7 Flower heads usually with more than 7 rays, these generally at least 8 mm long, sometimes much longer
      8 Larger leaf blades mostly more than 2 cm wide, sometimes more than 3 cm
        9 Leaf blades with nearly smooth margins, not distinctly toothed (plants often more than 1 m tall; rays white to pink, at least 15 mm long) . . . . *A. engelmannii*
ENGELMANN'S ASTER

        9 Leaf blades with prominent marginal teeth
          10 Plants to about 1 m tall, the stem usually single; involucres, stem, and leaves glandular-hairy, the glands stalked; slender lower portion of the corolla of disk flowers no longer than the broadened upper portion (mostly low to midmontane) . . . . *A. modestus*, pl. 85
GREAT NORTHERN ASTER

          10 Plants not often more than about 60 cm tall, usually with more than 1 stem; involucres, stems, and leaves not glandular-hairy; slender lower portion of the corolla of disk flowers much longer than the broadened upper portion . . . . *A. radulinus*
ROUGH-LEAVED ASTER

      8 Larger leaf blades not more than about 2 cm wide
       11 Each flowering stem usually with a single flower head at the tip (in *A. sibiricus* var. *meritus* the stems are sometimes branched, but the branches are not likely to have more than 1 flower head)
         12 Basal leaves not conspicuous and neither larger nor more prominent than those along the other portions of the stems; rays usually purple; slender lower portion of the corolla of disk flowers slightly longer than the broadened upper portion (mostly high montane, Brit. Col. to the Cascades of Wash. and eastward) . . . . *A. sibiricus* var. *meritus*
ARCTIC ASTER

         12 Basal leaves crowded, much larger and more prominent than those along the other portions of the stems; rays usually pinkish blue; slender lower portion of the corolla of disk flowers not as long as the broadened upper portion (montane and high montane)
           13 Achenes typically hairy for their entire length (in the Cascades from Linn Co., Oreg., southward; also in Calif. and Nevada) . . . . *A. alpigenus* var. *andersonii*
ANDERSON'S ALPINE ASTER

           13 Achenes typically hairy only in their upper portion (Olympic Mountains, Wash., and the Cascades from Wash. to Oreg.) . . . . *A. alpigenus* var. *alpigenus*, pl. 81
ALPINE ASTER

       11 Each flowering stem usually branched, the primary branches of some species with more than 1 flower head
         14 Lower phyllaries about as long as, but typically at least slightly wider than, the upper ones and sometimes gradually intergrading with leafy bracts nearest to the involucre

15 Plants typically less than 25 cm tall, the stems spreading outward with tips rising (phyllaries often with purple margins; high montane, in exposed habitats in the Cascades and eastward) . . . .
. . . . *A. foliaceus* var. *apricus*

15 Plants typically more than 25 cm tall, upright

  16 Lower phyllaries, especially on the uppermost head of an inflorescence, very much like the leafy bracts below the involucre; branches often with more than 1 flower head each (Olympic Mountains, Wash., and the Cascades, Brit. Col. to Wash.) . . . . *A. foliaceus* var. *foliaceus,* pl. 84
                                                                    LEAFY-BRACT ASTER

  16 Outer phyllaries somewhat distinct from the leafy bracts below the involucre; branches usually with 1 flower head each (in the Cascades and eastward) . . . . *A. foliaceus* var. *parryi*
                                                            PARRY'S LEAFY-BRACT ASTER

14 Phyllaries usually in at least 3 distinct series, those of successive series alternating and overlapping in much the same way as shingles on a roof (rays generally not more than 15 mm long)

  17 Leaves on the main stem, below the branched and many-flowered inflorescence, typically with tufts of crowded small leaves in their axils; outer phyllaries ending in a bristlelike tip (plants sometimes rather densely hairy; weed in some areas of Brit. Col.) . . . . *A. pilosus* var. *pilosus*
                                                       HAIRY ASTER (E North America)

  17 Leaves on the main stem without tufts of crowded small leaves in their axils; outer phyllaries not ending in a bristlelike tip

    18 Disk flowers with the slender lower portion of the corolla much longer than the broadened upper portion (rays white to purple, 8–13 mm long; involucres, stems, and leaves not glandular) . . . .
    . . . . *A. radulinus*
                                                         ROUGH-LEAVED ASTER

    18 Disk flowers with the slender lower portion of the corolla usually shorter than, but sometimes about equal to, the broadened upper portion

      19 Involucre (and usually also the stems and leaves) at least somewhat glandular

        20 Involucres, stems, and leaves densely glandular, the glands stalked; leaf blades to about 12 cm long, with toothed margins
        . . . . *A. modestus,* pl. 85
                                      GREAT NORTHERN ASTER

        20 Involucres (but not necessarily the stems and leaves) glandular but not densely so, the glands not conspicuously stalked

          21 Involucres, stems, and leaves slightly glandular; rays 8–14 mm long, white, aging to pink; leaf blades not often more than 4 cm long, the underside not cottony-hairy (Vancouver Island, Brit. Col., and Olympic Mountains, Wash., mostly above 4000 ft., 1220 m) . . . .*A. paucicapitatus*
                                   OLYMPIC MOUNTAINS ASTER

          21 Only the upper phyllaries obviously glandular; rays 12–20 mm long, usually violet or purplish; leaf blades to 7 cm long, the underside typically cottony-hairy (in the Cascades, usually well above 4000 ft., 1220 m, to Calif. . . . . *A. ledophyllus*
                                     CASCADES ASTER

      19 Involucre not obviously glandular

        22 Inflorescences usually with fewer than 10 flower heads (leaf blades slender, most of those on middle portions of the stems at least 7 times as long as wide; rays to about 15 mm long but commonly not more than 12 mm, usually violet; mostly montane in the Cascades, Brit. Col. to Calif.; also eastward) . . . *A. occidentalis*
                            WESTERN MOUNTAIN ASTER

Aster radulinus,
rough-leaved aster

22 Inflorescences usually with many flower heads (mostly in lowland habitats; the 3 species under this choice are extremely variable, but for typical specimens, the key should work)

    23 Involucres mostly 5–6 mm long, rarely 7 mm; rays not extending so much as 1 cm beyond the upper-most phyllaries, usually white or only tinged with pink or purplish (leaves rarely so much as 1 cm wide; phyllaries typically broadening conspicuously in their upper halves, then more or less rounded except for a projecting tip; Wash. to Oreg. in inland habitats, especially Puget Trough and Willamette Valley) . . . .*A. hallii*

HALL'S ASTER

    23 Involucres generally at least 6 mm long, sometimes 9–10 mm; rays commonly extending at least 1 cm beyond the uppermost phyllaries; rays blue to violet or purple (in coastal as well as inland habitats)

        24 Phyllaries typically broadening conspicuously in their upper halves, then more or less rounded except for a projecting tip; strictly coastal . . . . *A. chilensis*, pl. 82

PACIFIC ASTER

        24 Phyllaries typically broadening only slightly in their upper portions, then tapering gradually to pointed tips; in inland as well as coastal habitats (rays blue to violet or purple) . . . .*A. subspicatus*, pl. 86

DOUGLAS' ASTER

Balsamorhiza-Wyethia Complex

1 Leaves on the flowering stems usually substantial and of the same general form as the basal leaves, which are widest near the middle and several times as long as wide; pappus consisting of small teeth . . . . *W. angustifolia*, pl. 155

MULE'S EARS

1 Leaves on the flowering stems much smaller and very different from the basal leaves, whose blades are pinnately compound or approximately triangular and not often more than twice as long as wide; pappus absent

    2 Blades of basal leaves pinnately compound (leaflets silvery; SW Oreg. to Calif.) . . . . . . *B. sericea*, pl. 89

SILKY BALSAMROOT

    2 Blades of basal leaves approximately triangular, not compound

        3 Flowering stems often with more than 1 flower head (but the head at the top is usually larger than the ones below it); leaves usually green on both surfaces, even when young . . . . *B. deltoidea*, pl. 88

DELTOID BALSAMROOT

        3 Flowering stems with a single flower head; underside of leaves, and sometimes also the upper surface, white-woolly, at least when young (almost entirely E of the crest of the Cascades) . . . . *B. sagittata*

ARROW-LEAVED BALSAMROOT

Bidens

1 Plants aquatic, with 2 entirely different kinds of leaves: aquatic leaves divided into numerous hairlike, branched lobes; leaves above the waterline sessile, elongated-oval, to about 4 cm long, with coarsely toothed margins; rays of flower heads to 1.5 cm long . . . . *B. beckii*

BECK'S WATER MARIGOLD

    Bidens beckii has a wide distribution in E North America, and perhaps at least some populations in E Brit. Col., Wash., and Oreg. are native, but whether those W of the Cascades are native is not certain. Incidentally, some references resurrect the genus name *Megalodonta* for *B. beckii.* Either name is acceptable.

1 Plants usually growing in wet places but not truly aquatic, none of the leaves divided into hairlike lobes

    2 Flower heads usually with conspicuous rays

        3 Leaf blades toothed but not deeply lobed; flower heads usually nodding after they have begun to age . . . . *B. cernua*

NODDING BEGGAR-TICKS

3 Leaf blades deeply divided into 3 lobes, thus nearly compound; flower heads not nodding after they have begun to age (SE Vancouver Island and SW mainland of Brit. Col.) . . . . *B. amplissima*

2 Flower heads without rays or with only a few short, inconspicuous rays (*B. cernua*, first choice 3, sometimes lacks rays, but it is the only species in our region with leaves that are not compound nor deeply lobed)

4 Leaf blades divided into 3 lobes, the petiole broadly winged; achenes usually with 4 awns . . . *B. tripartita*
THREE-LOBED STICKTIGHT (E North America, Europe)

4 Leaf blades pinnately compound into 3 or 5 leaflets, the petiole not winged; achenes usually with 2 awns

5 Involucres usually with 5–8 outer (lower) phyllaries; achenes typically blackish . . . . *B. frondosa*
STICKTIGHT, LEAFY BEGGAR-TICKS

5 Involucre usually with 10–16 outer phyllaries; achenes typically greenish, brownish, or yellowish
. . . . *B. vulgata*
TALL BEGGAR-TICKS (E North America)

Brickellia

1 Flower heads generally single at the ends of branches; involucres 17–20 mm high; plants to about 50 cm tall, woody only near the base (Josephine Co., Oreg., to Calif.) . . . . *B. greenei*
GREENE'S BRICKELLBUSH

1 Flower heads distributed along the ultimate branches; involucres 12–14 mm tall; plants to more than 1.5 m tall, woody well above the base (Jackson and Josephine Cos., Oreg., to Calif.) . . . . *B. californica*
CALIFORNIA BRICKELLBUSH

Calycadenia

1 Rays yellow; a tack-shaped gland present on bracts below the involucre but not on the phyllaries (S Willamette Valley, Oreg., to Calif.) . . . . *C. truncata*
TACKWEED

1 Rays usually white, sometimes reddish or yellow; a least 1 tack-shaped gland present on most phyllaries as well as on the bracts below the involucre (Umpqua River valley, Oreg., to Calif.) . . . . *C. fremontii* (*C. ciliosa*)
FREMONT'S TACKWEED

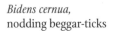
Bidens cernua,
nodding beggar-ticks

Bidens tripartita,
three-lobed sticktight

Carduus

1 Flower heads nodding; involucres stout, at least as wide as long and usually at least 3 cm long; phyllaries tapering abruptly to spinelike tips . . . .*C. nutans*
MUSK THISTLE (Europe)

1 Flower heads upright; involucres about twice as long as wide, rarely more than 2.5 cm long; phyllaries tapering gradually to sharp tips

    2 Phyllaries with dry, hardened, nongreen margins, the upper portions mostly smooth . . . . *C. tenuiflorus*
SLENDER-FLOWERED THISTLE (Europe, Asia)

    2 Phyllaries without dry, hardened, nongreen margins, the upper portions with numerous short prickles along the margins and on the outer surface . . . .*C. pycnocephalus*
ITALIAN THISTLE (Mediterranean region)

Centaurea-Acroptilon Complex

1 At least some phyllaries with spines more than 1 cm long at their tips

    2 Stems without wings but decidedly angled; pappus absent; corollas purple . . . .*C. calcitrapa*
PURPLE STAR THISTLE (S Europe)

    2 Stems with wings (these are extensions of the leaf bases); pappus well developed, at least on the central flowers of the head; corollas yellow

        3 Larger spines of the phyllaries thick and commonly 1–2 cm long; marginal flowers without a pappus (SW Oreg.) . . . .*C. solstitialis*, pl. 93
BARNABY'S THISTLE (Europe)

        3 Larger spines of the phyllaries slender and not often so much as 1 cm long; marginal flowers with a pappus . . . .*C. melitensis*
TOCALOTE (S Europe)

1 Phyllaries without spines so much as 1 cm long

    4 Pappus bristles prominent, some at least 8 mm long; perennial and spreading vegetatively by creeping rhizomes (pernicious weed) . . . .*A. repens* (*Centaurea repens*)
RUSSIAN KNAPWEED (central Asia)

    4 Pappus bristles, if present, not more than about 4 mm long; plants not spreading vegetatively

        5 At least some of the larger leaves deeply pinnately lobed

            6 Each phyllary with a stout spine about 3 mm long at its tip (in addition to this spine, there are a few shorter spines on both sides below it) . . . .*C. diffusa*
TUMBLE KNAPWEED (SE Europe, W Asia)

           6 Phyllaries without an especially prominent, stout spine at the tip (the upper part of each phyllary has slender teeth, however)

               7 Tips of the phyllaries conspicuously broadened (they are also toothed and darkened) . . . .
. . . .*C. nigrescens*
SHORT-FRINGED KNAPWEED (Europe)

               7 Tips of the phyllaries not conspicuously broadened

                  8 Phyllaries with 3 lengthwise lines; involucre to about 1 cm long . . . .*C. paniculata*
JERSEY KNAPWEED (Europe)

                  8 Phyllaries with 5 lengthwise lines; involucre usually more than 1 cm long . . . .
. . . .*C. stoebe* var. *micrantha* (*C. maculosa*)
SPOTTED KNAPWEED (Europe)

        5 Leaves smooth-margined or merely toothed, except perhaps for a few larger ones that may have a few shallow lobes

           9 Leaves narrow, usually less than 1 cm wide (corollas usually blue but sometimes purple, pink, or white; annual; commonly grown in gardens and often escaping) . . . .*C. cyanus*
BACHELOR'S BUTTON, CORNFLOWER (Europe)

9 Leaves, at least the larger ones, more than 1 cm wide

  10 Tips of phyllaries coarsely toothed or lobed (perennial)

    11 Tips of phyllaries with broad lobes, these with small teeth; corollas pink to purplish, occasionally white; achenes without a pappus . . . . *C. jacea*
                                          BROWN KNAPWEED (Europe)

    11 Tips of phyllaries toothed; corollas blue or white; achenes with pappus consisting of bristles less than 1 mm long . . . . *C. montana*
                                       MOUNTAIN BLUET (Europe)

  10 Most phyllaries other than the uppermost ones deeply divided into slender bristles; achenes with a pappus

    12 Outer flowers fertile, forming achenes; corollas all about the same size . . . . *C. nigra*
                                       BLACK KNAPWEED (Europe)

    12 Outer flowers sterile, not forming achenes; outer flowers distinctly larger than the ones in the central portion of the disk . . . . *C. ×pratensis* (a stable hybrid, *C. nigra × jacea*), pl. 92
                                       FIELD KNAPWEED

Cirsium

1 Involucre of flower heads mostly 1–1.5 cm high (sometimes 2 cm)

  2 Flower heads on a particular plant usually either pistillate or staminate; corollas usually purplish pink, occasionally white; plants perennial, reproducing vegetatively by creeping rhizomes (very aggressive weed) . . . . *C. arvense* var. *horridum*
                                       CANADA THISTLE (Europe)

  2 Flowers in each head with stamens and a pistil; corollas purplish; plants biennial, not reproducing vegetatively by creeping rhizomes . . . . *C. palustre*
                                        MARSH THISTLE (Europe)

1 Involucre of flower heads usually at least 2 cm high (all flowers in each head normally with stamens and a pistil)

Acroptilon repens,
Russian knapweed

Centaurea stoebe var. *micrantha,*
spotted knapweed

3 Stems winged by extensions of the leaf bases, the wings nearly or fully as long as the internodes ......
.... *C. vulgare*, pl. 99
BULL THISTLE (Europe)
3 Stems either not winged by extensions of the leaf bases, or the wings very short
  4 Phyllaries slightly broadened just below the base of the spine, the broadened portion somewhat fringed (corollas usually whitish or pale brownish) ....
.... *C. callilepis* (*C. remotifolium* var. *oregonense*), pl. 97
FRINGE-PHYLLARY THISTLE
  4 Phyllaries not broadened just below the base of the spine
    5 Upper half of most phyllaries with a lengthwise resinous ridge; usually in damp habitats (Josephine and Jackson Cos., Oreg., to Calif.) .... *C. douglasii* var. *breweri*
BREWER'S THISTLE, SWAMP THISTLE
    5 Phyllaries without a lengthwise resinous ridge; usually in dry habitats
      6 Upper third of the corolla not abruptly separated from the lower two-thirds; corollas usually crimson and very showy (Josephine and Jackson Cos., Oreg., to Calif.) ....
.... *C. occidentale* var. *venustum* (*C. pastoris*), pl. 98
VENUS THISTLE
      6 Upper third ("throat") of the corolla abruptly separated from the lower two-thirds ("tube"); corollas usually deep pink to rose-purple
        7 Styles either not projecting out of the corollas or projecting for not more than 1 mm ....
.... *C. brevistylum*, pl. 96
SHORT-STYLE THISTLE, INDIAN THISTLE
        7 Styles projecting conspicuously out of the corollas (Brit. Col. to Oreg., mostly near the coast and at low to moderate elevations in the Cascades and Coast Ranges) .... *C. edule*
EDIBLE THISTLE

Conyza
1 Involucre 3–4 mm tall, not conspicuously hairy; midveins of phyllaries brownish, resinous ....
.... *C. canadensis* var. *glabrata*, pl. 100
HORSEWEED
1 Involucre 4–6 mm high, conspicuously hairy; midveins of phyllaries green or purplish, not resinous ......
.... *C. floribunda* (tropical America)

Crepis
1 Achene with a prominent beak, this from one-third to about half as long as the body
  2 Stems and phyllaries with bristly yellowish hairs; achenes 3–5 mm long, the beak about half as long as the body .... *C. setosa*
BRISTLY HAWKSBEARD (Europe)
  2 Stems and phyllaries with bristly blackish hairs, otherwise with crowded, somewhat interwoven hairs; achenes 6–8 mm long, the beak about one-third as long as the body ..... *C. vesicaria* var. *taraxacifolia*
WEEDY HAWKSBEARD (Europe)
1 Achene merely tapering to the tip, or with a short, stout beak
  3 Involucre 5–8 mm long; achenes to 2.5 mm long (very common lowland weed) ... *C. capillaris*, pl. 103
SMOOTH HAWKSBEARD (Europe)
  3 Most involucres more than 8 mm long; achenes generally at least 3 mm long (except sometimes in *C. nicaeensis*)
    4 Leaves, stems, and phyllaries densely covered with long, gland-tipped hairs (involucre 18–24 mm long; achenes 5.5–9 mm long; S Oreg. to Calif.) .... *C. monticola*
MOUNTAIN HAWKSBEARD
    4 Leaves, stems, and phyllaries not densely covered with long, gland-tipped hairs (but there may be short hairs, and these may be glandular)

5 Most heads with 5–8 flowers
  6 Phyllaries either without hairs or with evenly distributed hairs; inflorescences sometimes with as many as about 100 flower heads . . . . ***C. acuminata***
            LONG-LEAVED HAWKSBEARD
  6 Phyllaries hairy along their margins but not along the midline; inflorescences with not more than about 40 flower heads . . . . ***C. pleurocarpa***
            NAKED-STEM HAWKSBEARD
5 Most heads with more than 10 flowers
  7 Involucre 8–10 mm long; phyllaries somewhat hairy but not glandular-hairy (achenes 2.5–4 mm long, 10-ribbed; annual or biennial weed, so far established in only a few places) . . . . ***C. nicaeensis***
            FRENCH HAWKSBEARD (Europe)
  7 Involucre usually at least 11 mm long; phyllaries often with gland-tipped hairs; achenes at least 6 mm long, usually with more than 10 ribs; perennial
    8 Leaves glandular-hairy; peduncles becoming noticeably dilated toward the flower heads; phyllaries glandular-hairy (Jackson Co., Oreg., E and N to Idaho, S to Calif.) . . . . ***C. bakeri***
            BAKER'S HAWKSBEARD
    8 Leaves not glandular-hairy; peduncles not becoming noticeably dilated toward the flower heads; phyllaries sometimes glandular-hairy (Jackson Co., Oreg., to Calif.; also E of the Cascades) . . . . ***C. occidentalis***
            WESTERN HAWKSBEARD
    Crepis occidentalis is variable and apparently linked genetically to several other species found in montane habitats.

Erechtites

1 Leaf blades with only teeth, no obvious lobes (coastal, Wash. to Calif.) . . . . ***E. minima*** (*E. prenanthoides*), pl. 104
            AUSTRALIAN FIREWEED (Australasia)
1 Leaf blades coarsely toothed and even pinnately lobed
  2 Involucres usually 5–7 mm high; leaf blades to 20 cm long, 7 cm wide (known in our region from only a few localities) . . . . ***E. hieracifolia*** var. ***hieracifolia*** (E North America, Caribbean region)
  2 Involucres usually 10–17 mm high; leaf blades to 15 cm long, 4 cm wide (coastal, Oreg., possibly also S Wash., to Calif.) . . . . ***E. glomerata*** (*E. arguta*)
            NEW ZEALAND FIREWEED (Australasia)

Ericameria-Pyrrocoma-Columbiadoria-Hazardia Complex

1 Flower heads without rays; plants commonly more than 1 m tall (younger stems covered with a feltlike covering of matted hairs, and usually with an unpleasant odor; phyllaries usually forming rather distinct vertical rows; SW Oreg. to Calif., also E of the Cascades) . . . . . ***E. nauseosa*** (*Haplopappus nauseosus*), pl. 105
            RABBIT BRUSH
1 All or most flower heads with at least a few ray flowers; plants not so much as 1 m tall
  2 Flower heads borne singly or in small clusters in the axils of the leaves
    3 Flower heads usually 1 in each leaf axil; phyllaries tapering gradually to pointed tips, not pressed down (Willamette Valley, Oreg., to Calif.) . . . . ***P. racemosa*** var. ***racemosa*** (*Haplopappus racemosus* var. *racemosus*)
            RACEMED GOLDENWEED
    3 Flower heads usually 2 or more in each leaf axil; phyllaries with rather blunt tips (except for a short point), typically pressed down (Douglas, Josephine, and Curry Cos., Oreg., to Calif.) . . . . ***P. racemosa*** var. ***congesta*** (*Haplopappus racemosa* subsp. *congesta*), pl. 141
            CROWDED GOLDENWEED
  2 Flower heads borne at the tips of branches of terminal inflorescences

4 Leaf blades with conspicuous marginal teeth; achenes not hairy (Josephine Co., Oreg., to Calif., mostly above 4000 ft., 1220 m) . . . . ***H. whitneyi*** (*Haplopappus whitneyi*)
WHITNEY'S GOLDENWEED

4 Leaf blades with smooth margins; achenes at least slightly hairy
  5 Plants very woody, low, not more than about 30 cm tall, rather freely branched (Siskiyou Mountain region of SW Oreg. and NW Calif., also E of the Cascades; not likely to be found below about 4000 ft., 1220 m) . . . . ***E. greenei*** (*Haplopappus greenei*)
GREENE'S GOLDENWEED

  5 Plants not especially woody except near the base, to about 50 cm tall, the main stems not much branched below the inflorescence (mostly along the E portion of the Columbia River Gorge, on both sides of the Cascades, and in the Calapooya Mountains, Oreg.) . . . . . . ***C. hallii*** (*Haplopappus hallii*)
HALL'S GOLDENWEED

Erigeron

Erigeron flagellaris var. *flagellaris,* not in this key, is distinctive in that some of its stems, slender and with only a few leaves, fall down and touch the ground. Its upright flowering stems typically bear a single flower head, this with at least 50 white, pink, or blue rays. It occurs in river valleys of southwestern British Columbia and has been found on at least one of the islands in the Strait of Georgia, but these localities are remote from its usual range east of the Cascades.

1 Leaves ternately divided 1 or more times into narrow lobes (plants not often more than 15 cm tall, very hairy and glandular; flower heads with or without ray flowers; rays, when present and well developed, to about 1 cm long, white to pink or blue; primarily montane and E of the crest of the Cascades but sometimes occurring on the W side, and in the Siskiyou Mountains of SW Oreg. and NW Calif.) . . . . ***E. compositus*** var. ***glabratus***
CUT-LEAVED DAISY

1 Leaves not ternately divided into narrow lobes
  2 Heads without ray flowers
    3 Upper stem leaves much smaller than those near the base; basal leaves generally still green at the time of flowering (Josephine and Jackson Cos., Oreg., to Calif.) . . . . ***E. bloomeri*** var. ***nudatus***
BLOOMER'S DAISY

    3 Upper stem leaves not much smaller than those near the base; basal leaves generally withered by the time flowering is in progress (Josephine and Jackson Cos., Oreg., to Calif.) . . . . . ***E. petrophilus***, pl. 110
ROCK DAISY

  2 Heads with well-developed ray flowers
    4 Rays bright yellow (high montane, Brit. Col. and Alberta to Wash.) . . . . ***E. aureus***, pl. 106
ALPINE YELLOW DAISY

    4 Rays not yellow
      5 Pappus of ray flowers consisting only of short bristles, these similar to the short bristles that are outside the long bristles of the pappus of disk flowers
        6 Leaf blades with conspicuously toothed margins; upper stem leaves not conspicuously smaller than those near the base (occasional weed) . . . . ***E. annuus***
ANNUAL DAISY (E United States)

        6 Leaf blades with nearly smooth margins; upper stem leaves conspicuously smaller than those near the base . . . . ***E. strigosus*** var. ***strigosus***
DAISY FLEABANE

      5 Pappus of ray flowers with long bristles similar to those of the disk flowers (there may also be short, stiff bristles outside the long bristles of the pappus of one or both types of flowers)
        7 Larger leaf blades narrow, mostly at least 10 times as long as wide

8 Blades of leaves on upper portions of the stems about the same size and shape as those near the base (S Oreg. to Calif.) . . . . *E. foliosus* **var.** *confinis*, pl. 108
LEAFY DAISY

8 Blades of leaves on upper portions of the stems much smaller than those near the base (lower leaves sometimes more than 7 cm long; Willamette Valley, Oreg., to Calif.) . . . .
. . . . *E. decumbens* **var.** *decumbens*, pl. 107
WILLAMETTE VALLEY DAISY

7 Larger leaf blades usually fairly broad (leaves on upper portions of the stems generally smaller, and often of different appearance, than those at or near the base)

  9 Leaves rather succulent; plants strictly limited to coastal bluffs (Oreg. to Calif.) . . . . *E. glaucus*, pl. 109
SEASIDE DAISY

  9 Leaves not succulent; plants not strictly coastal

    10 Rays not more than about 1 mm wide (and very numerous)

      11 Rays at least 5 mm long, spreading outward

        12 Rays usually 65–100, mostly about 1 mm wide, generally at least 10 mm long, deep violet; pappus consisting of 2 series of bristles . . . . *E. speciosus* **var.** *speciosus*, pl. 112
SHOWY DAISY

        12 Rays 150–400, less than 1 mm wide, not often more than 10 mm long, white to deep pink; pappus consisting of 1 series of bristles . . . . *E. philadelphicus*, pl. 111
PHILADELPHIA DAISY

      11 Rays (white to pink or purplish) not more than about 4 mm long, upright rather than spreading outward (montane, probably not often found below about 5000 ft., 1520 m) . . . .
. . . . *E. acris* **var.** *debilis*
NORTHERN DAISY

Erigeron acris is sometimes placed in the genus *Trimorpha*, partly because just inside the ray flowers, which are pistillate, there is another ring of strictly pistillate flowers that lack rays. *Erigeron acris* var. *debilis* typically has only 1 or a few flowers on each flowering stem and is not often much taller than 30 cm; var. *asteroides*, at high elevations from N Oreg. northward, typically has at least several flowers on each stem and may be more than 50 cm tall.

    10 Rays usually at least 1.5 mm wide

      13 Leaves on upper and middle portions of the stem only about twice as long as wide, not tapering to distinct petioles, the blades clasping (rays white, usually 25–40; Oreg. and Wash. in the Columbia River Gorge, also in Clackamas Co., Oreg.) . . . . *E. howellii*
HOWELL'S DAISY

      13 Leaves on upper and middle portions of the stem more than twice as long as wide, sometimes tapering to short petioles, the blades not clasping

        14 Plants generally more than 30 cm tall, the flowering stems distinctly upright

          15 Achenes with 2–4 lengthwise ridges; leaves densely hairy; involucres densely hairy above, conspicuously glandular below (rays generally 50–75, white to pink-purple; in the Olympic Mountains, Wash., and the Cascades, also in the Siskiyou Mountains of SW Oreg. and NW Calif.; not likely to be found below about 4000 ft., 1220 m). . . . . *E. aliceae*
ALICE EASTWOOD'S DAISY

Columbiadoria hallii,
Hall's goldenweed

15 Achenes with 4–7 lengthwise ridges; leaves at most only slightly hairy; involucre glandular and sometimes also hairy but not densely hairy above and glandular below (rays usually deep rose-purple but sometimes white; mostly above 4000 ft., 1220 m) . . . . *E. peregrinus*
PEREGRINE FLEABANE

Two varieties of *E. peregrinus*, vars. *peregrinus* and *callianthemus*, both sometimes divided further, occur in our region. In var. *peregrinus* the ray flowers are usually white; in var. *callianthemus* they are usually rose-purple.

14 Plants not often more than 30 cm tall, the stems usually spreading slightly outward before turning upward

16 Basal leaves coarsely toothed, the teeth mostly blunt; pappus bristles weak, tending to curl (rays white, bluish, or pink; in the Columbia River Gorge, Wash. and Oreg.) . . . . *E. oreganus*
GORGE DAISY

16 Basal leaves not toothed; pappus bristles stiff

17 Flowering stems with single flower heads (rays white; high montane in the Olympic Mountains, Wash.) . . . . *E. flettii*
FLETT'S DAISY

17 Flowering stems with 1 or more flower heads

18 Leaves on middle portions of flowering stems typically with distinct petioles; rays blue or pinkish purple (Siskiyou Mountains of SW Oreg. and NW Calif.) . . . . . . *E. cervinus* (includes *E. delicatus*)
SISKIYOU DAISY

18 Leaves on middle portions of flowering stems sessile; rays usually white (Calapooya Mountains and the Cascades, W-central Oreg.) . . . . *E. cascadensis*
CASCADES DAISY

Eriophyllum

1 Rays, if present, only 2–5 mm long; plants usually obviously woody near the base; flower heads densely clustered (along the seacoast, Coos Co., Oreg., to Calif.) . . . . *E. staechadifolium*, pl. 114
SEASIDE WOOLLY SUNFLOWER

1 Rays usually at least 7 mm long, sometimes more than 10 mm; plants not often obviously woody at the base; flower heads well separated . . . . *E. lanatum*
WOOLLY SUNFLOWER, OREGON SUNSHINE

Eriophyllum lanatum is variable, with several intergrading named varieties. Those in our region, with overlapping ranges, are keyed below.

2 Leaves equally densely white-hairy on both surfaces, the margins not rolled under (Curry, Josephine, and Jackson Cos., Oreg., to Calif.) . . . . *E. lanatum* var. *lanceolatum*

2 Leaves at least slightly less hairy on the upper surface than on the underside, the margins rolled under

3 Tips of leaf lobes often pointed; rays usually 8–10 mm long; achenes 2.5–3 mm long, conspicuously widening to the top (Lane, Douglas, Curry, Josephine, and Jackson Cos., Oreg., to Calif.; also E of the Cascades in S Oreg.) . . . . *E. lanatum* var. *achillaeoides*

3 Tips of leaf lobes usually blunt; rays usually more than 10 mm long; achenes usually 3–4 mm long, not conspicuously widening to the top (Brit. Col. to Curry, Josephine, and Jackson Cos., Oreg.; also E of the Cascades in Wash., Oreg., Idaho, and Montana) . . . . *E. lanatum* var. *lanatum*, pl. 113
Eriophyllum lanatum var. *integrifolium*, whose leaves are typically either not lobed or lobed only at the tip, has a wide distribution E of the Cascades and E of the Sierra Nevada.

Filago

1 Outer achene-producing flowers not closely surrounded by bracts, the achenes falling without any bracts attached to them; achenes straight

2 Larger leaves widest at the base or at least in the lower half; flower heads usually 20–50 in each dense cluster (phyllaries often red-tinged; plants to 35 cm tall, more or less regularly branched above the middle) . . . . *F. vulgaris*
COMMON FILAGO (Europe)

    2 Larger leaves widest in the upper half; heads in loose clusters of 3–30 ....
.... *F. pyramidata* **var.** *pyramidata* (Europe)
1 Outer achene-producing flowers closely surrounded by small bracts, these persisting around each achene after it falls away from the receptacle; achenes curved
    3 Single heads or clusters of heads in raceme- or paniclelike inflorescences; plants not branching dichotomously; plants usually about 30–40 cm tall but sometimes as tall as 70 cm (flower heads in clusters of as many as 12; entire plant usually whitish woolly-hairy) ....*F. arvensis*
                   FIELD FILAGO (Europe)
    3 Clusters of heads at the tips of stems and in the axils of branches; plants usually branching dichotomously, forming pairs of stems; plants not often more than 25 cm tall
      4 Flower heads in clusters of 2–14; leaves mostly 15–25 mm long, the slender blades often with inturned margins; clusters of heads usually shorter than the leaves surrounding them .....*F. gallica*
                   FRENCH FILAGO (Europe)
      4 Flower heads in clusters of 3–7; leaves mostly 4–10 mm long, the blades without inturned margins; clusters of heads usually longer than the leaves surrounding them ....*F. minima*
                   SMALL FILAGO (Europe)

Galinsoga

1 Pappus scales of disk flowers at least 8 times as long as wide, the upper half much more slender than the lower half; pappus scales of ray flowers about half as long as those of the disk flowers ....
.... *G. quadriradiata* (*G. ciliata*)
                   SHAGGY GALINSOGA (tropical America)
1 Pappus scales of disk flowers only about 4 times as long as wide, the upper half only slightly narrower than the lower half; pappus scales of ray flowers inconspicuous or lacking ....*G. parviflora*
                   SMALL-FLOWERED GALINSOGA (tropical America)

Gnaphalium

1 Pappus bristles joined at the base to form a ring, falling together
    2 Flower heads in a dense, nearly round inflorescence with several leaves beneath it (S Oreg., mostly near the coast, to Calif.) ....*G. japonicum*
                   JAPANESE CUDWEED (Asia, Australasia)
    2 Flower heads either in an elongated inflorescence or clustered at the top of the stem but not tightly packed together
      3 Inflorescence at least 3 times as long as wide; all phyllaries with pointed tips ...*G. purpureum*, pl. 117
                   PURPLE CUDWEED
      3 Inflorescence at the top of the stem, loosely branched, each branch with several heads; inner phyllaries somewhat squared-off at the tip ....*G. luteo-album*
                   WEEDY CUDWEED (Europe)
1 Pappus bristles not joined at the base, falling separately
    4 Involucres only 2–4 mm high; clusters of flower heads surrounded by bracts as conspicuous as the leaves at lower levels on the stems; plants usually not more than 20 cm tall
      5 Most larger leaves at least 6 times as long as wide; phyllaries without prominent white tips ....
.... *G. uliginosum*
                   MARSH CUDWEED (Europe)
      5 Most larger leaves not more than 5 times as long as wide; phyllaries typically with prominent white tips ....*G. palustre*, pl. 116
                   LOWLAND CUDWEED
    4 Involucres usually more than 4 mm high; clusters of flower heads not surrounded by bracts as conspicuous as the leaves at lower levels on the stems
      6 Leaves mostly green, not conspicuously woolly-hairy, slightly glandular on both surfaces (coastal, Lincoln Co., Oreg., to Calif.) ....*G. californicum*
                   CALIFORNIA CUDWEED

6 Leaves grayish, woolly-hairy on both surfaces, not glandular

    7 Bases of some leaves prolonged down the stems as narrow wings; upper portions of phyllaries sometimes brownish but not yellowish; perennial ....
.... *G. canescens* subsp. *thermale* (*G. microcephalum* subsp. *thermale*), pl. 115
SLENDER CUDWEED

    7 Bases of the leaves not prolonged down the stems as narrow wings; upper portions of phyllaries usually yellowish; annual or biennial .... *G. stramineum* (*G. chilense*)
COTTON-BATTING CUDWEED

Grindelia

In spite of many revisions, *Grindelia* remains troublesome because of intergradation and hybridization. Some plants of our region may not fit perfectly into any of the species to which the various choices lead.

1 Awns of pappus more than 0.3 mm wide, the margins with distinct small teeth; leaves slightly succulent (coastal, Alaska to Calif.) .... *G. stricta* var. *stricta*
COASTAL GUMWEED

1 Awns of pappus less than 0.3 mm wide, the margins smooth; leaves not noticeably succulent

    2 Lower phyllaries rolled back into complete circles; involucre not often more than 1 cm high ....
.... *G. nana*, pl. 119
SMALL GUMWEED

        In some specimens with small flower heads, presumed to be *G. nana*, none of the phyllaries are rolled back even to the extent that they form semicircles.

    2 Phyllaries upright, spreading slightly outward or rolled back only to the extent that they form semicircles, not complete circles; involucre usually more than 1 cm high

        3 Stems and flower peduncles conspicuously hairy; stems reddish; leaf blades, at least the larger ones, generally toothed (Josephine and Jackson Cos., Oreg., to Calif.) .... *G. hirsutula* var. *davyi*
DAVY'S GUMWEED

        3 Stems and flower peduncles only slightly hairy; stems generally not reddish; leaf blades sometimes with smooth margins, sometimes toothed (Puget Trough, Brit. Col. and Wash., and Willamette Valley, Oreg.) .... *G. integrifolia*, pl. 118
WILLAMETTE VALLEY GUMWEED

Helenium

1 Rays shorter than the disk, sometimes so short as to be inconspicuous; pappus scales to 1 mm long (in our region only occasional in Willamette Valley, Oreg.; also known from Klamath Co., Oreg.; more common and widespread in Calif.) .... *H. puberulum*, pl. 121
ROSILLA

1 Rays conspicuous, longer than the disk; pappus scales at least 1 mm long

    2 Flower heads several to many, on short peduncles (pappus scales 1–1.5 mm long) ...... *H. autumnale*
SNEEZEWEED

    2 Flower heads single or at most 2–3, on long peduncles

        3 Peduncles of flower heads hairy; pappus usually 3–4.5 mm long (in bogs, Coos Co., Oreg., to Calif.)
.... *H. bolanderi*
COAST SNEEZEWEED

        3 Peduncles of flower heads not hairy; pappus not so much as 3 mm long (in bogs, Curry and Josephine Cos., Oreg., to Calif.) .... *H. bigelovii*, pl. 120
TALL SNEEZEWEED

Helianthus-Helianthella Complex

1 Flower heads usually 1 at the end of each leafy stem; achenes of disk flowers markedly flattened and with thin edges (Douglas, Jackson, and Klamath Cos., Oreg., to Calif.) ...... *Helianthella californica* subsp. *nevadensis*
CALIFORNIA FALSE SUNFLOWER

1 Flower heads usually 2 or more on each leafy stem; achenes of disk flowers rather plump, often somewhat 4-angled

  2 Most leaves alternate

    3 Phyllaries abruptly narrowed to a slender tip; rays usually at least 2.5 cm long; achenes to more than 10 mm long . . . . ***Helianthus annuus***
        COMMON SUNFLOWER

    3 Phyllaries tapering more or less gradually to the tip; rays not so much as 2.5 cm long; achenes 3–4.5 mm long (S Oreg. to Calif.) . . . . ***Helianthus bolanderi***
        BOLANDER'S SUNFLOWER

  2 Most leaves opposite

    4 Phyllaries about 5 times as long as wide, tightly overlapping; disk flowers usually purple, sometimes yellow (reported from S Brit. Col., where probably introduced; sometimes cultivated in Calif., perhaps elsewhere) . . . . ***Helianthus rigidus*** var. ***subrhomboideus***
        RIGID SUNFLOWER (central and E North America)

    4 Phyllaries usually at least 6 times as long as wide, spreading outward to some extent, not tightly overlapping; disk flowers yellow (widespread E of the Cascades and from Brit. Col. to Calif.; plants reported from SW Brit. Col. probably introduced) . . . . ***Helianthus nuttallii*** var. ***nuttallii***
        NUTTALL'S SUNFLOWER

Hesperevax

1 Most flower heads in groups of many at the tips of stems; leaf blades narrowing to rather broad petioles, these broadened further where they attach to the stems (SW Oreg. to Calif.) . . . ***H. acaulis*** subsp. ***robustior***
    DWARF HESPEREVAX

1 Flower heads scattered along the stems as well as at the tips; leaves narrowed to slender petioles, these not broadened where they attach to the stems (Josephine and Curry Cos., Oreg., to Calif.) . . . . ***H. sparsiflora*** subsp. ***brevifolia***
    UPRIGHT HESPEREVAX

Hieracium

Hieracium, with more than 750 species, is represented in our region by more weeds than natives. Some of the aliens, however, have been encountered only one or a few times, and there are likely to be others whose presence has not yet been noted. To make identification simpler, the species likely to be weeds—those growing in urban areas and along well-traveled roads—are under the second choice 1. If you try both choices, you will probably soon see which is going to lead you in the right direction.

1 Native species

  2 Corollas white (very common in open woods) . . . ***H. albiflorum***
    WHITE-FLOWERED HAWKWEED

  2 Corollas yellow

    3 Leaves entirely basal

      4 Involucres with gray, star-shaped hairs and long, soft, black hairs, sometimes also with black glandular hairs (mostly E of the Cascades and not often found below about 5000 ft., 1520 m) . . . . ***H. gracile***
        LOW ALPINE HAWKWEED

      4 Involucres with only long, soft, gray hairs (montane, not often found below 5000 ft., 1520 m) . . . . ***H. triste***
        WOOLLY HAWKWEED

Hieracium albiflorum,
white-flowered hawkweed

3 Leaves present along the flowering stems, but they may become gradually smaller upward

  5 Leaves and stems of the lower portion of the plant densely covered with almost bristly hairs 5–10 mm long (Columbia River Gorge, Wash. and Oreg.) ....***H. longiberbe***
                LONG-BEARDED HAWKWEED

5 Hairs on leaves and stems of the lower portion not so much as 5 mm long

  6 Basal leaves small and typically shed before flowering begins (plants to about 1 m tall, at least the upper portions usually with some star-shaped hairs; leaf blades usually with a few conspicuous marginal teeth; involucres 6–13 mm tall, the phyllaries not obviously hairy; NW Oreg. eastward across much of North America) ....***H. umbellatum*** subsp. ***umbellatum***
                UMBELLATE HAWKWEED

6 Basal leaves substantial and usually persistent

  7 Leaf blades hairy on the margins and upper surface, but generally not obviously hairy on the underside (Josephine Co., Oreg., to Calif.) ....***H. bolanderi***
                BOLANDER'S HAWKWEED

7 Leaf blades usually hairy on both surfaces

  8 Peduncles and phyllaries of flower heads with gland-tipped hairs

    9 Peduncles and phyllaries densely covered with gland-tipped hairs (SW Oreg. to Calif.) ....***H. parryi***
                PARRY'S HAWKWEED

    9 Peduncles and phyllaries with relatively few gland-tipped hairs .... ***H. scouleri*** (*H. albertinum, H. cynoglossoides*)
                SCOULER'S HAWKWEED

  8 Peduncles and phyllaries without gland-tipped hairs

    10 Plants extremely hairy, the hairs unbranched, to about 2 mm long (E Lane and Douglas Cos., Oreg., to Calif.; mostly E of the crest of the Cascades and not likely to be found below 4000 ft., 1220 m) ....***H. horridum***
                SHAGGY HAWKWEED

    10 Plants with a feltlike, grayish covering of star-shaped hairs and also of unbranched hairs (montane, S Oreg. to Calif.) ....***H. greenei***
                GREENE'S HAWKWEED

1 Introduced (from Europe), weedy species

  11 Plants with creeping stolons, vegetatively forming colonies, these sometimes matlike; corollas orange or yellow

    12 Corollas orange

      13 Each inflorescence consisting of several crowded flower heads ....***H. aurantiacum***, pl. 125
                ORANGE HAWKWEED

      13 Each inflorescence consisting of only 2 flower heads ....***H. pilosella*** × ***aurantiacum***
                GARDEN HAWKWEED

    12 Corollas yellow

      14 Each flowering stem with only 1 flower head ....***H. pilosella***
                MOUSE-EAR HAWKWEED

      14 Each flowering stem with at least 2 flower heads

        15 Each flowering stem with only 2 heads, the branches bearing these about as long as the main stem .... ***H.*** ×***stoloniferum*** (*H. aurantiacum* × *pilosella*)

        15 Each flowering stem with 2 or more heads, these on short branches of the upper part of the main stem or in compact, umbel-like inflorescences

          16 Flower heads 2–6, on distinct branches of the upper part of the main stem

            17 Inflorescence rather crowded; involucres 5–7 mm long; leaf blades without star-shaped hairs .... ***H. lactucella***

17 Inflorescence rather loose; involucres 9–12 mm long; undersides of leaf blades with star-shaped hairs . . . . ***H. flagellare***

16 Flower heads usually 5 to many, on short peduncles and forming crowded, umbel-like inflorescences

  18 Upper surface of leaf blades usually somewhat bluish or grayish but not obviously hairy; underside of leaf blades with bristly hairs along the midrib . . . . ***H.*** ×***floribundum*** (*H. caespitosum* × *lactucella*)

  18 Upper surface of leaf blades obviously hairy but not at all bluish or grayish; underside of leaf blades usually with star-shaped hairs . . . . ***H. caespitosum*** (*H. pratense*)
YELLOW KING DEVIL

11 Plants without creeping stolons, not vegetatively forming colonies, individual plants distinct; corollas yellow

  19 Upper surface of leaf blades with purple spots or blotches (leaves in basal rosettes; stems with star-shaped white hairs and numerous glands) . . . . ***H. maculatum***
SPOTTED HAWKWEED

  19 Upper surface of leaf blades without purple spots or blotches

    20 Plants typically without basal leaves at the time of flowering (hairs on stems and undersides of leaves not branched, with bulbous bases) . . . . ***H. sabaudum***

    20 Plants with well-developed basal leaves at the time of flowering

      21 Margins of leaf blades either smooth or only with very small teeth

        22 Styles yellow; leaf blades somewhat bluish or grayish, either only slightly hairy or with long hairs, none of these star-shaped . . . . ***H. piloselloides*** (*H. florentinum, H. praealtum*)

        22 Styles dark; leaf blades not bluish or grayish, with long hairs, many of the hairs on the underside star-shaped . . . . ***H. caespitosum*** (*H. pratense*)
YELLOW KING DEVIL

      21 Margins of leaf blades coarsely toothed, at least at the base

        23 Leaf blades rounded, heart-shaped, or somewhat squared-off at the base, the petioles distinct . . . . ***H. murorum***
WALL HAWKWEED

        23 Leaf blades tapering gradually to the petioles

          24 Most hairs on stems and leaves not branched (there are relatively few star-shaped hairs) . . . . ***H. vulgatum***
COMMON HAWKWEED

          24 Most hairs on stems and leaves star-shaped (there are relatively few hairs that are not branched) . . . . ***H. lachenalii***
(*H. acuminatum* or *H. strumosum* of some references)

Hypochaeris

1 Leaves rough-hairy; flower heads usually about 3 cm wide, open whether or not there is sunshine; perennial . . . . ***H. radicata***
ROUGH CAT'S-EAR (Europe)

1 Leaves not obviously hairy; flower heads usually about 2 cm wide, open only when there is bright sunshine; annual . . . . ***H. glabra***
SMOOTH CAT'S-EAR (Europe)

Hieracium scouleri,
Scouler's hawkweed

Lactuca-Mycelis **Complex**

1 Flower heads with only 5 flowers (corollas yellow) . . . . *M. muralis*, pl. 138
WALL LETTUCE (Europe)

1 Flower heads with at least 8 flowers
    2 Achene without a slender beak; pappus bristles brownish; corollas usually cream or bluish . . . *L. biennis*
TALL BLUE LETTUCE (E United States)
    2 Achene with a slender beak as long as, or longer than, the body; pappus bristles white; corollas yellow
        3 Leaf blades more or less oblong, prickly along the margins and on the underside of the midrib . . . . . .
. . . . *L. serriola*
PRICKLY LETTUCE (Europe)
        3 Leaf blades rather slender, sometimes lobed but not prickly along the margins or on the underside
of the midrib . . . . *L. saligna*
WILLOW LETTUCE (Europe)

Lasthenia

1 Rays so short they may appear to be absent
    2 Phyllaries partly fused together; in vernal pools and other damp habitats . . . .*L. glaberrima*, pl. 130
SMOOTH GOLDFIELDS
    2 Phyllaries free of one another; on offshore rocks and islands populated by nesting seabirds . . . .
. . . . *L. maritima*
MARITIME GOLDFIELDS
1 Rays conspicuous
    3 Leaves neither lobed not coarsely toothed; involucre 5–10 mm high; pappus consisting of 1–7 slender
bristles; SW Oreg. to Calif. . . . . *L. californica* (*L. chrysostoma*), pl. 129
CALIFORNIA GOLDFIELDS
    3 At least some leaves lobed or coarsely toothed; involucre 4–6 mm high; pappus consisting of scales of 2
sizes, the shorter ones fringed; coastal in central and N Calif. but also known from 1 locality on Whid-
bey Island, Island Co., Wash. . . . . *L. minor*
WOOLLY GOLDFIELDS

Madia-Anisocarpus-Hemizonella-Kyhosia **Complex**

All the species in this complex in our region have long been assigned to *Madia*. Not all botanists would argue that
that four genera, three of them with a single species each in our region, are needed.

1 Achenes with a pappus; flower heads open in afternoon as well as morning; perennial or at least biennial
    2 Phyllaries 10–12 mm long; disk flowers with a pistil and stamens; anthers blackish (not often found
below 3500 ft., 1070 m; in our region mostly in SW Oreg.) . . . . *K. bolanderi* (*M. bolanderi*)
BOLANDER'S TARWEED
    2 Phyllaries 5–6 mm long; disk flowers strictly staminate; anthers yellow (usually in open woods) . . . .
. . . . *A. madioides* (*M. madioides*), pl. 71
WOODLAND TARWEED
1 Achenes without a pappus; flower heads of most species open only in the morning or evening; annual
    3 Heads not so much as 5 mm high
        4 Nearly all leaves opposite; each achene flattened in a plane at an angle of 90° to that of the ray of the
flower with which it is associated . . . . *H. minima* (*M. minima*)
LEAST TARWEED
        4 Most middle and upper leaves alternate; each achene flattened in a plane parallel to that of the ray
of the flower with which it is associated . . . .*M. exigua*
LITTLE TARWEED
    3 Heads usually at least 5 mm high

5 Only the ray flowers producing achenes (disk flowers strictly staminate)

  6 Plants to about 60 cm tall, the foliage lemon-scented; rays 4–10 mm long, greenish yellow; achenes triangular in cross section . . . .*M. citriodora*

                  LEMON-SCENTED TARWEED

  6 Plants to about 2 m tall, the foliage not lemon-scented; rays 10–20 mm long, yellow, often with a maroon blotch at the base; achenes conspicuously flattened . . . .*M. elegans*

                  COMMON MADIA

        In some references, the following varieties are recognized. They differ in habit of growth and time of flowering, but the distinctions are sometimes blurred.

    7 Basal rosette of leaves well developed (flowering summer to fall) . . . .*M. elegans* var. *densifolia*

    7 Basal rosette of leaves not well developed

      8 Flowering during summer . . . .*M. elegans* var. *elegans*, pl. 133

      8 Flowering during spring . . . .*M. elegans* var. *vernalis*

5 Disk flowers and ray flowers producing achenes (rays sometimes very short)

  9 Involucres spindle-shaped, usually more than twice as high as wide; tips of phyllaries scarcely differentiated (flower heads in dense clusters; unpleasantly aromatic) . . . .*M. glomerata*

                  STINKING TARWEED, MOUNTAIN TARWEED

  9 Involucres not more than 1.5 times as high as wide; tips of phyllaries slender and well differentiated

    10 Involucres rarely more than 10 mm high; herbage hairy and glandular in the inflorescence but not in the lower part of the plant; flower heads not in dense clusters . . . .*M. gracilis*, pl. 134

                  COMMON TARWEED

    10 Involucres to about 15 mm high; herbage hairy or glandular throughout; flower heads sometimes in dense clusters . . . .*M. sativa*

                  COAST TARWEED

Lactuca biennis,
tall blue lettuce

Madia exigua,
little tarweed

Matricaria

1 Flower heads without ray flowers; corollas 4-lobed (pineapple-scented; common and often weedy but probably native to the region) . . . . *M. discoidea* (*M. matricarioides*; *Chamomilla suaveolens* of some references), pl. 135
1 Flower heads with white ray flowers; disk corollas 5-lobed
    2 Receptacle not hollow when sliced open; achenes with 2 oil glands on one side near the top; plant not obviously aromatic . . . . *M. maritima* (*M. perforata* of some references)
        SCENTLESS MAYWEED (Europe)
    2 Receptacle hollow when sliced open; achenes without oil glands near the top; plant sweetly aromatic . . .
    . . . . *M. recutita* (*M. chamomilla* of many references)
        SWEET WILD CHAMOMILE (Europe)

Microseris-Nothocalais Complex

The flower heads of most species (other than *Nothocalais alpestris*) nod before opening.

1 Pappus consisting of numerous slender bristles, these with very small barbs
    2 Outer phyllaries much shorter than the upper ones; pappus bristles brownish (in sphagnum bogs) . . . .
    . . . . *M. borealis*
        NORTHERN MICROSERIS
    2 Outer phyllaries about the same length as the inner ones; pappus bristles whitish (montane and high montane) . . . . *N. alpestris*
        FALSE AGOSERIS
1 Pappus consisting of scales, each with a bristle, sometimes feathery or at least barbed, originating at the tip
    3 Corollas protruding, at most, only slightly beyond the involucre; pappus scales almost always 5; annuals
        4 Pappus scales usually 6–10 mm long, their bristles usually slightly shorter (SW Oreg. to Calif.) . . . . . .
        . . . . *M. acuminata*
        SIERRA FOOTHILLS MICROSERIS
        4 Pappus scales not so much as 6 mm long, their bristles about twice as long as the scales (scales nearly as long as the achenes; coastal) . . . . *M. bigelovii*
        BIGELOW'S MICROSERIS
    3 Corollas protruding well beyond the involucre; pappus, on most heads, consisting of more than 5 scales; perennials
        5 Pappus bristles about 15 or more, soft and feathery (SW Oreg. to Calif., also E of the crest of the Cascades) . . . . *M. nutans*
        NODDING MICROSERIS
        5 Pappus scales usually 6–10, stiff and slightly rough but not feathery
            6 Pappus scales about half as long as the bristles (Siskiyou Mountain region of SW Oreg. and NW Calif.) . . . . *M. howellii*
            HOWELL'S MICROSERIS
            6 Pappus scales much less than half as long as the slender bristles . . . . *M. laciniata*, pl. 137
            CUT-LEAVED MICROSERIS
        Several intergrading varieties of *M. laciniata* are recognized in some references.

Psilocarphus

1 Saclike bracts enclosing pistillate flowers about 3 mm long when achenes are mature; flower heads usually at least 6 mm high . . . . *P. brevissimus* (includes *P. elatior*)
        TALL WOOLLY-HEADS
1 Saclike bracts enclosing pistillate flowers about 2 mm long when achenes are mature; flower heads not more than 6 mm high
    2 Achenes widest above the middle; larger leaves usually at least 6 times as long as wide . . . . . *P. oregonus*
        OREGON WOOLLY-HEADS
    2 Achenes not wider above the middle than below; larger leaves not often more than 6 times as long as wide . . . . *P. tenellus* var. *tenellus*, pl. 140
        SLENDER WOOLLY-HEADS

Senecio

1 Plants sometimes more than 1 m tall, not noticeably hairy; larger leaf blades slightly succulent, the lower ones commonly more than 10 cm long and generally with smooth margins (but occasionally with a few teeth); inflorescence typically with numerous flower heads, the involucres to 8 mm high; rays, if present, few and not more than about 8 mm long (in damp montane habitats mostly E of the crest of the Cascades) . . . . *S. hydrophilus*
MARSH BUTTERWEED

1 Plants not in all respects as described in the other choice 1
  2 Rays either absent or inconspicuous (if present, only about 2 mm long and barely reaching beyond the phyllaries); most leaves pinnately lobed; annual weeds of gardens and waste places but sometimes found in more or less natural habitats
    3 Rays completely absent; small, erratically placed phyllaries at the base of the involucre with prominent black tips; number of larger phyllaries usually about 21 (given enough moisture, flowering throughout the year in milder portions of our region) . . . . *S. vulgaris*, pl. 146
COMMON GROUNDSEL (Eurasia)
    3 Rays present but only about 2 mm long; small phyllaries at the base of the involucre not black-tipped; number of larger phyllaries usually about 13 but sometimes as many as 21 . . . . *S. sylvaticus*
WOODLAND GROUNDSEL (Europe)

  2 Rays conspicuous; biennial or perennial
    4 General outline of blades of lower leaves narrowly triangular . . . . *S. triangularis*
TRIANGULAR-LEAVED SENECIO
Most specimens of *S. triangularis* in our region, with leaf blades about one-third as wide as long, fit into var. *triangularis*. Plants growing in coastal salt marshes in Wash. and Oreg. but otherwise not markedly different have been named var. *gibbonsii;* those growing in coastal sphagnum bogs and with proportionately more slender, often smooth-margined leaves have been named var. *angustifolius*.
    4 General outline of leaf blades not triangular
      5 Plants low, usually with at least several sprawling main branches, and not often more than about 15 cm tall (many leaf blades nearly or quite sessile, deeply toothed or shallowly lobed; high montane, often on rockslides) . . . . *S. fremontii* **var.** *fremontii*
FREMONT'S BUTTERWEED, DWARF MOUNTAIN BUTTERWEED
      5 Plants not low and sprawling, and usually much more than 15 cm tall
        6 True basal leaves usually falling before flowering time (all or almost all leaves deeply pinnately lobed)
          7 Plants sometimes more than 1 m tall; most larger leaves at least bipinnately lobed, the terminal primary lobe much larger than the lateral primary lobes; common weed on cleared land but also invading natural areas (noxious weed, toxic to livestock) . . . . *S. jacobaea*, pl. 144
TANSY RAGWORT (Europe)
          7 Plants not often more than about 60 cm tall; leaves not distinctly bipinnately lobed, the terminal primary lobe not conspicuously larger than most of the primary lateral lobes; native and usually found on serpentine soils (Siskiyou Mountains of SW Oreg. and NW Calif.) . . . . *S. eurycephalus*
CUT-LEAVED BUTTERWEED
        6 True basal leaves usually present at flowering time
          8 Blades of the basal leaves deeply pinnately lobed
            9 Plants not often more than 25 cm tall; high montane, often on rockslides (Olympic Mountains and the Cascades, Wash.) . . . . *S. flettii*
FLETT'S BUTTERWEED
            9 Plants generally more than 25 cm tall; not high montane (but sometimes low montane)

10 Phyllaries usually distinctly hairy; strictly coastal (S Wash. to Calif.) . . . . ***S. bolanderi* var. *bolanderi***
BOLANDER'S SENECIO

10 Phyllaries not hairy; not coastal (Columbia River Gorge and W Oreg.) . . . ***S. bolanderi* var. *harfordii***
HARFORD'S SENECIO

8 Blades of basal leaves not pinnately lobed (but they may be coarsely toothed)

11 Blades of basal leaves not much more than twice as long as wide; flowering stems with not more than 3 flower heads, often with only 1

12 Plants often with more than 1 flowering stem (rays usually 10–15 mm long; high montane in the Olympic Mountains, Wash.) . . . . ***S. neowebsteri*** (*S. websteri*)
OLYMPIC BUTTERWEED

12 Plants typically with a single flowering stem

13 Leaves distinctly hairy, sometimes densely so; flowering stem most commonly with 2–3 flower heads but sometimes only 1 (on serpentine soils, Josephine Co., Oreg.) . . . . . . ***S. hesperius***, pl. 143
SISKIYOU BUTTERWEED

13 Leaves not obviously hairy; flowering stem almost always with a single flower head, rarely 2 (rays 6–12 mm long; in the Cascades, mostly above 4000 ft., 1220 m) . . . . ***S. cymbalarioides***
ALPINE MEADOW BUTTERWEED

What has been called *S. cymbalarioides* in many earlier references is *S. streptanthifolius*, found E of the crest of the Cascades. Its flowering stems have several flower heads.

11 Blades of basal leaves usually decidedly more than twice as long as wide

14 Blades of basal leaves not sharply set off from the petioles because these are winged to the base (phyllaries conspicuously black-tipped; high montane, Olympic Mountains, Wash., and the Cascades of Brit. Col. but not of Wash., and eastward) . . . . ***S. lugens***
BLACK-TIPPED BUTTERWEED

14 Blades of basal leaves rather sharply set off from the petioles, these typically not winged to the base

15 Blades of larger leaves several times as long as wide . . . . ***S. macounii***, pl. 145
MACOUN'S SENECIO

15 Blades of most larger leaves not more than 3 times as long as wide

16 Plants not often more than 30 cm tall, typically with several flowering stems; leaves and stems woolly-hairy (SW Oreg. to Calif., also E of the Cascades) . . . . ***S. canus***
WOOLLY BUTTERWEED

16 Plants commonly more than 30 cm tall, with a single flowering stem; leaves and stem stiff-hairy, especially when young, but gradually becoming less hairy and not at any time woolly-hairy (mostly montane in the Cascades and eastward)

17 Rays white to cream . . . . ***S. integerrimus* var. *ochroleucus***
WHITE SINGLE-STEMMED BUTTERWEED

17 Rays yellow . . . . ***S. integerrimus* var. *exaltatus***
YELLOW SINGLE-STEMMED BUTTERWEED

Senecio integerrimus "var. *major*" (S Oreg. to Calif.) is scarcely different. Its phyllaries are more densely hairy than those of typical var. *exaltatus* and less likely to be conspicuously blackened at the tips.

Solidago-Euthamia Complex

1 Leaf blades hairy and grayish on both surfaces (plants to more than 1 m tall; in our region only in SW Oreg.) . . . . ***S. californica***
CALIFORNIA GOLDENROD

1 Leaf blades not hairy and grayish on both surfaces (they may, however, have some hairs on the underside and/or along the margins)

2 Inflorescence narrow (the branches are short), not often more than 4 cm wide; plants not often more than 60 cm tall

3 Plants resinous and rather aromatic; on backshores of sandy beaches on the coast . . . . ***S. simplex* subsp. *spathulata*** (*S. spathulata* subsp. *spathulata*)
DUNE GOLDENROD

3 Plants neither resinous nor especially aromatic; in inland habitats, widespread; also on Gulf Islands, Brit. Col., and San Juan Islands, Wash. .... *S. simplex* subsp. *neomexicana*, pl. 148
SPIKELIKE GOLDENROD

2 Inflorescence broad, the branches fairly long; plants often more than 1 m tall
    4 Most leaf blades more than 1 cm wide, without dark resinous dots ....
.... *S. canadensis* subsp. *salebrosa*, pl. 147
CANADA GOLDENROD

    4 Leaf blades rarely so much as 8 mm wide, with dark resinous dots (more common E than W of the crest of the Cascades) .... *E. occidentalis* (*S. occidentalis*)
WESTERN GOLDENROD

Sonchus

1 Involucres and peduncles with conspicuous, gland-tipped, sticky hairs (flower heads usually 3–5 cm wide; perennial, spreading aggressively by rhizomes) .... *S. arvensis*, pl. 149
PERENNIAL SOW THISTLE (Europe)

1 Involucres and peduncles without gland-tipped, sticky hairs
    2 Flower heads usually 3–5 cm wide; perennial .... *S. uliginosus*
WET-GROUND SOW THISTLE (Europe)

    2 Flower heads usually 1.5–2.5 cm wide; annual
        3 Lengthwise ribs of mature achenes without conspicuous, closely spaced bumps; general outline of basal lobes of upper leaves rounded (although toothed, they are not drawn out to a pointed tip) .....
.... *S. asper*
PRICKLY SOW THISTLE (Europe)

        3 Lengthwise ribs of mature achenes with conspicuous, closely spaced bumps; basal lobes of upper leaves drawn out to a pointed tip as well as toothed .... *S. oleraceus*
COMMON SOW THISTLE (Europe)

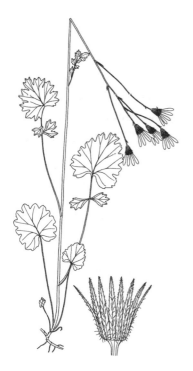

Senecio bolanderi var. *bolanderi*,
Bolander's senecio

Senecio canus,
woolly butterweed

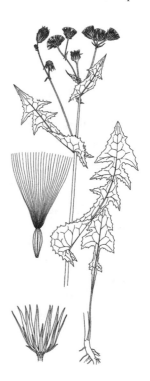

Sonchus asper,
prickly sow thistle

Stephanomeria

1 Inflorescence not obviously branched, with conspicuous leaves (generally more than 2 cm long) like those on lower portions of the stem (mostly above 3000 ft., 910 m; Lane Co., Oreg., to Calif.; also E of the crest of the Cascades) . . . . *S. lactucina*
LARGE-LEAVED STEPHANOMERIA

1 Inflorescence extensively branched, with only small leaves, if these have persisted to flowering time
    2 Each of the 5 sides of the achene with a narrow lengthwise groove (SW Oreg. to Calif.) . . . . *S. elata*
    SLENDER STEPHANOMERIA

    2 None of the 5 sides of the achene with a lengthwise groove (SW Oreg. to Calif.) . . . .
. . . . *S. virgata* subsp. *pleurocarpa*, pl. 150
VIRGATE STEPHANOMERIA

Tanacetum

1 Rays white, to about 8 mm long and much longer than the corolla tubes . . . .
. . . . *T. parthenium* (*Chrysanthemum parthenium*), pl. 152
FEVERFEW (Europe)

1 Rays, if present, yellow, not more than 3 mm long and not longer than the corolla tubes
    2 Heads usually at least 50 and in a nearly flat-topped inflorescence; stems upright and ribbed length-
    wise; common weed of roadsides and vacant lots . . . . *T. vulgare*
    TANSY (Europe)
    Caution: *Tanacetum vulgare* is toxic if eaten!

    2 Heads fewer than 20, the inflorescence not distinctly flat-topped; stems falling down, not ribbed length-
    wise; restricted to backshores and dunes of sandy beaches . . . . . . *T. camphoratum* (*T. douglasii*), pl. 151
    DUNE TANSY
    Another name that will be found in some references is *T. bipinnatum* var. *huronense*.

Tragopogon

1 Corollas purple . . . . *T. porrifolius*, pl. 153
VEGETABLE OYSTER, SALSIFY (Europe)

1 Corollas yellow
    2 Phyllaries usually at least 10, tapering gradually from their bases, mostly 3–4 cm long in the flowering
    stage, 4–7 cm long when achenes are ripe . . . . *T. dubius*
    LARGE YELLOW GOATSBEARD (Europe)

    2 Phyllaries usually 8, their basal portions distinctly wider than their abruptly narrower and gradually
    tapering terminal portions, mostly 1.5–2.5 cm long in the flowering stage, 2–4 cm long when achenes
    are ripe . . . . *T. pratensis*
    SMALL YELLOW GOATSBEARD (Europe)

BALSAMINACEAE Jewelweed Family

Most members of the jewelweed family are found in tropical areas, especially of Asia and Africa. Only one of the genera, *Impatiens,* is represented in our region, and only one or two of its species are natives here. The flowers, borne in the leaf axils, are slightly bizarre. There are three sepals; the lower one, saclike or cup-shaped, and sometimes with a spur within which nectar is secreted, is much larger than the two lateral ones. The corolla, consisting of five petals, is relatively small; the uppermost petal is free, but the two lateral ones on each side are joined together as decidedly unequal lobes. There are five stamens, with short, flattened filaments, and the fruit-forming portion of the pistil is above the level at which the sepals and petals are attached. The fruit is dry when mature.

Impatiens

1 Lowermost sepal without a saclike spur (sepals from pale yellow to orange; pouch of lowermost sepal rounded at the bottom; S Brit. Col. to NW Oreg., also E of the Cascades) . . . . *I. ecalcarata*
SPURLESS JEWELWEED
See note about hybridization of *I. ecalcarata* with *I. capensis* under the second choice 4.

1 Lowermost sepal with a prominent saclike spur

  2 Leaves opposite or in whorls; sepals mostly white, pale pink, or pale purple, with darker spots (garden plant, established at scattered localities, mostly near the coast) .... *I. glandulifera* (*I. roylei*), pl. 156

                                    POLICEMAN'S HELMET (Asia)

  2 Leaves alternate; sepals predominantly yellow or orange, one or more of them with darker spots

    3 Spur of lowermost sepal straight, pointed directly backward (sepals yellowish or whitish; lower sepal, including the spur, only about 1 cm long; garden plant, reported as a weed in SW Brit. Col.) .... *I. parviflora*

                          SMALL-FLOWERED TOUCH-ME-NOT (Asia)

    3 Spur of lowermost sepal conspicuously curved

      4 Sepals yellowish to bright yellow, the large lip of the lowermost one with brown, reddish brown, or purplish brown dots, these sometimes faint (Alaska to Oreg. but also in parts of central North America and in Eurasia) .... *I. noli-tangere*

                                      TOUCH-ME-NOT

      4 Sepals orange-yellow to orange, coarsely spotted with reddish brown (pouch of lowermost sepal tapering gradually to the bottom, where the spur originates; native to E North America and possibly to some parts of the Pacific Northwest; also cultivated and perhaps escaping) ...... *I. capensis*

                                    ORANGE BALSAM

        Impatiens capensis and I. ecalcarata (first choice 1) hybridize. The progeny show various combinations of shape of the lower sepal, the extent to which the spur, if present, is developed, and the degree to which the flowers are spotted.

BERBERIDACEAE Barberry Family

The barberry family is represented in our region by only a few species of shrubs and perennial herbs. The basic flower formula is as follows: six sepals, often petal-like, in two circles; six petals, also in two circles; six stamens; fruit dry or fleshy, with only one compartment for seeds. There are, however, exceptions, one of them the genus *Achlys*, whose flowers lack sepals and petals and have 6–13 stamens.

    The genus *Berberis* includes many shrubby species that are widely cultivated. One of the best for sunny gardens in our region is the native *B. aquifolium*, called Oregon grape; *B. nervosa* is valuable for shaded or partly shaded locations; and *B. repens*, from east of the crest of the Cascades, is often used where a shrub of low stature is desired. Among the herbaceous species, both species of *Achlys* and all three species of *Vancouveria* can be grown where there is shade and sufficient moisture.

1 Shrubs with evergreen, pinnately compound leaves, these with bristle-tipped marginal teeth .... *Berberis*

1 Perennial herbs, the leaves dying back before winter, the leaflets without bristle-tipped marginal teeth

  2 Leaves with 3 fan-shaped leaflets diverging from the top of the petiole; flowers small, with neither petals nor sepals, in dense spikes .... *Achlys*

  2 Leaves once or twice ternately compound; flowers rather conspicuous, in open racemes or open panicles, with 6 apparent sepals (in 2 series) and 6 petals, as well as some bracts .... *Vancouveria*

Impatiens noli-tangere, touch-me-not

Achlys

The distinction between *Achlys triphylla* and *A. californica*, which often coexist, is not sharp. Some botanists think that recognition of *A. californica* is not warranted.

1 Middle leaflet typically 4–11 cm long and with 3 lobes; stamens 3–4 mm long; fruit usually red-purple . . . . **A. triphylla** subsp. *triphylla*
THREE-LOBED VANILLA LEAF

1 Middle leaflet typically 7–16 mm long and with 6–8 lobes; stamens 4–6 mm long; fruit usually brownish . . . . **A. californica** (*A. triphylla* subsp. *californica*), pl. 157
SEVERAL-LOBED VANILLA LEAF

Berberis

The species of *Berberis* in our region have often been placed in a separate genus, *Mahonia*.

1 Leaflets usually 13–19 (sometimes as few as 11 or as many as 23), each generally with at least 3 rather prominent veins originating at the base; usually in shaded habitats . . . .**B. nervosa**, pl. 159
LONG-LEAVED OREGON GRAPE

1 Leaflets not more than 13, with only 1 prominent vein (the midrib) originating at the base; usually in sunny habitats
  2 Most stems upright, often more than 1 m tall; both surfaces of leaflets very shiny
    3 Leaflets 5–9, occasionally 11; terminal leaflet to 2.5 times as long as wide; petioles usually at least 2–3 cm long; leaves not especially crowded at the tops of the stems . . . .**B. aquifolium**, pl. 158
OREGON GRAPE, the state flower of Oregon
    3 Leaflets usually 7–11, sometimes 13; terminal leaflet usually not quite twice as long as wide; petioles not often so much as 2 cm long; leaves typically very crowded at the tops of the stems (Curry Co., Oreg., to Calif.) . . . .**B. pinnata** subsp. *pinnata*
CALIFORNIA BARBERRY
  2 Most stems spreading laterally, their upright portions not often more than 50 cm tall; only the upper surface, or neither surface, of the leaflets shiny
    4 Upper surface of leaflets shiny, the lower surface dull; leaflets 5–9, these with 6–12 teeth (usually 6–8) on each side (SW Oreg. to Calif.) . . . .**B. piperiana**
PIPER'S BARBERRY
    4 Both surfaces of leaflets dull; leaflets 3–9 (usually 5–6), with 2–10 teeth (usually 5–6) on each side (SW Oreg. to Calif.) . . . . **B. pumila**
DWARF WESTERN BARBERRY

> *Berberis pumila* has been confused with *B. repens,* which has a wide distribution E of the crest of the Cascades and which is characterized by thinner, flexible leaflets that may have more than 15 slender teeth on each side.

Vancouveria

1 Margins of leaflets thin, nearly membranous; foliage dying back before fruits have ripened completely; flower pedicels not glandular-hairy (petals 4–6 mm long, whitish; Wash. to Calif.) . . . . **V. hexandra**, pl. 161
INSIDE-OUT FLOWER

1 Margins of leaflets slightly thickened, usually whitish; foliage persisting until fruits have ripened, and sometimes until late fall; flower pedicels glandular-hairy at the base
  2 Flowers usually in a raceme (but the peduncle sometimes branched near the base); petals 4–6 mm long, the tips bent back, yellow (Josephine and Curry Cos., Oreg., to Calif.) . . . .**V. chrysantha**, pl. 160
YELLOW VANCOUVERIA
  2 Flowers in a panicle; petals 3–4 mm long, the tips not bent back, white or tinged with purple or lavender (Curry Co., Oreg., to Calif.) . . . .**V. planipetala**
SMALL INSIDE-OUT FLOWER

BETULACEAE Birch Family

The birch family is represented in our region by a hazelnut and several birches and alders. All are shrubs or trees with alternate, deciduous leaves. In alders and birches, both the pistillate and staminate flowers are in catkins. In hazelnuts, only the staminate flowers are in catkins; the pistillate flowers are produced singly or in clusters, but as a rule not more than two of a cluster mature as acornlike nuts.

Alders, like members of the pea family (Fabaceae) and many other plants, have nitrogen-fixing bacteria in nodules on their roots. These bacteria, with help from their hosts, are able to utilize atmospheric nitrogen gas in the synthesis of amino acids and proteins. Much of the nitrogen fixed by the bacteria becomes incorporated into the trees. Alder seedlings may therefore flourish on soils that are poor in ammonia and nitrates, the usual sources of nitrogen for plants. The symbiotic association accounts, in part, for the success of some alders on land that has been deforested. As the leaves decay, organic nitrogen is converted by various soil bacteria into ammonia and nitrates. This prepares the land for colonization by other plants, such as Douglas' fir. It is ironic that the increased acidity makes the soil unsuitable for succeeding generations of alders.

1 Most leaf blades with a slight indentation where the petiole joins the blade; pistillate flowers at the tips of branches, staminate flowers in drooping catkins; fruit a nut about 1.5 cm long, enclosed within a bottle-shaped involucre (this derived from a small bract beneath the flower) .... ***Corylus cornuta* var. *californica***
WESTERN HAZELNUT, CALIFORNIA HAZELNUT
Corylus avellana, the widely cultivated filbert, native to Europe, occasionally escapes from cultivation. Its nuts are commonly about 2 cm long.

1 Leaf blades without an indentation where the petiole joins the blade; pistillate and staminate flowers in catkins; each pistillate catkin producing numerous small, flattened nutlets (closely associated with the bracts of the catkin, thus not obvious)
  2 Pistillate catkins becoming woody, resembling conifer cones, retaining their integrity and usually persisting into the succeeding winter .... *Alnus*
  2 Pistillate catkins not becoming woody and usually falling apart when the fruits have ripened ... *Betula*

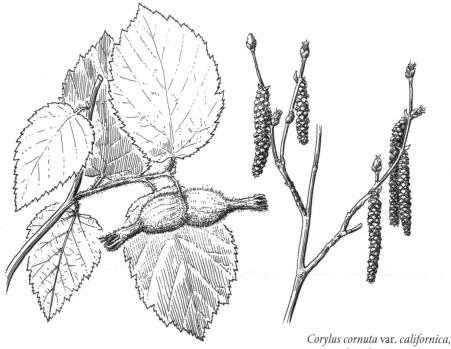

Corylus cornuta var. *californica,*
western hazelnut

Alnus

1 Trees to more than 20 m tall; leaf blades not distinctly double-toothed (either all teeth closely spaced and nearly the same size or the primary teeth coarse and with indistinct secondary teeth); pedicels of pistillate catkins not often more than 1 cm long

    2 Margins of leaf blades rolled under; primary marginal teeth coarse and not closely spaced; fruits, at the stage when they fall out of the pistillate catkins, with conspicuously winged margins . . . . . *A. rubra*
                                                       RED ALDER

    2 Margins of leaf blades not rolled under; marginal teeth usually all about the same size and closely spaced; fruits, at the stage when they fall out of the pistillate catkins, without conspicuously winged margins (mostly on lower slopes of the Cascades and eastward but also in SW Oreg.) . . . *A. rhombifolia*
                                                       WHITE ALDER

1 Shrubs or small trees not often more than 6 m tall; leaf blades distinctly double-toothed (each large tooth with several smaller, mostly acutely pointed teeth)

    3 Catkins appearing and flowering before leaves of the current season have developed; pistillate catkins on stout pedicels less than 6 mm long; lateral portions of fruits not thin and winglike (Alaska to Calif. and eastward, primarily montane and mostly E of the crest of the Cascades in Wash. and N Oreg. but found in the Siskiyou Mountains of SW Oreg. and and NW Calif.) . . . . *A. incana* subsp. *tenuifolia*
                                      THINLEAF ALDER, MOUNTAIN ALDER

    3 Catkins appearing and flowering as leaves of the current season are developing; most pistillate catkins on slender pedicels at least 2 cm long; lateral portions of fruits thin and winglike (mostly in the Cascades but also found in the Puget Trough, including some of the San Juan Islands, and close to the coast of S Oreg.) . . . .*A. viridis* subsp. *sinuata*, pl. 162
                                                       SITKA ALDER

        The leaves of some specimens of *A. viridis* found in coastal SW Oreg. and NW Calif. are not distinctly double-toothed. They have been referred to subsp. *fruticosa,* but the range of this is primarily from Alaska through Northwest Territories and N Brit. Col. to Alberta and Saskatchewan.

Betula

1 Shrubs, typically with several trunks and not more than 4 m tall (mostly restricted to bogs and other wet habitats)

    2 Leaf blades not often so much as 2.5 cm long; twigs with conspicuous resin glands than make them appear warty (Alaska to Calif. and eastward across North America) . . . .*B. glandulosa*
                                                  BOG BIRCH, RESIN BIRCH

    2 Leaf blades usually at least 2.5 cm long; twigs with small, inconspicuous resin glands, not obviously warty (Northwest Territories to Calif. and eastward across North America) . . . . *B. pumila*
                                                       DWARF BIRCH

        Betula glandulosa and *B. pumila* intergrade in areas where they coexist.

1 Trees, typically with a single trunk and to more than 10 m tall

    3 Bark peeling off in thin sheets; leaf blades typically with a rounded base, with not more than 9 pairs of lateral veins, and at least slightly hairy on the underside; central lobe of scales of pistillate catkins as long or longer than the lateral lobes (Alaska to Wash. and eastward across North America; the variety W of the Cascades in Brit. Col. and Wash. is *commutata*) . . . . *B. papyrifera*
                                                      PAPER BIRCH

    3 Bark peeling off in narrow strips; leaf blades typically with a broadly angular to wedge-shaped base, with as many as 18 pairs of lateral veins, and not hairy on the underside; central lobe of scales of pistillate catkins shorter than the lateral lobes (commonly cultivated and sometimes established in situations where it may appear to be native) . . . . *B. pendula*
                                    WEEPING BIRCH, WHITE BIRCH (Europe)

        Another cultivated European species that sometimes escapes is *B. pubescens,* silver birch. Its leaf blades are shaped like those of *B. pendula,* but the undersides are hairy.

BORAGINACEAE Borage Family

In members of the borage family, the inflorescences are often one-sided and at least slightly coiled in one plane, like the scroll of a violin. The calyx and corolla are typically five-lobed, and in some of the genera in our region the throat of the corolla tube has five outgrowths called crests. The five stamens, attached to the corolla tube, alternate with the lobes. The fruit-forming portion of the pistil is generally deeply divided into four lobes (sometimes only two) that separate into dry, one-seeded nutlets. In some species, however, only one or two of four prospective nutlets develop to maturity. Whether and how the nutlets are wrinkled, where their attachment scars are located, and whether they have prickles or wartlike outgrowths are extremely important in identification of species in certain genera. The foliage and stems of most of our species have bristly hairs. There are many deviations from the characteristics just stated, but after you have seen a few borages it should be easy to recognize others as members of the family.

Several Old World species are used for kitchen flavorings, herbal remedies, and dyes; others are cultivated for their value as ornamentals. Borage (*Borago officinalis*), two kinds of comfrey (*Symphytum*), and certain species of *Echium* and *Anchusa* are occasionally found in our region as escapes from gardens.

1 Corolla about 2 cm wide, deep blue, the lobes spreading widely, the tube so short that the lobes may appear to be completely separate petals (garden plant, often escaping) . . . . ***Borago officinalis***
BORAGE (Europe)

1 Corolla not so much as 1.5 cm wide and not in all other respects as described in the other choice 1

  2 Corolla markedly irregular, the 2 upper lobes much longer than the 3 lower ones; 4 of 5 stamens conspicuously protruding beyond the corolla (corolla usually blue, sometimes varying to pink or white; biennial garden plant, sometimes escaping) . . . . ***Echium vulgare***
BLUEWEED (Europe)

  2 Corolla not markedly irregular (very slightly irregular in 1 species of *Anchusa*); stamens all of similar length, none conspicuously protruding beyond the corolla)

    3 Nutlets, by the time they are nearly mature, spreading apart widely

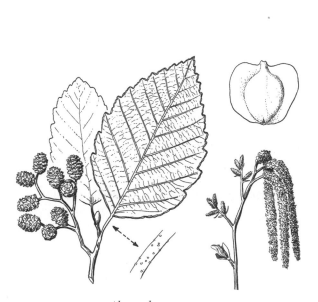

Alnus rubra,
red alder

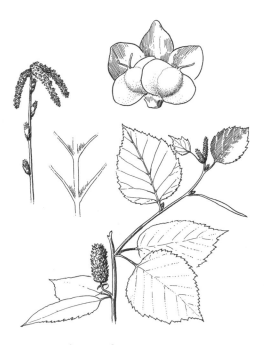

Betula papyrifera,
paper birch

> 4 Nutlets flattened, with hooklike prickles along their margins (SW Oreg. to Calif., also E of the Cascades) .... *Pectocarya pusilla*
> LITTLE PECTOCARYA
>> 4 Nutlets plump, with barb-tipped prickles over much of the surface .... *Cynoglossum*
> 3 Nutlets remaining more or less upright, not spreading apart widely (in certain species of some genera, not all 4 nutlets develop to maturity)
>> 5 Lower end of each nutlet encircled by a swollen, ringlike thickening, and leaving a pit on the receptacle after falling away
>>> 6 Corolla lobes spreading widely away from the tube .... *Anchusa*
>>> 6 Corolla lobes not spreading widely away from the tube .... *Symphytum*
>> 5 Lower ends of nutlets not encircled by a swollen, ringlike thickening, and not leaving a pit on the receptacle after falling away (in *Lithospermum* the bases of the nutlets are conspicuously concave, and the concavity is bordered by a rim, but there is not a ringlike thickening)
>>> 7 Nutlets attached by their bases to the receptacle
>>>> 8 Corolla lobes not spreading widely away from the tube .... *Mertensia*
>>>> 8 Corolla lobes spreading widely away from the tube
>>>>> 9 Attachment scar of each nutlet (only 1–2 of 4 may mature) as wide as the widest diameter of the nutlet and with a distinct rim; corolla yellow, white, or bluish white .... *Lithospermum*
>>>>> 9 Attachment scar of each nutlet much smaller than the widest diameter of the nutlet, without a distinct rim; corolla white or blue, often with a yellow throat .... *Myosotis*
>>> 7 Nutlets attached more or less obliquely to the receptacle, the attachment scar therefore on one side of the lower portion
>>>> 10 Nutlets with prickles bearing small barbs at their tips .... *Hackelia*
>>>> 10 Nutlets without prickles that bear barbs at their tips
>>>>> 11 Corolla yellow or orange .... *Amsinckia*
>>>>> 11 Corolla white (often with a yellow throat)
>>>>>> 12 Nutlets with a lengthwise ridge above the attachment scar .... *Plagiobothrys*
>>>>>> 12 Nutlets with a lengthwise groove above the attachment scar .... *Cryptantha*

Amsinckia

> 1 Margins of leaf blades with small teeth; 2 of the calyx lobes united for much more of their length than the others; nutlets 1–2 mm long (plants slightly succulent; branches often prostrate; on backshores and dunes of sandy beaches, Alaska to Calif.) .... *A. spectabilis* subsp. *spectabilis*
> SEASIDE FIDDLENECK
> 1 Margins of leaf blades smooth; all calyx lobes separated to the same extent; nutlets 2–4 mm long
>> 2 Corolla throat partly closed by hairy bulges; anthers of stamens well below the throat ... *A. lycopsoides*
>> BUGLOSS FIDDLENECK
>> 2 Corolla throat without hairy bulges; anthers of stamens reaching nearly to the throat
>>> 3 Corolla 2–3 mm wide, pale yellow .... *A. menziesii* var. *menziesii* (*A. micrantha*)
>>> MENZIES' FIDDLENECK
>>> 3 Corolla typically 4–6 mm wide, orange or orange-yellow ....
>>> .... *A. menziesii* var. *intermedia* (*A. intermedia*), pl. 163
>>> COMMON FIDDLENECK

Anchusa

> 1 Corolla lobes slightly unequal, and the tube slightly bent; stamens attached below the middle of the tube ....
> .... *A. arvensis*
> FIELD ALKANET (Europe)
> 1 Corolla lobes equal, the tube straight; stamens attached above the middle of the tube

2 Calyx lobes, when flowers are fresh, 6–9 mm long, longer than the tube (at the fruiting stage they are 8–12 mm long) . . . . *A. azurea*
BUGLOSS (Europe)

2 Calyx lobes, when flowers are fresh, 5–7 mm long, about half as long as the tube (at the fruiting stage they are 8–12 mm long) . . . . *A. officinalis*
COMMON ALKANET (Europe)

Cryptantha

In some species of *Cryptantha,* of the four nutlets that start to develop, only one or two may reach maturity.

1 Most bristlelike hairs on the calyx with conspicuously curved or even hooklike tips (S Willamette Valley and S coast of Oreg. to Calif.; also E of the Cascades) . . . . *C. flaccida*
WEAK-STEMMED CRYPTANTHA

1 Bristlelike hairs on the calyx without curved or hooklike tips

  2 Surface of at least some part of mature or nearly mature nutlets distinctly warty or wrinkled

    3 Corolla to about 5 mm wide; nutlets (1–2) roughened by small prickles on one side, smooth on the other (Curry and Josephine Cos., Oreg.) . . . . *C. fragilis*
BRITTLE CRYPTANTHA

    3 Corolla 4–8 mm wide (usually 5–6 mm); nutlets (1–4) warty on both sides (widespread from S Brit. Col. to Calif. and Baja Calif.) . . . . *C. intermedia* (*C. hendersonii*)
LARGE-FLOWERED CRYPTANTHA

  2 Surface of mature or nearly mature nutlets smooth and usually shiny, without warts, prickles, or coarse wrinkles

    4 Lengthwise attachment scar on nutlet shifted far to the right or left of the midline (corolla to about 2 mm wide; mostly montane and E of the crest of the Cascades but also in the Siskiyou Mountain region of SW Oreg. and NW Calif.) . . . . *C. affinis*
SLENDER CRYPTANTHA

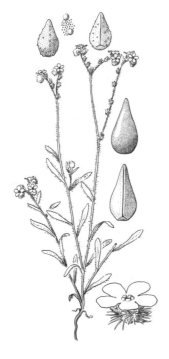

Cryptantha intermedia,
large-flowered cryptantha

Cryptantha affinis,
slender cryptantha

    4 Lengthwise attachment scar not shifted from the midline

      5 Most hairs on stems and leaves pressed down; nutlets (usually 3–4 maturing) tapering gradually to the tip and often spotted gray or darker brown; corolla to about 2.5 mm wide (mostly on backshores of sandy beaches, Curry Co., Oreg., to Calif.) . . . . ***C. leiocarpa***
SEASIDE CRYPTANTHA

      5 Most hairs on stems and leaves spreading outward; nutlets (usually only 1–2 maturing) drawn out to a rather slender tip and not spotted; corolla to about 4 mm wide (Josephine and Jackson Cos., Oreg., to Calif.) . . . . ***C. milobakeri***
MILO BAKER'S CRYPTANTHA

Cynoglossum

1 Inflorescence consisting of several flowering stems arising from the axils of upper leaves; corolla reddish purple . . . . ***C. officinale***
HOUND'S-TONGUE (Europe)

1 Inflorescence a single stem with short branches, each bearing a few flowers; corolla blue

    2 Larger leaves on middle and upper portions of the plant with conspicuous petioles, the blades widest near their bases . . . . ***C. grande***, pl. 164
GIANT HOUND'S-TONGUE

    2 Larger leaves on middle and upper portions of the plant without distinct petioles, usually clasping, the blades widest above the middle; corolla less than 1 mm wide (Jackson Co., Oreg., to Calif.; also E of the Cascades) . . . . ***C. occidentale***
WESTERN HOUND'S-TONGUE

Hackelia

1 Hairs on leaves less than 1 mm long, not conspicuous unless magnified; corolla (pink to blue) generally less than 7 mm wide, the tube reaching slightly beyond the tips of the calyx lobes (SW Oreg. to Calif.) . . . . ***H. micrantha*** (*H. jessicae*)
SMALL-FLOWERED STICKSEED

1 Most hairs on leaves, particularly along the margins, at least 1 mm long, conspicuous without magnification; corolla generally at least 9 mm wide when fully open, the tube not quite reaching the tips of the calyx lobes

    2 Corolla mostly blue, the throat whitish; prickles along the margins of the nutlets united by their bases to form a distinct flange; upper surface of nutlets with as many as about 12 prickles (SW Oreg. to Calif.) . . . . ***H. setosa***
BRISTLY STICKSEED

    2 Corolla white to pale blue, usually with yellow at the throat; prickles along the margins of the nutlets not united by their bases to the extent that there is a distinct flange; upper surface of nutlets with as many as 20 prickles or more (mostly E of the Cascades but in the Columbia River Gorge extending as far W as E Multnomah Co., Oreg.) . . . . ***H. diffusa***
DIFFUSE STICKSEED

Lithospermum

1 Small annual; corolla white or bluish white; nutlets brownish, their surfaces conspicuously wrinkled . . . . ***L. arvense***
CORN GROMWELL (Europe)

1 Stout perennial; corolla yellow; nutlets whitish, their surfaces smooth and shiny

    2 Most leaf blades at least 5 times as long as wide; pedicels of flowers 1–3 mm long; corolla 9–12 mm long (mostly E of the Cascades but also found in prairies in the Puget Sound region) . . . . ***L. ruderale***
WESTERN GROMWELL

    2 Most leaf blades 2–3 times as long as wide; pedicels of flowers 4–7 mm long; corolla 12–18 mm long (Josephine and Jackson Cos., Oreg., to Calif.) . . . . ***L. californicum***, pl. 165
CALIFORNIA GROMWELL

Mertensia

1 Corolla to about 10 mm long, widening gradually from the base (Lane Co., Oreg., to Calif.; not likely to be found below 3500 ft., 1070 m) . . . .*M. bella*
OREGON LUNGWORT

1 Corolla to about 15 mm long (but sometimes considerably shorter), beginning as a tube with parallel sides, then flaring outward rather abruptly
    2 Anthers usually 3.5–5 mm long (in lowland habitats, Puget Sound region of Wash. to Umpqua River valley, Oreg.) . . . .*M. platyphylla*, pl. 166
WESTERN LUNGWORT

    2 Anthers usually 2.2–3.5 mm long; Olympic Peninsula and the Cascades, Brit. Col. to Oreg.; also E of the crest of the Cascades; not likely to be found below 4000 ft., 1220 m) . . . .*M. paniculata* var. *borealis*
TALL LUNGWORT

It is difficult to separate *M. paniculata* var. *borealis* from *M. platyphylla* except on the basis of anther length and altitudinal range. Some plants of the former, however, become very large, more than 1 m tall, and may have numerous stems; *M. platyphylla* does not often reach a height of more than 60 cm and generally has only a few stems.

Myosotis

1 Calyx hairy, but the hairs not hooked
    2 Open corolla rarely more than 5 mm wide; calyx lobes about two-thirds as long as the tube (in wet places) . . . .*M. laxa*, pl. 168
SMALL FORGET-ME-NOT

    2 Open corolla commonly 6–10 mm wide; calyx lobes not more than one-third as long as the tube (common in woodlands to which it has escaped from cultivation, and also found in wet places) . . . .
. . . . *M. scorpioides*
FORGET-ME-NOT (Europe)

Hackelia diffusa,
diffuse stickseed

Lithospermum ruderale,
western gromwell

1 Calyx with at least some hooked hairs

    3 Corolla at first yellow, changing to blue .... *M. discolor*, pl. 167

            YELLOW-AND-BLUE SCORPION GRASS (Europe)

    3 Corolla blue or white from the beginning

        4 Calyx slightly asymmetrical, 2 of the lobes longer than the other 3; corolla white .... *M. verna*

            WHITE SCORPION GRASS

        4 Calyx symmetrical, all the lobes about the same length; corolla typically blue but sometimes white

            5 Corollas at least 4 mm wide, sometimes more than 8 mm .... *M. sylvatica*

                WOODLAND FORGET-ME-NOT

            5 Corollas not more than 3 mm wide

                6 Pedicels, by the time fruits have begun to develop, longer than the calyx lobes .... *M. arvensis*

                    COMMON FORGET-ME-NOT (Europe)

                6 Pedicels, by the time fruits have begun to develop, shorter than the calyx lobes .... *M. stricta*

                    SHORT-STALKED FORGET-ME-NOT (Europe)

Plagiobothrys

Plagiobothrys is a notoriously difficult genus. This key cannot be viewed as definitive, partly because the extent to which some species vary and the extent to which they intergrade are not known. It should work well for some members of the genus but probably not for others. The necessity to look carefully at microscopic characters of the seeds of certain species seems unavoidable.

1 Lower stem leaves (above the basal rosette) alternate

    2 Calyx not more than 4 mm long

        3 Calyx lobes not separating from the tube as the nutlets ripen; corolla about 3 mm wide when fully open; nutlets nearly as wide as long, cross-shaped, bumpy; plants rarely so much as 20 cm tall; leaves of basal rosette crowded, not often more than 2 cm long; sap not purple .... *P. tenellus*

            SLENDER POPCORN FLOWER

        3 Calyx lobes typically separating from the tube as the nutlet or nutlets ripen (usually only 1–2 nutlets mature); corolla usually 6–8 mm wide when fully open; nutlets considerably longer than wide, tapering to a point, not at all cross-shaped, irregularly ribbed; plants often robust, to more than 30 cm tall; leaves of basal rosette to about 5 cm long, those on flowering stems commonly 2–3 cm long; sap purple, the midrib and margins of leaves also purple or red .... *P. nothofulvus*, pl. 170

            RUSTY POPCORN FLOWER

    2 Calyx usually at least 4 mm long, especially after the nutlets have begun to ripen

        4 Bracts typically associated with at least some flowers of the inflorescence; calyx broadening to 4–5 mm near the base as the nutlets ripen; corolla 2 mm wide when open; nutlets with a deep, transverse, troughlike depression, this interrupted by the lengthwise ridge above the attachment scar; attachment scar shallow, much less than one-fifth as long as the nutlet (SW Oreg. to Calif.) .... *P. shastensis*

            SHASTA POPCORN FLOWER

        4 Inflorescence usually without bracts; calyx not broadening to 4–5 mm near the base as the nutlets ripen; corolla about 4 mm wide; nutlets without a deep, transverse, troughlike depression; attachment scar deeply concave, near the middle of the inner surface of the nutlet and about one-fourth as long as the nutlet (sap purple; SW Oreg. to Calif., also in Chile) .... *P. fulvus* (*P. campestris*)

            FULVOUS POPCORN FLOWER

1 Lower stem leaves opposite (there is often no distinct or persistent rosette of basal leaves)

    5 Attachment scar more or less triangular, about one-fourth to one-half as long as the nutlet (in our region likely to be found only in SW Oreg.)

        6 Nutlets with coarse transverse wrinkles but without prickles (Rogue River valley, Oreg., to Calif.) ....

        .... *P. glyptocarpus*

            SCULPTURED POPCORN FLOWER

6 Mature or nearly mature nutlets with prominent prickles, these covered with curved hairs; corolla not more than 2.5 mm wide

  7 Nutlets with numerous (about 50) slender prickles along the edges and on the side that faces outward; curved hairs on the prickles not so long as the prickles are wide at the base (SW Oreg. to Calif.) . . . . ***P. greenei***
                          GREENE'S POPCORN FLOWER

  7 Nutlets with not more than about 20 prickles, these rather stout and limited to the edges and midline region of the side that faces outward; curved hairs on the prickles mostly about as long as the prickles are wide at the base (Jackson Co., Oreg., to Calif.) . . . . ***P. austinae***
                          MS. AUSTIN'S POPCORN FLOWER

5 Attachment scar usually not triangular and not so much as one-fourth as long as the nutlet

  8 Hairs on stems and leaves spreading stiffly outward (outer surface of the nutlet with a lengthwise ridge reaching nearly to the base but otherwise only slightly wrinkled; in wet habitats, Umpqua and Rogue River valleys, Oreg.) . . . . ***P. hirtus***
                          ROUGH POPCORN FLOWER

8 Most hairs on stems and leaves pressed down

  9 Attachment scar distinctly above the base of the nutlet

    10 Lengthwise ridge on inner surface of nutlet occupying a conspicuous depression, this sometimes wider than the attachment scar . . . . ***P. reticulatus***
                          NETTED POPCORN FLOWER

    10 Lengthwise ridge on inner surface of nutlet either not in a distinct depression or the depression not so wide as the attachment scar

      11 Racemes either without bracts or with a bract only below the lowest flower; cross-ridges on outer surface of nutlet irregular, interrupted, and bumpy (in wet habitats, Brit. Col. to S Oreg.) . . . . ***P. figuratus***
                          FRAGRANT POPCORN FLOWER

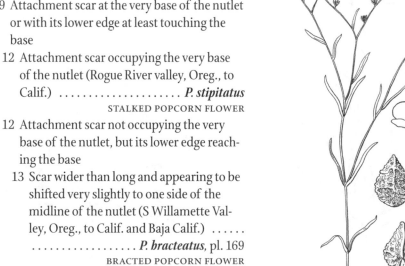

      11 Racemes typically with bracts below at least some flowers; cross-ridges on outer surface of nutlet rather regular, mostly continuous, and smooth . . . ***P. hispidulus***
             ROUGH-SEEDED POPCORN FLOWER

  9 Attachment scar at the very base of the nutlet or with its lower edge at least touching the base

    12 Attachment scar occupying the very base of the nutlet (Rogue River valley, Oreg., to Calif.) . . . . ***P. stipitatus***
           STALKED POPCORN FLOWER

    12 Attachment scar not occupying the very base of the nutlet, but its lower edge reaching the base

      13 Scar wider than long and appearing to be shifted very slightly to one side of the midline of the nutlet (S Willamette Valley, Oreg., to Calif. and Baja Calif.) . . . . ***P. bracteatus***, pl. 169
          BRACTED POPCORN FLOWER

      13 Scar at least slightly longer than wide

Plagiobothrys figuratus, fragrant popcorn flower

14 Plants typically upright, often more than 15 cm tall; corolla lobes to about 4 mm long; usually in habitats that are moist during much of the late spring and summer (W of the Cascades, S Brit. Col. to S Oreg.; apparently introduced in Alaska) . . . . *P. scouleri* **var. *scouleri*** (includes *P. granulatus*)
SCOULER'S POPCORN FLOWER

14 Plants typically sprawling, the tips of stems not often rising more than about 5 cm; corolla lobes to about 2 mm long; usually in habitats that are wet in winter and spring, and that later become very dry (sometimes growing in rock pools; Wash. to Calif.) . . . . *P. scouleri* **var. *penicillatus***

> Several other named species (*P. hispidulus, P. reticulatus, P. cognatus,* and *P. cusickii*) belong to the same complex as what are here called *P. scouleri* vars. *scouleri* and *penicillatus;* the relationships of these have not been clarified. It is not certain, in fact, that var. *penicillatus* is closer to var. *scouleri* than to some of the species listed above. Lumping some of the species together would be a practical solution, but it could lead to losing track of characters that later might help us better understand the systematics of the genus as a whole.

Symphytum

1 Stems with winglike lengthwise ridges that are continuous with the leaf bases; at least some hairs on stems markedly flattened (corolla blue, pink in bud stage; garden plant, sometimes escaping) . . . . *S. officinale*
COMFREY (Europe)

1 Stem without winglike ridges that are continuous with the leaf bases, or such ridges only very short; hairs on stems not markedly flattened

   2 Corolla generally faintly yellowish, sometimes bluish; surface of nutlets smooth (garden plant, sometimes escaping) . . . . *S. asperum*
ROUGH-STEMMED COMFREY (Europe)

   2 Corolla blue or purplish blue; surface of nutlets wrinkled . . . . *S.* ×*uplandicum* (believed to be *S. asperum* × *officinale*)
BLUE COMFREY, HYBRID COMFREY (Europe)

Plagiobothrys scouleri var. *scouleri*,
Scouler's popcorn flower

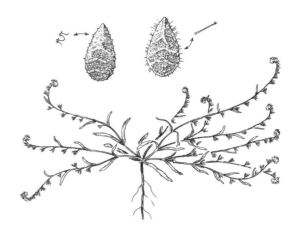

Plagiobothrys scouleri var. *penicillatus*

BRASSICACEAE Mustard Family

The mustard family has given us some important food plants as well as many attractive garden flowers. Among those we eat raw or cooked are cabbage, broccoli, cauliflower, bok choy, kohlrabi, radish, horseradish, and watercress. It is easy to recognize almost any member of the family when it is in flower. If there are four sepals, four petals, and six stamens, and if four of the stamens are longer than the other two, the plant is definitely in this family. The podlike fruit, furthermore, is usually partitioned lengthwise into two divisions. Certain genera or species deviate from the standard formula so far as the number of stamens and structure of the fruit are concerned, but after you have carefully looked at the flowers of a few typical representatives, you will be able to place a previously unfamiliar plant in this family.

Characteristics of the fruits are important in distinguishing genera and species of Brassicaceae. You will often need specimens with fruits that are developed to the extent that you can predict what their general shape will be when they are mature. The very first couplet of the key may, for at least a time, be the most troublesome one for you, because certain species of our region straddle the line between the two choices. Most plants, however, will fit clearly into one group or the other. Take what seems to be the best choice, and if this decision is not the right one, you will soon know.

Subularia aquatica var. *americana*, awlwort, is so distinctive and un-mustard-like that it is most conveniently dealt with here. It is a small annual with a few slender, somewhat grasslike but succulent basal leaves to about 5 cm long. It grows partly submerged along the edges of ponds and lakes, mostly at higher elevations and mostly east of the crest of the Cascades. The white petals are only about 1 mm long; the fruits, 2–3 mm long, are about twice as long as wide and slightly flattened at an angle of 90° to the partition that separates the valves.

1 Fruit conspicuously flattened, usually not so much as half as thick as wide and generally not more than 3.5 times as long as wide
  2 Fruit flattened at an angle of 90° to the partition that separates the 2 halves, so the location of the partition is visible externally on both flattened surfaces (in *Lobularia maritima*, under the other choice 2, there is a raised lengthwise line on both valves, but this is not the partition that separates the valves)

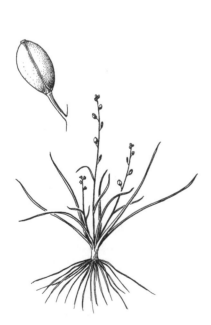

Subularia aquatica var.
americana, awlwort

Capsella bursa-pastoris,
shepherd's purse

3 Fruit nearly triangular, widest at the top (where there is shallow notch) and narrowing evenly to the pedicel (basal leaves pinnately lobed, upper leaves clasping the stems; petals white, mostly 2–3 mm long) . . . . ***Capsella bursa-pastoris***, p. 159
SHEPHERD'S PURSE (Europe)

3 Fruit not nearly triangular
  4 Fruit about 1.5–2 cm long, 3–4 times as long as wide, paddle-shaped, hanging down; petals 3–4 mm long, yellow; plants to about 1 m tall, with a rosette of petioled basal leaves and clasping leaves along the upright stem . . . . ***Isatis tinctoria***
DYER'S WOAD (Europe)

  4 Fruit and other aspects of the plant not as described in the other choice 4
    5 Fruit usually about 1.5 mm long, 2 mm wide, deeply divided lengthwise into 2 bulging halves, these with a networklike pattern (petals less than 1 mm long; stems trailing; leaves pinnately lobed, nearly compound) . . . . ***Coronopus didymus***
WART CRESS (Europe)

    5 Fruit more than 2 mm long, not deeply divided into 2 bulging halves (but it may be plump, and in *Cardaria draba* the right and left halves are often noticeably separated by a constriction between them)
      6 Fruit rather plump, definitely not thin
        7 Plants to about 50 cm tall, spreading by rhizomes; leaf blades clasping the stems; right and left halves of the fruit often noticeably separated by a lengthwise constriction; style about 1 mm long (perennial; petals white, 2–3 mm long) . . . . ***Cardaria draba***
HOARY CRESS (Europe)

        7 Plants not often more than 30 cm tall and not spreading by rhizomes; leaves not clasping the stems; right and left halves of the fruit not noticeably separated by a lengthwise constriction; style not more than 0.5 mm long (coastal, Alaska to Oreg.) . . . . ***Cochlearia officinalis***
SCURVY GRASS

      6 Fruit much flattened, thin
        8 Petals (white) decidedly unequal (2 about 2 mm long, 2 about 1 mm long); leaves entirely basal; plants usually not more than 15 cm tall (flowers sweetly fragrant) . . . .
. . . . ***Teesdalia nudicaulis***, pl. 182
SHEPHERD'S CRESS (Europe)

        8 Petals equal; leaves not entirely basal; plants often more than 15 cm tall
          9 Fruit with only 1 seed in each half; mature fruit not so much as 10 mm long . . . . . . ***Lepidium***
          9 Fruit with 2 or more seeds in each half; mature fruit in 1 species (a common weed) about 15 mm long, shorter in another species (native) . . . . ***Thlaspi***

2 Fruit flattened parallel to the partition that separates the 2 halves (the partition is usually visible along the narrow edges of the fruit but is sometimes obscure)
  10 Fruit usually 2–4 times as long as wide (petals white; in some forms of *D. verna* the fruit is only a little longer than wide—if, however, the plant has a rosette of basal leaves, is not more than 10 cm tall, and is in flower by February, this is probably the correct choice) . . . . ***Draba***
  10 Fruit not so much as twice as long as wide
    11 Petals 1.5–2 cm long, deep purple; mature fruit broadly oval, usually 3–4 cm long, raised up on a slender stalk above the level where the sepals and petals were attached (the stalk is 1–1.5 cm long)
. . . . ***Lunaria annua***, pl. 179
HONESTY (Europe)

    11 Petals less than 1 cm long, not purple (but they may be tinged with purple); mature fruit less than 2 cm long and not raised up on a stalk
      12 Flowers and fruits single on each upright stem arising from the base of the plant; leaves entirely basal (fruits to 8 mm long, broadly oval; seed with broad, thin margins; plants to about 15 cm tall; Jackson Co., Oreg., to Calif., and E of the Cascades) . . . . ***Idahoa scapigera***
SCALEPOD

12 Flowers and fruits at least several in each inflorescence
13 Fruit densely covered with hooked hairs . . . . *Athysanus pusillus*
SANDWEED
13 Fruit not covered with hooked hairs (but there may be straight hairs)
14 Fruit (usually hanging downward) with a broad winglike margin all around the swollen central portion, the margin sometimes with incisions or perforations (petals white or pinkish; racemes slender, usually with not more than 20 flowers) . . . . *Thysanocarpus*
14 Fruit without a broad winglike margin around a swollen central portion
15 Fruit lopsided or slightly twisted (Josephine Co., Oreg., to Calif.) . . . . *Heterodraba unilateralis*
15 Fruit symmetrical
16 Lower half of fruit wedge-shaped, less broadly rounded than the upper half (petals white to yellow) . . . . *Camelina*
16 Fruit almost perfectly oval or nearly circular, widest near the middle
17 Petals yellow; fruit without a raised lengthwise line on both valves . . . . *Alyssum*
17 Petals white or tinged with blue; fruit, at least when dry, usually with a slender, slightly raised lengthwise line on both valves (flowers with a sweet fragrance) . . . . *Lobularia maritima*
SWEET ALISON (Europe)
1 Fruit not conspicuously flattened (at least half as thick as wide), commonly, but not always, at least 4 times as long as wide (often with a stout beaklike prolongation derived from the persistent style of the pistil)
18 Fruit consisting of 2 unequal segments (not including the beaklike prolongation, if there is one), not divided by a lengthwise partition, and not splitting open lengthwise at maturity (look carefully to see if there are 2 segments, because the lower one may be short, resembling a pedestal for the much larger upper segment)
19 Upper segment of fruit nearly spherical, to about 1 cm long and containing only 1 seed; lower segment much shorter (petals cream, to about 1 cm long; foliage and stems not hairy; perennial; at the edges of sandy beaches, rarely encountered in our region) . . . . *Crambe maritima*
SEA KALE (Europe)
19 Upper segment of fruit longer than wide, cylindrical or somewhat angular (if cylindrical, then also usually becoming constricted between the seeds), tapering to a stout beak
20 Upper segment of fruit usually at least 5 times as long as wide, cylindrical, constricted between the seeds; plant as a whole not succulent . . . . *Raphanus*
20 Upper segment of fruit not so much as 3 times as long as wide, somewhat angular; plant as a whole succulent (restricted to backshores of sandy beaches) . . . . *Cakile*
18 Fruit not consisting of 2 unequal segments (but there may be a prominent beak, derived from a persistent style, at the tip), divided lengthwise by a partition, and splitting open lengthwise at maturity
21 Leaves not deeply lobed or compound (but they may be toothed)
22 Calyx somewhat urn-shaped, owing to a perceptible constriction before the tips of the sepals turn outward (petals narrow, with wavy margins; fruit slightly flattened parallel to the partition between the valves; in our region only in SW Oreg.) . . . . *Streptanthus*
22 Calyx not urn-shaped, the sepals either directed straight upward or spreading outward
23 Leaves at all levels of the plant without hairs (leaves above those at the base somewhat heart-shaped, sessile, and clasping the stem; stem usually single, sometimes more than 80 cm tall; petals white, greenish white, or cream) . . . . *Conringia orientalis*
HARE'S-EAR MUSTARD (Europe)
23 All or most leaves with at least some hairs

24 Annual (usually 20–30 cm tall) with a compact rosette of basal leaves and small sessile leaves along the flowering stem or stems; leaves and lower portions of the stems obviously hairy; petals white, about 3 mm long; fruits about 10–15 mm long, not more than 1 mm thick . . . . ***Arabidopsis thaliana***
WALL CRESS (Europe)

24 Plants, whether annual, biennial, or perennial, not meeting all criteria in the other choice 24

  25 Leaf blades (sometimes more than 15 cm long) at or near the base of the plant tapering gradually to a nearly cylindrical petiole (upper leaves sessile; petals usually 2–2.5 cm long, white to pink, rose, or pale purple; sweetly fragrant garden plant, sometimes escaping) . . . ***Hesperis matronalis***
SWEET ROCKET (Europe)

  25 Blades of leaves at or near the base of the plant, if not sessile, either distinctly set off from the petiole or tapering gradually to a flattened petiole or a flattened, nearly sessile base (the leaves at the very base may wither early)

    26 Blades of leaves at or near the base of the plant distinctly set off from the petiole (blades of lower leaves about as wide as long, with an indentation where the petiole is attached; petals about 6 mm long, considerably longer than the sepals, white; leaves and stems smelling like garlic; weed) . . . . ***Alliaria petiolata*** (*A. officinalis*)
GARLIC MUSTARD (widespread in Europe, N Africa, and other parts of the Old World)

    26 Blades of leaves at or near the base of the plant, if not sessile, tapering gradually to a flattened petiole or to a flattened, nearly sessile base

      27 Fruits about 2 mm long and only slightly wider, scarcely flattened, as a whole thus nearly round, and with a prominent networklike pattern; style about half as long as the fruit (petals pale yellow; plants upright, sometimes more than 75 cm tall, branching above; stem leaves sessile, with clasping bases; basal leaves usually withering by flowering time) . . . . ***Neslia paniculata***
BALL MUSTARD (Eurasia)

      27 Fruits elongated, usually more than 15 mm long; style much shorter than the fruit

        28 Petals distinctly yellow, orange, or slightly reddish; leaves above the base not clasping the stem; hairs, whether simple or branched, mostly oriented parallel to the long axes of the stems and sometimes of the leaves. . . . . ***Erysimum***

        28 Petals in most species pink to rose or purple, but white, cream, or pale yellow in some others; leaves above the base usually clasping the stem; hairs not obviously oriented parallel to the long axes of the stems . . . . ***Arabis***

21 At least some leaves deeply lobed or compound, usually in a pinnate pattern, but sometimes (in *Cardamine* spp.) in a pattern that is nearly palmate

  29 Mature fruit with a prominent beak derived from a persistent style whose thickness and length increase as the fruit matures (the beak is usually at least one-fourth as long as the mature fruit as a whole) . . . . ***Brassica-Eruca-Sinapis*** **complex**

  29 Mature fruit without a prominent beak (what may appear to be a beak is not much longer than the style on a young fruit, though it may be appreciably thicker—if you are in doubt about the prominence of the beak, try both choices 29; in succeeding couplets you will probably discover which choice is the correct one)

    30 Petals yellow

      31 Most leaves pinnately divided twice, occasionally 3 times (persistent style not so much as 1 mm long) . . . . ***Descurainia***

      31 None of the leaves deeply divided more than once

        32 Valves of the nearly or fully mature fruit with an obvious lengthwise ridge, this contributing to the 4-angled appearance of the fruit

33 Stems with prominent, rather stiff hairs, these mostly pointing downward (plants to more than 60 cm tall; petals pale yellow, to about 7 mm long; fruits 2–4 cm long, to about 1.5 mm thick, the style to 3 mm long) . . . . *Erucastrum gallicum*
HAIRY ROCKET (Europe)

33 Stems nearly or completely hairless . . . . *Barbarea*

32 Valves of the nearly or fully mature fruit without a lengthwise ridge, not noticeably 4-angled

34 Style barely or not at all evident but the stigma distinctly 2-lobed; fruits slender, usually not much thicker than the pedicels, straight or only slightly curved . . . . *Sisymbrium*

34 Style usually at least 0.5 mm long, sometimes as long as 2.5 mm, the stigma not 2-lobed; fruits obviously much thicker than the pedicels, and those of some species markedly curved . . . . . *Rorippa*

30 Petals white to pink or purplish

35 Plants aquatic, growing partly submerged in streams, ditches, or at the edges of ponds (larger leaves pinnately lobed; petals about 3–4 mm long, white, sometimes with purplish lines) . . . . *Rorippa*

35 Plants not aquatic (but some species of *Cardamine* grow in very wet places)

36 Annuals or perennials, if perennial not showing remnants of leaves of previous years, well represented in the lowlands, a few montane; at least some leaves pinnately or almost palmately lobed; petals white, pink, or purplish . . . . *Cardamine*

36 High-montane perennials, their lower portions usually showing numerous remnants of leaves of previous years; all or most leaf blades pinnately lobed (a few basal leaves may have only 3 lobes near the tip) petals white, often tinged with purple . . . . *Smelowskia*

Alyssum

1 Inflorescences not branching; petals cream to pale yellow; each chamber of the mature fruit with 2 seeds
. . . . *A. alyssoides*
YELLOW ALYSSUM (Europe)

1 Inflorescences branching; petals clear yellow; each chamber of the mature fruit with a single seed . . . .
. . . . *A. murale*
WALL ALYSSUM (Europe)

Arabis

Most of the species of *Arabis* in our region are either limited to southwestern Oregon or are montane, sometimes both. Making an unequivocal key seems to be just about impossible, due partly to variation and some hybridization, and also because experts have not agreed on the limits of several species. You are advised to try both choices of each couplet and see where it takes you; also, pay close attention to the geographic distributions and altitudinal ranges. The more difficult choices are those beginning with 4.

1 Mature fruits conspicuously flattened, usually 3–5 mm wide, sometimes slightly wider; seeds to more than 3 mm wide, including the membranous flange that almost completely encircles them

2 Fruits typically held more or less upright; stems usually with only 2–4 leaves above those crowded at the base; corolla 4–6 mm long, pale pink to pinkish purple or sometimes white (high montane in the Cascades, N Oreg., S to Calif.) . . . . *A. platysperma* var. *howellii*
HOWELL'S FLAT-SEED ROCK CRESS

2 Fruits typically hanging downward; stems generally with at least 5 leaves above those crowded at the base; corolla about 6 mm long, rose-purple (Siskiyou Mountains, Oreg., otherwise in the Cascades and E of the crest in Wash. and Oreg., and into Calif.) . . . . *A. suffrutescens* var. *suffrutescens*
WOODY ROCK CRESS

1 Mature fruits not conspicuously flattened, not more than about 3 mm wide; seeds usually not more than 2 mm wide, even when encircled partly or almost completely by a membranous flange

3 Basal leaves distinctly pinnately lobed, the terminal lobe the largest and usually rounded; leaves on flowering stems not clasping the stems and sometimes with distinct petioles (petals usually white, sometimes pale pink; montane in the Cascades; Alaska to N Wash.) .... *A. lyrata* var. *kamchatica*
KAMCHATKA ROCK CRESS

3 Basal leaves not distinctly pinnately lobed (but they may be coarsely toothed); leaves on flowering stems without petioles and in some species with a pair of basal lobes that clasp the stem

4 Blades of leaves above those near the base pinnately lobed (petioles of basal leaves becoming gradually and almost imperceptibly widened into blades, these, unless toothed, not more than 3 times as wide as the petioles; blades and petioles of basal leaves so densely covered by a fuzz of short, forked or several-branched hairs that the surfaces are nearly obscured; fruits hanging downward when mature or nearly mature; petals usually 8–10 mm long, deep pinkish red; Siskiyou Mountains of SW Oreg. and NW Calif.) .... *A. subpinnatifida*
KLAMATH ROCK CRESS, ASHY ROCK CRESS

4 Blades of leaves above those near the base not pinnately lobed

5 Fruits typically hanging downward

6 Pedicels of fruits rarely more than 6 mm long; corollas pink to purple (high montane, Brit. Col. to Calif.) .... *A. lemmonii* var. *lemmonii*
LEMMON'S ROCK CRESS

6 Pedicels of fruits usually at least 10 mm long, sometimes as long as 20 mm; corolla whitish to purplish (mostly montane, Brit. Col. to Wash. and eastward) .... *A. holboellii* var. *holboellii*
HOLBOELL'S ROCK CRESS
See note under *A.* ×*divaricarpa,* second choice 10.

5 Fruits typically directed outward or at least slightly upward (sometimes slightly downward in *A.* ×*divaricarpa*)

7 Relatively tall plants, usually with 1 or more upright stems usually at least 35 cm tall, sometimes much taller (but be sure to try the other choice 7)

8 Petals white or pale yellow; seeds not bordered by a winglike membrane

9 Plants commonly 50–80 cm tall, sometimes even taller; fruits not noticeably flattened; seeds in 2 rows on each side of the partition that divides the fruit lengthwise .... *A. glabra*
TOWER MUSTARD

9 Plants commonly 40–50 cm tall (not often more than 60 cm); fruits slightly flattened; seeds in 1 row on each side of the partition .... *A. hirsuta* var. *eschscholtziana*
HAIRY ROCK CRESS

8 Petals white to pink or pale purple; seeds bordered by a winglike membrane

10 Fruits with 2 rows of seeds on both sides of the lengthwise partition (corollas white or pale pink; montane, Brit. Col. to Calif. and eastward) .... *A. drummondii*
DRUMMOND'S ROCK CRESS

10 Fruits usually with a single row of seeds on both sides of the lengthwise partition but occasionally in 2 rows in some portions (lower leaves above the basal ones rather crowded, often overlapping conspicuously; most hairs on leaves and lower portions of stems 3-branched; fruits generally held slightly upright, spreading outward, or hanging slightly downward; petals pink to pale purple; montane in the Cascades) .... *A.* ×*divaricarpa*
SPREADING-POD ROCK CRESS

Arabis ×divaricarpa is believed to have originated many times and in many places by hybridization of *A. holboellii* (fruits with 1 row of seeds on both sides of the partition; fruits mostly hanging downward) and *A. drummondii* (seeds in 2 rows on both sides of the lengthwise partition; fruits mostly directed upward). Both presumed parents are often found where *A.* ×*divaricarpa* occurs.

7 Plants not often more than about 35 cm tall (but be sure to try the other choice 7)

11 Basal leaves all originating at about the same level, thus forming a rosette close to the ground (petals, at least their broader portions, usually richly colored, most commonly pink, rose, purple, or some related color, only occasionally white)

12 Blades of basal leaves nearly hairless except for simple hairs (sometimes to 1 mm long) arising from the tips of the marginal teeth; blades not often more than 1 cm wide; petals usually 8–10 mm long (Josephine Co., Oreg., to Calif.) . . . . ***A. macdonaldiana***

MACDONALD'S ROCK CRESS

12 Blades of basal leaves with simple and/or branched hairs on the upper and lower surfaces as well as along the margins; blades often to about 2 cm wide; petals usually at least 12 mm long

   13 Blades of basal leaves with only branched hairs (Josephine Co., Oreg., to Calif.) . . . . . . ***A. modesta***

ROGUE CANYON ROCK CRESS

   13 Blades of basal leaves with simple and branched hairs

      14 Hairs on margins of basal leaves almost all simple (Curry and Josephine Cos., Oreg., to Calif.) . . . .
. . . . ***A. aculeolata***, pl. 171

WALDO ROCK CRESS

      14 Hairs on margins of basal leaves mostly branched (Jackson and Josephine Cos., Oreg., to Calif.) . . . . ***A. oregana*** (*A. purpurascens*)

OREGON ROCK CRESS

11 Basal leaves, even if crowded, originating at different levels, not forming a neat rosette close to the ground

   15 Petals white (high montane in the Olympic Mountains, Wash., and Cascades, Wash. to Oreg.) . . . . . .
. . . . ***A. furcata***

CASCADE ROCK CRESS

   15 Petals usually pink to purple (occasionally white in *A. breweri* var. *breweri,* which is limited to a particular region)

      16 Blades of basal leaves scarcely if at all hairy (petals purple; in the Cascades, Brit. Col. to Wash. and eastward) . . . . ***A. lyallii*** var. *lyallii*

LYALL'S ROCK CRESS

      16 Blades of basal leaves distinctly hairy, sometimes densely so (most hairs with 3 or more branches originating at the base)

Arabis glabra,
tower mustard

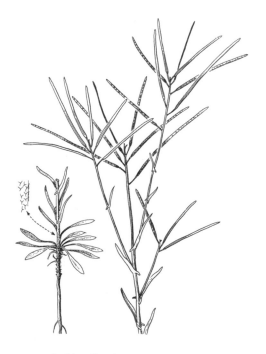

Arabis ×divaricarpa,
spreading-pod rock cress

17 Blades of basal leaves commonly more than 5 mm wide (and not much more than twice as long as wide); upper portion of flowering and fruiting stems typically hairy; corolla usually pink or purplish, sometimes white (Josephine and Jackson Cos., Oreg., to Calif.) . . . . *A. breweri* **var.** *breweri*
BREWER'S ROCK CRESS

17 Blades of most basal leaves not more than 5 mm wide

  18 Blades of basal leaves at least 3 times as long as wide; upper portion of flowering or fruiting stems usually not hairy (the flower pedicels, however, may be hairy); corolla generally purplish red (on serpentine soils, mostly below about 2500 ft., 760 m; Douglas, Josephine, and Jackson Cos., Oreg., to Calif.) . . . . *A. koehleri* **var.** *stipitata*, pl. 172
KOEHLER'S ROCK CRESS

  18 Blades of basal leaves usually not so much as 3 times as long as wide; upper portion of flowering or fruiting stems typically hairy; pedicels rarely more than 6 mm long; corolla pink to purple (mostly above 4500 ft., 1370 m; Brit. Col. to Calif.) . . . . *A. lemmonii* **var.** *lemmonii*
LEMMON'S ROCK CRESS

Barbarea

1 Style on mature fruit 2–3 mm long but not distinctly demarcated from the rest of the fruit, whose total length is about 2.5–3 cm . . . . *B. vulgaris*
COMMON WINTER CRESS, YELLOW ROCKET (Eurasia)

1 Style on fruit rarely more than 1.5 mm long

  2 Basal leaves usually with at least 10 lateral lobes; petals 6–8 mm long; fruits to 8 cm long . . . . . *B. verna*
EARLY WINTER CRESS (Eurasia)

  2 Basal leaves usually with not more than 10 lateral lobes; petals 3–5 mm long; fruits to 5 cm long . . . . *B. orthoceras*
AMERICAN WINTER CRESS

Brassica-Eruca-Sinapis **Complex**

1 Fruit (especially the seed-bearing portion) covered with flattened hairs (beak prominent, to about half as long as the fruit as a whole, flattened; petals whitish to pale yellow) . . . . *S. alba* (*Brassica hirta*)
WHITE MUSTARD (Europe)

1 Fruit not covered with conspicuous, flattened hairs

  2 Upper leaves sessile and clasping the stem (very common) . . . . *B. rapa* (*B. campestris*), pl. 173
FIELD MUSTARD, TURNIP (Europe)

        Brassica napus, rapeseed (Europe), is simlar to *B. rapa*. Its leaves, however, are noticeably slightly grayish or bluish instead of clear green, and its petals are on average slightly larger, 10–14 mm long instead of 6–11 mm.

  2 Upper leaves, if sessile, not clasping the stem

   3 Beak of fruit conspicuously flattened and bladelike (and to at least half as long as the rest of the mature fruit)

    4 Seeds in 2 rows on both sides of the lengthwise partition; petals 15–20 mm long, white to pale yellow, usually with violet lines (cultivated in gardens for salad and as a cooked vegetable; occasionally escaping) . . . . *E. vesicaria* **var.** *sativa*
GARDEN ROCKET

    4 Seeds in 1 row on both sides of the lengthwise partition; petals usually 9–12 mm long, yellow (fruit as a whole to about 3.5 cm long, the beak 1 cm long; significant weed, poisonous to livestock) . . . . *S. arvensis* (includes *B. kaber* vars. *kaber* and *pinnatifida*)
CHARLOCK (Europe)

   3 Beak of the fruit nearly cylindrical or only very slightly flattened, not bladelike

    5 Maturing fruits pressed to the stems of the inflorescence; fruit to 2 cm long, the beak usually 2–4 mm long . . . . *B. nigra*
BLACK MUSTARD (Europe)

    5 Maturing fruits not pressed to the stems of the inflorescence; fruit 3–5 cm long, the beak to 15 mm long . . . . ***B. juncea***
                                                   LEAF MUSTARD (Eurasia)

Cakile

1 Most leaf blades with a wavy or toothed margin, or shallowly lobed near the base; segments of the fruit separated by a simple constriction; petals about 6–8 mm long . . . . ***C. edentula* var. *edentula***
                                                      SEA ROCKET (E North America)

1 Most leaf blades pinnately lobed, some lobes separated nearly to the midrib; segments of the fruit separated by a raised V-shaped suture (properly part of the lower segment) that may be drawn out into a rather prominent horn on both sides; petals about 8–10 mm long . . . . ***C. maritima***, pl. 174
                                             HORNED SEA ROCKET (Europe)

Camelina

1 Stems and leaves conspicuously hairy, the unbranched hairs often longer than the branched hairs; mature fruits not often longer than 7 mm; seeds generally not more than 1 mm long . . . . ***C. microcarpa***
                                                 HAIRY FALSE FLAX (Eurasia)

1 Stems and leaves usually not conspicuously hairy, the unbranched hairs not longer than the branched hairs; mature fruits sometimes 9 mm long; seeds to 2 mm long . . . . ***C. sativa***
                                                 FALSE FLAX (Eurasia)

Cardamine

1 Leaves not compound or conspicuously lobed (plants not often more than 10 cm tall; petals white; high montane in the Cascades)

    2 Leaves, including the petioles, not often more than 2 cm long, the blades thin, with essentially regular margins (montane, Brit. Col. to Wash.) . . . . ***C. bellidifolia* var. *bellidifolia***
                                              ALPINE BITTER CRESS

    2 Leaves to about 3 cm long, the blades fleshy, with wavy margins (montane, Oreg. to Calif.) . . . .
    . . . . ***C. bellidifolia* var. *pachyphylla***
              THICK-LEAVED ALPINE BITTER CRESS

1 Leaves compound or at least conspicuously lobed

    3 Petals usually more than 7 mm long; style of pistil at least 3 mm long

        4 Most middle and upper leaves with at least 5 leaflets (usually 7–11), these arranged pinnately (in wet habitats, Willamette Valley, Oreg., to the coast) . . . . .
        . . . . ***C. penduliflora***
            WILLAMETTE VALLEY BITTER CRESS

        4 Most middle and upper leaves with 3 or 5 leaflets

          5 Lowermost leaves, arising from a rhizome or from tuberous thickenings of a rhizome, not compound (but they may be deeply lobed; Coast Ranges and coastal areas, Oreg. to Calif.) . . . . ***C. californica***
               (*Dentaria californica*, *C. integrifolia*)
                MILKMAIDS, TOOTHWORT
          Several intergrading subspecies or varieties of *C. californica* are recognized by some specialists.

Brassica juncea,
leaf mustard

5 Lowermost leaves, arising from a rhizome, compound, with 3 leaflets
    6 Most larger leaves on the upright stems, and also the leaves arising from the rhizomes, with angularly toothed leaflets not often more than twice as long as wide; plants sometimes more than 50 cm tall; rhizomes often extensively developed, so that some leaves originate several cm away from the bases of the upright stem . . . . *C. angulata*
        ANGLE-LEAVED BITTER CRESS
    6 Most larger leaves on the upright stems, and sometimes also the lowermost leaves, with leaflets more than twice as long as wide and without obvious teeth; plants not often more than 20 cm tall; rhizomes short, so that most leaves arising from them are close to the bases of the upright stems . . . . *C. nuttallii* (*C. pulcherrima* var. *tenella, Dentaria tenella*), pl. 175
        NUTTALL'S BITTER CRESS
        There are several intergrading subspecies or varieties of *C. nuttallii*.
3 Petals rarely more than 7 mm long; style of pistil rarely more than 2 mm long (except in *C. pattersonii*, which has a very restricted distribution)
    7 Each flower pedicel borne above a slender bract; petals pink; style of pistil 2–3 mm long (Saddle Mountain, Clatsop Co., Oreg.) . . . . *C. pattersonii*
        SADDLE MOUNTAIN BITTER CRESS
    7 Flower pedicels without bracts beneath them; petals white; style of pistil 0.5–2 mm long
        8 Petals 3–7 mm long; perennial, the upright stems arising from underground rhizomes (in wet habitats)
            9 At least some of the basal leaves simple; rhizomes not forming distinct tubers at the bases of the upright stems . . . . *C. breweri* var. *orbicularis*
                BREWER'S BITTER CRESS
            9 All basal leaves pinnately compound; rhizomes generally swelled to form tubers at the bases of the upright stems . . . . *C. occidentalis*
                WESTERN BITTER CRESS
        8 Petals 2–4 mm long; usually annual, sometimes biennial, the upright stems not connected to one another by underground rhizomes
            10 Stems typically branching mostly from the base; flowers usually with only 4 stamens, sometimes 5–6
                11 Fruits, when fully mature, with blunt tips (the most common small, weedy *Cardamine* in our region) . . . . *C. hirsuta*
                    HAIRY BITTER CRESS (Europe, Asia)
                11 Fruits, when mature, with sharply pointed tips . . . . *C. oligosperma*
                    LITTLE WESTERN BITTER CRESS
            10 Stems typically branching mostly from the leaf axils, rather than from the base; flowers usually with 6 stamens
                12 Leaves in the upper part of the plant compound, the leaflets attached to the rachis by slender stalks; outline of leaflets on upper leaves nearly circular; plants sometimes more than 40 cm tall . . . . *C. flexuosa*
                    WOOD BITTER CRESS (Europe, Asia)
                12 Leaves in the upper part of the plant not quite compound; outline of leaflets on upper leaves distinctly elongated, sometimes more than twice as long as wide; plants not often so much as 40 cm tall . . . . *C. pensylvanica*
                    PENNSYLVANIA BITTER CRESS

Descurainia

1 At least some leaves tripinnately lobed; mature fruits 2–3 cm long, usually with at least 20 seeds on each side of the partition . . . . *D. sophia*
    FLIXWEED (Europe)

1 Leaves not more than bipinnately lobed; mature fruits of plants in our region usually less than 1.5 cm long and usually with fewer than 15 seeds on each side of the partition (not often encountered W of the Cascades) . . . . ***D. pinnata***
TANSY MUSTARD

Several intergrading subspecies or varieties of *D. pinnata* have been named; plants recorded from W of the Cascades probably fit best in subsp. *filipes*.

Draba

1 Small annuals, not forming tight mats or cushions, usually with only a few flowering stems originating just above a rosette of basal leaves (some species under this choice may also be perennial, in which case they may branch more or less laterally at the base, but in general they do not form mats or cushions in which all branch stems have numerous, crowded leaves)

  2 Petals white, deeply divided at the tip into 2 conspicuous lobes; plants usually less than 7 cm tall, with a single flowering stem; all leaves strictly basal (one of the few herbaceous plants of our region that begin to flower as early as February) . . . . ***D. verna***
WHITLOW GRASS

  2 Petals not divided into 2 lobes; plants often more than 10 cm tall and usually with more than 1 flowering stem; flowering stems usually with at least 1–2 leaves but sometimes none

  3 Petals white; fruits generally 3–4 mm long, sometimes as long as 5 mm, about 3 times as long as wide; plant with hairs that divide at the base into 2–4 branches; lowest leaves few, not forming a distinct rosette . . . . ***D. brachycarpa***
SHORT-FRUITED WHITLOW GRASS

  3 Petals usually yellow or at least yellowish but sometimes white, especially after aging; fruits generally more than 5 mm long; hairs, if branched, not branching from the very base

  4 Flowering stems with only 1–2 leaves or none, but the basal rosette well developed (petals white; pedicels of mature or nearly mature fruits usually shorter than the fruits, which are generally not hairy) . . . . ***D. crassifolia***
THICK-LEAVED DRABA

  4 Flowering stems usually with more than 2 leaves

  5 Basal rosette not prominent, with only a few leaves; mature or nearly mature fruits usually about 3 times as long as wide, the pedicels about twice as long as the fruits . . . .
. . . . ***D. nemorosa***
WOODLAND WHITLOW GRASS

  5 Basal rosette typically prominent, with many leaves; mature or nearly mature fruits usually 4–5 times as long as wide, the pedicels not often more than about 1.5 times as long as the fruits

  6 Fruits hairy; petals white or cream . . . .
. . . . ***D. praealta***
TALL DRABA

  6 Fruits not hairy; petals yellow, at least when fresh . . . ***D. albertina*** (*D. stenoloba* var. *nana*)
SLENDER DRABA

Cardamine angulata,
angle-leaved bitter cress

1 Biennial or perennial plants either with a single unbranched stem with many crowded leaves at various levels near the base or forming tight mats or cushions in which there are at least several stems whose lower portions are typically densely covered with small leaves (if the plant appears to be a perennial but does not branch into several stems that, together with their crowded leaves, contribute to a tight mat or cushion, go back to the other choice 1, then to choice 3, which leads to *D. albertina, D. crassifolia,* and *D. praealta*)

  7 Plant with a single, upright stem with many crowded leaves near the base, the withered lower ones often persisting into subsequent seasons; upper portion of the stem and its flowering branches with scattered leaves; petals bright yellow; fruits to about 10 mm long, with prominent styles about 1 mm long; high montane, Wash. to Calif. . . . . *D. aureola,* pl. 176
                      GOLDEN DRABA

  7 Plant not in all respects as described in the other choice 7
    8 Style on fruits at least 1 mm long, sometimes as long as 3 mm (petals yellow, usually about 6–7 mm long; fruits 1 cm long; Siskiyou Mountains of SW Oreg. and NW Calif.) . . . . *D. howellii*
                      HOWELL'S DRABA

    8 Style on fruits not more than 1 mm long, usually much shorter and sometimes negligible
      9 Underside of leaf blades with long-stalked branched hairs, the branching sometimes in a starlike pattern . . . . *D. paysonii*
                      PAYSON'S DRABA

      9 Hairs on underside of leaf blades either not branched or the branches arising at or near the base
        10 Hairs on underside of leaves typically originating in pairs, each member of the pair then pinnately branched
          11 Leaf blades not more than 1.7 mm wide; hairs on leaves tightly pressed down (high montane in the Cascades and eastward) . . . . *D. oligosperma* var. *oligosperma*
                      FEW-SEEDED DRABA

          11 Leaf blades to 4 mm wide but sometimes less than 2 mm; hairs on leaves not tightly pressed down (high montane in the Olympic Mountains, Wash., Cascades, and eastward) . . . *D. incerta*
                      YELLOWSTONE DRABA

        10 Hairs on underside of leaves not branching in a pinnate pattern (they are either not branched or branched in a starlike pattern)
          12 Upper surface of leaves nearly hairless (high montane in the Cascades and eastward) . . . . *D. densifolia*
                      CROWDED-LEAF DRABA

          12 Upper surface of leaves, like the underside, conspicuously hairy (high montane in the Olympic Mountains, Wash., Cascades, and eastward) . . . . *D. lonchocarpa*
                      LANCE-FRUITED DRABA

Erysimum

1 Petals (pale yellow) to about 5 mm long; leaves not often more than 5 cm long, smooth-margined or with inconspicuous, widely spaced teeth; fruits 2–3 cm long; annual or biennial, usually branching at the base, sometimes above the base (widespread in Eurasia and possibly introduced in our region rather than native) . . . . *E. cheiranthoides*
                      WORMSEED MUSTARD

1 Petals more than 10 mm long (usually 15–25 mm); larger leaves commonly at least 5 cm long, often distinctly toothed; fruits more than 5 cm long (sometimes more than 10 cm); usually perennial, with upright stems that do not branch
  2 Lobes of the stigma decidedly longer than wide (petals yellow to red or brown; garden plant, sometimes escaping) . . . . *E. cheirii*
                      GARDEN WALLFLOWER (Europe)

  2 Lobes of the stigma no longer than wide

3 Petals pale yellow or cream; leaves noticeably succulent; fruit, when mature and dry, distinctly flattened; seeds winged along one or both sides as well as at the tip (plants rarely so much as 30 cm tall; strictly coastal, Curry Co., Oreg., to Calif.) . . . .*E. menziesii* **var. *concinnum***
PACIFIC WALLFLOWER

3 Petals bright yellow to deep orange, sometimes slightly reddish; leaves not noticeably succulent; seeds winged only at the tip or not at all

  4 Plants generally not more than about 30 cm tall when in flower; margins of blades of upper leaves coarsely toothed or obviously wavy; corollas bright lemon yellow; ripe fruits distinctly flattened and also alternately thickened and constricted

    5 Perennial, branching from the base; fruits not often more than 5 cm long (very high montane in the Olympic Mountains, Wash.) . . . .*E. arenicola* **var. *arenicola***
OLYMPIC WALLFLOWER

    5 Perennial (but probably mostly short-lived), typically with a single flowering stem; fruits to more than 10 cm long (high montane in the Olympic Mountains, Wash., and Cascades, Brit. Col. to Oreg.) . . . . *E. arenicola* **var. *torulosum***
CASCADES WALLFLOWER

    Erysimum arenicola vars. *arenicola* and *torulosum* are obviously not sharply distinct.

  4 Plants commonly more than 40 cm tall when in flower; margins of blades of upper leaves usually smooth but sometimes toothed; corollas bright yellow to orange or even reddish; fruits slightly flattened but nevertheless noticeably 4-sided, not alternately thickened and constricted (widespread biennial in lowland habitats) . . . .***E. capitatum*** (*E. asperum* of some references), pl. 177
WESTERN WALLFLOWER

    Erysimum capitatum is extremely variable, especially with respect to stature, size and form of the leaves, and corolla color. A further complication in our region is the presence, at high elevations in the Cascades, of perennial plants with yellow corollas and fruits that are flattened but also alternately thickened and constricted; these have sometimes been called *E. perenne* or *E. capitatum* var. *perenne*.

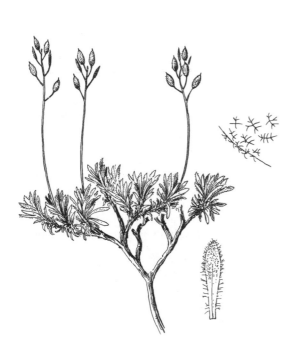

Draba incerta,
Yellowstone draba

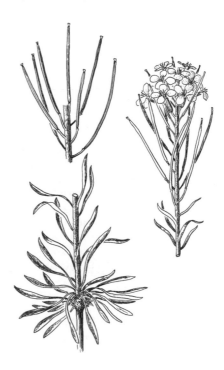

Erysimum capitatum,
western wallflower

Lepidium

1 Upper leaves clasping the stem
 2 Upper leaves usually less than twice as long as wide; basal leaves pinnately to bipinnately lobed; petals yellow . . . . ***L. perfoliatum***
                           SHIELD CRESS (Eurasia)
 2 Upper leaves 2–3 times as long as wide; basal leaves not often conspicuously lobed; petals white or only faintly yellowish
  3 Plants usually with a single upright stem; style not more than 0.6 mm long; anthers yellow; annual or biennial . . . . ***L. campestre***
                           FIELD CRESS (Europe)
  3 Plants usually with several upright stems; style about 1 mm long; anthers purple; perennial . . . .
  . . . . ***L. heterophyllum***
                  PERENNIAL FIELD CRESS (Europe)
1 Leaves not clasping the stem
 4 Sepals persisting until the fruit is nearly or fully mature (plants generally low, the stems typically spreading outward, close to the ground, from the center, thus forming a kind of rosette, but the inflorescences usually rising at least slightly) . . . . ***L. strictum***
                           PROSTRATE CRESS
 4 Sepals falling away early, or at least withering, about the same time as the petals and stamens
  5 Lobes of the fruit sharp-pointed (in alkaline soils; probably introduced where found in our region, as in Brit. Col.) . . . . ***L. oxycarpum***
                    SHARP-POD PEPPERGRASS
  5 Lobes of the fruit not sharp-pointed
   6 Pedicels distinctly flattened, about twice as wide as thick . . . . ***L. nitidum***
                  SHINING PEPPERGRASS
   6 Pedicels only slightly flattened, not so much as twice as wide as thick
    7 Plants typically with a single stem that does not branch except in the inflorescence; leaves below the inflorescence deeply pinnately divided, the lobes or leaflets generally toothed (occasionally cultivated as a salad vegetable and sometimes escaping) . . . . ***L. sativum***
                  GARDEN CRESS (Europe)
    7 Plants typically branching from the base and forming low, somewhat clumpy growths; leaves toothed or with a few lobes, but only some of the basal ones, if any, pinnately deeply divided . . . .
    . . . . ***L. virginicum***
                  VIRGINIA PEPPERGRASS

     Lepidium virginicum, widely distributed in North America, is divided into several intergrading varieties, of which 3 are native to our region: var. *menziesii* (pl. 178), Menzies' peppergrass, with hairy upper stems and pedicels and a few pinnately lobed leaves at or near the base, is found on backshores of sandy beaches and in other maritime habitats from Brit. Col. to S Oreg.; var. *pubescens,* also with hairy upper stems and pedicels but without clearly pinnately lobed leaves at the base, is found inland; var. *medium,* whose stems and pedicels are not obviously hairy, is also found inland. In all these, the fruits are as wide as long. Variety *virginicum,* native to E North America, is sometimes found in our region as a weed; its fruits are typically slightly longer than wide.

Raphanus

1 Fruit without distinct lengthwise grooves and ridges, not often with more than 3 seeds and not breaking apart at the constrictions between seeds; petals usually white, pink, or purplish, with darker veins . . . .
. . . . ***R. sativus***
                  WILD RADISH (Europe)
1 Fruit with regularly spaced lengthwise grooves and ridges, with 4–8 seeds and breaking apart at the constrictions between seeds; petals usually yellow, fading to white . . . . ***R. raphanistrum***
                  JOINTED CHARLOCK (Europe)

Rorippa

1 Petals white, sometimes with purplish lines (plants aquatic, growing partly submerged in streams, ditches, and ponds)

  2 Beak of fruit, if pronounced, not more than 1 mm long; seeds in 2 rows in each chamber of the fruit, with about 25 pits on each face (widespread in our region) . . . .***R. nasturtium-aquaticum***, p. 174

                                             WATERCRESS (Europe)

  2 Beak of fruit pronounced, typically at least 1 mm long; seeds essentially in just 1 row in each chamber of the fruit, with about 100 pits on each face (in our region known only from a few localities in Brit. Col.) . . . . ***R. microphylla***

                             ONE-ROW WATERCRESS (Europe)

1 Petals yellow (plants usually growing in wet habitats)

  3 Petals 3–5 mm long, longer than the sepals; perennial, spreading by rhizomes (Olympic Peninsula, Wash., and Willamette Valley, Oreg.; perhaps elsewhere) . . . .***R. sylvestris***

                        CREEPING YELLOW CRESS (Europe)

  3 Petals not often more than 2 mm long, about equal to the sepals; annual or biennial, not spreading by rhizomes

    4 Pedicels generally more than 5 mm long and many of them about as long as the mature fruits . . . .
. . . . ***R. palustris*** (*R. islandica*), pl. 180

                            MARSH YELLOW CRESS

        There are several named varieties of *R. palustris* that intergrade so much that it is difficult to characterize them.

    4 Pedicels not often more than 5 mm long and usually shorter than the mature fruits

      5 Fruits to 6 mm long, usually not more than 3 times as long as wide, curved only slightly if at all . . . .
. . . . ***R. obtusa***

                            PLUM-POD YELLOW CRESS

      5 Fruits to about 15 mm long, 1.5 mm wide, markedly curved . . . . ***R. curvisiliqua***

                            WESTERN YELLOW CRESS

        Two intergrading varieties of *R. curvisiliqua* in our region are keyed below.

Lepidium sativum,
garden cress

Raphanus sativus,
wild radish

    6 Sepals less than 1.5 mm long, petals not more than 1.5 mm long; plants low, with spreading branches . . . .*R. curvisiliqua* var. *lyrata*

    6 Sepals 1.5–2 mm long, petals to 2 mm long; plants upright . . . .*R. curvisiliqua* var. *glabrata*

Sisymbrium

1 Petals pale yellow, 3–4 mm long; fruits mostly about 1.5 cm long, pressed against the stem of the inflorescence . . . .*S. officinale*
                                        HEDGE MUSTARD (Eurasia)

1 Petals pale yellow or nearly white, at least 5 mm long; fruits more than 2 cm long, directed away from the stem of the inflorescence

    2 Pedicels slender, not half as thick as the fruits; fruits to about 3.5 cm long . . . .*S. loeselii*
                                     LOESEL'S TUMBLE MUSTARD (Eurasia)

    2 Pedicels stout, more than half as thick as the fruits; fruits commonly more than 3.5 cm long

        3 Leaves just below the inflorescences, if lobed, with a few rather broad lobes (some small leaves just below the inflorescences may not be lobed); petals usually 8–10 mm long . . . .*S. orientale*
                                  EASTERN TUMBLE MUSTARD (Eurasia)

        3 Leaves just below the inflorescences typically with at least several very slender lobes; petals usually 6–8 mm long . . . .*S. altissimum*
                                     TUMBLE MUSTARD (Eurasia)

Smelowskia

1 Petals 4–8 mm long; sepals typically shed early, before the fruits have developed to any great extent; mature fruits to about 4 times as long as wide; basal leaves sometimes with only 3 lobes (high montane in the Olympic Mountains, Wash., and Cascades, to Calif. and eastward) . . . .*S. calycina*
                                     ALPINE SMELOWSKIA

1 Petals 4–5 mm long; sepals typically persisting until the fruits have enlarged nearly to their maximum size; mature fruits about twice as long as wide; basal leaves usually like the upper leaves in being pinnately lobed (high montane in the Cascades, mostly E of the crest, to Calif.) . . . .*S. ovalis*
                                     OVAL-FRUIT SMELOWSKIA

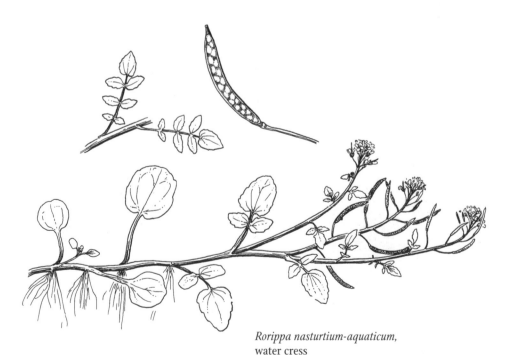

Rorippa nasturtium-aquaticum,
water cress

Streptanthus

1 Middle and upper portions of the stems without broad, clasping leaves; tips of petals dark purple; ripening fruits generally spreading outward or directed upward to some extent (Josephine Co., Oreg., to Calif.) . . . .
. . . . *S. howellii,* pl. 181
HOWELL'S STREPTANTHUS

1 Middle and upper portions of stems with broad, clasping leaves; tips of petals usually light, with purple veins; ripening fruits generally hanging downward to some extent (Curry Co., Oreg., to Calif.) . . . .
. . . . *S. tortuosus* **var.** *tortuosus*
MOUNTAIN STREPTANTHUS

A montane variety, *S. tortuosus* var. *orbiculatus,* not likely to be found below 5000 ft. (1520 m), occurs in the Cascades of S Oreg.

Thlaspi

1 Basal leaves absent or few and small, the stem leaves well developed; fruit to more than 1 cm wide, with broad winglike margins, the style barely evident in the apical notch; annual, and a common weed . . . .
. . . . *T. arvense*
FIELD PENNYCRESS (Europe)

1 Basal leaves usually numerous, the upper leaves small in comparison; fruit to about 5 mm wide, without winglike margins, the style prominent and in a broad, shallow notch; native perennials
2 Petioles of basal leaves rarely twice as long as the blades; pedicels of flowers mostly directed outward or slightly upward; flowering and fruiting stems sometimes more than 20 cm tall (in our region mostly montane, N Wash. to Calif.) . . . . *T. montanum* **var.** *montanum*
MOUNTAIN PENNYCRESS

Sisymbrium officinale,
hedge mustard

Smelowskia calycina,
alpine smelowskia

Thlaspi arvense,
field penny-cress

2 Petioles of basal leaves generally more than twice as long as the blades; pedicels of flowers mostly directed outward or slightly downward; flowering and fruiting stems not often more than 15 cm tall (Josephine Co., Oreg., at about 1500 ft., 460 m) . . . . *T. montanum* var. *siskiyouense*, pl. 183

SISKIYOU PENNYCRESS

While most montane specimens of *T. montanum* found at relatively low elevations in Josephine Co., Oreg., are decidedly different from those growing at or above 4000 ft. (1220 m) in the Cascades and other montane habitats, some plants are intermediate with respect to one or more of the key characters, the least useful of which is the way the flowers are oriented.

Thysanocarpus

1 Plant not conspicuously hairy; outer portions of fruit with clearly marked, slender ridges that radiate away from the swollen central portion; margins of fruit without prominent incisions (Umpqua River valley, Oreg., to Calif.) . . . . *T. radians*

RIBBED FRINGEPOD

1 Plant conspicuously hairy; outer portions of fruit without clearly marked, slender ridges (but there may be indistinct, broad ridges); margins of fruit sometimes with incisions . . . . *T. curvipes*, pl. 184

HAIRY FRINGEPOD

BUDDLEJACEAE Buddleja Family

Shrubs and trees belonging to the Buddlejaceae have opposite leaves. Their flowers are characterized by a bell-shaped, four-lobed calyx, a tubular, four-lobed corolla, and four stamens; the fruit-forming part of the pistil has two seed-producing divisions. *Buddleja davidii*, called summer lilac, is widely cultivated for its attractive purple or lilac flowers, borne in dense inflorescences as long as 40 cm. The leaf blades, as long as 25 cm, are dark green on the upper surface, white-woolly on the underside, and have toothed margins. This large shrub, a native of China, occasionally becomes established on vacant land.

Results of more recent studies strongly suggest that *Buddleja* should be transferred to Scrophulariaceae. See introduction to this assemblage, as it has traditionally been viewed, for a proposed regrouping of genera.

CABOMBACEAE Water-Shield Family

Plants of the Cabombaceae are rooted in mud of freshwater ponds, lakes, and sluggish streams. Some or all of them have circular, floating leaves to which the petiole is attached near the center. The flowers are borne singly and held above the surface of the water. The only species likely to be found in our region is *Brasenia schreberi* (pl. 185), called water shield. All its leaves have floating blades, these sometimes as much as or more than 8 cm long. The flowers have three reddish purple sepals and petals 10–15 mm long, 12–18 stamens, and 4–18 pistils. The tough, more or less egg-shaped fruits are as long as 8 mm.

Cabomba caroliniana, fanwort, a native of eastern North America, is commonly grown in aquaria and fish-ponds. It is reported to have become at least temporarily established in a few places in the region. Under ideal conditions, it too has some floating leaf blades (these have a circular outline, often with a notch), but its submerged leaves, opposite or in whorls, are divided into narrow lobes. The flowers, like those of *Brasenia*, have three sepals and petals (white, with yellow spots), but the number of stamens is fewer (three to six) and there are only two to four pistils.

CACTACEAE Cactus Family

The only cactus in our region is *Opuntia fragilis* (pl. 186), the brittle prickly pear. It has a wide distribution, California to British Columbia and eastward to the longitude of Texas, Wisconsin, and north-central Canada. In parts of this large area, however, its occurrence is spotty. In the Pacific Northwest, for instance, it is found mostly east of the Cascades, but there are populations on the San Juan Islands and Gulf Islands, and in a few other localities in the Puget Trough. The somewhat flattened stem segments are not often more than 5 cm long; the stout spines, two to seven in each cluster, sometimes reach a length of 3 cm. The many perianth segments—these are in several series, as in other cacti, and sepals cannot really be distinguished from petals—are as long as about 2 cm; the inner ones are bright yellow or greenish yellow. The numerous stamens have red filaments. The spiny fruit, usually a little more than 1 cm long, is unlike the prickly pears of most other species of the genus in that dries as it ripens.

CALLITRICHACEAE Water-Starwort Family

Water starworts, with slender and weak stems, are rooted in mud of shallow ponds and ditches. The leaves are opposite and have smooth margins. The flowers, borne in the leaf axils, are tiny and lack sepals and petals. Each one has a single stamen and a four-lobed pistil with two styles. When the fruit has matured and dried, the lobes, each with one seed, separate.

Callitriche

1 All leaf blades 1 to about 2.5 times as long as wide, none of them narrow (fruit bordered by a broad wing-like margin) . . . . *C. stagnalis*, pl. 187
                                         COMMON WATER STARWORT (Europe)
1 Some or all leaf blades proportionately narrow, several times as long as wide
  2 Pistillate flowers with pedicels at least 5 mm long (fruits bordered by a winglike margin; plants growing on wet soil, pressing fruits into the soil) . . . . *C. marginata*
                                WINGED WATER STARWORT
  2 Pistillate flowers sessile or nearly so, the pedicels scarcely apparent
    3 All leaf blades narrow, several times as long as wide . . . . *C. hermaphroditica*
                              NORTHERN WATER STARWORT
    3 At least a few leaves near the tips of the stems much wider than the lower leaves
      4 Fruits bordered by a winglike margin, at least above
        5 Winglike margin of the fruits of uniform width from the base to the tip (Oreg. to Calif.) . . . .
        . . . . *C. trochlearis*
                           WESTERN WATER STARWORT
        5 Winglike margin of the fruits wider above the middle than below . . . . *C. palustris* (*C. verna*)
                            MARSH WATER STARWORT
      4 Fruits not bordered by a winglike margin
        6 Fruits 0.8–1.4 mm long, usually broadest above the middle, the outline therefore somewhat heart- or egg-shaped . . . . *C. heterophylla* var. *bolanderi*
                              BOLANDER'S WATER STARWORT
        6 Fruits 0.6–0.8 mm long, usually broadest near the middle, the outline therefore nearly circular (except for the notch at the tip) . . . *C. heterophylla* var. *heterophylla* (*C. anceps* of some references)
                              DIVERSE-LEAVED WATER STARWORT

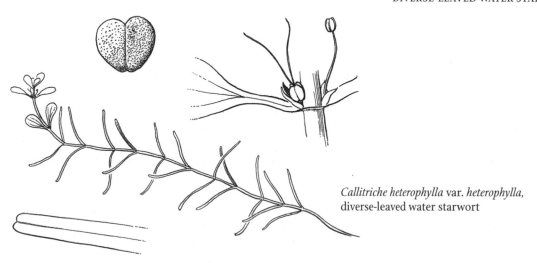

Callitriche heterophylla var. *heterophylla*,
diverse-leaved water starwort

CAMPANULACEAE Bluebell Family

Plants of the bluebell family generally have alternate, simple leaves. The calyx and corolla have five lobes, and the five stamens alternate with the corolla lobes. The pistil, whose fruiting portion is united to the calyx tube, has a single stigma, and the fruit, at maturity, is a dry capsule that opens by pores or splits apart lengthwise or crosswise.

In three of the genera found in our region—*Downingia, Howellia,* and *Lobelia*—the corolla is slightly to markedly irregular and usually conspicuously two-lipped. The filaments of the stamens, and sometimes also the anthers, are united to form a tubelike structure. For these reasons, the genera specified have often been segregated into a separate lobelia family (Lobeliaceae).

1 Plants aquatic in fresh water, mostly or entirely submerged
  2 All substantial leaves mostly 3–5 cm long, 2–3 mm wide, concentrated in a basal rosette; flowers few, in a long-stalked raceme that eventually reaches the surface of the water; corolla white or pale blue, markedly irregular, with 3 lobes forming an apparent lower lip, 2 lobes forming an apparent upper lip (Brit. Col. to N Oreg.) . . . . *Lobelia dortmanna,* pl. 196
                                                    WATER LOBELIA
  2 Leaves to about 4 cm long, 1.5 mm wide, scattered along stems branching from a leafless main stem; flowers originating in the axils of leaves; corolla, when present, shorter than the calyx, slightly 2-lipped, white or pale lavender (W Wash. and NW Oreg.; rare) . . . . *Howellia aquatilis*
           The corolla of *H. aquatilis* is often absent, especially in flowers that open early.
1 Plants essentially terrestrial although sometimes growing at the edges of ponds or in mud of drying vernal pools and ditches
  3 Corolla markedly irregular, with 3 lobes forming an apparent lower lip, 2 lobes forming an apparent upper lip (the lower lip is in fact the upper lip, and vice versa, but the position of the 2 lips is reversed by a twisting of the fruit-forming portion of the pistil)
    4 Plants very hairy, to more than 60 cm tall, upright; leaves to about 6 cm long, 2–2.5 times as long as wide, with toothed margins; flowers with distinct pedicels; corolla light blue; typically on dry soil (reported from SW Brit. Col.) . . . . *Lobelia inflata*
                                 WILD TOBACCO (central and E United States)
    4 Plants as a whole not obviously hairy, not often more than 30 cm tall, usually sprawling to at least some extent; leaf blades generally less than 2.5 cm long; flowers sessile; corollas usually deep blue, the lower lip with prominent bright markings; typically growing on mud of ditches and drying pools . . . . *Downingia*
  3 Corolla regular, with 5 equal lobes
    5 Flowers with obvious pedicels; perennial . . . . *Campanula*
    5 Flowers sessile or nearly so; annual
      6 Calyx lobes (usually at least 1 cm long), reaching far beyond the tips of the corolla lobes; most leaf blades much longer than wide (corolla mostly blue, the throat whitish) . . . .
       . . . . *Githopsis specularioides,* pl. 195
                                         BLUECUP
      6 Calyx lobes not reaching the tips of the corolla lobes; leaf blades nearly or fully as wide as long (except in *Triodanis biflora*)
        7 Corolla lobes blunt, separated for less than half the length of the corolla (corolla blue; uncommon W of the Cascades; most likely to be found at the edge of a pond or in some other moist habitat) . . . . *Heterocodon rariflorum* (*Specularia rariflorum*)
        7 Corolla lobes pointed, separated nearly to the base of the corolla (corolla deep blue to violet-blue or purple)
          8 Most leaf blades nearly or fully as wide as long, the upper ones generally clasping the stem; with as many as 5 flowers in each leaf axil; most flowers opening; fruit not noticeably constricted just below the calyx lobes . . . . *Triodanis perfoliata* (*Specularia perfoliata*)
                                   VENUS' LOOKING-GLASS

8 Leaf blades oval, decidedly longer than wide, none of them clasping the stem; rarely with more than 2 flowers in each leaf axil; flowers below those in the top 1–3 leaf axils usually not opening; fruit often noticeably constricted just below the calyx lobes (SW Oreg. to Calif., the Atlantic coast, and South America) . . . . *Triodanis biflora* (*Specularia biflora*)
SMALL VENUS' LOOKING-GLASS

Campanula

Besides the native species in this key, several garden campanulas from the Old World have been seen as escapes. Two especially common aliens are *Campanula medium*, Canterbury bells (biennial), and *C. rapunculoides*, creeping bellflower (perennial, spreading by rhizomes); both typically have blue flowers. *Campanula lactiflora*, European bellflower, is a rhizomatous perennial with white or pale blue flowers. All three species have large corollas and are commonly taller than 50 cm.

1 Corolla lobes about twice as long as the tube (corolla nearly or fully 15 mm long; leaves with prominent teeth; plants low, with rhizomes, the flowering stems not often more than 10 cm tall; endemic to the Olympic Mountains, Wash., and not likely to be found below 5000 ft., 1520 m) . . . . *C. piperi*, pl. 188
PIPER'S BELLFLOWER

1 Corolla lobes not much longer (and sometimes shorter) than the tube

  2 Corolla lobes wider than long and much shorter than the tube; style of pistil not obviously protruding beyond the corolla (corolla purplish blue) . . . . *C. rotundifolia*, pl. 190
COMMON BLUEBELL

  2 Corolla lobes longer than wide and usually slightly longer than the tube; style of pistil protruding well beyond the corolla

    3 Corolla bright blue; plants commonly more than 35 cm tall; all leaves sessile or nearly so (Polk Co., Oreg., to Calif.) . . . . *C. prenanthoides*, pl. 189
CALIFORNIA HAREBELL

    3 Corolla pale blue or nearly white; plants rarely more than 20 cm tall; lower leaves with distinct petioles, these sometimes longer than the blades . . . . *C. scouleri*, pl. 191
SCOULER'S HAREBELL

Downingia

1 Tube formed by the united anthers curving downward at an angle of more than 60° (sometimes nearly 90°) from the tube formed by the united filaments

  2 White field on lower lip of corolla with 2 oblong orange-yellow spots; lobes of lower lip nearly rounded but abruptly tapering to short, pointed tips (S Oreg. to Calif.) . . . . *D. bacigalupii*, pl. 192
BACIGALUPI'S DOWNINGIA

  2 White field of lower lip of corolla without yellow-orange spots; lobes of lower lip tapering gradually to pointed tips (Oreg. to Calif., also E of the Cascades, where it extends to Wash., Idaho, Nevada, and perhaps Brit. Col.) . . . . *D. elegans*, pl. 193
ELEGANT DOWNINGIA

1 Tube formed by united anthers curving downward at an angle of less than 45° from the tube formed by the united filaments (white field of lower lip of corolla with yellow, yellow-green, or yellow-orange spots; lobes of lower lip of corolla more or less rounded, then tapering abruptly to short, pointed tips)

  3 White field on lower lip of corolla with bright yellow, this usually in the form of 2 contiguous spots; inside of corolla tube not conspicuously hairy; none of the anthers with a bristle at the tip; fruit-forming portion of pistil with 1 seed-producing chamber (Wash. to Calif.) . . . *D. yina* (*D. willamettensis*), pl. 194
SPREADING DOWNINGIA

  3 White field on lower lip of corolla with 2 contiguous yellow-green spots; inside of corolla tube conspicuously hairy; 2 of the anthers with a bristle at the tip; fruit-forming portion of pistil with 2 seed-producing chambers (S Oreg. to Calif., also E of the Cascades) . . . . *D. bicornuta* var. *bicornuta*
TWO-HORNED DOWNINGIA

CAPRIFOLIACEAE Honeysuckle Family

All members of the honeysuckle family are perennial, and most are decidedly woody. Those in our region are vines, shrubs, and small trees. The leaves are opposite, and in honeysuckles (*Lonicera*) pairs of them may be united to form disklike structures that surround the stem. The calyx, usually small, has four or five lobes. The corolla, often with a substantial tube, may have four or five equal lobes, or it may be markedly two-lipped, in which case the upper lip has four lobes and the lower lip consists of a single large lobe. The stamens alternate with the corolla lobes and are attached to the tube. The fruiting portion of the pistil is below the level at which the corolla and calyx lobes originate. The fruit, with two to five seed-forming divisions, is fleshy in all representatives in our region other than *Linnaea borealis* var. *longiflora*.

1 Large shrubs or small trees with pinnately compound leaves .... *Sambucus*
1 Shrubs, vines, or herbaceous plants, the leaves not compound
    2 Low, trailing herbaceous plants to about 15 cm tall when in flower or fruit; leaf blades oval or slightly wedge-shaped, usually toothed in the upper half; flowers hanging down, borne in pairs on the peduncles; corolla regular, 5-lobed; stamens 4; fruits dry when mature ..... *Linnaea borealis* var. *longiflora*, pl. 197
                                              TWINFLOWER
    2 Plants not conforming to all criteria in the other choice 2
        3 Shrubs with toothed and/or lobed leaf blades (flowers in umbel-like inflorescences; corolla white; fruit orange or red) .... *Viburnum*
        3 Shrubs or vines, the leaf blades typically neither toothed nor lobed (in *Symphoricarpos albus* var. *laevigatus*, however, some leaves, especially on lush growth, may be deeply and irregularly lobed)
            4 Corolla (usually pink) regular (except for a slight bulge on the corolla tube); fruits white when ripe .... *Symphoricarpos*
            4 Corolla either markedly 2-lipped (the upper lip consisting of 4 lobes, the lower lip of 1 lobe) or apparently regular, but in that case with a perceptible bulge on the lower side of the tube; fruits not white when ripe .... *Lonicera*

Lonicera

In addition to the species of *Lonicera* in this key, there are several introduced species that have escaped from gardens. Of the vines, *L. etrusca*, Mediterranean honeysuckle, and *L. periclymenum*, woodbine, are perhaps the most commonly encountered; they are dealt with in this key. Two other species that have appeared where they could create problems are *L. japonica*, Japanese honeysuckle, and *L. tatarica*, Tartarian honeysuckle. The former, with white to yellow, often purple-tinged, two-lipped corollas to 4 cm long, is a climber or trailer; the latter, with white or pink, regular corollas to 2 cm long, is a shrub. *Lonicera pileata*, a small, rather stiff shrub with leaves only as long as about 2 cm, seems not to be so aggressive as the others, but it has survived in one or two places close to where it was probably planted.

1 Upright shrubs; flowers borne in pairs, but none of the leaves with blades united in such a way that they completely encircle the stem (corollas not 2-lipped except in *L. conjugialis*)
    2 Leaf blades often more than 10 cm long; each pair of flowers borne above 2 pairs of broad, leaflike bracts that become red (corollas yellow; fruits black when ripe; usually in wet habitats)
        3 Anthers reaching to or beyond the tips of the corolla lobes; corolla seldom more than 1.5 cm long (widespread in our region) .... *L. involucrata* var. *involucrata*
                                       BLACK TWINBERRY
        3 Anthers not reaching to the tips of the corolla lobes; corolla to 2 cm long (mostly along the coast, Lane Co., Oreg., to Calif.) .... *L. involucrata* var. *ledebourii*, pl. 199
                                       COAST TWINBERRY
    2 Leaf blades not often more than 6 cm long; each pair of flowers without bracts or with only a single pair of small, slender bracts

4 Bracts, if present, very small and inconspicuous; corollas 2-lipped, dark red or reddish purple; fruits red to blackish, fused together for at least half their length (montane, in the Cascades and Siskiyou Mountains, S to Calif.) . . . . *L. conjugialis*
MARRIED HONEYSUCKLE

4 Bracts small but obvious; corollas not 2-lipped, yellowish white to pale yellow; fruits red, fused together by their bases (in the Cascades, Olympic Mountains, and Siskiyou Mountains, not often below about 4500 ft., 1370 m; also E of the crest of the Cascades) . . . . *L. utahensis*
RED TWINBERRY

1 Vines; flowers in terminal inflorescences, with no tendency to form pairs or to be borne above bracts, but the blades of the pair of leaves nearest the inflorescence united (except in *L. periclymenum*), thus completely encircling the stem

  5 Corolla usually orange or orange-red (sometimes yellow), not 2-lipped, the tube about 3–4 times as long as the lobes . . . . *L. ciliosa*, pl. 198
ORANGE HONEYSUCKLE

  5 Corolla not orange or orange-red, distinctly 2 lipped, the lobes longer than the tube

    6 Corolla 3–5 cm long, pale yellow, tinged with purple (established in a few places, especially along the coast from Lane Co. to Curry Co., Oreg.) . . . . *L. etrusca*
MEDITERRANEAN HONEYSUCKLE (Europe)
Lonicera periclymenum, woodbine, is similar to *L. etrusca,* but the leaves of the pair below the inflorescence are not united.

    6 Corolla 1.5–2 cm long, mostly pinkish or purplish pink, yellowish within . . . . *L. hispidula* var. *hispidula*
PINK HONEYSUCKLE
Specimens of *L. hispidula* from S Oreg. and Calif. are often referred to var. *vacillans.* Many of them, however, are not clearly distinct from specimens found farther N in our region. Perhaps the division into varieties is not warranted.

Sambucus

1 Inflorescence not so tall as wide (often somewhat flat-topped); fruits bluish (nearly black if the powdery coating is rubbed off) . . . . *S. mexicana* (*S. caerulea*), pl. 200
BLUE ELDERBERRY

1 Inflorescence at least as tall as wide; fruits red (usually in wet habitats, such as the edges of marshes, streams, and ditches) . . . . *S. racemosa* var. *arborescens* (*S. callicarpa*), pl. 201
RED ELDERBERRY
A montane shrub with an inflorescence as tall as wide but with purplish black fruits is *S. racemosa* var. *melanocarpa* (*S. melanocarpa*), black elderberry. It is not likely to be found below about 5000 ft. (1520 m).

Symphoricarpos

1 Plants often more than 1 m tall, upright; leaf blades not hairy on the underside; corolla with a nectar gland below only 1 lobe; fruit usually 10–12 mm long . . . . *S. albus* subsp. *laevigatus*, pl. 202
SNOWBERRY

1 Plants rarely more than 50 cm tall, usually sprawling; leaf blades typically densely hairy on the underside; corolla with nectar glands below all 5 lobes; fruit 5–6 mm long (usually restricted to shaded, humid forests or to coastal areas) . . . . *S. mollis* (includes *S. mollis* var. *hesperius,* sometimes also called *S. hesperius*), pl. 203
CREEPING SNOWBERRY

Viburnum

1 Leaves not lobed; fruits red, not especially juicy . . . . *V. ellipticum*, pl. 204
OVAL-LEAVED VIBURNUM

1 Leaves shallowly 3-lobed above the middle; fruits red or orange, juicy

2 All flowers of the inflorescence similar and normally with stamens and a pistil (widespread from Alaska to N Oreg. but in our region rarely found below 1500 ft., 460 m; most likely to be encountered around bogs or swampy areas) . . . . *V. edule* (*V. pauciflorum*)
SQUASHBERRY

2 Marginal flowers of the inflorescence sterile and with enlarged corollas, these about 2 cm wide (occasionally escaping from gardens) . . . . *V. opulus* **subsp.** *opulus*
HIGHBUSH CRANBERRY (Europe)

Viburnum opulus subsp. *americanus,* scarcely different from subsp. *opulus,* extends across North America as far W as Brit. Col., Idaho, and Wash. but does not reach our region.

CARYOPHYLLACEAE Pink Family

Carnations, pinks, sweet William, and baby's breath are among the important garden plants that belong to the Caryophyllaceae. Some of the cultivated species have become more or less wild in a few places, adding to the already large number of native and weedy aliens that represent the family in our region. The leaves of almost all members of the group are opposite, and the nodes of the stems, where the leaves originate, are usually conspicuously swollen. The flowers typically have five sepals (or five calyx lobes, when the lower part of the calyx forms a cup or tube) and five petals; the petals are generally split into two or more lobes. In a few species, petals are lacking, at least on some flowers. The number of stamens is commonly five or ten, and the fruit, dry when mature, has from one to many seeds.

1 Leaves with membranous or somewhat silvery stipules
    2 Leaves alternate (plants slightly succulent; leaves to about 2 cm long, generally widest above the middle; stipules white; calyx only about 1 mm long, the lobes with white margins; petals white or pinkish, about as long as the calyx lobes; fruit purplish black, containing a single seed; uncommon weed) . . . . . .
. . . . *Corrigiola litoralis*
STRAPWORT (Europe)
    2 Leaves opposite
        3 Leaves and calyx lobes stiff, with sharp tips, the plants therefore very prickly; older stems freely breaking apart into short units that are painful to bare feet; petals extremely small and scalelike (plants forming prostrate mats; calyx lobes markedly unequal, the bristles at their tips about as long as the tube; on backshores of sandy beaches and on sandy soils around salt marshes; Wash. to South America) . . . . *Cardionema ramosissimum*, pl. 205
SAND MAT
        3 Leaves and calyx lobes or sepals, if with pointed tips, not prickly; stems not freely breaking apart into short units
            4 Calyx lobes slender, ending in bristlelike tips; petals absent; fruit containing a single seed (on hillsides near the coast, Curry Co., Oreg., to Calif.) . . . . *Paronychia franciscana*
SAN FRANCISCO WHITLOWWORT
            4 Sepals broad, usually only 2–3 times as long as wide, sometimes becoming slender toward the tips but these not bristlelike; petals usually present; fruit containing several seeds . . . .
. . . . *Spergula-Spergularia* **complex**
1 Leaves without stipules
    5 Calyx lobes equaling the tube, which is about 2 mm long, tightly encloses the fruit, and becomes markedly hardened and nutlike; petals absent; fruit containing a single seed (established along the coast in Curry Co., Oreg., and in the Willamette Valley) . . . . *Scleranthus annuus* **var.** *annuus*
GERMAN KNOTGRASS, KNAWEL (Europe)
    5 Calyx either consisting of separate sepals or lobed, in which case the lobes are usually shorter than the tube, which does not become markedly hardened and nutlike; petals usually present but sometimes extremely small or absent in certain species of *Cerastium* and *Stellaria;* fruit containing at least several seeds

6 Calyx with a distinct tube, this usually longer than the lobes

  7 Pistil with 2 styles

    8 Each flower with 1 or more pairs of bracts immediately below it, these bracts closely applied to the calyx . . . . *Dianthus*

    8 Flowers without bracts immediately below them

      9 Calyx about 2 mm long, 5-nerved (petals white, slightly longer than the calyx; garden plant, much used in the florist trade, occasionally escaping) . . . . *Gypsophila paniculata* var. *paniculata*

                                                               BABY'S BREATH (Europe and W Asia)

             In *G. scorzonerifolia*, also from Europe, the inflorescence is glandular-hairy, and the calyx teeth are longer (3–4 mm). It is known from a few localities in Brit. Col.

      9 Calyx at least 1 cm long, 10- to 20-nerved

        10 Each petal with a pair of slender outgrowths at the base of the broadened, spreading portion; calyx lobes unequal; petals white or pink (garden plant) . . . . *Saponaria officinalis*, pl. 210

                                                             BOUNCING BET (Europe)

        10 Petals without slender outgrowths; calyx lobes equal; petals pink . . . . *Vaccaria hispanica* (*V. segetalis*)

                                                             COW COCKLE (Europe)

  7 Pistil with 3 or 5 styles

    11 Petals (usually purplish red but sometimes clearly red or white) without outgrowths; calyx lobes longer than the tube (plants decidedly white-hairy) . . . . *Agrostemma githago*

                                                            CORN COCKLE (Europe)

    11 Petals usually with outgrowths near or above the middle (these outgrowths, however, are lacking or very small in certain species of *Silene*); calyx lobes shorter than the tube

      12 All flowers with stamens and a pistil

        13 Pistil with 3 styles; fruit splitting lengthwise into 6 divisions . . . . *Silene*

        13 Pistil with 5 styles; fruit splitting lengthwise into 5 divisions (tooth at the top of each division divided into 2 lobes; plants densely grayish hairy; calyx lobes twisted; petals crimson) . . . . *Lychnis coronaria*

                                                             ROSE CAMPION (Europe)

      12 Pistillate and staminate flowers on separate plants (pistil with 5 styles; fruit splitting lengthwise into 5 divisions)

        14 Petals white; flowers opening in the evening and closing about noon, very fragrant . . . . *Silene latifolia* subsp. *alba*

                                                        WHITE CAMPION (Eurasia)

        14 Petals crimson; flowers opening in the morning and remaining open all day . . . . . . *Silene dioica*

                                                         RED CAMPION (Eurasia)

              Silene latifolia subsp. *alba* and *S. dioica* hybridize to produce pink-flowered plants.

6 Sepals separate nearly or fully to the base, the lower portion of the calyx thus not a distinct tube

  15 Plants succulent, not at all hairy; flowers borne in the leaf axils (restricted to the backshores of sandy beaches) . . . . *Honckenya peploides*, pl. 208

                                                             SEA PURSLANE

  15 Plants not succulent, often hairy; flowers usually in cymes or umbels

    16 Petals distinctly, even if only shallowly, 2-lobed (petals often absent in *Stellaria crispa* and *S. borealis* subsp. *sitchana*)

      17 Pistil usually with 5 styles; fruit more or less cylindrical, splitting apart by teeth near the tip . . . . *Cerastium*

      17 Pistil usually with 3 styles (rarely 4); fruit more or less egg-shaped, splitting apart nearly or fully to the base by valves . . . . *Stellaria*

    16 Petals, if present, not distinctly lobed but sometimes either ragged or shallowly notched at the tip

18 Sepals and petals 4; fruit opening by 8 slits that appear in the upper portion (plants with crowded basal leaves, these very slender, and a few pairs of slightly broader leaves above; flowers few, the pedicels more than 2 cm long, sometimes as long as 6 cm; petals white, rounded at the tip, shorter than the sepals; occasional weed) . . . .*Moenchia erecta*
UPRIGHT CHICKWEED, MUNCHKIN CHICKWEED (Europe)

18 Sepals and petals usually 5; fruit splitting apart lengthwise into 3 or more divisions

  19 Flowers in umbels; petals (white or pale pink) with pointed, ragged tips . . . . . *Holosteum umbellatum*
UMBELLATE CHICKWEED (Eurasia)

  19 Flowers not in umbels; petals neither pointed nor ragged at the tip

    20 Pistil usually with as many styles as there are sepals and alternating with them . . . . *Sagina*

    20 Pistil with fewer styles than sepals . . . . *Arenaria-Minuartia-Moehringia* complex

Arenaria-Minuartia-Moehringia Complex

1 Most leaves at least 2 mm wide

  2 Stems 1–2 mm thick, weak, often falling down or supported by other vegetation; in wet habitats (Wash. to Calif. but rarely encountered) . . . .*A. paludicola*
MARSH SANDWORT

  2 Stems not more than 1 mm thick, firm and erect; in well-drained habitats

    3 Larger leaves at least 2 cm long, usually more than 3 times as long as wide, smooth-margined; stems with short, rough hairs . . . .*Moehringia macrophylla*, pl. 209
LARGE-LEAVED SANDWORT

    3 Larger leaves less than 1 cm long, rarely so much as 3 times as long as wide, with slightly bristly margins; stems smooth . . . . *A. serpyllifolia* subsp. *serpyllifolia*
THYME-LEAVED SANDWORT (Europe)

1 Leaves slender, often nearly needlelike, not more than 1.5 mm wide

  4 Plants forming dense mats or cushions, generally not more than 10 cm tall when flowering

    5 Tips of sepals bluntly rounded (mostly high montane, Alaska to Oreg. and eastward) . . . .
. . . . *Minuartia obtusiloba*
ALPINE SANDWORT

    5 Tips of sepals sharply pointed

      6 Petals usually shorter than the sepals or barely as long as the petals, sometimes absent (plants rarely more than 5 cm tall when flowering; axils of some pairs of primary leaves with bundles of secondary leaves; fruiting portion of pistil with 3 lengthwise sutures; SW Oreg. to Calif., also E of the Cascades) . . . .*Minuartia pusilla*
DWARF SANDWORT

      6 Petals usually about as long as the petals or slightly longer (stems glandular-hairy)

        7 Axils of some pairs of primary leaves with clusters of secondary leaves; sepals 3.5–7 mm long (SW Oreg. to Calif.) . . . .*Minuartia nuttallii* subsp. *gregaria*
NUTTALL'S SANDWORT

        7 Axils of primary leaves without clusters of secondary leaves; sepals 2–4 mm long (mostly high montane, Brit. Col. to Calif.) . . . .*Minuartia rubella*
NORTHERN SANDWORT

  4 Plants mostly upright, not forming dense mats or cushions

    8 Fruiting portion of pistil with 6 lengthwise sutures, these marking lines of separation of the 6 divisions of the fruit when this is ripe

      9 Sepals much less than twice as long as wide, the tips rather blunt or at least not sharply pointed (montane in the Olympic Mountains, Wash., and Cascades, Alaska to Oreg., and eastward) . . . .
. . . . *A. capillaris* var. *americana*
THREAD-LEAVED SANDWORT

9 Sepals at least twice as long as wide, the tips sharp-pointed (montane, SW Oreg. to Calif.; also E of the crest of the Cascades) . . . . *A. congesta* var. *suffrutescens*
CAPITATE SANDWORT

8 Fruiting portion of pistil with 3 lengthwise sutures, these marking lines of separation of the 3 divisions of the fruit when this is ripe

   10 Inflorescence not glandular-hairy

      11 Petals decidedly longer than the sepals (to about 1.5 times as long); sepals with green tips, the 3 veins inconspicuous, the lateral ones usually not reaching the apex; pedicels, by the time fruits are well developed, not often more than 15 mm long (on serpentine soils, Lane Co., Oreg., to Calif.) . . . . *Minuartia cismontana*
WESTERN-SLOPE SANDWORT

      11 Petals equal in length to the sepals or as much as about 1.25 times as long; sepals with membranous tips, conspicuously 3-nerved (sometimes 5-nerved), the lateral nerves distinct and reaching close to the apex; pedicels, by the time fruits are well developed, from 10 to more than 30 mm long (Josephine and Jackson Cos., Oreg., to Calif.) . . . . *Minuartia californica*
CALIFORNIA SANDWORT

   10 Inflorescence glandular-hairy

      12 Leaves to 1.5 mm wide at their bases, stiff and curving (seeds usually reddish, with a thin, winglike margin; Josephine Co., Oreg., to Calif.) . . . . *Minuartia howellii*
HOWELL'S SANDWORT

      12 Leaves not so much as 1 mm wide even at their bases, flexible and often curling

         13 Petals about twice as long as wide and about twice as long as the sepals (Rogue River valley, Oreg., to Calif. and Baja Calif.) . . . . *Minuartia douglasii*
DOUGLAS' SANDWORT

         13 Petals less than 1.5 times as long as wide and not much longer than the sepals (plants slender, the inflorescence usually less extensively branched than that of *M. howellii* and *M. douglasii;* Brit. Col. to NW Oreg.) . . . . *Minuartia tenella*
SLENDER SANDWORT

Cerastium

Cerastium tomentosum, called snow-in-summer and dusty miller, has occasionally escaped from gardens. Its stems and leaves are silvery due to a dense coating of woolly hairs.

1 Petals slightly more than 1 cm long, about twice as long as the sepals; most leaves narrow, at least 6 times as long as wide (perennial) . . . . *C. arvense*
FIELD CHICKWEED

1 Petals (sometimes absent in *C. glomeratum* and *C. nutans*) less than 1 cm long, not more than 1.5 times as long as the sepals; most leaves not so much as 6 times as long as wide

   2 Pedicels no longer than the sepals, the flowers therefore densely clustered (petals, when present, not quite as long as the sepals)

      3 Bracts of inflorescence green; petals, when present, notched for about one-fourth of their length (very common, widespread weed) . . . . *C. glomeratum* (*C. viscosum* of some references), pl. 206
STICKY MOUSE-EAR CHICKWEED (Europe)

      3 Bracts of inflorescence whitish, papery; petals shallowly 2-lobed (rather uncommon weed) . . . . *C. semidecandrum*
LITTLE MOUSE-EAR CHICKWEED (Europe)

   2 Pedicels usually distinctly longer than the sepals, the flowers therefore not so densely clustered as in the species under the other choice 2

4 Plants annual, upright, not forming mats or rooting at the nodes; flowers generally nodding; petals usually at least as long as the sepals (Brit. Col. to N Oreg.) . . . . *C. nutans*
NODDING CHICKWEED

4 Plants biennial or perennial, sprawling, often rooting at the nodes and forming mats; flowers not nodding; petals usually not quite as long as the sepals . . . .
. . . . *C. fontanum* var. *vulgare* (*C. vulgatum* or *C. holosteoides* of some references)
COMMON MOUSE-EAR CHICKWEED (Europe)

Dianthus

1 Plants not hairy; leaves 1–2 cm wide (petals white, pink, or red; commonly grown in gardens, occasionally becoming established in vacant lots and other places) . . . . *D. barbatus*
SWEET WILLIAM (Europe)

1 Plants usually hairy; leaves not often more than 5 mm wide
2 Flowers single or as many as 5 in each loose cyme; hairiness of leaves and stems rough to the touch; petals usually with long hairs near the base of the broadened portion (an escape from gardens) . . . . *D. armeria*
DEPTFORD PINK (Europe)

2 Flowers several in a congested cyme; hairiness of leaves and stems not rough to the touch; petals without hairs near the base of the broadened portion (an escape from gardens) . . . . *D. deltoides*, pl. 207
MAIDEN PINK (Europe)

Sagina

1 Sepals 4 (sometimes 5 in *S. procumbens;* annual)
2 Inflorescence glandular-hairy; petals absent or so small as to escape notice; stems mostly upright . . . . .
. . . . *S. apetala*
SMALL-FLOWERED PEARLWORT (Eurasia)

2 Inflorescence not glandular-hairy; petals (unless lacking) about half or three-fifths as long as the sepals; stems prostrate, rising at the tips (mostly coastal) . . . . *S. procumbens*
PROCUMBENT PEARLWORT (Eurasia)

1 Sepals 5
3 Fruits usually nodding (perennial; in wet places, usually above 3000 ft., 910 m) . . . . *S. saginoides*
ARCTIC PEARLWORT

3 Fruits upright
4 Pedicels and calyces somewhat glandular-hairy; leaves not succulent and not forming a basal rosette (annual) . . . . *S. decumbens* subsp. *occidentalis* (*S. occidentalis*)
WESTERN PEARLWORT

4 Pedicels and calyces not glandular-hairy; leaves succulent, and some of them forming a prominent basal rosette (perennial; in coastal habitats, Alaska to Calif.) . . . .
. . . . *S. maxima* subsp. *crassicaulis* (*S. crassicaulis*)
THICK-STEMMED PEARLWORT

Silene

Silene acaulis var. *subacaulescens,* not in this key, is easily identified because it forms low, cushionlike growths, generally less than 6 cm tall, that resemble some mosses. The leaves are about 10 mm long, 1 mm wide, and opposite. The flowers are borne singly on slender peduncles arising from the tips of the short stems. The calyx is usually about 5 mm long, and the corolla (white to pink or lavender) about 10 mm. This strictly high-montane perennial has a substantial woody root.

1 Pistil with 5 styles; fruit splitting apart by 5 bilobed teeth (annuals or short-lived perennials)
2 Petals white; flowers opening in the evening and closing by about noon . . . .
. . . . *S. latifolia* subsp. *alba* (*Lychnis alba*)
WHITE CAMPION (Europe)

2 Petals crimson; flowers opening in the morning and remaining open during the day . . . .
. . . . *S. dioica* (*Lychnis dioica*)
RED CAMPION (Eurasia)

Silene latifolia subsp. *alba* and *S. dioica* will hybridize and produce pink-flowered progeny.

1 Pistil with 3 styles; fruit splitting apart by 6 teeth
  3 Calyx tube with more than 10 lengthwise veins (some of these may be faint, and in *S. vulgaris* they are interconnected by branch veins)
    4 Calyx tube (this with about 15–20 nerves) becoming greatly inflated, the branches of the nerves forming a networklike pattern (outgrowths of petals reduced to 2 small bumps; perennial) . . . .
. . . . *S. vulgaris* (*S. cucubalus*)
BLADDER CAMPION (Europe)
    4 Calyx tube neither inflated nor with a networklike pattern of veins
      5 Petals (white to purplish) slightly toothed at the tip but not 2-lobed (calyx with 25–30 veins; annual) . . . . *S. conoidea*, p. 189
WEEDY CATCHFLY (Mediterranean Europe)
      5 Petals shallowly 2-lobed (annuals)
        6 Petals (white to pink) without outgrowths (calyx with 16–20 veins; Wash. and Oreg., where possibly introduced from Calif.) . . . . *S. multinervia*
MANY-VEINED CATCHFLY
        6 Petals (white to reddish) with outgrowths (calyx with about 30 veins) . . . . *S. conica*
STRIATED CATCHFLY (Europe)
  3 Calyx tube with 10 lengthwise nerves (some of these may be faint)
    7 Petals bright red (broadened portion of petals divided into 4 lobes, the 2 middle lobes often divided again; perennial; Josephine and Curry Cos., Oreg., to Calif.) . . . . *S. californica*, pl. 211
INDIAN PINK

    7 Petals not bright red (but they may be rose-pink in *S. hookeri*)

Cerastium nutans,
nodding chickweed

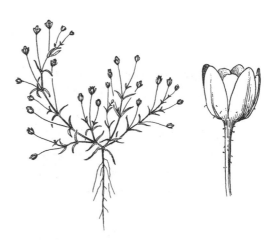

Sagina decumbens subsp. *occidentalis,*
western pearlwort

8 Broadened portion of petals either rounded or more or less abruptly squared-off, at most only very shallowly 2-lobed; annuals

  9 Outgrowths at the base of broadened portion of the petals inconspicuous, not so much as 0.5 mm long; internodes, especially in the upper portions of the plant, with broad, sticky bands (petals white to pink, extending beyond the calyx lobes for only 2–4 mm) . . . .*S. antirrhina*
SLEEPY CATCHFLY

  9 Outgrowths at the base of the broadened portion of the petals conspicuous, usually at least 1 mm long
   10 Plants somewhat bushy, not often more than 30 cm tall, obviously hairy; leaves sessile or nearly so (the petioles not very distinct) but not clasping the stems; petals white to pink or lavender, slightly twisted, much like the blades of a windmill (common weed) . . . . *S. gallica*, pl. 213
SMALL-FLOWERED CATCHFLY (Europe)

   10 Plants not bushy, commonly at least 30 cm tall, not at all hairy (or rarely slightly hairy); leaves sessile and more or less clasping the stems; petals pinkish lavender, not at all twisted . . . .*S. armeria*
SWEET WILLIAM CATCHFLY (Europe)

8 Broadened portion of petals deeply divided into 2 or more primary lobes

 11 Broadened upper portion of petals divided into 4–6 primary lobes, each of these divided into 2 secondary lobes (flowers with short pedicels, usually nodding; calyx somewhat inflated, generally sticky-glandular; corolla white; perennial, with at least several stems forming a bushy growth; Lane Co., Oreg., to Calif.) . . . . *S. campanulata* subsp. *glandulosa*, pl. 212
CAMPANULATE CAMPION

 11 Broadened upper portion of petals divided into only 2 or 4 lobes
  12 Broad upper portion of most petals divided into 4 lobes (sometimes only 2)
   13 All 4 lobes of the petals about the same length (flowers usually nodding; petals white to pink or pale yellow; Josephine and Jackson Cos., Oreg., to Calif.) . . . .*S. lemmonii*
LEMMON'S CAMPION

   13 Lateral lobes of petals distinctly shorter than those between them
    14 Basal leaves and those on lower portions of the flowering stems not often more than 6 mm wide
     15 Lower leaves rather conspicuously hairy on both surfaces; petals pink to rose or purplish (Curry, Josephine, and Jackson Cos., Oreg., to Calif.; not likely to be found below about 4000 ft., 1220 m) . . . .*S. grayi*
GRAY'S CATCHFLY

     15 Lower leaves not conspicuously hairy on either surface (there are, however, short hairs along the margins); corolla usually white or greenish, often purple-tinged (montane, in the Olympic Mountains, Wash., and Cascades, Brit. Col. to Wash.) . . . .*S. parryi*
PARRY'S CATCHFLY

    14 Basal leaves and those on the lower portions of the flowering stems usually more than 1 cm wide
     16 Plants low, compactly sprawling; corollas usually more than 2 cm wide when open, white, pale pink, deep rose-pink, violet, or purplish, the outgrowths at the bases of the broadened portions of the petals not toothed or lobed (perennial; Willamette Valley to SW Oreg. and Calif.) . . . .*S. hookeri* subsp. *hookeri*, pl. 214
HOOKER'S CATCHFLY, HOOKER'S PINK

     16 Plants upright, commonly more than 20 cm tall; corollas not often so much as 1.5 cm wide when open, greenish white to purplish, the outgrowths at the bases of the broadened portions of the petals irregularly toothed or lobed (lowermost portion of each petal with abundant hairs; perennial; Brit. Col. to Calif., mostly along the coast) . . . .
. . . . *S. scouleri* subsp. *grandis* (*S. scouleri* subsp. *pacifica*), pl. 215
SCOULER'S CATCHFLY, SEA-BLUFF CAMPION

Silene scouleri subsp. *scouleri,* found E of the crest of the Cascades, will perhaps occasionally be found on the W slope. Its leaves are less fleshy than those of subsp. *grandis,* and its petals do not have hairs on the lowermost portion.

12 Broad upper portion of most petals divided into only 2 lobes
  17 Broad upper portion of each petal divided into 2 lobes for more than half its length (plants annual, sometimes more than 75 cm tall, conspicuously hairy; larger lower leaves to about 8 cm long, 2.5 cm wide; broad upper portion of petals to 12 mm long, white to pink; style protruding prominently out of the corolla tube; some plants with mostly pistillate or staminate flowers) . . . . *S. dichotoma*
FORKING CATCHFLY (Eurasia)
  17 Broad upper portion of each petal not divided into 2 lobes for more than half its length
    18 Calyx lobes slender, at least 3 times as long as wide at the base; annual weed . . . . *S. noctiflora*
NIGHT-FLOWERING CATCHFLY (Europe)
    18 Calyx lobes not more than twice as long as wide at the base; native perennials
      19 Calyx usually not much more than 5 mm long, the lobes narrowing gradually to pointed tips and without membranous margins; petals white (Brit. Col. to Calif., also E of the Cascades and Sierra Nevada) . . . . *S. menziesii*
MENZIES' CAMPION
      19 Calyx usually 10–12 mm long, the lobes not much longer than wide
        20 Calyx lobes pointed at the tip; petals white or greenish, sometimes tinged with lavender (high montane in the Cascades, mostly E of the crest, Wash. to Oreg.) . . . . *S. suksdorfii*
SUKSDORF'S CATCHFLY
        20 Calyx lobes more or less rounded at the tip; petals white, greenish, pink, or purplish (NW Oreg. on coastal bluffs and on Saddle Mountain, Clatsop Co.) . . . . *S. douglasii* var. *oraria*
DOUGLAS' CATCHFLY

> *Silene douglasii* var. *douglasii* (here considered to include var. *monantha*), found E of the crest of the Cascades, perhaps occasionally enters our region in the W part of the Columbia River Gorge or on the W slope of the Cascades. Its leaves are less fleshy and more hairy than those of var. *oraria*.

Spergula-Spergularia Complex

1 Leaves (less than 1 mm wide) in whorls of about 8–10, most of the whorls farther apart than the length of the leaves; pistil with 5 styles (petals white, about 5 mm long; common weed) . . . . *Spergula arvensis*
CORN SPURREY (Europe)

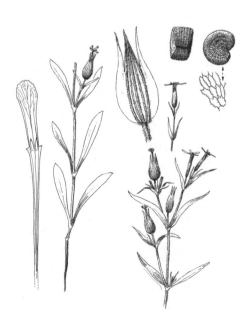

Silene conoidea,
weedy catchfly

Spergula arvensis,
corn spurrey

1 Leaves either strictly opposite or opposite and accompanied by 1 or more pairs of smaller leaves, thus forming what appear to be irregular whorls, these usually not much farther apart than the length of the leaves; pistil with 3 styles

  2 Stamens 2–5

    3 Tips of leaves with a short, nipplelike prolongation; sepals about twice as long as wide (at the edges of salt marshes) . . . . *Spergularia salina* var. *salina* (*S. marina*)
          SALT-MARSH SAND SPURREY

    3 Tips of leaves merely pointed, without a nipplelike prolongation; sepals at least 3 times as long as wide

      4 Stems and leaves sometimes glandular-hairy, sometimes not; leaves to about 4 cm long (around coastal salt marshes and mudflats) . . . . *Spergularia canadensis* var. *occidentalis*
            NORTHERN SAND SPURREY

      4 Stems and leaves always very glandular-hairy; leaves to about 1 cm long; occasional weed in waste places . . . . *Spergularia diandra*
            ALKALI SAND SPURREY (Europe)

  2 Stamens 7 or more

    5 Stipules almost as wide as long (less than 1.5 times as long as wide)

      6 Leaves to 5 cm long, the stipules 3–6 mm long; calyx not hairy (corolla white; around salt marshes) . . . . *Spergularia media*
            STOUT SAND SPURREY (Europe)

      6 Leaves to 2 cm long, the stipules 2–3 mm long; calyx glandular-hairy (corolla white to pink; sometimes at borders of salt marshes, sometimes in relatively dry, sandy, or hard-packed soils) . . . . *Spergularia bocconii*
            BOCCONE'S SAND SPURREY (Europe)

    5 Stipules decidedly longer than wide (petals pink)

      7 Leaves usually at least 15 mm long; petals 4–7 mm long; sepals 5–10 mm long; stamens almost always 10 (on seaside bluffs and around salt marshes) . . . . *Spergularia macrotheca* var. *macrotheca*, pl. 216
            BEACH SAND SPURREY

      7 Leaves to about 12 mm long; petals 2–5 mm long; sepals 3–5 mm long; stamens 6–10 (common weed) . . . . *Spergularia rubra*, pl. 217
            SAND SPURREY (Europe)

Stellaria

1 Stems, leaf petioles, and flower pedicels with hairs arranged in single lengthwise rows (leaves with prominent petioles; petals shorter than the sepals, divided nearly to the base; common weed) . . . *S. media*, pl. 219
            CHICKWEED (Eurasia)

1 Stems, petioles, and flower pedicels often hairy, but if so the hairs not arranged in single lengthwise rows

  2 Most larger leaves with wavy ("crisped") margins

    3 Plants usually with some more or less upright stems; most larger leaves at least 25 mm long, 13 mm wide, acutely pointed at the tip; flowers borne singly in the axils of the leaves; sepals with prominent membranous margins; petals, if present, much shorter than the sepals (in wet places) . . . . . . *S. crispa*
            CRISPED STARWORT

    3 Plants almost completely prostrate, with stems (commonly to about 50 cm long) occasionally rooting at the nodes; larger leaves rarely so much as 15 mm long, 6 mm wide, rounded or slightly pointed at the tip; flowers in inflorescences originating in the leaf axils; sepals without membranous margins; petals present, nearly or fully as long as the sepals and deeply divided into 2 lobes (weed in wet lawns but not widespread) . . . . *S. alsine*
            BOG STITCHWORT (Europe)

2 Margins of leaf blades not wavy

  4 Petals, if present, shorter than the sepals

    5 Plants annual, small, with a few to many nearly threadlike flowering stems (not often more than 15 cm long) originating from the basal portion; most leaves on flowering stems bractlike, less than 1 cm long (petals, when present, less than half as long as the sepals) . . . . *S. nitens*
                SHINING CHICKWEED

    5 Plants perennial, usually sprawling but with some stems becoming erect

      6 Larger leaf blades typically more than 3 cm long, elongated, 4–6 times as long as wide (petals, when present, from very small to not quite as long as the sepals) . . . . *S. borealis* subsp. *sitchana* (*S. calycantha* subspp. *sitchana* and *bongardiana*), pl. 218
                NORTHERN STARWORT

      6 Larger leaf blades typically less than 2.5 cm long, oval, not so much as 4 times as long as wide

        7 Tips of sepals blunt; largest leaves to about 12 mm long (petals absent; montane) . . . . *S. obtusa*
                BLUNT-SEPALED STARWORT

        7 Tips of sepals pointed; largest leaves to about 25 mm long (petals present or absent, montane) . . . . *S. calycantha*
                CUP-FLOWERED STARWORT

  4 Petals commonly present and as long as, or longer than, the sepals

    8 Leaves noticeably succulent; flowers originating singly in the leaf axils (in coastal salt marshes, Alaska to Lincoln Co., Oreg.) . . . . *S. humifusa*
                CREEPING CHICKWEED

    8 Leaves not obviously succulent; flowers in rather open inflorescences at the ends of the stems

      9 Leaf margins (when the underside of a leaf is viewed with a strong lens) appearing rough and bumpy (in meadows and on streambanks, mostly above 2000 ft., 610 m) . . . . *S. longifolia*
                LONG-LEAVED STARWORT

      9 Leaf margins smooth

        10 Margins of sepals with slender hairs; lobes of petals separated for nearly the full length of the petals (weed in lawns and fields) . . . . *S. graminea*
                LESSER STITCHWORT (Europe)

        10 Margins of sepals without obvious hairs; lobes of petals only about half as long as the petals (not likely to be found below about 4000 ft., 1220 m) . . . . *S. longipes* subsp. *longipes*
                LONG-STALKED STARWORT

CELASTRACEAE Staff-Tree Family

There are only two native representatives of the staff-tree family in our region. Both are shrubs with simple opposite leaves and flowers that are distinctive because the pistil is sunk into a disklike structure around whose edges the stamens are attached. This key gives more information concerning the flowers.

1 Evergreen; leaf blades to 3 cm long, more or less oval; flowers with 4 calyx lobes, 4 petals (about 2 mm long, brownish red), and 4 stamens; fruit slightly elongated, about 3–4 mm long, with a pointed tip (in our region mostly at moderate elevations in the Cascades and Siskiyou Mountains but abundant at scattered localities in the lowlands of the Puget Sound region, San Juan Archipelago, and adjacent areas; also in Calif.) . . . . *Paxistima myrsinites*, pl. 222
                OREGON BOXWOOD, FALSE BOXWOOD

1 Deciduous; leaves usually more than 5 cm long, narrowing to a slender tip; flowers with 5 calyx lobes, 5 petals (densely dotted with purplish brown), and 5 stamens; fruit 3-lobed, the seeds enclosed by orange tissue when the fruit cracks open (mostly from Lewis Co., Wash., to Calif., but also known to occur on Vancouver Island, Brit. Col.) . . . . *Euonymus occidentalis* var. *occidentalis*, pls. 220 & 221
                WESTERN BURNING BUSH, WESTERN WAHOO

CERATOPHYLLACEAE Hornwort Family

Hornworts belonging to the genus *Ceratophyllum* are submerged freshwater plants that could be confused with bladderworts (Lentibulariaceae) or water milfoils (*Myriophyllum*, Haloragaceae) because they are about the same size (stems to as long as 1 m or more) and because the leaves, arranged in whorls, are divided into slender lobes. Hornwort leaves, however, are stiff and, in our species, somewhat rough to the touch. The small flowers, sessile in the axils of the leaves, have neither a calyx nor a corolla, but there is a several-lobed involucre that resembles a calyx. Staminate flowers have numerous stamens; pistillate flowers have a pistil that develops into a one-seeded fruit about 5 mm long.

Ceratophyllum

1 Lobes of largest leaves commonly dividing only once or twice, rarely 3 times; plants somewhat rough to the touch because of small bumps on the leaves (common) . . . . *C. demersum*
ROUGH HORNWORT

1 Lobes of largest leaves dividing 3–4 times; plants not rough to the touch, the bumps on the leaves low or absent (Brit. Col. to Oreg.; relatively rare) . . . . *C. echinatum*
SMOOTH HORNWORT

CHENOPODIACEAE Goosefoot Family

The goosefoot family consists mostly of herbaceous plants, although some of its representatives are shrubs or near-shrubs. The leaves and stems are often mealy, owing to the presence of small scales, and some species are succulent. The flowers, usually clustered, are small and lack petals, and in certain genera there are staminate and pistillate flowers, sometimes on separate plants. Each fruit, dry at maturity, contains a single seed.

Spinach and the beet (whose cultivated forms include the sugar beet and Swiss chard) belong to this family. Other members of the group have been used as food and medicines by aboriginal peoples in various parts of the world.

1 Stems succulent, jointed; leaves reduced to scales (plants of salt marshes) . . . . *Salicornia*
1 Stems, if succulent, not jointed; leaves obvious, not scalelike (but they may be slender and/or spine-tipped)
  2 Leaves slender, most of them spine-tipped (upper leaves much shorter than the lower ones, which may be as long as about 5 cm; plants bushy, to 1 m tall; widely distributed weed but not often found in our region) . . . . *Salsola tragus* (*S. kali*), pl. 224
RUSSIAN THISTLE (Eurasia)
  2 Leaves not spine-tipped
    3 Leaves succulent, about as thick as wide, mostly 1–2 cm long (in coastal salt marshes, Alaska to Wash.) . . . . *Suaeda calceoliformis* (*S. maritima*)
SEA BLITE
    3 Leaves neither especially succulent nor as thick as wide
      4 Flowers (in short, dense inflorescences) more or less hidden in the axils of closely spaced, broad bracts; perianth represented by a single papery, scalelike structure, which is perhaps a sepal (plants to about 50 cm tall, upright; leaves narrow, to 5 cm long, 4 mm wide; 1 to a few flowers in the axil of each bract; flowers with 2 stamens, 1 pistil; fruit dark green to black, round, 3–4 mm wide; in our region, in sandy habitats along the Columbia River) . . . . *Corispermum hyssopifolium*
BUGSEED (Europe)
      4 Flowers not hidden in the axils of closely spaced, broad bracts (but in species of *Atriplex* the pistillate flowers have a pair of bracts below them; these bracts enlarge as the fruits develop, so the fruits become sandwiched between them); calyx, when present (it is often lacking in pistillate flowers), usually 5-lobed (but there are exceptions)

5 Flowers with either stamens or a pistil but not both (furthermore, staminate and pistillate flowers may be on separate plants); fruits sandwiched between a pair of bracts (these are small at the flowering stage) . . . . ***Atriplex***

5 All the flowers with stamens and a pistil; fruits not sandwiched between a pair of bracts . . . . ***Chenopodium***

Atriplex

1 Extensively branched, sprawling evergreen perennial forming a ground cover less than 25 cm tall; bracts enclosing fruit red, fleshy (leaf blades usually 1.5–2.5 cm long, about twice as long as wide, widest near the middle, with a wavy or indistinctly toothed margin and a mealy underside; in waste places, especially in saline and alkaline habitats; not yet so common in the Pacific Northwest as in central and S Calif.) . . . . ***A. semibaccata***
AUSTRALIAN SALTBUSH (Australia)

1 Annuals, usually upright and not forming an extensively branched ground cover; bracts enclosing fruit neither conspicuously fleshy nor red

  2 Pistillate flowers of 2 types: some lacking a perianth and enclosed by 2 oval bracts usually at least 1 cm long; others with a 3- or 5-lobed perianth and not enclosed by bracts (fruits developing in flowers with a perianth are squat, whereas those developing between bracts are flattened from side to side; plants to more than 1 m tall; largest leaves to more than 10 cm long, widest near the base; garden plant, occasionally escaping) . . . . ***A. hortensis***
GARDEN ORACHE (Europe)

  2 Pistillate flowers all alike, and all (whether with or without a perianth) enclosed by a pair of bracts

    3 Pistillate flowers with a lobed perianth and enclosed by a pair of oval, smooth-edged, mealy bracts about 2 mm long, these united for nearly all their length (leaf blades to about 3 cm long, widest near the middle, smooth-margined; not often encountered W of the Cascades) . . . . ***A. dioica***
RILLSCALE

    3 Pistillate flowers without a perianth, the bracts enclosing them usually more than 2 mm long, generally somewhat triangular or irregularly rhomboid, united for not more than half their length, and often with pointed marginal projections and/or with projections on the broad surfaces

      4 Leaves of the flowering branches, like those on lower portions of the plant, coarsely toothed and usually also gray-mealy, at least on the underside; larger leaf blades more or less triangular but not with a pair of pronounced lateral projections at the base (foliage often becoming reddish; bracts enclosing fruits triangular or arrowhead-shaped, the margins toothed and the broad surfaces with conspicuous projections; weed, not often found W of the Cascades) . . . . ***A. rosea***
RED ORACHE (Europe)

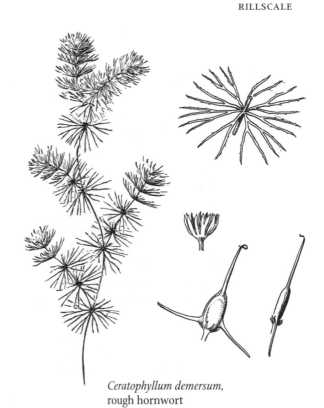

Ceratophyllum demersum,
rough hornwort

4 Leaves of the flowering branches not coarsely toothed, and the leaves, in general, greenish on both surfaces except for a powdery white deposit or slight mealiness; larger leaf blades often with a pair of prominent lateral projections at the base; seeds of 2 types, the black ones, on average, smaller than the brown ones (plants of salt marshes and other saline habitats; the 3 species under this choice vary extensively, and some plants may be difficult to identify with confidence)

  5 Bracts enclosing pistillate flowers slightly thickened near the base due to the presence of spongy tissue and becoming brown or blackish at maturity; stems often sprawling (margins of bracts enclosing pistillate flowers usually not toothed, the broad surfaces smooth or with a pair of small, blunt protuberances) . . . . ***A. prostrata***

             FAT HEN (probably introduced long ago from Eurasia)

  5 Bracts enclosing pistillate flowers not appreciably thickened near the base by the presence of spongy tissue and not becoming brown or blackish at maturity; plants usually upright

    6 Bracts enclosing fruits triangular or rhomboid, sharply angled and usually toothed and/or with sharp projections on the broad surfaces . . . . ***A. patula*** (*A. hastata* var. *patula*)

             SPEAR ORACHE (believed to have been introduced from Europe)

    6 Bracts enclosing fruits oval or triangular, sometimes slightly elongated but not sharply angled, toothed, or with sharp projections on the broad surfaces . . . . ***A. gmelinii*** (*A. patula* vars. *obtusa* and *zosterifolia*)

             GMELIN'S ORACHE

Chenopodium

1 Leaves and stems glandular, usually strongly scented (leaves often pinnately lobed, although the lobes are shallow)

  2 Plants sprawling; calyx without distinct lobes but with 3–5 inconspicuous teeth . . . . ***C. multifidum*** (*Roubieva multifida*)

             CUT-LEAVED GOOSEFOOT (South America)

  2 Plants upright; calyx with 5 distinct lobes

    3 Largest leaf blades rarely more than 2 cm long; flowers in nearly round, axillary clusters; calyx with yellow glands . . . . ***C. pumilio*** (*C. carinatum* of some references)

             LITTLE GOOSEFOOT (Australia)

    3 Largest leaf blades commonly at least 3 cm long, sometimes as long as 10 cm; flowers usually in several clusters on each axillary inflorescence

      4 Flowers on short but distinct pedicels; branches of inflorescence noticeably curved . . . . ***C. botrys***

             JERUSALEM OAK (Europe)

      4 Flowers sessile; branches of inflorescence straight . . . . ***C. ambrosioides***

             MEXICAN TEA (tropical America)

1 Leaves and stems not glandular (but the leaves are often scurfy or powdery, especially on the underside), sometimes unpleasantly scented

  5 Most or all fruits as long as or longer than wide, egg-shaped; calyx with 3 lobes (if there are some pumpkin-shaped fruits, the calyces enclosing these have 4–5 lobes)

    6 Most flowers in clusters on short, leafy branches of the main stems; calyx not becoming fleshy or decidedly red (it may become pinkish, however) . . . . ***C. rubrum***

             RED GOOSEFOOT

Atriplex patula,
spear orache

6 Most flowers in dense, round clusters (these are in fact short cymes) along the main stems; calyx becoming fleshy and red by the time the fruits are ripe

   7 Bracts absent beneath flowers near the tip of each head; flowers at the tops of the stems developing before those at progressively lower levels .... *C. capitatum*

                                    INDIAN INK, STRAWBERRY BLITE

   7 Bracts present throughout each flower head; flowers on the lower portions of the stems developing before those at progressively higher levels .... *C. foliosum*

5 Most or all fruits wider than long, somewhat pumpkin-shaped; calyx with 5 lobes

   8 Stems (especially the lower ones) mostly sprawling, the plants therefore not often so much as 30 cm tall (leaf blades pale green on the underside; fruit usually wider than long but sometimes longer than wide) .... *C. glaucum*

                                      OAK-LEAF GOOSEFOOT (Eurasia)

   8 Stems upright, the plants commonly at least 30 cm tall (usually much taller in *C. album* and *C. simplex*)

     9 Underside of leaf blades completely powdery white, the upper surface dull green .... *C. album*

                                     PIGWEED (probably Europe)

     9 Underside of leaf blades mealy or sparsely powdery, the upper surface shiny, dark green

       10 Leaf blades rarely more than 6 cm long, irregularly toothed for most of their length; flowers crowded in short inflorescences, conspicuously mealy or powdery .... *C. murale*

                                    WALL GOOSEFOOT (Europe)

       10 Leaf blades often more than 10 cm long, with only a few large teeth or shallow, pointed lobes, these mostly in the lower half; flowers in rather open, elongated racemes, these scarcely if at all mealy or powdery .... *C. simplex* (*C. hybridum* var. *simplex*)

                                     MAPLE-LEAVED GOOSEFOOT

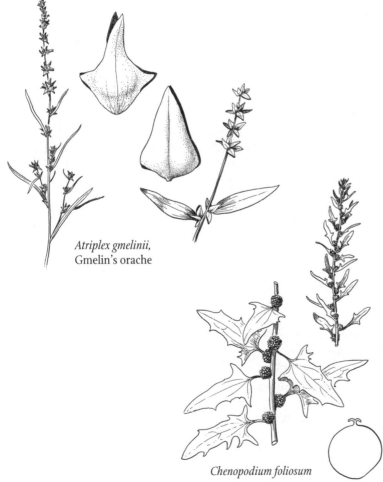

Atriplex gmelinii,
Gmelin's orache

Chenopodium foliosum

Chenopodium album,
pigweed

Salicornia

1 Middle flower in each group of 3 only slightly larger than the ones on both sides of it; perennial (common in almost all salt marshes) .... *S. virginica* (*S. ambigua, S. pacifica*), pl. 223
PICKLEWEED

1 Middle flower in each group of 3 about twice as tall as the ones on both sides of it; annual (usually turning bright red in fall; in salt marshes but not so commonly encountered as *S. virginica*) ....
.... *S. maritima* (*S. europaea*)
SAMPHIRE

> *Salicornia rubra,* red glasswort, a species found on alkaline soils inland, is occasionally encountered in our region but apparently not in salt marshes. The units into which its inflorescences are divided are only slightly longer than thick, whereas in *S. maritima* they are almost always obviously longer than thick. The seeds of *S. rubra* are only 1–1.2 mm long; those of *S. maritima* are at least 1.3 mm long, sometimes as long as 2 mm.

CONVOLVULACEAE Morning-Glory Family

Most members of the morning-glory family that are wild in our region are climbing or trailing plants with alternate leaves. The flowers have five separate or nearly separate sepals, a funnel-shaped corolla with five rather indistinct lobes, and five stamens that are attached to the corolla tube. The corolla is noticeably twisted when in the bud stage. The pistil, in our species, is partitioned lengthwise into two divisions, each of which normally produces two seeds.

Many morning glories of the genera *Convolvulus* and *Ipomoea* are valuable ornamental plants. The family has also given us the sweet potato, a species of *Ipomoea,* and the field bindweed, *C. arvensis,* a pest on farms and in gardens.

1 Corolla about 3 mm long, barely longer than the calyx and deeply divided into lobes (leaf blades with a kidney-shaped outline, 1–2 cm wide and not longer than wide; corolla whitish, the lobes rounded; creeping ground cover, native, but cultivated and escaping into habitats where it is not indigenous; coastal, Curry Co., Oreg., to Calif.) .... *Dichondra donnelliana*

1 Corolla more than 1 cm long, extending well beyond the calyx and not divided into distinct lobes
  2 Leaves thick, rather fleshy, the blades with a kidney-shaped outline; corolla mostly pink; limited to backshores of sandy beaches .... *Calystegia soldanella* (*Convolvulus soldanella*), pl. 226
BEACH MORNING GLORY
  2 Leaves neither thick nor fleshy, the blades more nearly triangular, arrowhead- or heart-shaped than kidney-shaped; not primarily on backshores of sandy beaches
    3 Bracts below each flower about twice as long as wide, so large as to nearly hide the calyx and originating immediately below the base of the calyx
      4 Leaf blades with a heart-shaped outline, owing to the presence of an indentation where the petiole is attached; corolla white to pink; trailing or climbing (widely distributed in temperate regions of the world; most populations in our region probably not native; several subspecies have been proposed) .... *Calystegia sepium* (*Convolvulus sepium*)
HEDGE BINDWEED
      4 Leaf blades more nearly triangular or arrowhead-shaped than heart-shaped, there being no conspicuous indentation where the petiole is attached; corolla white; mostly trailing, not climbing; in dry, well-drained habitats (Willamette Valley to SW Oreg., also in the Cascades of S Wash. and Oreg.) .... *Calystegia atriplicifolia* subsp. *atriplicifolia* (*Convolvulus nyctagineus,* in part)
NIGHT-BLOOMING MORNING GLORY
    3 Bracts below each flower at least 3 times as long as wide, not so large as to nearly hide the calyx and separated at least 1 mm from the base of the calyx

5 Bracts below each flower usually at least 5 mm long, originating 1–7 mm below the base of the calyx (corolla white to creamy yellow; Douglas Co., Oreg., to Calif.) . . . . ***Calystegia occidentalis* subsp. *occidentalis*** (*Convolvulus polymorphus*), pl. 225
PALE MORNING GLORY

5 Bracts below each flower rarely so much as 5 mm long, very slender, usually originating at least 10 mm (sometimes 20 mm) below the base of the calyx (corolla white or pink-tinged; common and pernicious weed) . . . . ***Convolvulus arvensis***
FIELD MORNING GLORY, SMALL BINDWEED (Europe)

CORNACEAE Dogwood Family

Members of the dogwood family native to North America have deciduous, opposite leaves. In certain species, however, successive pairs of leaves may be so close together that they appear to form a whorl. Furthermore, a few leaves just below the flower clusters of some species are conspicuously white, faintly yellowish, or pinkish and are often called petals by persons who do not realize that they are not even flower parts. The flowers themselves are small; each has four petals and four stamens, and the lower part of the four-lobed calyx is joined to the pistil and contributes to the fleshy, two-seeded fruit.

Some especially valuable cultivated plants belong to this family: *Cornus florida*, the so-called flowering dogwood of eastern North America, *C. kousa* of Asia, and certain species of *Aucuba*, also of Asia. Of the three dogwoods that grow wild in our region, *C. sericea* subsp. *occidentalis* is perhaps the most adaptable to cultivation, although it may require more moisture than some gardeners can give it. *Cornus nuttallii* is spectacular when in flower and when its foliage turns red in the fall, but it is susceptible to a serious disease caused by a fungus. *Cornus unalaschkensis*, like *C. canadensis*, its counterpart in eastern North America, is a marvelous ground cover for woodland habitats.

Cornus

1 Low, mostly herbaceous plants, rarely more than 20 cm tall, with a whorl of 4 or more substantial leaves at the top of the stem (lower leaves much reduced); flowers in a small cluster above 4 white bracts; fruits orange-red . . . . ***C. unalaschkensis***, pl. 230
DWARF DOGWOOD, BUNCHBERRY

Cornus unalaschkensis was long considered to be identical with *C. canadensis* of E North America. It is now believed to have originated as a hybrid between *C. canadensis* and *C. suecica* of N Europe, northern Asia, and extreme northwest North America.

Calystegia sepium,
hedge bindweed

Convolvulus arvensis,
field morning glory

1 Trees or shrubs
  2 Trees to about 20 m tall; flowers in a dense hemispherical cluster above several large, white or pale yellowish bracts; fruits orange-red .... *C. nuttallii*, pl. 228
     WESTERN DOGWOOD, the provincial flower of British Columbia
  2 Large shrubs, mostly less than 5 m tall; flowers in rather open cymes, these without any bracts directly beneath them; fruits white or bluish (young branches, and sometimes older stems, usually reddish)
    3 Leaf blades mostly 3–6 cm long, often slightly gray-green on at least the upper surface, paler on the underside; principal veins arranged in 3–4 pairs; not restricted to wet habitats (Jackson and Josephine Cos., Oreg., to Calif.) .... *C. glabrata*, pl. 227
     SMOOTH DOGWOOD
    3 Leaf blades mostly 5–10 cm long, green on both surfaces but paler on the underside; principal veins arranged in 4–7 (usually 5–6) pairs; usually in wet habitats, especially along streams ....
     .... *C. sericea* subsp. *occidentalis* (*C. stolonifera* var. *occidentalis*), pl. 229
     RED OSIER DOGWOOD

CRASSULACEAE Stonecrop Family

Most plants belonging to the stonecrop family are succulent perennials. The flowers usually have a calyx with five lobes or five separate sepals, five petals, five or ten stamens, and a pistil consisting of five divisions that may separate at maturity. The genus *Crassula*, however, is represented in our region by annual species whose flower parts are in threes or fours.

1 Small annuals, mostly less than 5 cm tall; flowers usually with 4 (sometimes 3) greenish sepals and 4 whitish petals, the latter not more than 2 mm long; stamens 4 .... *Crassula*
1 Substantial perennials, the flowering stems usually at least 10 cm tall; flowers with 5 sepals and 5 petals, the latter more than 2 mm long (usually more than 4 mm); stamens 10
  2 Leaves of basal rosettes to more than 5 cm long and 2 cm wide, somewhat pointed at the tip; leaves on the flowering stems much smaller and very different from those of the rosettes .... *Dudleya*
  2 Leaves of the rosettes, whether or not these have flowering stems, not so much as 2 cm wide and not pointed at the tip; leaves on the flowering stems smaller but not markedly different from those of the rosettes .... *Sedum*

Crassula

1 Sepals usually 3 (stems usually upright; sepals pointed at the tip, slightly longer than the petals; weed in open, usually disturbed areas) .... *C. tillaea*
    MOSS PYGMYWEED (Mediterranean region)
1 Sepals usually 4
  2 Plants upright; flowers in clusters; sepals pointed at the tip, usually longer than the petals; in open fields .... *C. connata* var. *connata* (*C. erecta*, *Tillaea erecta*), pl. 231
    ERECT PYGMYWEED
  2 Plants sprawling with stem tips rising; flowers single; sepals blunt at the tips, usually shorter than the petals; in muddy areas that dry out in summer .... *C. aquatica*
    PYGMYWEED

Dudleya

1 Pedicels of individual flowers usually 5–10 mm long, sometimes considerably longer (to about 30 mm); inflorescence as a whole usually rather loose (inland, Josephine Co., Oreg., to Calif.) .... *D. cymosa*, pl. 232
    INLAND DUDLEYA
1 Pedicels of individual flowers to 3 mm long, sometimes barely evident; inflorescence as a whole usually dense (on cliffs at the coast, Coos Co., Oreg., to Calif.) .... *D. farinosa*
    SEA-CLIFF DUDLEYA

Sedum

1 Most rosette leaves about as thick as wide and usually widest at or below the middle

    2 Leaves, including the ones on flowering stems, slender, often nearly 10 times as long as wide, pointed at the tip and with a prominent keel on the upper surface; midribs of decayed leaves often persisting on the stems (stems sometimes with bulblike reproductive buds in place of upper leaves and flowers; petals yellow; in our region on the Olympic Peninsula and a few places in the Willamette Valley, also Josephine and Jackson Cos., Oreg., to Calif.) . . . . *S. stenopetalum* **var.** *stenopetalum* (*S. douglasii*)

                                                                     NARROW-PETALED STONECROP

    2 Leaves rather stout, rarely more than 5 times as long as wide, blunt at the tip and without a keel on the upper surface; midribs of decayed leaves not persisting (but in *S. acre,* entire leaves persist after they have dried)

        3 Leaves commonly more than 1 cm long (petals usually 6–7 mm long, yellow)

            4 Leaves to 2 cm long, most with small bumps, those on the flowering stems scattered, usually not overlapping one another . . . . *S. lanceolatum* **var.** *lanceolatum* (*S. stenopetalum* of some references)

                                                       LANCE-PETALED STONECROP

            4 Leaves sometimes to 3 cm long, smooth, most of those on the flowering stems overlapping one another (along the coast, on islands of the San Juan Archipelago, and areas nearby) . . . . *S. lanceolatum* **var.** *nesioticum*, pl. 233

                                                           ISLAND STONECROP

                The slight differences between *S. lanceolatum* vars. *lanceolatum* and *nesioticum* are perhaps due to environmental influences.

        3 Leaves not often more than 1 cm long

            5 Petals (yellow to white) turned back; plants not mat-forming; annual or biennial (Jackson Co., Oreg., to Calif.) . . . . *S. radiatum*

            5 Petals not turned back; plants mat-forming; perennial (escapes from cultivation, often so well established that they may appear to be native)

                6 Petals yellow, about 6 mm long; leaves (slightly flattened on both surfaces) 3–6 mm long, bright green, usually persisting as membranous structures for a long time after withering . . . . *S. acre*

                                      WALL PEPPER (Europe)

                6 Petals white, 2–4 mm long; leaves (slightly flattened on the upper surface) 8–12 mm long, mostly dark green, separating cleanly from the stem, not persisting as membranous structures . . . . *S. album*

                         WHITE STONECROP (Europe)

1 Most leaves of the rosettes much wider than thick and widest above the middle

    7 Inflorescence usually with 3–4 main branches arising at about the same level on the flowering stems (petals yellow but sometimes becoming pink on aging)

        8 Most leaves on flowering stems opposite (petals yellow, about 3 times as long as the calyx lobes; Cascades and Olympic Mountains, not often below 3500 ft., 1070 m) . . . . *S. divergens*

                       CASCADES STONECROP

        8 Leaves on flowering stems alternate

Sedum stenopetalum var. *stenopetalum,* narrow-petaled stonecrop

9 Leaves usually with an obvious whitish coating; outer leaves of rosettes much larger than the inner ones; petals separate to the base, 7–10 mm long, not much more than twice as long as the calyx lobes; fruits spreading outward as they ripen, the persistent styles nearly or fully half as long as the fruits (the most common lowland *Sedum* of the region) . . . . *S. spathulifolium* subsp. *spathulifolium*, pl. 235
BROAD-LEAVED STONECROP

9 Leaves not often with an obvious whitish coating; outer leaves of rosettes about the same size as the inner ones; petals united at the base for about 2 mm, 8–13 mm long, 3–4 times as long as the calyx lobes; fruits remaining nearly upright as they ripen, the persistent styles about one-third as long as the fruits . . . . *S. oreganum*, pl. 234
OREGON STONECROP

7 Inflorescence paniclelike, the several (sometimes more than 10) main branches arising at distinctly different levels on the flowering stems

10 Leaves of rosettes spaced at least 2 mm apart, the internodes of the stems therefore evident; petals (cream to light yellow) united for a considerable distance above the base

11 Calyx lobes usually bluntly rounded at the tip; inflorescence usually with not more than 40 flowers (mostly above 3000 ft., 910 m; Jackson Co., Oreg., to Calif.) . . . .*S. obtusatum* subsp. *retusum*
SIERRA STONECROP

11 Calyx lobes usually somewhat pointed at the tip; inflorescence sometimes with as many as 70 flowers (mostly above 3000 ft., 910 m; Cascades and Siskiyou Mountains, Oreg. to Calif.) . . . . *S. oregonense*
CREAMY STONECROP

10 Leaves of rosettes so crowded that the internodes are not evident; petals separate to the base

12 Plants to about 20 cm tall when flowering; inflorescence (stem, branches, and leaves) obviously whitish; larger rosette leaves (sometimes slightly more than 3 cm long) at least 3.5 times as long as wide (petals cream to pale yellow; not likely to be found below 4000 ft., 1220 m; Jackson Co., Oreg., to Calif.) . . . . *S. oblanceolatum*
APPLEGATE STONECROP

12 Plants often more than 30 cm tall when flowering; inflorescence not obviously whitish; rosette leaves (these to 5 cm long) not often more than 3 times as long as wide

13 Pedicels, calyces, and petals with numerous small, gland-tipped outgrowths; petals yellow, to 12 mm long, united for about one-fourth their length, the free portions alternating with slender auxiliary structures; anthers of stamens not reaching the tips of the stigmas (Josephine Co., Oreg.) . . . . *S. moranii*
MORAN'S STONECROP

13 Pedicels, calyces, and petals without small, gland-tipped outgrowths; petals white to pale pink (occasionally yellow in *S. laxum* subsp. *laxum*), 8–10 mm long, united for about one-third their length, the free portions not alternating with slender auxiliary structures; anthers of stamens reaching beyond the tips of the stigmas

14 Leaves of flowering stems much longer than wide; rosette leaves to 5 cm long (but usually shorter); plants to 40 cm tall (petals sometimes yellow; Curry and Josephine Cos., Oreg., to Calif.) . . . . *S. laxum* subsp. *laxum*
LAX STONECROP

14 Leaves of flowering stems at most only slightly longer than wide; rosette leaves to about 3 cm long; plants to 25 cm tall (Curry and Josephine Cos., Oreg., to Calif.) . . . . *S. laxum* subsp. *heckneri*
HECKNER'S STONECROP

In SW Oreg. some specimens cannot definitely be assigned to *S. laxum* subsp. *laxum* or subsp. *heckneri*.

CUCURBITACEAE Gourd Family

The gourd family consists largely of plants that climb or trail and that have tendrils originating in the leaf axils. It includes many of our important food plants, including cucumbers, watermelons, cantaloupes, squashes, and pumpkins, and certain species that are sources of medicinal substances. Our only wild representative is *Marah oreganus* (pl. 236), called coast manroot, a perennial whose huge tuberlike root, sometimes more than 50 cm in diameter, lives for many years. The aboveground stems, appearing in spring, bear leaves whose somewhat irregularly lobed blades may be as wide as 30 cm. Staminate flowers, in conspicuous upright inflorescences, usually have five white petals alternating with five very small calyx lobes; the cuplike lower portion of the flower, which is here interpreted as a combined calyx-corolla tube, is united to the fruit-forming part of the pistil. There are three stamens. Arising from the same leaf axil that produces the staminate inflorescences is a single pistillate flower. The portion of the pistil located below the base of the calyx-corolla tube develops into a more or less egg-shaped, soft-spined fruit as long as 6 cm or more; this eventually dries out and cracks apart near the tip to release the one or two seeds, which are usually about 2 cm long.

Echinocystis lobata, prickly cucumber, an annual species introduced from central and eastern North America, has been found in southwestern British Columbia. Its leaf blades have five sharply angular lobes, and its staminate flowers usually have six petals. The fruits are more conspicuously bristly than those of *Marah oreganus,* and the seeds, about 1.5 cm long, are flattened.

CUSCUTACEAE Dodder Family

Dodders are rootless parasites with almost no chlorophyll (a little can be detected in the calyx) and greatly reduced leaves. They parasitize other flowering plants, penetrating the tissues of their hosts by specialized branches of their slender, twining stems. The small flowers typically have five calyx and corolla lobes and five stamens, which are attached to the corolla tube in line with the clefts between the lobes. The pistil, with two styles, develops into a small dry fruit with one or a few seeds. The stems of most dodders are yellow or orange, which makes them easy to see on the plants they parasitize. This offbeat group was for a long time included in the morning-glory family (Convolvulaceae).

Cuscuta

1 Corolla usually 4-lobed, the lobes rounded at the tip
.... *C. cephalanthi*
BUTTONBUSH DODDER
1 Corolla 5-lobed, the lobes pointed at the tip
  2 Corolla without a scale below each stamen
    3 Corolla lobes more or less upright or spreading outward; anthers less than 0.5 mm long, shorter than the filaments (Lane Co., Oreg., to Calif.)
.... *C. occidentalis*
WESTERN DODDER
    3 Corolla lobes turning back; anthers about 0.7 mm long, as long as the filaments
      4 Corolla tube not bulging outward between the stamens (Jackson Co., Oreg., to Calif.) ....
.... *C. californica* var. *californica*
CALIFORNIA DODDER
      4 Corolla tube bulging outward between the stamens (Jackson Co., Oreg., to Calif.) ....
.... *C. californica* var. *breviflora*
  2 Corolla with a fringed scale below each stamen (in some species the scales partly cover the filaments of the stamens)

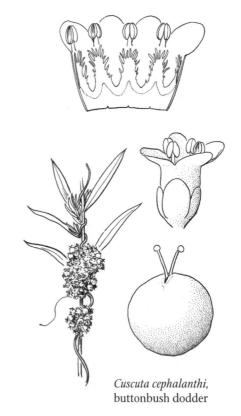

Cuscuta cephalanthi,
buttonbush dodder

    5 Corolla tube extending well beyond the tips of the calyx lobes ....*C. subinclusa*
LONG-FLOWERED DODDER

    5 Corolla not extending beyond the tips of the calyx lobes

      6 Stigmas slender, about half as long as the styles ....*C. epithymum*
THYME DODDER (Eurasia)

      6 Stigmas more or less globular, very stout

        7 Calyx lobes longer than wide (from late spring to summer, almost always present in salt marshes, where its usual host is *Salicornia virginica*) ....*C. salina* var. *major,* pl. 237
SALT-MARSH DODDER

        7 Calyx lobes about as long as wide or slightly wider than long ....*C. pentagona*
FIVE-ANGLED DODDER

DIPSACACEAE Teasel Family

In our region the teasel family is represented by two somewhat weedy biennial species of *Dipsacus* introduced from Europe. They grow stiffly to a height of more than 1 m. The stems are prickly, and the bases of the opposite leaves are fused in such a way that they form a cup in which water collects. The compact inflorescence is more or less thimble-shaped and has long spinelike bracts beneath it as well as shorter bracts around the small flowers. The whitish corolla tube, about 1 cm long, flares out into two larger lobes and two smaller lobes; the smaller lobes are usually pale purple. There are four stamens and a pistil that develops into an achene. Because of the way the spines on the small bracts around its individual flowers are curved downward, *D. sativus* has long been used in textile mills for raising the nap on woollen cloth.

Dipsacus

1 Bracts beneath the inflorescence curving upward and some of them longer than the inflorescence; bracts associated with individuals flowers ending in a straight spine .... *D. fullonum* (*D. sylvestris* or *D. fullonum* var. *sylvestris* of some references), pl. 238
COMMON TEASEL (Europe)

1 Bracts beneath the inflorescence directed outward, generally shorter than the inflorescence; bracts associated with individual flowers ending in a down-curved spine (known to be established in Douglas Co., Oreg., and perhaps found elsewhere in our region; more common in Calif.) .... *D. sativus* (*D. fullonum* of some references)
FULLER'S TEASEL (Europe)

DROSERACEAE Sundew Family

Sundews live in moist habitats, especially sphagnum bogs. Their basal leaves are covered with reddish hairs whose sticky tips trap insects. Longer hairs at the edges of the leaves turn inward to further immobilize the prey. The insects are slowly digested, and the soluble products are absorbed by the plant. The small flowers, with six white or pinkish petals, are on a leafless, upright stem.

Drosera

Hybrids of the two species in this key have been found in our region.

1 Leaf blades nearly circular ....*D. rotundifolia*
ROUND-LEAVED SUNDEW

1 Leaf blades decidedly elongated (rarely below 2000 ft., 610 m; mostly much higher) .... *D. anglica* (*D. longifolia*)
LONG-LEAVED SUNDEW

ELAEAGNACEAE Oleaster Family

The oleaster family consists of trees or shrubs whose undivided leaves are often coated, especially on the underside, with star-shaped or scalelike hairs. The only wild species in our region is *Shepherdia canadensis* (pl. 239;

Elaeagnus canadensis), called buffalo berry, soapberry, and soopolallie. This shrub has a wide distribution east of the Cascades, but it is also found in the southern portion of Vancouver Island and the Gulf Islands of British Columbia and on the San Juan Islands of Washington. The leaves are opposite, and the lower surfaces of the blades not only have brownish scales but also some whitish scurfiness. Staminate and pistillate flowers, neither of which have petals, are on separate plants. The staminate flowers have a calyx whose somewhat spreading lobes are as long as about 2 mm, greenish yellow at first, later brownish, and four stamens; the calyx lobes of pistillate flowers are more or less upright, and the fruit, developing below their bases, becomes a rather attractive berry—about 1 cm in diameter and red with small yellowish dots.

ELATINACEAE Waterwort Family

Waterworts found in our region are aquatic or semiaquatic annuals with opposite leaves. Their flowers, borne in the leaf axils, are small and inconspicuous. The numbers of sepals, petals, and stamens in the two species found in our region are very different and are best dealt with in this key. Both species, however, have a single pistil that develops into a dry fruit.

1 Plants forming small mats, the stems rarely so much as 10 cm tall; leaf blades several times as long as wide, about 1 cm long, tapering to an indistinct petiole; flowers with 2–3 sepals and petals, 3 stamens; sepals without hairs; fruit consisting of 2–3 chambers; stems neither hairy nor becoming hardened near the base; on mud (mostly E of the Cascades but found in a few places in our region) . . . . ***Elatine rubella*** (*E. triandra* of some references)
THREE-STAMENED WATERWORT

1 Plants to more than 20 cm tall; leaf blades more or less oval, usually 2–3 cm long, most of them with distinct petioles; flowers with 5 sepals and petals, 10 stamens; sepals with scattered, thick hairs; fruit divided lengthwise into 5 seed-producing chambers; stems glandular-hairy, their basal portions becoming slightly hardened; on wet ground (in our region known to occur along the lower Columbia River; S to Calif., E to Texas and Illinois) . . . . ***Bergia texana***
TEXAS BERGIA

Some flowers of *B. texana* do not really open until after they have been pollinated and the enlarging fruit forces the sepals, petals, and stamens apart.

Drosera rotundifolia,
round-leaved sundew

Elatine rubella,
three-stamened waterwort

EMPETRACEAE Crowberry Family

The only representative of the crowberry family in our region is *Empetrum nigrum* (pl. 240), black crowberry, found mostly on coastal bluffs and around sphagnum bogs. Although small, it qualifies as a shrub or subshrub because at least some portions of its stems, which may lie on the ground or be raised up about 10–15 cm, are woody. The slender leaves, grooved along the underside, are less than 1 cm long and mostly either alternate or arranged in whorls of four. The perianth of the small flowers consists of a lower whorl of three sepals and an upper whorl of three purplish brown petals. Beneath the sepals, and resembling them, are three bracts. There are usually two types of flowers: those that have three stamens and a pistil, and those in which the stamens are functional but the pistil is reduced. Normal pistils develop into fleshy, purplish black fruits about 5 mm wide; these contain several seeds.

ERICACEAE Heath Family

The heath family is interestingly diversified, for it includes a few trees, a wide variety of shrubs, and many herbaceous species, a substantial number of which lack chlorophyll and are specialized for life as saprophytes. Heaths, heathers, blueberries, rhododendrons, and azaleas are familiar garden plants that belong to this large assemblage, sometimes subdivided into several families. The flowers are regular or almost regular, typically (but not always) with a five-lobed calyx and a five-petaled or five-lobed corolla. Most commonly there are five or ten stamens, and the anther sacs of most species, instead of merely splitting open, release pollen through neat pores. The fruit, whether fleshy or dry at maturity, is usually divided lengthwise into five seed-producing chambers. In certain genera, including *Vaccinium*, which gives us blueberries and huckleberries, the fruit-forming portion of the pistil is below the level at which the calyx lobes and corolla originate.

Fungi associated with the roots of ericaceous plants make certain nutrients available to their hosts. Phosphorus is a particularly important element that enters the plants through fungi, whose threadlike, microscopic hyphae spread out widely through the soil. A dependence on fungal symbionts is especially pronounced in members of the family that lack chlorophyll; in most of these, the leaves are reduced to scales. Certain species of the genus *Pyrola* have two forms, one that has green leaves, another that is entirely saprophytic.

1 Plants saprophytic, without green leaves (in our region most species under this choice are restricted to coniferous forests)
    2 Plants (commonly to 35 cm tall, sometimes taller) almost entirely red, very fleshy; some upper leaves (these narrow) to about 10 cm long, the lower ones proportionately broader and mostly 2–4 cm long (Siskiyou Mountains of SW Oreg. to S Calif.; not likely to be found below 4000 ft., 1220 m) . . . . ***Sarcodes sanguinea***, pl. 266
                                                               SNOW PLANT
    2 Plants not almost entirely red (but they may be pink or pinkish, at least in part)
        3 Stems (to about 40 cm tall) with pink and white lengthwise stripes; flowers without a corolla . . . . ***Allotropa virgata***, pl. 241
                                                           SUGAR STICK
        3 Stems without pink and white lengthwise stripes (flowers with a corolla but calyx lacking in certain genera)
            4 Corolla lobed (that is, petals united for a substantial part of their length)
                5 Corolla narrowed near the top, the lobes very short, not hairy on their inner faces; sepals about half as long as the corolla, with a few short, thick, gland-tipped hairs . . . . ***Pterospora andromedea***, pl. 261
                                                        PINEDROPS
                5 Corolla not narrowed near the top, the lobes more than half as long as the tube, hairy on their inner faces; sepals nearly as long as the corolla, without gland-tipped hairs . . . . ***Hemitomes congestum***, pl. 253
                                                       GNOME PLANT

4 Corolla consisting of separate petals

  6 Corolla waxy-white (aging black); flowers single on each flowering stem . . . .
. . . . *Monotropa uniflora*, pl. 259
                                                                       INDIAN PIPE

  6 Corolla not waxy-white; flowers in inflorescences

    7 Corolla consisting of 5 petals, these opening widely; pistil extending conspicuously out of the co-rolla (and usually directed downward); plants not especially fleshy . . . .
. . . . *Pyrola* (see *Pyrola-Moneses-Orthilia* complex)
                In our region, the most common nongreen *Pyrola* is a nearly leafless form of *P. asari-folia* (pls. 262) but *P. picta* and *P. chlorantha* also have nongreen forms. See the key to the *Pyrola-Moneses-Orthilia* complex for species distinctions.

    7 Corolla usually consisting of 4 petals, not opening widely, therefore somewhat urn-shaped; pistil not extending out of the corolla; plants rather fleshy

      8 Inner faces of petals not hairy (but the margins of the petals are fringed with short, stout hairs) . . . . *Pleuricospora fimbriolata*
                                                      FRINGED PINESAP

      8 Inner faces of petals hairy

        9 Anthers longer than wide; sepals originating well above the bases of the petals; plants pink-ish or yellowish . . . . *Monotropa hypopitys* (*Hypopitys monotropa*)
                                         BROAD-LEAVED PINESAP

        9 Anthers wider than long; sepals originating at about the same level as the petals; plants whitish . . . . *Pityopus californicus*
                                        CALIFORNIA PINEFOOT

1 Plants with green leaves

  10 Leaves either (1) scalelike, not more than 5 mm long, and tightly arranged in 4 crowded rows along the stems, or (2) slender, more than 5 times as long as wide, and not more than about 15 mm long

    11 Leaves scalelike, less than 5 mm long and tightly arranged in 3 crowded rows along the stems; corolla bell-shaped, white (not often found below about 4500 ft., 1370 m) . . . *Cassiope-Harrimanella* complex

    11 Leaves slender, more than 5 times as long as wide and not more than about 15 mm long; corolla urn-shaped (distinctly narrowed at the neck) or bell-shaped, either pink to rose or yellowish white to greenish white (montane) . . . . *Phyllodoce*

  10 Leaves with proportionately broad blades, not slender or scalelike, usually at least 10 mm long (less than 10 mm in *Loiseleuria procumbens*)

    12 Petals separated to the base or nearly so

      13 Plants distinctly shrubby, woody almost throughout

        14 Flowers borne in clusters of many at the ends of stems; petals white, not more than 8 mm long . . . . *Ledum*

        14 Flowers borne singly in the axils of upper leaves; petals usually 10–12 mm long, with pinkish lengthwise streaks (Alaska to Oreg.; in our region at moderate to high elevations in the Cascades, Olympic Mountains, and Coast Ranges, but not common) . . . .
. . . . *Elliottia pyroliflora* (*Cladothamnus pyroliflorus*), pl. 250
                                                     COPPER BUSH

    13 Plants either herbaceous or woody only at the base, not often so much as 40 cm tall

      15 All substantial leaves concentrated at or near the base, the flowering stems without leaves or with only much-reduced leaves, and not branching . . . . *Pyrola-Moneses-Orthilia* complex

      15 Substantial leaves (sometimes in whorls) scattered along the upright stems, these branching near the base (petals pink to rose)

        16 Flowers with 5 petals, these opening widely and not turned back; fruit, when mature, dry and splitting apart; most leaves in whorls, the blades generally at least 2 cm long; usually in conifer-ous woods . . . . *Chimaphila*

16 Flowers with 4 petals, these usually turned back at least slightly; fruit fleshy, red when ripe; leaves not in whorls, the blades not often more than 1.5 cm long; in sphagnum bogs . . . . ***Vaccinium***

12 Petals united for a considerable portion of their length, a substantial portion of the corolla therefore usually bowl-, cup-, urn-, or funnel-shaped

  17 Corolla not constricted below the corolla lobes, therefore more nearly bell-shaped than urn-shaped, usually at least 15 mm wide (except in *Loiseleuria procumbens*)

    18 Some leaves nearly or perfectly opposite, the blades (stiff, with a very prominent, raised midrib and inrolled margins) to about 8 mm long; corolla less than 10 mm wide (pink, the lobes about as long as the tube and spreading outward slightly; Alaska to the Cascades of N Wash. but high montane in our region) . . . . ***Loiseleuria procumbens***
ALPINE AZALEA

    18 Leaves clearly alternate, the blades at least 10 mm long; corolla more than 10 mm wide

      19 Corolla at least 30 mm wide when open, the lobes at least as long as wide; large shrubs, sometimes more than 2 m tall . . . . ***Rhododendron***

      19 Corolla about 15 mm wide, shallowly bowl-shaped, the lobes wider than long; plants not often more than 30 cm tall

        20 Leaves to 25 mm long, without glandular dots on the underside; corolla pale pink to rose-purple, with 10 small lengthwise sacs (in sphagnum bogs) . . . . ***Kalmia microphylla*** subsp. *occidentalis*, pl. 254
WESTERN SWAMP LAUREL

        20 Leaves to about 20 mm long, with glandular dots on the underside; corolla rose, without lengthwise sacs . . . . ***Kalmiopsis***

  17 Corolla slightly constricted below the corolla lobes, thus urn-shaped, and not more than 10 mm wide

    21 Large evergreen tree (to more than 20 m tall; corolla yellow; fruit orange to red, covered with small bumps; leaf blades to about 10 cm in diameter; outer layers of bark peeling off in strips and large flakes; corolla white) . . . . ***Arbutus menziesii***, pl. 242
MADROÑO, MADRONE, ARBUTUS

        When Spanish explorers found this tree in Calif., they recognized its similarity to what was called madroño (*A. unedo*) in their homeland. Eventually, however, madroño (masculine) was corrupted to madrona (feminine). That word, in Spanish, has a very different meaning: an oversolicitous mother, a main irrigating ditch, or a main sewer.

    21 Shrubs, sometimes large but not conforming in all respects to the criteria given in the other choice 21

      22 Calyx and corolla 4-lobed; stamens 8; flowers and fruits in umbel-like clusters produced at the tips of the preceding year's growth (in other words, just below the shoots of the current year's growth), flowers urn-shaped, yellowish orange or yellowish red; calyx lobes fringed with hairlike outgrowths, fruit egg-shaped, dry when mature) . . . . ***Menziesia ferruginea***, pl. 258
RUSTYLEAF, FOOL'S HUCKLEBERRY

      22 Calyx and corolla 5-lobed; stamens 10; flowers and fruits in terminal inflorescences or in the axils of leaves of the current year's growth

        23 Flowers appearing in the axils of leaves of the current year's growth (fruit-forming portion of the pistil below the level at which the calyx lobes are attached) . . . . ***Vaccinium***

        23 Flowers borne in terminal inflorescences

          24 Calyx becoming fleshy and uniting with the fruit (the pistil is free of the 5-lobed calyx until the corolla falls away, but then the calyx envelops the pistil and becomes part of the fleshy fruit) . . . . ***Gaultheria***

          24 Calyx remaining separate from the pistil, not contributing to the dry or fleshy fruit

            25 Leaf blades (to about 4 cm long but usually only 1.5–2.5 cm) several times as long as wide, with slightly inrolled margins (corolla pale pink; fruit dry at maturity; N and mostly montane species inhabiting bogs; Alaska to Brit. Col. and eastward) . . . . . . ***Andromeda polifolia***
BOG ROSEMARY

            25 Leaf blades not often more than 3 times as long as wide, the margins not inrolled

26 Most leaf blades 3–6 cm long, elliptical, nearly or fully 3 times as long as wide, bracts on each pedicel membranous and whitish, not folded lengthwise; corolla white; fruit 5-lobed from the beginning of its development, dry when mature (Josephine and Curry Cos., Oreg., to Calif.) .... *Leucothoe davisiae*, pl. 257
WESTERN LEUCOTHOE

26 Leaf blades rarely so much as 6 cm long and not often more than twice as long as wide, except in some species with leaves only about 2–3 cm long; bract at the base of each pedicel broad, not membranous, usually slightly folded lengthwise; corolla white to pink; fruit either fleshy or with firm, only slightly juicy pulp, remaining so until drying out, but not-five lobed at any time during its development and not becoming a symmetrical dry fruit that persists for a few weeks .... *Arctostaphylos*

Arctostaphylos

Because of intergradation and hybridization, some *Arctostaphylos* plants are difficult to identify with certainty. One probable hybrid (*A. ?glandulosa* × *nevadensis*), found in Josephine and Curry Counties, Oregon, was named *A. parvifolia;* it is distinctive because its leaf blades, as long as about 2.5 cm, have a nearly circular outline. Others suspected of having a hybrid origin are *A. cinerea* and *A. oblongifolia;* these, also found in southwestern Oregon, are more or less intermediate between *A. viscida* and *A. canescens*.

1 Low shrubs or ground covers usually less than 30 cm tall; leaf blades not more than 3 cm long
  2 Leaf blades not often more than 2.5 cm long, the tips rounded or faintly notched; fruits bright red; plants of lowland habitats, widespread, especially in coastal habitats .... *A. uva-ursi*, pl. 246
KINNIKINNICK
  2 Leaf blades occasionally to 3 cm long, the tips with a noticeable point; fruits brownish red; in the Cascades, mostly above 2500 ft. (760 m), and also in the Siskiyou Mountains of SW Oreg. and NW Calif. ..
.... *A. nevadensis*
PINEMAT MANZANITA
    Intergrades between *A. uva-ursi* and *A. nevadensis* are occasionally encountered; see also the comment concerning hybridization of *A. uva-ursi* with *A. columbiana*, second choice 5.
1 Substantial, bushy shrubs, often more than 1 m tall; leaf blades of some species more than 3 cm long
  3 Plants (to about 2.5 m tall) usually with a substantial burl at the base (from which resprouting takes place after a fire; most bracts of the inflorescence 5–15 mm long; leaf blades green or slightly grayish; stems of young branchlets usually with short hairs, some of these glandular; fruit sticky; Coos Co., Oreg., to Calif.) .... *A. glandulosa* subsp. *glandulosa* (includes *A. intricata*), pl. 244
HAIRY MANZANITA
  3 Plants without a burl at the base (they do not resprout after a fire)
    4 Most bracts of the inflorescence 5–15 mm long
      5 Stems of youngest branchlets with short hairs, these often crowded but much less than 1 mm long and not glandular; leaf blades decidedly grayish; inflorescence, if branched, with not more than 3 branches; flower pedicels 5–9 mm long; plants to 2 m tall (Douglas Co., Oreg., to Calif.) ....
.... *A. canescens* subsp. *canescens*
HOARY MANZANITA
      Arctostaphylos canescens subsp. *canescens* is believed to hybridize with *A. viscida*.
      5 Stems of youngest branchlets with some hairs to about 1 mm long as well as shorter hairs, many of the hairs glandular; leaf blades dull green but not obviously grayish; inflorescences usually with at least 3 branches; flower pedicels 2–4 mm long; fruits, when mature, usually brownish orange (W side of the Cascades, on the Olympic Peninsula, on some islands of the San Juan Archipelago, and along the coast; to about 2.5 m tall in our region but much larger plants recorded in Calif.) .... *A. columbiana*, pl. 243
BRISTLY MANZANITA
      Arctostaphylos columbiana hybridizes with *A. uva-ursi*, first choice 2, the result a low, spreading plant to about 30 cm tall called *A.* ×*media*. Its leaves are dull green, more like those of *A. columbiana* than those of *A. uva-ursi*, but the fruits are red and similar to those of *A. uva-ursi*.

4 Most bracts of the inflorescence (except perhaps the lowest one) not often more than 5 mm long

    6 Flowers and their bracts well separated and rather evenly spaced; immature inflorescence upright, with an axis less than 1 mm thick; plants to about 2 m tall (Josephine and Curry Cos., Oreg., to Calif.) . . . . *A. hispidula*

          HOWELL'S MANZANITA

    6 Flowers and their bracts concentrated near the tip of the inflorescence; immature inflorescence nodding, with an axis about 1 mm thick

        7 Leaf blades with a distinctly grayish or whitish cast, often somewhat hairy or even glandular-hairy, not falling down and not rooting at the nodes; pedicels of inflorescence very glandular-hairy; plants to 3 m tall (Josephine and Jackson Cos., Oreg., to Calif.) . . . . *A. viscida* subsp. *pulchella*, pl. 247

             STICKY MANZANITA

        7 Leaf blades bright green, not at all hairy; stems falling down and sometimes rooting at the nodes; pedicels not hairy; plants to about 2 m tall (in the Cascades of Oreg. to Calif.) . . . . *A. patula*, pl. 245

             GREEN MANZANITA

Cassiope-Harrimanella Complex

1 Leaves alternate, mostly spreading away from the stem; flowers typically single at the tips of the stems and upright (high montane, Alaska to Brit. Col. and in the Cascades of N Wash.; not likely to be found below 5000 ft., 1520 m) . . . . *H. stelleriana* (*C. stelleriana*)

          ALASKAN MOUNTAIN HEATHER

1 Leaves opposite, mostly pressed against the stem; flowers typically 1 to a few along the upper portions of the stems but not at the tip

    2 Leaves with a distinct groove on the underside (high montane, Alaska to Brit. Col. and in the Cascades of N Wash.; not likely to be found as low as 5000 ft., 1520 m) . . . . *C. tetragona*

          FOUR-ANGLED MOUNTAIN HEATHER

    2 Leaves without a distinct groove on the underside (but there may be a groove on the upper surface)

        3 Leaves with somewhat papery margins and arranged in 4 distinct rows; branches, including leaves, to 4 mm thick (high montane) . . . . *C. mertensiana* var. *mertensiana*, pl. 248

             MERTENS' MOUNTAIN HEATHER

        3 Leaves without papery margins and not arranged in 4 distinct rows (although there are 4 leaves at each node, they do not line up clearly in rows); branches, including the leaves, about 2 mm thick (mostly Alaska to Brit. Col., typically rather high montane in the Cascades but known to occur as low as about 2000 ft., 610 m, in King Co., Wash.) . . . . *C. lycopodioides*

             CLUB-MOSS MOUNTAIN HEATHER

Chimaphila

1 Inflorescence usually with more than 3 flowers; most leaf blades about 3 times as long as wide, the veins without white borders . . . . *C. umbellata*, pl. 249

          PRINCE'S PINE

1 Inflorescence with only 1–3 flowers; most leaf blades about twice as long as wide, the veins often with white borders . . . . *C. menziesii*

          LITTLE PRINCE'S PINE

Gaultheria

1 Leaf blades less than 1 cm long; stems densely covered with thick, short hairs; corolla less than 3 mm long, with 4 calyx lobes; fruit white (N high-montane species, rarely if ever found in our region) . . . . *G. hispidula*

          CREEPING SNOWBERRY

1 Leaf blades typically more than 1 cm long; stems not densely covered with thick, short hairs; corolla usually more than 3 mm long, with 5 lobes

2 Larger leaves mostly 1–2 cm long, the margins smooth or indistinctly toothed; calyx not hairy (montane, not likely to be found below 3500 ft., 1070 m) . . . . ***G. humifusa***
ALPINE WINTERGREEN

2 Leaf blades at least slightly more than 2 cm long, the margins distinctly short-toothed; calyx usually noticeably hairy

   3 Larger leaf blades not so much as 4 cm long; calyx with conspicuous long, brownish hairs; corolla tube widest at the top (mostly montane but sometimes found as low as 2500 ft., 760 m) . . . .
. . . . ***G. ovatifolia***, pl. 251
WESTERN WINTERGREEN

   3 Larger leaf blades commonly at least 5 cm long; calyx glandular-hairy; corolla tube urn-shaped, usually glandular-hairy; common lowland species . . . . ***G. shallon***, pl. 252
SALAL

Kalmiopsis

In both species of *Kalmiopsis,* some flowers have stamens that reach far beyond the pistil, others have a pistil that reaches far beyond the stamens.

1 Flower pedicels not glandular-hairy; corolla generally 14–20 mm wide; lower portions of stamen filaments without crowded golden hairs (but there may be a few scattered hairs); fresh flowers secreting nectar but not fragrant (stems mostly upright; Siskiyou Mountains, Curry and Josephine Cos., Oreg., at 3000–6000 ft., 910–1830 m) . . . . ***K. leachiana***, pl. 255
LILLA LEACH'S KALMIOPSIS

1 Flower pedicels glandular-hairy; corolla generally 16–28 mm wide; lower portions of stamen filaments with crowded golden hairs; fresh flowers with a spicy-sweet fragrance but this not from nectar (stems often trailing; in the North Umpqua River drainage system, Douglas Co., Oreg., about 1700–3900 ft., 520–1190 m) . . . . ***K. "fragrans"*** (not yet formally described)
FRAGRANT KALMIOPSIS

Ledum

1 Upper surface of leaf blades dull, the underside with rust-colored, somewhat woolly hairs; in wet habitats, including sphagnum bogs, mostly near the coast and in the N Puget Trough of Brit. Col. and Wash. . . . .
. . . . ***L. groenlandicum***
LABRADOR TEA

1 Upper surface of leaf blades shiny, the underside greenish or whitish, without woolly hairs; in wet habitats mostly along the coast, S Wash. to Calif., but in Oreg. commonly found inland in Josephine and Curry Cos., especially in fens where *Darlingtonia* grows . . . . ***L. glandulosum*** subsp. ***columbianum***, pl. 256
PACIFIC LABRADOR TEA

Phyllodoce

Where the two species of *Phyllodoce* in this key occur together, hybrids named *P. ×intermedia* may also occur.

1 Corolla urn-shaped, yellowish or greenish white, externally glandular-hairy; sepals typically two-thirds as long as the corolla tube and glandular-hairy (not likely to be found below 4000 ft., 1220 m) . . . .
. . . . ***P. glanduliflora***
YELLOW MOUNTAIN HEATH

1 Corolla broadly bell-shaped, deep pink, not glandular-hairy; sepals not more than half as long as the corolla tube, hairy along the margins but not glandular-hairy (not likely to be found below 4000 ft., 1220 m) .
. . . . ***P. empetriformis***, pl. 260
PINK MOUNTAIN HEATH

Pyrola-Moneses-Orthilia **Complex**

Species of *Pyrola* known to have a nongreen and nearly leafless saprophytic phase are indicated as such.

1 Flower single at the top of the stem . . . .*M. uniflora* (*P. uniflora*)
1 Flowers in racemes
    2 Style of pistil straight, not directed downward or bent to one side
        3 Flowers concentrated on one side of the raceme . . . .*O. secunda* (*P. secunda, Remischia secunda*)

ONE-SIDED WINTERGREEN

        3 Flowers more or less equally distributed around the raceme . . . . **P. minor**

LESSER PYROLA

    2 Style of pistil directed downward or at least bent to one side
        4 Bracts at the bases of the flower pedicels longer than the pedicels; corolla pink, rose, or a related color
          . . . . *P. asarifolia*, pls. 262

LARGE PYROLA (has saprophytic phase)

In our region, green, leafy plants of 2 subspecies of *P. asarifolia* can be distinguished: subsp. *asarifolia* typically has smooth-margined, somewhat heart-shaped leaf blades; the leaf blades of subsp. *purpurea* are broadly oval, and their margins are studded with small, rather sharp teeth.

        4 Bracts at the bases of the flower pedicels shorter than the pedicels; corolla greenish, yellowish, cream, pink, or nearly purplish
          5 Inflorescences usually with not more than 8 flowers; corolla greenish or yellowish . . . .
          . . . . *P. chlorantha* (*P. virens*)

GREENISH WINTERGREEN (has saprophytic phase)

          5 Inflorescences usually with at least 10 flowers, sometimes more than 20; corolla greenish, cream, pink, or nearly purplish
            6 Leaf blades not more than twice as long as wide, at least some of them abruptly tapered to the petiole, which may be nearly as long as the blade, and with white lines along the main veins . . . . .
            . . . . *P. picta*

WHITE-VEINED PYROLA (has saprophytic phase)

            6 Leaf blades generally 2–3 times as long as wide, most of them tapered gradually to the petiole, which is much shorter than the blade, and without white lines along the main veins . . . *P. dentata*

Pyrola dentata has been placed in synonymy under *P. picta,* but it may be a good idea to keep in mind the distinctions and the fact that the 2 forms do not seem to intergrade, at least to any great extent. One who has seen both species in the field will appreciate that they look very different.

Rhododendron

1 Evergreen; leaf blades tough and somewhat leathery; corolla mostly pink to deep rose, the tube broadly funnel-shaped (stamens 10; Brit. Col. to Calif., in the Cascades, along the coast, and in portions of the Puget Sound region) . . . . *R. macrophyllum*, pl. 264

WESTERN RHODODENDRON, the state flower of Washington

1 Deciduous; leaf blades thin; corolla mostly white or cream, sometimes with pink and/or yellow, the tube narrowly funnel-shaped
    2 Stamens 5; corolla usually with a yellow blotch on the lower side and often with some pink; leaf blades with small marginal teeth, these tipped with hairs (typically in moist habitats, along the coast and along streams inland, Douglas, Coos, Curry, and Josephine Cos., Oreg., to Calif.) . . . . . . *R. occidentale*, pl. 265

WESTERN AZALEA

    2 Stamens 10; corolla usually white or cream throughout; leaf blades without marginal teeth but the margins sometimes slightly wavy (in the Cascades and Olympic Mountains, not often below about 3000 ft., 910 m; also in mountains E of the Cascades) . . . . *R. albiflorum*, pl. 263

WHITE RHODODENDRON

Vaccinium

Thanks to distribution of seeds by birds, the highbush blueberry, *Vaccinium corymbosum*, native to eastern North America, is sometimes found growing wild in areas where it is cultivated. Its leaves, pointed at the tip and to about 8 cm long and 5 cm wide, are larger than those of species native to the Pacific Northwest. The flowers are produced in racemes, so the fruits are clustered.

1 Corolla either (1) consisting of 4 separate petals, these usually turned back sharply, or (2) slightly urn-shaped and with 4 lobes, these about as long as the tube (fruit fleshy, red in all species under this choice)

  2 Corolla urn-shaped, with 4 lobes, these about as long as the tube, not turned back sharply; leaves to more than 8 cm wide (a circumboreal species, in our region known only from the W coast of S Vancouver Island, Brit. Col.) . . . . *V. vitis-idaea*
                                       LINGONBERRY, MOUNTAIN CRANBERRY

  2 Corolla consisting of 4 essentially separate petals, these usually turned back sharply; leaves not often more than 6 mm wide

    3 Two bracts on the pedicel of each flower 2–5 mm long, at least one-third as wide as long; fruit usually 1–1.5 cm wide (extensively cultivated in natural or man-made bogs in coastal areas of Brit. Col., Wash., and Oreg., and sometimes escaping) . . . . *V. macrocarpon* (*Oxycoccos macrocarpus*)
                                         CRANBERRY (E North America)

    3 Two bracts on the pedicel of each flower scarcely noticeable, slender, and not often so much as 2 mm long; fruit rarely more than 1 cm wide . . . .
    . . . . *V. oxycoccos* (*Oxycoccos oxycoccus*, *O. palustris*, *O. quadripetalus*), pl. 268
                                           WILD CRANBERRY

> The 2 main cranberries in our region, *V. macrocarpon* and *V. oxycoccos*, because of the structure of their corollas, are rather conspicuously different from most species of *Vaccinium*. Some references therefore place them in the genus *Oxycoccos*. *Vaccinium vitis-idaea* (first choice 2), however, is more or less intermediate, for its corolla is deeply 4-lobed, not shallowly 5-lobed as in most other species of the genus. Thus the segregation of *Oxycoccos* from *Vaccinium* is not sharp. You can decide for yourself which path to follow.

1 Corolla mostly somewhat urn-shaped, with 5 lobes, these much shorter than the tube (sometimes scarcely perceptible), often curving but not turned back sharply (in various habitats, including sphagnum bogs)

  4 Leaves evergreen, firm, the margins of the blades distinctly toothed (corolla white to pinkish; berry dark, blackish and shiny, usually without a whitish coating; plants to about 3 m tall; coastal and in portions of the Puget Sound region) . . . .
  . . . . *V. ovatum*, pl. 267
                         EVERGREEN HUCKLEBERRY

  4 Leaves deciduous, thin and flexible, the margins of the blades toothed in some species, not in others

    5 Mature fruits pink to red (young stems green or yellowish green, conspicuously angled lengthwise)

      6 Plants to more than 2 m tall, the branches not especially crowded; leaf blades rarely more than twice as long as wide, not often distinctly toothed except on young seedlings; fruit dull pink to reddish pink, the calyx lobes distinct and persisting; commonly growing out of decaying logs or stumps and abundant in most coniferous forests at low to moderate elevations . . . . *V. parvifolium*, pl. 269
                       RED HUCKLEBERRY

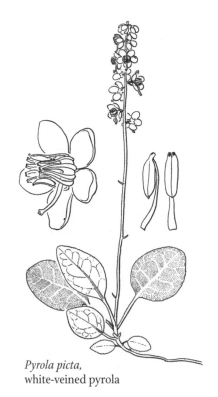

Pyrola picta,
white-veined pyrola

6 Plants rarely so much as 30 cm tall, the branches usually crowded together; most larger leaf blades at least twice as long as wide, distinctly toothed; fruit bright red, the calyx lobes scarcely noticeable (not likely to be found below 4000 ft., 1220 m) . . . . *V. scoparium*
GROUSEBERRY

5 Mature fruits blue or blackish, usually with a whitish coating

7 Flowers commonly in clusters of 2 or more (sometimes single); calyx lobes about as long as wide and persisting on the fruit (in sphagnum bogs, especially in coastal areas) . . . .
. . . . *V. uliginosum* subsp. *occidentale* (*V. occidentale*), pl. 270
BOG HUCKLEBERRY

7 Flowers borne singly; calyx lobes barely perceptible or absent

8 Leaf blades typically toothed rather evenly from the tip nearly to the base (mostly montane, not often found below 3000 ft., 910 m) . . . . *V. membranaceum*
THIN-LEAVED HUCKLEBERRY

8 Leaf blades typically toothed more conspicuously on the upper half than on the lower half, or vice versa

9 Leaf blades toothed more conspicuously on their upper than on their lower halves

10 Corolla tube nearly twice as long as wide (leaf blades with a conspicuous networklike arrangement of veins; mostly above 3000 ft., 910 m) . . . . *V. caespitosum*
DWARF BLUEBERRY

10 Corolla tube as wide as long and nearly globular (mostly above 3000 ft., 910 m) . . . *V. deliciosum*
CASCADES BLUEBERRY

9 Leaf blades toothed more conspicuously on their lower than on their upper halves

11 Corolla brownish pink, about as wide as long; pedicels usually becoming noticeably thicker just below the calyx; underside of leaf blades glandular along the midrib; style of pistil usually extending out of the corolla (Alaska to NW Oreg., in the Olympic Mountains, Cascades, and near the coast) . . . . *V. alaskaense*
ALASKA HUCKLEBERRY

11 Corolla pink, usually slightly longer than wide; pedicels not becoming noticeably thickened just below the calyx; underside of leaf blades often grayish but not hairy; style of pistil usually not extending out of the corolla (mostly above 3000 ft., 985 m, but occasionally found at low elevations near the coast) . . . . *V. ovalifolium*
OVAL-LEAVED HUCKLEBERRY

In some references, *V. ovalifolium* and *V. alaskaense* are considered to be the same, and the name *V. ovalifolium* is given priority.

EUPHORBIACEAE Spurge Family

The spurge family is a large assemblage of herbaceous, shrubby, and succulent plants. In southern Africa the succulent types are richly diversified, and many of them resemble cacti. The poinsettia, originating in Mexico, is perhaps the best-known species cultivated as a garden and pot plant. The family has given us some valuable sources of dyes and medicines, including castor oil, which is also used as a fuel for lamps and in the manufacture of soap, candles, varnish, and polishes. The seeds of certain species are so toxic that extracts of them have been used to disable fish in ponds, or applied to arrowheads for killing game animals. An attribute of some genera, including *Euphorbia* and *Chamaesyce,* both represented in our region, is a milky sap that may irritate the skin.

Spurges have relatively small flowers. None of ours has a corolla; in *Euphorbia* and *Chamaesyce,* in fact, a calyx is also lacking, although some bracts below a group of flowers could be mistaken for a calyx. When a true calyx is present as part of an individual flower, it is usually inconspicuous. Staminate flowers of *Euphorbia* and *Chamaesyce* have only one stamen, and pistillate flowers have only one pistil. The fruit-forming portion of the pistil is usually partitioned lengthwise into two or three divisions that crack apart at maturity; each division releases one or two seeds.

Mercurialis annua, annual mercury, a poisonous plant introduced from Europe and occasionally found as a weed, is described separately here. Its branching stems grow as tall as about 50 cm, and the sap is not milky. The leaves are alternate, with elongate-oval blades as long as about 5 cm and of a yellowish green color. Staminate and pistillate flowers are borne on separate plants. The staminate flowers, each with a three-lobed calyx and 8–20 stamens, are produced in clusters along an inflorescence about 2 cm long; the pistillate flowers, each with three sepals and a single pistil, appear in the axils of the leaves. The small dry fruit, bristly to the touch, has two divisions, each with one seed.

1 Sap not milky; leaves and stems very hairy, somewhat bristly to the touch, more gray than green, and with a strong odor; staminate and pistillate flowers separate, neither type borne within an involucre; calyx present in staminate flowers; fruit with a single seed-producing chamber (S Wash. to Baja Calif.) . . . . ***Eremocarpus setigerus***, pl. 272
TURKEY MULLEIN

1 Sap milky; stems and leaves not obviously hairy (except in *Chamaesyce maculata*, in which the stems and undersides of leaf blades are hairy, and in *Euphorbia oblongata*, which has hairy stems), not gray, and without a strong odor; flowers borne within a cup- or goblet-shaped involucre, the staminate flowers, each represented by 1 or more stamens, encircling a single pistillate flower; fruit consisting of 3 divisions

    2 Stems prostrate, the plants generally forming mats; leaves opposite . . . . ***Chamaesyce***

    2 Stems upright; leaves usually alternate (opposite in *E. lathyris*) . . . . ***Euphorbia***

Chamaesyce

1 Stems and undersides of at least some leaves hairy . . . ***C. maculata*** (*Euphorbia maculata, E. supina*), pl. 271
MILK SPURGE (E United States)

1 Stems and undersides of leaves not hairy (more common E than W of the Cascades)

    2 Involucres single in the leaf axils; seeds with 5–6 cross-ridges, these nearly at an angle of 90° to the long axis . . . . ***C. glyptosperma***
CORRUGATE-SEEDED MILK SPURGE

    2 Involucres usually 2 or more in the leaf axils; seeds with wrinkles but these not nearly at an angle of 90° to the long axis . . . . ***C. serpyllifolia*** subsp. *serpyllifolia* (*Euphorbia serpyllifolia*)
THYME-LEAVED SPURGE

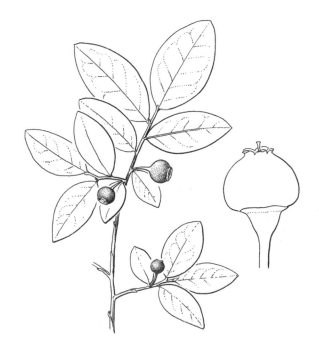

Vaccinium alaskaense,
Alaska huckleberry

Euphorbia esula,
leafy spurge

Euphorbia

1 Most leaves at least 4 times as long as wide (the leaves in the inflorescence or just beneath it may be proportionately much wider)

    2 All leaves opposite (the larger ones mostly more than 6 cm long) . . . . *E. lathyris*
                           CAPER SPURGE (Europe)

    2 Most or all leaves alternate

        3 Leaves of the inflorescence heart-shaped; larger leaves below the inflorescence usually 4–6 cm long (occasional W of the Cascades but a common and pernicious weed E of the Cascades) . . . . *E. esula*, p. 213
                           LEAFY SPURGE (Eurasia)

        3 Leaves of the inflorescence similar to those lower down but sometimes slightly larger; leaves below the inflorescence not often so much as 3 cm long

            4 Annual, branching from the base, the stems otherwise not branched except in the inflorescence; larger leaves mostly less than 2 cm long and typically directed upward, often overlapping . . . . *E. exigua*
                           DWARF SPURGE (Europe)

            4 Perennial, stems arising from creeping rhizomes, usually branched a few times below the inflorescence; larger leaves mostly at least 2 cm long and typically directed outward . . . . *E. cyparissias*
                           CYPRESS SPURGE (Europe)

1 Leaves not often more than 3 times as long as wide

    5 Most upper leaves, including those in the inflorescence, distinctly widest above the middle

        6 Most leaves of the inflorescence more than 1 cm wide, wider than the leaves below the inflorescence; fruit smooth . . . . *E. helioscopia*
                           SUN SPURGE (Europe)

        6 Leaves of the inflorescence not more than 1 cm wide, usually narrower than the leaves below the inflorescence; fruit with small projections (SW Oreg. to Calif.; also in central and S United States) . . . . *E. spathulata*
                           SPATULA-LEAVED SPURGE

    5 Most upper leaves, including those of the inflorescence, widest at or below the middle (the lower leaves, however, may be widest above the middle)

        7 Leaves of the inflorescence nearly or fully as wide as long; lower leaves without distinct petioles (Oreg. to Calif.) . . . . *E. crenulata*
                           WESTERN WOOD SPURGE

        7 Leaves of the inflorescence decidedly longer than wide; lower leaves with distinct petioles

            8 Annual, rarely more than 30 cm tall; stems not hairy; most leaves less than 3 cm long (very common weed) . . . . *E. peplus*, pl. 273
                           PETTY SPURGE (Europe)

            8 Perennial, to more than 50 cm tall; young stems hairy, especially at the nodes; leaves to 7 cm long . . . . *E. oblongata*
                         COMMON EUROPEAN SPURGE (Europe)

FABACEAE Pea Family

The pea family, as represented by natives in our region, consists mostly of herbaceous plants, but there are a few shrubs, and one species forms a small tree. Typically, the flowers have five sepals, five petals, ten stamens, and a pistil whose fruit-forming portion becomes a pod with a single row of seeds. The petals are arranged in a distinctive way: the two lower ones are fused, by their lower edges, to form a structure called the keel; the petals on both sides of the keel are called wings, and the upper petal, usually the largest, is called the banner. Except in one of the genera in our region, the filaments of at least nine of the ten stamens are united. The fruit, when dry, usually splits apart rather forcefully to scatter its seeds.

Amorpha fruticosa, a shrubby species native to the eastern United States and now established along the Columbia River in Oregon and Washington, does not fit the flower description just given. It has only one petal, corresponding to the banner. Nevertheless, in other respects, such as the arrangement of stamens, structure of the fruit, and the appearance of the leaves, it looks like a member of the pea family.

Many other species in our region are also alien. A few were introduced on purpose, but seeds of others were brought in accidentally. All the medicks (*Medicago*) and sweet clovers (*Melilotus*), and some of the true clovers (*Trifolium*), peas (*Lathyrus*), vetches (*Vicia*), and trefoils (*Lotus*), are of exotic origin. Especially noxious invaders are two shrubs, Scot's broom (*Cytisus scoparius*), and gorse (*Ulex europaea*), which have aggressively colonized large areas to the detriment of native vegetation.

Stipules are usually well developed in this family and must not be confused with leaves or leaflets. It would be easy to do this in the case of species in which the leaf is reduced to single tendril, as it is in *Lathyrus aphaca*, or when there are only one or two leaflets.

1 Woody shrubs, mostly more than 1.5 m tall
    2 Corolla only about 6 mm long, consisting only of a banner, this deep violet-blue (leaflets, calyces, and fruits conspicuously gland-dotted; larger leaf blades usually with at least 11 leaflets, alternate; plants sometimes more than 3 m tall; native to E United States and extensively cultivated in central United States; established along the Columbia River in Oreg. and Wash.) . . . . ***Amorpha fruticosa***
                    FALSE INDIGO
    2 Corolla usually about 1–2 cm long, with wings and keel as well as a banner, commonly yellow or white, occasionally reddish in some cultivars
        3 Branches (including short side branches) sharply pointed and functioning as thorns, the leaves also stiff and sharp-tipped . . . . ***Ulex europaea***
                    GORSE (Europe)
        3 Neither the branches nor the leaves with sharp tips (most leaves either small and simple or consisting of 3 or more leaflets)
            4 All leaves small and simple, and sometimes few and far between; stems (green or grayish green) essentially cylindrical, rushlike, not sharply angled (corolla about 2 cm long; occasionally colonizing disturbed habitats) . . . . ***Spartium junceum***
                    SPANISH BROOM
            4 At least some leaves with 3 leaflets; stems with distinct angular ridges
                5 Flowers borne in clusters at the ends of branches, these typically densely leafy (corolla about 1 cm long; occasionally colonizing coastal areas where winter temperatures are moderate) . . . .
                 . . . . ***Genista monspessulana*** (*Cytisus monspessulanus*)
                    FRENCH BROOM
                5 Flowers borne singly or in clusters in the leaf axils (most leaves with 3 leaflets but those on upper portions of the stem simple; corolla about 2 cm long; some branches, especially on older plants, may not have leaves; excessively common and perniciously invasive nuisance that should be prevented from gaining a foothold in areas where native plants are growing) . . . . . . ***Cytisus scoparius***
                    SCOT'S BROOM (Europe)
                      Cytisus multiflorus, called white Spanish broom (Europe), has white flowers about 1 cm long but is otherwise similar to *C. scoparius.* Various other species of *Cytisus,* and their cultivars, are grown in gardens and planted along highways.
1 Plants either completely or mostly herbaceous, at most woody only near the base
    6 Filaments of all 10 stamens separate
        7 Leaves pinnately compound, usually with at least 19 leaflets; corolla greenish white; fruit (rarely if ever produced by some populations) conspicuously constricted between successive seeds (Josephine Co., Oreg.) . . . . ***Sophora leachiana***, pl. 294
                    WESTERN SOPHORA, LILLA LEACH'S SOPHORA

7 Leaves palmately compound, with 3 leaflets; corolla yellow; fruit not conspicuously constricted between successive seeds .... ***Thermopsis***

6 Filaments of at least 9 stamens united

8 Filaments of all 10 stamens united, at least for a time (in *Rupertia physodes* the filament of 1 stamen may soon become mostly or completely free of the others; this species, however, is easily identified because of the glandular dots and black hairs on the calyx)

9 Leaves with 3 leaflets; calyx with greenish glandular dots and black hairs; anthers of all stamens about the same size .... ***Rupertia physodes*** (*Psoralea physodes*), pl. 293
CALIFORNIA TEA

9 Leaves typically with at least 5 leaflets, calyx without greenish glandular dots, and hairs, if present, not blackish; stamens of 2 types, those with smaller anthers alternating with those with larger anthers .... ***Lupinus***

8 Filaments of 9 stamens united, that of the tenth stamen free

10 Leaves with 3 leaflets; none of the leaves with tendrils

11 Leaflets palmately arranged, their stalks of equal length (except in *T. campestre*, a clover in which the stalk of the middle leaflet is longer than those of the lateral leaflets) .... ***Trifolium***

11 Stalk of the middle leaflet at least distinctly longer than those of the other 2 leaflets

12 Margins of leaflets smooth; fruits splitting apart lengthwise at maturity .... ***Lotus***

12 Margins of leaflets toothed; fruits not splitting apart at maturity

13 Fruits conspicuously curved or even coiled .... ***Medicago***

13 Fruits neither conspicuously curved nor coiled .... ***Melilotus***

10 Leaves usually with more than 3 leaflets unless some or all of them have become specialized as tendrils

14 Leaves represented by a single tendril, at the base of which are 2 conspicuous, leaflike stipules (corolla yellow) .... ***Lathyrus aphaca***, pl. 276
YELLOW PEA (Europe)

14 Leaves with at least some typical leaflets

15 Terminal leaflet specialized as a tendril

16 Style with a dense tuft or ring of hairs just below the stigma .... ***Vicia***

16 Style without a tuft or ring of hairs but flattened and hairy along about half of the lower side .... ***Lathyrus***

15 None of the leaflets specialized as a tendril

17 Leaves and stems covered with sticky, stalked glands; fruits covered with prickles 4–5 mm long .... ***Glycyrrhiza lepidota***, pl. 275
WILD LICORICE

17 Leaves and stems not covered with sticky, stalked glands; fruits not covered with prickles (but the fruits of *Onobrychis viciifolia* have a few stout, toothlike protuberances)

18 Flowers either borne singly or in umbel-like clusters

19 Tip of the keel protruding beyond the wings; mature fruits conspicuously constricted between seeds, breaking apart into 1-seeded segments (corollas pink or white; plants sprawling or sometimes climbing over other plants; garden plant, sometimes escaping) .... ***Securigera varia*** (*Coronilla varia*)
CROWN VETCH (Europe)

19 Tip of the keel not protruding beyond the wings; mature fruits not constricted between the seeds and not breaking apart into 1-seeded segments .... ***Lotus***

18 Flowers borne in racemes

20 Keel of corolla narrowed abruptly to a slender, forward-pointing beak (mostly in the mountains but also found near sea level in the San Juan Islands, Wash., and on some islands close to S Vancouver Island, Brit. Col.) .... ***Oxytropis monticola* subsp. *monticola*** (*O. campestris* subsp. *gracilis*), pl. 292
MOUNTAIN OXYTROPIS

20 Keel of corolla not narrowed to a slender, forward-pointing beak

  21 Fruits not much longer than wide, neither inflated nor constricted between seeds, with a few stout, toothlike protuberances, and with only 1–2 seeds (perennial; occasional weed) . . . ***Onobrychis viciifolia***
SANFOIN (Europe)

  21 Fruits usually considerably longer than wide, sometimes becoming either inflated or constricted between seeds, without toothlike protuberances

    22 Fruits, when mature, conspicuously constricted between seeds, not inflated, the 1-seeded segments eventually separating; corollas reddish pink to purplish (montane in the Cascades and Olympic Mountains, Wash., and eastward) . . . . ***Hedysarum occidentale***
WESTERN SWEET BROOM

    22 Fruits, when mature, not conspicuously constricted between seeds, sometimes much inflated or curved; corollas (of species in our region) whitish, yellowish, greenish, sometimes tinged with pale purple but not colorfully reddish pink or purple . . . . ***Astragalus***

Astragalus

1 Leaves not more than 4 cm long, the leaflets rarely more than 6 mm long; corolla whitish or lavender, sometimes tinged with pale purple; banner not more than 4 mm long; fruit not more than 5 mm long, broadly oval or nearly circular, almost as wide as long and without an obvious stalk; small annual (Jackson Co., Oreg., to Calif.) . . . . ***A. gambelianus***
BLACKISH MILK VETCH

1 Leaves generally much more than 4 cm long, the leaflets usually at least 8 mm long; corolla white, cream, greenish, or greenish yellow, not tinged with purple; banner at least 10 mm long; fruit at least 14 mm long, considerably longer than wide; perennial

  2 Fruit usually at least 2.5 cm long (to about 4 cm), at least 7 times as long as wide and conspicuously flattened from side to side (some plants markedly hairy, others scarcely hairy; stalk of fruit to 15 mm long; Jackson Co., Oreg., to Calif.) . . . . ***A. californicus***
CALIFORNIA MILK VETCH

  2 Fruit not often more than 2.5 cm long and not markedly flattened from side to side

    3 Banner 14–19 mm long; fruit several times as long as wide, becoming conspicuously curved as it dries, the stalk about 2 mm long (Josephine Co., Oreg., to Calif.; also at least once found in Yamhill Co., Oreg.) . . . . ***A. umbraticus***
BALD MOUNTAIN MILK VETCH

Hedysarum occidentale,
western sweet broom

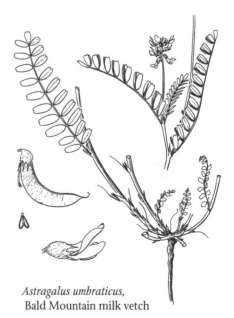

Astragalus umbraticus,
Bald Mountain milk vetch

3 Banner 10–14 mm long; fruit generally 2–3 times as long as wide, as a whole not conspicuously curved (but one margin may be curved more than the other), the stalk 6–12 mm long (Douglas Co., Oreg., to Calif.) . . . . *A. accidens* var. *hendersonii*, pl. 274

THICKET MILK VETCH

Leaflets of *A. accidens* var. *hendersonii* are usually notched at the tip. In *A. whitneyi* subsp. *siskiyouensis*, Siskiyou milk vetch, not likely to be found below about 5000 ft. (1520 m), the leaflets taper to the tip.

Lathyrus

1 Each leaf consisting only of its rachis and its continuation as a tendril (there are no leaflets, but there are 2 broad stipules below the base of the rachis; corolla yellow; annual) . . . . *L. aphaca*, pl. 276

YELLOW PEA (Europe)

1 Each leaf with at least 2 leaflets

  2 Each leaf with only 2 leaflets (in addition to stipules); often weedy species

    3 Corolla yellow (corolla 12–17 mm long; perennial; not common) . . . .*L. pratensis*

FIELD PEA (Europe)

    3 Corolla not yellow

      4 Corolla 25–30 mm long (corolla maroon, crimson, or rose-purple) . . . .*L. tingitanus*

TANGIER PEA (Europe)

      4 Corolla usually less than 20 mm long (but fully 25 mm long in *L. latifolius*, whose flower color is pink, rose, or occasionally white)

        5 Flowers usually solitary; the peduncle continued as a short tendril-like structure (leaflets slender, usually at least 15 times as long as wide; corolla about 1 cm long; annual)

          6 Peduncle usually at least 2 cm long (sometimes as much as 8 cm); corolla lavender or purplish; veins on fruit indistinct, forming a network . . . . *L. angulatus*

ANGLED PEA (Europe)

          6 Peduncle not often more than 2 cm long; corolla orange-red or vermilion; veins on fruit distinct and lengthwise . . . . *L. sphaericus*

GRASS PEA (Europe)

     5 Flowers usually 2 or more in each inflorescence

       7 Flowers usually 2–3 in each inflorescence

         8 Corolla 9–12 mm long, blue, purple, or reddish; leaves, stems, calyces obviously hairy, and fruits conspicuously hairy; lobes of calyx about as long as the calyx tube . . . .*L. hirsutus*

ROUGH PEA (Europe)

         8 Corolla 8–10 mm long, purple; leaves, stems, calyces, and fruits not obviously hairy; lobes of calyx about twice as long as the calyx tube . . . .*L. pusillus*

LOW VETCHLING (Europe)

       7 Flowers usually more than 3 in each inflorescence

         9 Most leaflets at least 10 times as long as wide; both lobes of stipules slender and not markedly different; corolla about 15 mm long, reddish . . . . *L. sylvestris*

FLAT PEA (Europe)

         9 Leaflets not often more than 6 times as long as wide; lobes of stipules of decidedly unequal length; corolla to 25 mm long, bright pink to rose, sometimes white . . . .*L. latifolius*

PERENNIAL PEA (Europe)

  2 Most leaves with at least 4 leaflets (in addition to stipules); native species

  10 Leaves without obvious tendrils but sometimes with a bristle or unbranched continuation of the rachis extending beyond the uppermost leaflets

    11 Flowers only 1–2 in each inflorescence; leaves with 10–16 leaflets . . . .*L. torreyi*

TORREY'S PEA

    11 Flowers generally at least 3 (usually 3–5) in each inflorescence; leaves with not more than 8 leaflets

12 Stems and leaves very hairy; corolla 12–18 mm long; on backshores of sandy beaches . . . .
. . . . *L. littoralis*, pl. 278
GRAY BEACH PEA

12 Stems and leaves not obviously hairy; corolla usually 15–25 mm long . . . . *L. nevadensis*, pl. 279
SIERRA NEVADA PEA

Lathyrus nevadensis varies and is often divided into several subspecies or varieties.

10 Leaves with obvious tendrils, these usually branched and clinging

13 Lateral 2 calyx lobes slender, at least 4 times as long as wide at the base (corolla usually white, sometimes with lavender streaks; Josephine and Curry Cos., Oreg., to Calif.) . . . . *L. delnorticus*
DEL NORTE PEA

13 Lateral 2 lobes of calyx not more than 3 times as long as wide at the base

14 Corolla mostly white, cream, faintly yellow, or faintly brownish (but sometimes tinged or streaked
with purplish or lavender)

15 Lateral lobes of calyx slightly broadened above the base (Wash. to Calif.) . . . .
. . . . *L. vestitus* subsp. *ochropetalus*
PACIFIC PEA

15 Lateral lobes of calyx tapering gradually to the tip, not distinctly broadened above the base

16 Corolla (when fresh) pale yellow to brownish orange (Josephine Co., Oreg., to Calif.) . . . .
. . . . *L. sulphureus*
SULFUR PEA, SNUB PEA

16 Corolla cream to pale yellow, the banner with purplish streaks (Oreg., especially in the Willa-
mette Valley) . . . . *L. holochlorus*
THIN-LEAVED PEA

14 Corolla commonly pink, rose, purple, blue, or some related color

17 Stipules arrowhead-shaped (almost strictly limited to backshores of beaches, relatively dry borders
of salt marshes, and other maritime habitats) . . . .
. . . . *L. japonicus* var. *maritimus* (*L. japonicus* var. *glaber*), pl. 277
BEACH PEA

Lathyrus sylvestris,
flat pea

Lathyrus polyphyllus,
leafy pea

17 Stipules not arrowhead-shaped
    18 Stipules not divided into 2 lobes and usually at least half the size of the largest leaflets of the same leaf . . . . *L. polyphyllus*, p. 219
                                                      LEAFY PEA

    18 Stipules divided into 2 lobes and much smaller than the largest leaflets of the same leaf
      19 Leaflets about 4 times as long as wide; strictly coastal . . . .*L. palustris*
                                                     MARSH PEA
      19 Leaflets not so much as 3 times as long as wide; not strictly coastal . . . .*L. nevadensis*, pl. 279
                                              SIERRA NEVADA PEA
             Lathyrus nevadensis varies and is often divided into several subspecies or varieties.

Lotus

1 Leaves with 5 leaflets, the 2 lowermost ones widely separated from the others and so close to the stem that they are sometimes considered to be stipules (common weeds in fields and along roadsides)
    2 Stems usually solid except perhaps near the base, where it may be hollow; inflorescence usually with not more than 8 flowers; calyx lobes not curving outward before flowers open . . . .*L. corniculatus*
                                         BIRD'S-FOOT TREFOIL (Europe)

    2 Stems hollow; inflorescence usually with 8–15 flowers; calyx lobes usually curving outward before flowers open . . . .*L. uliginosus*
                                    LARGE BIRD'S-FOOT TREFOIL (Europe)
          Lotus corniculatus and *L. uliginosus* are sometimes considered to be variants of a single species.

1 Leaves, if with 5 leaflets, without 2 that could be interpreted to be stipules (in other words, if stipules are present, they do not resemble the leaflets)
    3 Stipules recognizable but small and very different from the leaflets, often membranous
      4 Banner of corolla yellow, the wings pink, and the keel with a purplish tip; leaflets usually 5–7 (stems generally prostrate; almost strictly coastal) . . . .*L. formosissimus*, pl. 280
                                           SEASIDE LOTUS

      4 Corolla not so striking as that described in the other choice 4; most leaves with at least 9 leaflets
        5 Peduncle of inflorescence with a small, leaflike bract (this with as many as 5 leaflets) well below the flower cluster
          6 Peduncles of inflorescences as long or longer than most leaves; leaves with as many as 15 leaflets; inflorescence usually with 6–10 flowers; corolla 10 mm long, white to pink, becoming streaked as it ages; fruit to 5 cm long . . . .*L. aboriginus*
                                        THICKET LOTUS

          6 Peduncles of inflorescences shorter than most leaves; leaves with as many as 23 leaflets; inflorescence usually with at least 12 flowers; corolla usually 10–12 mm long, greenish to red or purplish red; fruit to 7 cm long . . . .*L. crassifolius* var. *crassifolius*
                                        THICK-LEAVED LOTUS

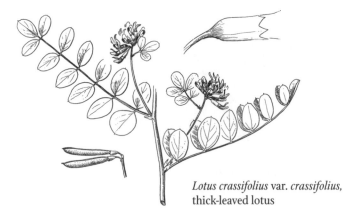

Lotus crassifolius var. *crassifolius*, thick-leaved lotus

5 Inflorescence without a prominent bract well below the flower cluster (if a small bract is present, it is just beneath the flower cluster)

  7 Leaflets usually 5 or 7 (not more than 7); banner and keel of corolla yellow, the wings white or yellow (mostly in bogs and other wet habitats, Wash. to Calif., also E of the Cascades) .... ***L. pinnatus***, pl. 282
                                        BOG LOTUS

  7 Leaflets usually 7 or 9 (sometimes 11); corolla usually pale yellow, but the banner sometimes reddish (usually along small streams but sometimes in other wet habitats, Lane, Josephine, and Curry Cos., Oreg., to Calif.) .... ***L. oblongifolius*** var. ***oblongifolius*** (*L. torreyi*, *L. oblongifolius* subsp. *torreyi*)
                                     NARROW-LEAVED LOTUS

3 Stipules either reduced to glands or not recognizable at all

  8 Rachis of leaves obviously flattened (this visible with low magnification)

    9 Flowers 1–2 in each leaf axil; corolla mostly cream to pale yellow but the tip of the banner purplish (leaves smooth to densely hairy; stems to more than 50 cm long, upright or falling down; in damp habitats, Brit. Col. to Calif.) ....***L. denticulatus***
                                     MEADOW LOTUS

    9 Flowers 1 in each leaf axil; corolla yellow, sometimes tinged with red

      10 Calyx lobes scarcely if at all longer than the tube (Umpqua River valley, Oreg., to Calif.) .... ***L. wrangelianus***, pl. 283
                                 HAIRY LOTUS, WRANGEL'S LOTUS

      10 Calyx lobes distinctly longer than the tube, often twice as long (Josephine and Jackson Cos., Oreg., to Calif.) ....***L. humistratus***
                                     HILL LOTUS

  8 Rachis of leaves not flattened

   11 Corolla (yellow, often tinged with orange or red) 8–10 mm long; body of fruit hairy, becoming conspicuously curved (often bending at an angle of more than 90°), not splitting apart at maturity (calyx hairy, the lobes about as long as the tube; Brit. Col. to Calif., on both sides of the Cascades) .... ***L. nevadensis*** var. ***douglasii***
                                     SIERRA NEVADA LOTUS

   11 Corolla not more than 8 mm long; body of fruit not hairy and not conspicuously curved (but the beak may be bent back)

     12 Leaflets usually 4–5, sometimes 3, not hairy; calyx not hairy, the lobes decidedly shorter than the tube; corolla 5–6 mm long, white, cream, or pale yellow, the buds and the back of the banner tinged pink, the flowers as a whole also becoming pink as they age ....***L. micranthus***, pl. 281
                                   SMALL-FLOWERED LOTUS

     12 Leaflets usually 3, sometimes 4–5, hairy; calyx hairy, the lobes longer than the tube; corolla 4–8 mm long, cream or pale yellow, often tinged with red .... ***L. purshianus*** (*L. unifoliolatus* var. *unifoliolatus*, misapplied)
                                     SPANISH CLOVER

Lupinus

In spite of much research on lupines of the Pacific Coast states, a definitive key to those of our region is difficult to make. A few species were described and named on the basis of apparently inadequate herbarium specimens. Other complications are variability within species and at least some hybridization between species. In large herbaria whose collections were built up over a period of many years, the identification of some specimens has been changed numerous times, from one species to another or from species to subspecies or variety and vice versa.

1 Prevailing color of corolla yellow (sometimes pale) or white, if white often becoming pale yellow after drying; fruits, except in *L. arboreus*, less than twice as long as wide (in some populations of *L. arboreus*, some
portions of the corolla, especially the banner, may be bluish or purplish)

  2 Plants obviously perennial, forming large bushes, commonly more than 1 m tall, many of the stems
woody, at least at the base; fruit elongated, generally 5–7 cm long, much longer than wide (leaflets
usually 7 or 11, typically with pointed tips; flowers about 15 mm long; coastal, on hillsides and on backshores of beaches, including sand dunes; native in Calif., introduced in Brit. Col., Wash., and Oreg. to
bind sand) . . . . *L. arboreus*, pl. 286
BUSH LUPINE (Calif.)

  2 Plants annual, not so much as 50 cm tall when flowering and not woody; fruits less than 2 cm long and
not much longer than wide (if the plant you are trying to identify has a mostly white corolla and fruits
that are much longer than wide, go to the second choice 1; it is probably a white-flowered form of a
prevailingly blue-flowered species)

    3 Stems generally spreading outward from the base; hairs on stems, petioles, undersides of leaflets, and
calyces mostly more than 3 mm long, sometimes 5 mm; leaflets 6–9, with pointed tips; corolla pale
yellowish or pure white when fresh except for dark dots on a small area of the banner (S Vancouver
Island and Gulf Islands, Brit. Col., and San Juan Islands, Wash.) . . . . *L. microcarpus* var. *scopulorum*
CHICK LUPINE

    3 Main stem or stems upright, the branching taking place mostly well above the base; hairs on stems,
petioles, undersides of leaflets, and calyces mostly less than 1 mm long (hairs on the mature fruit,
however, may be 4–5 mm long, as they are also in *L. microcarpus* var. *scopulorum*, first choice 3);
leaflets usually 6–7, typically with rounded tips; corolla decidedly yellow (Josephine, Jackson, and
Klamath Cos., Oreg., to Calif.) . . . . *L. luteolus*
INLAND YELLOW LUPINE

1 Corolla predominantly some shade of blue or purplish blue, with some white, but sometimes completely
white

  4 Relatively small annuals, rarely so much as 30 cm tall, often seeding in such a way as to form dense patches

    5 Leaflets to about 25 mm long, 8 mm wide; pedicels 2–5 mm long; flowers usually 10–13 mm long;
mature fruits usually 35–40 mm long (S Willamette Valley, Oreg., to Calif.) . . . .
. . . . *L. affinis* (*L. nanus* var. *carnosulus*)
FLESHY LUPINE

    5 Leaflets not often more than 2 mm long or more than 5 mm wide; pedicels only 1–3 mm long; flowers
usually less than 10 mm long; mature fruits not often so much as 25 mm long

      6 Flowers 6–9 mm long; banner bent backward at an angle of more than 60° from the midpoint of its
lower edge; upper surface of leaflets about as hairy as the underside . . . .
. . . . *L. bicolor* (*L. nanus* var. *apricus*), pl. 287
TWO-COLOR LUPINE

      6 Flowers 5–7 mm long; banner bent backward at an angle of less than 45° from the midpoint of its
lower edge; upper surface of leaflets only slightly hairy . . . *L. polycarpus* (*L. micranthus*, misapplied)
SMALL-FLOWERED LUPINE

        Lupinus bicolor and *L. polycarpus* intergrade to the extent that some botanists
would be content to put them under one name, which would, because of priority, be
L. bicolor.

  4 Perennials, often distinctly woody at the base and often much more than 30 cm tall (but certain
species, or at least some specimens, may be relatively small or form low growths because of their
sprawling habit)

    7 Plants low, with a woody base and sprawling stems that are also woody for much of their length,
forming dense mats; leaves and stems densely hairy, sometimes silvery; leaflets not often more than
1.5 cm long; inflorescence dense, commonly less than 4 cm long; flowers about 1 cm long, the corollas dark blue; at high elevations (well above 5000 ft., 1520 m) in the Siskiyou Mountains of SW Oreg.
and NW Calif., also other mountains in Calif. . . . . *L. breweri*
BREWER'S LUPINE

7 Plants not in all respects as described in the other choice 7

  8 Leaflets on larger leaves usually 10–15 (occasionally 17), to more than 12 cm long and sometimes more than 2 cm wide (racemes to about 40 cm long; free upper edges of keel, at least in plants of our region, without hairs; mature fruits usually 3–4 cm long, 7–8 mm wide) . . . . ***L. polyphyllus,*** pl. 291
                              LARGE-LEAVED LUPINE

          There are intergrading varieties of *L. polyphyllus;* the prevailing one in our region is var. *polyphyllus.*

  8 Leaflets rarely more than 10 and rarely so much as 10 cm long

    9 Plants strictly coastal, on backshores of beaches and adjacent hillside areas, sprawling and forming extensive mats, the upright flowering stems about 20–30 cm tall (stems conspicuously hairy, the hairs often especially dense at the nodes; leaflets mostly less than 3 cm long; mature fruits to 45 mm long by 7 mm wide) . . . . ***L. littoralis,*** pl. 290
                              SEASHORE LUPINE

    9 Inland species, usually not sprawling extensively or forming mats (2 that do sometimes sprawl, however, are *L. albicaulis* var. *shastensis* and *L. lepidus*)

      10 Free upper edges of keel without hairs

        11 When the banner is spread out, the upper one-third decidedly tapering to the tip rather than being evenly rounded (wings of corolla relatively narrow, only about half as wide as long, much of the widest part of the keel therefore exposed in flowers that have fully opened; 2 lobes of upper lip of calyx not so much as one-third as long as the lip as a whole; petals white to blue or purple, usually fading to brown)

          12 Flowers 12–16 mm long (Wash. to Calif.) . . . . ***L. albicaulis* var. *albicaulis***
                              SICKLE-KEELED LUPINE

          12 Flowers 8–11 mm long (plants often sprawling, only the flowering portions of the stems upright; Josephine Co., Oreg., to Calif.) . . . . ***L. albicaulis* var. *shastensis*,** pl. 284
                              SHASTA SPRINGS LUPINE

        11 When the banner is spread out, the upper third evenly rounded, except perhaps for a slight point at the very tip where the deep crease dividing the 2 halves lengthwise ends (most of the widest part of the keel covered by the wings in flowers that have fully opened)

          13 Two lobes of the upper lip of the calyx typically nearly one-third as long as the lip as a whole or even slightly more than one-third as long; petioles of leaves along the flowering stems not much more than 4 cm long; flowers usually at least 10 mm long, sometimes 14 mm (leaflets commonly 5–9 mm wide; corolla mostly pale purplish or some related color but occasionally pale yellowish; S Cascades of Oreg. to Calif.) . . . . ***L. adsurgens***
                              SILKY LUPINE

          13 Two lobes of the upper lip of the calyx much less than one-third as long as the lip as a whole; petioles of leaves along the flowering stems commonly more than 5 cm long, sometimes more than 8 cm; flowers usually 9–11 mm long (corolla blue or purplish; Puget Trough, Wash., and Willamette Valley to Douglas Co., Oreg.) . . . .
          . . . . ***L. oreganus***
                (*L. sulphureus* var. *kincaidii* of most references)
                      OREGON LUPINE

Lupinus oreganus,
Oregon lupine

10 Free upper edges of keel with hairs on at least a part of their length

 14 Upper lip of calyx divided for about half its length into 2 slender lobes

  15 Keel sickle-shaped and, except for its slender stalklike portion, at least 3 times as long as wide; back of the banner hairy; most of the keel hidden by the wings (banner usually blue, typically with a white or yellowish patch in the center, this darkening with age; fruit 3–5 cm long, 8–10 mm wide) ....*L. albifrons*, pl. 285

                         SILVER LUPINE

  15 Keel barely curved and, except for its slender stalklike portion, not so much 3 times as long as wide; back of banner not noticeably hairy; much of the keel exposed

   16 Racemes compact, less than 5 cm long and not so much as twice as long as wide; plants mostly high montane in the Olympic Mountains, Wash., and Cascades; usually not more than 10 cm tall ....*L. lepidus* var. *lobbii* (*L. lyallii*)

                         LOBB'S LUPINE

   16 Racemes usually much more than 5 cm long and more than twice as long as wide; plants not high montane; usually at least 20 cm tall when flowering ....*L. lepidus* var. *lepidus*, pl. 289

                       PRAIRIE LUPINE

      Plants in SW Oreg., N Calif., and eastward are often given the name *L. lepidus* var. *sellulus*. The flowers of var. *sellulus* (9–11 mm long) are generally slightly smaller than those of typical var. *lepidus* (11–13 mm long).

 14 Upper lip of calyx shallowly divided into 2 teeth

  17 Petioles of leaves along most portions of flowering stems not often more than 4 cm long; leaflets not often more than 3.5 cm long nor more than 7 mm wide (basal leaves generally absent or inconspicuous at flowering time, underside of leaflets white-hairy, the hairs not tightly pressed down; corolla mostly blue or blue-violet; widespread lowland species, Brit. Col. to Calif.) ....*L. rivularis*

                      RIVERBANK LUPINE

  17 Petioles of at least some leaves along flowering stems well over 5 cm long, sometimes more than 10 cm; leaflets commonly more than 3 cm long and more than 7 mm wide; basal leaves sometimes present at flowering time

   18 Tips of leaflets typically drawn out into a distinct process (mucron) 0.5–1 mm long; upper lip of calyx not conspicuously wider than the lower lip (leaflets commonly 30–45 mm long, sometimes 15 mm wide; underside of leaflets with pressed-down, whitish or brownish hairs; corolla violet or purplish blue but sometimes mostly white; Josephine Co., Oreg., to Calif.) ....
        ....*L. onustus* (*L. mucronulatus*, *L. sulphureus* var. *delnortensis*)

                     PLUMAS LUPINE

   18 Leaflets pointed at the tip but not drawn out into a distinct process so much as 0.5 mm long; upper lip of calyx usually conspicuously wider than the lower lip

    19 Hairs on leaves and stems sometimes conspicuous, many of them not pressed down; plants generally less than 25 cm tall; leaflets of larger leaves not often so much as 15 mm wide; high montane (Brit. Col. to Calif.)..
      ....*L. latifolius* var. *subalpinus* (sometimes called *L. arcticus* var. *subalpinus*)

                   HIGH-MONTANE LUPINE

    19 Hairs on stems and leaves mostly pressed down, rather than standing up; height usually considerably more than 25 cm tall; leaflets of larger leaves typically at least 15 mm wide, sometimes more than 20 mm wide (common in lowland and low to midmontane habitats, Brit. Col. to Wash.) ....*L. latifolius* var. *latifolius*, pl. 288

                   BROAD-LEAFLET LUPINE

      Much-branched and rather low-growing plants found in S Oreg. and N Calif. have slightly smaller flowers (8–10 mm long instead of 10–14 mm) than the widespread *L. latifolius* var. *latifolius*. These have been given the varietal name *viridifolius*.

Medicago

1 Corolla 6–11 mm long, usually blue or violet, sometimes pink, rarely white; stems upright (fruit spirally coiled, smooth) . . . .*M. sativa* subsp. *sativa*
ALFALFA, LUCERNE (Eurasia)

> *Medicago sativa* subsp. *falcata,* with corollas that are typically yellow and fruits that are curved but not coiled, will probably spread into our region; it is also of Eurasian origin.

1 Corolla generally less than 6 mm long, yellow or at least yellowish; stems usually sprawling to at least some extent

    2 Fruit not prickly, curved for less than 1 spiral turn . . . .*M. lupulina*
BLACK MEDICK (Europe)

    2 Fruit prickly, spirally coiled

        3 Most leaflets at least 1.5 cm long, with a central dark spot . . . .*M. arabica*
SPOTTED MEDICK (Europe)

        3 Most leaflets less than 1.5 cm long, without a dark spot . . . .*M. polymorpha*
BUR CLOVER (Europe)

Melilotus

1 Corolla white . . . .*M. albus*
WHITE SWEET CLOVER (Eurasia)

1 Corolla yellow

    2 Plants sometimes more than 1 m tall; corolla 4–6 mm long; leaflets usually toothed all around the margins . . . .*M. officinalis*
YELLOW SWEET CLOVER (Europe)

    2 Plants rarely so much as 1 m tall; corolla 2–3 mm long; most leaflets toothed above the middle . . . .
. . . . *M. indica*
SMALL YELLOW SWEET CLOVER (Europe)

Medicago lupulina,
black medick

Melilotus officinalis,
yellow sweet clover

Thermopsis

1 Stems conspicuously velvety-hairy, often silky (Josephine Co., Oreg., to Calif.) . . . .
. . . . *T. macrophylla* **var.** *macrophylla*
LARGE-LEAVED THERMOPSIS, FALSE LUPINE

1 Stems not conspicuously hairy (at lower elevations in the Coast Ranges and Cascades bordering the
Willamette Valley, Oreg., to Calif.) . . . . *T. gracilis*, pl. 295
SLENDER THERMOPSIS

> *Thermopsis gracilis* has also been treated as a variety (*venosa*) of *T. macrophylla;* fur-
> thermore, some specimens in our region are intermediate between *T. gracilis* and *T.*
> *macrophylla* var. *macrophylla*.

Trifolium

1 Each flower head with an involucre just beneath it (in most species the involucre is conspicuously toothed,
  and deeper clefts may separate groups of teeth into lobes; in *T. depauperatum,* however, the involucre is just
  a small cup without distinct teeth, and in *T. fragiferum* the involucre is poorly defined, consisting of only a
  few slender bracts that may be separate or connected at their bases)
  2 Involucre either cup-shaped, much smaller than the individual calyces and at most with only indistinct
    lobes, or consisting of a few slender bracts that may be separate or connected at their bases
    3 Involucre cup-shaped, sometimes with blunt, indistinct teeth; corolla reddish purple, becoming
      conspicuously inflated as it ages, but the calyx not obviously inflating; annual (SW Oreg. to Calif., also E
      of the Cascades; rarely found in W Brit. Col. or Wash.) . . . *T. depauperatum* **var.** *depauperatum,* pl. 298
      POVERTY CLOVER
    3 Involucre consisting of a few slender bracts that may be separate or connected at their bases; corolla
      pink to purplish, not inflating, but the calyx obviously becoming inflated, enclosing the corolla and
      becoming lopsided, 2 of the lobes much more prominent than the 3 small, bristlelike lobes; peren-
      nial, often rooting at the nodes . . . . *T. fragiferum*
      STRAWBERRY CLOVER (Europe)
  2 Involucre disklike, saucer-shaped, or bowl-shaped, usually divided into a few large teeth or into lobes
    consisting of a few to many small teeth
    4 Involucre shaped like a bowl or deep saucer, this enclosing the lower portions of the flowers (annual)
      5 Involucre distinctly lobed (each lobe with only 3–4 teeth), the separations between groups of teeth
        reaching almost half the distance to the attachment of the peduncle; calyx lobes much shorter than
        the tube, their membranous margins fringed with small teeth . . . . *T. microdon*
        VALPARAISO CLOVER
      5 Involucre with many small teeth, not distinctly lobed (if groups of teeth are slightly separated from
        one another, the separations are shallow and do not reach so much as one-fourth of the distance to
        the attachment of the peduncle); calyx lobes about as long as the tube, either with densely hairy
        margins or branched into a few stiff bristles
        6 Calyx lobes slender and hairy, not branched into stiff bristles; corolla dark purple (Curry and
          Josephine Cos., Oreg., to Calif.) . . . . *T. barbigerum*
          BEARDED CLOVER
        6 Calyx not hairy but divided into stiff bristles; corolla rose . . . . *T. cyathiferum*
          BOWL CLOVER
    4 Involucre nearly flat, not shaped like a bowl or deep saucer
      7 Involucral teeth numerous and separated to about the same depth so that the involucre is not dis-
        tinctly lobed (calyx lobes typically with 3 teeth but variable with respect to this character; annual)
        . . . . *T. willdenovii* (*T. tridentatum*), pl. 304
        TOMCAT CLOVER
      7 Involucre either rather distinctly divided into a few large teeth or into lobes that consist of groups
        of teeth
        8 Lobes of the involucre divided into a few conspicuous teeth (1 or more of these may be split into
          equal or unequal secondary teeth)

9 Lobes of the involucre hairy (flower heads about 1 cm wide) .... *T. microcephalum*
SMALL-HEADED CLOVER

9 Lobes of the involucre not hairy

  10 Flower heads about 1 cm wide, with not more than 15 flowers; corolla (white to pink or purplish) not becoming inflated on aging .... *T. oliganthum*
FEW-FLOWERED CLOVER

  10 Most flower heads at least 1.5 cm wide (sometimes as wide as 2.5 cm), with many flowers; corolla (cream, yellowish, sometimes distinctly yellow, but usually with considerable purple) becoming inflated on aging .... *T. fucatum* (*T. flavulum*), pl. 301
SOUR CLOVER

8 Involucre with numerous small teeth, groups of these sometimes forming separate lobes

  11 Plant as a whole soft-hairy and somewhat sticky; involucre, consisting of numerous teeth of varying size, not distinctly divided into lobes (annual; usually along streams; Douglas Co., Oreg., to Calif.) .... *T. obtusiflorum*
CLAMMY CLOVER

  11 Plant not noticeably hairy or sticky; involucre rather distinctly, even if irregularly, divided into lobes

    12 Calyx tube with more than 10 (usually about 15–20) lengthwise nerves; corolla purplish, often white-tipped; flower heads not often more than 1 cm long but sometimes considerably longer; annual or short-lived perennial .... *T. variegatum*
WHITE-TIP CLOVER

    12 Calyx tube with 10 lengthwise nerves; corolla reddish to purple; flower heads commonly at least 1.5 cm long; perennial .... *T. wormskjoldii* (includes *T. spinulosum* and *T. fimbriatum*)
COW CLOVER, WORMSKJOLD'S CLOVER

1 Flower head without an involucre beneath it

  13 Flower heads usually with only 3–6 fertile flowers, these with a yellowish, sometimes purple-tinged corolla 8–14 mm long and a calyx whose tube is purplish red and whose lobes are slender and green; as the fertile flowers age, a cluster of pale sterile flowers, each consisting of a calyx tipped with 4–5 pointed outgrowths, develops into a bur that wraps around the 1-seeded fruits; the bur typically is pressed into the ground by the lengthening peduncle (annual) .... *T. subterraneum*, p. 229
SUBTERRANEAN CLOVER (Europe, N Africa)

Trifolium cyathiferum,
bowl clover

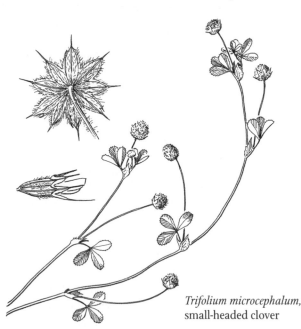

Trifolium microcephalum,
small-headed clover

13 Plant not as described in the other choice 13 (*T. glomeratum*, ball-head clover, native to Europe and an occasional weed in moist habitats, is not in the key—it is distinctive because its flower heads, borne in the axils of successive leaves, do not have a recognizable peduncle, and the pedicels of individual flowers are less than 1 mm long; the corollas are pink and slightly longer than the 10-ribbed calyx)

   14 Pedicels or bases of individual flowers accompanied by a slender, sometimes membranous bract

      15 Flower heads to about 4 cm long, 3 cm wide; individual flowers essentially sessile, the bracts accompanying them mostly at least 5 mm long, 1.5 mm wide, narrowing abruptly to a slender bristlelike tip; base of both wings of corolla with a bladderlike swelling; calyx with prominent ribs and becoming inflated (leaflets mostly 2–2.5 cm long; corolla white, aging to pink) . . . . **T. vesiculosum** var. **vesiculosum**
BLADDER CLOVER (Europe)

      15 Flower heads not so much as 2.5 cm long nor 2.5 cm wide; individual flowers with distinct pedicels, the bracts accompanying them not so much as 5 mm long or with a bristlelike tip; wings of the corolla without a bladderlike swelling; calyx without prominent ribs and not becoming inflated (wings without a bladderlike swelling at their bases)

         16 Flower heads mostly 1.5–2 cm long and broad; corolla white, sometimes pink-tinged; leaflets generally 1–2 cm long; plants generally low to the ground, spreading and rooting at the nodes, forming dense mats (common garden weed, often becoming established in places where it may appear to be native) . . . . **T. repens**
WHITE CLOVER (Europe)

         16 Flower heads not often more than 1 cm long or broad; corolla pale pink; leaflets generally less than 1.5 cm long; plants typically upright, not spreading or rooting at the nodes (not yet widespread in our region) . . . . **T. retusum** (Europe)

   14 Pedicels or bases of individual flowers not accompanied by a slender bract

      17 Flower heads sessile or on very short peduncles along the stems as well as at the tips; calyx lobes stiff bristles, the tube becoming inflated; corolla pink; plant as a whole very hairy . . . . . . **T. striatum**
SOFT TREFOIL (Europe)

      17 Flower heads not sessile or on very short peduncles (except in *T. albopurpureum* var. *dichotomum*, first choice 30, which does not fit all other criteria described in the other choice 17)

         18 Corolla bright yellow (small annual weeds)

            19 Most leaflets widest near the middle and not notched at the tip (flowers 5–6 mm long) . . . . **T. aureum** (*T. agrarium* of some references)
HOP CLOVER (Europe)

            19 Most leaflets widest near the tip and shallowly notched at the tip

               20 Each head with from a few to about 25–30 flowers, these mostly 3.5–4 mm long . . . . **T. dubium**, pl. 299
LEAST HOP CLOVER, SHAMROCK (Europe)

               20 Each head with at least 30 flowers, these mostly about 5 mm long . . . . **T. campestre** (*T. procumbens*)
LOW HOP CLOVER (Europe)

         18 Corolla white, cream, pale yellowish, pink, some shade of red, or purplish)

            21 Flower heads distinctly longer than wide, usually at least 1.5 times as long as wide

               22 Flower heads to about 2.5 cm long; corollas whitish to pale pink (most leaflets at least 4 times as long as wide, widest near the middle and pointed at the tip) . . . . **T. arvense**, pl. 297
RABBIT-FOOT CLOVER (Europe)

               22 Most flower heads more than 2.5 cm long, usually at least twice as long as wide; corollas bright red or pink

                  23 Corollas bright red; flower heads to about 4 cm long, about twice as long as wide; corollas bright red; leaflets not much longer than wide, widest near the tip, and shallowly notched at the tip . . . . **T. incarnatum**, pl. 302
CRIMSON CLOVER (Europe)

23 Corollas pink; flower heads to about 6 cm long, mostly at least 3 times as long as wide; corollas pink; leaflets to about 5 cm long and about 2 mm wide (hairs on stems and leaves pressed down) ....*T. angustifolium*, pl. 296

NARROW-LEAFLET CLOVER (Europe)

21 Flower heads not much, if at all, longer than wide

  24 Rachis of the flower head commonly (not necessarily always) continued beyond the uppermost flowers as a slender, sometimes branched projection

    25 Calyx lobes bordered by conspicuous, rather stout teeth (leaflets to about 3.5 cm long, widest near the middle, pointed at the tip; annual; corolla whitish to purple; Wash. to Calif.) ..... *T. ciliolatum*

TREE CLOVER

    25 Calyx lobes slender, smooth-margined

      26 Leaflets to 3 cm long, not often so much as 1.5 times as long as wide, widest near the tip and shallowly notched at the tip; corolla whitish to purple; annual ....*T. gracilentum*

PINPOINT CLOVER

      26 Leaflets to more than 4 cm long, most of them at least twice as long as wide, widest near the middle and pointed at the tip; corolla whitish or purple-tipped; perennial (in our region only in SW Oreg., also in the Cascades, to Calif.; not likely to be found below 3500 ft., 1070 m) .... *T. productum*

SHASTA CLOVER

  24 Rachis of the flower head not continued beyond the uppermost flowers

    27 Calyces (and usually also the rest of the plant) not at all hairy, but the margins of the calyx lobes and/or the margins of the leaflets may have bristlelike teeth (perennial; stems mostly upright, sometimes more than 40 cm tall; leaflets sometimes more than 5 cm long, 1.5–2 times as long as wide, widest near the middle, pointed or rounded at the tip; corolla white; Lane Co., Oreg., to Calif.) .... *T. howellii*, p. 230

HOWELL'S CLOVER

    27 Calyces (and usually at least some other parts of the plant) hairy

      28 Hairs on calyces restricted to the bases of the clefts between lobes (perennial; corolla usually pale pink, sometimes darker; common weed) ....*T. hybridum*

ALSIKE CLOVER (Europe)

Trifolium subterraneum,
subterranean clover

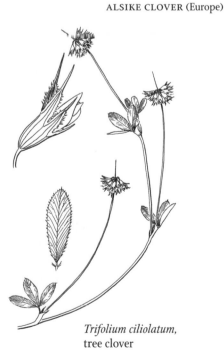

Trifolium ciliolatum,
tree clover

28 Hairs on calyces not restricted to the bases of the clefts between lobes

  29 Each calyx lobe with a few long, rather stout hairs, these longer and very different from the more crowded short hairs on the calyx tube (flower heads nearly or quite sessile, to about 3 cm long; calyx very hairy; corolla pink to purplish red, 1–2 cm long, twice as long as the calyx; perennial, commonly established along roadsides and in vacant lots) . . . . *T. pratense*, pl. 303

                                                    RED CLOVER (Europe)

  29 Calyx lobes without long, rather stout hairs that are very different from the hairs on the calyx tube

    30 Flower heads commonly borne in pairs above the uppermost leaves and often sessile (annual; corolla usually purplish but sometimes pink or nearly white, usually 6–9 mm long) . . . .

    . . . . *T. albopurpureum* var. *dichotomum* (*T. macraei*)

                                                TWIN-HEAD CLOVER

    30 Flower heads not commonly borne in pairs and on distinct peduncles, these generally at least 3 cm long

      31 Most leaflets 2.5–4 times as long as wide, widest near the middle, tapering gradually to the tip; marginal teeth crowded, about 10 within each 5-mm section of the edge (perennial and to a considerable extent montane, sometimes at high elevations) . . . . *T. longipes*

                                              LONG-STALKED CLOVER

        Several varieties of *T. longipes* have been named, but they intergrade so much that it is difficult to characterize them.

      31 Leaflets rarely more than 3 times as long as wide; marginal teeth rather widely spaced, only about 5 within each 5-mm section of the edge

        32 Flower heads dense, nodding by the time flowers are well developed, the peduncles bent down rather than remaining upright; most leaflets 2.5–4 times as long as wide, widest near the middle, tapering gradually to the tip; calyx conspicuously long-hairy; corolla yellowish, often purple-tinged . . . . *T. eriocephalum* var. *eriocephalum*, pl. 300

                                           WOOLLY-HEADED CLOVER

        32 Flower heads not nodding, the peduncles remaining upright (but individual flowers sometimes nodding after aging); most leaflets 1.5–3 times as long as wide, widest at or above the middle; calyx hairy but not conspicuously long-hairy

          33 Most leaflets 2–3 times as long as wide, very conspicuously notched at the tip (corolla usually pale pink; annual; S Oreg. to Calif., also E of the Cascades in Wash. and Oreg.) . . . .

          . . . . *T. bifidum* var. *decipiens*

                         NOTCH-LEAVED CLOVER, PINOLE CLOVER

          33 Most leaflets only slightly longer than wide, blunt or shallowly notched at the tip

            34 Flowers typically many in each dense head; stems and peduncles not especially slender; most or all individual flowers of the head sessile; corolla mostly purplish; annual . . .

            . . . *T. albopurpureum* var. *albopurpureum*

                     RANCHERIA CLOVER

            34 Flowers few (as many as about 10) in each loose head; stems and peduncles slender and delicate; individual flowers of the head with distinct pedicels; corolla cream to pink or rose; perennial (Josephine Co., Oreg., to Calif.) . . . . *T. breweri*

                     BREWER'S CLOVER

Trifolium howellii,
Howell's clover

Vicia

1 Flowers few in the axils of the leaves, not in a raceme with a distinct peduncle (annual)

  2 Corolla pale yellow, often either purple-tinged or with purple blotches

    3 Flowers 2–4 in each leaf axil; corolla not more than about 2 cm long, often with purple blotches . . . . ***V. pannonica***
                         HUNGARIAN VETCH (Europe)

    3 Flowers 1–3 in each leaf axil; corolla 2–3 cm long, often purple-tinged . . . . ***V. lutea***
                         YELLOW VETCH (Europe)

  2 Corolla typically deep pink, blue, purple, or some related color but sometimes white or nearly white (flowers 1–3 in each leaf axil)

    4 Corolla 5–6 mm long (lavender to pale blue, sometimes nearly white) . . . . ***V. lathyroides***
                         SPRING VETCH (Europe)

    4 Corolla at least 10 mm long

      5 Leaflets typically about 2–3 times as long as wide; calyx 10–15 mm long; corolla 18–30 mm long . . . . ***V. sativa* var. *sativa***
                         COMMON VETCH (Europe)

      5 Leaflets typically (but not always) more than 4 times as long as wide; calyx 7–10 mm long; corolla 10–18 mm long . . . . ***V. sativa* var. *angustifolia*** (*V. sativa* var. *nigra*), pl. 306
                         NARROW-LEAVED VETCH (Europe)

1 Inflorescence a raceme with a distinct peduncle (and sometimes with many flowers)

  6 Most leaves with at least 20 leaflets, plus the branching tendril (stems hollow; flowers as many as about 20 in each raceme; corolla dirty white to brownish orange, sometimes nearly clear orange or reddish; perennial) . . . . ***V. nigricans* var. *gigantea*** (*V. gigantea*), pl. 305
                         GIANT VETCH

  6 Leaves rarely with more than 18 leaflets, plus the branching tendril

    7 Most inflorescences with at least 18 flowers (racemes markedly 1-sided, the flowers facing in the same direction; corolla at least 1 cm long, usually deep purple, sometimes pale purple or white)

      8 Stems, leaves, and sepals distinctly hairy; base of calyx conspicuously lopsided, the upper portion forming a prominent bulge that protrudes back beyond the point of attachment of the pedicel; biennial . . . . ***V. villosa* var. *villosa***, pl. 307
                         WOOLLY VETCH (Europe)

      8 Stems, leaves, and sepals smooth or only slightly hairy; base of calyx not so lopsided that the upper portion forms a bulge that protrudes back beyond the point of attachment of the pedicel; perennial . . . . ***V. cracca***
                         BIRD VETCH (Europe)

            Some plants are intergrades that do not fit perfectly into either *V. villosa* var. *villosa* or *V. cracca*.

    7 Most inflorescences with fewer than 10 flowers

      9 Corolla at least 12 mm long, purple or rose and purple; perennial . . . . ***V. americana* var. *americana*** (*V. californica*)
                         AMERICAN VETCH

      9 Corolla not so much as 10 mm long, and not purple or rose and purple

        10 Most racemes with more than 3 flowers (to as many as 8); 3–4 mm long, whitish or pale blue; fruit conspicuously hairy . . . . ***V. hirsuta***
                         HAIRY VETCH (Europe)

        10 Racemes with not more than 3 flowers; annual

          11 Corolla 4–6 mm long, white to pale blue or pale lavender; tip of fruit with a small, hooklike remnant of the style on one side . . . . ***V. tetrasperma***, p. 233
                         SLENDER VETCH (Europe)

          11 Corolla 7–8 mm long, corolla white to lavender; tip of fruit tapering gradually to the remnant of the style (SW Oreg. to Calif.) . . . . ***V. hassei*** (*V. exigua*)
                         HASSE'S VETCH

FAGACEAE Oak Family

The oak family consists of trees and shrubs with alternate leaves. The staminate flowers, each with several sta-mens, are in elongated catkins; the pistillate flowers, each of which produces a nut, may be solitary (in oaks), in small clusters (in beeches), or in clusters at the bases of staminate catkins or on short separate pistillate catkins (in chestnuts and chinquapins).

Our representatives of the family are oaks (*Lithocarpus, Quercus*) and chinquapins (*Chrysolepis*). In oaks, the fruit is an acorn, consisting partly of a one-seeded nut derived from the pistil and partly of a scaly or bristly cup formed by bracts that were below the flower. In chinquapins, comparable bracts contribute to a spiny bur en-closing one to three nuts.

Oaks are notorious hybridizers. This does not present any special problems in British Columbia, Washing-ton, and northern Oregon, where there is only *Q. garryana*, but in southern Oregon and in California, where many areas have several species, hybrids are occasionally encountered.

1 Nuts (usually 1–2) enclosed within a spiny bur; leaf blades with golden scales on the underside, at least when young, but without lobes or marginal teeth (evergreen) ....*Chrysolepis*
1 Fruit an acorn (a nut partly enclosed within a cup); leaf blades not golden on the underside (except in *Quercus chrysolepis*, in which the undersides of the blades temporarily have golden hairs) but sometimes lobed or with marginal teeth
    2 Acorn cup with stout bristles, these spreading outward; staminate catkins stiffly upright (evergreen) ....*Lithocarpus*
    2 Acorn cup scaly, the scales pressed against the cup; staminate catkins usually drooping when well developed ....*Quercus*

Chrysolepis

1 Leaf blades (commonly 4–8 cm long) tapering to a blunt or only slightly pointed tip (the terminal portion is not elongated); bark of older specimens rather smooth (shrub rarely so much as 3 m tall; Jackson and Klamath Cos., Oreg., to Calif.) ....*C. sempervirens*
                                                      BUSH CHINQUAPIN
1 Leaf blades typically tapering gradually to a pointed tip (the terminal portion, in other words, is elongated); bark of older specimens usually rough and furrowed
    2 Large tree to more than 20 m tall; most leaf blades 7–9 cm long, flat (Wash. to Calif.) ....
    ....*C. chrysophylla* subsp. *chrysophylla*
                                                  GIANT GOLDEN CHINQUAPIN
    2 Large shrub or small tree, rarely more than 4 m tall; most leaf blades 3–4 cm long, noticeably folded at the midrib and usually with wavy or slightly upturned margins (Curry Co., Oreg., to Calif.) ....
    ....*C. chrysophylla* subsp. *minor*
                                                  SMALL GOLDEN CHINQUAPIN

Lithocarpus

1 Tree to more than 30 m tall; most leaf blades distinctly toothed and with a woolly coating on both surfaces when young, this coating easily rubbed off and much of it eventually shed, especially from the upper sur-face (Douglas, Jackson, Josephine, and Curry Cos., Oreg., to Calif.) ....
....*L. densiflorus* subsp. *densiflorus*, pl. 308
                                                  TANBARK OAK
1 Shrub to about 3 m tall; most leaf blades less than 5 cm long, either not toothed or with only an occasional tooth and not especially woolly on either surface, but both sides of the leaves nevertheless grayish (Josephine Co., Oreg., to Calif.) ....*L. densiflorus* subsp. *echinoides*, pl. 309
                                                  SMALL TANBARK OAK

Quercus

1 Leaf blades conspicuously lobed; deciduous

    2 Leaf lobes with bristle-tipped teeth; acorn enclosed by the cup for at least half its length (Lane Co., Oreg., to Calif.) . . . . *Q. kelloggii*

        KELLOGG'S OAK, CALIFORNIA BLACK OAK

    2 Leaf lobes without bristle-tipped teeth; acorn enclosed by the cup for much less than half its length

        3 Tree to 20 m tall; leaf blades to more than 10 cm long; winter buds only slightly woolly-hairy . . . .
        . . . . *Q. garryana* var. *garryana*, pl. 311

            GARRY'S OAK, WHITE OAK

        3 Shrub rarely more than 3 m tall; most leaf blades 5–7 cm long; winter buds gray, very woolly-hairy (on serpentine soils, Lane Co., Oreg., to Calif.) . . . . *Q. garryana* var. *breweri*

            BREWER'S OAK

1 Leaf blades not lobed (but they may be coarsely toothed); evergreen

    4 Most leaf blades at least 6 cm long (sometimes more than 12 cm long), rather evenly toothed (Douglas, Josephine, and Curry Cos., Oreg., to Calif., mostly above 2500 ft., 760 m) . . . . *Q. sadleriana*, pl. 312

        SADLER'S OAK, DEER OAK

    4 Most leaf blades less than 4 cm long, smooth-margined or toothed (often unevenly)

        5 Shrub or tree; leaf blades stiff, with golden hairs on the underside (these usually soon shed), either smooth-margined or with 1 or more sharp-tipped teeth (Douglas, Josephine, and Curry Cos., Oreg., to Calif.) . . . . *Q. chrysolepis*, pl. 310

            CANYON OAK

        5 Shrub not often so much as 2 m tall; leaf blades flexible, the underside without golden hairs, usually smooth-margined but sometimes with a few teeth that are not sharp-tipped (Josephine Co., Oreg., to Calif.) . . . . *Q. vaccinifolia*, pl. 313

            HUCKLEBERRY-LEAVED OAK

Vicia tetrasperma,
slender vetch

Chrysolepis chrysophylla subsp. *chrysophylla*,
giant golden chinquapin

Quercus kelloggii,
Kellogg's oak

FUMARIACEAE Bleeding-Heart Family

Bleeding hearts and their relatives are closely related to poppies and are sometimes placed in the same family, Papaveraceae. Many species of both groups, in fact, have the same characteristic smell when the foliage is bruised. In true poppies, however, the petals are all alike, and none of them has a spur at the base; the stamens, furthermore, are usually numerous. In members of the Fumariaceae, which have six stamens, two petals are different from other two, and the base of one or both of the outer ones has a saclike spur.

1 Both of the outer petals with a spur at the base; leaves strictly basal . . . . *Dicentra*
1 Only 1 of the outer petals with a spur at the base; leaves scattered along the stems
    2 Spur (when a flower is viewed with its long axis horizontal) bent slightly downward; corolla purplish, most intensely so at the tips of the petals; fruit nearly round; annual . . . . ***Fumaria officinalis***, pl. 317
                                                   FUMITORY (Europe)
    2 Spur not obviously bent downward; corolla yellow or some shade of pink, the color not especially intense at the tips of the petals; fruit at least somewhat elongated; biennial or perennial . . . . . . *Corydalis*

Corydalis

1 Lower stem leaves divided pinnately 2–4 times; corolla 20–30 mm long, pink, the spur 12–20 mm long (in moist habitats, mostly near the coast and at moderate elevations in the Coast Ranges and Cascades) . . . . . .
. . . . ***C. scouleri***, pl. 314
                                       WESTERN CORYDALIS
1 Lower stem leaves divided pinnately 4–6 times; corolla 12–20 mm long, pale to deep pink, often tinged with purple, the spur 9–11 mm long (along mountain streams, Clackamas and Multnomah Cos., Oreg., but only in a few localities; also on W slopes of the Cascades in S Wash.) . . . . ***C. aquae-gelidae***
                                       COLD-WATER CORYDALIS

Dicentra

1 Flower single at the top of the stem, this usually not more than 8 cm tall (corolla white to pale pink, but the inner petals usually with purplish tips (not likely to be found below 4500 ft., 1370 m) . . . . ***D. uniflora***
                                       ONE-FLOWERED DICENTRA
1 Flowers several on each flowering stem, this usually more than 15 cm tall
    2 Spurs of 2 outer petals 8–10 mm long, at least twice as long as wide at the base (corolla white to pale pink; mostly along banks of streams and rivers) . . . . ***D. cucullaria***
                                       DUTCHMAN'S-BREECHES
    2 Spurs of 2 outer petals bluntly saclike, not more than 4 mm long and no longer than wide
        3 Corolla purplish pink; leaves slightly but not conspicuously grayish . . . .
. . . . ***D. formosa*** subsp. ***formosa***, pl. 315
                                     WESTERN BLEEDING HEART
        3 Corolla whitish or yellowish, the tips of the 2 inner petals, in freshly opened flowers, tinged with rose; foliage conspicuously grayish (Josephine Co., Oreg., to Calif.) . . . . ***D. formosa*** subsp. ***oregana***, pl. 316
                                       OREGON BLEEDING HEART
            In *The Jepson Manual* the distinctive *D. formosa* subsp. *oregana* is mentioned in connection with *D. formosa* but is not given subspecific status.

GARRYACEAE Silk-Tassel Family

The shrubs called silk tassels have opposite, sessile or nearly sessile leaves. The flowers are in crowded inflorescences that resemble catkins, and pistillate and staminate flowers are on separate plants. In a staminate inflorescence the flowers are borne in groups of three above a pair of bracts; each flower has four stamens. In a pistillate inflorescence each flower has a single small bract beneath it. The fruit, when ripe, is somewhat fleshy inside but has a hard covering.

Garrya

1 Margins of leaf blades conspicuously wavy; dense hairiness on underside of leaf blades feltlike, the hairs interwoven, not conspicuously directed toward the tips of the blades (coastal, from Lincoln Co., Oreg., to Calif.) . . . .*G. elliptica*, pl. 318
COAST SILK TASSEL

1 Margins of leaf blades not conspicuously wavy; hairs, if present on the underside of leaf blades, pressed down and almost all directed toward the tips of the blades rather than interwoven

    2 Underside of leaf blades either without hairs or only sparingly hairy but even then soon shedding the hairs (in our region mostly in the Columbia River Gorge and SW Oreg., also on the W side of the Cascades from Linn Co., Oreg., to Calif., usually at elevations of at least 2000 ft., 610 m) . . . . . .*G. fremontii*
BEAR BUSH, FREMONT'S SILK TASSEL

    2 Underside of leaf blades rather densely hairy, almost silky, the hairs mostly pressed down and directed toward the tips of the blades (shrubs rarely more than 1.5 m tall; Josephine and Curry Cos., Oreg., to Calif.) . . . .*G. buxifolia*
BOXWOOD-LEAVED SILK TASSEL

GENTIANACEAE Gentian Family

Gentians and their relatives have opposite, sessile leaves. The calyx and corolla usually have five lobes, sometimes four, and the number of stamens is the same; the stamens are attached to the corolla tube. In the bud stage, the corolla lobes overlap one another with a slight twist. The fruit, when dry, splits apart lengthwise into two halves.

1 Corolla lobes much longer than the tube and opening widely; each corolla lobe with a conspicuous glandular pit bordered by a fringed membrane . . . .*Swertia*

1 Corolla lobes shorter, equal to, or only slightly longer than the tube, not opening widely (except in *Cicendia quadrangularis,* which is rarely more than 10 cm tall and has 4 yellow corolla lobes); corolla lobes without fringed glandular pits

    2 Plants rarely so much as 10 cm tall; stems rather sharply 4-angled; corolla bright yellow; calyx tube (cup-shaped, nearly as wide as long) with angular lengthwise ridges that reach to the 4 short, toothlike lobes (corolla closing at night and on dark, cloudy days; Willamette Valley, Oreg., to Calif.; also on the Pacific side of temperate South America) . . . .*Cicendia quadrangularis*
(*Microcala quadrangularis*)

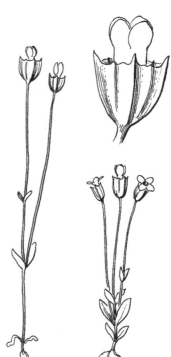

    2 Plants generally more than 10 cm tall; stems only slightly if at all angular; calyx tube without lengthwise ridges, the lobes substantial, not merely toothlike; corolla usually pink, blue, or violet, or at least tinged with one of these colors, sometimes white or salmon, generally 5-lobed (4-lobed in *Gentianopsis simplex* and sometimes in *Gentianella amarella*)

        3 Corolla usually bright pink (but sometimes white, yellowish, or salmon); corolla tube narrow, at least 5 times as long as wide; corolla lobes spreading widely . . . .*Centaurium*

        3 Corolla usually some shade of blue or violet (but sometimes only tinged with color); corolla tube not so much as 3 times as long as wide; corolla lobes not spreading widely outward . . . . . .
. . . . **Gentiana-Gentianella-Gentianopsis complex**

Cicendia quadrangularis

Centaurium

1 Most plants with several leaves forming a conspicuous rosette at the base; all flowers with a pair of bracts directly beneath them (in other words, they do not have distinct pedicels); biennial, now a common weed . . . . *C. erythraea* (*C. umbellatum* of some references), pl. 319
COMMON CENTAURY (Europe)

1 Leaves scattered along the stems, none of them forming a conspicuous rosette at the base; at least some flowers with distinct pedicels; annual

  2 Pedicels of some flowers at least 2 cm long and longer than the flowers themselves (in wet habitats, mostly E of the crest of the Cascades, only occasionally reported from our region) . . . . *C. exaltatum*
WESTERN CENTAURY

  2 Some flowers without pedicels (they arise directly above a pair of bracts), others with pedicels but these usually shorter than the flowers themselves . . . . *C. muehlenbergii*
MUEHLENBERG'S CENTAURY

Gentiana-Gentianella-Gentianopsis Complex

1 Annual, with a single stem bearing 1 flower; tips of corolla lobes bluntly rounded (in the Cascades of S Oreg. to Calif. and eastward) . . . . *Gentianopsis simplex*
ONE-FLOWERED GENTIAN

1 Perennial, with more than 1 flowering stem or the single stem usually with more than 1 flower; corolla lobes pointed at the tips

  2 Flowering stems arising from below a rosette of basal leaves

    3 Flowering stems usually at least 20 cm long; upper surface of corolla lobes deep blue, the outer surface usually green-tinged; pleats in line with the clefts between corolla lobes divided into 2–3 long, dark hairs (in fens or bogs, usually with *Darlingtonia*, Josephine Co., Oreg., to Calif.) . . . . *Gentiana setigera* (*G. bisetaea*), pl. 323
ELEGANT GENTIAN

    3 Flowering stems short, not often more than about 15 cm long; inside of corolla typically whitish and with green dots, the outside dark blue; pleats in line with the clefts between corolla lobes divided into 2 halves, these divided again into a few teeth tipped with slender hairs (montane and high montane, S Oreg. to Calif.) . . . . *Gentiana newberryi* var. *newberryi*, pl. 321
NEWBERRY'S GENTIAN

  2 Plants without a rosette of basal leaves, the stems arising directly from the root-crown

    4 Each flowering stem typically with 1 flower (leaves not often so much as twice as long as wide; pleats in line with clefts between corolla lobes ending in 2–3 narrowly triangular outgrowths; corolla usually 2–3.5 cm long, dark blue externally; in our region, widespread in the mountains but not often found below about 4500 ft., 1370 m) . . . . *Gentiana calycosa*, pl. 320
MOUNTAIN BOG GENTIAN

    4 Flowering stems usually with at least 2–3 flowers at or near the top, or with clusters of flowers in the axils of several pairs of leaves

      5 Corolla not more than 1.5 cm long; annual

        6 Lobes of the corolla nearly half as long as the tube, each with a fringe of long hairs originating at the base; corolla tube without pleats in line with the clefts between lobes . . . . *Gentianella amarella* subsp. *acuta* (*Gentiana amarella* subsp. *acuta*), pl. 324
NORTHERN GENTIANELLA

        6 Lobes of the corolla only about one-fourth as long as the tube, without a fringe of hairs at their bases; corolla with a pleat in line with the cleft between each 2 lobes, this pleat ending in 2 short outgrowths (in bogs, Alaska to N Wash., but rarely seen S of Brit. Col.) . . . . *Gentiana douglasiana*
DOUGLAS' GENTIAN

      5 Corolla at least 3 cm long; perennial

7 At least some leaves more than 3 times as long as wide; pleats in line with the clefts between corolla lobes squared-off at their free ends, without slender outgrowths (corolla usually 3–3.5 cm long; most commonly found in sphagnum bogs but occasionally in other wet places) . . . . *Gentiana sceptrum*, pl. 322
KING'S GENTIAN

7 Leaves generally not more than 2.5 times as long as wide; pleats in line with the clefts between corolla lobes with slender outgrowths

    8 Corolla 3.5–5 cm long, the margins of the lobes generally with a few small teeth; pleats in line with clefts between corolla lobes usually ending in several hairlike outgrowths (in wet mountain meadows, SW Oreg. to Calif.; not likely to be found below 3500 ft., 1070 m) . . . . *Gentiana plurisetosa*
KLAMATH GENTIAN

    8 Corolla usually 3–4 cm long, the margins of the lobes smooth; pleats in line with clefts between corolla lobes ending in a pair of triangular outgrowths (plants usually low and sprawling; in our region along the coast, Curry Co., Oreg., to Calif.) . . . . *Gentiana affinis* var. *ovata* (*G. menziesii*)
SPREADING GENTIAN

Swertia

1 Leaves on upper portions of flowering stems in whorls of 3–5; plants commonly about 50–100 cm tall; corollas 4-lobed, pale yellowish green, often tinged with green (on the W slope of the Cascades, Lane and Douglas Cos., Oreg., especially in the region of the tributaries of the Umpqua River) . . . .
. . . . *S. umpquaensis* (*Frasera umpquaensis*)
UMPQUA SWERTIA

1 Leaves on upper portions of flowering stems opposite; plants not often more than 60 cm tall; corollas 5-lobed, greenish white to pale blue, often with small darker dots (SW Oreg. to Calif.) . . . .
. . . . *S. albicaulis* var. *nitida*
WHITE-STEM SWERTIA

GERANIACEAE Geranium Family

Most plants of the geranium family have regular flowers; cultivated pelargoniums, with slightly irregular flowers, are exceptions. There are five separate sepals and petals, and usually 10 or 15 stamens. Some of the stamens may lack anthers, however, and the filaments are commonly at least slightly joined to one another at the base. The five styles of the pistil are bound together to form a long beak above the five-lobed seed-producing portion. When the fruit dries, the lobes separate, and each one, containing a single seed, retains its corresponding style. In *Erodium* the styles coil like corkscrews when they dry, but when they absorb moisture they straighten; the action of uncoiling literally drills the seeds into the soil. This family is represented in our region almost entirely by weeds. Some of these, however, are so well established in more or less wild areas that they may look like natives.

1 Leaves pinnately lobed or pinnately compound . . . . *Erodium*

1 Leaves palmately lobed (or, in the case of *G. robertianum*, palmately compound, the 3 primary divisions then pinnately but irregularly lobed) . . . . *Geranium*

Erodium

1 None of the leaves truly compound; fruit with a beak 5–7 cm long . . . . *E. botrys*
BROADLEAF FILAREE (Europe)

1 Most basal leaves pinnately compound, with at least 11 leaflets; fruit with a beak less than 5 cm long

    2 Sepals either acutely pointed or bristle-tipped; stipules pointed at the tip (the leaves of plants growing in relatively dry habitats generally form tight rosettes) . . . . *E. cicutarium*, pl. 325
COMMON STORKSBILL, REDSTEM FILAREE (Eurasia)

    2 Sepals neither acutely pointed nor bristle-tipped; stipules blunt at the tips . . . . *E. moschatum*
WHITESTEM FILAREE (Europe)

Geranium

1 Perennial to more than 60 cm tall; petals deep reddish purple, about 20 mm long (Wash. to Calif.) . . . .
. . . . *G. oreganum*, pl. 329
WESTERN GERANIUM

> *Geranium richardsonii,* Richardson's geranium, rarely encountered W of the Cascades, is similar to *G. oreganum* in size and growth habit, but its petals are slightly smaller (mostly about 15 mm long) and lighter (pale pink or white, with darker veins); the upper surfaces of the petals, furthermore, are conspicuously hairy for about half their length.

1 Annual or biennial, rarely more than 50 cm tall; petals not more than 15 mm long
  2 Petals at least 7 mm long
    3 Leaves shiny, not obviously hairy (larger leaves with only 5 lobes, these nearly as wide as long and with blunt teeth; sepals distinctly keeled; petals bright pink, 8–9 mm long) . . . . *G. lucidum*
                          SHINING CRANESBILL (Europe)
    3 Leaves obviously hairy
      4 Calyx glandular-hairy; leaves compound, the 3 primary divisions then pinnately but irregularly lobed (stems and leaves with a strong, rather unpleasant odor) . . . . *G. robertianum*, pl. 330
                          HERB ROBERT (Europe)
      4 Calyx not glandular-hairy; leaves deeply lobed but not quite compound (there are usually 5 primary lobes, these divided again; naturalized at a few localities) . . . . *G. columbinum*
                          LONG-STALKED GERANIUM (Europe)
  2 Petals less than 7 mm long
    5 Primary lobes of larger leaf blades not separated for more than two-thirds of the distance to the point where the petiole is attached
      6 Flowers with 10 anther-bearing stamens; fruit finely and irregularly cross-wrinkled but not obviously hairy . . . . *G. molle*, pl. 328
                          DOVE'S-FOOT GERANIUM (Europe)
      6 Flowers usually with 5 anther-bearing stamens (sometimes as many as 8); fruit not cross-wrinkled but with hairs, most of these pressed down . . . . *G. pusillum*, p. 16
                          SMALL-FLOWERED CRANESBILL (Europe)
    5 Primary lobes of larger leaf blades separated for more than two-thirds of the distance to the point where the petiole is attached
      7 Pedicels, by the time fruits have developed nearly to maturity, much longer than the calyx . . . .
. . . . *G. bicknellii* (includes subsp. *longipes*), pl. 326
                          BICKNELL'S GERANIUM
      7 Pedicels, by the time fruits have developed nearly to maturity, at most only slightly longer than the calyx
        8 Primary lobes of leaves separated nearly to the point where the petiole is attached . . . .
. . . . *G. dissectum*, pl. 327
                          CUTLEAF GERANIUM (Europe)
        8 Primary lobes of upper leaves not separated nearly to the point where the petiole is attached (the undivided portion of the blade is usually about 1 cm wide) . . . . *G. carolinianum*
                          CAROLINA GERANIUM

GROSSULARIACEAE Gooseberry Family

The shrubs we call gooseberries and currants, all belonging to the genus *Ribes*, have alternate and usually palmately lobed leaves. The flowers, in racemes, have five petals and five stamens. Much of the calyx is united with the pistil, so the fruit, which is fleshy, develops below the level at which the five calyx lobes are attached. The pistil has two styles, and the fruit has two seed-producing divisions.

Ribes

Do not mistake calyx lobes for petals; the petals are attached to the free portion of the calyx tube and, as a rule, are smaller than the calyx lobes.

1 Stems without prickles
  2 Free portion of the calyx tube more or less cylindrical, at least as long as wide
    3 Free portion of the calyx tube more than twice as long as the calyx lobes; leaf blades not often more than about 2.5 cm long (tips of anthers with a glandular depression; calyx and petals usually greenish, whitish, pink, or purplish; fruit red, at most only slightly glandular; montane and mostly E of the crest of the Cascades) . . . . *R. cereum* var. *cereum*, pl. 332
                                                      WAX CURRANT
    3 Free portion of calyx tube at most only slightly longer than wide; calyx lobes nearly or fully as long as the free portion of the tube; leaf blades usually at least 4 cm long
      4 Tips of anthers with a glandular depression; calyx usually whitish, greenish, or yellowish, often tinged with pink or purplish; petals white or slightly off-white
        5 Portion of calyx fused to the pistil conspicuously glandular and soft-hairy; ripe fruit (this blackish) without a whitish coating (montane and mostly E of the crest of the Cascades, Brit. Col. to Oreg.) . . . . *R. viscosissimum* var. *viscosissimum*
                                                 STICKY CURRANT
        5 Portion of calyx fused to the pistil neither conspicuously glandular nor obviously hairy; ripe fruit with a whitish coating (montane and mostly E of the crest of the Cascades, Oreg. to Calif.) . . . . . .
         . . . . *R. viscosissimum* var. *hallii*
                                                 HALL'S CURRANT
      4 Tips of anthers without a glandular depression; calyx and petals pale pink to deep reddish pink (rarely white)
        6 Sepals and petals bright pink to deep reddish pink (rarely white); underside of leaf blades sometimes so densely hairy as to be whitish . . . . *R. sanguineum* var. *sanguineum*, pl. 335
                                           RED-FLOWERING CURRANT
        6 Sepals and petals pale pink; underside of leaf blades sparsely hairy (along the coast, Lincoln Co., Oreg., to Calif.) . . . . *R. sanguineum* var. *glutinosum*
                  Ribes sanguineum vars. *sanguineum* and *glutinosum* intergrade, and some specimens cannot positively be assigned to one or the other.
  2 Free portion of the calyx tube cup-shaped, much broader than the portion fused to the pistil
    7 Inflorescences elongated, usually longer than the leaves below them, and generally with more than 15 flowers; bracts at the base of at least some pedicels fully as long as, or longer than, the pedicels (petals white; portion of the calyx fused to the pistil, and later the fruit, with glands and hairs but not gland-tipped hairs; ripe fruits whitish blue until the whitish coating is rubbed off; foliage with a strong, unpleasant odor; in moist forests, especially near the coast, also in the Coast Ranges, Olympic Mountains, and on the W slope of the Cascades) . . . . *R. bracteosum*, pl. 331
                                               STINK CURRANT
    7 Inflorescences usually shorter than the leaves above and below them, and not often with more than about 15 flowers; bracts at the bases of the pedicels much shorter than the pedicels; petals red, purplish, or some related color
      8 Racemes, at least when flowering, more or less upright; petals broadening gradually from near the base (portion of the calyx fused to the pistil, and later the ripening fruit, densely hairy; plants often falling down to some extent but the tips of the stems upright; mostly montane but also near the coast on the Olympic Peninsula, Wash.) . . . . *R. laxiflorum*
                                        TRAILING BLACK CURRANT
      8 Racemes, even when flowering, hanging down; petals broadening abruptly from a narrow stalk

9 Petals red; filaments of stamens much wider at the base than near the anthers; portion of calyx fused to the pistil, and later the ripening fruit, hairy; ripe fruit blackish with a powdery white coating (mostly montane in the Cascades, Brit. Col. to N Oreg., and in the Olympic Mountains, Wash.; also E of the Cascades) . . . .*R. acerifolium* (*R. howellii*)
MAPLE-LEAVED CURRANT

9 Petals reddish purple; filaments of stamens not conspicuously wider at the base than near the anthers; portion of calyx fused to the pistil, and later the ripening fruit, not glandular-hairy; ripe fruit red (montane, Alaska to Oreg. and eastward) . . . .*R. triste*
WILD RED CURRANT

1 Stems with prickles
　10 Stems with prickles between the nodes as well as at the nodes (fruit noticeably covered with glandular hairs)
　　11 Free portion of the calyx tube nearly saucer-shaped, much wider than deep; petals pinkish, about half as long as the calyx lobes . . . .*R. lacustre*, pl. 334
PRICKLY CURRANT

　　11 Free portion of the calyx tube about as deep as wide; petals white, pale pink, or yellowish, about two-thirds as long as the calyx lobes (near the coast, Douglas Co., Oreg., to Calif.) . . . .*R. menziesii*
COAST PRICKLY-FRUITED GOOSEBERRY

　10 Stems with prickles only at the nodes
　　12 Fruits not bristly; calyx green to reddish or purplish
　　　13 Stamens protruding about 2 mm beyond the tips of the calyx lobes (the calyx lobes turn back, however, soon after the flowers open); petals white to reddish . . . .*R. divaricatum* var. *divaricatum*, pl. 333
COAST BLACK GOOSEBERRY

　　　13 Stamens barely, if at all, extending beyond the tips of the calyx lobes; petals white (along the coast, Curry Co., Oreg., to Calif.) . . . .*R. divaricatum* var. *pubiflorum*
Ribes divaricatum vars. *divaricatum* and *pubiflorum* intergrade.

　　12 Fruits bristly; calyx red or purple
　　　14 Bristles on fruits crowded, less than 1 mm long, tipped with sticky glands (calyx lobes purplish red, petals white; mostly Josephine Co., Oreg., to Calif. but also in places on E and W sides of the Cascades in Wash. and Oreg.) . . . .*R. lobbii*
PIONEER GOOSEBERRY

　　　14 Bristles on fruits sharp-pointed, not tipped with glands (but in *R. roezlii* subsp. *cruentum* there are usually stalked glands between the bristles)
　　　　15 Free portion of calyx tube nearly as long as the calyx lobes; calyx crimson; petals white to pink; fruits usually with stalked glands between the bristles (Lane Co., Oreg., to Calif.) . . . . *R. roezlii* var. *cruentum*
SHINY-LEAVED GOOSEBERRY

　　　　15 Free portion of calyx tube less than half as long as the calyx lobes; calyx purplish red, petals white to bright yellow; fruits without stalked glands between the bristles (stems often spreading outward, touching the ground and rooting; Josephine and Jackson Cos., Oreg., to Calif.) . . . . .*R. marshallii*
MARSHALL'S GOOSEBERRY

HALORAGACEAE Water-Milfoil Family

Water milfoils are perennials rooted in mud of freshwater lakes and ponds. Those in our region, all belonging to the genus *Myriophyllum*, have feathery leaves divided into slender lobes. The inconspicuous flowers, with a cuplike, obscurely four-lobed calyx and sometimes four small petals, are borne in the axils of the submerged leaves or of the bracts that are part of an inflorescence raised above the water level. Staminate flowers, with four or eight stamens, are usually located above the pistillate flowers, which have one to four stigmas (often feathery) and which produce small fruits that split apart into four hard, one-seeded nutlets.

Myriophyllum

1 Flowers formed on submerged portions of stems, not on distinctly differentiated terminal inflorescences
....*M. farwellii*
FARWELL'S WATER MILFOIL

1 Inflorescences distinct from lower portions of stems and held above the waterline
  2 All leaves, and also the bracts of the inflorescence, most of which is held above the waterline, pinnately divided into slender, almost hairlike lobes ....*M. aquaticum* (*M. brasiliense, M. proserpinacoides*)
    PARROT'S FEATHER (South America)
  2 Bracts of the inflorescence, and also some other leaves, held above the waterline, toothed or lobed, but not similar to the lower leaves, which are divided into long, almost hairlike lobes
    3 Bracts of the inflorescence less than 3 mm long, shorter than the flowers, toothed or smooth-margined
      4 Most leaves with at least 30 slender lobes ....*M. spicatum*
        EURASIAN WATER MILFOIL (Eurasia)
      4 Leaves rarely if ever with more than 20 slender lobes ....
      ....*M. sibiricum* (*M. exalbescens* or *M. spicatum* subsp. *exalbescens* of some references)
        SIBERIAN WATER MILFOIL
    3 Bracts of the inflorescence at least 3 mm long, longer than the flowers, toothed or pinnately lobed
      5 Leaves partly opposite or in whorls, others alternate
        6 Submerged leaves usually with at least 15 slender lobes; divisions of fruit with numerous small warts ....*M. hippuroides*
          WESTERN WATER MILFOIL
        6 Submerged leaves usually with not more than 11 slender lobes; divisions of fruit smooth ....
        ....*M. pinnatum*
          GREEN PARROT'S-FEATHER
      5 Leaves strictly opposite or in whorls
        7 Bracts of the inflorescence (these 3–8 mm long) divided into slender lobes ......*M. verticillatum*
          WHORLED WATER MILFOIL
        7 Bracts of the inflorescence (at least the upper ones) merely toothed rather than lobed
          8 Most bracts of the inflorescence slender, much more than twice as long as wide ...*M. ussuriense*
            USSURIAN WATER MILFOIL
          8 Most bracts of the inflorescence, at least the upper ones, proportionately broad, at most only a little more than twice as long as wide ....*M. quitense*
            QUITO WATER MILFOIL

HIPPURIDACEAE Mare's-Tail Family

The Hippuridaceae is generally believed to have only a single species. This is *Hippuris vulgaris* (pl. 336), mare's tail, a partly submerged perennial rooted in mud in seepage areas and at the edges of lakes, ponds, and sluggish streams. It reaches a maximum height of about 40 cm and propagates itself vegetatively by creeping stems. The usually slender leaves, as long as 3 cm or more, are arranged in whorls and stand stiffly outward from the upright stems. The flowers, sessile in the axils of the leaves, are less than 2 mm long and lack petals. Most of them have a stamen as well as a pistil, but some have only one or the other. The fruit-forming part of the pistil is fused to the calyx, which has only rudimentary lobes. The fruit, about 2 mm long, is a one-seeded nutlike structure. This key distinguishes, strictly on the basis of vegetative characters, typical *H. vulgaris* from two other growth forms that some botanists consider to be distinct species.

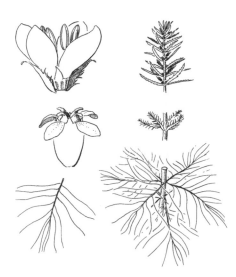

Myriophyllum hippuroides,
western water milfoil

Hippuris

1 Stems rarely more than 8 cm tall, 0.5 mm thick; leaves not often more than 6 mm long or 1 mm wide (montane at high elevations, Alaska to Wash. and eastward across northern North America; also E Asia) . . . .
. . . . *H. montana*
MOUNTAIN MARE'S TAIL

1 Stems commonly 20–30 cm tall (sometimes 40 cm), at least 1.5 mm thick; leaves usually more than 6 mm long, at least 1 mm wide
    2 Leaves slender, to more than 30 mm long, not more than about 2 mm wide, as many as 12 in each whorl . . . .*H. vulgaris*, pl. 336
COMMON MARE'S TAIL
    2 Leaves not more than about 15 mm long but comparatively broad, generally at least 3 mm wide, rarely more than 6 in each whorl (most commonly encountered in salt marshes and other saline habitats in the lowlands, Alaska to Brit. Col. and eastward across Canada) . . . .*H. tetraphylla*
FOUR-LEAVED MARE'S TAIL

HYDRANGEACEAE Hydrangea Family

Plants here placed in the hydrangea family have, in the past, been assigned to the saxifrage or gooseberry families, or to a family of their own, Philadelphaceae. They differ from saxifrages and gooseberries in having opposite leaves, and a distinctive feature of the flowers of one of our genera (*Philadelphus*) is the presence of numerous stamens. (Saxifrages do not have more than ten stamens, and gooseberries usually have five.)

1 Shrub to more than 2 m tall; leaf blades commonly 3–7 cm long; petals (white) 4, usually 1.5–2 cm long; stamens numerous . . . . *Philadelphus lewisii*, pl. 337
MOCK ORANGE

1 Low ground cover, the stems trailing and rooting at the nodes; leaf blades 1–2.5 cm long; petals (white) usually 5–6, about 4 mm long; stamens 8–12 (W Wash. and Oreg. to Calif.) . . . . *Whipplea modesta*, pl. 338
YERBA DE SELVA

HYDROPHYLLACEAE Waterleaf Family

The waterleaf family has representatives on all continents except Australia, but it is in western North America that there is an especially large number of species. Except for one shrub, *Eriodictyon californicum*, all that occur in our region are herbaceous. The flowers have five calyx and corolla lobes. The five stamens, attached to the corolla tube, alternate with its lobes. The pistil is partly or completely partitioned into two divisions. The inflorescence of some species is tightly coiled and one-sided. A few members of the genus *Phacelia*, especially *P. nemoralis*, have stinging hairs that may cause an unpleasant rash.

1 Evergreen shrub to about 2 m tall (leaf blades to more than 10 cm long, usually toothed, dark green, and shiny, the older ones often blackened by a fungus; corolla white or very pale blue; Josephine and Jackson Cos., Oreg., to Calif.) . . . .*Eriodictyon californicum*, pl. 339
YERBA SANTA
1 Herbs
    2 Flowers borne singly on peduncles originating in the axils of the leaves
        3 Leaves (mostly or entirely opposite) borne along sprawling stems, the blades deeply pinnately lobed; calyx with a slender, lobelike outgrowth originating between each 2 lobes . . . .*Nemophila*
        3 Leaves basal, the blades not lobed; calyx without a slender outgrowth originating between each 2 lobes (corolla pale blue or nearly white, with darker lines; Josephine and Jackson Cos., Oreg., to Calif. and eastward) . . . .*Hesperochiron pumilus*, pl. 340
DWARF HESPEROCHIRON

2 Flowers in distinct inflorescences
    4 Leaves mostly basal, the blades about as wide as long, often kidney-shaped in general outline and shallowly lobed . . . .*Romanzoffia*
    4 Stems with substantial leaves well above the base, and in most species the majority of the leaves pinnately lobed or pinnately compound
        5 Inflorescence rather compact and to a considerable extent branching dichotomously (that is, by twos); clusters of flowers on the ultimate branches of the inflorescence not in coiled, 1-sided aggregates that resemble the scroll of a violin; leaves pinnately lobed but not compound . . . . *Hydrophyllum*
        5 Inflorescence often elongated, not noticeably branching dichotomously; clusters of flowers on the ultimate branches of the inflorescence usually in coiled, 1-sided aggregates that resemble the scroll of a violin; leaves sometimes not lobed, sometimes with just 1–2 lobes but more commonly ranging from pinnately lobed to pinnately compound . . . .*Phacelia*

Hydrophyllum

1 Most leaflets or larger lobes with only 1–3 (rarely 4) teeth on each side (corolla white to pale lavender or purplish; stamens less than twice as long as the corolla; Marion and Polk Cos., Oreg., to Calif.; also E of the Cascades) . . . .*H. occidentale*, pl. 341
                                                        WESTERN WATERLEAF
1 Most leaflets or larger lobes with 3 or more teeth on each side
    2 Most leaf blades about as wide as long, usually with not more than 7 distinct lobes; stamens fully twice as long as the corolla; corolla generally green, greenish white, or cream, but deep blue or purple in populations on the N side of the Olympic Peninsula and extreme SW Wash. (common lowland species) . . . . *H. tenuipes*, pl. 342
                                                    SLENDER-STEMMED WATERLEAF
    2 Most leaf blades longer than wide, usually with at least 7 distinct lobes; stamens not quite twice as long as the corolla; corolla white or at least partly purplish (montane, mostly above 3500 ft., 1070 m) . . . . *H. fendleri* var. *albifrons*
                                                       FENDLER'S WATERLEAF

Nemophila

1 Corolla at least 1 cm wide (corolla white or bluish, the lobes with blackish dots from near the center toward the tips and edges, and sometimes also with blue veins; Willamette Valley and N coast of Oreg. to Calif.) . . . . *N. menziesii* var. *atomaria*, pl. 343
                                                      LARGE-FLOWERED NEMOPHILA
1 Corolla rarely more than 1 cm wide (corolla white or light blue, the lobes with or without darker veins, dots, or spots)
    2 Outgrowths between calyx lobes about half as long as the lobes; petals usually with darker veins, dots, or spots) . . . .*N. pedunculata*
                                                       MEADOW NEMOPHILA
    2 Outgrowths between calyx lobes rarely so much as one-third as long as the lobes; petals without darker veins, dots, or spots
        3 Lower leaves deeply 5- to 7-lobed, often nearly compound; corolla usually at least 4 mm long, sometimes nearly 10 mm (Rogue River valley, Oreg., to Calif.) . . . .*N. heterophylla*
                                                     VARIABLE-LEAF NEMOPHILA
        3 Lower leaves with 3–5 lobes separated about halfway to the midrib, never nearly compound; corolla not often more than 4 mm long . . . .*N. parviflora* var. *parviflora*, pl. 344
                                                    SMALL-FLOWERED NEMOPHILA

Phacelia

1 None of the leaf blades lobed and usually not even toothed

  2 Small upright annual (mostly less than 20 cm tall)

    3 Stems, leaves, and sepals very hairy but the hairs not glandular (corolla white to pale blue, 5–7 mm long, the lobes not spreading outward; Umpqua River valley, Oreg.) . . . . *P. verna*
                 SPRING PHACELIA

    3 Stems, leaves, and sepals glandular-hairy; corolla lobes spreading to at least some extent

      4 Corolla (4–5 mm long) bright violet-blue (Jackson, Josephine, and Klamath Cos., Oreg.; not likely to be found below 4000 ft., 1220 m) . . . . *P. peckii*
                 PECK'S PHACELIA

      4 Corolla lavender

        5 Corolla 2–3 mm long; style hairy below the level where it branches (Josephine Co., Oreg., to Calif.; not likely to be found below 4000 ft., 1220 m) . . . . *P. pringlei*
                 PRINGLE'S PHACELIA

        5 Corolla 3–6 mm long; style not hairy (Siskiyou and Trinity Cos., Calif., and perhaps to be expected in Josephine and Jackson Cos., Oreg.; not likely to be found, however, below 3500 ft., 1070 m) . . . . *P. leonis*
                 SISKIYOU PHACELIA

  2 Perennial, usually with at least several main stems originating at the base (leaves often at least somewhat silvery-hairy)

    6 Leaves sessile; larger blades slender, usually at least 10 times as long as wide (inflorescence consisting of only 2–3 corymbs, these crowded together to form a dense head; corolla white; on serpentine soils, interior of Coos Co., Oreg.) . . . . *P. capitata*
                 CAPITATE PHACELIA

    6 Leaves with distinct petioles, the larger blades fairly broad, not more than about 5 times as long as wide

      7 Larger blades only 1.5–2 times as long as wide (corolla white or very pale yellow; on backshores of sandy beaches, Curry Co., Oreg., to Calif.) . . . . *P. argentea*, pl. 345
                 SAND-DUNE PHACELIA

      7 Most larger blades 3–5 times as long as wide (corolla white to pale purplish; at moderate and high elevations in the Cascades) . . . . *P. hastata*
               Phacelia hastata, whose leaf blades sometimes have a pair of small lateral lobes, is dealt with in more detail in choice 16 under the second choice 1.

1 Blades of at least some leaves either coarsely toothed or with 1 or more pairs of lobes, sometimes both

  8 Leaf blades broad (and usually not so much as twice as long as wide), coarsely toothed, the larger teeth often with smaller teeth (in *P. bolanderi*, many leaves may also be divided into a large terminal lobe and a pair of small lateral lobes)

    9 Perennial, with stems to more than 1 m long and usually sprawling; larger leaves often divided into a large terminal lobe and a pair of small lateral lobes; calyx lobes all alike (corolla lavender, purplish, or bluish; primarily coastal, from Pacific and Wahkiakum Cos., Wash., to Calif., but the distribution not continuous; also inland in the Umpqua River valley and Siskiyou Mountains, Oreg. and NW Calif.) . . . . *P. bolanderi*, pl. 346
                 BOLANDER'S PHACELIA

    9 Annual, mostly somewhat bushy; leaf blades not divided into a large terminal lobe and a pair of small lobes; calyx lobes obviously unequal, 1–2 of them much wider than the others

      10 Stamens at least 5 mm long, protruding out of the corolla tube; corolla cream-white; stiff hairs on leaves and stems yellowish (strictly coastal, Curry Co., Oreg., to Calif.) . . . . *P. malvifolia*
                 MALLOW-LEAVED PHACELIA

      10 Stamens only 2–3 mm long, not protruding out of the corolla tube; corolla white to pale blue; stiff hairs on leaves and stems whitish or clear (Rogue River valley, Oreg., to Calif.; also E of the Cascades; usually close to streams) . . . . *P. rattanii*
                 RATTAN'S PHACELIA

8 Leaf blades either lobed bipinnately (most of the primary lobes with such slender connections to the rachis that they are nearly leaflets) or lobed in some other way

  11 Leaf blades lobed bipinnately, most of the primary lobes with such slender connections to the rachis that they are nearly leaflets; secondary lobes less deeply separated than the primary lobes but the foliage in general reminiscent of some ferns (corolla pale blue or purplish blue, 7–10 mm long and about as wide; annual; widespread in Calif., Arizona, and Baja Calif., and occasionally found in our region where commercial mixes of so-called wildflower seeds have been sown) . . . . *P. tanacetifolia*
TANSY PHACELIA

  11 Leaf blades not clearly bipinnately lobed (they are either somewhat irregularly divided into primary and secondary lobes or have 1 or more pairs of lobes or leaflets below a usually much larger terminal lobe)

    12 Leaf blades (often silvery due to hairs that are mostly pressed down) somewhat irregularly divided into primary and secondary lobes (corolla dark blue or purplish blue, about 6 mm long and wide; perennial; montane and in our region not likely to be found much below 5000 ft., 1520 m; Brit. Col. to Calif., also E of the Cascades) . . . .*P. sericea*
GRAY PHACELIA

    12 Some leaf blades with 1 or more pairs of lobes or leaflets below the terminal lobe

      13 Slender annual, to more than 40 cm tall, typically branched only above, not from the base (corollas lavender-blue, as wide or wider than long when fully open; mostly E of the crest of the Cascades but found in the Columbia River Gorge, and on the Gulf Islands and S Vancouver Island, Brit. Col.) . . . .*P. linearis*
SLENDER-LEAVED PHACELIA

      13 Biennial or perennial, generally branching at the base but sometimes with a single upright stem to much more than 40 cm tall

        14 Terminal lobe of the leaf blades not conspicuously larger than the lower lobes (or leaflets, when the connection to the rachis is very slender; plants often more than 1 m tall, with a single stem that is typically not branched except in the inflorescence; corolla usually 7–9 mm wide, slightly wider than long, greenish, cream, or brownish; in our region, in the Cascades at moderate elevations, Wash. to Calif., also E of the crest of the Cascades) . . . . *P. procera*
TALL PHACELIA

        14 Terminal lobe of the leaf blade typically much larger than the lower lobes (or leaflets)

          15 Leaf blades with not more than 1 pair of lobes below the terminal lobe (plants not often more than 50 cm tall, branching from the base; corolla to 7 mm long and wide, white to pale purplish)

            16 Low, compact, high-montane plants in the Cascades . . . . *P. hastata* var. *compacta*
TIMBERLINE PHACELIA

            16 Upright plants to more than 40 cm tall, mostly at moderate elevations in the Olympic Mountains, Wash., and Cascades, Brit. Col. to Oreg. . . . . *P. hastata* var. *leptosepala*
WHITE-LEAF PHACELIA

          15 Leaf blades commonly with 2 or more pairs of lobes or leaflets below the terminal lobe

            17 At least some leaves of the inflorescence lobed in the same way as the lower leaves (plants commonly more than 1 m tall, typically with a single main stem around which shorter stems have developed; stems and petioles with abundant stiff, straight hairs; corolla to about 7 mm long and wide, white to lavender) . . . . *P. heterophylla* subsp. *virgata*
VARIED-LEAF PHACELIA

            17 Leaves of the inflorescence not lobed

              18 Stems with abundant gland-tipped hairs but most of these shorter than the nonglandular hairs (plants low, not often more than 35 cm tall when flowering; inflorescences consisting of several corymbs originating at different levels; corolla white, to 7 mm long and wide; Josephine and Curry Cos., Oreg., to Calif.) . . . . *P. corymbosa*, pl. 347
SERPENTINE PHACELIA

18 Stems without gland-tipped hairs

    19 Plants commonly at least 1 m tall, the stems with bristly, often stinging hairs; leaves with as many as 7 lobes or leaflets; corolla greenish white to yellowish (Wash. to Calif.) . . . . ***P. nemoralis***
           BRISTLY PHACELIA

    19 Plants not often more than about 50 cm tall, the stems with hairs but these not stinging and many of them pressed down; leaves with not more than 3 lobes; corolla white, yellowish, or lavender (Wash. to Calif.) . . . . ***P. mutabilis***
           CHANGEABLE PHACELIA

Romanzoffia

1 Plants annual, not producing a bulblike structure consisting of bases of petioles of previous lower leaves; some lower leaves opposite; leaf blades rarely more than 7 mm long or wide, either not lobed or with not more than 5 lobes; corolla usually about 5.5 mm long and with a prominent dark spot below each lobe (plants delicate, the longest stems not often more than about 10 cm long; in the Cascades, from lower elevations to about 6000 ft., 1830 m, and in the Coast Ranges of Marion, Linn, Lane, and Douglas Cos., Oreg.) . . . . ***R. thompsonii***
           THOMPSON'S MIST MAIDEN

1 Plants perennial, producing a bulblike structure consisting of slightly to considerably thickened bases of petioles of previous lower leaves; none of the leaves opposite; larger leaf blades usually at least 1 cm long and wide, and commonly with at least 5 lobes; corolla usually at least 6 mm long and without a dark spot below each lobe

    2 Plants compact (the flowers typically not raised much above the longest basal leaves) and obviously hairy, the hairs multicellular; bulblike structure at base consisting of 2 rows of thickened petiole bases covered with matted, woolly hairs; tube of corolla as long as or longer than the lobes; strictly coastal, Brit. Col. to Calif. . . . . ***R. tracyi***
           SEA-CLIFF MIST MAIDEN

    2 Plants not especially compact (at least many of the flowers raised well above the longest basal leaves) and usually not very hairy, with only short, 1-celled hairs that bear a gland at the tip but sometimes also with multicellular hairs; tube of corolla as long as or longer than the lobes (except in *R. sitchensis* f. *greenei*); mostly inland, rarely on the coast itself

        3 Styles mostly 3.5–6 mm long, the basal portion distinctly hairy; mature fruits nearly twice as long as wide; thickened petiole bases forming a bulblike structure at the base of plant arranged in 2 vertical rows and mostly obscured by matted, woolly hairs; Coast Ranges, N Oreg. to Calif., also in the Cascades from N Lane Co., Oreg., to Calif. . . . . ***R. californica***
           CALIFORNIA MIST MAIDEN

        3 Styles mostly 3–5 mm long, the basal portion not hairy; mature fruits about 1.3 times as long as wide; thickened petiole bases forming a bulblike structure at the base of plant somewhat scalelike, arranged in a spiral pattern, the hairs that are present neither matted nor obscuring them; on seasonally wet rocks, mostly at low to moderate elevations, Alaska to Calif. . . . . ***R. sitchensis***, pl. 348
           SITKA MIST MAIDEN

           In some references, plants from the Columbia River Gorge, with hairless styles mostly 2–3 mm long and mature fruits about 1.6 times as long as wide, have been identified as *R. californica*. They conform to what had been described long ago as *R. suksdorfii*, but they are probably more closely related to typical *R. sitchensis*, and the best name for them at present is *R. sitchensis* f. *suksdorfii*. In plants from the Cascades westward, the corolla tube is no longer than the lobes, the styles are 3–5 mm long, and the mature fruits are about 1.3 times as long as wide. These, for the time being, can be called *R. sitchensis* f. *greenei*.

HYPERICACEAE Saint-John's-Wort Family

Members of the Saint-John's-wort family in our region are perennials with opposite, smooth-margined leaves that lack distinct petioles. The flowers have five sepals, five petals, and numerous stamens that are concentrated in three or more clusters. (In all species in this key, there are three clusters.) The pistil, usually with at least three styles, usually develops into a dry fruit with many seeds.

Only three of the species are native, and none of these is as commonly encountered as the European *Hypericum perforatum,* now a noxious weed. Several other introduced species have been found in British Columbia, Washington, and Oregon. Most of them are restricted to bogs where the cranberry is cultivated.

Omitted from this key are *Hypericum androsaemum,* called tutsan, and *H. calycinum,* the rose of Sharon, which are widely cultivated and occasionally escape. In both, the leaf blades generally exceed 5 cm long by 2.5 cm wide, and there are five clusters of stamens. The flowers of *H. androsaemum* are about 2 cm in diameter, and the fruits are fleshy, first red, then blackish purple; in *H. calycinum* the flowers are usually at least 5 cm in diameter, and the fruits are dry when mature.

In some references, the name Clusiaceae is given to a larger assemblage that includes *Clusia* and some other tropical genera as well as those here placed in Hypericaceae.

1 Petals yellow or orange-yellow; conspicuous orange or red glands not present between clusters of stamens
. . . . *Hypericum*
1 Petals pink, orange-pink, or purplish; conspicuous orange or red glands present between clusters of stamens (leaves mostly 2–4 cm long, usually less than twice as long as wide) . . . . *Triadenum fraseri*
MARSH SAINT-JOHN'S-WORT (E United States)

Hypericum

1 Upright portions of otherwise prostrate stems not often more than 10 cm tall (petals 3–4 mm long, pale yellow; plants forming mats at the edges of bogs, ponds, lakes, and other wet places) . . . .
. . . . *H. anagalloides*, pl. 349
BOG SAINT-JOHN'S-WORT
1 Upright stems, or upright portions of sprawling stems, commonly more than 20 cm tall
  2 Petals considerably longer than the sepals and with blackish dots (the leaves, sepals, and anthers may also have blackish dots)
    3 Leaves with crowded translucent dots on the underside, these sometimes exceeding 100 per leaf; sepals slender, less than 1.5 mm wide (petals with coarse, oval, black dots, these mostly close to the edges) . . . . *H. perforatum*, pl. 350
COMMON SAINT-JOHN'S-WORT, KLAMATH WEED (Europe)
    3 Leaves oval or elongated, with relatively few (usually not more than 30) translucent dots on the underside; sepals more or less oval, usually more than 1.5 mm wide
      4 Stems with 4 raised lines above each node (making the stems appear slightly 4-angled); edges of sepals smooth; petals with numerous coarse black dots, these not limited to the edges and often forming nearly distinct lines . . . . *H. maculatum* subsp. *obtusiusculum*
IMPERFORATE SAINT-JOHN'S-WORT (Europe)
      4 Stems with only 2 raised lines above each node; edges of sepals slightly ragged or with fine teeth; petals with small black dots, these at the edges (usually in ditches and other wet habitats) . . . .
. . . . *H. scouleri* subsp. *scouleri* (*H. formosum* subsp. *scouleri*)
WESTERN SAINT-JOHN'S-WORT
  2 Petals at most only 1–2 mm longer than the sepals and without blackish dots
    5 Leaves very slender, not often more than 3 mm wide and mostly at least 10 times as long as wide (petals orange-yellow, about 5 mm long) . . . . *H. canadense*
CANADIAN SAINT-JOHN'S-WORT (E North America)
    5 Leaves not especially slender, the larger ones more than 3 mm wide and mostly 3–6 times as long as wide

6 Petals mostly 6–7 mm long; pistil with single style (but this splits apart when the fruit dries and ruptures) . . . .*H. ellipticum*
PALE SAINT-JOHN'S-WORT (E United States)

6 Petals not more than 4 mm long; pistil with 3–4 styles
  7 Bracts beneath individual flowers or ultimate clusters of flowers mostly 2–3 times as long as wide
  . . . . **H. boreale**
  NORTHERN SAINT-JOHN'S-WORT (E North America)
  7 Bracts beneath individual flowers or ultimate clusters of flowers slender, at least 4 times as long as wide
    8 Larger leaves 2–3 times as long as wide; sepals mostly 2–3 mm long when fruits are well developed (2.5–3.5 mm long) . . . . *H. mutilum*
    SMALL-FLOWERED SAINT-JOHN'S-WORT (E North America)
    8 Larger leaves 3–4 times as long as wide; sepals 4.5–5.8 mm long when fruits are well developed (5–6 mm long) . . . .*H. majus*
    LARGER CANADIAN SAINT-JOHN'S-WORT (E North America)

LAMIACEAE Mint Family

The mint family gives us many species used in cooking, perfumery, and medicine. Rosemary, French lavender, thyme, marjoram, sage, and various mints are among the more important kinds that provide flavors or fragrances, and a packet of dry catnip will get the attention of almost any cat. Among the medicinal species, there are horehound, self-heal, and motherwort. While the majority of mints are aromatic, their fragrances are not always pleasing.

This family has a distinctive complex of characters. The stems are four-angled in cross section, and the leaves are opposite, with successive pairs at an angle of 90° to one another. The flowers are borne in the axils of the leaves; they are sometimes solitary but more often appear to be in whorls, and in certain genera the whorls are so crowded that the inflorescence is a continuous spike or a dense head. The five-lobed corolla is usually two-lipped, with two lobes generally forming the upper lip, three forming the lower lip. The five-lobed calyx may also be appreciably two-lipped. There are four stamens, in two pairs, but those of the upper pair often lack anthers. The fruiting part of the pistil is divided into four lobes, each of which becomes a one-seeded nutlet.

The mint family is large and diversified, so expect deviations from the formula just described. The flowers of some species are nearly regular rather than obviously two-lipped; others have such a small upper lip that this may seem to consist of only one lobe; in still others, the two lateral lobes of the lower lip appear to be part of the upper lip. In spite of such departures from the usual pattern, a little experience with some common mints will prepare you for placing almost any other species in the family.

1 Blades of lower leaves palmately lobed (flowers in dense clusters in the axils of upper leaves, which are mostly either 3-lobed or not lobed; corolla 1 cm long, pale pink, the upper lip consisting of a single, very hairy lobe; lower 2 calyx lobes directed downward; established in only a few localities in our region) . . . . *Leonurus cardiaca*
MOTHERWORT (Eurasia)

1 None of the leaf blades palmately lobed
  2 Corolla not obviously 2-lipped, appearing to consist of 4 nearly equal lobes (1–2 lobes, however, are appreciably wider than the others, and the largest lobe is often notched at the tip)
    3 Flowers with 2 anther-bearing stamens (there are also 2 sterile stamens); foliage, if bruised, not aromatic (flowers in clusters in the axils of the leaves; corollas white, or sometimes pinkish in *L. uniflorus*); plants of wet or marshy places) . . . . *Lycopus*
    3 Flowers with 4 anther-bearing stamens; foliage, if bruised, with a pleasing minty aroma
      4 Inflorescence a single dense cluster of flowers with 3 series of leafy bracts (lower, middle, and upper) below it . . . . *Monardella*
      4 Inflorescences elongated, with many flower clusters . . . . *Mentha*

2 Corolla decidedly 2-lipped, the upper lip consisting of 1–2 lobes, the lower lip usually consisting of 3 lobes (but in *Lamium* the middle lobe of the lower lip is notched, and the 2 lateral lobes are obscure, represented by a pair of slender, tooth- or filamentlike outgrowths. A few cultivated species sometimes escape: (1) In *Ajuga reptans,* the upper lip of the corolla is so short compared to the 3-lobed lower lip that it may seem to be lacking. This species, as tall as about 30 cm and usually with bronze-colored leaves and a congested inflorescence, spreads by creeping stolons. The corollas are usually blue, sometimes pink or white. (2) In *Salvia,* unique among the genera under this choice, there are only 2 stamens. At least 2 species of European origin have been found as escapes; in both, the upper lip of the corolla is long and arching, and is like a hood enclosing the stamens and pistil for much of their length. In *S. sclarea,* clary or clear eye, a bushy biennial that reaches a height of more than 1 m, the corolla is generally tinged with violet; the broad bracts in whose axils the flowers originate are papery and also tinged with violet or pink. In *S. glutinosa,* Jupiter's distaff, the corolla is pale yellow; the bracts are small and green.)

5 Calyx with 10 lobes, these slender, their tips somewhat spinelike and hooked . . . . ***Marrubium vulgare***
HOREHOUND (Europe)

5 Calyx with 5 lobes except in *Scutellaria,* in which the calyx has 2 lips, these not divided further

  6 Calyx (this with 2 lips, neither of which is divided into lobes) with a prominent curved ridge extending across its upper side; lower 2 stamens with only 1 functional pollen sac (corolla blue) . . . . ***Scutellaria***

  6 Calyx without a prominent curved ridge extending across its upper side; all 4 stamens normally with 2 pollen sacs

    7 Calyx distinctly 2-lipped, the upper lip with 3 lobes that are much shorter than the 2 lobes of the lower lip (in *Prunella vulgaris* the lobes of the upper lip are represented by 3 small teeth)

      8 Upper lip of calyx more or less squared-off, the lobes barely evident . . . . ***Prunella***

      8 Lobes of the upper lip of the calyx obvious, about one-fifth to one-third as long as those of the lower lip

        9 Low, mat-forming plants, with dense terminal inflorescences of small flowers; leaf blades about 1 cm long, nearly sessile; corolla 4–5 mm long, purple . . . . ***Thymus praecox*** subsp. ***arcticus*** (*T. serpyllum* of some references)
CREEPING THYME (Europe)

        9 Plants to about 1 m tall, the largest leaf blades often more than 5 cm long; flowers in clusters in the axils of the leaves; corolla 10–15 mm long, white to pale pink or pale blue . . . . ***Melissa officinalis***
LEMON BALM (SE Europe)

    7 Calyx not distinctly 2-lipped, the 5 lobes, whether equal or unequal, with similar proportions (the calyx may, however, be asymmetrical in the sense that the tips of the upper lobes may extend farther forward than those of the lower lobes)

     10 Upper lip of corolla consisting of a single lobe (calyx teeth nearly or quite equal)

      11 Base of lower lip of corolla with a pair of slender, upright projections (corolla white, pink, or purplish, with darker markings; annual) . . . . ***Galeopsis tetrahit***
COMMON HEMP NETTLE (Eurasia)

A slightly different species, variety, or hybrid introduced from Eurasia is *G. bifida,* in which the middle lobe of the lower lip of the corolla is notched and the dark markings on the lower lip do not extend to the margins.

      11 Base of lower lip of corolla without slender, upright projections

        12 Lobes of lower lip of corolla of nearly equal size, the middle lobe not notched; flowers borne singly in the axils of bracts of the main stem of the inflorescence or its branches (mostly E of the Cascades but occurring in the Columbia River Gorge and reaching the area of Portland, Oreg.) . . . . ***Physostegia parviflora***
WESTERN LION'S-HEART

12 Middle lobe of the lower lip of the corolla distinctly larger than the lateral lobes and sometimes notched (in species of *Lamium*, in which the middle lobe of the lower lip is notched, both lateral lobes are reduced to small toothlike outgrowths); flowers borne in clusters in the axils of leaves or bracts

    13 Corolla yellow with brownish markings (lateral lobes of lower lip well developed; perennial with creeping stolons, forming dense colonies; leaf blades usually 4–7 cm long, coarsely toothed, and in a common horticultural variant with a whitish or silvery blotch; only occasionally escaping from cultivation) . . . . ***Galeobdolon luteum*** (*Lamium galeobdolon*)
                                YELLOW ARCHANGEL (Europe)

    13 Corolla not yellow

      14 Middle lobe of the lower lip not notched (lateral lobes of the lower lip well developed) . . . ***Stachys***

      14 Middle lobe of the lower lip notched

        15 Lateral lobes of the lower lip smaller than the middle lobe but nevertheless obvious . . . . ***Dracocephalum parviflorum*** (*Moldavica parviflora*)
                                  AMERICAN DRAGONHEAD

        15 Lateral lobes of the lower lip represented only by small toothlike outgrowths . . . . ***Lamium***

10 Upper lip of corolla consisting of 2 distinct lobes or at least notched to the extent that there are 2 short lobes

    16 Upper lip of corolla divided for nearly all of its length into 2 lobes (stamens and pistil longer than the corolla and, on emerging from the tube, usually arching upward, then curving downward; nutlets rather firmly attached to one another) . . . . ***Trichostema***

    16 Upper lip of corolla notched into 2 short lobes

      17 Calyx obviously asymmetrical, its upper lobes projecting farther forward than the lower ones

        18 Plants low, creeping, rarely so much as 30 cm tall; leaf blades about as wide as long, rounded at the tip; flowers few in the axils of the leaf blades (corolla deep violet-blue, with purple spots) . . . . ***Glechoma hederacea***
                                  GROUND IVY (Europe)

        18 Plants upright, usually at least 30 cm tall when flowering; most leaf blades at least slightly longer than wide, pointed at the tip; flowers mostly in dense terminal inflorescences

          19 Margin of middle lobe of lower lip with several distinct, rounded teeth; corolla whitish, spotted with purple (occasional escape from cultivation) . . . . ***Nepeta cataria***
                                  CATNIP (Europe)

          19 Margin of middle lobe of lower lip without teeth; corolla whitish (montane, in our region not likely to be found below 4000 ft., 1220 m) . . . . ***Agastache urticifolia*** var. ***urticifolia***, pl. 351
                                  HORSEMINT

      17 Calyx not obviously asymmetrical, the upper lobes not projecting farther than the lower lobes (2 of the lobes, however, are slightly smaller than the other 3)

        20 Calyx tube noticeably swollen at the base (plants low, with spreading stems; leaf blades oval; flowers in a few crowded whorls; corolla 7–10 mm long, violet, with white markings on the lip; possibly established as a weed in a few places) . . . . ***Acinos arvensis*** (*Satureja acinos*)
                                  BASIL THYME (Europe)

        20 Calyx tube not noticeably swollen at the base

          21 Upright plants (from creeping rhizomes) generally more than 30 cm tall; all calyx lobes about the same size; flowers crowded in trichotomously branched inflorescences borne in the axils of the upper leaves (established in a few places) . . . . ***Origanum vulgare***
                                  WILD MARJORAM (Europe)

          21 Creeping plants, rooting at the nodes of prostrate stems, thus forming loose mats; flowers borne singly in the axils of the leaves; 2 calyx lobes smaller than the other 3 (aroma of bruised leaves very pleasing) . . . . ***Satureja douglasii***, pl. 359
                                  YERBA BUENA

        A hairy relative from Eurasia is *S. vulgaris,* wild basil, now a common weed in some areas of the Pacific Northwest. Its upright stems arise from creeping rhizomes, and the corollas are pink. Both species of *Satureja* are sometimes placed in *Clinopodium.*

Lamium

1 Leaf blades usually with a white mark along the midrib; corolla (purplish pink) 20–25 mm long, the upper lip at least 7 mm long; perennial . . . .*L. maculatum*
SPOTTED DEAD NETTLE (Europe)

1 Leaf blades without a white mark; corolla rarely more than 18 mm long, the upper lip not more than 5 mm long; annual
  2 Most upper leaves sessile, some of them clasping the stems, and none of the leaves purple-tinged; corolla reddish purple . . . .*L. amplexicaule*, pl. 352
HENBIT (Europe)
  2 All leaves with petioles, and at least the upper ones usually purple-tinged (in some populations in which the plants are very pale green, the leaves are not purple-tinged); corolla purplish pink . . . .
. . . . *L. purpureum*, pl. 353
RED DEAD NETTLE (Europe)
    Lamium ×incisum, believed to be a hybrid, *L. purpureum × moschatum*, has conspicuously sharp-toothed leaves. It is not so common in our region as *L. purpureum*.

Lycopus

1 Leaf blades pinnately lobed (the clefts between some of the lobes reaching at least halfway to the midrib)
  2 Upper surface of leaf blades with glandular dots but not hairy; calyx lobes not hairy; corolla white . . . .
. . . . *L. americanus*
CUT-LEAVED WATER HOREHOUND
  2 Upper surface of leaf blades hairy; calyx lobes hairy; corolla white with purple spots (uncommon weed in wet habitats) . . . . *L. europaeus*
GYPSYWORT (Europe)
1 Leaf blades toothed but not distinctly lobed
  3 Leaf blades rather evenly toothed, sessile; calyx lobes about twice as long as wide . . . .
. . . . *L. asper* (*L. lucidus* of some references)
WESTERN WATER HOREHOUND
  3 Leaf blades irregularly toothed, some of them tapering to a short, petiolelike base; calyx lobes not more than 1.5 times as long as wide . . . . *L. uniflorus*, pl. 354
BUGLEWEED

Mentha

1 Successive flower whorls distinctly separated, the internodes and leaves of the inflorescence clearly evident
  2 Larger leaves rarely more than 2 cm long; leaves beneath the flower clusters usually not extending much beyond the flowers and turned downward; corollas deep pink . . . .*M. pulegium*, pl. 356
PENNYROYAL (Europe)
  2 Larger leaves mostly 3–5 cm long; leaves beneath the flower clusters reaching well beyond the flowers and not turned downward; corollas usually pale blue or pale purple, sometimes pinkish or white (usually in fields in which the soil is damp throughout the year)
    3 Stems hairy, especially on the angles . . . .*M. arvensis*, pl. 355
FIELD MINT
    3 Stems not hairy . . . . *M. ×gracilis* (probably *M. arvensis × spicata*)
1 Successive flower whorls (at least the upper ones) so close together that the internodes and leaves of the inflorescence are mostly obscured (in *M. aquatica* there are usually only 2–3 whorls of flowers forming the main part of the inflorescence; if there are additional whorls on the same branch, these will be just above the uppermost leaves)
  4 Leaf blades (rarely so much as twice as long as wide) woolly-hairy on both surfaces, especially on the underside (corolla whitish, about 3 times as long as the calyx; established in only a few places) . . . .
. . . . *M. suaveolens* (*M. rotundifolia* of some references)
ROUND-LEAVED MINT (Europe)

4 Leaf blades not woolly-hairy (but they may be hairy, especially on the underside along the main veins)

    5 Leaves sessile or nearly so . . . . ***M. spicata***

                                     SPEARMINT (Europe)

    5 Leaves with distinct petioles

        6 Margins of calyx lobes conspicuously bristly-hairy; leaves without a lemonlike aroma . . . .

        . . . . ***M. ×piperita*** (generally thought to be *M. spicata × aquatica*)

                                       PEPPERMINT (Europe)

        6 Margins of calyx lobes not conspicuously bristly-hairy, but they may be hairy; leaves with a lemon-like aroma . . . . ***M. aquatica***

                            WATER MINT, LEMON MINT (Europe)

                Mentha aquatica has also been viewed as a hybrid and called *M. ×citrata.*

Monardella

In species of *Monardella,* each flower head has three series of bracts. The first choice in this key is based on the appearance of the four bracts of the lowermost series. After you get past this point, trouble begins, because monardellas are extremely variable and hybridize freely.

1 Lowermost bracts turned down, usually at least twice as long as wide and resembling the leaves below them, often to the extent that they have distinct petioles; bracts of the middle series not more than about 5 mm wide (Douglas, Josephine, and Curry Cos., Oreg.; to Calif.) . . . .
. . . . ***M. villosa* var. *villosa*** (*M. villosa* var. *subserrata*), pl. 357

                                    COYOTE MINT

        Monardella sheltonii (*M. villosa* var. *sheltonii*) is supposed to differ from *M. villosa* var. *villosa* in having calyces that are merely hairy, not glandular-hairy; furthermore, the hairiness on the underside of the leaf blades of *sheltonii* is not woolly, and the hairs on the stems do not exceed a length of 0.5 mm. The range of *M. sheltonii* extends from Jackson, Josephine, and Curry Cos., Oreg., to Calif., but in this region many specimens simply cannot be positively identified as *M. sheltonii* or *M. villosa.*

1 Lowermost bracts pressed against the middle bracts, not turned down, not resembling the leaves, not so much as twice as long as wide, and without distinct petioles; bracts of the middle series to about 8 mm wide

    2 Leaf blades typically smooth and shiny, not hairy (Josephine Co., Oreg., to Calif.) . . . . ***M. purpurea***

                                SISKIYOU MONARDELLA

    2 Leaf blades typically finely hairy, at least on the underside, and sometimes with a grayish tint, this not related to hairiness (mostly montane, Curry, Josephine, and Jackson Cos., Oreg., to Calif.; also E of the Cascades as far N as Wash.) . . . . ***M. odoratissima***

                            MOUNTAIN MONARDELLA

        The range of *M. odoratissima* extends from SE Brit. Col. to Calif. and eastward to Idaho, Colorado, and New Mexico, and several varieties have been named. In Wash. and Oreg. the distribution of *M. odoratissima* is mostly E of the crest of the Cascades. Assignment of specimens from the Siskiyou Mountain region to variety is difficult because of intergradation. In herbaria, most have been placed in var. *glauca,* the type of which was collected in SE Oreg., or var. *pallida,* originally collected in Nevada Co., Calif. There are also apparent hybrids between *M. odoratissima* and *M. purpurea.* You are here advised not to push your luck beyond the species level unless you have authenticated specimens for comparison.

Prunella

1 Blades of upper leaves usually about twice as long as wide; stems mostly prostrate . . . .
. . . . ***P. vulgaris* subsp. *vulgaris***

                          EUROPEAN SELF-HEAL, HEAL-ALL (Europe)

1 Blades of upper leaves usually about 3 times as long as wide; stems upright or at least substantial portions of them upright (considered to be native, and in our region probably more common than subsp. *vulgaris*)
. . . . ***P. vulgaris* subsp. *lanceolata*,** pl. 358

                              NARROW-LEAVED SELF-HEAL

Scutellaria

1 Flowers usually several to many in each axillary raceme; corolla 5–8 mm long (plants to more than 50 cm tall; leaf blades toothed) . . . . *S. lateriflora*
MAD-DOG SKULLCAP

1 Flowers borne singly in the leaf axils; corolla at least 12 mm long
  2 Leaf blades not twice as long as wide (most or all of them, including the upper ones, with low, rounded marginal teeth); plants not often more than 15 cm tall; hairs conspicuous, to 3 mm long (usually growing under shrubs; Curry, Josephine, and Jackson Cos., Oreg.; to Calif.) . . . . *S. tuberosa*, pl. 361
BLUE SKULLCAP
    Scutellaria tuberosa is unusual in that it produces a prominent underground tuber.
  2 Most leaf blades at least twice as long as wide; plants usually more than 20 cm tall; hairs not conspicuous and not more than 0.5 mm long
    3 Leaf blades commonly at least 3 cm long, sometimes as long as 5 cm, most of them with rounded marginal teeth; in wet habitats . . . . *S. galericulata*, pl. 360
MARSH SKULLCAP
    3 Leaf blades not often more than 3 cm long, most of them, especially those above the middle of the stem, with smooth margins; generally in dry habitats (Clark Co., Wash., and Willamette Valley, Oreg.; to Calif.; also E of the crest of the Cascades) . . . . *S. antirrhinoides*
SNAPDRAGON SKULLCAP

Stachys

1 Annual weed, not often more than about 30 cm tall (leaves and stems with rather stiff hairs; flowers usually in whorls of 4–6; corollas about 6–7 mm long, pale purple) . . . . *S. arvensis*
FIELD HEDGE NETTLE (Europe)

1 Perennial, generally more than 40 cm tall
  2 Leaves and stems thickly covered with long, soft hairs (corollas deep purplish blue, 6–12 mm long; garden plant, occasionally escaping) . . . . *S. byzantina*
LAMB'S EARS (Europe)
  2 Leaves and stems not thickly covered with long, soft hairs
    3 Corolla tube usually at least 15 mm long, sometimes more than 20 mm (plants often more than 1 m tall; corolla deep purplish red) . . . . *S. cooleyae* (*S. ciliata*), pl. 362
GREAT HEDGE NETTLE
    Stachys cooleyae is sometimes considered to be a variety of *S. chamissonis*.
    3 Corolla tube not so much as 15 mm long; corolla usually pink, sometimes purplish pink
      4 Upper leaves, including the 1–3 pairs below the lowest flower cluster, sessile or nearly so, the petioles generally not more than 7 mm long . . . . *S. rigida*
RIGID HEDGE NETTLE
      4 Upper leaves, including the 1–3 pairs below the lowest flower cluster, with petioles at least 1 cm long (mostly near the coast and often in shaded habitats) . . . . *S. mexicana*, pl. 363
NORTHWESTERN HEDGE NETTLE
        The first collection of *S. mexicana*, by a Spanish botanist, was probably at or near Nootka, Brit. Col. Its range does not extend to Mexico.

Trichostema

1 Leaves on well-developed plants (20 cm tall or larger) with distinct petioles, these mostly at least 1 cm long
  2 Corolla tube usually at least 5 mm long, protruding well beyond the calyx lobes and curving noticeably upward close to the throat; lower lip of corolla 4–7 mm long (plants with a distinctive odor; Douglas Co., Oreg., to Calif.) . . . . *T. laxum*
TURPENTINE WEED
  2 Corolla tube not more than 3 mm long, not protruding beyond the calyx lobes, curving only slightly and gradually upward; lower lip of corolla not more than 3 mm long (Josephine Co., Oreg., to Calif.) . . . . *T. simulatum*
SISKIYOU BLUE CURLS

1 Leaves, even on well-developed plants, without distinct petioles, or the petioles much less than 1 cm long
   3 Stamens usually 13–20 mm long; corolla tube, near the middle of its length, bent sharply upward (plants with a strong odor; on open, often weedy ground, Willamette Valley, Oreg., to Baja Calif.) . . . . *T. lanceolatum*, pl. 364
                                    VINEGAR WEED
   3 Stamens to about 6 mm long; corolla tube curving only slightly and gradually upward (mostly E of the Cascades but present in the Columbia River Gorge, reaching the Willamette Valley and extending S to Calif.) . . . . *T. oblongum*
                                      DOWNY BLUE CURLS

LAURACEAE Laurel Family

The laurel family is represented in our region by a single species, *Umbellularia californica* (pl. 365), the California bay laurel. Throughout much of its range, in southwestern Oregon and in coastal and mountainous parts of California, it forms a tree as tall as 30 m or more. In Josephine County, Oregon, and some other areas where soil is derived to a large extent from serpentine, it is more commonly a shrub. The rather tough blades of the alternate leaves are mostly 6–8 cm long and 2–3 cm wide. The flowers are small, with six yellowish green sepals about 6 mm long, nine stamens, and a pistil; there are no petals. In general, only one to three flowers in each cluster develop into fruits, which are fleshy, about 2.5 cm long, and have the shape of a plump olive. The fruits become purplish as they ripen, and each one contains a single large seed. The leaves of *U. californica* have an aroma much like that of *Laurus nobilis,* the European laurel, upon which humans have long depended for the "bay leaves" used for seasoning food. Its leafy branches were also used for making the laurel wreaths that crowned heroes and famous poets of long ago.

LENTIBULARIACEAE Bladderwort Family

Plants of the bladderwort family are either wholly aquatic or limited to wet habitats. The two genera in our region are very different in general appearance, but their flowers are similar. The lower lip of the corolla, with three lobes, has a conspicuous saclike spur; the upper lip is two-lobed. There are two stamens, attached to the lower part of the corolla tube.

1 Plants of bogs and other wet habitats; basal leaves well developed, the blades to about 5 cm long, 1.5 cm wide, slimy-glandular on the upper surface, trapping and digesting small insects; flowers single on leafless stems to 15 cm tall; corolla to 2.5 cm long, lavender . . . *Pinguicula macroceras* (*P. vulgaris* subsp. *macroceras*)
                                    GREATER BUTTERWORT
1 Plants of lakes and ponds, submerged except for the inflorescences; structures appearing to be leaves (they are in fact branch stems) divided into slender lobes; traps for capturing microscopic organisms borne on these branches or on branches of a different sort; flowers in racemes raised above the water level; corolla yellow, not more than 2 cm long . . . . *Utricularia*

Utricularia

1 Most bladders borne on branches separate from those bearing leaflike branches
   2 Lobes of leaflike branches conspicuously flattened, not so sharply pointed at the tip that they appear to end in a bristle; spur of lower lip of the corolla extending at a rather sharp angle away from the lip; corollas bright yellow . . . . *U. intermedia*
                                    MOUNTAIN BLADDERWORT
   2 Lobes of the leaves not conspicuously flattened, so sharply pointed that they appear to end in a bristle; spur of lower lip of corolla extending at an angle of nearly 90° away from the lip; corollas pale yellow . . . . *U. ochroleuca*
                                  BUFF-COLORED BLADDERWORT

1 Bladders typically borne on the lobes of the leaflike branches (lobes typically sharp-tipped)

    3 Leaflike branches with not more than 6 lobes altogether (usually only 2), these hairlike (inflorescence with 1–3 flowers; corolla 6–10 mm long) .... *U. gibba*

        SWOLLEN-SPUR BLADDERWORT (tropical America?)

    3 Leaflike branches usually with more than 10 ultimate lobes

        4 Leaflike branches to about 9 cm long, usually with 2 primary divisions, each of these divided several times, so there are many ultimate lobes; corolla usually about 15 mm long .... *U. macrorhiza* (*U. vulgaris* of some references, misapplied)

        COMMON BLADDERWORT

        4 Most leaflike branches not more than 3 cm long, with 3 primary divisions, each of these divided as many as 3 times; corolla 6–8 mm long .... *U. minor*

        LESSER BLADDERWORT

LIMNANTHACEAE Meadowfoam Family

The Limnanthaceae consists of only two genera, both limited to North America, and mostly found in the Pacific states. Only *Limnanthes* is found in our region. All the species are annuals with compound leaves, and they grow in habitats that are seasonally moist to very wet. The flowers typically have five sepals and five petals, ten stamens, and a pistil with five styles that correspond to the five divisions of the fruit-forming portion; each division becomes a one-seeded nutlet. *Limnanthes macounii* is an exception to the description of the flowers: it has four sepals, four petals, and eight stamens, and the pistil develops into four nutlets. *Limnanthes douglasii*, in cultivation since the mid-19th century and easily grown from seed, is a charming little plant for a garden in which there is wet, sunny place.

Limnanthes

1 Flowers with 4 sepals and 4 petals (petals white, 4–5 mm long, only slightly longer than the sepals; near Victoria, Brit. Col., and on at least one small island close to Victoria; also found in a field near the coast of San Mateo Co., Calif., where probably introduced, so by now there may be other populations S of Brit. Col.) .... *L. macounii*

    MACOUN'S MEADOWFOAM

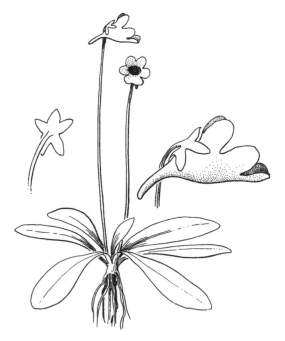

Pinguicula macroceras,
greater butterwort

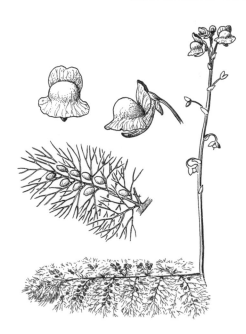

Utricularia macrorhiza,
common bladderwort

1 Flowers normally with 5 sepals and 5 petals
  2 Petals conspicuous and protruding well beyond the calyx; flowers opening widely
    3 Petals usually about 15 mm long, yellow with white tips (Douglas and Josephine Cos., Oreg.; widespread in Calif. as far S as San Benito and Santa Clara Cos.) . . . . *L. douglasii* subsp. *douglasii*, pl. 367
                                 MEADOWFOAM
    3 Petals, if so much as 15 mm long, not yellow with white tips
      4 Petals 8–10 mm long, completely white or with cream on the basal portion, sometimes becoming pinkish or pale purplish as they age; calyx not hairy (Josephine Co., Oreg.) . . . . *L. gracilis* subsp. *gracilis*, pl. 369
                                 SLENDER MEADOWFOAM
      4 Petals 10–15 mm long, white, the tips sometimes becoming pinkish or purplish as they age; calyx decidedly hairy (native to interior valleys in central Calif. but now well established in the Willamette Valley, Oreg., especially in Linn, Benton, and Lane Cos.) . . . . *L. alba* subsp. *alba*, pl. 366
                                 WHITE MEADOWFOAM

> *Limnanthes alba* subsp. *alba* was introduced to Oreg. with a view to producing large quantities of seed, which contain an oil used commercially.

  2 Petals (white, 6–8 mm long) inconspicuous, scarcely protruding beyond the calyx; flowers not opening widely
    5 Leaves and sepals not at all hairy (lower portion of each petal with 2 lengthwise rows of hairs; top of Upper and Lower Table Rock, Jackson Co., Oreg.) . . . . *L. floccosa* subsp. *pumila*
                                 TABLE ROCK MEADOWFOAM
    5 Leaves and inner surface of sepals hairy
      6 Leaves densely hairy; both surfaces of sepals densely hairy; petals 4.5–8.5 mm long, the lower portions without 2 lengthwise rows of hairs (Josephine and Jackson Cos., Oreg., to Calif.) . . . . *L. floccosa* subsp. *floccosa*, pl. 368
                                 HAIRY-LEAVED MEADOWFOAM
      6 Leaves only sparsely hairy; only the inner surface of the sepals densely hairy (the outer surface sparsely or not at all hairy); petals 7.5–9 mm long, the lower portions with 2 lengthwise rows of hairs (Jackson Co., Oreg.) . . . . *L. floccosa* subsp. *grandiflora*

> In Jackson Co., Oreg., *L. floccosa* subspp. *floccosa* and *grandiflora* may be found together around the same vernal pool; subsp. *grandiflora*, however, typically grows closer to the center of the drying pool and is in full flower when subsp. *floccosa* is mostly past the blooming stage.

LINACEAE Flax Family

The flowers of flaxes in our region have five nearly separate sepals, five separate petals (these may fall away early), and five stamens; the stamens alternate with the petals and are usually joined together at the base, thereby forming a low collar. The pistil is partitioned lengthwise into five divisions, each of which produces two flattened seeds. After the fruit has ripened and dried, its wall generally splits apart into ten valves.

The common flax, *Linum usitatissimum*, whose species name means "of maximum usefulness," has been cultivated for many centuries. Linen cloth, made from its long fibers, is probably the oldest known textile. Flax fibers have also been used in making nets and ropes. The seeds are pressed to obtain linseed oil, which is incorporated into paints, inks, varnishes, and linoleum. The solid material left after the oil has been squeezed out is sometimes fed to cattle.

1 Plants commonly at least 30 cm tall; pistil with 5 styles; petals typically blue (occasionally white), at least 8 mm long; margins of sepals with small teeth but these not glandular . . . . *Linum*
1 Plants not often more than 20 cm tall; pistil with 2–3 styles; petals white, pale pink, pink-streaked, or yellow, rarely more than 4 mm long; margins of sepals usually with slender, glandular teeth

2 Leaves alternate and smooth-margined; petals white, pale pink, or pink-streaked; styles 3 (Josephine Co., Oreg., to Calif.) . . . . **Hesperolinon micranthum** (*Linum micranthum*)
DWARF FLAX

2 Leaves opposite, those just below the inflorescence with toothed margins; petals yellow; styles 2 (Douglas Co., Oreg., to Calif., in the Cascades and Siskiyou Mountains; not likely to be found below 3000 ft., 910 m) . . . . *Sclerolinon digynum*
NORTHWESTERN YELLOW FLAX

Linum

1 Petals 8–10 mm long; leaf blades (with 3 main veins) not often more than 2 cm long (common weed, perhaps partly because of seed being incorporated into so-called wildflower mixes) . . . .
. . . . *L. bienne* (*L. angustifolium*), pl. 370
NARROW-LEAVED FLAX (Europe)

1 Petals typically at least 10 mm long
2 Leaf blades with a single main vein (the midrib); petals usually 15–20 mm long, commonly blue, sometimes white . . . . *L. lewisii* **subsp.** *lewisii* (*L. perenne* subsp. *lewisii*), pl. 371
LEWIS' FLAX

2 Leaf blades with 3 main veins; petals usually 12–15 mm long, blue or white (occasionally escaping from cultivation) . . . . *L. usitatissimum*
COMMON FLAX (Europe)

LOASACEAE Blazing-Star Family

There are numerous species of Loasaceae in California and other southwestern states, and a few in the region east of the Cascades. Only one, however, has been found within the range covered by this book. That is *Mentzelia laevicaulis* (pl. 372), blazing star or great mentzelia, whose wide distribution barely extends to southwestern Oregon, where it is known only from Jackson and Josephine Counties. It is a biennial as tall as about 1 m, with somewhat silvery stems and leaves. The flowers have five shiny, bright yellow petals 3–8 cm long. The calyx has five rather slender lobes, and its elongated tube is united with the fruit-forming portion of the pistil. The many stamens originate just below the 5 calyx lobes; a few of the outer ones, because of their broadened filaments, resemble petals, although they are much narrower. The mature fruit, a dry pod, releases its seeds through an opening at the top.

LYTHRACEAE Loosestrife Family

The loosestrifes common in our region are wetland plants belonging to the genus *Lythrum*. Their flowers, borne singly or in clusters in the axils of the leaves, are concentrated in an elongated inflorescence. The calyx, tubular and ribbed lengthwise, has five to seven lobes, these alternating with slender, toothlike outgrowths. Originating from the top of the calyx tube, in line with the toothlike outgrowths, are five to seven petals. The filaments of the stamens, equal in number to the petals, are attached to the lower part of the calyx tube. The pistil, free of the calyx tube but usually tightly enclosed by it, is partitioned lengthwise into two seed-producing divisions. *Rotala ramosior*, toothcup, rarely encountered, has four calyx lobes, four petals, four stamens, and a pistil with four divisions. The flower structure of many members of the family, some important in horticulture, deviate significantly from the formulas just described.

1 Plants sprawling and rooting at the nodes (stems 4-angled in cross section; leaves opposite, with short petioles, the blades oval, about 1.5 cm long; flowers about 1 mm wide, borne singly in the axils of the leaves; petals, if present, lilac; weedy in ditches and other wet, mostly muddy habitats but not yet common in the region) . . . . *Lythrum portula*
PURSLANE LOOSESTRIFE (Europe)

1 Plants growing upright, not sprawling and/or rooting at the nodes

2 Leaves opposite; sepals, petals, and stamens 4 (annual, to about 15 cm tall; flowers usually solitary in the leaf axils; petals white, about 1 mm long; widely distributed in North America, Mexico, and the West Indies but rare in our region) . . . . ***Rotala ramosior***
TOOTHCUP

2 Leaves mostly alternate (some lower leaves may be opposite); sepals, petals, and stamens 5–7

   3 Petals rose-purple, 7–10 mm long; plants to more than 1 m tall (perennial; grown in water gardens and now widely established in marshes and along ditches and lake margins, where it may displace native wetland vegetation and create problems for some animals) . . . . ***Lythrum salicaria***, pl. 373
PURPLE LOOSESTRIFE (Europe)

   3 Petals pink, to about 2.5 mm long; plants to about 50 cm tall (annual, introduced in wet places, especially near the coast) . . . . ***Lythrum hyssopifolium***
HYSSOP LOOSESTRIFE (Europe)

MALVACEAE Mallow Family

The flowers of mallows have five separate petals that are usually rolled up in the bud stage, a five-lobed calyx, and numerous stamens whose filaments are united to form a tube around the pistil. The anthers may be concentrated at the top of the filament tube or scattered along part of its length. The pistil is partitioned into several seed-producing divisions, which typically separate after the fruit has dried.

Among the mallows with which most of us are familiar are the hollyhock, probably a native of China, various tropical species of *Hibiscus*, and several European species of *Malva* that have become established as weeds. Our region does, however, have an interesting assemblage of native species, mostly belonging to the genus *Sidalcea*.

1 Flowers without bracts directly beneath the calyx (but there may be a bract at the base of each pedicel; native species) . . . . ***Sidalcea***

1 Each flower with 1 or more bracts directly beneath the calyx (except for *Iliamna latibracteata*, all species under this choice are introduced)

   2 Leaf blades, if palmately lobed, not with triangular lobes . . . . ***Malva***

   2 Leaf blades (these to 20 cm wide) palmately lobed, the general outline of the lobes triangular (petals 2–3 cm long, rose-purple; along streams, Douglas Co., Oreg., to Calif.) . . . . ***Iliamna latibracteata***
BROAD-BRACTED GLOBE MALLOW

Malva

1 Upper leaves divided into many narrow lobes (petals white or pink, 2–3 cm long; an escape from gardens) . . . . ***M. moschata***
MUSK MALLOW (Europe)

1 All leaves shallowly lobed but the lobes neither numerous nor narrow

   2 Petals mostly 15–25 mm long, bluish purple (plants usually biennial or perennial, to more than 1 m tall) . . . . ***M. sylvestris***
COMMON MALLOW (Europe)

   2 Petals not more than 13 mm long; white, pale pink, or pale lavender

      3 Petals (8–13 mm long, white or pale lavender) at least twice as long as the calyx lobes; divisions of the ripe fruits not markedly wrinkled . . . . ***M. neglecta***, pl. 374
DWARF MALLOW (Eurasia)

      3 Petals (4–5 mm long, white, pale pink, or pale lavender) scarcely if at all longer than the calyx lobes (sometimes shorter); divisions of the ripe fruits markedly wrinkled

         4 Narrow lower portion of each petal without a fringe of hairs . . . . ***M. parviflora***
SMALL-FLOWERED MALLOW (Europe)

         4 Narrow lower portion of each petal with a fringe of hairs . . . . ***M. rotundifolia*** (*M. pusilla* of some references)
SMALL MALLOW (Europe)

Sidalcea

Some species and subspecies of *Sidalcea* are difficult to distinguish because of variation, intergradation, and hybridization. Authoritative keys, based to a large extent on the nature of the hairs on the plants, are not likely to be useful to persons who do not already have considerable experience with the region's species. Most of the sidalceas of British Columbia, Washington, and northern and coastal Oregon are rather well marked and should be easy to identify. There will be more problems in the interior of southwestern Oregon, where subspecies of *S. malviflora* co-occur with a subspecies of *S. oregana,* whose distribution is mostly limited to areas in or east of the Cascades. Two kinds of flowers—those with a pistil and stamens, and slightly smaller ones in which stamens, at least functional ones, are absent—may occur on the same plant or on separate plants of a population.

1 Leaves on upper portions of stems similar to those on the lower part of the plant (the separations between the lobes of upper leaves do not extend more than half the distance to the attachment of the petiole); divisions of fruit without beaks (petals 7–12 mm long, white or tinged with purple; Curry Co., Oreg., to Calif.) . . . . *S. malachroides*
MAPLE-LEAF SIDALCEA

1 Upper leaves much more deeply lobed than the lower leaves; divisions of fruit, in some species, with beaks
  2 Petals usually very pale pink or pinkish lavender, sometimes nearly white (plants upright, commonly more than 1 m tall; calyx to 9 mm long; petals to 2 cm long; Willamette Valley, Oreg.) . . . . *S. campestris*, pl. 375
MEADOW SIDALCEA

  2 Petals bright to deep pink or pinkish lavender
    3 Petals not often more than 12 mm long; calyx 5–7 mm long; beak on each division of mature fruit less than 0.5 mm long (plants often sprawling; racemes commonly 2–3 on each flowering stem, congested, most of the flowers touching; calyx lobes usually purplish, Clark Co., Wash., and Multnomah to Linn, Benton, and Tillamook Cos., Oreg.) . . . . *S. nelsoniana*
NELSON'S SIDALCEA

    3 Petals commonly more than 12 mm long; calyx generally more than 7 mm long; beak on each division of fruit at least 0.5 mm long
      4 Inflorescence less than twice as long as wide, usually congested, the flowers touching one another; corolla deep pink; divisions of fruit 3.5–4 mm long; hairs on stems and petioles conspicuous, 1–2 mm long (Clark and Lewis Cos., Wash., to Clatsop, Tillamook, and Lincoln Cos., Oreg.) . . . . *S. hirtipes*, pl. 378
BRISTLY-STEMMED SIDALCEA

      4 Plants not as described nor with the range given in the other choice 4
        5 Plants to more than 1 m tall; stems, petioles, stipules, and calyces tinged with purple; stems not conspicuously hairy, sometimes nearly smooth; petals usually deep pink; divisions of fruit 4 mm long, the beaks 0.8–1.3 mm long; growing close to tidelands, especially salt marshes (Brit. Col., including SE Vancouver Island, and Puget Sound region and coastal Wash. and Oreg. as far S as Douglas Co.) . . . . *S. hendersonii*, pl. 377
HENDERSON'S SIDALCEA

        5 Plants not as described nor with the distribution given in the other choice 5

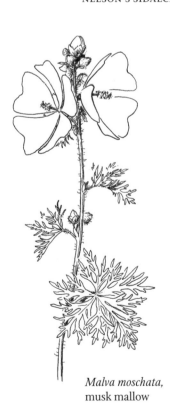

Malva moschata,
musk mallow

6 Calyx lobes (often purplish) usually very slightly wider just above the base than at the base; pedicels usually less than 3 mm long (plants to more than 1 m tall; calyx to about 9 mm long; petals to 18 mm long; Willamette Valley to S Lane Co., Coquille River valley, and Umpqua River valley, Oreg.) . . . . *S. cusickii*, pl. 376

CUSICK'S SIDALCEA

6 Calyx lobes widest at the base

   7 Plants generally upright, the stems not falling down and taking root; pedicels not often more than 3 mm long (the inflorescence therefore nearly spikelike); calyx rarely so much as 6 mm long; petals usually lavender or light purple; divisions of fruit smooth or with a faint networklike pattern (leaves often distinctly grayish; Jackson, Josephine, and Klamath Cos., Oreg., to Calif.; also E of the crest of the Cascades in Oreg.) . . . . *S. oregana* subsp. *spicata*

OREGON SIDALCEA

   7 Plants generally with stems that fall down and sometimes take root; pedicels at least 3 mm long, sometimes as much as 10 mm; calyx usually at least 8 mm long; petals usually bright to deep pink, divisions of mature fruit with a prominent networklike pattern . . . . *S. malviflora*

MALLOW SIDALCEA

In our region, 3 intergrading subspecies of *S. malviflora* can be distinguished, sometimes with difficulty. From the N Willamette Valley to Josephine Co. and in the Coast Ranges of Oreg., and in at least Thurston Co., Wash., there is subsp. *virgata* (pl. 379), which typically has an elongate inflorescence with as many as 40–50 flowers, these with petals to 25 mm long. In some references it is given the rank of species. The inflorescences of subsp. *patula*, found along the coast from Curry Co., Oreg., to Calif., usually have fewer than 25 flowers; the calyces of these are bristly hairy (some of the hairs 1 mm long), and the petals are not often so much as 20 mm long. Most plants in the interior of Curry Co. and in Josephine and Jackson Cos., Oreg., seem to fit best in subsp. *asprella*, to which subspp. *elegans* and *nana* should probably be referred. Like subsp. *patula*, they have fewer and smaller flowers than subsp. *virgata*; the leaves, furthermore, may be slightly grayish. It should be kept in mind that flowers without functional stamens are typically slightly smaller than those with functional stamens.

MENYANTHACEAE Buckbean Family

Buckbeans grow in bogs and in shallow water at the edges of lakes and ponds. The rhizomatous stems produce alternate leaves whose simple or compound blades are held above the waterline together with the upright racemes of flowers. The calyx and corolla are usually five-lobed, sometimes six-lobed. The corolla is distinctive because of the hair- or scalelike outgrowths that cover the inner surfaces of its lobes. The stamens, attached to the corolla tube, alternate with the lobes. The lower part of the fruit-forming portion of the pistil is united to the calyx tube; the fruit is a capsule that eventually cracks open or disintegrates to release its seeds.

Fauria crista-galli, deer cabbage

1 Leaves compound, with 3 leaflets, these without marginal teeth; corolla lobes covered with more or less evenly distributed hairlike outgrowths (in bogs, swamps, and shallow water at the edges of lakes and ponds; widespread) . . . . *Menyanthes trifoliata*, pl. 380

BUCKBEAN

1 Leaves not compound or lobed, the margins with blunt teeth; corolla lobes with 3 ridges of scalelike outgrowths (in bogs, swamps, and other wet habitats, Alaska to Vancouver Island, Clallam Co. to Grays Harbor Co., Wash., and more recently found in the Cascades of Linn Co., Oreg.) . . . . *Fauria crista-galli* (*Nephrophyllidium crista-galli*)

DEER CABBAGE

MOLLUGINACEAE Carpetweed Family

Carpetweeds and their relatives, some of which have in the past been placed in Aizoaceae, are mostly found in warmer regions. Our only representative, *Mollugo verticillata,* probably introduced from South America, forms low mats, especially on sandy soils along rivers. At each stem node there are typically four to six slender leaves to about 3 cm long; the petioles are not very distinct. There are a few flowers at each node. The five sepals, usually about 2 mm long, are whitish on the upper surface. There are commonly three stamens and a single pistil whose fruit-forming portion, partitioned into three divisions, becomes a plump capsule 3–4 mm long. The curvature of the small seed is decorated by several delicate, parallel ridges.

MYRICACEAE Wax-Myrtle Family

Wax myrtles and their relatives make up a small family of trees and shrubs, mostly inhabiting regions with warm climates. The leaves, in whose axils the catkins are located, are usually at least slightly aromatic. In the species in our region, both of the genus *Myrica,* each flower in a staminate catkin consists of a few stamens above a bract. Each flower in a pistillate catkin, with two styles, also has a small bract beneath it; it develops into a one-seeded fruit.

Myrica

1 Evergreen shrub or tree; leaf blades commonly at least 6 cm long, usually widest near the middle, the margins toothed for most of their length; pistillate and staminate catkins on the same plant; along the coast, on backshores, in woods and thickets, and around bogs, primarily S Wash. to Calif. but known from the region of Tofino and Ucluelet, Brit. Col. . . . . ***M. californica,*** pl. 381
CALIFORNIA WAX MYRTLE

1 Deciduous shrub; leaf blades rarely so much as 5 cm long, usually widest above the middle, either with smooth margins or with only a few teeth near the tip; pistillate and staminate catkins on separate plants; around bogs, swamps, and slow streams, inland as well as at the coast . . . . ***M. gale,*** pl. 382
SWEET GALE

NYCTAGINACEAE Four-o'clock Family

In the four-o'clock family, which consists of herbaceous plants with opposite leaves, the flowers lack a corolla, but the five-lobed, bell-shaped or tubular calyx, often white or colored, resembles a corolla. Bracts below each flower or flower cluster may also be colored and are sometimes united to form an involucre. The number of stamens in the species in our region is five, and the pistil is single. The calyx tube is not united to the pistil, although it may adhere to the one-seeded fruit as this dries to form what is essentially an achene. Two species, belonging to the genus *Abronia,* grow on backshores of sandy beaches; a third, belonging to *Mirabilis,* occurs in the Siskiyou Mountain region of southwestern Oregon and northwestern California.

Mollugo verticillata,
carpetweed

1 Fruit ribbed lengthwise but not with prominent winglike outgrowths; bracts united to form a funnel-like tube with 5–6 lobes; stems mostly upright, to more than 50 cm tall (involucre usually 3–3.5 cm long, with about 7–10 flowers; calyx about 4 cm long, mostly greenish and purplish to magenta; Jackson Co., Oreg., to Calif.) . . . . ***Mirabilis greenei***
SISKIYOU FOUR-O'CLOCK

1 Fruit with prominent winglike outgrowths; bracts not united; stems mostly prostrate
    2 Corolla yellow, the tube 8–10 mm long; body of fruit, when ripe, considerably thicker than the width of the winglike outgrowths . . . . ***Abronia latifolia***, pl. 383
YELLOW SAND VERBENA

    2 Corolla pink or purplish pink, the tube 6–8 mm long; body of fruit, when ripe, about as thick as the width of the winglike outgrowths . . . . ***Abronia umbellata*** subsp. ***breviflora***, pl. 384
PINK SAND VERBENA

NYMPHAEACEAE Water-Lily Family

Water lilies are aquatic perennials whose leaves have nearly circular blades that float or are raised slightly above the waterline. The thick stems, rooted in mud, spread laterally, producing new clusters of leaves and flowers at intervals. The number of sepals, petals, and stamens varies according to species, and even within a species. Furthermore, in some species, sepals can easily be mistaken for petals. The single pistil, whose flattened or concave style has numerous barlike stigmas arranged in a circle, becomes a large fruit consisting of several seed-producing divisions.

1 Flowers usually with 4 green sepals, these external to several larger yellow sepals that could be mistaken for petals; true petals numerous, small, greenish yellow or purple-tinged, shorter than the reddish or purplish stamens; leaf blades sometimes raised above the water level . . . . ***Nuphar lutea*** subsp. ***polysepala*** (*N. polysepala*), pl. 385
YELLOW POND LILY

1 Flowers with only 4 sepals, these green; petals white, often tinged with pink, or yellow, much larger than the sepals and stamens; leaf blades floating
    2 Petals yellow (escaped from cultivation on Vancouver Island, Brit. Col., perhaps elsewhere) . . . . ***Nymphaea mexicana***
YELLOW WATER LILY (Mexico)

    2 Petals white or tinged with pink
        3 Petals usually 20–30; sepals 3–6 cm long; flowers fragrant (cultivated and sometimes becoming established in the wild) . . . . ***Nymphaea odorata***
WHITE WATER LILY, FRAGRANT WATER LILY (E United States)

        3 Petals usually 7–15; sepals 2–3 cm long; flowers not fragrant (widely distributed in E Asia, E Canada, and the N United States, from Michigan eastward; in our region, present in coastal Brit. Col. and once collected at a locality in W Whatcom Co., Wash.) . . . . ***Nymphaea tetragona***
PYGMY WATER LILY

OLEACEAE Olive Family

Besides the olive, *Olea europaea*, the olive family includes many other shrubs or trees that are widely cultivated. Among them are ashes (*Fraxinus*), *Forsythia*, jasmines (*Jasminum*), lilacs (*Syringa*), and privets (*Ligustrum*). Persons who appreciate the extreme diversity shown by all those just mentioned may wonder what holds them together in the same family. The following complex of characters may help: leaves almost always opposite; calyx usually with four lobes; corolla, if present, usually four-lobed or consisting of four free petals; stamens usually two; pistil one, its fruit-forming portion usually with two divisions, each usually producing two seeds. Note the emphasis on "usually." This obviously means that not all members of the family adhere to all the criteria. The nature of the ripe fruit, furthermore, varies greatly; it may be fleshy (as in the olive and privets), a dry capsule (as in lilacs and *Forsythia*), or a winged dry fruit, as in ashes.

The only native representative of the family in our region is *Fraxinus latifolia* (pl. 386), Oregon ash, most commonly found along streams. It is a tree to more than 20 m tall, with opposite, pinnately compound leaves; the leaflets are smooth-margined. Staminate and pistillate flowers, lacking petals, are in separate inflorescences. The staminate flowers almost always have two stamens, below which is a small bractlike calyx. Pistillate flowers have a more obvious four-lobed calyx, and the style of the pistil is longer than the fruit-forming portion, which develops into a one-seeded, winged fruit that is generally about 3 cm long.

Ligustrum vulgare, the common privet, an important garden shrub introduced from Europe, occasionally becomes established in waste places. Its leaves, mostly opposite, have oval blades about 4–5 cm long. The flowers, with white or pale purplish corollas about 5 mm long, are numerous in each branched, terminal inflorescence. This species has shiny black fruits to 8 mm long.

ONAGRACEAE Evening-Primrose Family

The Onagraceae consists almost entirely of herbaceous plants; garden fuchsias, native to Central and South America, and a few others may become woody. The fruit-forming portion of the pistil is united to the tube of the calyx; the other flower parts—typically four sepals, four petals, and eight stamens—are attached to the top of the calyx tube, sometimes extended slightly above the top of the future fruit. (In this key, the extension is called the flower tube.) There are exceptions, however, to each of these criteria, other than the position of the developing fruit with respect to the calyx and other flower parts. One or more garden species of *Fuchsia*, especially *F. magellanica*, have escaped from cultivation in coastal areas of Oregon.

1 Flowers without petals (stamens 4; sepals 4, persisting on the fruits, which are about 3–4 mm long; plants forming mats in wet places) . . . . **Ludwigia palustris**
WATER PURSLANE

1 Flowers with 2, 4, 5, or 6 sepals and petals (4 in most species)
    2 Flowers with 2 sepals and 2 petals (1–1.5 mm long, 2-lobed, white), and 2 stamens; fruit covered with hooked hairs . . . . **Circaea alpina** subsp. *pacifica*, pl. 391
ENCHANTER'S NIGHTSHADE
    2 Flowers usually with 4–5 (sometimes 6) sepals and petals; fruit not covered with hooked hairs
        3 Petals and sepals usually 5, sometimes 6, the sepals persisting on the fruit (petals yellow, 1–2 cm long; plants growing in shallow water or in very wet places) . . . .
        . . . **Ludwigia hexapetala** (*Jussiaea uruguayensis*)
SIX-PETALED WATER PRIMROSE (S America)
        3 Petals and sepals 4, the sepals not persisting on the fruit
            4 Seeds with a tuft of long hairs at one end (the hairs can usually be seen on seeds taken from fruits that are still not quite mature) . . . .
            . . . . **Epilobium-Chamerion complex**
            4 Seeds without a tuft of long hairs at one end
                5 Stamens in line with the petals fertile, the others sterile; fruit somewhat egg-shaped (only about twice as long as wide), not splitting lengthwise when mature and containing only 1–2 seeds (Jackson Co., Oreg., to Calif. but not seen in Oreg. for many years) . . . . . .
        . . . . **Clarkia heterandra** (*Gaura heterandra*), pl. 396
ALTERNATING-STAMENED CLARKIA

Ludwigia hexapetala, six-petaled water primrose

5 All stamens fertile; fruit not at all egg-shaped, more than twice as long as wide, splitting lengthwise at maturity, usually containing at least several seeds

  6 Fruit consisting of 2 chambers, each with 1 row of seeds—caution: because the fruit breaks apart by 4 valves, one could mistakenly assume that there are 4 chambers (sepals turned back; branch stems very slender; mostly above 2000 ft., 610 m) . . . . *Gayophytum humile* (*G. nuttallii*)
DWARF GROUND SMOKE

  6 Fruit consisting of 4 chambers, each with 1–2 rows of seeds

    7 Petals yellow . . . . *Camissonia-Oenothera* complex

    7 Petals not yellow

      8 Flowers sessile or on very short pedicels; calyx lobes upright; petals white or some shade of pink . . . . *Epilobium-Chamerion* complex

      8 Flowers on conspicuous pedicels; calyx lobes turned back; petals white or mostly pink or purple, sometimes with red blotches near or below the center . . . . *Clarkia*

Camissonia-Oenothera Complex

1 Plants upright, the leafy stems sometimes more than 1 m tall; petals usually at least 2 cm long; stigma 4-lobed

  2 Petals 2.5–5 cm long; stigma raised well above the anthers . . . . *O.* ×*glazioviana* (*O.* ×*erythrosepala*, *O. biennis*), pl. 406
BIENNIAL EVENING PRIMROSE (Europe; generally believed to have been derived by hybridization of 2 American spp.)

  2 Petals not so much as 2.5 cm long; stigma not raised above the anthers

    3 Petals decidedly shorter than the sepals; plants rarely so much as 1 m tall (mostly coastal, S Oreg. to Calif.) . . . . *O. wolfii*
WOLF'S EVENING PRIMROSE

    3 Petals about the same length as the sepals; plants commonly more than 1 m tall . . . . *O. villosa* subsp. *strigosa*
STRIGOSE EVENING PRIMROSE

1 Plants either with such short stems that the leaves are essentially basal or with spreading, prostrate stems; petals not so much as 2 cm long; stigma not 4-lobed

  4 Plants with short stems, all leaves essentially basal; flower single on each long peduncle; fruit not conspicuously curved or coiled

    5 Leaves with distinct petioles, the blades to more than 5 cm long, about twice as long as wide; petals usually about 1.5 cm long, only slightly longer than the sepals; fruit less than 1 cm long, without winglike flanges (Douglas Co., Oreg., to Calif.) . . . . *C. ovata* (*O. ovata*), pl. 389
SUNCUP

    5 Leaves sessile, the blades generally 4–6 cm long and about 10 times as long as wide; petals usually 1 cm long, about twice as long as the sepals; fruit 1–3 cm long, with 4 winglike flanges (Josephine Co., Oreg., to Calif.) . . . . *C. graciliflora*
SLENDER-FLOWERED EVENING PRIMROSE

  4 Plants with spreading, prostrate stems; flowers nearly or quite sessile (what may look like a peduncle is the fruit-forming portion of the flower); fruit, when mature, conspicuously curved or coiled

    6 Fruit 4-angled, not becoming obviously bumpy as it dries; leaf blades on flowering stems oval, less than twice as long as wide, differing from the much longer and more slender basal leaves (on backshores of sandy beaches, Coos Co., Oreg., to Calif.) . . . . *C. cheiranthifolia* subsp. *cheiranthifolia*, pl. 387
BEACH EVENING PRIMROSE

    6 Fruit cylindrical, becoming bumpy as it dries; leaf blades on flowering stems more than 10 times as long as wide, similar to the basal leaves (S Vancouver Island and Gulf Islands, Brit. Col., and San Juan Islands, Wash., and along the Columbia River; otherwise mostly E of the Cascades and in Calif.) . . . . *C. contorta*, pl. 388
CONTORTED-POD EVENING PRIMROSE

Clarkia

1 Each petal divided into 3 lobes (flowers with 4 fertile stamens; mostly E of the crest of the Cascades and in the E portion of the Columbia River Gorge but reportedly collected long ago in Multnomah Co., Oreg.) . . . . *C. pulchella*
BEAUTIFUL CLARKIA

1 Petals not divided into lobes

  2 Each petal with a slender, stalklike lower portion, this about half as long as the broader upper portion (petals 6–12 mm long, pink or pinkish lavender, sometimes red at the base; Willamette Valley, Oreg., to Calif.; also widespread E of the Cascades) . . . . *C. rhomboidea*, pl. 399
TONGUE CLARKIA

  2 Petals without a slender, stalklike lower portion

    3 Sepals separating from one another after turning back; fruiting portion of the pistil 4-grooved while petals are present; fruits, at maturity, 4-angled (the subspecies of *C. purpurea*, differentiated in the key below, vary extensively in flower color and other characters, and they also intergrade)

      4 Most leaves less than 5 times as long as wide; flowers crowded in the inflorescence (petals lavender to purple or purplish red, frequently with a darker spot near the tip; Douglas Co. and probably E Coos Co., Oreg., to Calif.) . . . . *C. purpurea* subsp. *purpurea* (*C. purpurea*)
PURPLE CLARKIA

      4 Most leaves more than 6 times as long as wide; flowers usually not crowded in the inflorescence

        5 Petals 1.5–2.5 cm long; stamens shorter than the stigma, not adhering to it; anthers maturing before the stigma (petals pinkish, lavender, or purple, typically with a darker spot near the tip) . . . . *C. purpurea* subsp. *viminea*, pl. 398
LARGE CLARKIA

        5 Petals less than 1.5 cm long; stamens about as long as the stigma, adhering to it; anthers maturing at the same time as the stigma (petals lavender to purple or purplish red, frequently a deep wine red, when light in color often with a dark purple spot near the middle or close to the tip; widespread from Brit. Col. to Baja Calif., mostly W of the crests of the Cascades and Sierra Nevada) . . . . *C. purpurea* subsp. *quadrivulnera* (*C. quadrivulnera*), pl. 397
WINE-CUP CLARKIA

    3 Sepals usually adhering to one another and turned to one side below the rest of the flower; fruiting portion of the pistil usually cylindrical while petals are present, not 4-grooved

      6 Tips of flowering stems, with unopened flowers, drooping

        7 Petals generally 1–2 cm long, usually almost uniformly pink but sometimes a little darker at the base (Willamette Valley, Oreg., to Calif.; also E of the Cascades in Wash. and Oreg., and E of the Sierra Nevada in Calif.) . . . . *C. gracilis* subsp. *gracilis*, pl. 395
SUMMER'S DARLING

        7 Petals 2–4 cm long, mostly pink but with a bright red central spot (Douglas and Josephine Cos., Oreg., to Calif.) . . . . *C. gracilis* subsp. *sonomensis*
SLENDER CLARKIA

      6 Tips of flowering stems, with unopened flowers, upright

        8 Petals less than 2 cm long; stigma not raised above the stamens

          9 Petals usually 10–15 mm long, pink with red markings near the base; all 8 stamens usually fertile; fruit elongated, usually 2–3 cm long, with numerous seeds, and splitting open lengthwise at maturity (mostly along the coast of Oreg., in the Columbia River Gorge, and on the Olympic Peninsula, San Juan Islands, and Vancouver Island) . . . . *C. amoena* subsp. *caurina*, pl. 392
PACIFIC CLARKIA

          9 Petals 5–6 mm long, uniformly pink; with 4 fertile stamens (these in line with the petals) and 4 sterile stamens; fruit more or less egg-shaped, with only 1–2 seeds, not splitting open when mature (Jackson Co., Oreg., to Calif. but not seen in Oreg. for many years) . . . . *C. heterandra* (*Gaura heterandra*), pl. 396
ALTERNATING-STAMENED CLARKIA

8 Petals usually more than 2 cm long; stigma raised above the stamens

    10 Large plants rather bushy; petals 2.5–4 cm long, mostly pink and usually but not always with a red central spot or some less conspicuous red mark; fruit typically longer than the internode above the node to which it is attached (mostly in the Puget Trough of Brit. Col. and Wash., Willamette Valley, and Douglas and Josephine Cos., Oreg.) . . . . *C. amoena* **subsp.** *lindleyi*, pl. 394
FAREWELL-TO-SPRING

    10 Plants slender; petals 1.5–3 cm long, pink or lavender, usually with a red central spot; fruit typically shorter than the internode above the node to which it is attached (Josephine, Jackson, and Curry Cos., Oreg., to Calif.) . . . . *C. amoena* **subsp.** *huntiana*, pl. 393
HUNT'S CLARKIA

Epilobium-Chamerion **Complex**

In all species of *Epilobium*, except the last four in this key, the seeds have a tuft of long hairs at one end; these can usually be seen on seeds within a fruit that is close to mature. Because most species can be keyed without reference to this character, it is not used until near the end, to segregate species whose seeds lack a tuft of hairs and that were formerly assigned to *Boisduvalia*. Beginning with the second choice 3, the key is likely to become difficult for those who have not already worked with this group of plants. Positive identification often requires careful study of seeds, which may not be mature enough on the specimens observed. Furthermore, there is considerable variation within some species. While certain of them are here broken down into subspecies or varieties, attempts at identification below the species level may be discouraging.

1 Flower tube about 20 mm long, bright red like the petals and sepals (Curry Co., Oreg., to Calif.) . . . .
. . . . *E. canum* **subsp.** *latifolium* (*Zauschneria californica* var. *latifolia, Z. latifolia*)
BROAD-LEAVED CALIFORNIA FUCHSIA

    Plants with white or pink flowers, such as are propagated by gardeners and commercial establishments, are rarely encountered in the wild.

1 Flower tube generally less than 10 mm long, sometimes less than 1 mm, and neither it nor the petals and sepals scarlet

    2 Corolla pale yellow (leaves opposite; stigma protruding well beyond the petals; perennial; widespread in the mountains but not likely to be found below 3000 ft., 910 m) . . . .*E. luteum*
YELLOW-FLOWERED WILLOW HERB

    2 Corolla white to pink, rose, or purplish rose

        3 Petals with a narrow lower portion, becoming rather abruptly wider, not distinctly notched at the tip; upper 2 petals appreciably smaller than the lower 2, the corolla therefore slightly irregular (perennial commonly more than 1 m tall; larger leaf blades sometimes more than 15 cm long; petals usually 10–15 mm long, pink or purplish pink, rarely white) . . . . . *C. angustifolium* (*E. angustifolium*), pl. 390
FIREWEED

        3 Petals widening gradually from the base and notched into 2 lobes at the tip; all petals the same size

            4 Stigma conspicuously 4-lobed (petals usually at least 1 cm long)

                5 Stems not often more than 30 cm long, often partly lying down, with the tips upright (petals usually 15–20 mm long, pink; mostly in dry habitats, including dry streambeds, SW Oreg. to Calif.) . . . . *E. rigidum*, pl. 404
SISKIYOU WILLOW HERB, RIGID WILLOW HERB

                5 Stems upright, commonly more than 40 cm tall (perennial)

                    6 Leaves and at least the upper portions of stems conspicuously hairy; leaf blades with rather evenly and closely spaced teeth; petals usually at least 15 mm long, purplish rose (garden plant, occasionally escaping, usually to wet habitats; locally common now in the Columbia River Gorge) . . . . *E. hirsutum*
HAIRY WILLOW HERB (Europe)

6 Leaves and stems not conspicuously hairy (hairs, when present, usually pressed down); leaf blades without evenly and closely spaced teeth; petals mostly 10–15 mm long but sometimes smaller, pink to purplish rose (around bogs and in other wet places, SW Oreg. to Calif.) ....
.... *E. oreganum* (*E. exaltatum*), pl. 402
OREGON FIREWEED

4 Stigma more or less globular, at most only indistinctly 4-lobed
  7 Flower tube proportionally conspicuous, sometimes as much as 9 mm long, usually about equal to the petals (plants often extensively branched, sometimes more than 1 m tall; stems of lower portion peeling; petals usually 4–6 mm long but occasionally nearly 10 mm long, white to rose; common on dry soils; annual) .... *E. brachycarpum* (*E. paniculatum*), pl. 400
TALL ANNUAL WILLOW HERB

  7 Flower tube rarely so much as 3 mm long, shorter than the petals
    8 Seeds without a tuft of long hairs at one end; leaves alternate except at or near the base (annual)
      9 Leaves nearly or quite hairless (whatever hairs are present are usually limited to the underside of the midrib); stems only slightly hairy; each of the 4 chambers of the fruit with 2 rows of seeds; fruit (5–9 mm long) very stiff, usually not splitting to the base (in moist places, including drying borders of ponds) .... *E. pygmaeum* (*Boisduvalia glabella*), pl. 403
PYGMY WILLOW HERB

      9 Leaves, except perhaps some upper ones, decidedly hairy; stems also hairy; each chamber of the fruit with a single row of seeds; fruit not especially stiff, usually splitting apart for its full length
        10 Fruit (4–11 mm long), just before splitting, without a distinct beaklike prolongation (petals 4–6 mm long, deep pink) .... *E. densiflorum* (*Boisduvalia densiflora, B. salicina*)
DENSELY FLOWERED WILLOW HERB

        10 Fruit, just before splitting, with a distinct beaklike prolongation
          11 Sepals about 2 mm long; petals 2–4 mm long, deep pink; fruit 8–13 mm long; seeds in 4 straight rows in each chamber; leaves with smooth margins ..... *E. torreyi* (*Boisduvalia stricta*), pl. 405
TORREY'S WILLOW HERB

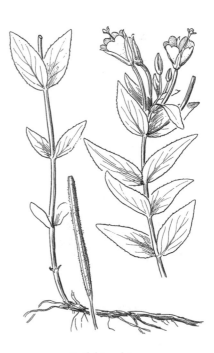

          11 Sepals 2–6 mm long; petals 4–11 mm long, pale pink; fruit 14–19 mm long, the seeds alternating on opposite sides of each chamber (Douglas Co., Oreg., to Calif.) ....
.... *E. pallidum* (*Boisduvalia pallida*)
PALE WILLOW HERB

    8 Seeds with a tuft of hairs at one end (see note before the beginning of the key); at least some of the leaves, especially those on lower portions of the plant, opposite (except in *E. foliosum*)
      12 Plants not often more than 30 cm tall; petals not more than 5 mm long; annual (the two choices 12 are not unequivocal except for the comparison of annual versus perennial; if you follow both, however, you will probably arrive at a satisfactory determination)
        13 Lower leaves mostly alternate, the upper ones in clusters; flowers crowded in the inflorescence; plants to about 40 cm tall; surface of seeds with small, low bumps ..... *E. foliosum*
LEAFY WILLOW HERB

Epilobium luteum,
yellow-flowered willow herb

13 Almost all leaves opposite, the blades flat; flowers loosely scattered along the inflorescence; plants rarely more than 25 cm tall; surface of seeds with a networklike pattern (in general, probably more common in damp than in dry habitats) . . . . *E. minutum*, pl. 401

TINY WILLOW HERB

Compare with the description of *E. oregonense* in the second choice 12.

12 Plants commonly more than 25 cm tall, sometimes more than 1 m; petals often more than 5 mm long; perennial, and in certain species producing bulblike offsets from the underground stems (*E. oregonense*, a high-montane species restricted to marshy habitats and mostly E of the crest of the Cascades, is easiest to deal with here—it is a perennial that spreads by slender stolons and forms mats, and the stems that rise up and produce inflorescences are usually 20–30 cm tall and have sessile, opposite leaves; the internodes of the inflorescence are much longer than the bracts of the same part of the plant; the petals are pale pink to violet, 5–8 mm long)

14 Seeds with close-set lengthwise ridges (this is the most reliable character but can be seen only on fully developed seeds and requires use of high magnification; do not confuse numerous small, evenly spaced ridges with 2–3 coarse ridges that develop on seeds that have shriveled); inflorescences generally upright; petals sometimes more than 10 mm long; pedicels of nearly ripe fruits generally less than 20 mm long, sometimes negligible . . . . *E. ciliatum*

COMMON WILLOW HERB

The 3 subspecies of *E. ciliatum* vaguely distinguished below intergrade.

15 Petals rarely more than 6 mm long and sometimes as short as 2 mm, white to pink . . . . *E. ciliatum* subsp. *ciliatum*

15 Petals 4–15 mm long, pale pink to rose or purplish rose

16 Inflorescence more or less flat-topped . . . . *E. ciliatum* subsp. *watsonii*

16 Inflorescence somewhat elongated . . . . *E. ciliatum* subsp. *glandulosum*

14 Seeds without close-set lengthwise ridges (they are either smooth, have a networklike pattern, or have a surface that looks (under magnification of at least 30×) like fine sandpaper

17 Surface of seeds smooth, even when examined with high magnification; petals varying considerably in length, sometimes only 3 mm long, sometimes as long as 12 mm; pedicels of ripe fruits usually not more than 2 cm long (stolons not producing bulblets)

18 Stems to more than 75 cm long; leaves to 7 cm long; fruit generally 5–7 cm long . . . . *E. glaberrimum* subsp. *glaberrimum*

SMOOTH WILLOW HERB

18 Stems not often more than 35 cm tall; leaves not more than 3.5 cm long; fruit generally less than 5 cm long . . . . *E. glaberrimum* subsp. *fastigiatum*

17 Surface of seeds either resembling that of fine sandpaper or with a networklike pattern; petals not more than 7 mm long; pedicels of ripe or nearly ripe fruits usually more than 2 cm long

19 Surface of seeds (when examined at a magnification of at least 30×) resembling that of fine sandpaper; inflorescences usually nodding; stolons producing small bulblets; plants commonly at least 50 cm tall; corolla white to pink . . . . *E. halleanum*

HALL'S WILLOW HERB

19 Surface of seeds with a networklike pattern; inflorescences upright; stolons not producing bulblets; plants usually less than 50 cm tall; corolla generally white, occasionally pink (montane, not likely to be found below 4000 ft., 1220 m) . . . . *E. lactiflorum* (*E. alpinum* var. *lactiflorum*)

WHITE-FLOWERED WILLOW HERB

OROBANCHACEAE Broomrape Family

Broomrapes are parasites attached to the roots of other flowering plants. They are not green and have no typical leaves, but there are reduced, scalelike leaves along the lower portions of the stems. The flowers have a five-lobed calyx and a two-lipped corolla, three lobes forming the lower lip and two lobes forming the upper one. The four stamens are attached to the corolla tube. The fruit is dry at maturity and has a single seed-producing chamber.

At various times in the past, it has been proposed that several genera conventionally placed in Scrophulariaceae should become part of the Orobanchaceae. More recent studies strongly support this idea. The genera involved, all partial parasites, are itemized in the discussion of Scrophulariaceae in connection with the way the genera of that family may be redistributed.

1 Inflorescence somewhat resembling the cone of a conifer in being compact and unbranched, and in having broad, blunt bracts . . . . *Boschniakia*
1 Flowers either in a loose raceme, in a panicle, or borne singly; the bracts, when present, narrow and pointed . . . . *Orobanche*

Boschniakia

1 Aerial portion of plant usually less than 10 cm tall; largest bracts usually less than 1 cm wide, pointed at the tip; anthers hairy only at their bases; usually parasitic on *Gaultheria shallon* and *Arctostaphylos uva-ursi* (color of the plant as a whole usually yellowish or purplish brown; mostly at the coast, Brit. Col. to Calif., and in the region of the Puget Trough, including the Gulf Islands, Brit. Col., and San Juan Islands, Wash.) . . . . *B. hookeri*, pl. 407
SMALL GROUND CONE
1 Aerial portion of plant commonly more than 10 cm tall; largest bracts more than 1 cm wide, blunt at the tip; usually parasitic on *Arbutus menziesii* and *Arctostaphylos* spp. (Josephine Co., Oreg., to Calif.) . . . . *B. strobilacea*, pl. 408
LARGE GROUND CONE

Orobanche

1 Calyx completely divided into 2 segments, each of these usually divided again into 2 lobes (established around Portland and at several other localities in northern Oreg., probably elsewhere in our region; parasitic on species of *Trifolium*) . . . . *O. minor*
CLOVER BROOMRAPE (Europe)
1 Calyx divided into 5 nearly equal lobes
  2 Each flower on a pedicel not more than 3 cm long and with a pair of bracts below the calyx (inflorescence a panicle)
    3 Calyx not more than 8 mm long, the lobes not obviously longer than the tube; corolla mostly yellowish, with brown markings (Cascades and Siskiyou Mountains; has been found attached to roots of *Holodiscus discolor* but perhaps also parasitizes other hosts) . . . . *O. pinorum*
PINE-FOREST BROOMRAPE
    3 Calyx usually more than 10 mm long, the lobes decidedly longer than the tube; corolla generally violet, purplish, or purplish brown, or at least tinged with one of these colors . . . . *O. californica*, pl. 409
CALIFORNIA BROOMRAPE
        Orobanche californica is extremely variable. In some floras it is subdivided into several subspecies, at least 2 of which occur in our region. The distinctions between them are fuzzy, however. Plants parasitizing species of *Grindelia* at low elevations from Brit. Col. to Calif. have been called subsp. *californica;* those parasitizing various species of *Aster* and *Erigeron,* especially above 3000 ft. (910 m), have been called subsp. *grayana.*
  2 Each flower on a pedicel at least 3 cm long and without a pair of bracts below the calyx
    4 Plants usually with more than 5 flowers, these on pedicels about as long as the aboveground portion of the stem; calyx lobes about as long as the tube (corolla usually light purple; on various host plants) . . . . *O. fasciculata*
CLUSTERED BROOMRAPE

4 Plants usually with only 1–3 flowers (sometimes more, however), these on pedicels much longer than the aboveground portion of the stem; calyx lobes distinctly longer than the tube (corolla mostly violet to dark purple; usually parasitizing species of *Sedum* and *Saxifraga*) . . . . *O. uniflora*, pl. 410

NAKED BROOMRAPE

> For distinguishing *O. fasciculata* and *O. uniflora*, the relative lengths of the calyx lobes and calyx tube are perhaps more reliable than the number of flowers and the relative lengths of the pedicels to the aboveground portion of the stem. In other words, some specimens with more than 5 flowers and a moderately long aboveground stem seem to be closer to *O. uniflora* than to *O. fasciculata*. The matter needs study.

OXALIDACEAE Oxalis Family

Three members of the oxalis family are native to the region covered by this book; the others are weeds introduced from other parts of the world. All belong to the genus *Oxalis*. The family is characterized by leaves that resemble those of clovers in having three leaflets at the tip of the petiole, and by fleshy underground rhizomes that make some of the weedy species difficult to eradicate. The calyx is five-lobed; the five petals, however, are separate, and before the flowers open they overlap one another and have a slight twist. There are ten stamens, the filaments of which are united at the base. The fruit-forming part of the pistil is partitioned lengthwise into five seed-producing divisions.

Oxalis

1 Petals white, pink (or pink-veined), sometimes rose or lilac; all substantial leaves basal
  2 Flowering stems with a single flower; petals 12–20 mm long, not notched at the tip, white, pink (or pink-veined), sometimes rose or lilac (especially in a robust form, var. *smalliana*, from Curry Co., Oreg.) . . . . *O. oregana*, pl. 411

REDWOOD SORREL

  2 Flowering stems with several flowers; petals about 10 mm long, notched at the tip, white or pink-tinged (plants to more than 40 cm tall when in flower; Coast Ranges and W slopes of the Cascades; rarely found below 1000 ft., 300 m) . . . . *O. trilliifolia*, pl. 413

GREAT OXALIS

1 Petals yellow; flowering stems, whether upright or prostrate, leafy
  3 Each peduncle usually with 1 flower (sometimes 2–3); petals usually about 10 mm long, sometimes longer (Clark Co., Wash., to Calif.) . . . . *O. suksdorfii*, pl. 412

WESTERN YELLOW OXALIS

  3 Most peduncles with at least 3 flowers; petals to 9 mm long
    4 Hairs on stems and petioles partitioned into units and blunt-tipped . . . . *O. europaea* (*O. stricta* of some references)

UPRIGHT YELLOW SORREL

> *Oxalis europaea* is a weed in our region but probably native to parts of North America as well as Europe and E Asia.

    4 Hairs on stems and petioles neither partitioned into units nor pointed at the tip
      5 Stems mostly prostrate, the tips becoming upright; stems and leaves usually brownish, purplish, or reddish; seeds wrinkled crosswise but the crests of the ridges not white (very common weed in gardens) . . . . *O. corniculata*

TRAILING YELLOW SORREL (Europe)

      5 Stems mostly upright but sometimes prostrate to some extent; stems and leaves usually green; seeds wrinkled crosswise, the crests of the ridges white (weed, not common in our region) . . . . . *O. dillenii*

DILLEN'S OXALIS (Europe)

PAEONIACEAE Peony Family

The peony family, with a single genus and about 30 species, is closely related to the buttercup family (Ranunculaceae). In peonies, however, the numerous stamens and the two to five pistils are joined to a fleshy disk, and the innermost stamens are the first to produce pollen; buttercups and their relatives do not have the fleshy disk, and it is the outermost stamens that produce pollen first. The number of petals ranges from five to ten. *Paeonia brownii*, western peony, is the only species in the Pacific Northwest. In our region it is occasionally found in Josephine and Jackson Counties of southwestern Oregon. From there it extends into California and into the area east of the Cascade crest, where its range, from northern Washington eastward and southward, is considerable. Plants reach a height of more than 50 cm and have attractive leaves, typically with three deeply lobed leaflets. The flowers are produced singly at the ends of the stems. There are five greenish to purple-tinged sepals, usually 1–1.5 cm long and differing a little in exact size and shape. The five brownish red or brownish purple petals are about the same size as the sepals. In our region, this interesting plant is not often seen below 3000 ft. (910 m).

PAPAVERACEAE Poppy Family

The flowers of poppies have four or more separate, similar petals, and usually two, sometimes three, sepals. The number of stamens ranges from several to many, and the fruiting portion of the pistil, although initially partitioned lengthwise into two or more seed-producing divisions, ripens as a single unit. An exception is creamcups, *Platystemon californicus*, in which the several divisions separate before the fruit is mature.

1 Petals 4, generally more than 2 cm long
  2 Sepals united, forming a cap over the petals before the flowers open, then falling away as a unit . . . . *Eschscholzia*
  2 Sepals not united, falling away separately after the flowers open . . . . *Papaver*
1 Petals generally 6 (sometimes 7 in *Platystemon californicus*), not more than 1.5 cm long (plants rarely so much as 30 cm tall when in flower)
  3 Petals (these to about 1 cm long) cream with yellow at the base; stamens many more than 12; fruit consisting of at least 6 divisions, these separating early and usually constricted into beadlike units (Rogue River valley and along the coast of Coos and Curry Cos., Oreg., to Calif.) . . . . . *Platystemon californicus*, pl. 417
                                        CREAMCUPS

  3 Petals white or cream but without yellow at the base; stamens 16 or fewer; fruit consisting of only 3 divisions, these remaining firmly attached to one another until the fruit cracks open to release the seeds . . . . *Meconella*

Eschscholzia

1 Receptacle funnel-shaped, longer than wide, with a broad, collarlike rim at the top; petals 2–6 cm long, usually orange or yellow but sometimes of other colors in horticultural forms; native from southernmost Wash. to Baja Calif. but widely cultivated and also established where planted along roadsides and in open fields) . . . .
. . . . *E. californica* subsp. *californica*, pl. 415
      CALIFORNIA POPPY, the state flower of California
1 Receptacle not longer than wide, with only an inconspicuous rim at the top; petals to 2.5 cm long, yellow (N Josephine Co., Oreg.; also Calif.) . . . .
. . . . *E. caespitosa*, pl. 414
    SLENDER CALIFORNIA POPPY

Paeonia brownii, western peony

Meconella

1 Petals to about 5 mm long, white; stamens usually 3–6, rarely more; leaf blades to about 1 cm long, more or less oval (widely distributed but rare, perhaps most common on SE Vancouver Island, Brit. Col., and in the Willamette Valley, Oreg.; small, easily overlooked, and flowering in late March or early April, before most wildflower enthusiasts are in the field) . . . .*M. oregana*, pl. 416
WHITE MECONELLA

1 Petals 5–10 mm long, white or cream, stamens 8–16; leaf blades to more than 4 cm long, narrow (coast of Curry Co., Oreg., to Calif.) . . . . *M. californica*
NARROW-LEAVED MECONELLA

Papaver

The species in this key have been in cultivation for a long time, and variants from the wild types have been selected for propagation. Thus the petal color of plants that have escaped from gardens varies considerably.

1 Upper leaves clasping the stem; leaf blades lobed but the lobes not separated nearly to the midrib (plants to about 1 m tall; petals usually orange but ranging from white to purple) . . . . *P. somniferum*
OPIUM POPPY (Europe)

1 None of the leaves clasping the stem; leaf blades deeply pinnately lobed, some lobes separated nearly to the midrib
  2 Leaves once-pinnately lobed, the lobes not again deeply divided (petals usually scarlet, sometimes white, orange, or pink, with a dark spot at the base) . . . .*P. rhoeas*
CORN POPPY (Europe)

  2 Leaves bipinnately lobed
    3 Fruits more than twice as long as wide, bristly-hairy; petals red, generally with a dark spot at the base
. . . .*P. argemone*
PRICKLY-HEADED POPPY (Europe)

    3 Fruits not so much as twice as long as wide, not hairy; petals red or orange, usually without a dark spot at the base . . . . *P. dubium*
BLINDEYES (Europe)

PARNASSIACEAE Parnassia Family

The small parnassia family is closely related to the saxifrage family (Saxifragaceae) and has usually been included in that group. Its flowers, however, are distinctly different in that they have, in addition to five anther-bearing stamens, five sterile stamens that originate at the bases of the petals. The sterile stamens are typically divided at their tips into fingerlike projections, which are sometimes long and slender. A curious feature of *Parnassia cirrata* is the presence of a fringe of long hairs on both sides of the lower half of each petal.

Parnassia

1 Both sides of lower half of each petal with a fringe of long hairs (montane, in bogs and other wet habitats, Alaska to Calif., also E of the Cascades, mostly above 4000 ft., 1220 m) . . . .
. . . . *P. cirrata* var. *intermedia* (*P. fimbriata* var. *intermedia*), pl. 418
FRINGED GRASS-OF-PARNASSUS

1 Lower portions of petals without marginal outgrowths
  2 Peduncle of flower with a small, leaflike bract (this about the same size as the sepals) well above the middle; sterile stamens usually with at least 15 (sometimes as many as 25) fingerlike projections (in bogs, Josephine Co., Oreg., to Calif.) . . . . *P. californica* (*P. palustris* var. *californica*)
CALIFORNIA GRASS-OF-PARNASSUS

  2 Peduncle of flower with a broad, leaflike bract, much larger than the sepals, well below the middle; sterile stamens not often with more than 15 fingerlike projections (montane, in wet habitats, mostly above 3500 ft., 1070 m) . . . . *P. palustris*
NORTHERN GRASS-OF-PARNASSUS

In some references, the widespread and variable *P. palustris* is divided up into subspecies or varieties.

1. *Asplenium trichomanes* subsp. *trichomanes,* maidenhair spleenwort (Aspleniaceae)

3. *Woodwardia fimbriata,* giant chain fern (Blechnaceae)

2. *Blechnum spicant,* deer fern (Blechnaceae)

4. *Athyrium filix-femina* var. *cyclosorum,* lady fern (Dryopteridaceae)

5. *Dryopteris arguta,* coastal wood fern (Dryopteridaceae)

6. *Dryopteris expansa,* wood fern (Dryopteridaceae)

7. *Polystichum californicum,* California shield fern (Dryopteridaceae)

8. *Polystichum munitum,* western sword fern (Dryopteridaceae)

9. *Botrychium pumicola,* pumice grape fern (Ophioglossaceae), Wilbur L. Bluhm

10. *Polypodium glycyrrhiza,* licorice fern (Polypodiaceae)

11. *Adiantum aleuticum,* five-finger fern (Pteridaceae)

12. *Aspidotis densa,* Indian's dream (Pteridaceae)

13. *Cheilanthes gracillima,* lace fern (Pteridaceae), Wilbur L. Bluhm

14. *Pellaea andromedifolia,* coffee fern (Pteridaceae)

15. *Pteridium aquilinum* subsp. *pubescens,* bracken (Pteridaceae)

16. *Azolla mexicana*, Mexican mosquito fern (Azollaceae)

18. *Equisetum telmateia* subsp. *braunii*, giant horsetail (Equisetaceae)

17. *Equisetum hyemale* subsp. *affine*, common scouring rush (Equisetaceae)

19. *Diphasiastrum sitchense*, Sitka club moss (Lycopodiaceae), Wilbur L. Bluhm

20. *Lycopodium clavatum*, ground pine (Lycopodiaceae)

21. *Selaginella oregana*, Oregon selaginella (Selaginellaceae)

22. *Selaginella wallacei*, Wallace's selaginella (Selaginellaceae)

23. *Chamaecyparis lawsoniana*, Lawson's cypress (Cupressaceae)

24. *Chamaecyparis nootkatensis*, yellow cypress (Cupressaceae)

25. *Juniperus communis*, common juniper (Cupressaceae)

26. *Juniperus scopulorum*, Rocky Mountain juniper (Cupressaceae)

27. *Thuja plicata*, western red cedar (Cupressaceae)

28. *Abies grandis*, grand fir (Pinaceae)

29. *Picea sitchensis*, Sitka spruce (Pinaceae)

30. *Pinus attenuata*, knobcone pine (Pinaceae)

31. *Pinus contorta* subsp. *contorta*, shore pine (Pinaceae)

32. *Pinus monticola*, western white pine (Pinaceae)

33. *Pinus ponderosa* var. *ponderosa*, western yellow pine (Pinaceae)

34. *Pseudotsuga menziesii* var. *menziesii*, Douglas' fir (Pinaceae)

35. *Tsuga heterophylla*, western hemlock (Pinaceae)

36. *Taxus brevifolia*, western yew (Taxaceae)

37. *Sequoia sempervirens,* coast redwood (Taxodiaceae)

38. *Acer circinatum,* vine maple (Aceraceae)

39. *Acer glabrum* var. *douglasii,* Douglas' maple (Aceraceae)

40. *Carpobrotus chilensis,* sea fig (Aizoaceae)

41. *Rhus trilobata,* skunkbush (Anacardiaceae)

42. *Toxicodendron diversilobum,* poison oak (Anacardiaceae)

43. *Glehnia littoralis* subsp. *leiocarpa,* beach silvertop (Apiaceae)

44. *Heracleum maximum*, cow parsnip (Apiaceae)

45. *Lomatium triternatum* subsp. *triternatum*, narrow-leaved lomatium (Apiaceae)

46. *Lomatium utriculatum*, spring gold (Apiaceae)

47. *Oenanthe sarmentosa*, water parsley (Apiaceae)

48. *Osmorhiza berteroi*, sweet cicely (Apiaceae)

49. *Perideridia gairdneri* subsp. *borealis*, Gairdner's yampah (Apiaceae)

50. *Sanicula arctopoides*, footsteps-of-spring (Apiaceae)

51. *Sanicula bipinnatifida*, purple snakeroot (Apiaceae)

52. *Sanicula crassicaulis*, snakeroot (Apiaceae)

53. *Sanicula peckiana*, Peck's snakeroot (Apiaceae)

54. *Scandix pecten-veneris*, shepherd's needle (Apiaceae)

55. *Apocynum androsaemifolium*, bitter dogbane (Apocynaceae)

56. *Apocynum cannabinum*, Indian hemp (Apocynaceae)

57. *Vinca minor*, common periwinkle (Apocynaceae)

58. *Aralia californica*, elk clover (Araliaceae)

59. *Oplopanax horridus,* devil's club (Araliaceae)

60. *Asarum caudatum,* western wild ginger (Aristolochiaceae)

61. *Asclepias fascicularis,* narrowleaf milkweed (Asclepiadaceae)

62. *Asclepias speciosa,* showy milkweed (Asclepiadaceae)

63. *Achillea millefolium,* yarrow (Asteraceae)

64. *Ageratina occidentalis,* western ageratina (Asteraceae)

65. *Agoseris apargioides* var. *maritima,* seaside agoseris (Asteraceae)

66. *Agoseris aurantiaca* var. *aurantiaca*, orange agoseris
(Asteraceae), Linda H. Beidleman

67. *Agoseris grandiflora*, large-flowered agoseris (Asteraceae)

68. *Ambrosia chamissonis* var. *bipinnatisecta*, beach bur
(Asteraceae)

69. *Ambrosia chamissonis* var. *chamissonis*, silvery beachweed
(Asteraceae)

70. *Anaphalis margaritacea*, pearly everlasting (Asteraceae)

71. *Anisocarpus madioides*, woodland tarweed (Asteraceae)

73. *Antennaria suffrutescens,* evergreen everlasting (Asteraceae)

74. *Arctium minus,* small burdock (Asteraceae)

72. *Antennaria rosea,* rosy pussytoes (Asteraceae), Wilbur L. Bluhm

76. *Arnica cordifolia,* heart-leaved arnica (Asteraceae), Wilbur L. Bluhm

75. *Arnica amplexicaulis,* streambank arnica (Asteraceae), Wilbur L. Bluhm

77. *Arnica discoidea,* rayless arnica (Asteraceae)

79. *Artemisia campestris*, northern wormwood (Asteraceae)

78. *Arnica spathulata*, Klamath arnica (Asteraceae)

83. *Aster curtus*, short white-topped aster (Asteraceae)

80. *Artemisia suksdorfii*, coastal mugwort (Asteraceae)

81. *Aster alpigenus* var. *alpigenus*, alpine aster (Asteraceae), Wilbur L. Bluhm

82. *Aster chilensis*, Pacific aster (Asteraceae)

84. *Aster foliaceus* var. *foliaceus*, leafy-bract aster (Asteraceae)

85. *Aster modestus*, great northern aster (Asteraceae), Wilbur L. Bluhm

86. *Aster subspicatus*, Douglas' aster (Asteraceae)

87. *Baccharis pilularis*, chaparral broom (Asteraceae)

88. *Balsamorhiza deltoidea*, deltoid balsamroot (Asteraceae)

89. *Balsamorhiza sericea*, silky balsamroot (Asteraceae)

90. *Bellis perennis*, English daisy (Asteraceae)

91. *Blepharipappus scaber* (Asteraceae)

92. *Centaurea ×pratensis,* field knapweed (Asteraceae)

93. *Centaurea solstitialis,* Barnaby's thistle (Asteraceae)

94. *Chaenactis douglasii* var. *douglasii,* hoary pincushion (Asteraceae)

95. *Cichorium intybus,* chicory (Asteraceae)

96. *Cirsium brevistylum,* short-style thistle (Asteraceae)

97. *Cirsium callilepis,* fringe-phyllary thistle (Asteraceae)

98. *Cirsium occidentale* var. *venustum,* Venus thistle (Asteraceae)

99. *Cirsium vulgare,* bull thistle (Asteraceae)

100. *Conyza canadensis* var. *glabrata*, horseweed (Asteraceae)

101. *Coreopsis tinctoria* var. *atkinsoniana*, Columbia coreopsis (Asteraceae)

102. *Cotula coronopifolia*, brass buttons (Asteraceae)

103. *Crepis capillaris*, smooth hawksbeard (Asteraceae)

104. *Erechtites minima*, Australian fireweed (Asteraceae)

105. *Ericameria nauseosa*, rabbit brush (Asteraceae)

106. *Erigeron aureus*, alpine yellow daisy (Asteraceae)

107. *Erigeron decumbens* var. *decumbens*, Willamette Valley daisy (Asteraceae)

108. *Erigeron foliosus* var. *confinis,* leafy daisy (Asteraceae)

109. *Erigeron glaucus,* seaside daisy (Asteraceae)

110. *Erigeron petrophilus,* rock daisy (Asteraceae)

111. *Erigeron philadelphicus,* Philadelphia daisy (Asteraceae)

112. *Erigeron speciosus* var. *speciosus,* showy daisy (Asteraceae)

113. *Eriophyllum lanatum* var. *lanatum,* woolly sunflower (Asteraceae)

114. *Eriophyllum staechadifolium,* seaside woolly sunflower (Asteraceae)

115. *Gnaphalium canescens* subsp. *thermale,* slender cudweed (Asteraceae)

116. *Gnaphalium palustre,* lowland cudweed (Asteraceae)

117. *Gnaphalium purpureum,* purple cudweed (Asteraceae)

118. *Grindelia integrifolia,* Willamette Valley gumweed (Asteraceae)

119. *Grindelia nana,* small gumweed (Asteraceae)

120. *Helenium bigelovii,* tall sneezeweed (Asteraceae)

121. *Helenium puberulum,* rosilla (Asteraceae)

122. *Hemizonia fitchii,* Fitch's spikeweed (Asteraceae)

123. *Heterotheca oregona,* Oregon golden aster (Asteraceae)

124. *Heterotheca villosa* var. *villosa*, hairy golden aster (Asteraceae)

125. *Hieracium aurantiacum*, orange hawkweed (Asteraceae)

126. *Hulsea nana*, dwarf hulsea (Asteraceae), Wilbur L. Bluhm

127. *Jaumea carnosa* (Asteraceae)

128. *Lapsana communis*, nipplewort (Asteraceae)

129. *Lasthenia californica*, California goldfields (Asteraceae)

130. *Lasthenia glaberrima*, smooth goldfields (Asteraceae)

131. *Lessingia filaginifolia* subsp. *californica*, beach lessingia (Asteraceae)

132. *Luina hypoleuca*, silverback (Asteraceae)

134. *Madia gracilis*, common tarweed (Asteraceae)

133. *Madia elegans* var. *elegans*, common madia (Asteraceae)

135. *Matricaria discoidea*, pineapple weed (Asteraceae)

137. *Microseris laciniata*, cut-leaved microseris (Asteraceae)

136. *Micropus californicus* var. *californicus*, slender cottonweed (Asteraceae)

138. *Mycelis muralis,* wall lettuce (Asteraceae)

139. *Petasites frigidus* subsp. *palmatus,* coltsfoot (Asteraceae)

140. *Psilocarphus tenellus* var. *tenellus,* slender woolly-heads (Asteraceae)

141. *Pyrrocoma racemosa* var. *congesta,* crowded goldenweed (Asteraceae)

142. *Rudbeckia californica* var. *glauca,* California coneflower (Asteraceae)

143. *Senecio hesperius,* Siskiyou butterweed (Asteraceae)

144. *Senecio jacobaea,* tansy ragwort (Asteraceae)

145. *Senecio macounii*, Macoun's senecio (Asteraceae)

146. *Senecio vulgaris*, common groundsel (Asteraceae)

147. *Solidago canadensis* subsp. *salebrosa*, Canada goldenrod (Asteraceae)

148. *Solidago simplex* subsp. *neomexicana*, spikelike goldenrod (Asteraceae)

149. *Sonchus arvensis*, perennial sow thistle (Asteraceae)

150. *Stephanomeria virgata* subsp. *pleurocarpa*, virgate stephanomeria (Asteraceae)

151. *Tanacetum camphoratum,* dune tansy (Asteraceae)

152. *Tanacetum parthenium,* feverfew (Asteraceae)

153. *Tragopogon porrifolius,* salsify (Asteraceae)

154. *Uropappus lindleyi,* narrow-leaved uropappus (Asteraceae)

155. *Wyethia angustifolia,* mule's ears (Asteraceae), Wilbur L. Bluhm

156. *Impatiens glandulifera,* policeman's helmet (Balsaminaceae)

157. *Achlys californica,* several-lobed vanilla leaf (Berberidaceae)

158. *Berberis aquifolium*, Oregon grape (Berberidaceae)

160. *Vancouveria chrysantha*, yellow vancouveria (Berberidaceae)

159. *Berberis nervosa*, long-leaved Oregon grape (Berberidaceae)

161. *Vancouveria hexandra*, inside-out flower (Berberidaceae)

163. *Amsinckia menziesii* var. *intermedia*, common fiddleneck (Boraginaceae)

162. *Alnus viridis* subsp. *sinuata*, Sitka alder (Betulaceae)

164. *Cynoglossum grande*, giant hound's-tongue (Boraginaceae)

165. *Lithospermum californicum*, California gromwell (Boraginaceae)

166. *Mertensia platyphylla*, western lungwort (Boraginaceae)

167. *Myosotis discolor*, yellow-and-blue scorpion grass (Boraginaceae)

168. *Myosotis laxa*, small forget-me-not (Boraginaceae)

169. *Plagiobothrys bracteatus*, bracted popcorn flower (Boraginaceae)

170. *Plagiobothrys nothofulvus*, rusty popcorn flower (Boraginaceae)

171. *Arabis aculeolata*, Waldo rock cress (Brassicaceae)

172. *Arabis koehleri* var. *stipitata*, Koehler's rock cress (Brassicaceae)

173. *Brassica rapa*, field mustard (Brassicaceae)

174. *Cakile maritima*, horned sea rocket (Brassicaceae)

175. *Cardamine nuttallii*, Nuttall's bitter cress (Brassicaceae)

176. *Draba aureola*, golden draba (Brassicaceae), Wilbur L. Bluhm

177. *Erysimum capitatum*, western wallflower (Brassicaceae)

178. *Lepidium virginicum* var. *menziesii*, Menzies' peppergrass (Brassicaceae)

179. *Lunaria annua*, honesty (Brassicaceae)

180. *Rorippa palustris*, marsh yellow cress (Brassicaceae)

181. *Streptanthus howellii,* Howell's streptanthus (Brassicaceae)

182. *Teesdalia nudicaulis,* shepherd's cress (Brassicaceae)

183. *Thlaspi montanum* var. *siskiyouense,* Siskiyou pennycress (Brassicaceae)

184. *Thysanocarpus curvipes,* hairy fringepod (Brassicaceae)

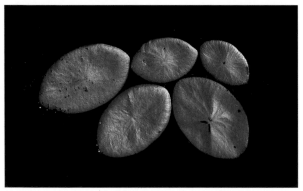

185. *Brasenia schreberi,* water shield (Cabombaceae)

186. *Opuntia fragilis,* brittle prickly pear (Cactaceae)

187. *Callitriche stagnalis,* common water starwort (Callitrichaceae)

188. *Campanula piperi,* Piper's bellflower (Campanulaceae)

189. *Campanula prenanthoides,* California harebell (Campanulaceae)

190. *Campanula rotundifolia,* common bluebell (Campanulaceae)

191. *Campanula scouleri,* Scouler's harebell (Campanulaceae)

192. *Downingia bacigalupii,* Bacigalupi's downingia (Campanulaceae)

193. *Downingia elegans,* elegant downingia (Campanulaceae)

194. *Downingia yina,* spreading downingia (Campanulaceae)

195. *Githopsis specularioides,* bluecup (Campanulaceae), Wilbur L. Bluhm

196. *Lobelia dortmanna,* water lobelia, photographed underwater (Campanulaceae)

197. *Linnaea borealis* var. *longiflora*, twinflower (Caprifoliaceae)

198. *Lonicera ciliosa*, orange honeysuckle (Caprifoliaceae)

199. *Lonicera involucrata* var. *ledebourii*, coast twinberry (Caprifoliaceae)

200. *Sambucus mexicana*, blue elderberry (Caprifoliaceae)

201. *Sambucus racemosa* var. *arborescens*, red elderberry (Caprifoliaceae)

202. *Symphoricarpos albus* subsp. *laevigatus*, snowberry (Caprifoliaceae)

203. *Symphoricarpos mollis*, creeping snowberry (Caprifoliaceae)

204. *Viburnum ellipticum*, oval-leaved viburnum (Caprifoliaceae)

205. *Cardionema ramosissimum,* sand mat (Caryophyllaceae)

206. *Cerastium glomeratum,* sticky mouse-ear chickweed (Caryophyllaceae)

207. *Dianthus deltoides,* maiden pink (Caryophyllaceae)

208. *Honckenya peploides,* sea purslane (Caryophyllaceae)

209. *Moehringia macrophylla,* large-leaved sandwort (Caryophyllaceae)

210. *Saponaria officinalis,* bouncing Bet (Caryophyllaceae)

211. *Silene californica,* Indian pink (Caryophyllaceae)

212. *Silene campanulata* subsp. *glandulosa,* campanulate campion (Caryophyllaceae)

213. *Silene gallica,* small-flowered catchfly (Caryophyllaceae)

214. *Silene hookeri* subsp. *hookeri,* Hooker's catchfly (Caryophyllaceae)

215. *Silene scouleri* subsp. *grandis,* Scouler's catchfly (Caryophyllaceae)

216. *Spergularia macrotheca* var. *macrotheca,* beach sand spurrey (Caryophyllaceae)

217. *Spergularia rubra,* sand spurrey (Caryophyllaceae)

218. *Stellaria borealis* subsp. *sitchana,* northern starwort (Caryophyllaceae)

219. *Stellaria media,* chickweed (Caryophyllaceae)

220. *Euonymus occidentalis* var. *occidentalis,* western burning bush, in flower (Celastraceae)

221. *Euonymus occidentalis* var. *occidentalis,* western burning bush, with fruit and seeds (Celastraceae)

222. *Paxistima myrsinites,* Oregon boxwood (Celastraceae)

223. *Salicornia virginica,* pickleweed (Chenopodiaceae)

224. *Salsola tragus,* Russian thistle (Chenopodiaceae)

225. *Calystegia occidentalis* subsp. *occidentalis,* pale morning glory (Convolvulaceae)

226. *Calystegia soldanella,* beach morning glory (Convolvulaceae)

227. *Cornus glabrata,* smooth dogwood (Cornaceae)

228. *Cornus nuttallii,* western dogwood (Cornaceae)

229. *Cornus sericea,* red osier dogwood (Cornaceae)

230. *Cornus unalaschkensis,* dwarf dogwood (Cornaceae)

231. *Crassula connata* var. *connata,* erect pygmyweed (Crassulaceae)

233. *Sedum lanceolatum* var. *nesioticum,* island stonecrop (Crassulaceae)

232. *Dudleya cymosa,* inland dudleya (Crassulaceae)

234. *Sedum oreganum,* Oregon stonecrop (Crassulaceae)

235. *Sedum spathulifolium* subsp. *spathulifolium*, broad-leaved stonecrop (Crassulaceae)

236. *Marah oreganus*, coast manroot (Cucurbitaceae)

237. *Cuscuta salina* var. *major*, salt-marsh dodder (Cuscutaceae)

238. *Dipsacus fullonum*, common teasel (Dipsacaceae)

239. *Shepherdia canadensis*, buffalo berry (Elaeagnaceae)

240. *Empetrum nigrum*, black crowberry (Empetraceae)

241. *Allotropa virgata*, sugar stick (Ericaceae)

242. *Arbutus menziesii*, madroño (Ericaceae)

243. *Arctostaphylos columbiana*, bristly manzanita (Ericaceae)

244. *Arctostaphylos glandulosa* subsp. *glandulosa*, hairy manzanita (Ericaceae)

245. *Arctostaphylos patula*, green manzanita (Ericaceae)

246. *Arctostaphylos uva-ursi*, kinnikinnick (Ericaceae)

247. *Arctostaphylos viscida* subsp. *pulchella*, sticky manzanita (Ericaceae)

248. *Cassiope mertensiana* var. *mertensiana*, Mertens' mountain heather (Ericaceae), Michael Fahey

249. *Chimaphila umbellata*, prince's pine (Ericaceae)

250. *Elliottia pyroliflora*, copper bush (Ericaceae), Wilbur L. Bluhm

251. *Gaultheria ovatifolia*, western wintergreen (Ericaceae), Wilbur L. Bluhm

252. *Gaultheria shallon*, salal (Ericaceae)

253. *Hemitomes congestum*, gnome plant (Ericaceae)

254. *Kalmia microphylla* subsp. *occidentalis*, western swamp laurel (Ericaceae)

255. *Kalmiopsis leachiana*, Lilla Leach's kalmiopsis (Ericaceae), Wilbur L. Bluhm

256. *Ledum glandulosum* subsp. *columbianum*, Pacific Labrador tea (Ericaceae)

258. *Menziesia ferruginea*, rustyleaf (Ericaceae)

257. *Leucothoe davisiae*, western leucothoe (Ericaceae)

259. *Monotropa uniflora*, Indian pipe (Ericaceae)

261. *Pterospora andromedea*, pinedrops (Ericaceae)

260. *Phyllodoce empetriformis*, pink mountain heather (Ericaceae), Michael Fahey

262. *Pyrola asarifolia*, large pyrola, green-leaved and leafless saprophytic phases (Ericaceae)

263. *Rhododendron albiflorum*, white rhododendron (Ericaceae), Linda H. Beidleman

264. *Rhododendron macrophyllum*, western rhododendron (Ericaceae)

265. *Rhododendron occidentale*, western azalea (Ericaceae)

266. *Sarcodes sanguinea*, snow plant (Ericaceae)

267. *Vaccinium ovatum*, evergreen huckleberry (Ericaceae)

268. *Vaccinium oxycoccos*, wild cranberry (Ericaceae)

269. *Vaccinium parvifolium*, red huckleberry (Ericaceae)

270. *Vaccinium uliginosum* subsp. *occidentale*, bog huckleberry (Ericaceae)

271. *Chamaesyce maculata*, milk spurge (Euphorbiaceae)

272. *Eremocarpus setigerus*, turkey mullein (Euphorbiaceae)

273. *Euphorbia peplus*, petty spurge (Euphorbiaceae)

274. *Astragalus accidens* var. *hendersonii*, thicket milkvetch (Fabaceae)

275. *Glycyrrhiza lepidota*, wild licorice (Fabaceae), Wilbur L. Bluhm

276. *Lathyrus aphaca*, yellow pea (Fabaceae)

277. *Lathyrus japonicus* var. *maritimus*, beach pea (Fabaceae)

278. *Lathyrus littoralis*, gray beach pea (Fabaceae)

279. *Lathyrus nevadensis*, Sierra Nevada pea (Fabaceae)

280. *Lotus formosissimus*, seaside lotus (Fabaceae)

281. *Lotus micranthus*, small-flowered lotus (Fabaceae)

282. *Lotus pinnatus*, bog lotus (Fabaceae)

283. *Lotus wrangelianus,* hairy lotus (Fabaceae)

284. *Lupinus albicaulis* var. *shastensis,* Shasta Springs lupine (Fabaceae)

285. *Lupinus albifrons,* silver lupine (Fabaceae)

286. *Lupinus arboreus,* bush lupine (Fabaceae); pl. 287 on next page

288. *Lupinus latifolius* var. *latifolius,* broad-leaflet lupine (Fabaceae)

289. *Lupinus lepidus* var. *lepidus,* prairie lupine (Fabaceae)

290. *Lupinus littoralis,* seashore lupine (Fabaceae)

291. *Lupinus polyphyllus,* large-leaved lupine (Fabaceae), Wilbur L. Bluhm

287. *Lupinus bicolor,* two-color lupine (Fabaceae); pls. 288–291 on previous page

292. *Oxytropis monticola* subsp. *monticola,* mountain oxytropis (Fabaceae)

293. *Rupertia physodes,* California tea (Fabaceae)

294. *Sophora leachiana,* western sophora (Fabaceae)

295. *Thermopsis gracilis,* slender thermopsis (Fabaceae)

297. *Trifolium arvense,* rabbit-foot clover (Fabaceae)

296. *Trifolium angustifolium,* crimson clover (Fabaceae)

298. *Trifolium depauperatum* var. *depauperatum*, poverty clover (Fabaceae)

299. *Trifolium dubium*, shamrock (Fabaceae)

300. *Trifolium eriocephalum* var. *eriocephalum*, woolly-headed clover (Fabaceae)

301. *Trifolium fucatum*, sour clover (Fabaceae)

302. *Trifolium incarnatum*, crimson clover (Fabaceae)

303. *Trifolium pratense*, red clover (Fabaceae)

304. *Trifolium willdenovii*, tomcat clover (Fabaceae)

305. *Vicia nigricans* var. *gigantea*, giant vetch (Fabaceae)

306. *Vicia sativa* var. *angustifolia*, narrow-leaved vetch (Fabaceae)

307. *Vicia villosa* var. *villosa*, woolly vetch (Fabaceae)

308. *Lithocarpus densiflorus* subsp. *densiflorus*, tanbark oak (Fagaceae)

309. *Lithocarpus densiflorus* subsp. *echinoides*, small tanbark oak (Fagaceae)

310. *Quercus chrysolepis*, canyon oak (Fagaceae)

311. *Quercus garryana* var. *garryana*, Garry's oak (Fagaceae)

312. *Quercus sadleriana*, Sadler's oak (Fagaceae)

313. *Quercus vaccinifolia*, huckleberry-leaved oak (Fagaceae)

314. *Corydalis scouleri,* western corydalis (Fumariaceae)

315. *Dicentra formosa* subsp. *formosa,* western bleeding heart (Fumariaceae)

316. *Dicentra formosa* subsp. *oregana,* Oregon bleeding heart (Fumariaceae)

317. *Fumaria officinalis,* fumitory (Fumariaceae)

318. *Garrya elliptica,* coast silk tassel (Garryaceae)

319. *Centaurium erythraea,* common centaury (Gentianaceae)

320. *Gentiana calycosa,* mountain bog gentian (Gentianaceae), Michael Fahey

321. *Gentiana newberryi* var. *newberryi*, Newberry's gentian (Gentianaceae), Wilbur L. Bluhm

322. *Gentiana sceptrum*, king's gentian (Gentianaceae)

323. *Gentiana setigera*, elegant gentian (Gentianaceae)

324. *Gentianella amarella* subsp. *acuta*, northern gentianella (Gentianaceae)

325. *Erodium cicutarium*, common storksbill (Geraniaceae)

326. *Geranium bicknellii*, Bicknell's geranium (Geraniaceae)

327. *Geranium dissectum*, cutleaf geranium (Geraniaceae)

328. *Geranium molle*, dove's-foot geranium (Geraniaceae)

329. *Geranium oreganum*, western geranium (Geraniaceae)

330. *Geranium robertianum*, herb Robert (Geraniaceae)

331. *Ribes bracteosum*, stink currant (Grossulariaceae)

334. *Ribes lacustre*, prickly currant (Grossulariaceae)

332. *Ribes cereum* var. *cereum*, wax currant (Grossulariaceae), Linda H. Beidleman

333. *Ribes divaricatum* var. *divaricatum*, coast black gooseberry (Grossulariaceae)

335. *Ribes sanguineum* var. *sanguineum*, red-flowering currant (Grossulariaceae)

336. *Hippuris vulgaris*, mare's tail (Hippuridaceae)

337. *Philadelphus lewisii*, mock orange (Hydrangeaceae)

338. *Whipplea modesta*, yerba de selva (Hydrangeaceae)

339. *Eriodictyon californicum*, yerba santa (Hydrophyllaceae)

340. *Hesperochiron pumilus*, dwarf hesperochiron (Hydrophyllaceae), Wilbur L. Bluhm

341. *Hydrophyllum occidentale*, western waterleaf (Hydrophyllaceae)

342. *Hydrophyllum tenuipes*, slender-stemmed waterleaf (Hydrophyllaceae)

343. *Nemophila menziesii* var. *atomaria*, large-flowered nemophila (Hydrophyllaceae)

344. *Nemophila parviflora* var. *parviflora*, small-flowered nemophila (Hydrophyllaceae)

345. *Phacelia argentea*, sand-dune phacelia (Hydrophyllaceae)

346. *Phacelia bolanderi*, Bolander's phacelia (Hydrophyllaceae)

347. *Phacelia corymbosa*, serpentine phacelia (Hydrophyllaceae)

349. *Hypericum anagalloides*, bog Saint-John's-wort (Hypericaceae)

348. *Romanzoffia sitchensis*, Sitka mist maiden (Hydrophyllaceae)

350. *Hypericum perforatum,* common Saint-John's-wort (Hypericaceae)

351. *Agastache urticifolia* var. *urticifolia,* horsemint (Lamiaceae), Wilbur L. Bluhm

352. *Lamium amplexicaule,* henbit (Lamiaceae)

353. *Lamium purpureum,* red dead nettle (Lamiaceae)

354. *Lycopus uniflorus,* bugleweed (Lamiaceae)

355. *Mentha arvensis,* field mint (Lamiaceae)

356. *Menth pulegium,* pennyroyal (Lamiaceae)

357. *Monardella villosa* var. *villosa,* coyote mint (Lamiaceae)

358. *Prunella vulgaris* subsp. *lanceolata*, narrow-leaved self-heal (Lamiaceae)

359. *Satureja douglasii*, yerba buena (Lamiaceae)

360. *Scutellaria galericulata*, marsh skullcap (Lamiaceae)

361. *Scutellaria tuberosa*, blue skullcap (Lamiaceae)

362. *Stachys cooleyae*, great hedge nettle (Lamiaceae)

363. *Stachys mexicana*, northwestern hedge nettle (Lamiaceae)

364. *Trichostema lanceolatum*, vinegar weed (Lamiaceae)

365. *Umbellularia californica,* California bay laurel (Lauraceae)

366. *Limnanthes alba* subsp. *alba,* white meadowfoam (Limnanthaceae)

367. *Limnanthes douglasii* subsp. *douglasii,* meadowfoam (Limnanthaceae)

368. *Limnanthes floccosa* subsp. *floccosa,* hairy-leaved meadowfoam (Limnanthaceae)

369. *Limnanthes gracilis* subsp. *gracilis,* slender meadowfoam (Limnanthaceae)

370. *Linum bienne,* narrow-leaved flax (Linaceae)

371. *Linum lewisii* subsp. *lewisii,* Lewis' flax (Linaceae)

372. *Mentzelia laevicaulis,* blazing star (Loasaceae)

373. *Lythrum salicaria*, purple loosestrife (Lythraceae)

375. *Sidalcea campestris*, meadow sidalcea (Malvaceae)

376. *Sidalcea cusickii*, Cusick's sidalcea (Malvaceae)

374. *Malva neglecta*, common mallow (Malvaceae)

377. *Sidalcea hendersonii*, Henderson's sidalcea (Malvaceae)

378. *Sidalcea hirtipes*, bristly-stemmed sidalcea (Malvaceae)

379. *Sidalcea malviflora* subsp. *virgata*, mallow sidalcea (Malvaceae)

380. *Menyanthes trifoliata*, buckbean (Menyanthaceae)

381. *Myrica californica*, California wax myrtle (Myricaceae)

382. *Myrica gale*, sweet gale (Myricaceae)

383. *Abronia latifolia*, yellow sand verbena (Nyctaginaceae)

384. *Abronia umbellata* subsp. *breviflora*, pink sand verbena (Nyctaginaceae)

385. *Nuphar lutea* subsp. *polysepala*, yellow pond lily (Nymphaeaceae)

386. *Fraxinus latifolia*, Oregon ash (Oleaceae)

387. *Camissonia cheiranthifolia* subsp. *cheiranthifolia*, beach evening primrose (Onagraceae)

388. *Camissonia contorta,* contorted-pod evening primrose (Onagraceae)

389. *Camissonia ovata,* suncup (Onagraceae)

390. *Chamerion angustifolium,* fireweed (Onagraceae)

391. *Circaea alpina* subsp. *pacifica,* enchanter's nightshade (Onagraceae)

392. *Clarkia amoena* subsp. *caurina,* Pacific clarkia (Onagraceae)

393. *Clarkia amoena* subsp. *huntiana,* Hunt's clarkia (Onagraceae)

394. *Clarkia amoena* subsp. *lindleyi,* farewell-to-spring (Onagraceae)

395. *Clarkia gracilis* subsp. *gracilis*, summer's darling
(Onagraceae)

396. *Clarkia heterandra*, alternating-stamened clarkia
(Onagraceae)

397. *Clarkia purpurea* subsp. *quadrivulnera*, wine-cup clarkia
(Onagraceae)

398. *Clarkia purpurea* subsp. *viminea*, large clarkia
(Onagraceae)

399. *Clarkia rhomboidea*, tongue clarkia (Onagraceae)

400. *Epilobium brachycarpum*, Siskiyou willow herb
(Onagraceae)

401. *Epilobium minutum*, tiny willow herb (Onagraceae)

402. *Epilobium oreganum,* Oregon fireweed (Onagraceae)

403. *Epilobium pygmaeum,* pygmy willow herb (Onagraceae)

404. *Epilobium rigidum,* Siskiyou willow herb (Onagraceae),
Wilbur L. Bluhm

405. *Epilobium torreyi,* Torrey's willow herb (Onagraceae)

406. *Oenothera ×glazioviana,* biennial evening primrose
(Onagraceae)

407. *Boschniakia hookeri,* small ground cone (Orobanchaceae)

408. *Boschniakia strobilacea,* large ground cone
(Orobanchaceae)

409. *Orobanche californica*, California broomrape (Orobanchaceae)

410. *Orobanche uniflora*, naked broomrape (Orobanchaceae)

411. *Oxalis oregana*, redwood sorrel (Oxalidaceae)

412. *Oxalis suksdorfii*, western yellow oxalis (Oxalidaceae)

413. *Oxalis trilliifolia*, great oxalis (Oxalidaceae)

414. *Eschscholzia caespitosa*, slender California poppy (Papaveraceae)

415. *Eschscholzia californica* subsp. *californica*, California poppy (Papaveraceae)

416. *Meconella oregana*, white meconella (Papaveraceae)

417. *Platystemon californicus*, creamcups (Papaveraceae)

419. *Plantago erecta*, California plantain (Plantaginaceae)

418. *Parnassia cirrata* var. *intermedia*, fringed grass-of-Parnassus (Parnassiaceae), Michael Fahey

420. *Plantago maritima*, seaside plantain (Plantaginaceae)

422. *Limonium californicum*, sea lavender (Plumbaginaceae)

421. *Armeria maritima* subsp. *californica*, sea pink (Plumbaginaceae)

423. *Collomia grandiflora*, large-flowered collomia (Polemoniaceae)

424. *Collomia heterophylla*, varied-leaved collomia (Polemoniaceae)

425. *Gilia capitata* subsp. *capitata*, globe gilia (Polemoniaceae)

427. *Leptosiphon bicolor*, bicolored leptosiphon (Polemoniaceae)

426. *Ipomopsis aggregata* subsp. *formosissima*, skyrocket (Polemoniaceae), Michael Fahey

428. *Leptosiphon minimus*, tiny leptosiphon (Polemoniaceae)

429. *Microsteris gracilis*, annual phlox (Polemoniaceae)

430. *Navarretia leucocephala* subsp. *leucocephala*, white-flowered navarretia (Polemoniaceae)

431. *Navarretia squarrosa*, skunkweed (Polemoniaceae)

432. *Phlox adsurgens,* woodland phlox (Polemoniaceae)

433. *Phlox diffusa* subsp. *diffusa,* spreading phlox (Polemoniaceae)

434. *Phlox speciosa,* showy phlox (Polemoniaceae)

435. *Polemonium carneum,* great polemonium (Polemoniaceae)

436. *Polemonium pulcherrimum* subsp. *pulcherrimum,* showy polemonium (Polemoniaceae), Wilbur L. Bluhm

437. *Polygala californica,* milkwort (Polygalaceae)

438. *Chorizanthe membranacea*, pink spineflower (Polygonaceae)

440. *Eriogonum marifolium*, Sierra buckwheat (Polygonaceae), Wilbur L. Bluhm

439. *Eriogonum compositum* subsp. *compositum*, composite buckwheat (Polygonaceae)

441. *Eriogonum nudum* subsp. *nudum*, naked buckwheat (Polygonaceae)

442. *Eriogonum ternatum*, ternate buckwheat (Polygonaceae)

443. *Eriogonum umbellatum*, sulfur-flowered buckwheat (Polygonaceae)

444. *Eriogonum vimineum*, wicker buckwheat (Polygonaceae)

445. *Polygonum amphibium* var. *emersum,* swamp knotweed (Polygonaceae)

446. *Polygonum arenastrum,* common knotweed (Polygonaceae)

451. *Rumex acetosella,* sheep sorrel (Polygonaceae)

447. *Polygonum convolvulus,* morning-glory bindweed (Polygonaceae)

448. *Polygonum paronychia,* beach knotweed (Polygonaceae); pls. 449–450 on next page

452. *Rumex crispus,* curly-leaved dock (Polygonaceae)

453. *Rumex salicifolius* subsp. *salicifolius,* willow-leaved dock (Polygonaceae)

449. *Polygonum persicaria*, lady's thumb (Polygonaceae)

450. *Reynoutria ×bohemica*, Bohemian giant knotweed (Polygonaceae); pls. 451–453 on previous page

454. *Calandrinia ciliata*, redmaids (Portulacaceae)

455. *Claytonia exigua* subsp. *exigua*, pale miner's lettuce (Portulacaceae)

456. *Claytonia lanceolata*, western spring beauty (Portulacaceae)

457. *Claytonia perfoliata* subsp. *perfoliata*, miner's lettuce (Portulacaceae)

458. *Claytonia sibirica*, candyflower (Portulacaceae)

459. *Lewisia columbiana* var. *columbiana*, Columbia lewisia (Portulacaceae)

460. *Lewisia cotyledon* var. *cotyledon,* Siskiyou lewisia (Portulacaceae)

461. *Lewisia oppositifolia,* opposite-leaved lewisia (Portulacaceae)

462. *Lewisia pygmaea,* alpine lewisia (Portulacaceae), Linda H. Beidleman

463. *Montia linearis,* slender-leaved montia (Portulacaceae)

464. *Anagallis arvensis,* scarlet pimpernel (Primulaceae)

465. *Dodecatheon hendersonii,* Henderson's shooting star (Primulaceae)

466. *Douglasia laevigata* subsp. *laevigata,* smooth-leaved douglasia (Primulaceae), Wilbur L. Bluhm

467. *Glaux maritima,* sea milkwort (Primulaceae)

468. *Lysimachia ciliata,* fringed loosestrife (Primulaceae)

469. *Lysimachia thyrsiflora,* tufted loosestrife (Primulaceae)

471. *Aconitum columbianum* subsp.
columbianum, Columbia monkshood
(Ranunculaceae), Wilbur L. Bluhm

472. *Actaea rubra,* baneberry
(Ranunculaceae)

474. *Anemone drummondii* var.
drummondii, Drummond's anemone
(Ranunculaceae), Wilbur L. Bluhm

470. *Trientalis latifolia,* broad-leaved starflower (Primulaceae)

473. *Anemone deltoidea,* white anemone (Ranunculaceae)

475. *Anemone lyallii,* little mountain anemone (Ranunculaceae)

476. *Anemone occidentalis,* western pasqueflower (Ranunculaceae), Linda H. Beidleman

477. *Anemone oregana* var. *oregana,* Oregon anemone (Ranunculaceae)

478. *Aquilegia formosa,* western columbine (Ranunculaceae)

480. *Cimicifuga elata,* tall bugbane (Ranunculaceae)

479. *Caltha leptosepala,* white marsh marigold (Ranunculaceae), Michael Fahey

481. *Delphinium menziesii* subsp. *menziesii,* Menzies' larkspur (Ranunculaceae)

486. *Ranunculus aquatilis* var. *aquatilis,* white water buttercup (Ranunculaceae); pl. 487 below

482. *Delphinium nudicaule,* red larkspur (Ranunculaceae)

483. *Delphinium nuttallii* subsp. *ochroleucum,* white rock larkspur (Ranunculaceae)

484. *Delphinium trolliifolium,* poison larkspur (Ranunculaceae)

485. *Myosurus minimus,* least mousetail (Ranunculaceae); pl. 486 above

487. *Ranunculus austro-oreganus,* southern Oregon buttercup (Ranunculaceae)

488. *Ranunculus californicus* var. *cuneatus,* California buttercup (Ranunculaceae)

489. *Ranunculus flammula,* creeping spearwort (Ranunculaceae)

490. *Ranunculus macounii,* Macoun's buttercup (Ranunculaceae)

491. *Ranunculus occidentalis* var. *occidentalis,* western buttercup (Ranunculaceae)

492. *Ranunculus repens,* creeping buttercup (Ranunculaceae)

493. *Ranunculus uncinatus,* woodland buttercup (Ranunculaceae)

494. *Thalictrum occidentale,* western meadow rue (Ranunculaceae)

495. *Trautvetteria carolinensis,* false bugbane (Ranunculaceae)

496. *Trollius albiflorus,* globeflower (Ranunculaceae), Linda H. Beidleman

497. *Ceanothus cuneatus,* common buckbrush (Rhamnaceae)

498. *Ceanothus integerrimus,* deer brush (Rhamnaceae)

499. *Ceanothus pumilus,* Siskiyou mat (Rhamnaceae)

500. *Ceanothus sanguineus,* redstem ceanothus (Rhamnaceae)

501. *Ceanothus thyrsiflorus,* blueblossom (Rhamnaceae)

502. *Rhamnus californica* subsp. *occidentalis,* serpentine coffee berry (Rhamnaceae)

503. *Rhamnus purshiana,* cascara (Rhamnaceae)

504. *Amelanchier alnifolia* subsp. *semiintegrifolia*, serviceberry (Rosaceae)

505. *Aphanes arvensis,* field parsley piert (Rosaceae)

506. *Aruncus dioicus,* goatsbeard (Rosaceae)

507. *Cercocarpus betuloides* var. *betuloides,* birch-leaved mountain mahogany (Rosaceae)

508. *Crataegus douglasii* var. *douglasii,* Douglas' hawthorn (Rosaceae)

509. *Crataegus monogyna,* hawthorn (Rosaceae)

510. *Dryas octopetala* subsp. *hookeriana,* mountain avens (Rosaceae)

511. *Geum macrophyllum* var. *macrophyllum*, large-leaved avens (Rosaceae)

512. *Holodiscus discolor*, ocean spray (Rosaceae)

513. *Malus fusca*, Pacific crabapple (Rosaceae)

514. *Oemleria erasiformis*, osoberry (Rosaceae)

515. *Physocarpus capitatus*, ninebark (Rosaceae)

516. *Potentilla anserina* subsp. *pacifica*, Pacific cinquefoil (Rosaceae)

517. *Potentilla glandulosa* var. *glandulosa*, sticky cinquefoil (Rosaceae)

518. *Potentilla gracilis* var. *gracilis*, slender cinquefoil (Rosaceae)

519. *Potentilla palustris,* marsh cinquefoil (Rosaceae)

520. *Potentilla villosa* var. *parviflora,* arctic cinquefoil (Rosaceae)

521. *Prunus emarginata* var. *mollis,* bitter cherry (Rosaceae)

522. *Prunus virginiana* subsp. *demissa,* chokecherry (Rosaceae)

523. *Rosa gymnocarpa,* wood rose (Rosaceae)

524. *Rosa nutkana* subsp. *nutkana,* Nootka rose (Rosaceae)

525. *Rosa pisocarpa,* clustered wild rose (Rosaceae)

526. *Rubus parviflorus,* thimbleberry (Rosaceae)

527. *Rubus spectabilis*, salmonberry (Rosaceae)

528. *Sanguisorba annua*, western burnet (Rosaceae)

529. *Sanguisorba canadensis*, Canada burnet (Rosaceae)

530. *Sorbus scopulina* var. *cascadensis*, western mountain ash (Rosaceae), Wilbur L. Bluhm

531. *Sorbus sitchensis* var. *grayi*, Sitka mountain ash (Rosaceae), Wilbur L. Bluhm

532. *Spiraea betulifolia* var. *lucida*, white spiraea (Rosaceae)

533. *Spiraea densiflora*, mountain spiraea (Rosaceae), Linda H. Beidleman

534. *Spiraea douglasii* subsp. *douglasii*, Douglas' hardhack (Rosaceae)

535. *Spiraea pyramidata*, pyramidal spiraea (Rosaceae)

536. *Galium andrewsii*, Andrews' bedstraw (Rubiaceae)

537. *Galium aparine*, cleavers (Rubiaceae)

538. *Sherardia arvensis*, field madder (Rubiaceae)

539. *Comandra umbellata* subsp. *californica*, bastard toadflax (Santalaceae)

542. *Chrysosplenium glechomifolium*, western golden saxifrage (Saxifragaceae)

540. *Darlingtonia californica*, California pitcher plant (Sarraceniaceae); pl. 541 on next page

543. *Elmera racemosa* var. *puberulenta*, hairy elmera (Saxifragaceae), Linda H. Beidleman

544. *Lithophragma affine*, woodland starflower (Saxifragaceae)

541. *Boykinia occidentalis*, slender boykinia (Saxifragaceae); pl. 542 on previous page

545. *Saxifraga caespitosa*, tufted saxifrage (Saxifragaceae)

546. *Saxifraga integrifolia*, grassland saxifrage (Saxifragaceae)

547. *Saxifraga rufidula*, red-wool saxifrage (Saxifragaceae), Wilbur L. Bluhm

548. *Saxifraga tolmiei*, Tolmie's saxifrage (Saxifragac), Wilbur L. Bluhm

549. *Tellima grandiflora*, fringecups (Saxifragaceae)

550. *Tiarella trifoliata* var. *trifoliata*, three-leaflet coolwort (Saxifragaceae)

551. *Tolmiea menziesii*, piggyback plant (Saxifragaceae)

552. *Antirrhinum vexillo-calyculatum* subsp. *breweri*, Brewer's snapdragon (Scrophulariaceae)

554. *Castilleja attenuata*, valley tassels (Scrophulariaceae)

555. *Castilleja elata*, slender paintbrush (Scrophulariaceae)

553. *Castilleja ambigua* subsp. *ambigua*, Johnny-nip (Scrophulariaceae)

556. *Castilleja hispida* var. *hispida*, harsh paintbrush (Scrophulariaceae)

557. *Castilleja levisecta*, golden paintbrush (Scrophulariaceae)

559. *Castilleja rubicundula* subsp. *litho-spermoides*, cream-sacs Scrophulariaceae)

560. *Collinsia grandiflora*, large-flowered blue-eyed Mary (Scrophulariaceae)

558. *Castilleja miniata* var. *dixonii*, Dixon's paintbrush (Scrophulariaceae)

561. *Collinsia parviflora*, small-flowered blue-eyed Mary (Scrophulariaceae)

562. *Cordylanthus maritimus* subsp. *palustris*, salt-marsh bird's-beak (Scrophulariaceae)

563. *Cordylanthus tenuis* subsp. *viscidus*, sticky bird's-beak (Scrophulariaceae)

564. *Euphrasia stricta,* eyebright (Scrophulariaceae)

565. *Gratiola ebracteata,* bractless hedge hyssop (Scrophulariaceae)

566. *Mimulus alsinoides,* chickweed monkey flower (Scrophulariaceae)

567. *Mimulus aurantiacus,* bush monkey flower (Scrophulariaceae)

568. *Mimulus cardinalis,* scarlet monkey flower (Scrophulariaceae)

569. *Mimulus douglasii,* Douglas' monkey flower (Scrophulariaceae), Michael Fahey

570. *Mimulus guttatus,* common monkey flower (Scrophulariaceae)

571. *Mimulus lewisii,* Lewis' monkey flower (Scrophulariaceae), Wilbur L. Bluhm

572. *Mimulus moschatus*, musk monkey flower
(Scrophulariaceae)

573. *Mimulus tricolor*, tricolor monkey flower
(Scrophulariaceae), Wilbur L. Bluhm; pl. 574 below

575. *Parentucellia viscosa*, yellowweed
(Scrophulariaceae)

576. *Pedicularis attolens*, little elephant's-
head (Scrophulariaceae), Linda H.
Beidleman

578. *Pedicularis densiflora*, Indian warrior
(Scrophulariaceae)

574. *Orthocarpus bracteosus*, rosy owl's clover
(Scrophulariaceae)

577. *Pedicularis contorta*, curved-beak lousewort
(Scrophulariaceae), Michael Fahey

579. *Pedicularis groenlandica*, elephant's-head (Scrophulariaceae), Linda H. Beidleman

580. *Penstemon azureus*, azure penstemon (Scrophulariaceae)

583. *Penstemon roezlii*, Roezl's penstemon (Scrophulariaceae); pl. 584 below

581. *Penstemon cardwellii*, Cardwell's penstemon (Scrophulariaceae)

582. *Penstemon davidsonii* var. *davidsonii*, creeping penstemon (Scrophulariaceae), Wilbur L. Bluhm

584. *Penstemon rupicola*, rock penstemon (Scrophulariaceae), Linda H. Beidleman

585. *Penstemon serrulatus*, spreading penstemon (Scrophulariaceae)

586. *Scrophularia californica* subsp. *californica*, California figwort (Scrophulariaceae)

587. *Synthyris missurica*, western mountain synthyris (Scrophulariaceae)

588. *Synthyris reniformis*, snow queen (Scrophulariaceae)

589. *Triphysaria eriantha* subsp. *eriantha*, yellow Johnny-tuck (Scrophulariaceae)

590. *Triphysaria pusilla*, dwarf owl's clover (Scrophulariaceae)

591. *Verbascum blattaria*, moth mullein (Scrophulariaceae)

592. *Solanum physalifolium*, hairy nightshade (Solanaceae)

593. *Daphne laureola*, spurge laurel (Thymelaeaceae)

594. *Urtica dioica* subsp. *gracilis,* American nettle (Urticaceae)

595. *Plectritis congesta,*
rosy plectritis (Valerianaceae)

596. *Valeriana scouleri,* Scouler's valerian (Valerianaceae)

597. *Verbena hastata,* blue verbena (Verbenaceae)

598. *Viola adunca,* western blue violet (Violaceae)

599. *Viola douglasii,* Douglas' violet (Violaceae)

600. *Viola glabella,* smooth woodland violet (Violaceae)

601. *Viola hallii,* Hall's violet (Violaceae)

602. *Viola howellii*, Howell's violet (Violaceae)

603. *Viola lobata* subsp. *lobata*, lobe-leaved pine violet (Violaceae)

604. *Viola ocellata*, two-eyed violet (Violaceae)

605. *Viola praemorsa* subsp. *praemorsa*, upland yellow violet (Violaceae)

606. *Viola primulifolia* subsp. *occidentalis*, western bog violet (Violaceae)

607. *Arceuthobium campylopodum*, western dwarf mistletoe (Viscaceae)

608. *Phoradendron villosum*, western mistletoe (Viscaceae)

609. *Sagittaria latifolia*, wapato (Alismataceae)

610. *Lysichiton americanus,* yellow skunk cabbage (Araceae)

611. *Bolboschoenus maritimus* subsp. *paludosus,* marsh bulrush (Cyperaceae)

612. *Carex lenticularis,* lenticular sedge (Cyperaceae); pl. 613 below

614. *Carex obnupta,* slough sedge (Cyperaceae)

616. *Eleocharis palustris,* common spike rush (Cyperaceae); pls. 617–618 on next page

619. *Schoenoplectus tabernaemontani,* great bulrush (Cyperaceae)

613. *Carex macrocephala,* big-head sedge; pistillate (Cyperaceae)

615. *Cyperus eragrostis,* tall cyperus (Cyperaceae)

617. *Eriophorum chamissonis*, Chamisso's cotton grass (Cyperaceae)

618. *Eriophorum crinigerum*, fringed cotton grass (Cyperaceae); pl. 619 on previous page

620. *Iris bracteata*, Siskiyou iris (Iridaceae)

621. *Iris chrysophylla*, slender-tubed iris (Iridaceae)

622. *Iris douglasiana*, Douglas iris (Iridaceae)

623. *Iris innominata*, golden iris (Iridaceae)

624. *Iris tenax* var. *tenax*, tough-leaved iris (Iridaceae)

625. *Iris tenuis*, Clackamas iris (Iridaceae)

626. *Iris ×thompsonii,* Thompson's iris (Iridaceae)

628. *Sisyrinchium bellum,* blue-eyed grass (Iridaceae)

627. *Olsynium douglasii* var. *douglasii,* Douglas' grass widows (Iridaceae)

629. *Sisyrinchium californicum,* golden-eyed grass (Iridaceae)

630. *Sisyrinchium hitchcockii,* Hitchcock's blue-eyed grass, right, and *S. idahoense* var. *idahoense,* Idaho blue-eyed grass, left (Iridaceae)

631. *Juncus bolanderi,* Bolander's rush (Juncaceae)

632. *Juncus effusus* subsp. *pacificus,* Pacific rush (Juncaceae)

633. *Juncus oxymeris*, pointed rush (Juncaceae)

634. *Luzula comosa*, Pacific wood rush (Juncaceae)

635. *Lemna minor*, common duckweed (Lemnaceae)

636. *Allium acuminatum*, Hooker's onion (Liliaceae)

637. *Allium amplectens*, paper onion (Liliaceae)

638. *Allium bolanderi*, Bolander's onion (Liliaceae)

639. *Allium cernuum*, nodding onion (Liliaceae)

640. *Allium falcifolium*, sickle-leaved onion (Liliaceae)

641. *Allium unifolium*, clay onion (Liliaceae)

642. *Brodiaea coronaria* subsp. *coronaria*, harvest brodiaea (Liliaceae)

643. *Brodiaea elegans* subsp. *elegans*, elegant brodiaea (Liliaceae)

644. *Brodiaea terrestris* subsp. *terrestris*, dwarf brodiaea (Liliaceae)

645. *Calochortus tolmiei*, cat's-ear mariposa lily (Liliaceae)

646. *Calochortus uniflorus*, meadow mariposa lily (Liliaceae); pls. 647–652 on next page

653. *Clintonia uniflora*, white bead-lily (Liliaceae)

654. *Dichelostemma congestum*, ookow (Liliaceae)

647. *Camassia howellii,* Howell's camas (Liliaceae)

648. *Camassia leichtlinii* subsp. *leichtlinii ,* great white camas (Liliaceae)

649. *Camassia leichtlinii* subsp. *suksdorfii,* Suksdorf's camas (Liliaceae)

650. *Camassia quamash* subsp. *maxima,* common camas (Liliaceae)

651. *Chlorogalum pomeridianum* var. *pomeridianum,* soap plant (Liliaceae), Linda H. Beidleman

652. *Clintonia andrewsiana,* pink bead-lily (Liliaceae); pls. 653–654 on previous page

655. *Dichelostemma ida-maia,* firecracker flower (Liliaceae)

656. *Erythronium citrinum,* lemon fawn lily (Liliaceae)

657. *Erythronium grandiflorum* subsp. *grandiflorum*, yellow fawn lily (Liliaceae)

660. *Erythronium oregonum*, Oregon fawn lily (Liliaceae); pl. 661 on next page

658. *Erythronium hendersonii*, Henderson's fawn lily (Liliaceae)

659. *Erythronium montanum*, avalanche lily (Liliaceae), Wilbur L. Bluhm

662. *Fritillaria affinis* subsp. *affinis*, mission bells (Liliaceae)

663. *Fritillaria gentneri*, Gentner's fritillary (Liliaceae); pls. 664–665 on next page

666. *Hastingia alba*, white rush lily (Liliaceae)

667. *Hastingia bracteosa*, large-flowered rush lily (Liliaceae)

661. *Erythronium revolutum*, pink fawn lily (Liliaceae); pls. 662–663 on previous page

664. *Fritillaria glauca*, Siskiyou fritillary (Liliaceae)

665. *Fritillaria recurva*, scarlet fritillary (Liliaceae); pls. 666–667 on previous page

668. *Lilium bolanderi*, Bolander's lily (Liliaceae)

669. *Lilium columbianum*, Columbia lily (Liliaceae)

670. *Lilium occidentale*, western lily (Liliaceae)

671. *Lilium washingtonianum* subsp. *purpurascens*, Washington's lily (Liliaceae), Linda H. Beidleman

672. *Narthecium californicum,* bog asphodel (Liliaceae)

673. *Prosartes hookeri,* fairy bells (Liliaceae)

674. *Scoliopus hallii,* fetid adder's-tongue (Liliaceae), Wilbur L. Bluhm

675. *Streptopus amplexifolius,* large twisted-stalk (Liliaceae)

676. *Trillium albidum,* white trillium (Liliaceae)

677. *Trillium kurabayashii,* Kurabayashi's trillium (Liliaceae), Michael Fahey

678. *Trillium ovatum* subsp. *ovatum,* western trillium (Liliaceae)

679. *Trillium rivale,* creek trillium (Liliaceae)

680. *Triteleia grandiflora,* large-flowered triteleia (Liliaceae); pls. 681–682 on next page

683. *Veratrum californicum* subsp. *californicum,* California false hellebore (Liliaceae), Wilbur L. Bluhm

684. *Veratrum viride* subsp. *eschscholtzii,* green false hellebore (Liliaceae), Linda H. Beidleman

685. *Xerophyllum tenax,* bear grass (Liliaceae), Linda H. Beidleman

686. *Zigadenus venenosus* subsp. *venenosus,* meadow death camas (Liliaceae)

687. *Calypso bulbosa* subsp. *occidentalis,* calypso (Orchidaceae)

688. *Cephalanthera austinae,* phantom orchid (Orchidaceae), Linda H. Beidleman

681. *Triteleia hyacinthina*, hyacinth triteleia (Liliaceae)

682. *Triteleia ixioides* subsp. *anilina*, pretty face (Liliaceae); pls. 683–688 on previous page

689. *Corallorhiza maculata*, spotted coralroot (Orchidaceae)

690. *Corallorhiza striata* var. *striata*, striped coralroot (Orchidaceae)

691. *Cypripedium californicum*, California lady's slipper (Orchidaceae)

692. *Epipactis gigantea*, giant helleborine (Orchidaceae)

693. *Epipactis helleborine*, helleborine (Orchidaceae)

694. *Piperia elegans* subsp. *elegans*, elegant rein orchid (Orchidaceae)

695. *Piperia unalascensis*, short-spurred rein orchid (Orchidaceae)

696. *Spiranthes romanzoffiana*, hooded lady's tresses (Orchidaceae); pl. 697 below

698. *Anthoxanthum odoratum*, sweet vernal grass (Poaceae)

699. *Briza maxima*, big quaking grass (Poaceae)

700. *Bromus madritensis* subsp. *rubens*, foxtail chess (Poaceae)

701. *Cynosurus echinatus*, dogtail (Poaceae); pls. 702–704 on next page

697. *Ammophila arenaria* subsp. *arenaria*, European beach grass (Poaceae); pl. 698 above

705. *Poa bulbosa* subsp. *vivipara*, bulbous bluegrass (Poaceae)

702. *Dactylis glomerata*, orchard grass (Poaceae)

703. *Hordeum murinum* subsp. *leporinum*, hare barley (Poaceae)

704. *Leymus mollis* subsp. *mollis*, dune grass (Poaceae); pl. 705 on previous page

706. *Poa confinis*, beach bluegrass (Poaceae)

707. *Polypogon monspeliensis*, rabbit-foot grass (Poaceae)

710. *Typha latifolia*, broadleaf cattail (Typhaceae)

708. *Potamogeton natans*, floating pondweed (Potamogetonaceae)

709. *Smilax californica*, California greenbrier (Smilacaceae)

PLANTAGINACEAE Plantain Family

All plantains of our region—some native, others introduced—belong to a single genus, *Plantago*. It is recognizable by a dense terminal inflorescence in which the flowers have four sepals, a somewhat papery four-lobed corolla, and two or four stamens. The fruit is partitioned lengthwise into two chambers, each producing one or more seeds. In all but one of the species in our region, the leaves are basal.

Certain genera of Scrophulariaceae are now thought to be more closely related to those of Plantaginaceae than to other Scrophulariaceae, so we may expect Plantaginaceae to become a much larger and more diverse family. See the discussion of Scrophulariaceae for a list of genera that are likely to be transferred to Plantaginaceae.

Plantago

1 Leaves opposite at intervals along the upright stems (there are no basal leaves); inflorescences borne on peduncles arising in the axils of the leaves (uncommon weed in our region) .... *P. psyllium*
SAND PLANTAIN (Eurasia)

1 Leaves basal; inflorescences terminal on peduncles arising from the base of the plant
  2 Leaf blades pinnately lobed (annual or biennial weed, rather strictly coastal in our region) ....
.... *P. coronopus*
CUTLEAF PLANTAIN (Eurasia)

  2 Leaf blades not pinnately lobed (in some species, however, the margins of the blades may be toothed)
    3 Bracts of the inflorescence to more than 2 cm long, reaching far beyond the flowers (annual or short-lived perennial weed) .... *P. aristata*
BRISTLY PLANTAIN (E United States)

    3 Bracts of the inflorescence usually less than 5 mm long, not reaching far beyond the flowers
      4 Most leaf blades at least one-third as wide as long
        5 Most leaf blades about half as wide as long, tapered abruptly to the petiole (common perennial weed) .... *P. major*
COMMON PLANTAIN (Europe)

        5 Most leaf blades about one-third as wide as long, tapering gradually to the petiole

Parnassia californica,
California grass-of-Parnassus

Plantago major,
common plantain

6 Inflorescences to more than 20 cm long, slender, usually more than 10 times as long as wide; leaves and stems not often conspicuously hairy (on coastal bluffs, in salt marshes, and in some other coastal wet places, Tillamook Co., Oreg., to Mexico) . . . . *P. subnuda* (includes *P. hirtella*)
TALL COAST PLANTAIN

6 Inflorescences not more than about 10 cm long and not more than 5 times as long as wide; leaves and stems typically conspicuously hairy (flowers fragrant; uncommon perennial weed, known to occur in Brit. Col.) . . . .*P. media*
HOARY PLANTAIN (Eurasia)

4 Leaf blades not so much as one-third as wide as long
  7 Stamens 2; annual
    8 Plants commonly more than 10 cm tall when in flower; corolla usually with 1 upright lobe, 3 spreading lobes; fruit usually with more than 4 seeds (mostly on bluffs and beaches along the coast, also inland around vernal pools and in alkaline habitats) . . . . *P. elongata* var. *elongata* (includes *P. bigelovii*)
ANNUAL PLANTAIN

    8 Plants less than 10 cm tall; corolla usually with all 4 lobes upright; fruit with only 4 seeds (weed recorded from widely scattered localities in our region; not primarily coastal or associated with saline or alkaline habitats) . . . . *P. pusilla*
SLENDER PLANTAIN (E United States)

  7 Stamens 4; perennial (except *P. erecta*)
    9 Outer 2 calyx lobes (those nearest the bract below each flower) united; inflorescence, especially when young, conical, widest at the base (leaves to more than 25 cm long and more than 3 cm wide; common weed) . . . . *P. lanceolata*
ENGLISH PLANTAIN (Europe)

    9 All 4 calyx lobes separate; inflorescence, even when young, not obviously conical or widest at the base
      10 Crown, where the basal leaves originate, brown-woolly; inflorescence to more than 15 cm long in the fruiting stage (widespread in North America but in our region reported only from Coos and Curry Cos., Oreg.) . . . . *P. eriopoda*
SALINE PLANTAIN

      10 Crown not brown-woolly; inflorescence rarely more than 10 cm long in the fruiting stage
        11 Leaves obviously succulent (leaf blades usually smooth-margined and not more than 5 mm wide, but if wider, sometimes with a few teeth) . . . . *P. maritima*, pl. 420
SEASIDE PLANTAIN

Two varieties or subspecies are recognized in some references: *juncoides* is the one typically found at the edges of salt marshes and in other moist maritime habitats; *californica* is characteristic of drier situations, such as bluffs overlooking the coast.

        11 Leaf blades not succulent
          12 Plants annual, relatively small, the leaves rarely so much as 12 cm long, very slender and conspicuously hairy (S Oreg. to Calif.) . . . . *P. erecta* (*P. hookeriana*), pl. 419
CALIFORNIA PLANTAIN

          12 Robust perennial, the leaves sometimes more than 20 cm long, the blades often more than 2 cm wide, not obviously hairy (in our region mostly in coastal bogs from Lincoln Co., Oreg., northward) . . . . *P. macrocarpa*
NORTH PACIFIC PLANTAIN

PLUMBAGINACEAE Leadwort Family

In plants of the leadwort family, the flowers have a five-lobed calyx (the tube of which is usually ribbed lengthwise) and a five-lobed, somewhat papery corolla; the lobes of the corolla may be separated so deeply that they may appear to be free petals. There are five stamens, and these are attached to the corolla tube, in line with the lobes. The pistil, with five styles, develops into a dry fruit containing a single seed.

1 Flowers in clusters on a branched panicle, each cluster with scalelike bracts beneath it; corolla lobes on a long tube; basal leaves usually at least 30 mm wide (near the high-tide line in salt marshes, Coos Co., Oreg., to Calif.) . . . . *Limonium californicum*, pl. 422
SEA LAVENDER

1 Flowers in dense heads at the ends of unbranched stems, each head with broad, papery bracts beneath it; corolla lobes (bright pink) separated nearly to the base; basal leaves not more than 3 mm wide

  2 Outer bracts of the flower head (not the bracts below these, which are turned back and form a sheath around the stem) slender and longer than the inner ones (usually on bluffs and hillsides above rocky shores but sometimes on backshores of sandy beaches; occasionally on prairies of the Puget Trough in Thurston and Lewis Cos., Wash.) . . . . *Armeria maritima* subsp. *californica*, pl. 421
SEA PINK, SEA THRIFT

  2 Outer bracts of the flower head oval and usually shorter than the inner ones; mostly inland and montane
. . . . *Armeria maritima* subsp. *sibirica*
MOUNTAIN THRIFT

      Armeria maritima occurs across northern North America, Europe, and Asia, and varies considerably with respect to the characteristics given in the couplet of choice 2. Even some plants in our region may not fit perfectly into subsp. *californica* or subsp. *sibirica*.

POLEMONIACEAE Phlox Family

Except for species of *Phlox* and one *Leptosiphon*, members of the Polemoniaceae in our region are herbaceous plants, mostly annuals. Both the calyx and corolla usually have five lobes, and there are usually five stamens (these attached to the corolla) and a pistil that is divided lengthwise into three seed-producing chambers. Some species of *Navarretia* deviate from this formula, and in certain other genera, flowers with four calyx and corolla lobes may be mixed with those that have the typical number of five.

1 Leaves pinnately compound, the larger ones with at least 11 leaflets to about 1 cm wide (a few of the divisions of a leaf may technically be lobes because they are broadly attached to the rachis) . . . . . . *Polemonium*
1 Leaves, if divided, merely lobed, not compound
  2 Leaves not lobed
    3 Leaves alternate . . . . *Collomia*
    3 Most leaves, at least the lower ones, opposite
      4 Delicate plants (generally less than 30 cm tall) with very slender leaves, the lower ones opposite; all or most peduncles with just 1 flower; corolla 5–8 mm long, white to lavender (Josephine Co., Oreg., to Calif.; also in the Cascades and E of the Cascades) . . . .
      . . . . *Navarretia sinistra* subsp. *sinistra* (*Gilia sinistra* var. *sinistra*)
GILIA-LIKE NAVARRETIA
      4 Plants not especially delicate, the leaves either proportionately broad (2 to several times as long as wide) or stiff and somewhat needlelike . . . . *Phlox-Microsteris* complex
  2 Most leaves lobed
    5 Stamens attached to the corolla at various levels (leaves irregularly pinnately lobed; corolla 1–1.5 cm long, bright pink) . . . . *Collomia heterophylla*, pl. 424
VARIED-LEAVED COLLOMIA
    5 Stamens attached to the corolla at about the same level (but the stamens may be of unequal length)
      6 Calyx lobes of obviously unequal length (leaf lobes sharp-tipped, prickly) . . . . *Navarretia*
      6 Calyx lobes of equal length (at least not obviously unequal); leaf lobes not sharp-tipped or prickly
        7 Leaves mostly opposite, at least in the lower part of the plant, and palmately divided into slender, sometimes almost needlelike lobes . . . . *Leptosiphon*
        7 Leaves alternate, at least the lower ones usually lobed pinnately or bipinnately (there may, however, be only 1–2 lobes on each side . . . . *Gilia-Allophyllum-Ipomopsis* complex

Collomia

1 Most leaves irregularly pinnately lobed (corolla usually 10–15 mm long, bright pink, sometimes lavender or white) . . . . *C. heterophylla*, pl. 424

          VARIED-LEAVED COLLOMIA

1 Leaves not lobed

  2 Corolla (usually pale yellow, salmon, or pinkish, sometimes white) usually 20–25 mm long, the lobes to 10 mm long (plants commonly more than 20 cm tall, not branching from near the base but often with a few short upper branches) . . . . *C. grandiflora*, pl. 423

          LARGE-FLOWERED COLLOMIA

  2 Corolla not more than 15 mm long, the lobes not more than 3 mm long

    3 Filaments of all stamens about the same length but attached to the corolla tube at distinctly different levels; corolla white to pink or bluish; plants to more than 40 cm tall (more common E than W of the crest of the Cascades) . . . . *C. linearis*

          NARROW-LEAF COLLOMIA

    3 Filaments of stamens of very different lengths but attached to the corolla tube at about the same level; corolla lobes pink to lavender but the tube often reddish; plants not often more than 15 cm tall (if bruised, exuding a sap that stains yellow; Josephine and Jackson Cos., Oreg., to Calif.; widespread E of the Cascades) . . . . *C. tinctoria*

          YELLOW-STAINING COLLOMIA

Gilia-Allophyllum-Ipomopsis Complex

1 Corolla about 3 cm long, bright red (plants commonly at least 50 cm tall; Lane Co., Oreg., to Calif.; also E of the Cascades) . . . . *I. aggregata* subsp. *formosissima* (*G. aggregata*), pl. 426

          SKYROCKET

1 Corolla not so much as 3 cm long and not bright red

  2 Larger leaves usually with as many as 7 lobes, rarely as many as 11 (corolla tube and lobes violet-blue or purple; Rogue River valley, Oreg., to Calif.) . . . . *A. gilioides*

          PURPLE ALLOPHYLLUM

  2 Most larger leaves with more than 7 lobes, sometimes many lobes

    3 Flowers not in dense, round heads, but they may be clustered (Lincoln Co., Oreg., to Calif.) . . . . *G. millefoliata* (*G. multicaulis* var. *millefoliata*)

          SAN FRANCISCO GILIA

    3 Flowers in dense, nearly round heads (plants not often branching from the base)

      4 Flower heads densely white-hairy at the base (coastal, S Oreg. to Calif.) . . . . *G. capitata* subsp. *tomentosa*

      4 Flower heads not densely white-hairy at the base (they may, however, be slightly glandular)

        5 Corolla lobes less than 1 mm wide; seeds usually 1–6 in each fruit . . . . *G. capitata* subsp. *capitata*, pl. 425

          GLOBE GILIA, BLUE FIELD GILIA

        5 Corolla lobes 1–2 mm wide; seeds 10–25 in each fruit (coastal, Coos Co., Oreg., to Calif.) . . . . *G. capitata* subsp. *pacifica*

Leptosiphon

Most of the species of *Leptosiphon* in our region have, until relatively recently, been placed in *Linanthus*.

1 Corolla tube more than twice as long as the calyx

  2 Lobes of bracts beneath flowers conspicuously white-hairy, most of the hairs 1–1.5 mm long (corolla lobes pink, often with a darker spot at the base; Jackson and Josephine Cos., Oreg., to Calif.) . . . . *L. ciliatus*

          WHISKER BRUSH, BRISTLY-BRACTED LEPTOSIPHON

2 Lobes of bracts beneath flowers not conspicuously white-hairy, few if any of the hairs more than 1 mm long

    3 Corolla conspicuously bicolored or even tricolored, the throat yellow, the lobes usually with white near the throat, then pink to purplish; tube of corolla usually at least 20 mm long; calyx with sparse, almost bristlelike hairs, these not so plentiful as to form a whitish fuzz . . . . ***L. bicolor***, pl. 427
               BICOLORED LEPTOSIPHON

    3 Corolla mostly white or cream, not conspicuously bicolored; tube of corolla 10–15 mm long; calyx with crowded short hairs that form a whitish fuzz . . . . . ***L. minimus*** (*Linanthus bicolor* var. *minimus*), pl. 428
               TINY LEPTOSIPHON

1 Corolla tube scarcely if at all longer than the calyx

    4 Extensively branched perennial, woody at the base (corolla lobes white, the throat and sometimes the tube yellow; montane and almost entirely E of the crest of the Cascades, Wash. to Calif. and eastward) . . . . ***L. nuttallii*** **subsp.** ***nuttallii*** (*Linanthastrum nuttallii*)
               NUTTALL'S LEPTOSIPHON

    4 Typically single-stemmed annuals, only occasionally branched

        5 Calyx 4–6 mm long; corolla (with a yellow throat, otherwise white, pink, or purplish) usually about 10–12 mm long, with a ring of hairs encircling the inside of the tube; corolla lobes decidedly shorter than the tube (Jackson and Josephine Cos., Oreg., to Calif.) . . . . ***L. bolanderi***
               BOLANDER'S LEPTOSIPHON

        5 Calyx not so much as 4 mm long; corolla (white, pale pink, lilac, or violet) barely longer than the calyx, without a ring of hairs encircling the tube; corolla lobes about as long as the tube (Jackson Co., Oreg., to Calif.; also E of the crest of the Cascades to Wash.) . . . . ***L. harknessii***
               HARKNESS' LEPTOSIPHON

Navarretia

1 Leaves not lobed (delicate plants, generally less than 30 cm tall, with very slender opposite leaves, the lower ones opposite; all or most peduncles with a single flower; corolla 5–8 mm long, white to lavender; Josephine Co., Oreg., to Calif.; also in the S Cascades and E of the crest of the Cascades) . . . .
         . . . . ***N. sinistra*** **subsp.** ***sinistra*** (*Gilia sinistra* var. *sinistra*)
               GILIA-LIKE NAVARRETIA

1 Most leaves lobed

    2 Bracts beneath the inflorescence broad, the width at the middle (not including the lobes) sometimes more than 6 mm (corolla white, yellowish, purplish, or bluish; hairs on main stems, many of them gland-tipped, directed outward, not pressed down; Rogue River valley, Oreg., to Calif.) . . . . ***N. atractyloides***
               HOLLY-LEAVED NAVARRETIA

    2 Bracts (not including the lobes) not more than 4 mm wide (usually much less than 4 mm)

        3 Much of the plant covered with gland-tipped hairs

            4 Middle lobe of each bract with just 1 secondary lobe; stigmas 3 (corolla light blue; plant with an odor much like that of a skunk) . . . . ***N. squarrosa***, pl. 431
               SKUNKWEED

            4 Middle lobe of each bract with several secondary lobes on both sides; stigmas 2 (corolla light to bright blue; Douglas, Jackson, and Josephine Cos., Oreg., to Calif.) . . . .
            . . . . ***N. pubescens***
               DOWNY NAVARRETIA

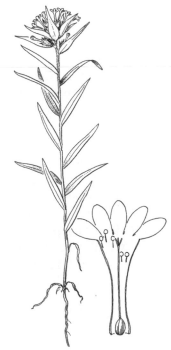

Collomia linearis,
narrow-leaf collomia

   3 Hairs, where present, not gland-tipped

     5 Some stamens attached to the corolla tube at a very different level than others

       6 Two calyx lobes usually very different from the others in being larger and in having a tooth or short lobe on both sides; successive lateral lobes of bracts well separated (corolla white to blue, and rather frequently with 4 lobes instead of 5; stigmas 2; Jackson Co., Oreg., to Calif.) . . . . ***N. heterandra***
TEHAMA NAVARRETIA

       6 Calyx lobes not all the same length but all alike in not having a tooth or lobe on both sides; lobes of bracts (usually 5, counting the long middle lobe) all originating close together at the base (corolla white to blue or pinkish, sometimes with a yellow throat; stigmas 3; Jackson and Josephine Cos., Oreg., to Calif.; also E of the Cascades; not likely to be found below about 4000 ft., 1220 m) . . . .
. . . . ***N. divaricata*** subsp. ***divaricata***
MOUNTAIN NAVARRETIA

     5 All stamens attached to the corolla tube at about the same level

       7 Calyx lobes 3-pronged (lower portions of bracts densely hairy but the hairs mostly not more than 1 mm long; corolla usually pale blue; stigmas 3) . . . . ***N. tagetina***
MARIGOLD NAVARRETIA

       7 Calyx lobes not divided; stigmas 2

         8 Lower portions of bracts (at least the inner ones) bordered by a distinct membrane (plants sometimes very compact; corolla white; usually growing on drying mud around ponds and lakes or in fields that are wet in winter; Douglas Co., Oreg., to Calif.) . . . .
. . . . ***N. leucocephala*** subsp. ***leucocephala***, pl. 430
WHITE-FLOWERED NAVARRETIA

         8 Lower portions of bracts not bordered by a membrane

           9 Bracts conspicuously woolly-hairy, the hairs sometimes more than 3 mm long; corolla white to pale blue . . . . ***N. intertexta*** subsp. ***intertexta***
NEEDLE-LEAVED NAVARRETIA

           9 Bracts not conspicuously woolly-hairy; corolla pink to lavender (flowering when the soil of wetland areas, especially small pools, dries out in summer; Benton and Lane Cos., Oreg.) . . . .
. . . . ***N. willamettensis***
WILLAMETTE VALLEY NAVARRETIA

Phlox-Microsteris Complex

1 Annual, rarely so much as 20 cm tall; corolla lobes rarely more than 3 mm long (larger leaves usually 20–25 mm long, 4–5 mm wide; corolla tube white or yellowish, the lobes pink, lavender, or blue, sometimes white) . . . . ***M. gracilis*** (*P. gracilis*), pl. 429
ANNUAL PHLOX

1 Perennial, much-branched and usually at least slightly woody at the base; corolla lobes at least 5 mm long, in some species more than 10 mm

   2 Leaves slender, generally not more than 2 mm wide or 15 mm long, stiff and tapering to sharp tips (plants usually forming small, dense, matlike growths; corolla pink, lilac, or white, the lobes commonly 6–10 mm long)

     3 Corolla lobes not often more than 8 mm long and usually about twice as long as wide; styles of pistil typically 2–4 mm long (Siskiyou Mountain region of SW Oreg. and NW Calif., also in the Cascades)
. . . . ***P. diffusa*** subsp. ***diffusa***, pl. 433
SPREADING PHLOX

     3 Corolla lobes commonly 8–10 mm long, nearly or fully as wide as long; styles of pistil typically 5–6 mm long (Olympic Mountains, Wash., and the Cascades; also E of the crest of the Cascades) . . . .
. . . . ***P. diffusa*** subsp. ***longistylis***
Some plants will not fit cleanly into *P. diffusa* subsp. *diffusa* or subsp. *longistylis*, and some botanists recommend not trying to go beyond species.

2 Leaves commonly at least 3 mm wide, slender or proportionately broad, not stiff

    4 Most larger leaves 2–3 cm long, about twice as long as wide; corolla lobes rounded at the tip (corolla pink; in the Cascades from Linn Co., Oreg., to Calif., and also in the Siskiyou Mountain region of SW Oreg. and NW Calif.) . . . . ***P. adsurgens***, pl. 432
                                                                                          WOODLAND PHLOX

    4 Most larger leaves several times as long as wide (commonly about 30 mm long by 3 mm wide); corolla lobes notched at the tip (corolla usually pink, sometimes white; Josephine, Jackson, and Curry Cos., Oreg., to Calif.; also E of the Cascades) . . . . ***P. speciosa***, pl. 434
                                                                                       SHOWY PHLOX

          In some treatises, 2 varieties or subspecies of *P. speciosa* are recognized for our region: *occidentalis,* in which the leaves, stems, and calyces have short hairs, these sometimes gland-tipped, and *nitida,* which lacks hairs.

Polemonium

1 Corolla lobes less than half as long as the tube (plants glandular and smelling of skunk)

    2 Leaflets typically not lobed but occasionally some with shallowly separated lobes; calyx about 5 mm long, the lobes nearly as long as the tube; corolla (including the lobes) to about 14 mm long (high montane in the Cascades and eastward) . . . . ***P. elegans***
                                                                           ELEGANT POLEMONIUM

    2 Leaflets conspicuously divided into 3–5 lobes; calyx at least 8 mm long (sometimes more than 12 mm), the lobes about one-third as long as the tube; corolla generally 20–30 mm long (high montane in the Cascades and eastward) . . . . ***P. viscosum***
                                                                           SKUNK POLEMONIUM

1 Corolla lobes at least as long as the tube (plants not conspicuously glandular or smelling of skunk)

    3 Calyx usually at least 8 mm long when flowers are open; corolla (including the lobes) usually 2–2.5 cm long, white, yellow, salmon, lavender, purple, or rarely blue (widespread from Wash. to Calif. and occurring from sea level to moderate elevations in the mountains but the localities scattered) . . . . ***P. carneum***, pl. 435
                                                                           GREAT POLEMONIUM

Navarretia intertexta subsp. *intertexta,* needle-leaved navarretia

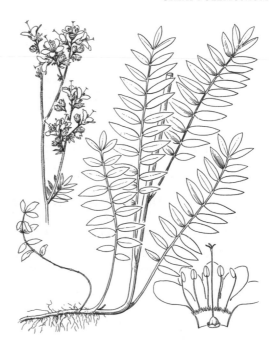

Polemonium occidentale subsp. *occidentale,* western polemonium

3 Calyx not more than 8 mm long; corolla not so much as 2 cm long, primarily blue, blue with yellow in the tube, or white (when the corolla lobes are blue, the tube is generally lighter than the lobes)

    4 Plants not bushy, the upright flowering stems being continuations of horizontal rhizomes, not branches from a tough, persistent stem located directly above a taproot (mostly montane and mostly E of the crest of the Cascades) . . . .*P. occidentale* subsp. *occidentale*, p. 279
                         WESTERN POLEMONIUM

    4 Plants somewhat bushy, with several major branches originating from a tough, persistent stem located just above a taproot

        5 Leaflets not often more than 1 cm long, the terminal 3 leaflets on each leaf generally clearly separate; plants very compact, rarely more than 20 cm tall (Alaska to Calif., mostly montane but occasionally found at lower elevations, as in the San Juan Islands, Wash.) . . . . *P. pulcherrimum* subsp. *pulcherrimum*, pl. 436
                         SHOWY POLEMONIUM

        5 Leaflets more than 1 cm long, sometimes as long as 3 cm, the terminal 3 leaflets on each leaf often united; plants not especially compact, the flowering stems to more than 40 cm tall (montane, Wash. to Calif.) . . . . *P. californicum* (*P. calycinum*, *P. pulcherrimum* var. *calycinum*)
                         CALIFORNIA POLEMONIUM

POLYGALACEAE Milkwort Family

The irregular flowers of milkworts superficially resemble those of the pea family (Fabaceae), mostly because two of the five sepals—those at the sides of the flower—are usually colored like the petals and therefore resemble the lateral petals of peas; the lowermost petal, furthermore, looks much like the keel formed by two united petals in the flower of a pea. The only species native in our region, *Polygala californica* (pl. 437), found in Josephine and Curry Counties, Oregon, and much of California, is a bushy, slender-stemmed perennial, often somewhat woody at the base. It is generally not more than 20 cm tall but occasionally reaches a height of 30 cm and has oblong or elliptical, short-petioled leaves 1–4 cm long. The flowers, sometimes single, sometimes in an inflorescence of two to four, are bright to deep pink. There are three petals, joined to one another at the base. The keel-like petal encloses the eight stamens and the pistil. A further specialization is the union of the filaments of the stamens to form an incomplete tube, which is attached to the bases of the lateral petals.

A garden *Polygala* that sometimes escapes is *P. vulgaris*, European milkwort or common milkwort. Its inflorescences are racemes with about eight or ten flowers; the color of the corolla and lateral sepals ranges from white to pink or blue.

The genus name *Polygala* means "much milk" and is thought to be based on an old idea that some plants of this group, if eaten by cows, stimulate the production of milk. "Milkwort" is also tied to this notion.

POLYGONACEAE Buckwheat Family

The Polygonaceae, which includes the two species of cultivated buckwheats, are mostly herbaceous, but there are also shrubby representatives. The inflorescences are usually conspicuous, but the individual flowers are generally small. The perianth, commonly with four to six lobes, is not clearly differentiated into calyx and corolla, but it may be white or brightly colored. The number of stamens ranges from three to nine. The fruit, at maturity, is dry, and most of it is filled up by the single seed. In two of the genera in our region, *Eriogonum* and *Chorizanthe*, the flowers originate, singly or in clusters, within more or less cup-shaped and lobed involucres. In *Chorizanthe*, in fact, each involucre surrounds a single flower. In keying, it is important not to confuse these structures.

1 Leaves without stipules; flowers single to several or many in each cup-shaped, lobed involucre, the lobes sometimes spine-tipped

    2 Involucres usually with more than 1 flower, not tipped with spines; leaves with broad blades and usually with distinct petioles (plants, especially perennial species, often shrubby) . . . . *Eriogonum*

2 Involucre with 1 flower, rarely 2; each lobe of the involucre tipped with a curved spine; leaves (the upper ones mostly opposite) essentially sessile, slender, mostly 2–3 cm long (upright, somewhat woolly-hairy annual, often more than 50 cm tall and sometimes branching dichotomously in the upper portion; involucres 6-lobed, usually hairy externally and with white margins, crowded into dense heads at the tips or near the tips of the branches, fewer in the axils of leaves in lower portions of the plant; perianth white to rose; Jackson Co., Oreg., to Calif.) . . . .
. . . . ***Chorizanthe membranacea*** (*Eriogonella membranacea*), pl. 438
PINK SPINEFLOWER

1 Leaves with stipules, these united and forming sheaths than encircle the stems; flowers not in involucres
   3 Leaf blades with a notch where the petiole is attached, otherwise rounded, about as wide as, or even wider than, long; leaves mostly basal except for 1 below the inflorescence on most flowering stems; flowers with 4 perianth lobes, 2 of them much broader than the other 2 (in our region strictly montane and not often found below about 5000 ft., 1520 m) . . . . ***Oxyria digyna***
MOUNTAIN SORREL
   3 Leaf blades, if with a notch at the base, not otherwise rounded or as wide as long; leaves often at least several on each flowering stem; flowers with 3, 5, or 6 perianth lobes
      4 Perianth with 6 lobes (3 inner, 3 outer), often greenish; leaves often mostly basal; flowers in racemes or panicles . . . . ***Rumex***
      4 Perianth with 5 lobes, generally not greenish; leaves usually not mostly basal; flowers in racemes or in the axils of leaves
         5 Plants commonly at least 1 m tall, sometimes more than 2 m; outer 3 perianth lobes, by the time the fruit has developed, with winglike expansions (most leaf blades more than 10 cm long; perennial, escaping from cultivation and often forming dense thickets) . . . . ***Reynoutria***
         5 Plants rarely so much as l m tall, and stems of some species prostrate; outer 3 perianth lobes without winglike expansions . . . . ***Polygonum***

Eriogonum

1 Leaf blades commonly more than 10 cm long, sometimes more than 15 cm (and usually 2–3 times as long as wide); blades hairy on the underside but not densely white-woolly (petioles usually about as long as, or slightly longer than, the blades; perianths white when fresh; Rogue River valley, Oreg., to Calif.; also E of the Cascades) . . . . *E. elatum*
TALL BUCKWHEAT

1 Leaf blades not often more than 8 cm long; blades densely white-woolly on the underside
   2 Most of the aboveground portion of the plant consisting of a repeatedly branched inflorescence; annual (involucres sessile or nearly so, borne singly along the branches and in the forks between branches; perianths white or yellowish to deep pink)
      3 Outline of leaf blades nearly circular; branches of inflorescence white-woolly (Josephine and Jackson Cos., Oreg., to Calif.; also E of the Cascades) . . . . *E. vimineum*, pl. 444
WICKER BUCKWHEAT

Oxyria digyna,
mountain sorrel

3 Leaf blades elongated, sometimes twice as long as wide; branches of the inflorescence not obviously hairy (Rogue River valley, Oreg., to Calif.) . . . . *E. roseum* (*E. virgatum* of some references)

ROSY BUCKWHEAT

2 Stem of inflorescence typically branching only in its upper portion, the flowers therefore concentrated in umbels or in clusters on a few branches near the top; perennial

4 Inflorescence loosely branched 2 or more times above the middle of the stem, the flower clusters therefore at the tips of several branches rather than in a simple umbel or compound umbel (in *E. pyrolifolium* var. *coryphaeum*, first choice 8, the inflorescence is sometimes 2-branched)

5 Branches of the inflorescence white-hairy; bracts at forks of the inflorescence leaflike; ultimate branches ending in a single involucre, this, and also the perianths of the several flowers within it, woolly-hairy; most larger leaf blades at least twice as long as wide (Josephine Co., Oreg., to Calif.) . . . . *E. pendulum*

WALDO BUCKWHEAT

5 Branches of the inflorescence not conspicuously hairy; bracts at forks of inflorescence inconspicuous, almost scalelike (the margins hairy); ultimate branches ending in a cluster of several involucres, these, and the perianths of flowers within them, only slightly hairy and mostly along the margins (S Willamette Valley, Oreg., to Calif.; also E of the Cascades) . . . . . *E. nudum* subsp. *nudum*, pl. 441

NAKED BUCKWHEAT

4 Inflorescence a single, simple or compound umbel

6 Leaf blades commonly 4–8 cm long (and to about twice as long as wide); perianths white to yellowish, often changing to rose (lobes of involucres broadly triangular; Umpqua River valley, Oreg., to Calif.; also E of the Cascades and in the Columbia River Gorge) . . . . *E. compositum* subsp. *compositum*, pl. 439

COMPOSITE BUCKWHEAT

6 Leaf blades not often more than 4 cm long

7 Plants, when flowering, to more than 50 cm tall; most larger leaf blades 2.5–4 cm long; perianths white to pink (strictly coastal, Curry Co., Oreg., to Calif.) . . . . *E. latifolium*

COAST BUCKWHEAT, TIBINAGUA

7 Plants, when flowering, rarely so much as 30 cm tall; larger leaf blades generally not more than about 3 cm long

8 Inflorescence (this sometimes compact, sometimes with 2 branches) with only 2 bracts beneath it; perianths white, greenish, pink, or red, but not yellow (leaf blades more or less oval, woolly-hairy on the underside; high montane in the Cascades) . . . . *E. pyrolifolium* var. *coryphaeum*

ALPINE BUCKWHEAT

8 Inflorescence typically with 3 or more bracts just beneath it (the bracts may be small, especially in *E. ovalifolium* var. *nivale*, so look carefully)

9 Leaf blades (not often more than 15 mm long) densely white-hairy on both surfaces (low, compact cushionlike plants; perianths white to yellowish, often tinged with red or purple, sometimes distinctly yellow; high montane in the Olympic Mountains, Wash., and in the Cascades, Brit. Col. to Oreg.; also eastward and in Calif.) . . . . *E. ovalifolium* var. *nivale*

CUSHION BUCKWHEAT

9 Leaf blades densely white-hairy on the underside but usually only slightly white-hairy on the upper surface (perianths yellow, sometimes streaked with red or changing to red)

10 Lobes of involucre turned back; umbels sometimes compound (bracts beneath primary umbels well developed, leaflike) . . . . *E. umbellatum*, pl. 443

SULFUR-FLOWERED BUCKWHEAT

Eriogonum umbellatum, a buckwheat with a wide geographic and altitudinal range, has more than 20 named varieties in W North America, and several in our region. It will be difficult to identify those you encounter unless you can devote considerable time to comparing material you have collected with herbarium specimens that bear labels annotated by an expert.

10 Lobes of involucre upright, not turned back; umbels rarely compound

    11 All flowers normally with stamens and a pistil; styles of pistil about 3 mm long (Josephine Co., Oreg., to Calif.) . . . . ***E. ternatum***, pl. 442

        TERNATE BUCKWHEAT

    11 Functionally pistillate and staminate flowers on separate plants (but some flowers on pistillate plants may lack a pistil and have a few reduced stamens instead); styles of pistil not more than 0.5 mm long (not likely to be found below 4000 ft., 1220 m; Cascades of S Oreg. to Calif.) . . . . ***E. marifolium***, pl. 440

        SIERRA BUCKWHEAT

Polygonum

1 Leaf blades distinctly widest near the base, sometimes more or less triangular or heart-shaped, usually at least 2 cm long

  2 Annual weeds, sprawling, trailing on the ground, or climbing into other plants

    3 Most leaf blades with an indentation at the base, therefore heart-shaped; stems trailing on the ground or climbing into other plants (if not flowering, could be mistaken for a morning glory) . . . . ***P. convolvulus***, pl. 447

        MORNING-GLORY BINDWEED (Europe)

    3 Leaf blades without an indentation at the base, therefore more nearly triangular than heart-shaped; stems sprawling but not climbing into other plants . . . . ***P. nepalense***

        NEPALESE KNOTWEED (Asia)

  2 Perennials, the stems upright, often growing in mountain rockslides (the 3 species under this choice have also been placed in the genus *Aconogonum*)

    4 Leaves to more than 10 cm long, most of the larger ones 2–3 times as long as wide; flowers numerous in each several-branched, open panicle (high montane, often in rockslides) . . . . . . ***P. phytolaccifolium***

        ALPINE KNOTWEED

    4 Leaves not often more than 6 cm long, most of the larger ones not much more than twice as long as wide; flowers in small clusters originating in the axils of upper leaves

Eriogonum pyrolifolium var. *coryphaeum*, alpine buckwheat

Polygonum phytolaccifolium, alpine knotweed

5 Larger leaf blades about twice as long as wide, sometimes slightly longer; petioles, when obvious, not much more than 5 mm long (high montane, Siskiyou Mountains of SW Oreg. and NW Calif.) . . . . *P. davisiae*

MS. DAVIS' KNOTWEED

5 Larger leaf blades usually not quite twice as long as wide; petioles usually more than 5 mm long, sometimes more than 10 mm (high montane, in rockslides and deposits of pumice, Wash. to Oreg.) . . . . *P. newberryi*

NEWBERRY'S KNOTWEED

Plants in the Olympic Mountains, Wash., and E of the crest of the Cascades in Wash. tend to be much less hairy than those in the Cascades of Oreg., E of the Cascades there, and in Calif.; the former are sometimes placed in var. *glabrum* and the latter in var. *newberryi.*

1 Leaf blades not distinctly widest near the base, therefore not triangular or heart-shaped

6 Flowering stems with a single upright terminal raceme in which the flowers are so crowded that the bracts (except those at the base) are obscured (plants of wet places or completely aquatic and with some floating leaves)

7 Petioles of lower leaves about as long as the blades; upper leaves sessile, clasping the stems (inflorescence 1–6 cm long, the perianths white or pink) . . . . *P. bistortoides*

MOUNTAIN-MEADOW KNOTWEED

7 Petioles of lower leaves much shorter than the blades; upper leaves with at least short petioles (leaves with floating blades have long petioles)

8 Plants mostly under water, the blades of upper leaves, by the time flowers are produced, floating; inflorescence not often more than 3 cm long . . . . *P. amphibium* subsp. *stipulaceum*

SHORE KNOTWEED

8 Plants of wet habitats and sometimes partly under water but without floating leaves; inflorescence usually 3–10 cm long . . . . *P. amphibium* var. *emersum* (*P. coccineum, P. hartwrightii*), pl. 445

SWAMP KNOTWEED

6 Flowering stems not with a single terminal raceme in which the flowers are so crowded that the bracts are obscured (in some species under this choice, the inflorescences are dense, but they are not single and terminal)

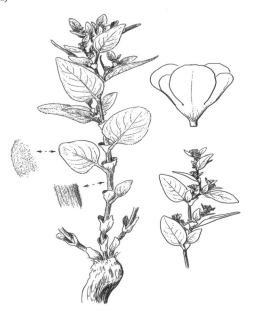 

Polygonum newberryi
vars. *newberryi,* left, and *glabrum,* right

Polygonum bistortoides,
mountain-meadow knotweed

9 Inflorescences (usually at least 2 cm long) at the ends of main stems, branch stems, or on peduncles originating in the leaf axils

10 Perianths with glandular dots

11 Perianth to 4 mm long, greenish with pink or whitish tips; plants to about 60 cm tall (inflorescences typically nodding; occasional weed, especially in moist areas) . . . .*P. hydropiper*
SMARTWEED, WATER PEPPER (Europe)

11 Perianth to 3 mm long, greenish or brownish green, with whitish tips; to about 1 m tall (in marshy areas) . . . . *P. punctatum*
WATER SMARTWEED

10 Perianths without glandular dots (plants to more than 80 cm tall)

12 All or most leaf blades with a conspicuous dark blotch (larger leaves usually 3–10 cm long, with a short petiole; racemes not often more than about 2.5 cm long; perianth pink or purplish) . . . .
. . . .*P. persicaria*, pl. 449
LADY'S THUMB (Europe)

12 Leaf blades without a dark blotch (larger leaves 3–20 cm long, sessile or with short petioles; racemes generally more than 2.5 cm long, sometimes as long as about 7 cm)

13 Racemes (on long peduncles) borne in the axils of upper leaves of the main stem or stems (racemes elongated, loose, the flowers not quite touching one another; perennial; around shallow ponds and in swamps) . . . .*P. hydropiperoides*
MILD WATER PEPPER

13 Racemes mostly borne on branches of the main stem or stems

14 Branches of main stem terminating in single, rather loosely flowered racemes (mostly E of the crest of the Cascades but occasionally in montane habitats on the W slope; Wash. to Calif. and eastward) . . . . *P. majus*
PALOUSE KNOTWEED

14 Branches of main stem usually bearing at least 2–3 dense racemes, most flowers touching one another

15 Racemes only about twice as long as wide, usually upright; flowers pink . . . . . *P. pensylvanicum*
PINKWEED

15 Racemes at least 5–6 times as long as wide, some or all usually drooping; flowers greenish to white or pink (weed) . . . .*P. lapathifolium*
WILLOWWEED (Europe)

9 All flowers produced singly or in small clusters in the axils of leaves that may be gradually reduced upward but that are not so abruptly reduced to small bracts that there are sharply delimited inflorescences (in other words, at least the lower flower clusters are usually in the axils of well-developed leaves)

16 Plants forming mats on backshores of sandy beaches, somewhat woody at the base, the stems mostly prostrate but the flowers produced in small clusters in the axils of leaves at the tips of upright portions (midrib of leaf blades raised prominently on the underside; brownish remains of stipules obvious on the stems) . . . . *P. paronychia*, pl. 448
BEACH KNOTWEED

16 Plants not growing on sandy beaches (but some species are around salt marshes or otherwise close to salt water)

17 Flowers sessile and usually solitary (sometimes 2) in the leaf axils (plants upright, to about 40 cm tall; largest leaf blades to 4 cm long, 4 mm wide) . . . . *P. californicum*
CALIFORNIA KNOTWEED

17 Flowers on short pedicels and mostly in clusters of 2 or more

18 Leaves (mostly 5–7 mm long) stiff, with prickly tips (plants forming small, compact cushions; on sandy flats and beds of dried-out pools and streams, Josephine Co., Oreg., to Calif.) . . . . *P. parryi*
PRICKLY KNOTWEED

18 Leaves not stiff, the tips not prickly

 19 Stems not sharply angled lengthwise, but they may have at least several delicate ribs (stems mostly prostrate but sometimes partly upright; weeds, especially prevalent on hard-packed soils of roadsides and paths)

  20 Perianth lobes pink or greenish white, separated for about half the length of the perianth; fruits (achenes) with 3 more or less equal concave surfaces . . . .*P. arenastrum,* pl. 446
   COMMON KNOTWEED, DOORWEED (Europe)

  20 Perianth lobes pink, purple, or white, separated almost to the base of the perianth; fruits with 2 convex surfaces, 1 concave surface . . . .*P. aviculare*
   KNOTWEED (Europe)

 19 Stems (or at least portions of them) distinctly angled lengthwise and sometimes with ribs between the angles

  21 Flowers nodding by the time the perianth opens (perianth generally 2.5–3.5 mm long, the lobes greenish, sometimes with white or reddish margins; achenes conspicuously 3-angled lengthwise, black and shiny; plants usually 15–25 cm tall) . . . . *P. douglasii* var. *douglasii*
   DOUGLAS' KNOTWEED

  21 Flowers not nodding

   22 Perianth usually 3–4 mm long, pink, pinkish, or faintly bluish, each lobe with a greenish midrib; plants usually less than 10 cm tall; common on dry, grassy or mossy hillsides, especially close to salt water, on the Gulf Islands, Brit. Col., and San Juan Islands, Wash., but also found in similar habitats in many other portions of our region; flowering in September–October) . . . .
   . . . . *P. douglasii* subsp. *spergulariiforme* (*P. spergulariaeforme*)
   FALL KNOTWEED

   22 Perianth 1.5–2.5 mm long, and plants not in all other respects as described in the other choice 22

    23 Tips of stems with crowded leaves, reduced leaves (bracts), and flowers

     24 Bracts associated with flowers with conspicuous white margins; achenes usually dull, with a lengthwise groove (lowland and montane, W and E of the crest of the Cascades) . . . .
     . . . . *P. polygaloides* var. *confertiflorum* (*P. confertiflorum*)
     CLOSE-FLOWERED KNOTWEED

     24 Bracts associated with flowers without white margins; achenes usually shiny, without a lengthwise groove (montane, mostly E of the crest of the Cascades) . . . .
     . . . . *P. polygaloides* var. *kelloggii* (*P. kelloggii*)
     KELLOGG'S KNOTWEED

    23 Tips of stems without especially crowded leaves and bracts

     25 Most larger leaves 8–10 times as long as wide (Brit. Col. to NW Oreg.) . . . . *P. nuttallii*
     NUTTALL'S KNOTWEED

     25 Leaf blades elongate-oval, the larger ones not much more than 3 times as long as wide (perianth about 2–3 mm long)

      26 Perianth usually green with paler margins, the lobes distinctly longer than the tube; achenes black, shiny, protruding only slightly, if at all, beyond the perianth lobes . . . *P. sawatchense*
      SAWATCH KNOTWEED

      26 Perianth white or greenish (sometimes with pink margins but not primarily pink)

       27 Lobes of the perianth about as long as the tube; achenes yellowish, protruding well beyond the perianth lobes (primarily at the edges of salt marshes where the forest comes close to the shore) . . . .*P. fowleri*
       FOWLER'S KNOTWEED

       27 Lobes of the perianth about half as long as the tube; achenes, when mature, black or nearly black (mostly high montane, Brit. Col. to Calif. and eastward) . . . . *P. minimum*
       LEAFY KNOTWEED

Reynoutria

1 Leaf blades more than twice as long as wide, widest near the middle; base of blade wedge-shaped rather than notched or squared-off (mostly in coastal areas) . . . . *R. polystachya*
HIMALAYAN KNOTWEED (Asia)

1 Leaf blades not so much as twice as long as wide, usually slightly wider near the base than near the middle; base of blade either notched or more or less squared-off

  2 Leaf blades sometimes to 35 cm long, about 1.5 times as long as wide, the notch at the base conspicuous, its depth often one-tenth that of the blade length; tips of blades not drawn out into slender points; inflorescences much shorter than the leaf blades; plants often more than 3 m tall . . . . *R. sachalinensis*
GIANT KNOTWEED (Japan and Russian islands N of Japan)

  2 Leaf blades not often more than 25 cm long, nearly squared-off at the base or with just a shallow notch; tips of blades drawn out into slender points; inflorescences sometimes as long as, or longer than, the leaf blades; plants not often so much as 3 m tall

    3 Base of leaf blades squared-off; inflorescences as long or longer than the leaf blades . . . . *R. cuspidata*
JAPANESE KNOTWEED (Asia)

    3 Base of leaf blades with a shallow notch; inflorescences shorter than the leaf blades . . . .
. . . . *R. ×bohemica* (*R. cuspidata × sachalinensis*), pl. 450
BOHEMIAN GIANT KNOTWEED

Rumex

1 Pistillate and staminate flowers on separate plants (leaf blades arrowhead-shaped)

  2 Plants not spreading by rhizomes; upright stems to about 1 m tall; blades of lower leaves to about 10 cm long, the basal corners not conspicuously diverging; each pedicel with a joint well below the flower; occasionally cultivated and sometimes escaping . . . .*R. acetosa*
GARDEN SORREL (Eurasia)

  2 Plants spreading by rhizomes; upright stems not often more than 30 cm tall; blades of lower leaves to about 4 cm long, the basal corners often conspicuously diverging; each pedicel with a joint just below the flower

    3 Larger leaf blades to about 4 times as long as wide, the margins not obviously turned under (common and pernicious weed) . . . . *R. acetosella*, pl. 451
SHEEP SORREL (Europe)

    3 Larger leaf blades to 6–7 times as long as wide, the margins obviously turned under (occasional weed) . . . .
. . . . *R. tenuifolius*
SLENDER-LEAVED SORREL (Europe)

1 Pistillate and staminate flowers on the same plant

  4 Inner 3 perianth segments ("valves") of pistillate flowers with conspicuous marginal teeth or bristlelike outgrowths, these at least 1 mm long

    5 All 3 of the inner perianth segments of pistillate flowers with a prominent swelling ("callosity"); annual or biennial

      6 Swelling on inner perianth segments at least 0.5 mm wide; none of the marginal teeth on the perianth segments as long as the segments; coastal . . . . *R. persicarioides*
SEASHORE DOCK (Eurasia)

      6 Swelling on inner perianth segments rarely so much as 0.5 mm wide; longest marginal teeth on the perianth segments as long as the segments; coastal and inland . . . . *R. maritimus*
GOLDEN DOCK

Rumex maritimus, golden dock

5 Only 1 or sometimes 2 of the inner perianth segments with a prominent swelling; perennial

    7 Pedicels jointed at or near the middle; surface of swelling on inner perianth segments coarsely warty . . . . *R. pulcher*
                                        FIDDLE DOCK (Europe)

    7 Pedicels jointed decidedly below the middle; surfaces of swellings on inner perianth segments smooth or only slightly wrinkled . . . . *R. obtusifolius*
                                       BROAD-LEAVED DOCK (Europe)

4 Margins of inner perianth segments of pistillate flowers sometimes roughened but without distinct marginal teeth or bristlelike outgrowths

    8 Stems branching from the base; leaf blades narrowing gradually to the petioles (inner perianth segments not often more than 3 mm long, any or all or none of them with conspicuous thickenings) . . . . *R. salicifolius* subsp. *salicifolius*, pl. 453
                                       WILLOW-LEAVED DOCK

    8 Stems not branching from the base (but there may be branches on the upper parts of the stems); blades of basal and lower stem leaves narrowing abruptly to the petioles, and sometimes with a notch where the petiole is attached

        9 None of the inner perianth segments with a prominent swelling (blades of basal and lower leaves sometimes notched where the petiole is inserted; usually in wet habitats, including edges of salt marshes) . . . . *R. aquaticus* var. *fenestratus* (*R. occidentalis*)
                                       WESTERN DOCK

        9 At least 1 of the inner perianth segments with a prominent swelling

          10 Inflorescence dense, successive whorls of flowers on the main stem and branches pressed tightly together

              11 Leaf blades conspicuously crisp-margined; inner perianth segments not distinctly notched at the base, usually longer than wide and not more than about 5 times as wide as the swelling (very common large weed) . . . . *R. crispus*, pl. 452
                                         CURLY-LEAVED DOCK (Europe)

Rumex pulcher,
fiddle dock

Rumex obtusifolius,
broad-leaved dock

11 Leaves not conspicuously crisp-margined; inner perianth segments distinctly notched at the base, usually about as wide as long and much more than 5 times as wide as the swelling . . . . ***R. patientia***
PATIENCE DOCK (Eurasia)

10 Inflorescence not so dense that successive whorls of flowers are pressed tightly together

12 All 3 inner perianth segments of pistillate flowers with a swelling, this nearly twice as long as wide . . . . ***R. conglomeratus***
CLUSTERED DOCK (Europe)

12 Only 1 or sometimes 2 of the inner perianth segments with a swelling, this about 1.5 times as long as wide . . . . ***R. sanguineus***
RED-VEINED DOCK (Europe)

PORTULACACEAE Purslane Family

The flowers of most purslanes are distinctive in having only two sepals. The number of petals varies from five to more than 15, but in *Claytonia, Calandrinia,* and *Montia,* the genera that account for the majority of species in our region, there are typically five. The pistil is single, and there are usually at least three stamens. The fruit, dry when mature, encloses several to many seeds.

1 Flowers generally with at least 6 petals, sometimes as many as 13, occasionally 5 in *L. triphylla* . . . . . ***Lewisia***

1 Flowers almost always with 5 petals (rarely 6)

2 Petals yellow (rather succulent annual with prostrate stems; petals attached to the calyx, which consists of 2 sepals united at the base; common garden weed but not often found in our region except in S Oreg.) . . . . ***Portulaca oleracea***
COMMON PURSLANE (Europe)

2 Corolla not yellow

3 Corolla uniformly deep purplish red (rarely white); individual flowers borne in the axils of leaves similar to those on lower portions of the stems; stamens generally more than 6 but ranging from 3 to 15 . . . . ***Calandrinia ciliata*** (includes var. *menziesii*), pl. 454
REDMAIDS

3 Corolla not uniformly purplish red (but it may have red lines or other markings); individual flowers usually borne in the axils of small bracts or independent of bracts (but in *M. fontana* sometimes borne in the axils of substantial leaves); stamens 3 or 5 . . . . *Claytonia-Montia* **complex**

Claytonia-Montia **Complex**

This is a difficult group, to a considerable extent because some of the species recognized in more recent revisions of *Claytonia* and *Montia* intergrade and/or are interfertile.

1 Leaves on flowering stems opposite (the members of a pair, may, however, be joined together, and the union may be so complete as to form a disklike structure around the stem)

2 Stems on which inflorescences originate with at least 2 pairs of leaves, the upper ones not markedly reduced when compared with the lower ones

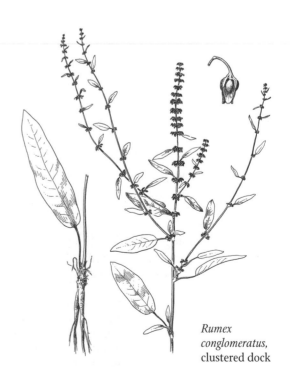

Rumex conglomeratus, clustered dock

3 Stems on which inflorescences originate typically upright, with several pairs of leaves, these to about 5 cm long; plants producing nearly leafless stolons from their bases; petals white or pink, 5–8 mm long (perennial; in wet habitats) . . . .***M. chamissoi***
TOAD LILY

3 Stems on which inflorescences originate sprawling, the leaves not often more than 2 cm long; plants not producing stolons from their bases; petals white, mostly 1–1.5 mm long (annual; in wet habitats, and often floating in shallow water) . . . .***M. fontana*** (*M. hallii*)
WATER MONTIA

2 Stems arising from the central portion of the plant with only 1 pair of conspicuous leaves below the inflorescence (the leaves from whose axils flowers originate are smaller and bractlike); annual

4 One pair of leaves beneath the inflorescence united to form a nearly circular, disklike structure around the stem

5 Blades of basal leaves typically narrow, at least several times as long as wide, tapering gradually to the petiole . . . .***C. parviflora*** subsp. ***parviflora***
SMALL-LEAVED CLAYTONIA

5 Blades of basal leaves typically only 1–2 times as long as wide, tapering abruptly to the petiole . . . . .
. . . .***C. perfoliata*** subsp. ***perfoliata***, pl. 457
MINER'S LETTUCE

4 Leaves beneath the inflorescence, if united, not joined to the extent that they form a nearly circular, disklike structure around the stem

6 Leaves beneath the inflorescence not united; petals at least 7 mm long, sometimes more than 12 mm (perennial, or some plants of *C. sibirica* annual)

7 Leaves beneath the inflorescence typically at least 4 times as long as wide; stems growing from an underground tuber 1–2 cm in diameter (corolla white with pink or rose lines to deep pink, sometimes with a yellow center; in our region not common below 4000 ft., 1220 m, but E of the Cascades often found at lower elevations) . . . .***C. lanceolata***, pl. 456
WESTERN SPRING BEAUTY

7 Leaves beneath the inflorescence typically about as wide as long; stems not growing from a tuber but the stem at the base may be thickened, and in *C. cordifolia* the stems usually arise at intervals from an underground rhizome

8 Blades of basal leaves commonly heart-shaped; only the lowest flower of the inflorescence originating above a small bract (Siskiyou Mountains of SW Oreg. and NW Calif., otherwise mostly E of the crest of the Cascades) . . . .***C. cordifolia*** (*Montia cordifolia*)
BROAD-LEAVED CLAYTONIA

8 Blades of basal leaves oval; at least 2–3 flowers of the inflorescence originating above small bracts . . . .***C. sibirica*** (*M. heterophylla, M. sibirica*), pl. 458
CANDYFLOWER

6 Leaves of the pair beneath at least some inflorescences partly united, often asymmetrically; petals not more than 5 mm long

9 Plants commonly at least 10 cm tall (sometimes more than 20 cm) when flowering . . . .
. . . .***C. washingtoniana***
WASHINGTON CLAYTONIA

9 Plants generally less than 10 cm tall when flowering

10 Blades of most basal leaves oval or somewhat triangular, distinct from the petioles; leaves of the pair beneath the inflorescence about as wide as long . . . .***C. rubra***
RED-STEM MINER'S LETTUCE

Two subspecies or varieties of *C. rubra* are sometimes recognized. In subsp. *rubra* the blades of the basal leaves are somewhat triangular, widest near the base, whereas in subsp. *depressa* they are more or less oval, widest near the middle; in subsp. *depressa*, furthermore, the number of chromosomes in cells is 2 or 3 times that characteristic of subsp. *rubra*.

10 Blades of basal leaves slender, scarcely distinct from the petioles; leaves beneath the inflorescence, if not partly or wholly united, longer than wide

  11 Pair of leaves beneath the inflorescence either free of one another or united only on one side (in that case appearing to be 2 lobes of a single leaf); petals to about 5 mm long . . . .
. . . . *C. exigua* subsp. *exigua*
(includes *M. spathulata* vars. *exigua, spathulata, rosulata,* and *tenuifolia*), pl. 455
PALE MINER'S LETTUCE

  11 Pair of leaves beneath the inflorescence completely united to form a cup; petals not more than 2 mm long (almost all aboveground parts of the plant, except the white petals, often reddish)
. . . . *C. exigua* subsp. *glauca* (*M. perfoliata* f. *glauca*)
GLAUCOUS MINER'S LETTUCE

1 Leaves above the base of the plant alternate

  12 Each cluster of a few flowers produced in the axil of a stipulelike bract opposite the base of a narrow but conspicuous leaf (sepals to about 1.5 mm long, the petals, white, shorter; some stems falling down and rooting at the nodes) . . . . *M. howellii*
HOWELL'S MONTIA

  12 Flowers borne in racemelike inflorescences, these often mostly 1-sided

    13 Petals (pink or white) 7–15 mm long (perennial; plants usually connected by underground rhizomes and also producing slender stolons that may bear reproductive bulblets; mostly on wet rocks) . . . . . .
. . . . *M. parvifolia* (includes vars. *parvifolia* and *flagellaris*)
MOISTURE-LOVING MONTIA

    Plants whose leaf blades are more or less oval, longer than wide are sometimes separated as var. *parvifolia;* in var. *flagellaris,* found mostly in coastal habitats, the leaf blades have a nearly circular outline.

    13 Petals (usually white, sometime pinkish) not more than 5 mm long

      14 Leaf blades, especially those of basal leaves, about as wide as long and commonly more than 5 mm wide; stamens 5; perennial . . . . *M. diffusa*
DIFFUSE MONTIA

      14 Leaf blades slender, rarely so much as 3 mm wide; stamens usually 3; annual

        15 Plants rarely more than 8 cm tall, sometimes only 2–3 cm; sepals about 2 mm long
. . . . *M. dichotoma*
DWARF MONTIA

        15 Plants to about 20 cm tall; sepals usually 3–6 mm long . . . . *M. linearis,* pl. 463
SLENDER-LEAVED MONTIA

Lewisia

1 Basal leaves usually disappearing by the time flowers have developed (flowering stem or stems to about 10 cm tall, usually with 2–3 conspicuous slender leaves, these generally 3–4 cm long and all originating at about the same level; petals 5–9, commonly 4–6 mm long, pink or white with pink lines; lower portion of each stem delicate and easily separating from an underground tuber 5–10 mm in diameter; in the Siskiyou Mountains, Oreg. and NW Calif., but not likely to be found below 4000 ft., 1220 m; also E of the crest of the Cascades) . . . . *L. triphylla*
THREE-LEAVED LEWISIA

Montia parvifolia,
moisture-loving montia

1 Basal leaves at least several, well developed, and forming a persistent rosette; leaves on flowering stems bractlike, much smaller than the basal leaves

    2 Blades of most basal leaves broadening to a width of at least 2 cm near the tip (petals generally 12–15 mm long, usually pink or orangish pink, with darker lines, but sometimes white with pink lines)

        3 Margins of blades of basal leaves not wavy or toothed (Josephine and Jackson Cos., Oreg., to Calif.; mostly above 3000 ft., 910 m) . . . .*L. cotyledon* **var.** *cotyledon,* pl. 460
                                                                 SISKIYOU LEWISIA, IMPERIAL LEWISIA

        3 Margins of leaf blades conspicuously wavy or somewhat toothed (Curry and Josephine Cos., Oreg., to Calif.) . . . .*L. cotyledon* **var.** *howellii*
                                                                HOWELL'S LEWISIA

    2 Blades of basal leaves not so much as 1 cm wide

        4 Flowering stems rarely so much as 10 cm long, usually no longer than the basal leaves (flowering stems with a single pair of bractlike leaves; petals generally 6–12 mm long, white, somewhat greenish, or pink; mostly above 5000 ft., 1520 m, in the Cascades and Olympic Mountains, Brit. Col. to Calif.; also E of the Cascades and Sierra Nevada) . . . . *L. pygmaea,* pl. 462
                                                                 ALPINE LEWISIA

        4 Flowering stems at least 10 cm tall, much longer than the basal leaves

            5 Flowering stems with 1 or more pairs of conspicuous slender leaves, these opposite and resembling the persistent basal leaves; petals 8–11, 12–17 mm long, white or pink (Josephine Co., Oreg., to Calif., mostly in pine forests, often where damp, at 1500–4000 ft., 460–1220 m) . . . .
            . . . . *L. oppositifolia,* pl. 461
                                                           OPPOSITE-LEAVED LEWISIA

            5 Leaves on flowering stems bractlike, much smaller than the persistent basal leaves; flowers usually at least several; petals usually 7–9, occasionally as many as 11, white with pink lines to very deep pink (at a few scattered montane localities in our region; rare below 4000 ft., 1220 m) . . . .
            . . . . *L. columbiana* **var.** *columbiana,* pl. 459
                                                              COLUMBIA LEWISIA

        The subspecific or varietal name *rupicola* has been applied to plants from the Cascades, Saddle Mountain, Clatsop Co., Oreg., and the Olympic Mountains, Wash. The basal leaves of these plants are usually rounded at the tip, and the bractlike leaves on the lower portions of the flowering stems typically have glandular teeth. These characters are less commonly noted in specimens from E of the crest of the Cascades.

PRIMULACEAE Primrose Family

Most members of the primrose family are herbaceous plants with simple leaves. These may be entirely basal, distributed along the stems, or in a whorl at the top of the stem. The flowers are sometimes solitary, sometimes in racemes or umbel-like inflorescences. The calyx and corolla have a cup-shaped or tubular lower portion, but the lobes, of which there are usually five, are well developed. The stamens, also generally five, are attached to the corolla tube. A conspicuous exception to the standard formula is the genus *Trientalis,* in which the number of calyx lobes, corolla lobes, and stamens commonly varies from five to seven, even on the same plant. In *Dodecatheon,* flowers with four stamens and four-lobed calyces and corollas may be found on some specimens of certain species. In the representatives of Primulaceae in our region, the pistil, which develops into a many-seeded dry fruit, is free of the calyx tube. An interesting feature of the fruits of two of our genera is the way they open: separating into two halves crosswise instead of splitting apart lengthwise.

Many garden plants, including species of *Primula, Soldanella, Androsace,* and *Cyclamen,* belong to this family. A common weed in gardens is the scarlet pimpernel, *Anagallis arvensis,* whose flowers open only in sunshine. *Trientalis latifolia,* called starflower, a common wildflower in wooded areas, is perhaps the easiest species to establish in a garden of native plants, but it spreads so rapidly by underground stems that one may soon have too much of it.

It has been proposed that three of the genera represented in our region—*Trientalis, Anagallis,* and *Lysimachia*—be transferred to Myrsinaceae. That family, as long understood, is mostly confined to subtropical and tropical areas, and consists entirely of woody plants. Time will tell whether the transfer will be generally approved.

1 Mat-forming plants with cushions of small leaves; corolla rose-pink, fading to lavender, 10–12 mm long, the tube longer than the lobes (perennials, uncommon at lower elevations except as noted) . . . . . ***Douglasia***
1 Plants neither mat-forming nor with cushions of small leaves
  2 Leaves (except for small bracts beneath the inflorescence) entirely basal
    3 Corolla lobes more than twice as long as the tube, turned sharply back; stamens protruding conspicuously and pressed tightly to the pistil . . . . ***Dodecatheon***
    3 Corolla lobes less than twice as long as the tube, not bent back (corolla white) . . . . ***Androsace***
  2 Leaves not entirely basal
    4 Flowers sessile in the leaf axils
      5 Leaves mostly opposite; petals absent (but the sepals, 3–4 mm long, white to pale pink, resemble petals); fruit splitting lengthwise into 5 valves; perennial, mostly in salt marshes at the coast but sometimes in inland marshes) . . . . ***Glaux maritima***, pl. 467
                                                                              SEA MILKWORT
      5 Leaves mostly alternate; petals present, about 1.5 mm long, white or pale pink; top half of the fruit separating from the bottom half; annual, mostly on moist ground or around drying freshwater ponds . . . . ***Centunculus minimus*** (sometimes called *Anagallis minima*)
                                                                         CHAFFWEED
    4 Flowers with distinct peduncles
      6 Leaves less than 2 cm long; corolla usually pinkish scarlet (rarely blue); top half of the fruit breaking away from the bottom half (flowers opening only in bright sunshine; plants sprawling; common annual weed) . . . . ***Anagallis arvensis***, pl. 464
                                                                    SCARLET PIMPERNEL (Europe)

      6 Leaves more than 2 cm long; corolla not scarlet; fruit splitting apart lengthwise into valves
        7 Stems usually less than 20 cm long; most leaves in a whorl at the top of the stem, just below the several flowers (others, if present, much reduced); corolla lobes usually 5–7, pink or white . . . . ***Trientalis***
        7 Stems usually at least 30 cm long; leaves opposite, scattered along the stems; corolla lobes 5 (rarely 6), pale to clear yellow . . . . ***Lysimachia***

Androsace

1 Leaf blades abruptly narrowed to the petiole; calyx usually about 2 mm long (in our region only in the N Willamette Valley; rare and local) . . . . ***A. filiformis***
                                            SLENDER ANDROSACE
1 Leaf blades tapering gradually to the petiole; calyx 3.5–5 mm long (Jackson Co., Oreg., to Calif.) . . . . ***A. elongata*** subsp. ***acuta***
                                           LONG-STEMMED ANDROSACE

Androsace filiformis,
slender androsace

Dodecatheon

1 Corolla white with dark markings at the base; leaves with coarsely toothed margins (in our region only in the Columbia River Gorge, usually in at least partly shaded, moist habitats; widespread on the E slopes of the Cascades from Brit. Col. to N Oreg.) . . . . *D. dentatum*
WHITE SHOOTING STAR

1 Corolla usually pink, rose, purplish, or some related color (rarely white), yellow at the base; leaves with smooth margins
  2 Stigma globular, distinctly thicker than the style; filaments of stamens not much more than 1 mm long, free of one another for at least half their length (mostly montane, in our region not often found below 3000 ft., 910 m) . . . . *D. jeffreyi*
JEFFREY'S SHOOTING STAR

  2 Stigma slender, no thicker than the style; filaments of stamens usually at least 2 mm long and united into a tube for all or most of their length
    3 Leaf blades usually not so much as twice as long as wide, narrowing abruptly to the petiole . . . . *D. hendersonii*, pl. 465
HENDERSON'S SHOOTING STAR

    3 Leaf blades usually more than 3 times as long as wide, narrowing gradually to the petiole . . . . *D. pulchellum* (*D. pauciflorum*)
FEW-FLOWERED SHOOTING STAR

Several varieties of *D. pulchellum* have been named; the prevailing one in our region would be called *pulchellum* or *macrocarpum*.

Douglasia

1 Margins of leaf blades not toothed and not obviously hairy (in Wash. in the Cascades and Olympic Mountains, and in the Columbia River Gorge, sometimes at low elevations) . . . . *D. laevigata* subsp. *laevigata*, pl. 466
SMOOTH-LEAVED DOUGLASIA

1 Margins of leaf blades somewhat toothed and conspicuously hairy (on Saddle Mountain, Clatsop Co., Oreg., in the Columbia River Gorge, and in the Cascades, mostly above 4000 ft., 1220 m) . . . . *D. laevigata* subsp. *ciliolata*

Lysimachia

1 Flowers in terminal or axillary racemes
  2 Racemes terminal on the main stems; flowers widely separated; corolla lobes about 3 times as long as wide (in a few bogs to which *Vaccinium oxycoccos,* the cultivated cranberry, has been introduced) . . . . . *L. terrestris*
BULB-BEARING LOOSESTRIFE (E North America)

  2 Racemes originating in the axils of the leaves; flowers crowded, individually inconspicuous; corolla lobes slender, more than 10 times as long as wide (in sphagnum bogs and other wet habitats, often partly submerged) . . . . *L. thyrsiflora*, pl. 469
TUFTED LOOSESTRIFE

1 Flowers solitary in the leaf axils
  3 Stems mostly flat on the ground, rooting at the nodes; leaf blades broadly oval, usually scarcely longer than wide (escaping from gardens) . . . . *L. nummularia*
CREEPING JENNY (Europe)

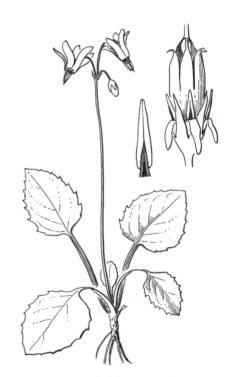

Dodecatheon dentatum,
white shooting star

3 Stems upright; most leaves at least twice as long as wide
  4 Most leaf blades about twice as long as wide; tips of the corolla lobes reaching well beyond the tips of the calyx lobes (along the Columbia River as far W as Multnomah Co., Oreg., otherwise E of the Cascades) . . . . *L. ciliata* (*Steironema ciliatum*), pl. 468
  FRINGED LOOSESTRIFE
  4 Most leaf blades at least 4 times as long as wide; tips of corolla lobes barely reaching the tips of the calyx lobes (marshes of Josephine Co., Oreg.; widespread in North America, including Oreg. and Wash. E of the Cascades) . . . . *L. lanceolata* (*Steironema lanceolatum*)

Trientalis

1 Corolla pink; largest leaves usually at least 5 cm long; common woodland plant . . . .
  . . . . *T. latifolia* (*T. borealis* subsp. *latifolia*), pl. 470
  BROAD-LEAVED STARFLOWER
1 Corolla white; largest leaves usually less than 5 cm long; restricted to sphagnum bogs and some other wet habitats . . . . *T. arctica* (*T. europaea* subsp. *arctica*)
  NORTHERN STARFLOWER

RANUNCULACEAE Buttercup Family

Most plants belonging to the buttercup family are herbaceous and have alternate leaves. (The only ones that have woody stems and opposite leaves are vines of the genus *Clematis*.) Although stamens are typically numerous, the number of pistils and their seed production vary. In some genera, there are many separate pistils, each becoming a dry fruit that encloses a single seed; in others, there are only a few pistils that mature as dry fruits containing many seeds. In only one of the representatives in our region, *Actaea spicata*, baneberry, does the single pistil become a fleshy fruit. When both sepals and petals are present, there are commonly five of each, but a few species have more than five petals. Petals are sometimes lacking, and the sepals are sometimes very small. When there are no petals, the sepals are generally white or brightly colored. In *Aquilegia*, columbines, the five petals have long, hollow spurs that extend backward between the sepals; in *Delphinium*, larkspurs, which have only four petals, the upper two have spurs that fit into a spur on one of the sepals.

Staminate and pistillate flowers are sometimes separate, but even when this is the case a few flowers may have stamens as well as pistils. It should also be noted that in certain species found in our region, not all petals develop normally on all flowers. These flowers are, however, essentially regular. In *Delphinium*, flowers are really irregular because the two upper petals are distinctly different from the two lower ones.

The Ranunculaceae is a remarkably diverse assemblage, but after a little experience with a few common species you should be able to decide that even an unfamiliar new discovery belongs to this family.

Lysimachia nummularia,
creeping Jenny

1 Flowers with sepals and substantial petals, but there may be fewer petals than sepals, and in *Actaea rubra* the sepals usually fall away early

  2 Flowers irregular

    3 Flowers with 5 sepals and 4 petals (in 2 pairs); uppermost sepal not greatly enlarged but with a long spur . . . . *Delphinium*

    3 Flowers with 5 sepals and 2 petals (2 poorly developed lower petals are also sometimes present); uppermost sepal greatly enlarged, forming a hood over the petals (sepals and petals mostly deep bluish purple; upper leaf axils sometimes producing bulblets instead of flowers; in our region not often found below about 3000 ft., 910 m) . . . . . *Aconitum columbianum* subsp. *columbianum*, pl. 471

            COLUMBIA MONKSHOOD

  2 Flowers regular (unless l or more petals are abortive, which is often the case in certain species of *Ranunculus*)

    4 Petals with spurs; sepals and spurs of petals red . . . . *Aquilegia formosa*, pl. 478

            WESTERN COLUMBINE

    4 Petals without spurs

      5 Pistil single, developing into a fleshy, very shiny red or white fruit; petals white (the sepals, which usually fall away early, are also sometimes white) . . . . *Actaea rubra*, pl. 472

            BANEBERRY

      5 Pistils at least several, developing into dry fruits; petals usually yellow but white in some aquatic and wetland species) . . . . *Ranunculus*

1 Flowers either without petals (in which case the sepals may be petal-like) or the petals less noticeable than the sepals (in *Coptis* the petals may be longer than the sepals, but they are very slender and, like the sepals, usually disappear early)

  6 Flowers borne singly on each leafless stem about 5–10 cm tall; pistils (usually at least 100) tightly packed on the slender receptacle, forming a spikelike structure to more than 2 cm long; sepals with spurs; petals usually present, whitish, about as long as the sepals but very slender and soon disappearing; all leaves basal, with narrow blades . . . . *Myosurus minimus*, pl. 485

            LEAST MOUSETAIL

  6 Plants not conforming in all respects to the description in the other choice 6

    7 Vines, the older stems woody (leaves pinnately compound, usually with 5 leaflets; sepals about 1 cm long, cream; style persisting as a long, plumelike structure) . . . . *Clematis*

    7 Plants herbaceous

      8 Each flowering stem with a single flower, the peduncle of this originating above a whorl of leaves (there are usually 3 leaves in each whorl; sepals petal-like, white, pink, or blue) . . . . *Anemone*

      8 Flowers, if borne singly, not on a peduncle originating above a whorl of leaves

        9 Leaves not compound or lobed (in bogs and other very wet habitats) . . . . *Caltha*

        9 Leaves compound or deeply lobed

          10 Plants evergreen, low, spreading by rhizomes; leaves pinnately compound (or nearly bipinnately compound), with more than 3 ultimate leaflets or lobes; flowers 1 or a few on leafless stems arising near the base of the plant; sepals whitish, usually falling early; petals present, very slender, with a prominent gland near the base, soon disappearing . . . . *Coptis*

          10 Plants deciduous and not conforming to all other criteria described in the other choice 10 (petals absent)

            11 Flowers either borne singly or in umbel-like inflorescences

              12 Flowers borne singly or in umbel-like inflorescences; petals absent; sepals white to pink or rose but often falling early; stamens distinctly dilated near the middle or above the middle . . . . *Enemion*

12 Flowers borne singly; petals (yellow) 15 or more but not often more than 5 mm long and partly hidden by the stamens; sepals white in freshly opened flowers, usually greenish or yellowish in buds; stamens not distinctly dilated at or above the middle; mostly montane . . . .
. . . . *Trollius albiflorus* (*T. laxus* var. *albiflorus*), pl. 496
GLOBEFLOWER

> The structures called petals in *T. albiflorus* have also been interpreted to be sterile stamens.

11 Flowers usually numerous in each raceme, panicle, or corymb

  13 Most or all flowers either strictly staminate or strictly pistillate . . . . *Thalictrum*

  13 Flowers with 1 or more pistils and numerous stamens

    14 Flowers in elongated racemes, these branched below, so there are secondary racemes; flowers with only 1 pistil; leaves bipinnately compound . . . . *Cimicifuga elata*, pl. 480
TALL BUGBANE

    14 Flowers in corymbs; flowers with several pistils; leaves palmately lobed . . . .
. . . . *Trautvetteria carolinensis*, pl. 495
FALSE BUGBANE

Anemone

1 Leaves (usually at least 3 cm long) in the whorl below the flower peduncle toothed or with 1 or more shallow incisions but not compound or even conspicuously lobed (sepals white, usually about 2 cm long; W of the Cascades, King Co., Wash., to Calif.) . . . . *A. deltoidea*, pl. 473
WHITE ANEMONE, WINDFLOWER

1 Leaves in the whorl below the flower peduncle deeply lobed or compound, sometimes with many ultimate divisions

  2 Flowering stems with not more than 1 leaf at the base (when present, this is similar to the leaves in the whorl below the flower); leaves in the whorl below the flower with 3 separate leaflets, 1 or more of these sometimes so deeply divided as to form nearly secondary leaflets but not deeply divided further

    3 Sepals not more than about 1 cm long, white, rarely pale pinkish or bluish; leaflets to about 2.5 cm long, not divided so deeply that there are nearly secondary leaflets . . . . *A. lyallii*, pl. 475
LITTLE MOUNTAIN ANEMONE

    3 Sepals more than 1 cm long, white, pinkish, blue, bluish purple, or reddish purple; leaflets often more than 2.5 cm long, often divided so deeply that there are nearly secondary leaflets

      4 Most leaflets or nearly secondary leaflets with at least 5 prominent teeth or shallowly divided lobes (Coast Ranges and the Cascades, Wash. to Calif.; also the Siskiyou Mountain region of SW Oreg. and NW Calif.) . . . . *A. oregana* var. *oregana*, pl. 477
OREGON ANEMONE

      4 Most leaflets with not more than 5 prominent teeth or distinct lobes (usually close to the coast, especially in sphagnum bogs; Wash. to N Oreg.) . . . . *A. oregana* var. *felix*
> Some specimens do not fit cleanly into either *A. oregana* var. *oregana* or var. *felix*.

  2 Flowering stems with at least several basal leaves; each leaf in the whorl below the flower either deeply divided into 3 lobes (these again just shallowly lobed) or deeply divided 2 or more times, the ultimate lobes sometimes small (in *A. multifida* the flowering stems are commonly branched, with a whorl of leaves below one or more of the flower peduncles as well as at the point of branching)

    5 Basal leaves with 3 leaflets, these shallowly lobed or merely toothed (leaves in the whorl beneath the flower peduncle divided into 3 lobes, these only shallowly lobed again; sepals not often more than 15 mm long, white or tinged with blue) . . . . *A. parviflora*
SMALL-FLOWERED ANEMONE

    5 Basal leaves either pinnately compound (the primary leaflets divided into secondary leaflets and lobes) or ternately divided into lobes and secondary lobes

6 Basal leaves pinnately compound, the primary leaflets divided into secondary leaflets and lobes; sepals (white or sometimes tinged with purple on the outer surface) usually 2–3 cm long; styles, on aging flowers, 2–3.5 cm long, covered with long, somewhat silky hairs (montane and not likely to be found below about 4500 ft., 1370 m) . . . . *A. occidentalis*, pl. 476
WESTERN PASQUEFLOWER

6 Basal leaves ternately compound or nearly compound, the leaflets or primary lobes again deeply lobed 1–2 times; sepals not more than 2 cm long; styles not covered with long hairs (the achenes, however, are very hairy)

    7 Flowering stems rarely branched; styles (usually yellow) from half to fully as long as the achenes; sepals to 20 mm long, white, but the outer surface commonly tinged with blue (montane and in our region not likely to be found below about 5000 ft., 1520 m) . . . . *A. drummondii* var. *drummondii*, pl. 474
DRUMMOND'S ANEMONE

    7 Flowering stems commonly branched; styles (usually pink or reddish) not so much as half as long as the achenes; sepals to 15 mm long, typically yellowish, sometimes white, the outer surface tinged with some shade of red, purple, or blue (montane and in our region not likely to be found below about 5000 ft., 1520 m) . . . .*A. multifida*
CUT-LEAVED ANEMONE

In some references, 2 varieties of *A. multifida* are recognized: var. *multifida* is as tall as about 60 cm, with each main stem bearing as many as 7 flowers, whereas var. *saxicola* is not often more than 30 cm tall, with each main stem bearing not more than 3 flowers.

Caltha

1 Sepals yellow; most flowers borne on the rising tips of sprawling stems, these sometimes rooting at the nodes (flowering stems with as many as 3 flowers and 3 leaves; in wet, boggy or marshy habitats, in our region strictly coastal except where planted or probably planted) . . . . *C. palustris* var. *palustris* (*C. asarifolia*)
YELLOW MARSH MARIGOLD

1 Sepals white; flowering stems (these usually with 1 leaf) upright, arising from a short, leafy base (leaf blades about as long as wide, the basal lobes touching or overlapping; flowering stems usually with 2 flowers; not often found below about 2000 ft., 610 m) . . . . *C. leptosepala* (*C. leptosepala* var. *biflora, C. biflora*), pl. 479
WHITE MARSH MARIGOLD

Clematis

Clematis tangutica, golden clematis, native to Asia, is known to escape from cultivation; its sepals are commonly 2.5–3 cm long and bright yellow. In the two species that are commonly found in our region, the sepals are white.

1 All flowers with stamens and pistils; leaflets usually smooth-margined or the upper leaflets of the blade with 1–2 lobes on each side (well established in many places) . . . .*C. vitalba*
VIRGIN'S BOWER (Europe)

1 Flowers either strictly staminate or strictly pistillate; all leaflets usually coarsely toothed . . .*C. ligusticifolia*
WESTERN CLEMATIS

Coptis

1 Leaves with 3 leaflets, these toothed but not deeply lobed; flowers borne singly; petals prolonged scarcely beyond the nectar gland . . . . *C. laciniata*
THREE-LEAFLET GOLDTHREAD

1 Primary divisions of leaflets deeply divided again into secondary leaflets or lobes; flowers usually 2–3 on each flowering stem; petals prolonged for at least 5–6 mm beyond the nectar gland, the prolongation very slender (Alaska to Snohomish Co., Wash., and in our region not likely to be found below 3000 ft., 910 m) . . . . *C. asplenifolia*
FERN-LEAVED GOLDTHREAD

Delphinium

The European larkspur, *Consolida ambigua,* whose flowers may be blue, purple, pink, or white, occasionally escapes from gardens. It can easily be distinguished from the native species of *Delphinium* because most or all its leaves are repeatedly divided into slender lobes.

1 Sepals and petals red or orange-red, rarely yellow (Curry, Josephine, and Jackson Cos., Oreg., to Calif.) . . . .
. . . . *D. nudicaule*, pl. 482
RED LARKSPUR

1 Sepals and petals not red or orange-red
  2 Sepals mostly whitish, cream, or pale yellow, often tinged with blue or with bluish tips, but in general giving the impression that the flower as a whole is more nearly white than blue
    3 Sepals 10–12 mm long (upper petals light blue, the lower ones whitish; mostly in rocky habitats, Clackamas and Yamhill Cos., Oreg.) . . . .
. . . . *D. nuttallii* subsp. *ochroleucum* (*D. leucophaeum, D. ochroleucum*), pl. 483
WHITE ROCK LARKSPUR

    3 Sepals usually 15–20 mm long
      4 Plants usually at least 60 cm tall; widest leaf lobes more than 1 cm wide; pedicels of flowers to about 8 cm long (Willamette Valley, Oreg., especially Clackamas, Polk, and Benton Cos.) . . . .
. . . . *D.* ×*pavonaceum* (believed to be *D. trolliifolium* × *D. menziesii* subsp. *pallidum*)
PEACOCK LARKSPUR

      4 Plants not so much as 60 cm tall; widest leaf lobes less than 1 cm wide; pedicels of flowers not often more than 5 cm long (NW Oreg.) . . . .*D. menziesii* subsp. *pallidum*
PALE LARKSPUR

  2 Sepals and petals (and therefore the flowers as a whole) mostly blue or purple
    5 Flowering stems commonly at least 1 m tall (sometimes more than 1.5 m), generally at least 2 arising from the root crown, usually branched and with at least 40 flowers (stems and leaves scarcely if at all hairy but usually with a slightly grayish tint; in the Cascades, the Olympic Mountains, Wash., and the Siskiyou Mountains, Oreg. to Calif., otherwise mostly E of the Cascades or N of our region) . . . .
. . . . *D. glaucum*
GRAYISH LARKSPUR

Delphinium glaucum is unusual in that at flowering time, the root crowns already have buds of future flowering stems.

Coptis laciniata,
three-leaflet goldthread

Clematis ligusticifolia,
western clematis

    5 Flowering stems rarely more than about 60 cm tall (except *D. trolliifolium*), typically only 1 arising from the root crown (except sometimes in *D. glareosum*), with fewer than 40 flowers, and in most species without branches other than the pedicels of individual flowers

      6 Plants commonly more than 60 cm tall, sometimes more than 1 m; sepals generally 18–20 mm long, sometimes slightly longer (SW Wash. and NW Oreg., including the Columbia River Gorge) . . . . ***D. trolliifolium***, pl. 484
                                    POISON LARKSPUR

      6 Plants rarely if ever 60 cm tall; sepals rarely so much as 15 mm long

        7 Plants commonly only 20–30 cm tall, occasionally with more than 1 stem, the stem or stems sometimes branched; leaves somewhat succulent; mostly among loose rocks of high-montane areas in the Cascades, Brit. Col. to Oreg., and in the Olympic Mountains, Wash. . . . . ***D. glareosum***
                                      ROCKSLIDE LARKSPUR

        7 Plants commonly more than 30 cm tall, usually with a single stem, this without branches other than the flower pedicels; leaves not at all succulent; lowland or low-montane species

          8 Racemes commonly with as many as about 20 flowers; spur of upper sepal not often more than 12 mm long and usually not obviously longer than the sepal; sepals not spreading widely outward, the calyx therefore somewhat cup-shaped (Pierce Co., Wash., to N Oreg.; also the Columbia River Gorge) . . . . ***D. nuttallii*** subsp. ***nuttallii***
                                      NUTTALL'S LARKSPUR

          8 Racemes usually with not more than about 15 flowers; spur of upper sepal usually at least 13 mm long (sometimes 20 mm in *D. nuttallianum*), often distinctly longer than the sepal; sepals spreading nearly flat outward

            9 Leaves and stems often glandular; lower petals typically divided into 2 lobes for about one-third of their length (mostly E of the crest of the Cascades, especially where *Pinus ponderosa* grows, but present in the Columbia River Gorge and also in SW Oreg.; not in the Olympic Mountains, Wash.; an extremely variable species) . . . . ***D. nuttallianum***
                                      UPLAND LARKSPUR

            9 Leaves and stems not glandular; lower petals typically divided into 2 lobes for not more than about one-fifth of their length (common and widespread below about 2500 ft., 760 m, W of the Cascades) . . . . ***D. menziesii*** subsp. ***menziesii*** (*D. oreganum*), pl. 481
                                        MENZIES' LARKSPUR

             Delphinium menziesii subsp. menziesii is here interpreted to include specimens in Josephine and Jackson Cos., Oreg., that have been identified as *D. decorum*. The latter, according to the treatment of the genus in *Flora of North America*, does not occur N of Calif.

Enemion

    1 Plants not often so much as 20 cm tall; flowers borne singly on stems that scarcely rise above the leaves; sepals less than 1 cm long (Yamhill, Polk, Benton, and Jackson Cos., Oreg., S to Calif., but the distribution in Oreg. not necessarily continuous) . . . . ***E. stipitatum*** (*Isopyrum stipitatum*)
                                        DWARF RUE ANEMONE

    1 Plants commonly at least 20 cm tall; flowers as many as 10 in each umbel-like inflorescence, this raised well above the leaves; sepals about 1 cm long (Puget Trough and Willamette Valley, from Thurston and Lewis Cos., Wash., to Marion Co., Oreg.; also along the coast of Oreg. at least as far S as Tillamook Co.) . . . . ***E. hallii*** (*Isopyrum hallii*)
                                        HALL'S RUE ANEMONE

Ranunculus

    1 Petals white (sometimes yellow at the base in *R. aquatilis* vars. *aquatilis* and *diffusus*); plants submerged, except for flowers and floating leaves, but sometimes exposed after the water level drops

      2 Submerged leaves divided into slender, nearly hairlike lobes, the blades of floating leaves with 3 rather broad lobes . . . . ***R. aquatilis*** **var.** ***aquatilis*** (*R. aquatilis* var. *hispidulus*), pl. 486
                                        WHITE WATER BUTTERCUP

2 All leaves divided into slender, hairlike lobes

   3 Submerged leaves usually divided 3 times; each flower usually producing at least 10 achenes . . . .
. . . . *R. aquatilis* **var.** *diffusus* (includes vars. *capillaceus* and *subrigidus*)

   3 Submerged leaves divided not more than twice; each flower usually producing 2–7 achenes . . . .
. . . . *R. lobbii*
LOBB'S WATER BUTTERCUP

1 Petals yellow; plants terrestrial or growing in wet places, sometimes becoming submerged when the water level rises; none of the leaves divided into slender, nearly hairlike lobes

   4 Blades of at least some leaves, especially those at the base of the plant, compound (that is, with completely separate leaflets)

      5 At least some leaves with as many as 5 leaflets, these deeply lobed (petals usually 10–15 mm long; beak of achenes 2.5–4 mm long, straight) . . . . *R. orthorhynchus* **var.** *orthorhynchus*
BIRD'S-FOOT BUTTERCUP

      5 Leaves with not more than 3 leaflets (the terminal leaflet may, however, be so deeply divided that its lobes are nearly leaflets)

         6 Beak of achenes distinctly hooked (the curvature exceeding an angle of 90°)

            7 Beak of achenes 0.7–1.2 mm long; plants with prostrate stems rooting at the nodes (petals usually 10–13 mm long, sometimes doubled, that is, with petaloid stamens; common and very aggressive weed, especially in lawns and along ditches) . . . . *R. repens*, pl. 492
CREEPING BUTTERCUP (Europe)

            7 Beak of achenes 0.3–0.6 mm long; plants upright, sometimes more than 50 cm tall (petals usually 10–12 mm long; common weed) . . . . *R. acris*
TALL BUTTERCUP (Europe)

         6 Beak of achenes straight or curved but not hooked (the curvature less than an angle of 90°)

            8 Beak of achenes directed sharply away from the long axis of the body (flat surfaces of achenes usually with a few to many small bumps; scale at the base of each petal nearly squared-off at its upper edge; petals usually 7–9 mm long) . . . . *R. sardous*
HAIRY BUTTERCUP (Europe)

            8 Beak of achenes not directed sharply away from the long axis of the body

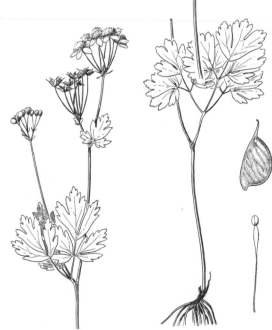

               9 Achenes with numerous hooked bristles (petals to about 2 mm long but as a rule only some of the 5 developing normally, and sometimes none of them evident; mostly E of the Cascades but occasionally found in W Oreg. and in the Columbia River Gorge) . . . .*R. hebecarpus*
DOWNY BUTTERCUP

               9 Achenes without hooked bristles

                  10 Petals commonly at least 7 mm long, sometimes more than 10 mm (underground base of plant swollen, bulblike; uncommon weed) . . . . *R. bulbosus*
BULBOUS BUTTERCUP (Europe)

                  10 Petals rarely more than 7 mm long (in wet habitats)

                     11 Petals to about 4 mm long; aggregate of maturing achenes to about 1 cm high, and higher than wide (plants very hairy) . . . .*R. pensylvanicus*
BRISTLY BUTTERCUP

Enemion hallii,
Hall's rue anemone

11 Petals to about 7 mm long; aggregate of maturing achenes not so much as 1 cm high, and not higher than wide .... *R. macounii*, pl. 490
MACOUN'S BUTTERCUP

4 None of the leaf blades fully compound (but they may be deeply lobed)
12 Leaf blades not lobed (plants of very wet places, sometimes rooting at the nodes or spreading by stolons, and sometimes becoming submerged)
13 Blades of larger leaves much less than twice as long as wide (sometimes scarcely or not at all longer than wide)
14 Plants spreading by stolons
15 Aggregate of maturing achenes considerably higher than wide; achenes with a short, nearly straight, often blunt beak; petals 5 or more .... *R. cymbalaria* var. *saximontanus*
FIGWORT BUTTERCUP
15 Aggregate of maturing achenes about as high as wide; achenes with a sharp-tipped, hooked beak; petals 5 (montane in the S Cascades of Oreg., and Klamath and Siskiyou Mountains of SW Oreg. and NW Calif.; not likely to be found below about 4500 ft., 1370 m) ..... *R. gormanii*
GORMAN'S BUTTERCUP
14 Plants not spreading by stolons
16 Achenes blunt at the tip, without a beak; petals at least 7 .... *R. ficaria*
LESSER CELANDINE (Europe)
16 Achenes with a prominent, slightly curved beak; petals usually 5 (montane, in our region not likely to be found as low as 4000 ft., 1220 m) .... *R. populago*
MOUNTAIN BUTTERCUP
13 Blades of most larger leaves at least twice as long as wide
17 Stems rooting at the nodes, the plants thereby forming mats, these often partly or completely submerged; flowering stems usually less than 10 cm tall and not often with more than 3 flowers in each inflorescence; petals rarely more than 5 mm long (but occasionally to nearly 10 mm) .....
.... *R. flammula*, pl. 489
CREEPING SPEARWORT
Varieties of *R. flammula* have been named, but they intergrade so much that any one specimen may be difficult to identify precisely.
17 Stems not rooting at the nodes; flowering stems usually at least 20 cm tall (sometimes more than 30 cm), with at least 3 flowers in each inflorescence; petals more than 6 mm long (usually 10 mm)
.... *R. alismifolius*
PLANTAIN-LEAVED BUTTERCUP
The treatment of *R. alismifolius* in *Flora of North America* recognizes 6 varieties, 3 of which are found in our region. For what it is worth, the key below summarizes the differences between them.
18 Margins of leaf blades with small teeth; stems 3.5–8 mm thick; mostly in lowland habitats ....
.... *R. alismifolius* var. *alismifolius*
18 Margins of leaf blades smooth; stems only 1–3 mm thick; mostly in montane habitats
19 Leaf blades oval or slightly elongated, not so much as 3 times as long as wide ....
.... *R. alismifolius* var. *alismellus*
19 Leaf blades proportionately slender, usually 4–6 times as long as wide ....
.... *R. alismifolius* var. *hartwegii*
12 Blades of larger leaves distinctly lobed, sometimes very deeply (the primary lobes, moreover, may be again deeply lobed)
20 Larger leaf blades with a nearly circular outline, the primary lobes separated nearly to the attachment of the petiole and divided into secondary and tertiary lobes; furthermore, the primary lobes may be so crowded that some of them form a layer under the others (petals 7–15, much narrower than the 5 sepals and not appreciably longer; achenes with lengthwise ridges and a sharply curved beak; montane, typically growing where snow prevails well into the summer) .... *R. cooleyae*
GRACE COOLEY'S BUTTERCUP

20 Larger leaf blades not with a nearly circular outline and the plants in general not in all respects as described in the other choice 20

  21 Aggregate of maturing achenes distinctly higher than wide and often more than 1 cm high (plants only slightly if at all hairy; blades of most larger leaves deeply lobed nearly to the base; flat surfaces of achenes with crosswise ridges, the beak a short, rounded protuberance; now a weed in streams and wet fields) . . . . ***R. sceleratus*** var. ***sceleratus***

                            CELERY-LEAVED BUTTERCUP (E North America)

        In *R. sceleratus* var. *multifidus*, native in W North America, including our region, the flat surfaces of the achenes do not have crosswise ridges.

  21 Aggregate of maturing achenes not higher than wide and not so much as 1 cm high

    22 Flat surfaces of mature or nearly mature achenes spiny or bristly

      23 Most primary leaf lobes considerably longer than wide; beak of achenes nearly or fully 3 times as long as wide at the base, nearly straight (spines on body of achene stout, the tips curved or hooked; occasional weed) . . . . ***R. arvensis***

                                    FIELD BUTTERCUP (Europe)

      23 Primary leaf lobes broad, about as wide as long; beak of achenes not obviously more than about twice as long as wide at the base

        24 Petals at least 4 mm long, sometimes as long as 10 mm; spines on achenes stout, not arising from bumps and at most only slightly curved . . . . ***R. muricatus***

                                PRICKLE-SEED BUTTERCUP

        24 Petals to only about 2 mm long; bristles on achenes arising from small bumps and distinctly curved or even hooked at the tip . . . . ***R. parviflorus***

                          SMALL-FLOWERED BUTTERCUP (Europe)

    22 Flat surfaces of mature or nearly mature achenes not spiny (but they may be hairy)

      25 Flowers with 9–17 petals, these usually 10–15 mm long (beak of achenes markedly hooked; not often found N of Oreg.; see note) . . . . ***R. californicus*** var. ***cuneatus***, pl. 488

                                  CALIFORNIA BUTTERCUP

        Some specimens with 9 or more petals from near Victoria, Vancouver Island, Brit. Col., the Gulf Islands of Brit. Col., and the San Juan Islands of Wash. are believed to be *R. californicus* var. *cuneatus,* which may have been introduced; others are apparently hybrids between this buttercup and *R. occidentalis* var. *occidentalis.*

      25 Flowers commonly with 5–8 petals (unless some of them have not developed fully)

        26 Petals (5) not often more than 4 mm long, 1 or more of them often abortive; usually in habitats that are at least partly shaded; beak of mature achenes so markedly curved that the tip points back at the body . . . . ***R. uncinatus***, pl. 493

                                WOODLAND BUTTERCUP

        26 Petals (5 or more) at least 6 mm long, sometimes more than 15 mm, typically all normally developed; usually in open, sunny habitats

          27 Beak of mature achenes nearly straight; petals 5–8, to 15 mm long and typically widest near the tip and nearly or fully as wide as long; leaves and most portions of stems (except perhaps in the inflorescence) not conspicuously hairy (mostly at rather high elevations) . . . . ***R. eschscholtzii***

                                ESCHSCHOLTZ' BUTTERCUP

          27 Beak of mature achenes straight or curved; petals typically 5, occasionally 6, about twice as long as wide; leaves and most portions of stems conspicuously hairy

            28 Outer (lower) surface of petals with prominent reddish to purplish markings (beak of achenes straight or slightly curved; Jackson Co., Oreg.) . . . . ***R. austro-oreganus***, pl. 487

                          SOUTHERN OREGON BUTTERCUP

              Although *R. austro-oreganus* is very distinctive and restricted to a small area of Oreg., it is possibly part of the *R. occidentalis* vars. *howellii–dissectus* complex; see notes under choice 29.

            28 Outer (lower) surface of petals without prominent reddish to purplish markings

29 Beak of achenes curved (common throughout our region) . . . . . ***R. occidentalis* var. *occidentalis***, pl. 491

WESTERN BUTTERCUP

Ranunculus occidentalis var. *ultramontanus,* found above about 4000 ft. (1220 m) in the Cascades of S Oreg. and S to Calif., has especially narrow petals (not so much as 3 mm wide) and stems that tend to lie on the ground.

29 Beak of achenes straight (SW Oreg. to N Calif.) . . . . ***R. occidentalis* var. *howellii***

HOWELL'S BUTTERCUP

Ranunculus occidentalis var. *dissectus,* with a distribution from NE Oreg. to NW Calif., scarcely differs from var. *howellii;* the ultimate lobes of its leaves are said to be somewhat lance-shaped rather than elliptic.

Thalictrum

1 Mature achenes (these flattened), usually about 1.5 times as long as wide (not including the style), usually slightly lopsided (mostly E of the Cascades but also found from SW Oreg. to Calif.) . . . . ***T. polycarpum***

TALL MEADOW RUE

1 Mature achenes about 3 times as long as wide, sometimes slightly curved, but not markedly lopsided (widespread, Wash. to Willamette and Umpqua River valleys, Oreg.) . . . . ***T. occidentale***, pl. 494

WESTERN MEADOW RUE

RESEDACEAE Mignonette Family

The mignonettes occasionally found wild in our region are European species cultivated in gardens. All three are assigned to the genus *Reseda*. Their flowers, borne in elongated inflorescences, have several sepals and petals. The petals are usually of unequal size or form, or both, but the irregularity of the flowers is also pronounced because the stamens, of which there are usually at least ten, are concentrated on one side. In the few species most likely to be encountered there is a single pistil that produces many seeds; in others, however, there is a starlike cluster of pistils, each of which becomes a one-seeded fruit.

Thalictrum polycarpum,
tall meadow rue

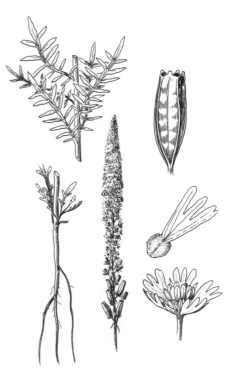

Reseda alba,
white mignonette

Reseda

1 Petals 4, yellowish, the uppermost one obviously larger than the others; leaves not lobed (used for many centuries as a source of a yellow dye) . . . . *R. luteola*

DYER'S ROCKET, WELD (Europe)

1 Petals usually 5–6, yellowish, greenish white, or white, all nearly the same size; leaves deeply lobed

   2 Petals white or greenish white; larger leaves usually with 10–14 more or less regularly paired lobes in addition to the terminal lobe . . . . *R. alba*

WHITE MIGNONETTE, UPRIGHT MIGNONETTE (Europe)

   2 Petals yellowish; larger leaves usually with 3–7 lobes . . . . *R. lutea*

WILD MIGNONETTE (Europe)

RHAMNACEAE Buckthorn Family

In our region the buckthorn family is represented by a tree and several shrubs belonging to the genera *Rhamnus* and *Ceanothus.* The individual flowers of these are small, but in some species of *Ceanothus* the inflorescences are showy, and they may also be fragrant. The calyx generally has five lobes, sometimes four, and unless petals are lacking there is a corresponding number of these as well as of stamens. The stamens originate at the edge of the cup formed by the basal part of the calyx. They are in line with the calyx lobes but alternate with the petals. There is a single pistil. In *Rhamnus* this is free of the calyx and becomes a fleshy fruit, but in *Ceanothus* it is usually united with the calyx and develops into a dry fruit.

Of the many species of *Ceanothus* in the Pacific states, especially California, several are widely cultivated. Of those in our region, *C. thyrsiflorus*, the blueblossom, whose natural range includes the coastal portion of southern Oregon, is the best known.

1 Trees or shrubs; leaf blades without a pair of lateral veins as prominent as the midrib; petals small, greenish, the inflorescence therefore not showy; fruit not lobed, fleshy . . . . *Rhamnus*

1 Shrubs (sometimes large, sometimes low and prostrate); leaf blades of some species with 2 lowest lateral veins as prominent as the midrib; petals white, pinkish, lavender, or blue, spoon-shaped owing to the narrow basal portion and broad terminal portion; fruit 3-lobed, dry at maturity . . . . *Ceanothus*

Ceanothus

1 Prostrate-stemmed shrubs, usually forming matted growths (leaves opposite; flowers lavender or blue, often becoming white on aging)

   2 Leaf blades usually with smooth margins or a few teeth at the tip but not often with any prominent marginal teeth; each lobe of fruit smooth or with only a low bump; Josephine and Curry Cos., Oreg., to Calif. . . . . *C. pumilus*, pl. 499

SISKIYOU MAT, DWARF CEANOTHUS

Ceanothus prostratus,
mahala mat

2 Leaf blades usually with prominent teeth around the margins but sometimes with teeth only at the tip; each lobe of fruit with a conspicuous wavy-edged, hornlike outgrowth; occasionally found in Josephine and Curry Cos. but more common in Klamath Co., Oreg., and with a wide distribution in Brit. Col., Wash., and Oreg. E of the crest of the Cascades) . . . . *C. prostratus*, p. 305

MAHALA MAT

Ceanothus prostratus, C. pumilus, and the much larger *C. cuneatus,* first choice 3, are known to hybridize.

1 Substantial upright shrubs

3 Leaves opposite, the blades generally oblong, often notched at the tip, and without lateral veins as prominent as the midrib (evergreen; flowers white, in rounded inflorescences; each lobe of fruit with a conspicuous outgrowth; most branches narrowing to the tip but not thornlike; Willamette Valley, Oreg., at one time as far north as Clackamas Co., to Calif.) . . . . *C. cuneatus*, pl. 497

COMMON BUCKBRUSH

See note under *C. prostratus,* second choice 2.

3 Leaves alternate, the 2 lateral veins at the base of the blade nearly or fully as prominent as the midrib

4 Shrubs usually not much more than 1 m tall, densely branched, with many short branches becoming sharp-tipped thorns (evergreen; leaf blades oval; flowers white; each lobe of the fruit with a prominent ridge; mostly above 3000 ft., 910 m; Douglas, Jackson, Josephine, and Curry Cos., Oreg., to Calif.) . . . . *C. cordulatus*

SNOW BRUSH

4 Shrubs commonly at least 1 m tall; none of the branches becoming sharp-tipped thorns

5 Leaf blades to more than 7 cm long, usually more than half as wide as long; upper surfaces of blades, especially when young, slightly sticky, appearing to have been varnished, and fragrant when rubbed (evergreen; flowers white)

6 Leaf blades typically with velvety hairiness on the underside (Brit. Col. to Calif., mostly E of the crest of the Cascades) . . . . *C. velutinus* var. *velutinus*

TOBACCO BRUSH, STICKY LAUREL

6 Leaf blades without velvety hairiness on the underside (coastal, Brit. Col. to Calif., and also in the Puget Sound–Hood Canal region of Wash.) . . . . *C. velutinus* var. *hookeri*
(*C. velutinus* var. *laevigatus*)

5 Leaf blades, if as much as 7 cm long, not more than half as wide as long; upper surfaces of blades neither sticky nor appearing to have been varnished, and not fragrant when rubbed

7 Evergreen; young branches conspicuously angled lengthwise; leaf blades rarely so much as 4 cm long; flowers usually light to deep blue (occasionally white in *C. thyrsiflorus*)

8 Leaf blades with 3 main veins arising at the base (Douglas, Coos, and Curry Cos., Oreg., to Calif.; widely grown in gardens; occasional specimens found in uncultivated places outside the natural range probably introduced) . . . . *C. thyrsiflorus*, pl. 501

BLUEBLOSSOM

Ceanothus velutinus var. *velutinus*, tobacco brush

8 Leaf blades pinnately veined from the midrib but the lateral veins often becoming less prominent on older leaves (native to NW Calif.; colonies in W Lane Co., Oreg., may also be native) . . . . *C. parryi*
LADY-BLOOM; PARRY'S CEANOTHUS

7 Deciduous, or partly evergreen in *C. integerrimus;* young branches not angled lengthwise; leaf blades usually at least 4 cm long; flowers white, pale blue, or pinkish
  9 Leaf blades usually not more than twice as long as wide, with fine marginal teeth; young stems often reddish; flowers white . . . . *C. sanguineus*, pl. 500
REDSTEM CEANOTHUS, TEA TREE
  9 Leaf blades usually at least twice as long as wide, without marginal teeth, except sometimes in the upper half; young stems not reddish; flowers usually pale blue, sometimes white or slightly pinkish (Douglas Co., Oreg., to Calif. but widely distributed in Wash. and Oreg. E of the crest of the Cascades)
. . . . *C. integerrimus*, pl. 498
DEER BRUSH

Rhamnus

1 Substantial tree, commonly more than 5 m tall; deciduous (but small specimens, to about 1 m tall, often retaining their leaves through the winter); leaf blades dark green, rarely more than twice as long as wide . . .
. . . . *R. purshiana*, pl. 503
CASCARA

1 Shrub to about 2.5 m tall; evergreen; leaf blades yellowish green, generally about 2.5–3 times as long as wide (on serpentine soils, Josephine Co., Oreg., to Calif.) . . . . *R. californica* subsp. *occidentalis*, pl. 502
SERPENTINE COFFEE BERRY
    Rhamnus californica subsp. *californica*, California coffee berry, which does not grow on serpentine soils and is limited to Calif., is similar in general appearance to subsp. *occidentalis,* but its leaves are dark green on the upper surface and usually more green than yellow-green on the underside. Furthermore, its fruits typically have 2 seedlike stones, whereas those of subsp. *occidentalis* usually have 3.

ROSACEAE Rose Family

The rose family is of great economic importance, for it includes many trees and shrubs that produce edible fruit (and seeds, in the case of almonds) as well as many that are cultivated for their ornamental value. This is a large and diversified assemblage, difficult to define concisely. The arrangement of pistils and the structure of the fruit are particularly variable features. Nevertheless, after you have learned to recognize some of the common genera, such as *Rubus* (blackberries and raspberries), *Rosa* (roses), *Prunus* (cherries), *Fragaria* (strawberries), and *Potentilla* (cinquefoils), you will probably be able to place relatives of these plants in the same family.

The characteristics summarized here apply to members of the rose family that grow wild in the region. The leaves are alternate and often have stipules. The calyx has five lobes, and sometimes there is an accessory outgrowth between the lobes. There are normally either five petals or none. The stamens usually number at least 15; like the petals, they are attached to the cuplike portion of the calyx. There may be a single pistil or several to many of them. When there is just one, it may be fused to the calyx cup, which explains why the calyx lobes of an apple or pear are situated at the free end. When there are many pistils, each may become a one-seeded dry fruit (in a cinquefoil), or it may become a one-seeded fleshy fruit attached to a conical receptacle (as in a blackberry or strawberry). In a strawberry, the receptacle is fleshy, but the many fruits embedded in it are of the one-seeded dry type; the little brownish projections scattered over the surface of a strawberry are remains of the styles of the pistils.

Omitted from this key are shrubs of the genera *Pyracantha* (with thorns) and *Cotoneaster* (without thorns), commonly grown in gardens. They are becoming more and more abundant in areas that otherwise may seem to be natural. They have nearly round, red or orange-red fruits, mostly about 8–10 mm long. Birds make use of the berries and thus serve as agents of dispersal.

1 Trees, shrubs, or vines that are to a considerable extent woody and whose stems may also have prickles or thorns (prickles, characteristic of roses, are outgrowths of the epidermis; thorns are short, sharp-tipped spur branches)—caution: some members of the family, because of their relatively large size, could be mistaken for shrubs even though they are nonwoody plants that die back each winter

  2 At least some branches with prickles or short, sharp-tipped spurs functioning as thorns

    3 At least some branches with prickles, but none with sharp-tipped spurs functioning as thorns

      4 Fruit an aggregate of fleshy, 1-seeded fruits, either like a raspberry (the aggregate freely separating from the conical receptacle) or a blackberry (the aggregate not separating from the receptacle) .... ***Rubus***

      4 Fruit a rose "hip," an urn-shaped or nearly round structure whose fleshy outer portion is derived from the calyx (this is fused to the pistil, in which the seeds are formed) .... ***Rosa***

    3 At least some branches with sharp-tipped spurs functioning as thorns (see note in the second choice 2, concerning *Malus fusca*)

      5 Fruit, whether mature or immature, usually with a 5-lobed calyx persisting at its tip (the fruit, in other words, is like a very small apple); leaf blades deeply lobed or rather coarsely toothed, especially in the upper half .... ***Crataegus***

      5 Calyx, at the base of the fruit when it starts to develop, soon shed (the mature fruit, in other words, is like a cherry or plum); leaf blades smooth-margined or with evenly spaced small teeth almost to the petiole .... ***Prunus***

  2 None of the branches with prickles or sharp-tipped spur branches functioning as thorns (in *Malus fusca* some branches may form leafless spur shoots, but these are generally blunt-tipped when compared with those of *Crataegus* and certain species of *Prunus*)

    6 Leaves pinnately compound (flowers numerous, in corymbs, these sometimes nearly flat-topped; fruits orange or red when ripe) .... ***Sorbus***

    6 Leaves not compound

      7 Leaf blades palmately lobed and with a palmate arrangement of principal veins

        8 Most leaf blades at least 8 cm wide; flowers usually 3–7 in each inflorescence; petals (white) usually at least 15 mm long; fruit a raspberry, red when ripe .... ***Rubus parviflorus***, pl. 526
                                                THIMBLEBERRY

        8 Leaf blades not often more than 6 cm wide; flowers usually at least 10 in each inflorescence; petals (white) about 4 mm long; fruit dry, consisting of 3–5 pistils that are only partly united .... ***Physocarpus capitatus***, pl. 515
                                                NINEBARK

      7 Leaf blades not palmately lobed (but they may be pinnately lobed) and without a palmate arrangement of principal veins

        9 Most leaf blades (these to more than 7 cm long) with several lobes on both sides, the lobes toothed (shrub; flowers about 5 mm wide, numerous in each panicle; petals whitish; pistils usually 5, developing into dry achenes) .... ***Holodiscus discolor***, pl. 512
                                                OCEAN SPRAY

             Holodiscus dumosus var. *glabrescens,* with leaf blades not more than about 2 cm long and with inflorescences that usually do not branch more than once, is montane and mostly E of the crest of the Cascades but has been found on the W side in Oreg.

        9 Leaf blades either not lobed or with only 1–2 lobes

          10 Some leaf blades with 1–2 small, pointed lobes (if 2, these usually unequal); petals white to pink, 9–14 mm long; fruit about 1–1.5 cm long, yellowish, brownish, or purplish red, resembling an apple in general form) .... ***Malus fusca*** (*Pyrus fusca, P. rivularis*), pl. 513
                                                PACIFIC CRABAPPLE

             One cultivar or another of the domestic apple, *M. pumila* (*M. domestica, Pyrus malus*), and pear (*P. communis*), both native to Europe, may occasionally be found growing wild. Cultivars of *M. floribunda,* Japanese flowering crabapple, have also been reported as escapes.

      10 Leaf blades not lobed
         11 Leaves stiff, evergreen; flowers without petals; fruit a dry achene, retaining a feathery stigma usually at least 5 cm long . . . . ***Cercocarpus***
         11 Leaves neither stiff nor evergreen; flowers with petals; fruit fleshy or dry, without a long, feathery stigma
            12 Leaf blades toothed (at least near the tip)
               13 Flowers many, in dense compound corymbs; petals less than 3 mm long; pistils generally 5 (but not all necessarily develop into fruits); fruits dry at maturity . . . . ***Spiraea***
               13 Flowers few to many, in clusters, racemes, corymbs, or panicles; petals usually at least 4 mm long; pistil 1; fruits fleshy
                  14 Most leaf blades (about 3–4 cm long) toothed in the upper half or two-thirds (petals white, 1–2 cm long, often slightly twisted; fruits about 1 cm, dark purplish) . . . . ***Amelanchier***
                  14 Most leaf blades toothed almost all around their margins (flowers in racemes, corymbs, or panicles) . . . . ***Prunus***
            12 Leaf blades not toothed, usually about 3 times as long as wide
               15 Large shrub; leaf blades mostly about 8–12 cm long, the petioles slender; staminate and pistillate flowers on separate plants, a few flowers in each nodding raceme; petals white, about 5–6 mm long; pistils usually 5; fruits fleshy (but not all pistils become fruits), orange to bluish black (very common lowland shrub) . . . . ***Oemleria cerasiformis*** (*Osmaronia cerasiformis*), pl. 514
                              OSOBERRY, INDIAN PLUM
               15 Small, very low shrub; leaf blades mostly about 2 cm long, tapering gradually to broad petioles; flowers in very dense racemes to about 4 cm long; all flowers with stamens and a pistil; petals white, about 2 mm long; pistils usually 5; fruits dry, splitting open lengthwise (Olympic Mountains, Wash.; not often found below about 5000 ft., 1520 m) . . . . ***Petrophytum hendersonii***
                              HENDERSON'S ROCKMAT
1 Plants either herbaceous (but sometimes so large as to be mistaken for shrubs) or low, often mat-forming shrubs whose woodiness may not be readily apparent
    16 Leaf blades fully bipinnately compound (plants commonly more than 1 m tall; flowers in panicles usually more than 20 cm long; staminate and pistillate flowers separate, but the pistillate flowers have vestigial stamens; petals about 1 mm long; pistils usually 3) . . . . . ***Aruncus dioicus*** (*A. sylvester*), pl. 506
                              GOATSBEARD
    16 Leaf blades either not compound or only once-pinnately compound (in *Sanguisorba annua*, first choice 18, however, the leaflets are so deeply lobed that the leaves may seem to be bipinnately compound)
       17 Flowers (these individually small and inconspicuous) without petals; calyx 4-lobed (because the lobes alternate with small bracts, they could be mistaken for petals)
          18 Flowers sessile, densely crowded on the axis of a terminal inflorescence that is usually at least slightly longer than wide; leaves pinnately compound, sometimes nearly bipinnately compound; calyx tube, fused to the achene-forming portion of the pistil, becoming 4-angled (in certain species an inflorescence may have separate pistillate and staminate flowers) . . . . ***Sanguisorba***
          18 Flowers on distinct, even if short, pedicels, not densely crowded on the axis of an inflorescence; leaf blades either more or less fan-shaped or somewhat rounded, with several shallow lobes; calyx tube not becoming 4-angled . . . . ***Alchemilla-Aphanes*** **complex**
       17 Flowers with petals

19 Plants commonly more than 1 m tall; leaf blades pinnately compound, but the 1–2 pairs of lower leaflets small and sometimes inconspicuous, the terminal leaflet to more than 12 cm wide and palmately lobed, the lobes toothed; flowers in nearly flat-topped inflorescences; petals about 6 mm long, white; fruit a dry achene, flattened, hairy, the body of it about 4 mm long when fully mature, the persistent style nearly as long (known from along the Trask, Wilson, and Tillamook Rivers, Tillamook Co., Oreg., a few other localities in NW Oreg., and along the Naselle River, Pacific Co., Wash.) . . . .
. . . . *Filipendula occidentalis*
QUEEN-OF-THE-FOREST

19 Plants not conforming in all respects to the description in the other choice 19

  20 Petals (yellow) deeply 3- or 5- lobed at the tip (stamens 20–25; pistils numerous, becoming achenes embedded in the fleshy, strawberrylike receptacle but this not very juicy; garden plant, sometimes escaping) . . . . *Duchesnea indica*
INDIAN STRAWBERRY (India)

  20 Petals not deeply lobed at the tip

    21 Flowers borne singly on short, leafless stems; petals 7–10, white; pistils numerous, the styles that persist on the dry achenes becoming long and featherlike; leaf blades to about 3 cm long, 2–3 times as long as wide, the upper surface somewhat corrugated, the margins, with rounded teeth, typically rolled under; plants evergreen, forming mats that hug the ground (high montane, mostly well above 6000 ft., 1830 m, Alaska to the Cascades of Brit. Col. and Wash.; also eastward) . . . .
. . . . *Dryas octopetala* subsp. *hookeriana*, pl. 510
MOUNTAIN AVENS

    21 Plants not in all respects as described in the other choice 21

      22 Leaves regularly with 3 leaflets or lobes; plants low, sometimes spreading by stolons, often forming mats

        23 Fruits achenes, these developing singly in each of several pistils, neither fleshy nor becoming embedded in a fleshy receptacle (petals hairy, pale yellow; montane, mostly above 5000 ft., 1520 m, in our region) . . . . *Sibbaldia procumbens*

        23 Fruits either numerous achenes sunken in a fleshy receptacle like that of a strawberry or few, fleshy, 1-seeded, and forming an aggregate fruit like that of a raspberry or blackberry; petals not yellow

          24 Fruits achenes, these sunken into a fleshy receptacle, the whole mass becoming a strawberry
. . . . *Fragaria*

          24 Fruits small, fleshy, and 1-seeded, forming an aggregate like that of a raspberry or blackberry
. . . . *Rubus*

      22 Leaves either with more than 3 leaflets or lobes, or the plants upright, not spreading by stolons

        25 Calyx tube bearing a ring of numerous hooked bristles just below the lobes (plants sometimes to more than 1 m tall; leaf blades pinnately compound, with some leaflets much larger than others; inflorescence an elongated raceme, each flower originating above a small, lobed bract; petals to 4 mm long, yellow; pistils 2; achenes enclosed within the calyx tube, which becomes hardened and grooved) . . . . *Agrimonia*

        25 Calyx tube not bearing a ring of numerous hooked bristles

          26 Stamens 10 (leaves pinnately compound, the leaflets sometimes deeply divided) . . . . *Horkelia*

          26 Stamens more than 10, sometimes numerous

            27 Leaf blades to about 2 cm long, somewhat fan-shaped, divided once or twice into 3 slender-lobed portions, the lobes with pointed tips; petals 3–4 mm long, white; low, mat-forming, evergreen subshrub (inflorescences borne on upright stems 15–20 cm tall; in our region not often found below about 4500 ft., 1370 m, except on isolated peaks) . . . . . . *Luetkea pectinata*
PARTRIDGE FOOT

27 Leaf blades generally more than 2 cm long, pinnately or palmately divided into lobes, these not slender; petals often more than 5 mm long, not white; perennials dying down each winter, not at all shrubby

    28 Leaflets of larger basal leaves, in general, increasing gradually in size from the base of the leaf nearly to the tip . . . . *Geum*

    28 Leaflets of larger basal leaves not increasing markedly in size from the base nearly to the tip (furthermore, the leaflets of some species are palmately arranged) . . . . *Potentilla*

Agrimonia

1 Calyx tube conspicuously hairy (garden plant, sometimes escaping from cultivation) . . . . *A. eupatoria*
                                                          AGRIMONY (Europe)

1 Calyx tube, if at all hairy, with only a few stiff hairs near the base (mostly E of the Rocky Mountains but present in Calif., SW Oreg., and in some other places in W North America) . . . . *A. gryposepala*
                                                          TALL AGRIMONY

Alchemilla-Aphanes Complex

1 Plants perennial, commonly at least 30 cm tall; leaf blades rounded, with several shallow, rather evenly toothed lobes, and with a deep notch where the petiole is inserted; flowers in cymes or panicles at the ends of the stems (garden plant, occasionally established in natural areas) . . . . *Alchemilla subcrenata* (*A. vulgaris* of some references)
                                                         LADY'S MANTLE (Europe)

1 Plants annual, rarely so much as 10 cm tall; leaf blades more or less fan-shaped, not much more than 1 cm long, with a few proportionately deep lobes, and with a wedge-shaped base; flowers extremely small, borne in the axils of the leaves

    2 Leaf blades not more than 5 mm long; calyx surrounding mature fruit not more than 1.8 mm long . . . .
    . . . . *Aphanes microcarpa*
                                              SMALL-FRUITED PARSLEY PIERT (Europe)

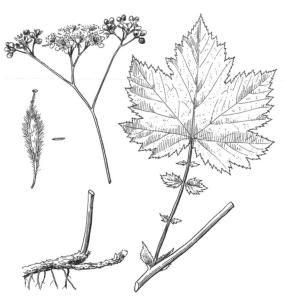

Filipendula occidentalis,
queen-of-the-forest

Luetkea pectinata,
partridge foot

2 Leaf blades to 8 mm long; calyx surrounding mature fruit to 2.5 mm long . . . .
. . . . **Aphanes arvensis** (*A. occidentalis, Alchemilla occidentalis*), pl. 505

FIELD PARSLEY PIERT

The name *A. occidentalis* was applied to what was believed to be a native species, and it may indeed be indigenous. It is not, however, easily separable from European *A. arvensis,* although it is true that this plant, on average, is more robust (to 20 cm tall) and has slightly larger leaf blades (to 10 mm long). Perhaps a definitive study of the relationship of *A. occidentalis* and *A. arvensis* will appear. In the meantime, *A. occidentalis* is a perfectly acceptable name for plants in our region.

Amelanchier

1 Pistil usually with 2–4 styles (occasionally 5); leaf blades pale, somewhat grayish green, the upper and lower surfaces, including midribs and veins, with abundant hairs (SW Oreg. to Calif., also extending far E of the Cascades) . . . .*A. utahensis* (includes *A. pallida*)

UTAH SERVICEBERRY

1 Pistil usually with 5 styles; leaf blades green, the upper and lower surfaces without hairs or with only widely scattered hairs

2 Petals commonly 11–15 mm long; upper portion of fruit-forming part of the pistil usually not conspicuously hairy (widespread W of the Cascades, also found in some habitats E of the Cascades) . . . .
. . . . *A. alnifolia* subsp. *semiintegrifolia* (*A. florida*), pl. 504

SERVICEBERRY

2 Petals rarely more than 12 mm long; upper portion of the fruit-forming part of the pistil usually very hairy (W of the Cascades in Wash. and Brit. Col.) . . . . *A. alnifolia* subsp. *humptulipensis*

Cercocarpus

1 Leaf blades 2–3 cm long, 3–4 times as long as wide, not toothed, the margin rolled under (in our region limited to the Siskiyou Mountains, and there mostly above 3000 ft., 910 m; widespread E of the Cascades, and also in Calif.) . . . .*C. ledifolius* var. *ledifolius*

MOUNTAIN MAHOGANY

1 Leaf blades commonly 3–5 cm long, rarely so much as twice as long as wide, toothed above the middle, the margin not rolled under

2 Leaf blades to 4 cm long, more or less oval except for the wedge-shaped basal portion, with 4–7 lateral veins (in our region found only in SW Oreg., also in Calif.) . . . . *C. betuloides* var. *betuloides*, pl. 507

BIRCH-LEAVED MOUNTAIN MAHOGANY, PLUME TREE

2 Leaf blades to 8 cm long, rather distinctly rhomboid in outline, with 6–12 lateral veins (in our region found only in SW Oreg., also in Calif.) . . . . *C. betuloides* var. *macrourus*

Many specimens do not fit perfectly into *C. betuloides* var. *betuloides* or var. *macrourus.*

Crataegus

1 Leaf blades conspicuously lobed; fruits red

2 Leaf blades with 3–7 lobes; fruits usually with only 1 stone (this, like the stone of a peach, plum, or apricot, consists of the seed and the hardened inner portion of the fruit) . . . . *C. monogyna*, pl. 509

HAWTHORN (Europe)

See note under *C. douglasii,* choice 3.

2 Leaf blades with 3–5 lobes; fruits usually with 2 stones . . . . *C. laevigata* (*C. oxyacantha*)

QUICKSET HAWTHORN (Europe, N Africa, W Asia)

1 Leaf blades coarsely toothed but not often truly lobed; fruits blackish

3 Most flowers with 10 stamens; leaf blades (especially those on short side branches) sometimes distinctly lobed (in our region mostly in the Puget Trough; widespread E of the Cascades) . . . .
. . . . *C. douglasii* var. *douglasii*, pl. 508

DOUGLAS' HAWTHORN, BLACK HAWTHORN

3 Most flowers with 20 stamens; leaf blades, even those on short side branches, coarsely toothed but rarely distinctly lobed) .... ***C. douglasii* var. *suksdorfii***
SUKSDORF'S HAWTHORN

Crataegus douglasii vars. *douglasii* and *suksdorfii* may also be viewed as separate species. Apparent hybrids of *C. monogyna* and *C. douglasii* var. *suksdorfii* have been noted in areas where these occur together.

Fragaria

Fragaria virginiana and *F. vesca* vary so much that no attempt is made here to distinguish named varieties. Furthermore, the two species intergrade to some extent. *Fragaria chiloensis* is probably more stable, but it also intergrades with the others and its genes have in fact been used, along with those of *F. virginiana,* to create the cultivated strawberry, sometimes called *F.* ×*ananassa.*

1 Plants limited to backshores and bluffs at the coast; leaves thick, somewhat leathery .... ***F. chiloensis***
COAST STRAWBERRY, BEACH STRAWBERRY

On some specimens (subsp. *lucida*) the hairs on the stems and leaf petioles are pressed down; on others (subsp. *pacifica*) the hairs stand straight outward.

1 Plants not usually found on backshores and bluffs at the coast; leaves neither especially thick nor leathery
2 Leaflets slightly bluish green, the upper surface not obviously hairy; terminal tooth of each leaflet usually much smaller than the teeth on both sides of it; usually in open places ....
.... ***F. virginiana*** (includes vars. *glauca* and *platypetala*)
WESTERN STRAWBERRY
2 Leaflets green, the upper surface obviously hairy; terminal tooth of each leaflet usually at least as long as the teeth on both sides of it; usually in somewhat shaded habitats ....
.... ***F. vesca*** (includes vars. *americana, bracteata,* and *californica*)
WOOD STRAWBERRY

Geum

1 Calyx lobes remaining more or less upright; petals not often more than 4 mm long, pale yellow, sometimes tinged with pink or reddish purple; style only slightly bent near the hairy tip, until the tip falls off (on Saddle Mountain, Clatsop Co., Oreg., and the Olympic Peninsula, Wash.; also in Calif.) ....
.... *G. triflorum* subsp. *campanulatum*
WESTERN RED AVENS

1 Calyx lobes turning downward soon after the flowers open; petals at least 4 mm long, bright yellow; style on achenes with a U-shaped bend before continuing as a short, hairy tip
2 Stipules of leaves on middle and upper portions of the stems decidedly longer than wide, much smaller than the larger leaflets or lobes of the blades, at most with only a few teeth and usually tapering to a point; petals generally 5–9 mm long and with a slight indentation at the tip; receptacles, at the time fruits are well developed, with few hairs, these less than 1 mm long
..... *G. macrophyllum* var. *macrophyllum,* pl. 511
LARGE-LEAVED AVENS

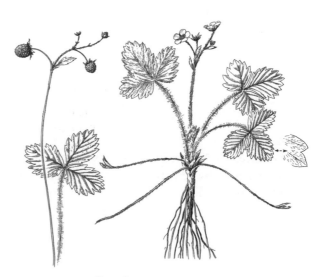

Fragaria vesca,
wood strawberry

2 Stipules on leaves of middle and upper portions of stems nearly or fully as wide as long, often at least half as wide as the larger leaflets or lobes of the blades, extensively toothed and rounded at the tip; petals generally 4–6 mm long and without an indentation at the tip; receptacles, at the time fruits are well developed, with crowded hairs at least 1 mm long (weed) .... *G. urbanum*
WOOD AVENS (Europe)

Horkelia

1 Leaflets of lower leaves divided at the tip into 2–3 teeth (flowers usually in dense, headlike inflorescences)
  2 Petals not obviously longer than the sepals and not conspicuously broadened near the tip, only about 1 mm wide (Douglas, Jackson, and Josephine Cos., Oreg., to Calif.) .... *H. tridentata* var. *tridentata*
THREE-TOOTHED HORKELIA, CLUSTERED HORKELIA
  2 Petals longer than the sepals and conspicuously broadened to a width of at least 2 mm (sometimes 4 mm) near the tip
    3 Teeth at the tips of lower leaves 2 to several times as long as wide (Willamette Valley to S Oreg.) .... *H. congesta* var. *congesta*
DENSE-FLOWERED HORKELIA
    3 Teeth at the tips of lower leaves scarcely if at all longer than wide (Josephine Co., Oreg., to Calif.) .... *H. congesta* var. *nemorosa*
Horkelia congesta vars. *congesta* and *nemorosa* intergrade.
1 Most leaflets of lower leaves deeply divided into 2 to several lobes
  4 Stipules divided into several nearly hairlike segments
    5 Leaflets divided into several lobes, these about 1 mm wide, and some of them separated nearly to the base (Jackson Co., Oreg., to Calif.) .... *H. daucifolia*
CARROT-LEAVED HORKELIA
    5 Leaflets divided for as much as two-thirds of their length into 2–3 lobes (Josephine and Curry Cos., Oreg., to Calif.) .... *H. sericata*
SILKY HORKELIA
  4 Stipules not divided into nearly hairlike segments (but they may be divided into a few lobes)
    6 Primary leaflets only shallowly divided into short lobes; leaves so hairy as to appear white- or gray-silky (high montane, Jackson Co., Oreg., to Calif.) .... *H. hendersonii*
HENDERSON'S HORKELIA
    6 Primary leaflets deeply divided into slender lobes; leaves not so hairy as to appear white- or gray-silky (in the Cascades of Oreg., mostly above 3000 ft., 910 m) .... *H. fusca*
PINE-WOODS HORKELIA
Specimens found on the W slope of the Cascades fit best in *H. fusca* var. *filicoides;* other varieties occur on the E side of the crest.

Potentilla

1 Petals reddish or purple; receptacle somewhat spongy, slightly resembling a strawberry that has not developed normally (leaves pinnately compound; restricted to marshes and bogs) ....
.... *P. palustris*, pl. 519
MARSH CINQUEFOIL
In many references the distinctive *P. palustris* is placed in a separate genus, *Comarum.*

Horkelia congesta var. *congesta,* dense-flowered horkelia

1 Petals usually some shade of yellow, sometimes white or cream; receptacle not spongy

  2 Leaves palmately compound

    3 None of the leaves with more than 3 leaflets

      4 Plants somewhat shrubby, the flowering stems to about 25 cm long and usually to at least some extent upright; basal leaves only slightly hairy, green on both surfaces (montane in the Olympic Mountains, Wash., and Cascades, mostly above 4000 ft., 1220 m) .... *P. flabellifolia*
FANLEAF CINQUEFOIL

      4 Plants tufted, low, the flowering stems rarely longer than 15 cm and generally not upright; basal leaves densely hairy, especially on the underside, which is conspicuously whitish or grayish (on coastal bluffs and rocks above the shore, Alaska to S Brit. Col., and inland in the Cascades and Olympic Mountains, Wash., mostly well above 4000 ft., 1220 m) ... *P. villosa* var. *parviflora*, pl. 520
ARCTIC CINQUEFOIL

    3 At least the basal leaves with 5 or more leaflets

      5 Flowers usually with 4 petals and 4 sepals (sometimes 5 of each); stems long, at first upright, then falling down, sometimes rooting at the nodes .... *P. anglica*
ENGLISH CINQUEFOIL (Europe)

        Potentilla anglica is apparently the plant called *P. procumbens* in some references dealing with the flora of our area. It was described by John Sibthorp in 1794 and is not the same as the *P. procumbens* based on Linnaeus' *Sibbaldia procumbens* of 1753 (p. 310).

      5 Flowers with 5 petals and 5 sepals; stems not prostrate

        6 Petals usually dull cream-yellow; stamens usually more than 20; leaflets 5–7; mature achenes with a pattern of raised ridges .... *P. recta*
PALE CINQUEFOIL (Europe)

        6 Petals usually clear, bright yellow; stamens usually 20; leaflets 5–9; mature achenes nearly smooth
.... *P. gracilis*
SLENDER CINQUEFOIL

        Of the several varieties of *P. gracilis* that have been named, at least 3 are in our region. You can try to separate them by the key below.

       7 Lobes or teeth of leaflets separated for not more than about half the distance to the midrib

        8 Underside of leaflets typically densely white-hairy, the upper surface green and scarcely hairy
.... *P. gracilis* var. *gracilis*, pl. 518

        8 Underside of leaflets only slightly hairy, about as green as the upper surface ....
.... *P. gracilis* var. *fastigiata*

       7 Lobes of leaflets separated for at least three-fourths the distance to the midrib

        9 Some lobes of leaflets typically with a few teeth .... *P. gracilis* var. *flabelliformis*

        9 Lobes of leaflets not toothed .... *P. gracilis* var. *elmeri*

  2 Leaves pinnately compound

  10 Plants shrubby, with shredding bark; leaflets (these silky-hairy) not divided into lobes; fruit-forming portion of pistils densely hairy, the hairs persisting on the mature achenes (in the Olympic Mountains, Wash.; also in the Cascades but mostly E of the crest and mostly above 4000 ft., 1220 m) ... *P. fruticosa*
SHRUBBY CINQUEFOIL

      Potentilla fruticosa is sometimes placed in the genus *Pentaphylloides* because it is shrubby and its achenes are hairy. Furthermore, as early as 1813, North American specimens were given the species name *floribunda,* although they seem not to be conspicuously distinct from Eurasian plants.

  10 Plants not shrubby; leaflets divided into lobes; neither the fruit-forming portion of the pistils nor the achenes hairy

    11 Flowers borne singly on stems that are leafless except at the base; plants spreading by stolons that root at the nodes; in wet places, including seepage areas, borders of salt marshes, and bogs ....
.... *P. anserina* subsp. *pacifica* (*P. pacifica*), pl. 516
PACIFIC CINQUEFOIL

11 Flowers borne in branched inflorescences; plants not spreading by stolons; not necessarily in wet places

  12 Pistils with the style attached close to the tip

    13 Basal leaves typically with 2 pairs of lateral leaflets, those of the lower pair originating so close to the upper pair that the leaf as a whole is nearly palmately lobed (Olympic Mountains, Wash., and the Cascades, mostly E of the crest) ....*P. diversifolia* var. *diversifolia*
                                                      DIVERSE-LEAVED CINQUEFOIL

    13 Basal leaves with at least leaflets or lobes, these pinnately arranged, the pairs well separated

      14 Lateral leaflets (usually 8–12; the blade as a whole about twice as long as wide) white-hairy, usually appearing silky (montane, mostly E of the crest of the Cascades except in SW Oreg.)
      .... *P. drummondii* var. *breweri*
                                                   BREWER'S CINQUEFOIL

      14 Leaflets hairy but not silky hairy

        15 Leaflets gray-hairy, typically overlapping (SW Oreg.) ....*P. drummondii* var. *bruceae*
                                                MRS. BRUCE'S CINQUEFOIL

        15 Leaflets green, usually not overlapping (montane, in the Olympic Mountains, Wash., SW Oreg., and in the Cascades, but mostly E of the Cascades) .... *P. drummondii* var. *drummondii*
                                                DRUMMOND'S CINQUEFOIL

  12 Pistils with the style attached at about the middle or below the middle

    16 Pistils with the style attached at about the middle; branches of the inflorescence typically bunched together (corolla white to pale yellow; montane and mostly E of the crest of the Cascades) ....
    .... *P. arguta* var. *convallaria*
                                                   TALL CINQUEFOIL

    16 Pistils with the style attached well below the middle; branches of the inflorescence not bunched together (stems sometimes densely glandular-hairy; common lowland species, well represented W of the Cascades) .... *P. glandulosa*
                                                  STICKY CINQUEFOIL

        Potentilla glandulosa is conventionally divided into varieties, several of which are in our region. Considering the extent to which they intergrade, use the key below with caution.

    17 Petals no longer than the sepals, often distinctly shorter

      18 Petals usually 5–7 mm long, nearly as wide as long, cream or pale yellow ....
      .... *P. glandulosa* var. *glandulosa*, pl. 517

      18 Petals usually 3–5 mm long, distinctly longer than wide, yellow ...... *P. glandulosa* var. *reflexa*

    17 Petals typically at least 1 mm longer than the sepals

      19 Petals 8–10 mm long, clear yellow (S Oreg. to Calif.) .... *P. glandulosa* var. *ashlandica*

      19 Petals 4–8 mm long, cream (rather high montane) .... *P. glandulosa* var. *nevadensis*

Prunus

Prunus avium (sweet cherry), *P. cerasus* (sour cherry), *P. domestica* (garden plum), *P. cerasifera* (cherry plum), and *P. persica* (peach), all widely cultivated, occasionally turn up in places where they have not intentionally been planted. These trees, at least some of them familiar to most persons, have not been included in this key.

1 Flowers usually more than 30 in each elongated raceme (leaves to about 10 cm long, twice as long as wide, drawn out into a point at the tip; petals 4–6 mm long; fruits red to purplish black) ....
.... *P. virginiana* subsp. *demissa*, pl. 522
                                                   CHOKECHERRY

        Two species of *Prunus* introduced from Europe also have elongated racemes with many flowers. One of them is *P. laurocerasus*, cherry laurel, commonly grown as a small tree or in the form of a hedge; it is evergreen, with large, stiff leaf blades that are not much more than twice as long as wide. The other is *P. serotina*, black cherry, a large tree with deciduous leaves whose thin blades may be nearly 3 times as long as wide. The fruits of both species are purplish black when ripe.

1 Flowers not more than about 12 in each inflorescence, sometimes only 1–4

  2 Stems bearing sharp-tipped side branches functioning as thorns

    3 Most larger leaf blades about twice as long as wide; plants typically very thorny; fruits to about 15 mm long, too sour to be eaten; occasionally intentionally planted and sometimes escaping . . . . . *P. spinosa*
                                                   BLACKTHORN (Europe)

    3 Most larger leaf blades much less than twice as long as wide; plants typically with only a few thorns; fruits to about 20 mm long, sweet when ripe (in our region largely restricted to the Willamette Valley from Marion Co. to the Umpqua River valley and some other areas of S Oreg.; also in Calif.) . . . . *P. subcordata*
                                             WESTERN PLUM, SIERRA PLUM

  2 Stems not bearing sharp-tipped side branches functioning as thorns

    4 Petals 5–7 mm long; fruit about 1 cm long, red or purple (leaf blades about 5 cm long, twice as long as wide, blunt at the tip; typically a tree with a single main trunk) . . . . . *P. emarginata* var. *mollis,* pl. 521
                                                        BITTER CHERRY

        Prunus emarginata var. *emarginata,* which typically forms several-stemmed, somewhat shrubby growths, is found in the Olympic Mountains and E of the crest of the Cascades, perhaps occasionally W of the crest. There may be no compelling reason to bother with the varietal names.

    4 Petals usually 6–10 mm long

      5 Leaves pointed at the tip; flowers as many as about 12 in each inflorescence; fruits 6–8 mm long, red to nearly black (used as a stock for bud grafts of cherries and occasionally becoming established in situations where it may appear to be native) . . . . *P. mahaleb*
                                         SAINT LUCIE'S CHERRY (Europe)

      5 Leaves not pointed at the tip; flowers usually only 2–3 in each cluster; fruit about 2 cm long, usually dark red or reddish purple (in our region largely restricted to the Willamette Valley from Marion Co. S to the Umpqua River valley and to some other areas of S Oreg.; also in Calif.) . . . . *P. subcordata*
                                           WESTERN PLUM, SIERRA PLUM

Rosa

1 At least some sepals fringed with slender lobes (prickles conspicuously down-curved, with stout bases; sepals very glandular; escapes from cultivation)

  2 Undersides and edges of leaflets, also petioles, with abundant stalked glands; petals 2 cm long, pink (foliage fragrant) . . . . *R. eglanteria*
                                        SWEETBRIER, EGLANTINE (Europe)

  2 Undersides of leaflets sometimes hairy, especially along the midrib, but not conspicuously glandular; petals 2–2.5 cm long, white to pink . . . . *R. canina*
                                                  DOG ROSE (Europe)

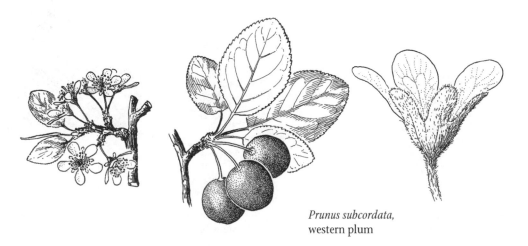

Prunus subcordata,
western plum

1 Sepals not fringed with slender lobes (in *R. gymnocarpa* the sepals are shed soon after the fruit has partly developed)

  3 Prickles crowded, slender to stout, not down-curved; petals about 5 cm long, purplish pink (escaping from cultivation) . . . . **R. rugosa**
                                                                                  JAPANESE BRIER (Asia)

  3 Plants, if with crowded straight prickles, not with petals so much as 5 cm long (native species)

    4 Prickles slender, numerous, scattered all along the stems; sepals shed early, even before the fruit has reached its full size, about 1 cm long (petals to about 1.5 cm long, dark pink, often not evenly colored; mature fruits bright red; usually in partly shaded habitats) . . . . **R. gymnocarpa**, pl. 523
                                                             WOOD ROSE, BALD-HIP ROSE

    4 Prickles, whether slender or stout, usually widely scattered; sepals persisting on mature fruits

      5 Some or all prickles enlarging gradually to bases that are at least half as wide as the prickles are long

        6 Tips of prickles straight; flowers generally solitary; petals usually about 2.5 cm long; mature fruits orange or orange-red . . . . **R. nutkana** subsp. **nutkana**, pl. 524
                                                            NOOTKA ROSE

        6 Tips of at least some prickles curving downward; flowers generally clustered; petals to 2 cm long; mature fruits red (in our region only in Josephine and Jackson Cos., Oreg.; to Calif.) . . . . . . **R. californica**
                                                           CALIFORNIA ROSE

    5 Prickles slender for most of their length, their bases generally much less than half as wide as the prickles are long

      7 Plants commonly more than 1.5 m tall; prickles restricted to the nodes and sometimes absent from a considerable portion of the plant; teeth of leaflet margins without secondary teeth; petals to 2 cm long; fruits usually longer than wide, without stalked glands (often growing in or near wet habitats) . . . . **R. pisocarpa**, pl. 525
                                                            CLUSTERED WILD ROSE

      7 Plants rarely more than 50 cm tall; prickles not restricted to the nodes and generally present throughout the plant; teeth of leaflet margins usually with secondary teeth; petals to 1.5 cm long; fruits spherical, typically with stalked glands (Lane Co., Oreg., to Calif.) . . . . **R. spithamea** subsp. **spithamea**
                                                          DWARF ROSE, GROUND ROSE

Rubus

1 Mat-forming plants without prickles, or prickly vines with slender, trailing or clambering stems not so much as 5 mm thick

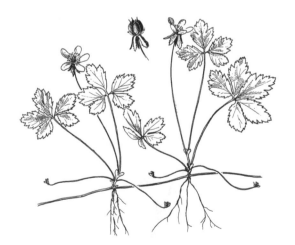

Rubus pedatus,
strawberry bramble

Rubus nivalis,
snow bramble

2 Plants without prickles, spreading by stolons and forming mats; all or most flowers with both stamens and pistils (pistils fleshy but cohering only slightly when ripe)

    3 Leaf blades consisting of only 3 leaflets; pistils usually 7–15 (mostly montane, at low and moderate elevations) . . . . ***R. lasiococcus***
       HAIRY-FRUITED DWARF BRAMBLE

    3 Most leaf blades consisting of 5 leaflets; pistils usually 3–6 (from the lowlands to rather high elevations in the mountains) . . . . ***R. pedatus***
       STRAWBERRY BRAMBLE

2 Plants with curved prickles, creeping or vining but not producing stolons; staminate and pistillate flowers on separate plants

    4 Deciduous vine, trailing or climbing into shrubs; most leaves compound, with 3 leaflets; blackberry with numerous individual fruits . . . . ***R. ursinus*** (*R. vitifolius*)
       DEWBERRY, TRAILING BLACKBERRY

    4 Creeping evergreen vine; leaf blades ranging from heart-shaped to 3-lobed or even divided into 2–3 separate leaflets (stipules about half as wide as long; petals pink to dull purple; blackberry with only a few relatively large, 3-mm, individual fruits; mostly in the mountains but occasionally as low as 1000 ft., 300 m) . . . . ***R. nivalis***
       SNOW BRAMBLE

1 Shrub usually at least 1 m tall, or coarse, woody vine with some stems at least 1 cm thick

  5 Shrub with most stems upright; aggregate of fruits forming a raspberry (when picked, the aggregate separates cleanly from the receptacle)

    6 Leaves palmately lobed (stems without prickles; petals white, usually about 2 cm long; raspberry about as wide as long, pinkish red when ripe) . . . . ***R. parviflorus***, pl. 526
       THIMBLEBERRY

    6 Leaves compound, most of them with 3 leaflets

      7 Petals deep purplish red; stems with straight prickles or none, and without a whitish or purplish coating; raspberry yellow to orange or red, longer than wide; plants usually forming thickets in moist habitats . . . . ***R. spectabilis***, pl. 527
       SALMONBERRY

      7 Petals (often not developing equally) white; stems with stout, down-curved prickles and with a whitish or purplish coating; raspberry purplish blue to nearly black, about as wide as long; usually growing in sunny, relatively dry habitats . . . . ***R. leucodermis*** subsp. *leucodermis*
       BLACKCAP

Rubus leucodermis subsp.
leucodermis, blackcap

Rubus laciniatus,
evergreen blackberry

5 Coarse, woody vine with sprawling, rather than upright, stems; aggregate of fruits forming a blackberry (when picked, it does not separate from the receptacle; at least many leaves with 5 or more leaflets; prickles pointing downward)

    8 Leaflets deeply lobed; most leaves usually persisting through the winter ....*R. laciniatus*, p. 319
                                           EVERGREEN BLACKBERRY (Europe)

    8 Leaflets toothed but not lobed; leaves deciduous

        9 Leaves not so hairy on the underside as to appear grayish or whitish (introduced in a few localities)
          .... *R. macrophyllus*
                                      LARGE-LEAVED BLACKBERRY (Europe)

        9 Leaflets so hairy on the underside that they appear whitish

           10 Inflorescence without stalked glands (very common, aggressive, and generally undesirable but nevertheless producing a lot of berries for jam and pie makers) ....
              ....*R. armeniacus* (*R. discolor* or *R. procerus* of some references)
                                   HIMALAYAN BLACKBERRY (Asia)

           10 Inflorescence (especially the pedicels) with stalked glands (not yet common) ....*R. vestitus*
                                     BLACKBERRY (Europe)

               Rubus allegheniensis var. *allegheniensis,* mountain blackberry or Allegheny blackberry, native to the E United States, is reported to have been introduced in Brit. Col. Like *R. vestitus,* its pedicels have stalked glands, but its berries are distinctly elongated rather than round, and its leaflets are more slender, sometimes fully twice as long as wide.

Sanguisorba

1 Leaflets deeply divided into narrow lobes, most of these less than 2 mm wide; stamens 2; annual or biennial
    ....*S. annua* (*S. occidentalis*), pl. 528
                                       WESTERN BURNET, ANNUAL BURNET

1 Leaflets coarsely toothed but not deeply divided into lobes; stamens at least 4; perennial

    2 Leaflets generally 1–1.5 cm long; each head with many separate staminate and pistillate flowers (the staminate flowers mostly below the pistillate ones); stamens 12 (established at scattered localities) ....
          ....*S. minor* **subsp.** *muricata*
                                      GARDEN BURNET (Europe)

    2 Most leaflets at least 2 cm long; all flowers with pistils and stamens; stamens 4

        3 Filaments of stamens about as long as the sepals, not becoming flattened and wider above the middle (in bogs and other wet habitats, especially along the coast in our region, but with a wide distribution in N North America, Europe, and Asia) ....*S. officinalis* (*S. microcephala*)
                                      GREAT BURNET, RED BURNET

        3 Filaments of stamens 2–3 times as long as the sepals, becoming flattened and wider above the middle

           4 Sepals conspicuously reddish or purplish; filaments of stamens about twice as long as the sepals (in coastal bogs and other wet habitats, Alaska to Wash.) ....*S. menziesii*
                                      MENZIES' BURNET

           4 Sepals greenish or slightly reddish; filaments of stamens nearly or fully 3 times as long as the sepals (in wet habitats, mostly in the mountains, Alaska to Oreg. and eastward; also in Asia) ....
          ....*S. canadensis* (*S. sitchensis*), pl. 529
                                    CANADA BURNET, SITKA BURNET

Sorbus

1 Substantial tree; leaves with 11–17 leaflets (commonly planted in towns and cities, and sometimes escaping to natural areas) ....*S. aucuparia*
                                      ROWAN (Europe)

               This tree, often called European mountain ash, is not a true ash, but then neither are the next 2 species.

1 Large shrubs or small trees; leaves with 7–13 leaflets (montane, W slopes of the Cascades in Brit. Col. and Wash., and in the Olympic Mountains, Wash., and not likely to be found below 4000 ft., 1220 m)

2 Leaves with as many as 13 leaflets, these usually about 3 times as long as wide and pointed at the tip; pistils with 3–4 styles; fruits orange to bright red, rather shiny .... *S. scopulina* **var.** *cascadensis*, pl. 530
WESTERN MOUNTAIN ASH

2 Leaves with as many as 11 leaflets, these at most only slightly longer than wide, not pointed at the tip; pistils with 2–3 styles; fruits red but dull, with a slightly grayish or bluish tinge ... *S. sitchensis* **var.** *grayi*, pl. 531
SITKA MOUNTAIN ASH

Spiraea

1 Inflorescence a nearly flat-topped corymb
    2 Inflorescence usually not more than 4 cm in diameter; petals pink to rose (montane, mostly well above 2500 ft., 760 m) .... *S. densiflora*, pl. 533
MOUNTAIN SPIRAEA

    2 Inflorescence commonly 4–8 cm in diameter; petals white or with only a faintly pinkish or lavender tint .... *S. betulifolia* **var.** *lucida*, pl. 532
WHITE SPIRAEA

1 Inflorescence a rounded or elongated corymb
    3 Petals white or pale pink; inflorescence pyramidal, not often so much as twice as long as wide ....
.... *S. pyramidata*
(probably *S. betulifolia* subsp. *lucida* × *S. douglasii* subsp. *menziesii* or subsp. *douglasii*), pl. 535
PYRAMIDAL SPIRAEA

    3 Petals deep pink or rose; inflorescence elongated, usually more than twice as long as wide
        4 Leaf blades densely grayish hairy on the underside (common in the lowlands W of the Cascades) ....
.... *S. douglasii* **subsp.** *douglasii*, pl. 534
DOUGLAS' HARDHACK

        4 Leaf blades, if hairy on the underside, not densely so (mostly at low to moderate elevations W of the crest of the Cascades, and widespread E of the crest) .... *S. douglasii* **subsp.** *menziesii*
MENZIES' HARDHACK

Many specimens cannot positively be assigned to *S. douglasii* subsp. *douglasii* or subsp. *menziesii*.

RUBIACEAE Madder Family

The large madder family includes coffee, cinchona (the source of quinine), and gardenia, all of which are substantial shrubs. The species growing wild in Oregon, Washington, and British Columbia, however, are either completely herbaceous or only slightly woody at the base. Their leaves appear to be in whorls, but in fact they are in pairs; the whorled arrangement is due to the presence of stipules that resemble the true leaves. The flowers, with few exceptions, have a four-lobed, tubular corolla and four stamens. The portion of the pistil that develops into the fruit is united with the calyx and is below the level at which the petals and stamens originate. Calyx lobes are poorly developed or absent. In most of the species in our region, the fruit consists of two lobes, which eventually separate as dry, one-seeded nutlets. Almost all belong to the genus *Galium*. The fruits of some of them are covered with hooked bristles that cling to clothing, especially socks and pant legs. The four-angled stems of galiums are also often studded with bristles that engage clothing. In this key, no distinction is made between stipules and true leaves; all members of a whorl are called leaves.

Kelloggia galioides, characterized by opposite instead of whorled leaves and by a white or pink corolla that has a conspicuous tube, is common in montane areas east of the crest of the Cascades. There are only a few reports of it crossing over to the western slope.

1 Corolla pale pink or pale blue, the tube longer than the 4 lobes, these directed upward as much as outward (weed common in lawns, orchards, vacant lots, and other disturbed habitats) .... *Sherardia arvensis*, pl. 538
FIELD MADDER (Mediterranean region)

1 Corolla white, greenish, yellowish, or purplish, the 3–4 lobes longer than the tube and spreading outward
.... *Galium*

Galium

1 Most or all corollas with 3 lobes (plants sometimes annual, sometimes perennial)

 2 Leaves 2–4 at each node; flowers usually single at each node; stems smooth .... *G. bifolium*
LOW MOUNTAIN BEDSTRAW

 2 Leaves 4–6 at each node; flowers usually at least 2–3 at each node, sometimes many; stems usually roughened by downward-pointed prickles along the angles (corolla about 1.5 mm wide; fruit smooth; in wet habitats) ....*G. trifidum* subsp. *columbianum* (*G. trifidum* subsp. *pacificum, G. cymosum*)
SMALL BEDSTRAW

   Plants of high-montane meadows, which form rather tight mats or tufts instead of straggly growths typical of *G. trifidum* subsp. *columbianum,* can be segregated as *G. trifidum* var. *pusillum.*

1 Most or all corollas with 4 lobes

 3 Leaves in whorls of 4

  4 All flowers with stamens and a pistil; fruit consisting of a pair of nutlets (leaves oval, to 3 cm long, about twice as long as wide; nutlets densely covered with hooked hairs; in moist woods, generally above 1500 ft., 460 m; Wash. to Calif.) ....*G. oreganum*
OREGON BEDSTRAW

  4 Staminate and pistillate plants separate; fruit fleshy

   5 Plants forming low, often dense mats, the tips of the stems usually not rising so much as 5 cm; leaves slender, more than 7 times as long as wide

    6 Leaves not often more than 10 mm long, rather sharp-tipped; flowers about 2 mm wide (Josephine Co., Oreg., to Calif.) ....*G. andrewsii,* pl. 536
ANDREWS' BEDSTRAW

    6 Leaves to about 15 mm long, tapering to a point but not sharp-tipped; flowers about 3 mm wide (Josephine and Jackson Cos., Oreg., to Calif.) ....*G. ambiguum* subsp. *siskiyouense*
SISKIYOU BEDSTRAW

   5 Plants generally with some substantial upright or climbing stems; leaves oval or narrowly oval, not so much as 4 times as long as wide

    7 Stems with short prickles, these of assistance in climbing (S Oreg. to Calif. and Baja Calif.) ......
....*G. porrigens* subsp. *porrigens*
CLIMBING BEDSTRAW

    7 Stems without prickles and not climbing

     8 Leaves of one pair in each whorl usually distinctly smaller than those of the other pair; stems and leaves not obviously hairy (Jackson Co., Oreg., to Calif.) ....*G. bolanderi*
BOLANDER'S BEDSTRAW

     8 All 4 leaves in each whorl of the same or nearly the same size; stems and leaves usually obviously hairy (Josephine Co., Oreg., to Calif.) ....*G. californicum* subsp. *californicum*
CALIFORNIA BEDSTRAW

 3 Leaves in whorls of 5–8, at least on the main stems (sometimes 4 on smaller branches of *G. mollugo,* sometimes 10 on *G. odoratum;* plants generally upright)

  9 Leaves not often so much as 10 mm long

   10 Most leaves in whorls of 6; fruit with hooked hairs ....*G. parisiense*
WALL BEDSTRAW (Mediterranean region)

   10 Number of leaves in each whorl varying from 5 to 8; fruit without hooked hairs ....*G. divaricatum*
LAMARCK'S BEDSTRAW (Mediterranean region)

  9 Leaves mostly more than 15 mm long

   11 Leaves regularly in whorls of 6; flowers regularly 3 at each node (fruit with hooked hairs; mostly in woods) ....*G. triflorum*
FRAGRANT BEDSTRAW

   11 Leaves mostly in whorls of 6–8 (sometimes 4 on smaller branches of *G. mollugo,* sometimes 10 on *G. odoratum*); flowers not regularly 3 at each node

12 Most inflorescences with at least 10 flowers, sometimes many; stems smooth (except for bristles at the stem nodes in *G. odoratum*)

  13 Leaves not often more than 25 mm long nor more than 4 mm wide; flowers to 4 mm wide; fruits smooth, often becoming black as they age; stems smooth .... ***G. mollugo***
                                                       WILD MADDER (Europe)

  13 Leaves to more than 40 mm long and more than 10 mm wide; flowers 6–7 mm wide; fruits densely covered with hooked hairs; stems with bristles at the nodes (garden plant with sweetly scented flowers, sometimes escaping) .... ***G. odoratum*** (*Asperula odorata*)
                                            SWEET WOODRUFF (Europe)

12 Inflorescences typically with 3–5 flowers; stems with downward-pointing prickles

  14 Fruit roughened by small bumps but without hooked hairs; pairs of nutlets usually slightly more than 4 mm wide; pedicels of ripening fruits turning downward ....
    .... ***G. tricornutum*** (*T. tricorne* of some references)
                            ROUGH-FRUITED CORN BEDSTRAW (Europe)

  14 Fruit either smooth or with hooked hairs; pairs of nutlets usually not more than 4 mm wide (exclusive of the hooked hairs); pedicels of fruits not turning downward

    15 Corollas white, usually 1.6–2 mm wide; fruits typically with hooked hairs, rarely smooth, the pairs of nutlets (exclusive of the hooked hairs) about 4 mm wide .... ***G. aparine***, pl. 537
                                              CLEAVERS

    15 Corollas slightly greenish or yellowish, not more than about 1.5 mm wide; fruit typically smooth but sometimes with hooked hairs, the pairs of nutlets not more than about 3 mm wide (uncommon weed) .... ***G. spurium***
                                          FALSE CLEAVERS (Eurasia)

Galium oreganum,
Oregon bedstraw

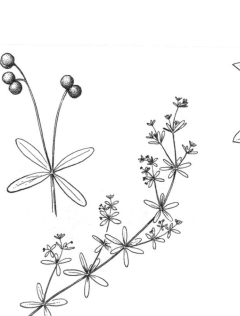

Galium trifidum subsp. *columbianum,*
small bedstraw

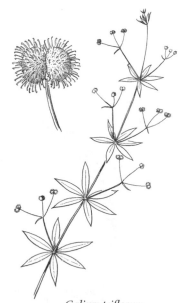

Galium triflorum,
fragrant bedstraw

SALICACEAE Willow Family

Both genera of the willow family are represented west of the Cascades by native trees and shrubs. The leaves are alternate and deciduous, and the flowers are borne in staminate and pistillate catkins, which are on separate plants. There are no petals or sepals, but below each flower in a catkin there is a scalelike bract. In the genus *Populus* (cottonwoods, quaking aspen), the pistil or stamens are borne on a disklike structure; in *Salix* (willows), this is replaced by one or two small glands. The staminate catkins are short-lived, but the pistillate catkins persist until the fruits that develop from the pistils have ripened. The seeds, when released, have long hairs that facilitate dispersal by wind.

1 Leaf blades not more than 1.5 times as long as wide, broadest close to the base, and sometimes heart-shaped, owing to a slight notch at the base; catkins hanging down .... *Populus*
1 Most leaf blades at least twice as long as wide and rarely broadest close to the base (except in *S. rigida*); catkins upright .... *Salix*

Populus

1 Most leaf blades 3–10 cm long; leaf petioles not much more than half as long as the blades, only slightly flattened .... *P. balsamifera* subsp. *trichocarpa*
BLACK COTTONWOOD

1 Most leaf blades 2–4 cm long; leaf petioles nearly or fully as long as the blades and markedly flattened (the leaves therefore trembling when there is wind) .... *P. tremuloides*
QUAKING ASPEN

Salix

This key is based to a large extent on vegetative characters that, though less reliable than catkins, are accessible over a long growing season. It is important to use mature shoots for identification, and to avoid those that come up as suckers, sprouting from the bases of main stems, especially when these have been cut back to the ground. The leaves of such sucker shoots often deviate markedly from the typical form. Catkins are, however, referred to in certain couplets, and it will be helpful if some can be found. Pistillate catkins usually persist on the shrub or tree much longer than the staminate catkins.

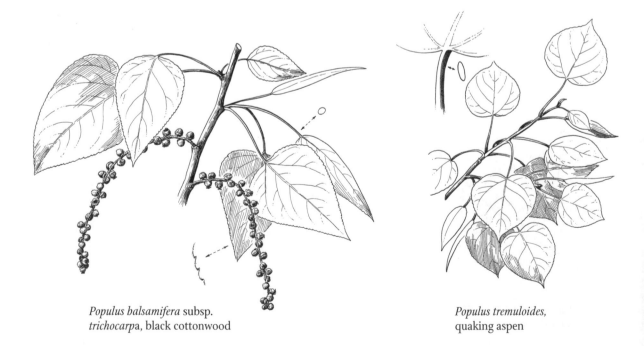

Populus balsamifera subsp. *trichocarp*a, black cottonwood

Populus tremuloides, quaking aspen

The classification of some of the willows in our region is now reasonably stable, but that of others continues to be in a state of flux. The difficulties are due to the enormous range of variation within some species, and also to hybridization. Note that some species, because of their variability, are in the key twice.

If a particular couplet seems not to be unequivocal, follow both choices. You will probably soon discover that one lead is better than the other. Please pay attention to information provided with respect to geographic ranges and habitats, which are likely to help confirm identification. Incidentally, the only lowland species of our region that commonly grows away from standing water or very wet habitats is *Salix scouleriana*, which often forms very large trees.

The key does not include the corkscrew willow, *Salix matsudana,* nor the weeping willow, *S. babylonica.* The white willow, *S. alba,* and some of its hybrids, also cultivated for their general appearance or attractive catkins, are mentioned briefly in connection with the native shining willow, *S. lucida* var. *lasiandra.* Some of these garden plants are occasionally found in situations where they may appear to be wild.

1 Low shrubs of high-montane habitats, rarely so much as 15 cm tall (staminate flowers with 2 stamens, as in most willows of our region)

  2 Bract below each flower of a staminate or pistillate catkin not obviously hairy (leaf blades to about 2.5 cm long, the underside with a whitish coating; in the Olympic Mountains, Wash., and Cascades, Brit. Col. to Wash. and eastward) . . . .*S. nivalis*
                                                      SNOW WILLOW

  2 Bract below each flower of a staminate or pistillate catkin conspicuously hairy all over

    3 Larger leaf blades to about 2.5 cm long and about 3 times as long as wide, the tips generally pointed (dry leaves often persisting for at least another growing season; in the Cascades, Brit. Col. to Wash., and eastward) . . . .*S. cascadensis*
                                                CASCADES WILLOW

    3 Larger leaf blades to about 5 cm long, generally not so much as 2.5 times as long as wide, the tips blunt or pointed (bracts below individual flowers of a catkin dark brown to nearly black; underside of leaf blades usually with a whitish coating and a few long, straight hairs; Olympic Mountains, Wash., and the Cascades, Brit. Col. to Wash. and eastward) . . . .*S. arctica*
                                                ARCTIC WILLOW

Salix arctica,
arctic willow

Salix lucida subsp. *lasiandra,*
shining willow

1 Trees or shrubs at least 1 m tall
    4 Petioles and bases of leaf blades with a few conspicuous glandular swellings; staminate flowers with 3–8 (usually 5) stamens; leaf blades (these to more than 15 cm long, generally about 5 times as long as wide) drawn out into a tail-like tip (common and widespread) ....
.... *S. lucida* **subsp.** *lasiandra* (*S. lasiandra*), p. 325
SHINING WILLOW

> *Salix lucida* subsp. *caudata,* if present W of the Cascades, is certainly not common. The undersides of its leaf blades lack the whitish cast of those of subsp. *lasiandra.* In subsp. *caudata,* furthermore, microscopic stomates are typically present on both surfaces of the blades, whereas in subsp. *lasiandra* they are generally restricted to the underside or at least much more abundant on the underside. *Salix alba,* the white willow (Europe), and *S. ×rubens* (*S. alba × fragilis*) are similar to *S. lucida* subsp. *lasiandra* in the shape of the leaf blades and also because the upper portions of the petioles have glandular swellings. In these garden plants, however, both sides of the blades are usually hairy throughout the growing season, whereas in *S. lucida* subsp. *lasiandra* the hairiness generally disappears early. Some of the weeping willows, with drooping, yellow stems, are not wild-type *S. babylonica* but hybrids, *S. babylonica × S. alba* or *fragilis.*

    4 Petioles and bases of leaf blades without conspicuous glandular swellings (but there may be small glands on the petioles or margins of the leaf blades); staminate flowers with only 1–2 stamens; leaf blades not drawn out into a tail-like tip except in *S. prolixa* and *S. geyeriana* subsp. *meleina*
        5 Staminate flowers with only 1 stamen; undersides of leaf blades typically silky-hairy throughout the growing season (leaf blades usually 2–2.5, occasionally as much as 3, times as long as wide and widest above the middle, but sometimes slightly more elongate and widest near the middle; pistillate catkins to about 7.5 mm wide; common and widespread) ....*S. sitchensis*
SITKA WILLOW

        5 Staminate flowers with 2 stamens; undersides of leaf blades usually not silky-hairy throughout the growing season, but they may be conspicuously white-hairy, the hairs not pressed down (in certain species, leaves that are not fully developed may be silky-hairy, but as a rule this type of hairiness soon disappears)
           6 Most larger leaf blades more than 4 times as long as wide
               7 Plants producing new shoots from the roots, thereby forming dense colonies
                   8 Mature leaf blades with numerous pressed-down hairs on both surfaces, the underside about as green as the upper surface; fruits on pistillate catkins hairy (Brit. Col. to Oreg., at least as far S as the Umpqua River valley) ....*S. sessilifolia*
SOFT-LEAVED WILLOW

                   8 Mature leaf blades usually without pressed-down hairs but the underside usually somewhat whitish when compared with the upper surface; fruits on pistillate catkins not hairy ....
.... *S. melanopsis* (*S. exigua* var. *melanopsis*)
DUSKY WILLOW

> *Salix fluviatilis,* river willow, at least so far as our region is concerned, is here tentatively considered to be the same as *S. melanopsis.*

               7 Plants not producing shoots from the roots, thus not colonial
                   9 Petioles not often more than 5 mm long; pistillate catkins not more than about 1.5 cm long (larger leaf blades usually drawn out into tail-like tips) ....*S. geyeriana* **subsp.** *meleina*
GEYER'S WILLOW

                   9 Petioles often more than 5 mm long; pistillate catkins about 3–4 cm long
                      10 Bases of leaf blades narrowly wedge-shaped; leaf blades not drawn out into tail-like tips (in our region mostly in SW Oreg.; widespread E of the Cascades and in Calif.) ....
.... *S. lasiolepis* (includes *S. tracyi*)
ARROYO WILLOW

10 Bases of leaf blades rounded or only very slightly angled, sometimes notched where the petiole is attached; larger leaf blades usually drawn out into tail-like tips ....
.... **S. prolixa** (*S. mackenzieana, S. rigida* subspp. *mackenzieana* and *macrogemma*)
MACKENZIE'S WILLOW

6 Blades of larger leaves not more than 4 (usually not more than 3) times as long as wide

11 At least the underside of the leaf blades persistently white-hairy throughout the growing season (blades usually 2–2.5 times as long as wide, widest near the middle)

12 Both surfaces of the leaf blades usually persistently hairy throughout the growing season (petioles sometimes with glands; leaf blades sometimes with glands on the marginal teeth; high montane in the Cascades of Oreg., to Calif. and eastward) .... *S. eastwoodiae*
ALICE EASTWOOD'S WILLOW, SIERRA WILLOW

Salix eastwoodiae is extremely variable. The leaves of some specimens believed to be S. eastwoodiae have nearly hairless leaf blades.

12 Only the underside of the leaf blades persistently white-hairy (see note concerning *S. hookeriana* var. *piperi,* after second choice 13)

13 Leaf blades not often more than 8 cm long, generally only 3–5 cm long, widest at or above the middle, rounded or pointed at the tip, typically not stiff or leathery (along streams in inland areas where there is serpentine rock, Josephine Co., Oreg., to Calif.) .... *S. delnortensis*
DEL NORTE WILLOW

13 Leaf blades commonly 8–10 cm long, sometimes larger, usually widest near the middle, pointed at the tip, somewhat stiff and leathery (typically growing as a large shrub or tree less than 4 m tall, generally around freshwater seeps, ponds, and lakes that are close to salt water, not only along the open coast but around Puget Sound, the Strait of Georgia, and other large bays) ....
.... *S. hookeriana*, p. 328
HOOKER'S WILLOW

A slightly different form, sometimes distinguished as *S. hookeriana* var. *piperi,* has proportionately longer leaf blades that lose the white hairiness on the underside as they age. This form occurs in wet habitats remote from salt water. When *S. scouleriana,* especially one that has been cut down, produces sucker shoots at the base, the abnormally large leaf blades on these resemble those of *S. hookeriana* in shape and in being densely white-hairy on the underside.

Salix sitchensis, Sitka willow

Salix geyeriana subsp. *meleina,*
Geyer's willow

11 Underside of leaf blades not persistently white-hairy (whatever hairs are present on young leaves typically disappear or become sparse by the time the leaves have matured)

  14 Most larger leaf blades typically widest well above the middle

    15 Large tree to more than 10 m tall, often with several trunks, and not restricted to wet habitats; leaf blades with whitish hairs on the underside when young, but these rarely persisting into late spring or summer; margins of blades not rolled under; fruiting pistils hairy (widespread, and the only large lowland willow likely to be found away from fresh water) . . . . **S. scouleriana**
                                                                   SCOULER'S WILLOW

    15 Shrub or small tree; leaf blades whitish on the underside, even when no hairs are present; margins of blades often rolled under; fruiting pistils not hairy (Oreg. to Calif.) . . . .
      . . . . **S. lasiolepis** (includes var. *tracyi*)
                                                           ARROYO WILLOW

  14 Most leaf blades typically widest near the middle (see note concerning *S. hookeriana* var. *piperi*, after second choice 13; although the underside of its large leaf blades, when mature, are not conspicuously hairy, the variety is more conveniently dealt with in connection with *S. hookeriana* than here)

    16 Larger leaf blades commonly drawn out into slender, tail-like tips; pedicels of fruits on pistillate catkins at least 4–5 mm long (bases of leaf blades usually rounded, sometimes notched where the petiole is attached) . . . **S. prolixa** (*S. mackenzieana, S. rigida* subspp. *mackenziana* and *macrogemma*)
                                                           MACKENZIE'S WILLOW

    16 Leaf blades often pointed but not drawn out into tail-like tips; pedicels of fruits on pistillate catkins much less than 4 mm long

      17 Shrubs not often much more than 1 m tall, growing in bogs; stems touching down and rooting, the plants thus forming extensive colonies; style of pistillate flowers negligible, usually only 0.1–0.2 mm long (bracts beneath individual flowers of pistillate catkins not hairy) . . . . **S. pedicellaris**
                                                           BOG WILLOW

      17 Shrubs more than l m tall or small trees, not typically in bogs; not forming colonies; style of pistillate flowers at least 0.3 mm long, sometimes more than 1 mm

Salix hookeriana,
Hooker's willow

Salix scouleriana,
Scouler's willow

18 Larger leaf blades narrowly wedge-shaped at the base (fruits of pistillate flowers hairy) . . . *S. lemmonii*
LEMMON'S WILLOW

18 Most larger leaf blades either rounded at the base or broadly angled, definitely not narrowly wedge-shaped

   19 Bracts beneath individual pistillate flowers dark long-hairy (style of pistillate flowers 0.5–1.5 mm long; leaf blades, before becoming fully developed, cottony-hairy; not likely to be found below about 3500 ft., 1070 m) . . . . *S. commutata*
VARIABLE WILLOW

   19 Bracts beneath individual pistillate flowers not hairy

      20 Underside of leaf blades whitish (mostly high montane) . . . .*S. barclayi*
BARCLAY'S WILLOW

      20 Underside of leaf blades about as green as the upper surface (mostly high montane) . . . . *S. boothii*
BOOTH'S WILLOW

SANTALACEAE Sandalwood Family

There is just one member of the sandalwood family in our region. This is *Comandra umbellata* subsp. *californica* (pl. 539), called bastard toad-flax, widespread west of the Cascades from British Columbia to California but not often encountered. It is a perennial that is mostly herbaceous, but it has a tough, almost woody base. Underground, it is connected to the root system of a shrub or tree that provides some nutritional support. The upright stems, not often more than 30 cm tall, have alternate, almost sessile leaves. Most of these are about 2–3 cm long, but a few of the lower ones are small and scalelike. The flowers are borne in small inflorescences arising in the axils of the upper leaves. They lack a corolla but have a calyx that is usually about 5 mm long, five-lobed, greenish white to white or purplish; the lobes have prominent hairs on their inner faces. There are five stamens. The fruit-forming part of the pistil is united with the calyx tube. The sepals persist on the top of the fruit, which is eventually dry, commonly 5–8 mm long, purplish or brownish, and encloses a single seed. *Comandra umbellata* subsp. *pallida* and *Geocaulon lividum* (*C. livida*) are similar species found east of the Cascades.

SARRACENIACEAE Pitcher-Plant Family

Pitcher plants, restricted to marshes and bogs, are most conspicuously characterized by their tubular leaves, into which water is secreted. Insects that drown in the water are digested by action of bacteria, and some of the soluble nutrients are absorbed the plant. The nodding flowers are borne singly on long peduncles. When petals are present, there are five, and they soon fall off; the sepals, larger than the petals, persist. There is a ring of stamens and a pistil that develops into a dry fruit with three or more chambers.

The only western representative of this remarkable family is *Darlingtonia californica* (pl. 540), the California pitcher plant or cobra lily, with leaves sometimes more than 50 cm long. The tubular portion of each leaf is a modified petiole; it ends in a hood, which has many transparent windows and whose opening faces downward. The two-lobed "tongue of the cobra" hanging down from the hood corresponds to the blade of the leaf. There are nectar glands on this as well as in the petiolar portion; furthermore, there are downward-directed hairs in the petiolar portion to discourage insects from moving upward and out of the trap. The flowers have yellowish, purple-veined sepals about 4 cm long, purple petals, short stamens, and a five-chambered pistil.

Darlingtonia is found from Tillamook County, Oregon, to northern California. Near the coast it usually grows in sphagnum bogs; in inland areas, however, it is partial to shallow troughs and pockets on serpentine slopes. Such habitats, characterized by a flow of water and lower acidity than is typical of sphagnum bogs, are called fens, and these are numerous in parts of Curry and Josephine Counties, Oregon. Some of the plants associated with *Darlingtonia* in serpentine fens are not found anywhere else.

SAXIFRAGACEAE Saxifrage Family

Most plants of the saxifrage family are perennials that die back each fall. The principal leaves are concentrated at the base of the plant, and upper leaves, if present, are usually reduced. In the flowers, the five lobes of the calyx originate at the rim of a cuplike lower portion. The petals (usually five) and stamens (usually five or ten) are also attached to the rim of the calyx cup. The fruit-forming portion of the pistil may be completely free of the calyx cup or partly united with it. Either way, after the fruit has ripened and dried, it splits open lengthwise. (In *Bensoniella oregona*, however, the fruit splits open while it is still green.)

1 Flowers without petals but with 4 greenish or yellowish calyx lobes that could be mistaken for petals (forming mats in wet places; stems rooting at the nodes; leaves mostly opposite except on the upper portions of upright stems; stamens 8, these alternating with fleshy glands; fruit 2-lobed) . . . . ***Chrysosplenium glechomifolium***, pl. 542
WESTERN GOLDEN SAXIFRAGE

1 Petals usually present, but if these are lacking, there are 5 calyx lobes
  2 Most leaf blades at least 20 cm wide (sometimes more than 30 cm), the petiole attached close to the center of a nearly circular blade rather than at the edge or in a notch (plants with tough rootstocks, these usually anchored between rocks in mountain streams; petals white, about 7 mm long, soon shed; Coast Ranges, Benton Co., Oreg., to Calif.) . . . . ***Darmera peltata*** (*Peltiphyllum peltatum*)
GREAT SHIELD LEAF

  2 Leaf blades rarely so much as 10 cm wide, the petiole attached at the edge or in a notch, as in most leaves
    3 Petals divided into lobes, these sometimes so slender as to be nearly hairlike
      4 Pistil with 3 styles (petals white to pink) . . . . ***Lithophragma***
      4 Pistil with 2 styles (petals mostly white or greenish, at least at first, but sometimes becoming pink, crimson, brownish, or purplish as they age)
        5 Stamens 10 (petals about 1.5 mm wide at the base, the upper portions broader, spreading outward, and divided at the tip into about 7 slender lobes, these usually becoming pink or crimson as they age) . . . . ***Tellima grandiflora***, pl. 549
FRINGECUPS

        5 Stamens 5
          6 Petals divided pinnately into 4 or more well-separated lateral lobes (these, like the lobe at the tip, slender and almost hairlike; in *M. ovalis* there may be only 2 lateral lobes, but they are well below the tip) . . . . ***Mitella***
          6 Petals divided at or close to the tip into 3 or more lobes
            7 Petals divided at the very tip into 3 lobes, these either very slender and projecting forward or fingerlike and spreading apart slightly; calyx tube tapering to the base . . . . ***Mitella***
            7 Petals typically divided into a cluster of 3–7 fingerlike lobes, not all of these originating at the same level; calyx tube nearly squared-off at the base (Olympic Mountains, Wash., and on the W and E slopes of the Cascades but not often below about 5000 ft., 1520 m) . . . . ***Elmera racemosa*** var. ***puberulenta***, pl. 543
HAIRY ELMERA

    3 Petals not divided into lobes
      8 Petals 4 (slender, about twice as long as the calyx lobes, brownish); stamens 3 (1 shorter than the other 2) in line with the 3 upper calyx lobes, which are larger than the 2 lower calyx lobes (reproducing vegetatively from buds at the bases of some of the leaf blades; the new plants take root when they touch the soil) . . . . ***Tolmiea menziesii***, pl. 551
PIGGYBACK PLANT, YOUTH-ON-AGE

      8 Petals normally 5; stamens 5 or 10 (but 1 or more of them may not be fully developed)
        9 Stamens 5 (but 1 or more of them may not be fully developed)
          10 Stamens less than half as long as the petals
            11 Petals 1.2–2.5 mm long, persisting even after withering; calyx lobes about as long as the tube; plants rarely more than 25 cm tall, producing stolons that root at the nodes, where new plants originate (wet cliffs along the Willamette River, Oreg., and in the Columbia River Gorge) . . . . ***Sullivantia oregana***
OREGON SULLIVANTIA

11 Petals usually 4–7 mm long, falling away before withering; calyx lobes shorter than the tube; plants often more than 30 cm tall, without stolons . . . . ***Boykinia***

10 Stamens at least half as long as the petals (sometimes as long as, or even longer than, the petals)

  12 Petals slender and nearly hairlike for their entire length; fruits breaking open while still green, exposing the seeds (Josephine and Curry Cos., Oreg., to Calif.; not likely to be found below 4000 ft., 1220 m) . . . . ***Bensoniella oregana*** (*Bensonia oregana*)

  12 Petals not nearly hairlike for their entire length (if slender, they are at least much wider at the base than at the tip)

    13 Petals dark purple, slender, narrowing gradually from the base to the tip; calyx lobes 6–10 mm long, several times as long as wide; plants of wet banks or cliffs (SW Wash. to NW Oreg.) . . . .
. . . . ***Bolandra oregona***
                                                             OREGON BOLANDRA

    13 Petals (these are sometimes absent) white or greenish, usually broader in the upper half than below; calyx lobes not so much as 5 mm long, less than 3 times as long as wide; mostly plants of well-drained, often rocky habitats . . . . ***Heuchera***

9 Stamens 10

14 Plants with crowded leaves, forming dense clumps or mats; leaves (including petioles, if these are present) less than 2 cm long . . . . ***Saxifraga***

14 Plants not forming dense clumps or mats; most leaves more than 2 cm long (except in *Saxifraga nuttallii*)

  15 Leaves palmately lobed or palmately compound . . . . ***Tiarella***

  15 Leaves neither palmately lobed nor palmately compound

    16 Petals only about one-third as wide as the calyx lobes; 2 divisions of the pistil separate nearly to the base (not likely to be found below 4000 ft., 1220 m) . . . . ***Leptarrhena pyrolifolia***
                                                 FALSE SAXIFRAGE

    16 Petals nearly always substantially wider than the calyx lobes; 2 divisions of the pistil united for much of their length

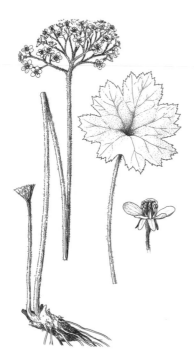

Darmera peltata,
great shield leaf

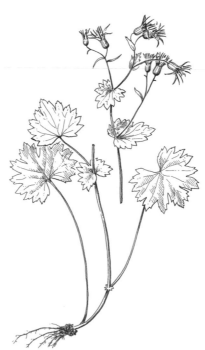

Bolandra oregona,
Oregon bolandra

17 Leaves with a distinct joint separating the blade from the petiole, the blades usually falling before the petioles; lower portions of styles, at flowering time, tightly touching one another (all substantial leaves basal; leaf blades wedge-shaped in the lower half to two-thirds, coarsely toothed near the tip; plants with woody rootstocks; SW Oreg. to Calif., also E of the crest of the Cascades in Wash.; not likely to be found anywhere below 5000 ft., 1520 m) . . . . *Saxifragopsis fragarioides*
JOINT-LEAVED SAXIFRAGE

17 Leaves without a distinct joint separating the blade from the petiole, the blades not falling before the petioles; lower portions of styles not tightly touching one another . . . . *Saxifraga*

Boykinia

1 Stipules leaflike, to more than 1.5 cm long, usually with toothed margins; blades of larger leaves to more than 15 cm wide . . . . *B. major*
LARGE-LEAVED BOYKINIA

1 Stipules not leaflike, consisting mostly of a few brownish bristles; blades of larger leaves not often more than 8 cm wide . . . . *B. occidentalis* (*B. elata*), pl. 541
SLENDER BOYKINIA

Heuchera

1 Styles and stamens not protruding beyond the calyx lobes
  2 Stems and petioles of flowering shoots densely hairy, the hairs brownish, to 5 mm long (mostly E of the crest of the Cascades but found in the Olympic Mountains, Wash., and to some extent on the W slope of the Cascades) . . . . *H. chlorantha*
NARROW-FLOWERED ALUMROOT
  2 Stems and petioles of flowering shoots only slightly hairy, the hairs whitish (in our region only in SW Oreg., also E of the Cascades) . . . . *H. cylindrica* subsp. *glabella*
LAVA ALUMROOT

1 Styles and stamens protruding well beyond the calyx lobes

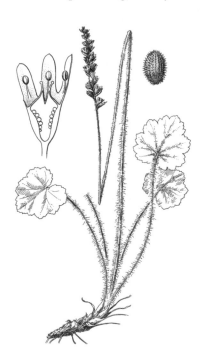

Heuchera chlorantha,
narrow-flowered alumroot

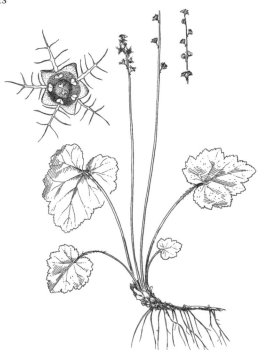

Mitella pentandra,
five-point mitrewort

3 Pedicels shorter than the calyces; inflorescences dense, the flowers crowded (stems, petioles, and leaf blades very hairy; petioles to about 20 cm long; coastal, Tillamook Co., Oreg., to Calif.) . . . *H. pilosissima*
SHAGGY ALUMROOT

Heuchera merriamii, which is only slightly hairy and whose petioles are rarely longer than 5 cm, extends from Josephine Co., Oreg., to Calif. but is not likely to be found below 4500 ft. (1370 m).

3 Pedicels much longer than the calyces; inflorescence as a whole loose, the flowers widely scattered
    4 Undersides of leaf blades sparsely if at all hairy; seeds 3–4 times as long as wide (mostly near the coast and in the mountains) . . . . *H. glabra*
SMOOTH ALUMROOT

    4 Undersides of leaf blades decidedly hairy
        5 Leaf blades typically about as wide as long, shallowly lobed, the marginal teeth not conspicuously pointed (the lobes therefore not jagged-edged); petioles and flowering stems varying in the extent of hairiness and sometimes smooth . . . . *H. micrantha* var. *micrantha*
SMALL-FLOWERED ALUMROOT

        5 Leaf blades typically longer than wide, at least some of the lobes separated for about one-third the distance to the midrib, the marginal teeth pointed (the lobes therefore jagged-edged); petioles and flowering stems conspicuously hairy . . . . *H. micrantha* var. *diversifolia*

Heuchera micrantha var. *diversifolia* seems to be the more common variety in our region. It and var. *micrantha* intergrade, however.

Lithophragma

1 Basal leaves divided less than halfway to the base of the blade
    2 Calyx tube rounded at the base, much less than half of the fruit-forming part of the pistil attached to the rounded portion (Curry, Josephine, Jackson, and Klamath Cos., Oreg., to Calif.) . . . .
      . . . . *L. campanulatum* (*L. heterophyllum* var. *campanulatum*)
BELL-STAR

    2 Calyx tube conical at the base, at least half of the fruit-forming part of the pistil attached to the conical portion (Curry, Josephine, and Jackson Cos., Oreg., to Calif.) . . . . *L. affine*, pl. 544
WOODLAND STAR

        Plants from SW Oreg. usually show some degree of intergradation with *L. parviflorum*, first choice 4.

1 Basal leaves palmately compound or at least divided more than halfway to the base of the blade
    3 Calyx tube about as long as wide (mostly E of the Cascades but occurring in our region on S Vancouver Island and Gulf Islands, Brit. Col., and on the Olympic Peninsula and San Juan Islands, Wash.) . . . .
      . . . . *L. glabrum* (includes *L. bulbiferum*)
ROCKET STAR

    3 Calyx tube (including the portion that is united to the fruit-forming part of the pistil) distinctly longer than wide
        4 Calyx tube nearly or fully twice as long as wide (and broadening rather evenly upward from the base), the lobes at least as long as wide; most petals with 3 lobes . . . . *L. parviflorum* var. *parviflorum*
PRAIRIE STARFLOWER

        4 Calyx tube not more than about 1.5 times as long as wide; most petals with 5 lobes (almost entirely E of the crest of the Cascades) . . . . *L. tenellum*
SLENDER WOODLAND STAR

Mitella

1 Flowering stems with 1–3 well-developed leaves similar to the basal leaves . . . . *M. caulescens*
LEAFY-STEMMED MITREWORT

1 Flowering stem without well-developed leaves (at most, there is 1 much reduced leaf)
    2 Stamens in line with the petals, alternating with the calyx lobes (not likely to be found below 4000 ft., 1220 m) . . . . *M. pentandra*
FIVE-POINT MITREWORT

    2 Stamens in line with the calyx lobes, alternating with the petals
       3 Petals divided at the tip into 3–5 teeth or lobes
          4 Leaf lobes somewhat angular and mostly smooth-margined; teeth at tips of the petals deeply separated and slender, almost threadlike . . . . *M. diversifolia*
ANGLE-LEAVED MITREWORT

          4 Leaf lobes rounded and with distinct teeth; lobes (usually 3) at tips of the petals shallowly separated, not slender or threadlike . . . . *M. trifida*
THREE-TOOTHED MITREWORT

       3 Petals pinnately lobed
          5 Leaf blades longer than wide . . . . *M. ovalis*
OVAL-LEAVED MITREWORT

          5 Leaf blade as wide or wider than long, often somewhat kidney-shaped
             6 Flowers with 10 stamens (Alaska to N Wash., from the lowlands into the mountains) . . . *M. nuda*
COMMON MITREWORT

             6 Flowers with 5 stamens (montane, not likely to be found below 4000 ft., 1220 m) . . . . . *M. breweri*
FEATHERY MITREWORT, BREWER'S MITREWORT

Saxifraga

All the species of *Saxifraga* in this key are perennial, but most die down each winter. A weedy annual saxifrage, native to Europe but noticed at Victoria, British Columbia, is *S. tridactylites*. It grows to a height of about 15 cm, and its stems, branching and usually reddish, are glandular-hairy. Most of the leaves are three-lobed. The white petals are 2–3 mm long (about twice as long as the sepals) and notched at the tip.

1 Plants with crowded leaves, forming dense clumps or mats; leaf blades (these without distinct petioles) not more than 2 cm long (usually considerably less than 2 cm)
    2 Petals (these to 9 mm long) pinkish purple; leaves distinctly opposite (not more than about 5 mm long); plants, even when flowering, not more than about 2.5 cm tall (Alaska to Wash., not likely to be found below about 5000 ft., 1520 m) . . . . *S. oppositifolia*
PURPLE MOUNTAIN SAXIFRAGE

    2 Petals not primarily pinkish purple (but they may have purplish spots); leaves alternate
       3 Most leaves with 3 lobes at the tip (occasionally 2 or as many as 7); petals white . . . . *S. caespitosa*, pl. 545
TUFTED SAXIFRAGE

       3 Leaves not lobed; petals white or white spotted with purple
          4 Leaves more or less spoon-shaped, blunt at the tip, and bristles, if present, limited to the narrow lower portion; petals white (not often found below about 5000 ft., 1520 m) . . . . . . *S. tolmiei*, pl. 548
TOLMIE'S SAXIFRAGE

          4 Leaves pointed at the tip and with bristly margins for their entire length; petals white or pale yellow, with purple spots (widely distributed from the lowlands to high elevations)
             5 Most leaves tapering gradually from the base to the tip (in our region mostly in the Cascades) . . . . *S. bronchialis* var. *austromontana*
SPOTTED SAXIFRAGE

             5 Most leaves tapering abruptly from above the middle to the tip (in our region mostly in the Cascades and westward) . . . . *S. bronchialis* var. *vespertina*
MATTED SAXIFRAGE

1 Plants not forming dense clumps or mats; leaves (these usually basal except for bracts of the flowering stems, often with distinct petioles) more than 2 cm long (except in *S. nuttallii*, whose small leaves are scattered along the stems)
      6 Petals yellow (outline of leaf blades somewhat kidney-shaped; annual; introduced at a few localities in the northern Willamette Valley, Oreg., perhaps elsewhere) . . . . *S. sibthorpii*
YELLOW SAXIFRAGE (Europe)

6 Petals not yellow

   7 Stems slender, trailing (most leaves about 1.5 cm long, usually with 3 shallow lobes, sometimes 2, 4, or 5 lobes; petals white with pink veins; S Wash. to Calif.; wet banks on the W slope of the Cascades, in the Coast Ranges, and along the coast in Lincoln and Lane Cos., Oreg.; also in the Rogue River valley in Curry Co., Oreg.) . . . . ***S. nuttallii***
NUTTALL'S SAXIFRAGE

   7 Stems rather stout, not trailing

     8 Leaf blades about as wide as long, often nearly circular in general outline, shallowly lobed and/or toothed, with or without a notch where the petiole is attached

       9 Plants usually with not more than 3 basal leaves (leaf blades with a deep notch where the petiole is attached; petals 3.5 mm long, white; some of the flowers usually replaced by vegetative reproductive bulblets, and the axils from which the basal leaves originate also often with bulblets; Alaska to Calif., in wet cliffside habitats from the Cascades to the coast) . . . . ***S. mertensiana***
MERTENS' SAXIFRAGE

       9 Plants usually with more than 3 basal leaves

      10 Leaf blades without an obvious indentation where the petiole is attached

        11 Petioles scarcely if at all longer than the blades (montane, mostly above 4000 ft., 1220 m) . . . . ***S. lyallii***
LYALL'S SAXIFRAGE

        11 Petioles of most leaves to more than twice as long as the blades . . . . . ***S. odontoloma*** (*S. arguta*)
STREAM SAXIFRAGE

      10 Leaf blades with an obvious indentation where the petiole is attached (the indentation is at least slightly deeper than the separations between lobes)

        12 Inflorescence a slender raceme, often with just 1 normally developed flower (with white petals to about 1 cm long) at the tip; some of the lower flowers replaced by vegetative reproductive bulblets, some the axils from which the basal leaves originate also with bulblets (mostly in rockslides, Alaska to N Wash., in our region high montane in the Cascades) . . . . ***S. cernua***
NODDING SAXIFRAGE

Saxifraga bronchialis var. *austromontana*, spotted saxifrage

Saxifraga marshallii, Marshall's saxifrage

12 Inflorescence freely branched, about as wide as long, with numerous normal flowers with white to pink petals to about 4 mm long; none of the flowers replaced by vegetative bulblets (montane, mostly above 4000 ft., 1220 m) . . . . *S. nelsoniana* var. *cascadensis* (*S. punctata*)
CASCADE SAXIFRAGE

8 Leaf blades generally approximately oval, usually decidedly longer than wide, without a notch where the petiole is attached

13 Filaments of some or all stamens widening from the base, then narrowing to the tip (leaf blades toothed)

14 Petals with 2 yellow spots near the base (wet habitats near the coast from Lane Co., Oreg., to Calif.; farther N in Oreg. gradually intergrading with 1 or more of the species under the other choice 14)
. . . . *S. marshallii* (*S. hallii*), p. 335
MARSHALL'S SAXIFRAGE

14 Petals without yellow spots near the base

15 Inflorescence somewhat flat-topped (petals and filaments of stamens often purple-tinged; in our region W of the Cascades from Brit. Col. to NW Oreg., also in the Columbia River Gorge)
. . . . *S. rufidula* (*S. occidentalis* var. *rufidula*), pl. 547
RED-WOOL SAXIFRAGE

15 Inflorescence pyramid-shaped

16 Leaf blades narrowed to a distinct petiole that is usually about as long as the blade (Columbia River Gorge to the coast, then S to Tillamook Co., Oreg.) . . . . . . *S. gormanii* (*S. occidentalis* var. *dentata*)
GORMAN'S SAXIFRAGE

16 Leaf blades (very hairy) narrowed to an indistinct petiole that is nearly or fully half as wide as the blade (on mountain peaks in Clatsop and Tillamook Cos., Oreg.) . . . .
. . . . *S. hitchcockiana* (*S. occidentalis* var. *latipetiolata*)
BROAD-PETIOLED SAXIFRAGE

Although *S. hitchcockiana* keys out here, it is believed to be closely related to some of the species below.

13 Filaments of stamens either widest near the base or not obviously widened at any level

17 Fruit-forming portion of the pistil, when flowers are fresh, nearly or completely free of the calyx

18 Three petals with pairs of dark spots on their wider portions; some plants producing bulblets on the inflorescence . . . . *S. ferruginea*
RUSTY SAXIFRAGE

18 None of the petals with dark spots; plants not producing bulblets on the inflorescence (valleys of the Coquille River, lower Umpqua River, and Rogue River, Oreg., to Calif.) . . . . *S. howellii*
HOWELL'S SAXIFRAGE

17 Lower half of the fruit-forming portion of the pistil united with the calyx but becoming free of the calyx by the time the fruit is nearly mature

19 Most leaf blades at least 10 cm long, tapering to a broad, indistinct petiole; in bogs, marshes, or wet seepage areas . . . . *S. oregana*
OREGON SAXIFRAGE

19 Leaf blades not often so much as 10 cm long, tapering to a distinct petiole; not in bogs, marshes, or wet seepage areas

20 Leaf blades with prominent teeth (Josephine and Jackson Cos., Oreg., to Calif.) . . . *S. californica*
CALIFORNIA SAXIFRAGE

20 Leaf blades without prominent teeth (the margins are typically smooth, except perhaps near the tip)

21 Inflorescence not especially crowded, the clusters of flowers on the lateral branches typically not pressed close to one another or to the cluster at the tip of the main stem (mostly if not entirely E of the crest of the Cascades, N Wash. to S Oreg.) . . . .
. . . . *S. nidifica* var. *claytoniifolia* (*S. integrifolia* var. *claytoniaefolia*)
MEADOW SAXIFRAGE

21 Inflorescence crowded, the flowers of few short lateral branches pressed close to those at the tip of the main stem

    22 Flowering stem and its branches, and also the leaves, conspicuously glandular-hairy (bases of flowering stems sometimes producing bulblets; in the lowlands and at low elevations in the mountains, mostly W of the crest of the Cascades) . . . . *S. integrifolia*, pl. 546
                        GRASSLAND SAXIFRAGE

    22 Flowering stem and its branches with only sparse glandular hairs, the leaves also not obviously glandular-hairy (montane and mostly above 5000 ft., 1520 m; Josephine Co., Oreg., to Calif.). . . . . *S. aprica*
                        ALPINE SAXIFRAGE

Tiarella

1 Leaves compound, with 3 leaflets, these again divided nearly to their bases (Vancouver Island, Brit. Col., to Oreg.) . . . . *T. trifoliata* var. *laciniata* (*T. laciniata*)
                        CUTLEAF FOAMFLOWER

1 Leaves either compound, with 3 leaflets that are not divided nearly to their bases, or merely lobed
    2 Leaves compound, with 3 leaflets that are again divided into lobes for as much as about half their length . . . . *T. trifoliata* var. *trifoliata*, pl. 550
                        THREE-LEAFLET COOLWORT

    2 Leaves deeply 3- or 5-lobed but not compound . . . . *T. trifoliata* var. *unifoliata*
                        SUGAR SCOOP, WESTERN COOLWORT

SCROPHULARIACEAE Snapdragon Family

Among the many representatives of the snapdragon family in our region, most are herbaceous, but there are some shrubs. The corolla is typically two-lipped, with the upper lip divided into two lobes and the lower lip divided into three lobes. This pattern, however, is not adhered to by all members of the group. In *Verbascum* the corolla has five nearly equal lobes and is not obviously two-lipped; in *Synthyris* and *Veronica* the corolla has four lobes, the uppermost one, generally largest, believed to be comparable to the two-lobed upper lip of most genera. The calyx is commonly five-lobed, four-lobed in some species. The arrangement of stamens is also variable. The following patterns predominate: two pairs of anther-bearing stamens, sometimes accompanied by a sterile stamen; one pair of anther-bearing stamens, no sterile stamens; five anther-bearing stamens. The fruit-forming portion of the pistil, free of the calyx tube, is partitioned lengthwise into two seed-producing halves. The fruit splits open after it has matured and dried.

Some of the representatives of this large assemblage in our region, especially those under the first choice 1 in this key, are partial parasites. While they have green leaves and can synthesize much of their food, their roots are joined to those of various other plants, which provide them with additional nutritional support.

While we are used to the idea that Scrophulariaceae is a cohesive group, results of more recent research indicate that only a few of the genera traditionally assigned to it should remain in it; the rest should be placed in other families. So far as the genera in our region are concerned, the proposed distribution is given below. Note that Plantaginaceae, up to now with only a few genera of its own, is supposed to absorb most of the genera of Scrophulariaceae, and that *Buddleja*, now in Buddlejaceae, seems to belong in genuine Scrophulariaceae:

Scrophulariaceae: *Buddleja, Scrophularia, Verbascum*

Orobanchaceae: *Castilleja, Cordylanthus, Euphrasia, Orthocarpus, Parentucellia, Pedicularis, Rhinanthus, Triphysaria*

Phrymaceae: *Mazus, Mimetanthe, Mimulus*

Plantaginaceae: *Antirrhinum, Collinsia, Cymbalaria, Digitalis, Gratiola, Keckiella, Kickxia, Limosella, Linaria, Lindernia* (?), *Nothochelone, Penstemon, Synthyris, Tonella, Veronica*

1 Upper lip of corolla modified to form a narrow hood or beaklike structure (galea) that usually encloses the stamens and at least much of the pistil (in *Euphrasia stricta* the hoodlike form of the upper lip is not so well marked as it is in other species under this choice)

  2 Leaves opposite (the bracts in whose axils the flowers originate may be alternate, however)

    3 Calyx, after flowers have opened, inflated (it becomes even more obviously inflated and balloonlike after the fruit has started to develop; corolla yellow) . . . . *Rhinanthus borealis*
YELLOW RATTLE

    3 Calyx not becoming obviously inflated

      4 Plants rarely branched; corolla yellow; leaf blades glandular-hairy, usually with 5–7 teeth on each side (common weed) . . . . *Parentucellia viscosa*, pl. 575
YELLOWWEED (Europe)

      4 Plants branched; corolla white to pale violet, with dark blue or purple veins; leaf blades not hairy, with only 2–5 teeth, these bristle-tipped, on each side (occasional weed) . . . . *Euphrasia stricta* (*E. officinalis*), pl. 564
EYEBRIGHT (Europe)

  2 Leaves alternate

    5 Each stamen with 2 equal anther sacs; most leaf blades, whether basal or on the flowering stems, pinnately lobed (except in *P. racemosa*, in which the blades are merely toothed, and in *P. howellii*, in which some leaves may not be lobed or may only have 3 lobes); upper lip of corolla often sharply curved upward or downward . . . . *Pedicularis*

    5 Each stamen with only 1 anther sac or with 2 very unequal anther sacs; leaves with not more than 4 pairs of pinnately arranged lobes

      6 Calyx shaped like an upside-down boat, notched at the tip (each stamen with 1 anther sac or 2 unequal anther sacs) . . . . *Cordylanthus*

      6 Calyx with a tube and distinct lobes

        7 Tip of upper lip of corolla closed, the stigma and stamens therefore not projecting out of it (furthermore, the tip may also have a cylindrical, downward projection; each stamen with 2 unequal anther sacs) . . . . *Orthocarpus*

        7 Tip of upper lip of corolla open, the stigma and stamens often projecting out of it

          8 Each stamen with 2 unequal anther sacs . . . . *Castilleja*

          8 Each stamen with only 1 anther sac . . . . *Triphysaria*

1 Upper lip of corolla not modified to form a hood or beaklike structure that encloses the stamens and at least much of the pistil (the upper lip may consist of 2 lobes or it may be undivided; in certain species, moreover, the corolla, with 5 nearly equal lobes, may appear to be regular)

  9 Corolla with 5 nearly equal lobes, at first glance appearing to be regular; flowers with 5 anther-bearing stamens (plants biennial, with prominent basal leaves) . . . . *Verbascum*

  9 Corolla usually distinctly irregular, with 5 or apparently 4 lobes, often 2-lipped; flowers with fewer than 5 anther-bearing stamens

    10 Corolla tube with a sac or slender spur on the lower side at the base . . . . *Linaria-Antirrhinum-Cymbalaria-Kickxia* complex

    10 Corolla tube without a sac or spur at the base

      11 Flowers with 4 fertile stamens and 1 sterile stamen (this may be reduced to a small flaplike structure at the base of the upper lip of the corolla—look carefully!)

        12 Lobes of upper lip of the corolla projecting farther forward than those of the lower lip, and the middle lobe of the lower lip directed downward; sterile stamen reduced to a small flap at the base of the upper lip; herbaceous plants (stems 4-angled; leaves coarsely toothed; corolla mostly maroon or yellowish green and maroon) . . . . *Scrophularia*

        12 Corolla either with 5 nearly equal lobes or distinctly 2-lipped, none of the 3 lobes of the lower lip directed downward; sterile stamen well developed, sometimes longer than the fertile ones; shrubby plants

13 Filaments of fertile stamens separating from the corolla tube at different levels and not hairy near the base . . . . *Penstemon*

13 Filaments of all fertile stamens separating from the corolla tube at the same level and conspicuously hairy near the base

  14 Anthers of fertile stamens with woolly hairs; plants to 1 m tall, the aboveground stems not woody and dying down each winter; corolla about 25–30 mm long, pink-purple (usually in rocky, forested habitats, widespread) . . . . ***Nothochelone nemorosa***

  14 Anthers of fertile stamens not hairy; plants not often so much as 1 m tall, the aboveground stems at least slightly woody and persisting through the winter; corolla to 15 mm long, mostly brownish purple, but the lower lip pale yellow with dark lines (Jackson Co., Oreg., to Calif.) . . . ***Keckiella lemmonii***
                                                                   LEMMON'S KECKIELLA

11 Flowers with 4 or 2 stamens, these with functional anthers (there are no obvious filaments without anthers)

 15 Flowers with 2 anther-bearing stamens

  16 Leaves mostly basal, the leaves on flowering stems much reduced and alternate . . . . *Synthyris*

  16 Leaves scattered along the stems, opposite (but bracts of the inflorescence may be alternate)

   17 Corolla with scarcely any tube and not distinctly 2-lipped, but the lowermost lobe the smallest and the uppermost lobe often larger than the 2 lateral lobes . . . . *Veronica*

   17 Corolla with a substantial tube, 2-lipped, the lower lip with 3 lobes, the upper lip not lobed

    18 Sterile stamens either absent or recognizable only on the lower side of the base of the corolla tube . . . . *Gratiola*

    18 Sterile stamens evident as 2 slight projections on the lower lip of the corolla (in wet habitats) . . .
  . . . .*Lindernia dubia*
                                                        FALSE PIMPERNEL

Two varieties of *L. dubia* are recognized in some references: *dubia,* with flower pedicels no longer than the leaves in whose axils they originate, and with all or most leaf blades tapering gradually to the base; *anagallidea,* with most flower pedicels much longer than the leaves in whose axils they originate, and with all or most leaf blades broadly rounded at the base. These varieties intergrade, and specimens fitting the characteristics of both are sometimes found at the same locality.

Nothochelone nemorosa

Lindernia dubia vars. *dubia,* left, and *anagallidea,* right

15 Flowers with 4 anther-bearing stamens

  19 Plants woody shrubs to about 1 m tall (corolla dull yellow or orange; leaves somewhat sticky glandular; coastal Curry Co., Oreg., to Calif.) . . . . ***Mimulus aurantiacus***, pl. 567

                      BUSH MONKEY FLOWER

  19 Plants herbaceous (but sometimes large)

    20 Calyx consisting of almost completely separate sepals, these of different lengths (plants typically tall, often more than 1 m, unbranched except for the pedicels of flowers; corolla generally at least 4 cm long, commonly purplish red but sometimes white or nearly white; escaping from cultivation in gardens and now firmly established along roadsides and in fields and vacant lots) . . . . ***Digitalis purpurea***

                      FOXGLOVE (Europe)

    20 Calyx consisting of a tube and lobes

      21 Leaves entirely basal, with petioles much longer than the blades; corolla inconspicuous, with 5 equal lobes (on muddy shores of lakes and ponds) . . . . ***Limosella aquatica***

                      MUDWORT

      21 Leaves scattered along the stems, the petioles, if present, much shorter than the blades; corolla irregular, usually obviously 2-lipped (except in *Tonella tenella*, in which the corolla is only slightly 2-lipped)

        22 Middle lobe of the lower lip of the corolla much smaller than the lateral ones, somewhat boat-shaped, enclosing the stamens and the style of the pistil . . . . ***Collinsia***

        22 Middle lobe of the lower lip of the corolla neither boat-shaped nor enclosing the stamens and style of the pistil

          23 Corolla only slightly 2-lipped, its tube not obviously longer than the calyx; stigma not divided . . . . ***Tonella tenella***

                      SMALL-FLOWERED TONELLA

          23 Corolla conspicuously 2-lipped, the tube much longer than the calyx (except in *Mazus japonicus*)

            24 Flowers in terminal racemes, these with a small bract below each flower; calyx lobes equal . . . . ***Mazus japonicus***

                      JAPANESE MAZUS (Asia)

            24 Flowers borne in the axils of the upper leaves, which are rather well developed, the inflorescence thus more or less leafy; calyx lobes sometimes unequal . . . . ***Mimulus***

Limosella aquatica,
mudwort

Tonella tenella,
small-flowered tonella

Castilleja

1 Bracts of inflorescence green; upper lip of corolla (beak) reaching not more than 2 mm beyond the lower lip (annual)

  2 Corolla usually 12–20 mm long, white or yellowish; stigma not reaching the tip of the upper lip of the corolla; lower lip of corolla about 2 mm deep . . . . *C. tenuis* (*Orthocarpus hispidus*)
                                                    HAIRY OWL'S CLOVER

  2 Corolla usually at least 20 mm long, yellow, the lower lip often with 2 purple spots; stigma just reaching the tip of the upper lip of the corolla; lower lip of corolla 4–6 mm deep (SW Oreg. to Calif.) . . . .
      . . . . *C. rubicundula* subsp. *lithospermoides* (*Orthocarpus lithospermoides*), pl. 559
                                                    CREAM-SACS

1 Bracts of inflorescence colored (at least at their tips) with yellow, orange, red, purple, or related colors

  3 Small annuals, the main stem not branching as low as ground level

    4 Stigma not reaching the tip of the upper lip of the corolla; corolla 10–25 mm long, whitish, the lower lip usually with purple dots; in inland habitats . . . . *C. attenuata* (*Orthocarpus attenuatus*), pl. 554
                                                    VALLEY TASSELS

    4 Stigma projecting beyond the tip of the upper lip (beak) of the corolla; corolla 15–25 mm long, mostly pale yellow, pink, or purplish; plants of upper levels of salt marshes

      5 Calyx lobes and tips of bracts pale yellow; corolla yellow, with some purplish markings . . . .
      . . . . *C. ambigua* subsp. *ambigua* (*Orthocarpus castillejoides*), pl. 553
                                                   JOHNNY-NIP

      5 Calyx lobes and tips of bracts purplish; corolla pink or purplish (Coos Co., Oreg., to N Calif.) . . . . . .
      . . . . *C. ambigua* subsp. *humboldtiensis* (*Orthocarpus castillejoides* subsp. *humboldtiensis*)

  3 Perennials, most of the main branches originating at ground level from a base that is usually at least somewhat woody

    6 Most hairs on stems, leaves, and bracts branched (leaves below inflorescence to about 5 cm long but not often more than 4 mm wide and not lobed; tips of bracts of the inflorescence bright red; SW Oreg. to Calif.) . . . . *C. pruinosa*
                                                   FROSTED PAINTBRUSH

    6 Hairs, if present on stems, leaves, or bracts, not branched

      7 Most leaves, including those on the lower portion of the stem, with distinct lobes (*C. applegatei* var. *applegatei*, occurring at high elevations, above 6000 ft., 1830 m, in Douglas and Klamath Cos., Oreg., and eastward, could fit either here or under the other choice 7, depending on the specimen—it is distinctive because its stems, leaves, and bracts have crowded glandular hairs and are very sticky; the leaves, moreover, have wavy margins; the tips of the bracts are bright red, and the corolla, whose upper lip is about as long as the tube, is sometimes more than 35 mm long; the calyx lobes and lobes of the bracts are pointed; several other varieties of *C. applegatei* occur E of the crest of the Cascades and in Calif.)

        8 Upper lip (beak) of the corolla not more than half as long as the corolla tube

          9 Upper lip of the corolla about half as long as the corolla tube and much longer than the lower lip (tips of bracts of the inflorescence yellow to nearly orange; lobes mostly limited to the upper third of the leaf blades; Brit. Col. to Linn Co., Oreg.) . . . . *C. levisecta*, pl. 557
                                                GOLDEN PAINTBRUSH

          9 Upper lip of the corolla less than half as long as the corolla tube and only slightly longer than the lower lip (stems and leaves densely woolly-hairy; tips of bracts dull red or yellowish; mostly above 5000 ft., 1520 m, in the Cascades and Siskiyou Mountains of SW Oreg. to Calif.) . . . .
        . . . . *C. arachnoidea*
                                                COBWEBBY PAINTBRUSH

        8 Upper lip of the corolla decidedly more than half as long as the corolla tube

          10 Upper lip of the corolla about three-fourths as long as the corolla tube (because of intergradation it is perhaps impossible to make an unequivocal key to the varieties of *C. parviflora;* those in our region are not often found below 4000 ft., 1220 m)

11 Corolla 20–25 mm long (bracts red to deep rose but sometimes whitish; calyx lobes usually blunt; in the Cascades, mostly E of the crest, Wash. to Oreg.) . . . . *C. parviflora* var. *oreopola*
ROSY PAINTBRUSH

11 Corolla not more than 20 mm long

   12 Bracts some shade of pink, rose, purplish red, or purple; calyx lobes usually blunt (Olympic Mountains, Wash.) . . . . *C. parviflora* var. *olympica*
OLYMPIC PAINTBRUSH

   12 Bracts usually white or tinged with purplish pink, sometimes almost completely purplish pink; calyx lobes usually pointed (in the Cascades, Brit. Col. to Wash.) . . . . . . *C. parviflora* var. *albida*
WHITISH PAINTBRUSH

10 Upper lip of the corolla as long or longer than the tube; bracts usually red or orange-red (but sometimes yellow or at least yellowish in *C. hispida*)

   13 Upper lip of the corolla about as long as the tube when flowers are well developed, not more than half of it protruding out of the calyx; stems and leaves conspicuously bristly-hairy, many of the hairs 1 mm long or longer; calyx lobes and lobes of bracts generally rather blunt (bracts with greenish glands on short stalks)

      14 Stems and leaves glandular-hairy (the gland-tipped hairs, however, are generally much shorter than the nonglandular hairs); the uppermost lateral leaf lobes usually less than 1 cm long (bracts usually red, sometimes yellow; Josephine Co., Oreg., to Calif.) . . . . *C. hispida* var. *brevilobata*
SHORT-LOBED PAINTBRUSH

      14 Stems and leaves decidedly hairy but not conspicuously glandular-hairy; uppermost lateral leaf lobes commonly more than 1 cm long (bracts usually red, occasionally yellow; common and widely distributed W of the Cascades) . . . . *C. hispida* var. *hispida*, pl. 556
HARSH PAINTBRUSH

   13 Upper lip of the corolla longer than the tube when flowers are well developed, much of it protruding out of the calyx; stems and leaves either with rather short hairs or not obviously hairy; calyx lobes and lobes of bracts usually pointed, but sometimes blunt

      15 Stems and leaves usually distinctly hairy; lowest lateral lobes of bracts often originating well below the middle of the blade; tips of bracts bright red (in the Cascades, Brit. Col. to Lane Co., Oreg., mostly above 4000 ft., 1220 m, and E of the crest) . . . . *C. rupicola*
CLIFF PAINTBRUSH

      15 Leaves and stems not noticeably hairy but the bracts slightly hairy, especially along the margins and midribs; lowest lateral lobes of bracts usually originating at about the middle of the blade; tips of bracts pale reddish orange to bright red (often yellowish orange after fading; on mountain peaks, Clatsop Co., Oreg.) . . . . *C. chambersii*
CHAMBERS' PAINTBRUSH

7 Leaves on the lower portion of the stem, and sometimes all leaves below the inflorescence, without lobes

16 Most leaves (rounded, thick and somewhat succulent) less than twice as long as wide (strictly coastal, Curry Co., Oreg., to Calif.) . . . . *C. mendocinensis*
MENDOCINO PAINTBRUSH

16 Most leaves at least 3 times as long as wide (the uppermost leaves sometimes only about twice as long as wide)

   17 Calyx lobes bluntly rounded

      18 Tips of bracts and calyx lobes pinkish orange to pinkish purple (in wet habitats, including fens in which *Darlingtonia* grows, Josephine Co., Oreg., to Calif.) . . . . *C. elata* (*C. miniata* subsp. *elata* in some references), pl. 555
SLENDER PAINTBRUSH

      18 Tips of bracts and calyx lobes bright red to crimson

         19 Bracts typically not lobed, the tips crimson rather than bright red; stems rarely branched; upper leaves rarely lobed (midmontane in the Cascades, Brit. Col. to N Wash.) . . . . *C. elmeri*
ELMER'S PAINTBRUSH

19 Bracts typically lobed, bright red; stems sometimes branched; upper leaves sometimes lobed (coastal, mostly on bluffs, dunes, and in sandy, thinly forested areas, Oreg. to Calif.) . . . .*C. affinis* **var.** *litoralis* (*C. litoralis*)

PACIFIC PAINTBRUSH

17 Calyx lobes pointed at the tip (tips of bracts of inflorescence bright red)

  20 Leaves below the inflorescence, unlike the lower ones, 3-lobed; stems usually somewhat scattered, the plants spreading by rhizomes (in the Cascades, Wash. to Oreg., mostly above 5000 ft., 1520 m) . . . .*C. suksdorfii*

SUKSDORF'S PAINTBRUSH

  20 Leaves below the inflorescence, like the lower ones, usually not lobed; stems generally clustered, the plants typically not spreading by rhizomes (common and widespread, not restricted to higher elevations) . . . .*C. miniata*

COMMON PAINTBRUSH

In a phase of this species found only close to the shore, Alaska to Wash., the stems and leaves are somewhat succulent ("crisp"), easily snapped. Although this has been given the name *C. miniata* var. *dixonii* (pl. 558), Dixon's paintbrush, its distinctive character is perhaps due to environmental influences.

Collinsia

1 Inflorescence as a whole glandular-hairy

  2 Lateral lobes of the lower lip of the corolla like the lobes of upper lip in being somewhat squared-off at the tip; pedicels, after the fruits have begun to mature, not turning downward; most leaves in whose axils individual flowers originate not especially reduced . . . .*C. rattanii*

RATTAN'S BLUE-EYED MARY

  2 Lateral lobes of the lower lip of the corolla rounded at the tip; pedicels, after the fruits have begun to mature, turning downward; most leaves in whose axils individual flowers originate much reduced, essentially bractlike (SW Oreg. to Calif.) . . . .*C. torreyi*

TORREY'S BLUE-EYED MARY

1 Inflorescence as a whole not glandular-hairy

  3 Filaments of upper 2 stamens with sparse but obvious hairs; middle lobe of the lower lip of the corolla distinctly hairy (Lane Co., Oreg., to Calif.; also E of the Cascades) . . . .*C. sparsiflora* **var.** *bruceae* (*C. bruceae*)

MRS. BRUCE'S BLUE-EYED MARY

  3 Filaments of all 4 stamens not hairy; middle lobe of the lower lip of the corolla not hairy

    4 Corolla generally at least 10 mm long, sometimes as long as 17 mm; axis of the corolla tube forming an angle of nearly 90° to the axis of the calyx tube . . . .*C. grandiflora*, pl. 560

LARGE-FLOWERED BLUE-EYED MARY

    4 Corolla commonly 4–8 mm long, rarely as long as 10 mm; axis of the corolla tube forming an angle of about 45° to the axis of the calyx tube . . . .*C. parviflora*, pl. 561

SMALL-FLOWERED BLUE-EYED MARY

Plants assigned to *C. parviflora* are extremely variable in habit of growth and appearance of the flowers. Colonies in well-drained, mossy or grassy habitats sometimes consist of plants only about 5 cm tall.

Cordylanthus

1 Plants not often more than 20 cm tall, as a whole hairy but not glandular or sticky; larger leaves mostly 2–2.5 cm long, 4–5 mm wide; corolla pale purplish or whitish (in coastal salt marshes, Coos Co., Oreg., to Calif.) . . . .*C. maritimus* **subsp.** *palustris*, pl. 562

SALT-MARSH BIRD'S-BEAK

1 Plants usually at least 20 cm tall, as a whole glandular-hairy, very sticky; larger leaves mostly 3–3.5 cm long, not so much as 2 mm wide; corolla mostly reddish brown, the tip of the beak greenish yellow (Jackson and Josephine Cos., Oreg., to Calif.) . . . . *C. tenuis* **subsp.** *viscidus*, pl. 563

STICKY BIRD'S-BEAK

After accumulating dust, hair, and other windblown detritus on its sticky stems and leaves, *C. tenuis* subsp. *viscidus* becomes a candidate for the Pacific Northwest's most forlorn-looking plant.

Gratiola

1 Flowers with a pair of small bracts associated with the calyx lobes (these bracts are so similar to the calyx lobes that there may appear to be 7 lobes instead of 5; in wet places) . . . . *G. neglecta*

OBSCURE HEDGE HYSSOP

1 Flowers without a pair of small bracts closely associated with the calyx (in wet places) . . . .
. . . . *G. ebracteata*, pl. 565

BRACTLESS HEDGE HYSSOP

Linaria-Antirrhinum-Cymbalaria-Kickxia **Complex**

Antirrhinum majus, snapdragon, a garden plant known to almost everyone, is not in this key. In the wild form of the species, native to Europe, the corolla is typically 3–4 cm long and purplish red with a yellow throat, sometimes pale yellow all over; in cultivated forms that are occasionally seen as escapes from gardens, however, almost any corolla color is possible. In most species of *Linaria,* scattered through the key, milky juice exudes from the stems and leaves when these are cut or broken.

1 Corolla (this with a slender spur) mostly yellow (but there may be orange in the throat, or the upper lip and throat may be purplish, or the entire corolla may be tinged with purple)
  2 Leaves in whorls (plants usually sprawling, the flowering stems commonly branched; corolla, including the spur, about 2 cm long, the yellow in the throat usually more orangish than on the tube or lips; annual; occasional weed in the Willamette Valley, Oreg., probably elsewhere) . . . . *L. supina*

SMALL BUTTER-AND-EGGS (Europe)

  2 Leaves either alternate, or alternate above, opposite below
    3 Leaves (with more or less oval blades) clasping the stems (occasional weed) . . . .
. . . . *L. genistifolia* **subsp.** *dalmatica*

DALMATIAN TOAD-FLAX (Europe)

    3 Leaf blades not clasping the stems
      4 Plants upright, the flowering stems not often branched; leaves practically sessile, most blades at least 8 times as long as wide, generally not obviously hairy; corolla, including the spur, 25–30 mm long, typically conspicuously orange in the throat; perennial; cultivated in gardens, now a widespread weed . . . . *L. vulgaris*

BUTTER-AND-EGGS (Europe)

      4 Plants sprawling, the flowering stems branched; leaves with distinct petioles, the blades not much longer than wide, often somewhat arrowhead-shaped, hairy; corolla not so much as 2 cm long, usually yellowish except for the violet upper lip (sometimes bluish all over); annual; occasional weed
. . . . *K. elatine*

SHARP-LEAVED FLUELLIN (Europe)

1 Corolla not mostly yellow
  5 Corolla with a short sac (this not so much as twice as long as wide) near the base
    6 Most leaves about as wide as long, 5- or 7-lobed (corolla 1–1.5 mm long, mostly pale lilac or violet, with some yellowish on the lower lip; sac at the base of the corolla conical, 1–3 mm long; weedy, colonizing rock walls in many localities) . . . . *C. muralis* (*L. muralis*)

KENILWORTH IVY (Mediterranean region)

    6 Leaves much longer than wide, not lobed

7 Main stem and branches not slender or weak (corolla purplish pink with a yellow throat; occasionally escaping from cultivation) .... *A. orontium*
LESSER SNAPDRAGON (Europe)

7 Main stem and branches very slender, weak, the plants often supported by other vegetation (corolla lavender or dull purple, with darker veins, Douglas Co., Oreg., to Calif.) ....
.... *A. vexillo-calyculatum* subsp. *breweri* (*A. breweri*), pl. 552
BREWER'S SNAPDRAGON

5 Corolla with a slender spur at the base
  8 Spur of corolla straight or nearly so (corolla, including the spur, usually 15–30 mm long, purplish, with a nearly white spot in the throat but variously colored in plants grown in gardens or introduced from so-called wildflower seed mixes .... *L. maroccana*
  MOROCCAN TOAD-FLAX (N Africa)

  8 Spur of corolla distinctly curved
    9 Plants annual or biennial, not often more than 50 cm tall, sometime with several short, sprawling stems forming a rosette at the base; corolla violet to blue, often with white ridges in the throat .....
    .... *L. canadensis*
    BLUE TOAD-FLAX

    9 Plants perennial, commonly at least 50 cm tall, not forming a rosette of short stems at the base; inflorescence usually very crowded; corolla usually violet or lavender-purple, darker on the swelling at the throat (occasional weed, perhaps started with seed from a so-called wildflower mix) ....
    .... *L. purpurea*
    PURPLE TOADFLAX (Europe)

Mimulus

1 Woody shrub to about 1 m tall (corolla dull yellow or orange; leaves somewhat sticky-glandular; coastal Curry Co., Oreg., to Calif.) .... *M. aurantiacus*, pl. 567
BUSH MONKEY FLOWER

1 Plants herbaceous, not often so much as 75 cm tall
  2 Calyx not markedly 5-angled, the midribs of the lobes not obvious (stems and leaves conspicuously hairy; plants with an unpleasant odor; corolla 5–9 mm long, yellow, sometimes with maroon spots; in our region known to occur in Josephine and Jackson Cos., Oreg.; widespread in Calif. and also occasionally found E of the crest of the Cascades in Wash. and Oreg.) ...... *M. pilosus* (*Mimetanthe pilosa*)
  DOWNY MONKEY FLOWER

  2 Calyx markedly 5-angled, the midribs of the lobes raised and prominent
    3 Corolla mostly yellow (but often with red or maroon spots)
      4 Corolla to about 14 mm long, with a conspicuous reddish brown blotch at the base of the middle lobe of the lower lip; plants rarely so much as 15 cm tall .... *M. alsinoides*, pl. 566
      CHICKWEED MONKEY FLOWER

      4 Corolla usually more than 15 mm long (except sometimes in *M. moschatus*), without a single large blotch at the base of the middle lobe of the lower lip
        5 Uppermost calyx lobe decidedly larger than the others (in wet places)
          6 Each stem bearing not more than 5 flowers, the pedicels of these typically originating in the axils of leaves that are the largest or nearly the largest (strictly montane, not often found below about 4000 ft., 1220 m) .... *M. tilingii*
          TILING'S MONKEY FLOWER, YELLOW MOUNTAIN MONKEY FLOWER

          6 Each stem usually bearing at least 5 flowers, the pedicels of these typically originating in the axils of bracts that are much smaller than the lower leaves (very common in wet lowland and montane habitats) .... *M. guttatus*, pl. 570
          COMMON MONKEY FLOWER

          Mimulus guttatus includes several named, intergrading varieties and also plants that have previously been identified as *M. nasutus.*

5 Uppermost calyx lobe not decidedly longer than the others

  7 Plants forming low mats that hug the ground, the flowering stems, each usually with only 1 flower, generally not much more than 5 cm tall; corolla not distinctly 2-lipped (montane and especially above 5000 ft., 1520 m; rare below 4000 ft., 1220 m) . . . .*M. primuloides* var. *primuloides*

             PRIMROSE MONKEY FLOWER

  7 Plants generally more than 10 cm tall, not forming mats that hug the ground, the flowering stems usually with several flowers; corolla distinctly 2-lipped

    8 Leaves and stems very hairy, becoming slimy when handled; corolla 1–3 cm long (in wet places) . . . . *M. moschatus* (includes vars. *moschatus* and *sessilis*), pl. 572

             MUSK MONKEY FLOWER

    8 Leaves and stems hairy but not becoming slimy when handled; corolla 2.5–4 cm long (in wet places, mostly at the coast and in the Coast Ranges) . . . .*M. dentatus*

             COAST MONKEY FLOWER

3 Corolla mostly some shade of red, orange, pink, rose, or purple

  9 Corolla red or orange-red, except for dull yellow at the throat and in the tube (plants commonly more than 40 cm tall; corolla usually 4–5 cm long, the lobes tending to curve backward; SW Oreg. to Calif. and eastward to Utah) . . . .*M. cardinalis*, pl. 568

             SCARLET MONKEY FLOWER

  9 Corolla predominantly pink, purplish pink, rose, or purple

  10 Substantial perennial commonly at least 30 cm tall (corolla usually 3–4 cm long, purplish pink or rose-red, with some yellow; montane and mostly E of the crest of the Cascades, not often found below about 4000 ft., 1220 m) . . . .*M. lewisii*, pl. 571

             LEWIS' MONKEY FLOWER

  10 Small annuals not more than about 15 cm tall, often much smaller

    11 Lower lip of the corolla much reduced, as if it had been cut off, its 3 lobes scarcely apparent (plants not more than about 5 cm tall even when in flower; corolla primarily purple but the throat streaked with yellow, the tube usually at least 25 mm long; Josephine and Jackson Cos., Oreg., to Calif.) . . . .*M. douglasii*, pl. 569

             DOUGLAS' MONKEY FLOWER

    11 Lower lip of the corolla well developed, its 3 lobes conspicuous

      12 Pedicels typically at least as long as the calyces (sometimes slightly shorter but not much shorter); plants generally slender (corolla pink, purplish, or purplish red, often with yellow spots, the tube to about 8 mm long; mostly E of the crest of the Cascades) . . . .*M. breweri*

             BREWER'S MONKEY FLOWER

      12 Pedicels distinctly shorter than the calyces; plants generally rather compact

        13 Corolla mostly dull reddish purple, with a yellow, red-spotted area in the throat, the tube about 1 cm long (Josephine, Jackson, and Klamath Cos., Oreg., to Calif.) . . . .*M. jepsonii*

             JEPSON'S MONKEY FLOWER

        13 Corolla mostly purple, with a darker spot on each lobe of the lower lip and with a yellow, red-spotted area in the throat, the tube usually more than 2 cm long (Polk Co., Oreg., to Calif.) . . . .*M. tricolor*, pl. 573

             TRICOLOR MONKEY FLOWER

Orthocarpus

1 Lateral lobes of bracts of inflorescence smaller than the middle lobe but their bases usually at least half as wide as the middle lobe; transition from 3-lobed upper leaves to bracts gradual, the bracts not hiding the corollas (corollas usually 15–20 mm long, typically pinkish purple, sometimes white; tip of the beaklike upper lip with a downward projection) . . . . *O. bracteosus*, pl. 574

             ROSY OWL'S CLOVER

1 Lateral lobes of bracts of inflorescence very small compared to the middle lobe; transition from upper leaves to bracts abrupt, the bracts sometimes mostly hiding the corollas

2 Tip of beaklike upper lip of the corolla with a small, cylindrical downward projection; corollas usually 10–12 mm long, purplish, usually with a whitish lower lip (and mostly hidden by the bracts) . . . . *O. imbricatus*
MOUNTAIN OWL'S CLOVER

2 Tip of beaklike upper lip of the corolla without a cylindrical downward projection; corollas at least 12 mm long, usually purplish pink
  3 Corolla commonly about 20 mm long, the beaklike upper lip extending at least 3 mm beyond the lower lip; pouches of the lower lip 4–5 mm deep (Jackson and Klamath Cos., Oreg., to Calif.) . . . . *O. cuspidatus* subsp. *cuspidatus*
SISKIYOU OWL'S CLOVER
  3 Corolla commonly 12–15 mm long, the beaklike upper lip not extending so much as 3 mm beyond the lower lip; pouches of the lower lip not much more than 3 mm deep (Josephine and Jackson Cos., Oreg., to Calif.) . . . . *O. cuspidatus* subsp. *copelandii*
COPELAND'S OWL'S CLOVER

The subspecies of *O. cuspidatus* intergrade to the extent that some specimens cannot definitely be assigned to subsp. *cuspidatus* or subsp. *copelandii*.

Pedicularis

1 Leaf blades with toothed margins but none of them obviously lobed; calyx with only 2 lobes (corolla whitish, usually conspicuously tinged with pink or purple, the upper lobe abruptly down-curved and sickle-shaped; in our region not often found below 3500 ft., 1070 m) . . . . *P. racemosa* var. *racemosa*
SICKLE-TOP LOUSEWORT

1 At least many of the leaf blades lobed; calyx with 5 lobes
  2 Lower leaf blades on flowering stems usually with only 1–2 pairs of lateral lobes, these typically much narrower than the terminal lobe; basal leaves, these with as many as about 17 lobes, withering by the time of flowering (corollas mostly white to pale yellowish but the beaklike upper lip sometimes deep pink; Josephine Co., Oreg., to Calif., in our region rare below 5000 ft., 1520 m) . . . . *P. howellii*
HOWELL'S LOUSEWORT
  2 Lower leaf blades on flowering stems usually with at least several pairs of lateral lobes, these not conspicuously narrower than the terminal lobe; basal leaves usually present at the time of flowering, except in *P. bracteosa*
    3 Upper lip of corolla a slender beak that is curved upward or downward
      4 Beaklike upper lip of corolla curved downward (corolla white or yellowish, usually tinged or dotted with pink or purple; mostly E of the crest of the Cascades and in our region rare below 5000 ft., 1520 m) . . . . *P. contorta*, pl. 577
CURVED-BEAK LOUSEWORT
      4 Beaklike upper lip of corolla curved upward, resembling a raised elephant's trunk (lateral lobes of lower lip of corolla resembling an elephant's ears; corolla pink to reddish purple)
        5 Beaklike upper lip of corolla at least 7 mm long, sometimes more than 15 mm; calyces with only short hairs (in our region rare below 3500 ft., 1070 m) . . . . *P. groenlandica*, pl. 579
ELEPHANT'S-HEAD
        5 Beaklike upper lip of corolla not more than about 5 mm long; calyces conspicuously long-hairy (Oreg. to Calif., not likely to be found below 4500 ft., 1370 m) . . . . *P. attolens*, pl. 576
LITTLE ELEPHANT'S-HEAD
    3 Upper lip of corolla not a slender beak that is curved upward or downward
      6 Plants not often so much as 50 cm tall, the stems often sprawling to some extent; stem leaves few, less conspicuous than the basal leaves, which persist through the time of flowering; lower lip of corolla inconspicuous, not more than one-fourth as long as the upper lip, the 3 lobes often scarcely distinct (corollas generally deep purplish red but sometimes orange or yellow; Josephine, Jackson, and Klamath Cos., Oreg., mostly above 3500 ft., 1070 m, to Calif.) . . . . *P. densiflora*, pl. 578
INDIAN WARRIOR

6 Plants commonly at least 50 cm tall, the flowering stems upright; stem leaves about as well developed as the basal leaves, which usually wither by the time flowering is underway; lower lip of corolla conspicuous, about half as long as the upper lip, the 3 lobes obvious . . . .*P. bracteosa*
BRACTED LOUSEWORT

In our region, 3 intergrading varieties of *P. bracteosa,* none of them common below about 4000 ft. (1220 m), can be distinguished; they are keyed below.

7 Calyx typically glandular-hairy, the glands dark; corolla usually deep purplish red but sometimes yellow (Olympic Mountains, Wash.) . . . .*P. bracteosa* var. *atrosanguinea*
7 Calyx not glandular-hairy and sometimes not at all hairy
  8 Free portions of paired lateral sepals much shorter than the fused portion below, which is typically about as wide as long (corolla yellow to deep purplish red; Cascades from Pierce Co., Wash., to Brit. Col.) . . . .*P. bracteosa* var. *latifolia*
  8 Free portions of paired lateral sepals about as long as the fused portion below, which is typically longer than wide; corolla greenish yellow, often red-tinged, sometimes almost completely reddish (Cascades and Siskiyou Mountains, Oregon and Calif.) . . . .*P. bracteosa* var. *flavida*

Penstemon

If the fertile stamens of the plant you are keying depart from the corolla tube at the same level, and if their filaments are hairy at the base, go back to the key to Scrophulariaceae, to choice 14, which separates *Nothochelone nemorosa* and *Keckiella lemmonii.* These two species are so similar in other respects to *Penstemon* that even experienced botanists may assume that they are in this genus.

1 Anthers of fertile stamens with long, tangled hairs visible without magnification
  2 Plants at least partly upright, sometimes to about 40 cm tall; most leaf blades more than 3 cm long
    3 Corolla bright rose-purple to blue-violet; margins of leaf blades with distinct teeth (in the Cascades, Coast Ranges, and Siskiyou Mountains, mostly above 2000 ft., 610 m) . . . .*P. cardwellii,* pl. 581
CARDWELL'S PENSTEMON
    3 Corolla lavender-blue to pale purple; margins of leaf blades (in this variety) more often smooth than toothed (mostly E of the crest of the Cascades) . . . .*P. fruticosus* var. *fruticosus*
SHRUBBY PENSTEMON
  2 Plants forming low mats, the upright flowering branches rarely so much as 10 cm tall; leaf blades not often more than 1.5 cm long
    4 Corolla deep pink to rose-purple; leaf blades slightly grayish and sometimes hairy (mostly montane but occasionally found at relatively low elevations in the Columbia River Gorge) . . . . *P. rupicola,* pl. 584
ROCK PENSTEMON
    4 Corolla blue-lavender to bluish purple; leaf blades not grayish and not at all hairy (both sides of the Cascades, to Calif., but not likely to be found below 3000 ft., 910 m) . . . . . .*P. davidsonii* var. *menziesii*
CREEPING PENSTEMON

Penstemon davidsonii var. *davidsonii* (pl. 582), apparently not so common as var. *menziesii* W of the crest of the Cascades, differs from the latter in having smooth-margined rather than toothed leaf blades.

1 Anthers of fertile stamens not covered with tangled hairs (but there may inconspicuous straight hairs)
  5 Leaf blades without marginal teeth or lobes
    6 Sterile stamen hairy near the tip (corollas usually purplish blue, sometimes yellowish in *P. procerus* var. *tolmiei*)
      7 Slender tips of the calyx lobes about as long as the basal portion; corollas usually at least 11 mm long; pollen sacs 0.6–1 mm long (in our region, S Wash. and N Willamette Valley, Oreg., otherwise E of the crest of the Cascades) . . . .*P. rydbergii* var. *hesperius*
TALL PENSTEMON, RYDBERG'S PENSTEMON

Penstemon euglaucus, midmontane in the Cascades from Wash. to Oreg. but mostly E of the crest, is similar to *P. rydbergii* var. *hesperius* except for the fact that its leaves and stems consistently have a grayish tinge.

7 Slender tips of the calyx lobes much shorter than the basal portion; corollas usually 7–11 mm long; pollen sacs 0.3–0.7 mm long

    8 Plants generally not more than 15 cm tall; flowering stems usually with a single whorl of flowers (corollas sometimes yellowish instead of purplish blue; mostly above 5000 ft., 1520 m, Olympic Mountains, Wash., and the Cascades, Brit. Col. to Wash.) . . . . *P. procerus* var. *tolmiei*
                TOLMIE'S PENSTEMON

    8 Plant generally at least 15 cm tall, sometimes as tall as 30 cm; flowering stems usually with at least 2 whorls of flowers (mostly above 5000 ft., 1520 m, in the Cascades, especially E of the crest, Oreg. to Calif.) . . . . *P. procerus* var. *brachyanthus*
                SMALL-FLOWERED PENSTEMON

6 Sterile stamen not hairy near the tip

    9 Calyces, corollas, and branches of inflorescence usually distinctly glandular-hairy (but sometimes not in *P. laetus* var. *sagittatus*); blades of larger leaves typically narrow, at least 10 times as long as wide

      10 Corolla at least 20 mm long, sometimes more than 30 mm, purplish pink to violet; calyx 5–8 mm long (Josephine, Jackson, and Klamath Cos., Oreg., to Calif.) . . . . *P. laetus* var. *sagittatus*
                GAY PENSTEMON

      10 Corolla 13–22 mm long but rarely more than 20 mm, usually purplish blue; calyx 3.5–6 mm long (Josephine and Jackson Cos., Oreg., to Calif.; also E of the Cascades) . . . . *P. roezlii*, pl. 583
                ROEZL'S PENSTEMON

    9 Calyces, corollas, and branches of inflorescence not glandular-hairy; blades of larger leaves less than 4 times as long as wide

      11 Plants often more than 30 cm tall; corolla usually 20–35 mm long, usually deep blue but sometimes purplish pink; anthers commonly at least 2 mm long, sometimes as long as 3 mm (Josephine and Jackson Cos., Oreg., to Calif.) . . . . *P. azureus*, pl. 580
                AZURE PENSTEMON

      11 Plants not often so much as 30 cm tall; corolla 14–20 mm long, violet-blue or blue; anthers to 1.8 mm long (Jackson Co., Oreg., to Calif.) . . . . *P. parvulus*
                SMALL AZURE PENSTEMON
            Penstemon azureus and *P. parvulus* intergrade.

5 Most leaf blades, at least the lower ones, with marginal teeth or pointed lobes

12 Corolla predominantly off-white or faintly yellowish (almost strictly limited to the region E of the crest of the Cascades except for 1 or more localities in Lane Co., Oreg.) . . . . *P. deustus* var. *deustus*
                HOT-ROCK PENSTEMON

12 Corolla predominantly some shade of lavender, blue, or purple

    13 Leaf blades with pointed lobes or coarse teeth of uneven size, the separations between the lobes or teeth often extending more than halfway to the midrib (corolla 22–32 mm long, bright lavender with darker streaks on the inner surface of the lower lip; at lower elevations in the Cascades and some other areas W of the Cascades, S Brit. Col. to N Oreg.) . . . . . *P. richardsonii* var. *richardsonii*
                CUT-LEAVED PENSTEMON

    13 Leaf blades with marginal teeth but these of rather even size and never so deeply separated that they can be called lobes

Penstemon deustus var. *deustus*, hot-rock penstemon

14 Corolla without any hairs inside or outside (corolla usually 17–25 mm long, blue to blue-purple; S Brit. Col. to Lane Co., Oreg., in the Cascades and Coast Ranges) . . . . *P. serrulatus,* pl. 585
SPREADING PENSTEMON

14 Corolla with hairs inside or outside, or both
  15 Lower lip of the corolla not hairy (but the floor of the inside of the tube may be hairy); sterile stamen only sparsely hairy (corolla usually 13–18 mm long, light blue to bluish purple or violet-purple; SW Oreg. to Calif.) . . . . *P. anguineus*
TONGUE-LEAVED PENSTEMON

  15 Lower lip of the corolla hairy, at least near the throat; sterile stamen densely hairy
    16 Sterile stamen reaching barely to the throat of the corolla (corolla 15–22 mm long, glandular-hairy externally, blue or bluish purple, the tube usually paler than the lips; S Brit. Col. to N Oreg.) . . . .
. . . . *P. ovatus*
BROAD-LEAVED PENSTEMON

    16 Sterile stamen reaching well beyond the throat of the corolla (corolla usually 18–30 mm long, mostly blue-violet, light purple, or lavender, but the inside of the tube often whitish; SW Oreg. to Calif.) . . . . *P. rattanii* var. *rattanii*
RATTAN'S PENSTEMON

Scrophularia

1 Sterile stamen more or less club-shaped, distinctly longer than wide and usually purplish brown (W of the Cascades, especially near the coast) . . . . *S. californica* subsp. *californica,* pl. 586
CALIFORNIA FIGWORT

1 Sterile stamen somewhat fan-shaped, distinctly wider than long and usually yellowish green (W and E of the crest of the Cascades) . . . . *S. lanceolata*
LANCE-LEAVED FIGWORT

Synthyris

1 Leaf blades deeply pinnately divided, nearly pinnately compound (endemic to the Olympic Mountains, Wash., and not likely to be found as low as 5000 ft., 1520 m) . . . . *S. pinnatifida* var. *lanuginosa*
CUT-LEAF SYNTHYRIS

1 Leaf blades toothed to shallowly lobed but not deeply divided
  2 Corolla lobes about as long as the tube (Lewis Co., Wash., to Calif.) . . . . *S. reniformis,* pl. 588
SNOW QUEEN, ROUND-LEAVED SYNTHYRIS

  2 Corolla lobes decidedly longer than the tube
    3 Corolla lobes not divided (in the Columbia River Gorge from Skamania Co., Wash., and Hood River Co., Oreg., E to Idaho) . . . . *S. missurica* (includes *S. stellata*), pl. 587
WESTERN MOUNTAIN SYNTHYRIS

    3 Corolla lobes split into slender, almost threadlike divisions (Saddle Mountain, Clatsop Co., Oreg., Olympic Mountains of Wash., and a few localities between) . . . . *S. schizantha*
FRINGED SYNTHYRIS

Triphysaria

1 Plants (with purplish brown stems and leaves) not often more than 15 cm tall, branching from the base, so there is not a distinct main stem; corolla purplish or purplish red, 4–6 mm long . . . .
. . . . *T. pusilla* (*Orthocarpus pusillus*), pl. 590
DWARF OWL'S CLOVER

1 Plants commonly more than 15 cm tall, usually branching well above the base, so there is a distinct main stem; corolla at least 10 mm long
  2 Leaves and stems purplish, usually obviously hairy; upper lip (beak) of corolla purplish, the middle lobe of the lower lip yellow, the lateral lobes white (coastal, Curry Co., Oreg., to Calif.) . . . .
. . . . *T. eriantha* subsp. *eriantha* (*Orthocarpus erianthus*), pl. 589
YELLOW JOHNNY-TUCK

2 Leaves and stems yellowish, greenish, or brownish, usually not obviously hairy; corolla mostly white or yellow, the pouch of the lower lobe with purple dots

   3 Corolla mostly white (coastal, SE Vancouver Island, Brit. Col.; otherwise Lane Co., Oreg., to Calif.)
     . . . . ***T. versicolor* subsp. *versicolor*** (*Orthocarpus versicolor*)
                    WHITE OWL'S CLOVER

   3 Corolla mostly yellow (Douglas Co., Oreg., to Calif.) . . . .
     . . . . ***T. versicolor* subsp. *faucibarbata*** (*Orthocarpus faucibarbatus*)
                    YELLOW OWL'S CLOVER

Verbascum

1 Leaves green, the plants not woolly-hairy (but they may have some glandular hairs, especially above); flower pedicels 10–15 mm long (corollas usually yellow, occasionally white) . . . . ***V. blattaria***, pl. 591
                    MOTH MULLEIN (Eurasia)

1 Leaves grayish, the plants as a whole woolly-hairy; flower pedicels not so much as 3 mm long

   2 Margins of corolla lobes smooth; leaves, except on upper portions, with distinct petioles; corollas yellow (common weed) . . . . ***V. thapsus***
                    COMMON MULLEIN (Eurasia)

   2 Margins of corolla lobes somewhat crinkly; leaves, at almost all levels, without distinct petioles; corollas usually yellow or orange-yellow, sometimes white (occasional weed in SW Brit. Col. and nearby areas of W Wash.) . . . . ***V. phlomoides***
                    WOOLLY MULLEIN (Eurasia)

Veronica

1 Flowers either concentrated in a single unbranched terminal inflorescence that is a continuation of a main stem and in which each flower is nearly sessile in the axil of a bract, or nearly sessile and single in the axils of leaves

   2 Annuals, not spreading by rhizomes, not forming mats, but sometimes crowded

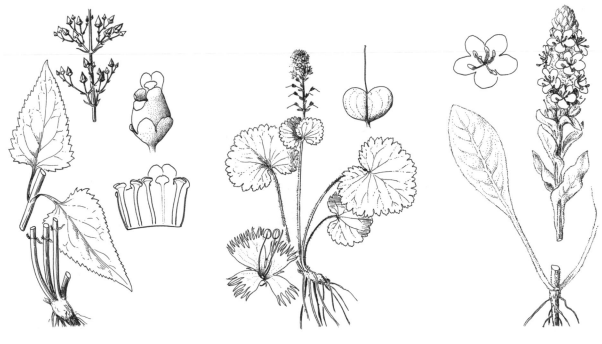

Scrophularia lanceolata,
lance-leaved figwort

Synthyris schizantha,
fringed synthyris

Verbascum thapsus,
common mullein

3 Blades of larger leaves not more than twice as long as wide, distinctly toothed; corolla blue-violet, only 2–2.5 mm wide when fully open . . . . *V. arvensis*

FIELD SPEEDWELL (Europe)

3 Blades of larger leaves mostly 3–10 times as long as wide, not distinctly or evenly toothed; corolla white or nearly so

   4 Inflorescence and fruits glandular-hairy . . . . *V. peregrina* var. *xalapensis*

PURSLANE SPEEDWELL

   4 Inflorescence and fruits not glandular-hairy (uncommon weed) . . . .
. . . . *V. peregrina* var. *peregrina* (believed to be from E North America)

2 Perennials spreading by shallowly buried rhizomes, thereby forming mats

  5 Style of pistil 6–10 mm long, about as long as the fully developed fruit; filaments of stamens 4–8 mm long; leaf blades about twice as long as wide; corolla (deep violet-blue) to 12–13 mm wide (S Brit. Col. to Oreg. and eastward; in our region in the Olympic Mountains and Cascades, not likely to be found below 5000 ft., 1520 m) . . . . *V. cusickii*

CUSICK'S SPEEDWELL

  5 Style of pistil not more than about 3.5 mm long and only about half as long as the fully developed fruit; filaments of stamens not more than 4 mm long; leaf blades generally more than twice as long as wide; corolla not more than 10 mm wide

   6 Fruit distinctly longer than wide (filaments of stamens 1–1.5 mm long; corolla to 10 mm wide, violet-blue but usually lighter than that of *V. cusickii*, first choice 5; not likely to be found below about 5000 ft., 1520 m) . . . . *V. wormskjoldii*

WORMSKJOLD'S SPEEDWELL

   6 Fruit as wide or wider than long

    7 Corolla white or pale blue, with darker blue lines; stem of inflorescence not obviously more hairy or glandular than the leafy part; filaments of stamens 1–2.5 mm long (occasional weed) . . . .
. . . . *V. serpyllifolia* var. *serpyllifolia*

THYME-LEAVED SPEEDWELL (Europe)

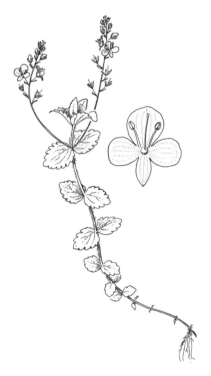

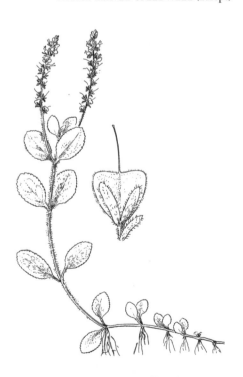

Veronica chamaedrys,
germander speedwell

Veronica officinalis,
common speedwell

7 Corolla typically bright blue; stem of inflorescence considerably more hairy and glandular than the leafy part; filaments of stamens 2–4 mm long (in our region mostly montane and not likely to be found below 4000 ft., 1220 m) . . . . *V. serpyllifolia* var. *humifusa*

1 Flowers either with long pedicels and borne singly in the axils of leaves or bracts, or on branches originating in the axils of leaves below the tips of the main stems

  8 Flowers borne singly in the axils of leaves or bracts

    9 Stems rooting at the nodes, the plants thereby forming mats; calyx lobes not fringed with long hairs (corolla usually pale blue or lavender-blue) . . . . *V. filiformis*
    SLENDER SPEEDWELL, CREEPING SPEEDWELL (Asia Minor)

    9 Stems not rooting at the nodes, the plants not forming mats (but individual plants may be crowded); calyx lobes fringed with long hairs

      10 Leaf blades with 3–5 rather distinct lobes, often as wide as long and usually squared-off at the base; corolla pale blue . . . . *V. hederifolia*
      IVY-LEAVED SPEEDWELL

      10 Leaf blades with toothed margins but not distinctly lobed, usually longer than wide and not squared-off at the base; corolla bright blue with prominent purplish lines and a white center . . . . *V. persica*
      PERSIAN SPEEDWELL (Eurasia)

  8 Flowers in racemelike branches originating in the axils of the leaves (all of which are opposite)

    11 Plants obviously hairy; not ordinarily growing in wet places

      12 Leaves sessile, usually with 5–11 teeth on each side (mostly in lawns) . . . . *V. chamaedrys*
      GERMANDER SPEEDWELL (Europe)

      12 Most leaves with petioles, the blades usually with 12–20 teeth on each side (common weed along roadsides and paths, and also in open woods) . . . . *V. officinalis*
      COMMON SPEEDWELL (Eurasia)

    11 Plants scarcely if at all hairy (except sometimes in *V. scutellata*, which is distinctive in having leaves that are usually at least 8 times as long as wide); plants usually growing in wet places

Veronica scutellata,
marsh speedwell

Veronica anagallis-aquatica,
water speedwell

13 All leaves with short but distinct petioles (in wet places) .... *V. americana*
AMERICAN BROOKLIME

> *Veronica americana* is sometimes—and perhaps correctly—called *V. beccabunga* var. *americana*.

13 Most leaves (especially those in the middle and upper regions of the plant) sessile

  14 Fruit conspicuously flattened, wider than long, and markedly notched at the tip; larger leaves usually at least 8 times as long as wide (in wet places) .... *V. scutellata*, p. 353
MARSH SPEEDWELL

  14 Fruit not conspicuously flattened and only slightly if at all notched at the tip; leaves not often more than 5 times as long as wide

    15 Leaves to 3 times as long as wide; fruits about as long as wide; corolla blue or violet (in wet places) .... *V. anagallis-aquatica*, p. 353
WATER SPEEDWELL

    15 Leaves usually 3–5 times as long as wide; fruits a little wider than long; corolla white, pink, or pale blue (in wet places) .... *V. catenata*
CHAIN SPEEDWELL

SOLANACEAE Nightshade Family

To the nightshade family we owe some very important food plants and flavorings: potato, tomato, tomatillo, eggplant, sweet pepper, and chili pepper (but not black pepper, which belongs to the Piperaceae, not represented in our region). The family also includes tobacco and some medicinal plants, including black henbane and deadly nightshade, which are just two of the species whose fruits or leaves are poisonous. Many species have become established as weeds in North America, and we have our share of these in British Columbia, Washington, and Oregon.

Both the calyx and corolla are five-lobed, and there are usually five stamens, which are attached to the corolla tube. The fruit, partitioned lengthwise into two or four seed-producing divisions, is sometimes dry when mature, sometimes a fleshy berry.

Physalis pubescens, low hairy ground-cherry, grown in vegetable gardens, is not in this key. A native of the eastern United States, it is usually more than 50 cm tall, and its flowers and fruits resemble those of various species of *Solanum*. A distinctive feature of the genus to which it belongs, however, is the inflated calyx that completely encloses the fruit.

1 Corolla with only a short tube (sometimes so short that there may seem to be none) .... *Solanum*
1 Corolla with a definite and sometimes long tube

  2 Corolla (white or tinged with purple) trumpet-shaped, 6–10 cm long, flaring outward to a width of 3–5 cm, each shallow lobe tipped with a slender, toothlike projection (fruit 3–5 cm long, with numerous soft spines before drying out and splitting lengthwise; leaves to more than 15 cm long, the blades shallowly lobed or coarsely toothed) .... *Datura stramonium*
JIMSONWEED (Europe)

  2 Corolla neither trumpet-shaped nor so much as 3 cm long, and not flaring conspicuously, the lobes rounded

    3 Leaf blades sessile, shallowly divided into nearly triangular lobes; corolla usually yellowish green, with purple lines and purple throat, about as long as the calyx; calyx closely covering the fruit, which separates crosswise into 2 sections when dry (rarely encountered as a weed W of the Cascades) .... *Hyoscyamus niger*
BLACK HENBANE (Europe)

    3 Leaves with petioles, the blades not lobed; corolla purplish, greenish, or yellowish, about twice as long as the calyx; calyx lobes spreading away from the fleshy black fruit (1.5–2 cm wide) .... *Atropa belladonna*
DEADLY NIGHTSHADE (Europe)

Solanum

1 Stems and leaves spiny

    2 Corolla yellow; fruit dry at maturity, completely enclosed by the calyx, this covered with slender spines to 1 cm long . . . . *S. rostratum*

          BEAKED NIGHTSHADE (Great Plains region of United States)

    2 Corolla usually bluish or pale violet; fruit fleshy, yellow when ripe, not completely enclosed by the calyx, which is not spiny (established E of the Cascades and perhaps in a few places W of the Cascades) . . . . *S. carolinense*

          CAROLINA HORSE NETTLE (central and E United States, Mexico)

1 Stems and leaves not spiny

    3 Corolla lobes (bluish purple) very shallow, much wider than long (plants shrubby, to about 1 m tall; fruit usually 7–9 mm in diameter; none of the leaves lobed; Curry, Josephine, and Jackson Cos., Oreg., to Calif.) . . . . *S. parishii*

          PARISH'S NIGHTSHADE

    3 Corolla lobes at least as long as wide

        4 Perennial vine climbing over shrubs; some leaves 3-lobed; corolla deep blue or violet; fruit red when ripe; usually in wet places . . . . *S. dulcamara*

          BITTERSWEET, BITTERSWEET NIGHTSHADE (Europe)

        4 Plants not conforming in all respects to criteria in the other choice 4

          5 Inflorescence usually branched into 2 umbel-like flower clusters (plants to about 1 m tall but the stems often falling down; corolla white or pale violet; fruit usually about 15 mm wide, dark purple when ripe; perennial; near the coast in Curry Co., Oreg., to Calif.) . . . . *S. furcatum*

          FORKED NIGHTSHADE (South America)

          5 Inflorescence usually consisting of a single umbel-like flower cluster

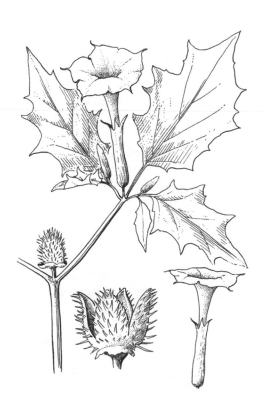

Datura stramonium,
jimsonweed

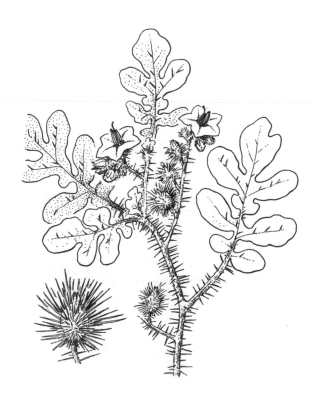

Solanum rostratum,
beaked nightshade

6 Stems and calyx very hairy; calyx becoming slightly enlarged and partly covering the fruit, the lobes approximately triangular; fruit yellow when ripe . . . .*S. physalifolium*, pl. 592

HAIRY NIGHTSHADE (South America)

Solanum sarrachoides, whose presence in our region has not yet been documented, is similar to *S. physalifolium;* its calyx lobes, however, are elongated and reach to or beyond the tip of the mature fruit, and there are typically only 4 flowers in an inflorescence.

6 Stems and calyx only slightly if at all hairy; calyx not becoming enlarged or partly covering the fruit; fruit black or dark purple when ripe

7 Corolla (with yellow spots below the base of the lobes) about 10 mm wide; calyx lobes not turned back when the fruit is ripe; usually annual . . . .*S. nigrum*

BLACK NIGHTSHADE (Europe)

7 Corolla 3–6 mm wide; calyx lobes turned back when the fruit is ripe; annual or perennial . . . .
. . . .*S. americanum* (*S. nodiflorum*)

SMALL-FLOWERED NIGHTSHADE (South America)

The name *S. americanum* var. *nodiflorum* is sometimes applied to plants reported as weeds in our region.

THYMELAEACEAE Daphne Family

Most members of the daphne family are shrubs whose calyx, with four lobes, usually resembles a corolla; true petals are absent or reduced to small, scalelike structures. There are eight or ten stamens, the filaments of these attached to the tubular portion of the calyx, and a single pistil that may develop into a fleshy or dry fruit, depending on the genus.

Gardeners will be familiar with several attractive species of *Daphne,* some of which have fragrant flowers. One European species of the genus, however, is becoming a nuisance. This is *D. laureola* (pl. 593), called spurge laurel. It is a pleasant-looking evergreen shrub, with elongated, shiny leaves to more than 10 cm long. Clusters of greenish yellow, unscented flowers, produced in the axils of leaves near the tops of the stems, appear in March. The egg-shaped, fleshy fruits, about 1 cm long, are nearly black. They are poisonous, so one would imagine that the seeds are not spread by birds. They are, however, effectively disseminated in one way or another, and this plant is becoming extremely common in some areas, especially southwestern British Columbia, including the Gulf Islands, and the Puget Sound region of Washington. It may be a good idea to eradicate it, partly because its fruits could entice children to taste them, and partly because it could compete aggressively with native vegetation.

URTICACEAE Nettle Family

The nettles in our region, members of the genus *Urtica,* are herbaceous annuals or perennials with opposite leaves. The flowers are concentrated in clusters that originate in the leaf axils. Each flower has either four stamens or a pistil that produces a single seed. The calyx of staminate flowers is four-lobed, that of pistillate flowers is either four- or two-lobed. Petals are absent. Stinging hairs are present on the stems and leaves, and contact with them will probably result in a prickly sensation that may last a few hours.

Urtica

1 Plants annual, rarely more than 50 cm tall; leaf blades not often so much as 4 cm long, usually widest near the middle and without an indentation where the petiole is attached (garden, orchard, and barnyard weed, and, of nettles in our region, the one with the most potent sting) . . . .*U. urens*

DWARF NETTLE (Europe)

1 Plants perennial, to more than 1 m tall; leaf blades commonly more than 5 cm long, usually widest below the middle and sometimes with a slight indentation where the petiole is attached

2 Staminate and pistillate flowers on separate plants; both surfaces of the leaf blades with abundant stinging hairs (known from scattered localities in Brit. Col., SW Wash., and NW Oreg.) . . . .
. . . . *U. dioica* subsp. *dioica*

EUROPEAN NETTLE (Europe)

2 Staminate and pistillate flowers usually present on the same plant (but those of one or the other type are generally more numerous on a particular plant); stinging hairs mostly restricted to the undersides of the leaf blades

    3 Stems with a rather dense covering of short, soft hairs as well as stinging hairs; underside of leaf blades with abundant white hairs (sometimes almost woolly-hairy) in addition to stinging hairs (extreme SW Oreg. to Calif.; also in and E of the Cascades and Sierra Nevada) . . . . *U. dioica* subsp. *holosericea*

        HOARY NETTLE

    3 Stems with scattered stiff hairs, these mostly pressed down and pointing in the same direction, as well as stinging hairs; underside of leaf blades smooth or with only sparse short hairs in addition to stinging hairs (widespread over much of North America and the prevailing nettle of Brit. Col., W Wash. and Oreg., and coastal Calif.) . . . . *U. dioica* subsp. *gracilis* (*U. dioica* var. *lyallii*), pl. 594

        AMERICAN NETTLE

VALERIANACEAE Valerian Family

Representatives of the valerian family in our region are herbaceous perennials with opposite leaves and crowded inflorescences. The corolla, with five lobes, is usually at least slightly two-lipped and generally has a perceptible to prominent saclike spur originating from the lower side of the proportionately long tube. The calyx tube is united to the fruit-forming portion of the pistil; in the genus *Valeriana,* the calyx lobes are conspicuous as well as considerably modified, but in *Plectritis* they are so much reduced that for all practical purposes they are missing. Three stamens are attached to the inside of the corolla tube. The fruit, containing a single seed, is dry when mature.

Not all members of the family conform to the formula just described. For instance, the red valerian, *Centranthus ruber,* commonly grown in gardens, has essentially equal corolla lobes; the tube, however, does have an obvious spur. This plant often escapes and becomes so well established in some places that it may seem to be a native.

Solanum nigrum,
black nightshade

Urtica urens,
dwarf nettle

1 Some leaves pinnately lobed; calyx, at the time of flowering, consisting of several to many inrolled, feather-like bristles that expand and become conspicuous as the fruits begin to develop; perennial (corolla white or pale pink) .... *Valeriana*

1 None of the leaves compound; calyx without obvious bristles at any stage; annual (corolla white to dark pink) .... *Plectritis-Valerianella* **complex**

Plectritis-Valerianella Complex

1 Stems usually branching dichotomously at least once; corolla without an obvious saclike spur (corolla white or pale blue; *P. brachystemon*, first choice 5, usually has only a short spur, sometimes no spur at all)

  2 Fruit less than twice as long as wide, with a lengthwise corky mass .... *V. locusta* (*V. olitoria*)
      EUROPEAN CORN SALAD (Europe)

  2 Fruit less than twice as long a wide, without a lengthwise corky mass (not yet widespread in our region) .... *V. carinata*
      KEELED CORN SALAD (Europe)

1 Stem rarely branching (branches, if developing at all, opposite); corolla usually with an obvious saclike spur (but the spur is short or sometimes even absent in *P. brachystemon*)

  3 Corolla only very slightly 2-lipped, white to pale pink (spur nearly as wide as the corolla tube; corolla 2–3.5 mm long) .... *P. macrocera*
      LONGHORN PLECTRITIS

  3 Corolla decidedly 2-lipped, usually pale to deep pink, sometimes white

    4 Spur about as long as the corolla tube, slender and tapering to a point; corolla (usually deep pink) with 1–2 darker spots at the base of the lower lip (Josephine Co., Oreg., to Calif.) ... *P. ciliosa* subsp. *ciliosa*
      LONGSPUR PLECTRITIS

    4 Spur, if evident, less than one-fourth as long as the corolla tube; corolla without darker spots at the base of the lower lip

      5 Corolla to 3.5 mm long, white to pale pink; spur short, often reduced to a small swelling, or absent .... *P. brachystemon* (*P. anomala, P. aphanoptera, P. congesta* var. *major, P. magna* var. *nitida*)
      PALE PLECTRITIS

      5 Corolla 4.5–9.5 mm long, pale to dark pink or reddish pink; spur distinct (but not much longer than wide) .... *P. congesta*, pl. 595
      ROSY PLECTRITIS, SEA BLUSH

      In some references, *P. congesta* is divided into 2 varieties, *congesta* and *major,* the latter the same as what is here called *P. brachystemon.*

Valeriana

1 Basal leaves persisting and pinnately divided into a least 7 lobes (sometimes more than 17), the terminal one not obviously larger than the lateral ones (garden plant, sometimes escaping) .... *V. officinalis*
  COMMON VALERIAN, GARDEN HELIOTROPE (Eurasia)

1 Basal leaves (when persisting) not often divided into more than 5 lobes, the terminal lobe typically much larger than the lateral ones

  2 Basal leaves (when persisting) not often larger than the leaves higher on the stems; leaflets of lower leaves (and also of upper leaves) usually coarsely toothed, sometimes shallowly lobed; fruits usually 5–6 mm long; plants sometimes more than 1 m tall; in the Cascades above 3000 ft. (910 m) but not farther W .... *V. sitchensis*
      NORTHERN VALERIAN

  2 Basal leaves often larger than the leaves higher on the stems; leaflets usually not coarsely toothed and generally not toothed at all; fruits usually 4–5 mm long; plants not often more than 70 cm tall; from near sea level to about 4000 ft. (1220 m) in the mountains .... *V. scouleri*, pl. 596
      SCOULER'S VALERIAN

      In some references, *V. sitchensis* and *V. scouleri* are considered to be subspecies of *V. sitchensis.*

VERBENACEAE Verbena Family

In verbenas and their relatives, the leaves are opposite or whorled, and the flowers are in elongated inflorescences or dense heads. The stems are usually four-angled, as in mints, teasels, and a few other families. In *Verbena*, the only genus growing wild in our region, the calyx is tubular and five-lobed. The corolla is also five-lobed and sometimes perceptibly two-lipped. There are four stamens, arranged as two pairs, and a single pistil. When ripe, the fruit breaks apart into four nutlets, each containing a single seed. In other genera, there may be significant deviations from the formula given here for *Verbena*.

1 Plants prostrate, forming tight mats; leaf blades to 2 cm long, usually toothed along the margins of the upper half; inflorescence to about 1 cm long, on a peduncle 1.5 cm long or longer; calyx with 2–4 lobes; corolla 4–5 mm long, pink or white (widely grown in warmer areas of North America for erosion control or for lawns; an uncommon weed in our region) . . . . ***Phyla nodiflora*** (*Lippia nodiflora*)
LEMON VERBENA (South America)

1 Plants not prostrate nor forming tight mats (but the stems may sprawl); leaf blades mostly at least 3 cm long, toothed or lobed for most of their length; inflorescence large, branched; calyx with 5 lobes; corolla more than 5 mm long, usually blue, lavender, violet, or purple, occasionally white . . . . ***Verbena***

Verbena

1 Bracts of the inflorescence at least 5 mm long, often more than 10 mm, much longer than the flowers themselves; leaves mostly 3–5 cm long (the blades deeply divided into 3 or 5 lobes); corolla white to lavender (widespread in North America, including portions of the Pacific Northwest E of the Cascades, but only occasionally encountered in our region) . . . . ***V. bracteata***
BRACTED VERBENA

1 Bracts of the inflorescence not so much as 5 mm long, shorter than the flowers; lower leaves usually more than 5 cm long; corolla blue, violet, or purple

   2 Blades of upper leaves deeply lobed; plants often sprawling (Douglas Co., Oreg., to Calif.) . . . . ***V. lasiostachys*** subsp. *lasiostachys*
WESTERN VERBENA

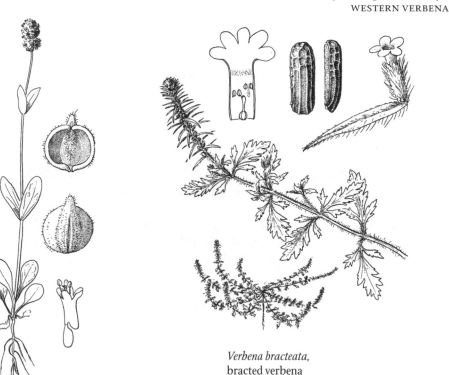

Plectritis macrocera,
longhorn plectritis

Verbena bracteata,
bracted verbena

2 Blades of upper leaves coarsely toothed but not deeply lobed; plants mostly stiffly upright (sometimes more than 1 m tall)

    3 Most or all leaves with distinct petioles at least 1 cm long .... *V. hastata,* pl. 597
                                                                 BLUE VERBENA

    3 Most or all leaves completely sessile, often clasping the stems (garden plant, occasionally escaping)
       .... *V. bonariensis*
                                  CLUSTER-FLOWERED VERBENA (South America)

VIOLACEAE Violet Family

Violets have irregular flowers, the two upper petals, two lateral petals, and lower petal obviously different. The lower petal is especially distinctive because it has a saclike spur near its base. The sepals, separate from one another, are also unequal, and each one has, where it is attached to the receptacle, a small flaplike appendage. There are five stamens, the two lower ones having winglike lobes that go down into the spur of the lower petal. The fruit-forming portion of the pistil is not partitioned lengthwise into chambers, but its wall consists of three valves that separate when the dry fruit is mature; in certain species the valves crack apart with enough force to scatter the seeds. In many violets, some of the flowers, especially those appearing late in the season, differ from typical flowers because they remain closed; they may nevertheless produce normal fruits through self-pollination.

Viola

1 Stipules well developed, about the same size as the leaf blades and pinnately lobed; introduced species, most likely to be found near habitations

    2 Petals typically cream or pale yellow tinged with blue-violet; spur of lowermost petal about as long as the flaplike appendages of the sepals; annual .... *V. arvensis*
                                                  FIELD PANSY (Europe)

    2 Petals mostly deep blue-violet with some white and yellow (occasionally mostly yellow, however); spur of the lowermost petal longer than the flaplike appendages of the sepals; usually annual or biennial, sometimes perennial .... *V. tricolor*
                            WILD PANSY, HEART'S-EASE (Europe)

1 Stipules not well developed, much smaller than the leaf blades, smooth-margined or toothed but not lobed (perennial native species)

    3 Flowers conspicuously bicolored, the 2 upper petals dark violet, the other 3 petals cream or pale yellow, with dark lines (Willamette Valley, Oreg., to Calif.; more common in SW Oreg. than in the Willamette Valley) .... *V. hallii,* pl. 601
                                                    HALL'S VIOLET

    3 Flowers not distinctively bicolored in the way described in the other choice 3

        4 Leaf blades deeply lobed (color of inner faces of petals primarily pale yellow, yellow, or orange)

            5 Lateral petals without hairs at their bases (leaf blades more or less palmately lobed, some of the primary lobes with small secondary lobes; Jackson Co., Oreg., to Calif., also E of the Cascades; in our region not likely to be found below 3000 ft., 910 m) .... *V. sheltonii*
                                                  SHELTON'S VIOLET

            5 Lateral petals with short, club-shaped hairs at their bases

                6 Leaf blades regularly pinnately lobed, the ultimate lobes slender; petals orange-yellow (Josephine and Jackson Cos., Oreg., to Calif.) .... *V. douglasii,* pl. 599
                                                  DOUGLAS' VIOLET

                6 Leaf blades lobed in a nearly palmate pattern, the primary lobes broad, sometimes with small secondary lobes; petals yellow (Josephine Co., Oreg., to Calif.) ... *V. lobata* subsp. *lobata,* pl. 603
                                          LOBE-LEAVED PINE VIOLET

                  Viola lobata subsp. lobata intergrades with subsp. integrifolia, first choice 15.

        4 Leaf blades not lobed (but they may have conspicuous teeth)

7 Both lateral petals white, cream, or yellow, with a dark purple spot formed by coalescence of dark lines near the base

  8 Leaf blades with wedge-shaped bases, therefore not heart-shaped (Lane, Douglas, Josephine, and Curry Cos., Oreg., to Calif.) . . . . ***V. cuneata***
                       WEDGE-LEAVED VIOLET

  8 Leaf blades heart-shaped (Douglas, Josephine, and Curry Cos., Oreg., to Calif.) . . . ***V. ocellata***, pl. 604
                       TWO-EYED VIOLET

7 Inner surface of lateral petals, if white, cream, yellow, or yellow-orange, without a dark purple spot near the base

  9 Inner surface of all petals mostly yellow, with dark lines

    10 Leaf blades with a notch at the base, mostly heart-shaped or with a nearly circular outline, not much longer than wide

      11 Plants robust, to more than 20 cm tall, mostly upright; deciduous . . . . ***V. glabella***, pl. 600
                       SMOOTH WOODLAND VIOLET

      11 Plants low, generally less than 7 cm tall when in flower, evergreen or at least partly so

        12 Plants with stolons that take root and produce new plants, thus generally forming mats; leaf blades heart-shaped, somewhat pointed at the tip; common lowland and low-montane species . . . . ***V. sempervirens***
                       EVERGREEN YELLOW VIOLET

        12 Plants with underground rhizomes but not stolons, and not obviously mat-forming; leaf blades typically with a nearly circular outline; mostly montane but sometimes found below about 1000 ft. (300 m) . . . . ***V. orbiculata***
                       ROUND-LEAVED VIOLET

    10 Leaf blades without a notch at the base, distinctly longer than wide

      13 Larger leaf blades usually more than 1.5 times as long as wide, their margins smooth or somewhat erratically toothed; backs of upper 2 petals, when fresh, at most only slightly brownish or purplish

        14 Leaf blades conspicuously hairy, the margins often toothed but more erratically than regularly; backs of upper 2 petals, when fresh, slightly brownish or purplish; primarily a lowland species of well-drained, often rocky or gravelly habitats W of the Cascades . . . . ***V. praemorsa*** subsp. ***praemorsa*** (*V. nuttallii* subsp. *praemorsa*), pl. 605
                       UPLAND YELLOW VIOLET

        14 Leaf blades at most only slightly hairy, the margins smooth; backs of upper 2 petals not noticeably darkened by brown or purple; S Cascades and Siskiyou Mountain region of SW Oreg. and NW Calif.) . . . . ***V. bakeri*** (*V. nuttallii* var. *bakeri*)
                       BAKER'S VIOLET

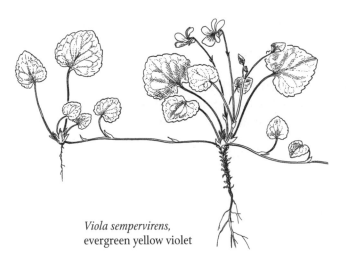

Viola sempervirens,
evergreen yellow violet

13 Larger blades not often more than 1.5 times as long as wide, their margins usually conspicuously and evenly toothed; backs of upper 2 petals, when fresh, decidedly brownish or purplish

    15 Leaves and stems not often tinged with purple; lower internodes of the stems much longer than the upper ones; flowers restricted to the uppermost portions of the stems (Josephine Co., Oreg., to Calif.) . . . . *V. lobata* subsp. *integrifolia*

        Viola lobata subsp. *integrifolia* intergrades with subsp. *lobata*, second choice 6.

    15 Leaves usually tinged with purple; lower internodes of the stems not much longer than the upper ones; flowers not restricted to the uppermost portions of the stems (Siskiyou Mountains of SW Oreg. and NW Calif., also E of the Cascades) . . . . *V. purpurea* subsp. *purpurea*
                                                        PURPLE-TINGED VIOLET

        Plants conforming to *V. purpurea* subsp. *purpurea* are also found E of the crest of the Cascades from S Oreg. to Calif.; another subspecies, *venosa,* is limited to the area E of the crest of the Cascades from N Wash. to Oreg.

9 Inner surface of some or all petals white, blue, or purple

  16 Leafy flowering stems rising well above the base of the plant and usually bearing at least 2–3 flowers

    17 Petals white except for some yellow at their bases and purplish lines on the lower 3 petals; leaf blades heart-shaped, decidedly longer than wide, tapering to slender tips (Brit. Col. to N Oreg., in montane and some lowland habitats, and E to the Midwestern states and provinces) . . . .
      . . . . *V. canadensis* subsp. *rugulosa*
                                                          CANADA VIOLET

    17 Petals either mostly blue or violet-blue except for white or yellow at the bases of the lower 3 petals, which also have dark lines, or mostly white with purple lines on the lower 3 petals; leaf blades either wider than long or only slightly longer than wide, not decidedly longer and not tapering to slender tips.

      18 Blades of basal leaves kidney-shaped, wider than long; bases of 3 lower petals with considerable yellow, as well as dark lines (leaf blades usually hairy on the underside and with purplish veins on the upper surface; in crevices and between loose rocks, Olympic Mountains, Wash., mostly above about 4500 ft., 1370 m) . . . . *V. flettii*
                                        OLYMPIC VIOLET, FLETT'S VIOLET

      18 Blades of basal leaves not kidney-shaped, mostly about as long as or longer than wide and somewhat pointed at the tip; bases of lower 3 petals white and with dark lines but without appreciable amounts of yellow (widespread lowland species)

        19 Corolla spur longer than wide; petals usually deep violet-blue, rarely white; sepals smooth-margined, without a pair of lobes at their bases . . . . *V. adunca,* pl. 598
                                        WESTERN BLUE VIOLET

        19 Corolla spur no longer than wide; petals usually pale blue, sometimes dark blue or white; sepals often with fringed margins and with a pair of small lobes at their bases . . . . . *V. howellii,* pl. 602
                                        HOWELL'S VIOLET

  16 Flowers borne singly on leafless peduncles arising from the base of the plant (the peduncles may have a pair of small bracts)

    20 Petals usually blue or violet (but some may be partly white)

      21 Plants with leafy, more or less erect stems that usually bear more than 1 flower; not spreading by stolons (in bogs and other wet places, mostly near the coast, Alaska to Oreg.) . . . . . . *V. langsdorfii*
                                        LANGSDORF'S VIOLET

      21 Plants without leafy, erect stems, the flower peduncles arising from the base; spreading by stolons (along streams and in other wet habitats) . . . . *V. palustris*
                                        MARSH VIOLET

    20 Petals white except for dark lines on the lower 3

22 Leaf blades more or less heart-shaped but with a more nearly circular outline, about as wide as long, not often more than 3 cm long; flower peduncles commonly less than 6 cm long (but variable); petals usually less than 10 mm long (in bogs and other wet habitats; not often found below about 2000 ft., 610 m, but recorded from a few low-elevation coastal localities) ...... *V. macloskeyi* subsp. *macloskeyi*
MACLOSKEY'S VIOLET, SMALL WHITE VIOLET

22 Leaf blades elongated, generally more than 5 cm long; peduncles of typical flowers commonly at least 10 cm long (but variable)

23 Larger leaf blades usually 2–3 times as long as wide, petals usually 10–12 mm long (sometimes a little shorter), the 2 lateral ones conspicuously bearded; plants not known to produce closed flowers (in bogs, Josephine and Curry Cos., Oreg., to Calif.) .... *V. primulifolia* subsp. *occidentalis,* pl. 606
WESTERN BOG VIOLET

23 Larger leaf blades usually 5–6 times as long as wide; petals usually 6–8 mm long, the 2 lateral ones at most only inconspicuously bearded; plants commonly producing closed flowers, these usually nodding and on much shorter peduncles than the typical flowers (leaf petioles commonly reddish; found in wet habitats, especially coastal bogs where cranberries are grown, in W Wash. and SW Brit. Col., remote from the region where *V. primulifolia* subsp. *occidentalis* is native; to be expected, however, in cranberry bogs in Oreg.; almost certainly introduced) .... *V. lanceolata* subsp. *lanceolata*
LANCE-LEAVED VIOLET (E North America)

VISCACEAE Mistletoe Family

The mistletoes of our region are perennials that parasitize trees and shrubs. The leaves, which are opposite, may be conspicuous, somewhat leathery structures, or they may be reduced to small scales. The flowers are of two types. Those that produce pollen have a perianth consisting of three or four lobes, each with a stalkless anther at its base; in pistillate flowers the fruit-forming part of the pistil is enveloped by the cup of the two- or three-lobed perianth. The ripe fruit is a sticky or mucilaginous berry containing a single seed. Fruits of some species of *Arceuthobium* expel their seeds explosively.

Phoradendron juniperinum,
juniper mistletoe

1 Leaves with well-developed blades, these usually about 2 cm long, dull green; parasitic on *Quercus* spp., especially *Q. garryana,* occasionally on other nonconiferous trees and shrubs (Washington Co., Oreg., to Calif.) . . . . ***Phoradendron villosum***
(*P. flavescens* var. *villosum*), pl. 608
WESTERN MISTLETOE

1 Leaves scalelike; parasitic on coniferous trees
   2 Fruits on distinct pedicels; stems and leaves reddish, brownish, yellow, olive, or greenish, the color often apparently depending on the host that is parasitized . . . . *Arceuthobium*
   2 Fruits sessile; stems and leaves usually yellow-green or green (parasitic on *Calocedrus decurrens, Juniperus occidentalis,* and *J. scopulorum*) . . . . ***Phoradendron juniperinum*** (*P. libocedri*), p. 363
JUNIPER MISTLETOE

Arceuthobium

The species of *Arceuthobium* are keyed partly on the basis of recognizable differences, partly on the basis of the plants they parasitize. The species and varieties listed here scarcely differ from one another and from *A. campylopodum* except in stem length, degree of bushiness, and coloration (yellow, yellow-green, reddish, etc.). They are therefore commonly lumped with *A. campylopodum:*

> *Arceuthobium abietinum:* parasitic on *Abies* spp.
> *Arceuthobium californicum:* parasitic on *Pinus lambertiana*
> *Arceuthobium cyanocarpum:* parasitic on *Pinus albicaulis,* and perhaps *P. monticola* and *Picea breweriana*
> *Arceuthobium monticola:* parasitic on *Pinus monticola*
> *Arceuthobium siskiyouense:* parasitic on *Pinus attenuata*
> *Arceuthobium tsugense* var. *mertensiana:* parasitic on *Tsuga mertensiana*
> *Arceuthobium tsugense* var. *tsugense:* parasitic on *Tsuga heterophylla*

1 Stems not more than 3 cm long, the internodes not often more than 1 mm thick; branches of primary stems generally few (and all those originating from a single stem are in the same plane); parasitic on *Pseudotsuga menziesii* . . . . ***A. douglasii***
DOUGLAS' FIR LEAFLESS MISTLETOE
1 Stems commonly more than 3 cm long, the internodes commonly more than 1 mm thick; primary stems generally with abundant branches
   2 Branches originating in whorls, not all in the same plane; parasitic on *Pinus albicaulis* and *P. contorta* subsp. *murrayana* E of the crest of the Cascades . . . . ***A. americanum***
LODGEPOLE PINE DWARF MISTLETOE
   2 Branches in the same plane as the stem from which they originate, a well-developed stem therefore somewhat fanlike; parasitic on *Pinus contorta, P. jeffreyi,* and *P. ponderosa* . . . . ***A. campylopodum***, pl. 607
WESTERN DWARF MISTLETOE

VITACEAE Grape Family

The grape family consists of woody vines with branching tendrils. The small greenish flowers are borne in clusters whose stalks originate opposite the petioles of the leaves. There are usually four or five petals, sepals, and stamens; the petals fall early. The juicy fruits have two seed-producing divisions. The cultivated grape, *Vitis vinifera,* grown for many centuries in Europe and now in many parts of the world, is probably a native of western Asia. Virginia creeper, *Parthenocissus quinquefolia,* of eastern North America, and Japanese ivy, *P. tricuspidata,* native to China and Japan, are other well-known representatives of the family; both occasionally escape from cultivation.

Vitis californica, California wild grape, grows as far north as Douglas and Coos Counties, Oregon. Its fruits, 6–10 mm wide and purplish when ripe, are probably not sweet enough to be popular even with small children. The leaves, to 12 cm wide, turn red in fall. *Vitis riparia,* June grape or riverbank grape, with a range extending from Nova Scotia to New Mexico, is sometimes cultivated for its red autumn foliage; like *V. vinifera* it occasionally becomes firmly established on waste ground or abandoned homesites.

Monocotyledonous Families

ACORACEAE Sweet-Flag Family

The genus *Acorus*, represented in North America by two species that may not be easy to separate, has long been placed in Araceae, but it is now fashionable to give it a family of its own, Acoraceae. In its habit of growth, an *Acorus* slightly resembles a cattail (*Typha*, Typhaceae) because of its narrow leaves, sometimes more than 1 m long, and the stalked, club-shaped inflorescence, the spadix, usually 5–8 cm long. The spadix, however, is accompanied by a narrow, leaflike spathe. The flowers, tightly crowded onto the spadix, normally have a pistil and six stamens in addition to six short perianth segments. The leaves, pleasingly aromatic when bruised, are distinctive because the most conspicuous vein is off to one side of the midline.

Acorus

1 Most conspicuous vein and 1 or more other veins raised above the upper surface of the leaf blade; plants fertile, producing fruits (introduced into W North America) ....*A. americanus*
   AMERICAN SWEET FLAG (E North America, possibly also Siberia)
1 Most conspicuous vein of leaf blade prominently raised above the upper surface, but the other veins not raised; plants sterile, therefore not producing fruits ....*A. calamus*
   SWEET FLAG (probably native to Asia)
   Acorus calamus is now found throughout much of the world. It is used in medicine and perfumery, and for flavoring.

ALISMATACEAE Water-Plantain Family

Plants of the water-plantain family are rooted in mud and usually partly submerged for at least part of the growing season. The leaves are basal; in some species the blades are broad and arrowhead-shaped, but in others they are merely oval, or very slender, or not developed at all. The numerous flowers are arranged in whorls on a branched inflorescence. Each flower has three sepals and three petals. In certain species in our region, some flowers are strictly staminate, others strictly pistillate or with stamens and pistils. The number of stamens and pistils ranges from several to many. The fruiting portion of each pistil, dry when mature, is joined tightly to the seed it encloses.

The first key will not be very helpful if flowers or fruits are not present or not in good condition. The keys to species of *Alisma* and *Sagittaria* are based to a considerable extent on the form of the leaves, and if you try both genera you may be able to determine the species.

1 Pistils (and later the fruits) arranged spirally in a nearly globular mass; stamens, when present, usually 7–9 or many; petals white ....*Sagittaria*
1 Pistils (and later the fruits) in a single whorl; stamens usually 6; petals white or tinged with pink, lilac, or purplish ....
.... *Alisma*

Acorus calamus,
sweet flag

Alisma

1 Leaf blades indistinct but usually recognizable on at least some leaves as a slightly broadened (to 5 mm wide) upper portion . . . .***A. gramineum***
NARROWLEAF WATER PLANTAIN

> The form of the leaves of *A. gramineum* varies greatly, and some plants may show no distinct blades, in which case they could resemble *Sagittaria subulata* var. *gracillima.*In the latter, however, the pistils, and eventually also the fruits, are arranged spirally in a globular cluster, whereas in *A. gramineum* they are arranged in a circle.

1 Leaf blades distinct, oval or elongated-oval, not more than about 6 times as long as wide

2 Leaf blades oval, rarely more than 3 times as long as wide . . . . ***A. triviale*** (*A. plantago-aquatica* subsp. *americanum*)
WATER PLANTAIN

2 Leaf blades elongated-oval, mostly at least 4 times as long as wide . . . . ***A. lanceolatum***
LANCELEAF WATER PLANTAIN (Eurasia, N Africa)

Sagittaria

1 Relatively delicate plants, the leaves slender, not more than 3 mm wide, nearly cylindrical, without blades, and tapering to the tip; stamens usually 7–9 (not yet widespread) . . . .***S. subulata* var. *gracillima***
SLENDERLEAF WATER PLANTAIN (E United States)

1 Relatively stout plants, the blades of most leaves arrowhead-shaped, with pointed basal lobes; stamens, when present, usually at least 15

2 Bracts beneath whorls of flowers generally 10–25 mm long, slender and tapering to a pointed tip, not at all boat-shaped; stamens, when present, usually about 15–25; staminate and pistillate flowers separate but on the same plant . . . . ***S. cuneata***
ARUM-LEAF ARROWHEAD

2 Bracts beneath whorls of flowers not often more than 10 mm long, blunt-tipped and somewhat boat-shaped; stamens, when present, more than 20; some plants with only staminate or only pistillate flowers, others with flowers of both types and/or with flowers that have stamens and pistils . . . .
. . . . ***S. latifolia***, pl. 609
WAPATO

Alisma triviale,
water plantain

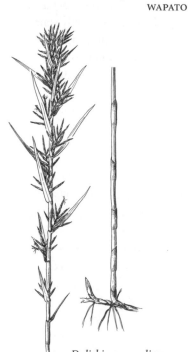

Dulichium arundinaceum,
three-way sedge

ARACEAE Arum Family

Calla lilies (*Zantedeschia*), from Africa, and species of *Anthurium* and *Philodendron,* from tropical America, are familiar examples of the Araceae. The small flowers are crowded onto a clublike inflorescence, called the spadix. Originating below the inflorescence, and sometimes surrounding it almost completely, is the spathe, essentially a large bract, often richly colored. All flowers may have a few stamens and a pistil, or the staminate flowers may be concentrated in the upper part of the spadix, the pistillate ones in the lower portion. Small scalelike structures, if present, are the only perianth parts. In many members of this large family, the inflorescence produces unpleasant odors to attract insects that normally lay their eggs in dead animals, dung, or other ill-smelling situations. The odors trick insects into entering the spathe and pollinating the flowers.

1 Leaf blades oval, to more than 80 cm long, sometimes more than 1 m, without whitish veins; spathe yellow; fruits, when ripe, greenish, so compactly arranged on the spadix that they are not easily separated; plants, if bruised, with an odor resembling that of a skunk (limited to marshy habitats; usually beginning to flower in late February) . . . . *Lysichiton americanus*, pl. 610
YELLOW SKUNK CABBAGE
1 Leaf blades arrowhead-shaped, rarely more than 20 cm long, with whitish veins; spathe pale yellowish or whitish green; fruits about 1 cm long, orange-red when ripe, easily separated; plants, if bruised, without a skunklike odor . . . . *Arum italicum*
ITALIAN ARUM (Europe)
Arum italicum occasionally escapes from cultivation. Children should be cautioned not to put the attractive fruits into their mouths—the tissue contains microscopic, needlelike crystals of calcium oxalate, which will penetrate the mucous membranes and cause painful sensations that will not quickly disappear.

CYPERACEAE Sedge Family

In general, sedges and their relatives are partial to wet habitats, where they often predominate. They resemble grasses in their growth form and the appearance of their leaves, and also because their florets are mostly greenish, inconspicuous, and clustered (see p. 369). The stems of sedges, however, are usually three-angled. The florets are concentrated in spikelets, each floret arising above a specialized bract, here called a scale. (Do not confuse these with any bracts that may be present below the spikelets.) When a perianth is present, this consists of bristlelike elements that do not resemble petals or sepals of most flowering plants. An individual floret may have both a pistil and stamens, or it may have only one or the other. The fruit-forming part of the pistil and the seed it encloses develop together into a dry achene.

In *Carex,* the largest genus in the family, a specialized, somewhat flask-shaped bract, called the perigynium, envelops the pistil and subsequently the achene. The tip of the perigynium is open, allowing the stigmas and sometimes a portion of the style to protrude. Special directions for identifying species of *Carex* are given before the key to that genus.

1 Achene developing on each floret enveloped by a perigynium, a sac open only at the tip (the stigmas of the pistil, and sometimes a portion of the style, protrude through the opening) . . . . *Carex*
1 Achene not enveloped by a perigynium
  2 Scales of each spikelet arranged in 2 vertical rows
    3 Perianth absent; plants mostly with basal leaves, the inflorescence terminal, with a cluster of leaflike bracts beneath it; stems 3-angled . . . . *Cyperus*
    3 Perianth present in the form of 6–9 bristles; each stem with numerous scattered leaves, the axils of the upper ones bearing inflorescences; stems cylindrical . . . . *Dulichium arundinaceum*
THREE-WAY SEDGE
Because of its cylindrical stems and general appearance, *D. arundinaceum* could easily be mistaken for a grass.
  2 Scales of each spikelet arranged in a spiral

4 Style of the pistil distinctly thickened at the base, the thickened portion persisting on the achene as a caplike or conical structure

    5 Each flowering stem with at least several spikelets consisting of scales, but fertile florets (or fruits that have developed in the florets) present in the axils of only 1–2 of the scales; perianth of each floret consisting of 10–12 bristles (scales of spikelets whitish) . . . . *Rhynchospora alba*
                WHITE BEAK RUSH

    5 Each flowering stem with a single spikelet, this with several fertile florets (or achenes that have developed in the florets); perianth of florets either absent or consisting of not more than 6 bristles
. . . . *Eleocharis*

4 Style of pistil not thickened at the base to form a caplike or conical structure (but the style may persist as a slender projection)

    6 Each achene with a single hyaline, scalelike structure between it and the scale in whose axil it has developed; plants usually annual; stamen generally 1 . . . . *Hemicarpha micrantha*
                COMMON HEMICARPHA

    6 Each achene usually with 1 to many bristles in addition to the scale in whose axil it has developed; plants usually perennial; stamens usually 3, sometimes 2

        7 Each of the several to many florets with a perianth consisting of several to many bristles, these long and conspicuous, older inflorescences therefore resembling balls of cotton or clumps of brownish fur . . . . *Eriophorum*

        7 Each floret either without a perianth, or the perianth consisting of not more than 6 bristles, these usually no longer than the scales of the spikelet . . . .
. . . . *Scirpus-Schoenoplectus-Bolboschoenus-Isolepis-Trichophorum* complex

Rhynchospora alba,
white beak rush

Carex

In our region, *Carex* is represented by more species than any other genus of higher plants. It has some messy clusters of species whose members, often showing considerable variation and intergradation, are difficult to separate with conviction. The problem is exacerbated by hybridization.

In some species, an inflorescence consists of a single spikelet of florets; in most, however, there are at least two or three spikelets. A particular spikelet may be strictly pistillate or strictly staminate, but it is also common for a spikelet to have staminate florets above the pistillate ones, or pistillate florets above the staminate ones. The structure of staminate florets is rarely invoked in keys for identification, but much emphasis is placed on the pistillate florets, so the general structure of these requires thorough understanding. The pistil of each pistillate floret is enclosed by a saclike bract called the perigynium. This is open at the tip, allowing the stigmas, and sometimes also a portion of the style, to protrude. As the achene (consisting of the seed and remnant of the pistil) develops, it remains within the perigynium. Just below each perigynium, there is, on the axis of the spikelet, a bract called the scale. This usually persists along with its corresponding perigynium. At the base of the spikelet, there is typically another type of bract, sometimes rather leaflike, sometimes much like an enlarged scale. Before using this key, be sure you know exactly what is meant by perigynium, scale, and bract.

Perigynium is the term that is used most frequently in the key, and it must be stated frankly that some details of perigynial structure cannot easily be seen with a hand lens. Furthermore, some choices in the key require you to measure carefully to fractions of a millimeter.

1 Each flowering stem with a single spikelet at the tip, the staminate and pistillate spikelets either on separate plants or the staminate florets above the pistillate florets in the spikelet (the staminate florets may be shed early, so look carefully for traces of them; furthermore, be sure you are really dealing with a single spikelet, because in some species under the other choice 1, 2 or more separate spikelets may be pressed together very tightly)

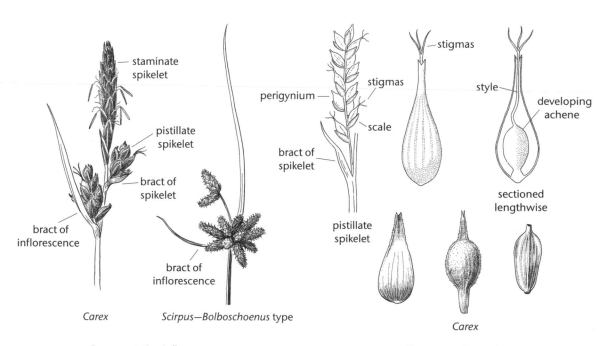

Carex   Scirpus—Bolboschoenus type

Representative Inflorescences

Carex

Representative perigynia

Cyperaceae

2 Staminate and pistillate spikelets on separate plants (inflorescences up about 40 cm tall, much longer than the leaves; leaf blades flat, 2–3 mm wide; perigynia about 20–40 on each pistillate spikelet, about twice as long as wide, brown to blackish brown, both sides hairy; stigmas usually 3, sometimes 4; in wet, open areas, SW Oreg. to Calif.) . . . . *C. scabriuscula* (*C. gigas*)
CASCADES SEDGE

Carex scabriuscula and certain other species in which pistillate and staminate spikelets are on separate plants are dealt beginning with the second choice 19.

2 Staminate florets above the pistillate florets in the same spikelet
  3 Scales below the perigynia of pistillate portions of spikelets shed early; perigynia 5–6 times as long as wide, hanging downward (staminate florets shed early; pistillate florets usually only 3–5; in sphagnum bogs, Alaska to N Wash.) . . . . *C. pauciflora*
FEW-FLOWERED SEDGE

  3 Scales below the perigynia persisting as the achenes ripen; perigynia less than 5 times as long as wide
    4 Leaf blades (flat) mostly 2–3 mm wide (scales below perigynia mostly dark brown, sometimes nearly black; montane, not likely to be found below about 3500 ft., 1070 m) . . . . *C. nigricans*
BLACKISH SEDGE

    4 Leaves, whether flat or folded, less than 2 mm wide
      5 Leaves folded or slightly rolled up, thus sometimes appearing to be cylindrical (bracts below 2–3 lowest perigynia longer than the perigynia and sometimes even longer than the entire spikelet; perigynia about 2.5 times as long as wide, widest near the middle; plants sometimes more than 50 cm tall, usually forming dense tufts; SW Oreg. to Calif.) . . . . *C. multicaulis*
MANY-STEMMED SEDGE

      5 Leaves typically flat
        6 Perigynia (4.5–6 mm long) about 4 times as long as wide, tapering gradually to the tip (coastal, Alaska to Wash.) . . . . *C. circinata*
COILED SEDGE

        6 Perigynia not more than 3 times as long as wide
          7 Perigynia with a spongy, stalklike lower portion that is about one-fourth or one-half as long as the egg-shaped portion that encloses the achene

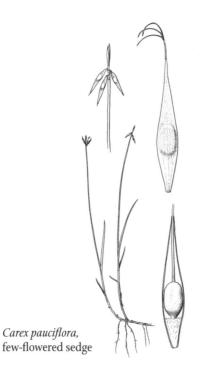

Carex pauciflora,
few-flowered sedge

Carex circinata,
coiled sedge

8 Perigynia 5–7 mm long, the stalklike lower portion about half as long as the egg-shaped portion . . . . *C. geyeri*
GEYER'S SEDGE

8 Perigynia less than 5 mm long, the stalklike lower portion about one-fourth as long as the egg-shaped portion (in sphagnum bogs) . . . . *C. leptalea*
BRISTLE-STALKED SEDGE

7 Perigynia without a spongy, stalklike lower portion that is so much as one-fourth as long as the egg-shaped portion that encloses the achene

9 Plants forming dense tufts, not spreading by rhizomes; stigmas 2–3 (montane and not likely to be found below about 4000 ft., 1220 m) . . . . *C. nardina*
NARD SEDGE

9 Plants with 1 or a few stems arising at intervals from a spreading rhizome; stigmas 3 (in the Cascades, N Oreg. to Calif.; mostly above 6000 ft., 1830 m) . . . . *C. breweri*
BREWER'S SEDGE

1 Each flowering stem with 1 or more spikelets below the one at the tip (look carefully, because all the spikelets may be tightly pressed together)

10 Pistillate inflorescences (usually on plants separate from those bearing staminate inflorescences) commonly 3–4 cm thick, sometimes even thicker, consisting of several spikelets tightly crowded together; on backshores of sandy beaches (stigmas 3; perigynia usually 10–15 mm long, the beak, about as long as the swollen portion, divided at the tip into 2 painfully sharp teeth; new stems sprouting up at intervals from rhizomes, thus often forming distinct lines of plants; the most easily identifiable sedge in our region; Alaska to Oreg., also in N Asia) . . . . *C. macrocephala*, pl. 613
BIG-HEAD SEDGE

Carex kobomugi, sea isle Japanese sedge, from E Asia, has been widely used in E United States for stabilizing sand dunes. It was once found at Portland, Oreg., where it was presumably introduced with ballast material. In general appearance it is similar to *C. macrocephala,* although its pistillate inflorescences do not get much thicker than 2.5 cm, and its flowering stems are not so sharply angled as those of this species. The awns of the scales below the perigynia, furthermore, are longer than those of *C. macrocephala:* 4–6.5 mm instead of 4 mm or less.

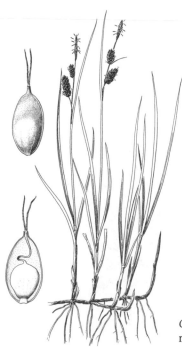

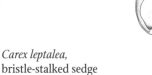

Carex leptalea,
bristle-stalked sedge

Carex saxatilis,
russet sedge

10 Pistillate inflorescences (or pistillate portions of inflorescences) much less than 3 cm thick

   11 Plants growing on backshores of sandy beaches and with spreading rhizomes along which new plants are formed at intervals; inflorescences dense, to about 2 cm thick, and made up of spikelets that have staminate florets above, pistillate florets below, or sometimes only pistillate florets; perigynium 3–4.2 mm long, with a distinct basal stalk as well as a prominent beak; stigmas 2 (some plants may be strictly staminate or strictly pistillate; Wash. to Calif.) . . . . ***C. pansa***
SAND-DUNE SEDGE

> *Carex pansa* and *C. macrocephala* are the only species of *Carex* likely to be found on sandy beaches where the sand shifts to a considerable extent (but see note concerning *C. kobomugi* under the first choice 10). Other species, however, may be expected where the sand is hard-packed or where depressions fill with water.

   11 Plants not in all respects, including habitat, as described in the other choice 11

     12 Style persisting on the achene, usually longer than the achene itself and becoming bent or contorted (the stigmas, however, may not persist; to see the style it is necessary to open the perigynium)

       13 Undersides of leaf blades with soft hairs (there are also hairs on at least the upper portions of the leaf sheaths; scales below the individual perigynia with rough-edged awns; in very wet places, mostly E of the crest of the Cascades, but possibly reaching Jackson Co., Oreg.) . . . . . ***C. atherodes***
ROUGH-AWNED SEDGE

       13 Undersides of leaf blades not hairy

         14 Stigmas 2; achene lens-shaped, the opposite sides convex; perigynia usually with only 2 prominent veins, these on the narrow edges; beak of perigynia short, slightly if at all 2-toothed (scales below individual perigynia without awns; mostly montane but occasionally found at least as low as about 3000 ft., 910 m) . . . . ***C. saxatilis***, p. 371
RUSSET SEDGE

         14 Stigmas 3; achene 3-angled; perigynia with several equally prominent nerves; beak of perigynia prominent, with conspicuous teeth

           15 Pistillate spikelets nodding (scales below perigynia with rough-edged awns; teeth on beak of perigynia 1.5–3 mm long, the tips spread widely apart; plants forming tufts; in wet habitats) . . . . ***C. comosa***
BRISTLY SEDGE

Carex comosa,
bristly sedge

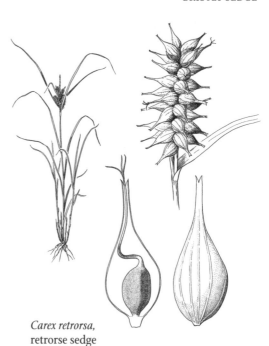

Carex retrorsa,
retrorse sedge

15 Pistillate spikelets more or less upright

  16 Plants mostly forming tufts, spreading only to a slight extent by short rhizomes; perigynia usually at least slightly more than twice as long as wide

    17 Perigynia 4–8 mm long, usually about 2.5 times as long as wide, more or less upright, not spreading apart at maturity . . . . *C. vesicaria*
          INFLATED SEDGE

    17 Perigynia 6–10 mm long, usually fully 3 times as long as wide, conspicuously spreading apart at maturity, some of them, especially the lower ones, turning slightly downward . . . . . *C. retrorsa*
          RETRORSE SEDGE

  16 Plants spreading by rhizomes; perigynia about twice as long as wide

    18 Upper surface of leaf blades with numerous small wartlike bumps (not common) . . . . ***C. rostrata***
          BEAKED SEDGE

    18 Upper surface of leaf blades without small wartlike bumps (an especially common and widespread species) . . . . *C. utriculata* (*C. rostrata* of some references, misapplied)
          SAC SEDGE

12 Style not persisting on the achene after the style withers (at most, the achene will have just a short prolongation at the tip)

  19 Stigmas 2; achenes almost always lens-shaped but one side usually more convex than the other

    20 Spikelets usually more than 2 cm long and separate (in other words, what looks like a spikelet is just that, not a cluster of smaller spikelets); uppermost spikelet of the inflorescence consisting of staminate florets, the lower ones of pistillate florets (one must be a little flexible in dealing with this choice —the terminal spikelet sometimes has a few pistillate florets at the tip or at the base, and there may be 1–2 wholly or partly staminate spikelets below it; the rest of the spikelets, however, will normally be strictly pistillate)

      21 Pistillate spikelets with not more than 20 perigynia, these not crowded together and often becoming more widely spaced as some fall away without ripening; leaflike bract beneath the lowest spikelet with a sheath at least 5 mm long, sometimes more than 10 mm (the blade as long as, or longer than, the inflorescence; perigynia usually becoming orange or yellow-brown before falling; mostly montane but sometimes at lower elevations) . . . . ***C. aurea***
          GOLDEN-FRUITED SEDGE

Carex utriculata,
sac sedge

Carex aurea,
golden-fruited sedge

21 Pistillate spikelets (at least the larger ones) with more than 20 perigynia, sometimes many, and usually crowded tightly together; leaflike bract beneath the lowest spikelet without a distinct sheath

  22 At least the lower spikelets (these either strictly pistillate or with some staminate florets above) noticeably nodding

    23 Lower spikelets nearly or quite sessile, commonly at least 5 cm long, sometimes more than 8 cm (abundant, widespread) . . . . *C. obnupta*, pl. 614
        SLOUGH SEDGE

    23 Lower spikelets with obvious peduncles

      24 Perigynia without a beak and rounded at the base (coastal, especially in salt marshes) . . . *C. lyngbyei*
        LYNGBYE'S SEDGE

      24 Perigynia with a distinct beak and tapering to the base, sometimes forming an indistinct stalk (from the coast to the W slope of the Cascades, in very wet places) . . . . *C. aquatilis* subsp. *dives* (*C. sitchensis*)
        SITKA SEDGE

  22 Lower spikelets more or less upright

    25 Perigynia thick and hard, difficult to puncture (SW Oreg. to Calif.) . . . . *C. barbarae*
        SANTA BARBARA SEDGE

    25 Perigynia thin, easily punctured

      26 Veins on perigynia distinct, even if sometimes not prominent

        27 Perigynia usually more than twice as long as wide; not abruptly narrowed at the base to form a distinct stalk

          28 Perigynia with 1–3 lengthwise veins on both broad surfaces (in wet habitats but not among rocks along swift streams; S Wash. to Calif.) . . . . *C. angustata* (*C. eurycarpa*)
            NARROW-FRUITED SEDGE

          28 Perigynia with 3–9 lengthwise veins, at least on one surface (along swift streams, at levels that are likely to be under water at least at times; S Wash. to Calif.) . . . . *C. nudata*
            TORRENT SEDGE

        27 Perigynia not more than twice as long as wide, abruptly narrowed at the base to form a distinct stalk, this usually 0.2–0.4 mm long (scales below perigynia dark blackish brown except for a greenish midline streak)

          29 Plants spreading extensively by rhizomes; leaves mostly not reaching beyond the inflorescences, often much shorter (occasional weed in Brit. Col.) . . . . *C. nigra*
            BLACK SEDGE (E North America, Eurasia)

          29 Plants forming dense tufts, not spreading extensively by rhizomes; leaves mostly reaching well above the inflorescences . . . . *C. lenticularis*, pl. 612
            LENTICULAR SEDGE

             The 3 subspecies of *C. lenticularis* found in our region are keyed below, but they vary and intergrade to the extent that individual specimens may be difficult to identify.

            30 Lowest spikelet of the inflorescence 4–6 mm wide; stalk of the perigynium 0.4–0.7 mm long (in wet freshwater habitats near the coast) . . . . *C. lenticularis* subsp. *limnophila*

            30 Lowest spikelet of the inflorescence 3–4 mm wide; stalk of the perigynium 0.1–0.5 mm wide

              31 Upper half of the perigynium typically with purplish brown spots (the beak completely purplish brown) and with 1–3 veins on the side that faces the axis of the spikelet . . . . *C. lenticularis* subsp. *impressa*

              31 Perigynium purplish brown only on the tip of the beak and with 5–7 veins on each side . . . . *C. lenticularis* subsp. *lipocarpa*

      26 Veins on perigynia not distinct

        32 Perigynia at least half as thick as wide (S Brit. Col. to Oreg., also E of the crest of the Cascades) . . . . *C. aperta*
        COLUMBIA SEDGE

32 Perigynia not so much as half as thick as wide

    33 Perigynia not more than 2 mm long and tightly enclosing the achene (in wet habitats, including streams) . . . . *C. interrupta*
                                                      GREEN-FRUITED SEDGE

    33 Perigynia at least 2.5 mm long, only loosely enclosing the achene

        34 Bract below the lowest spikelet usually reaching at least to the tip of the inflorescence (usually in very wet habitats) . . . . *C. aquatilis* subsp. *aquatilis*
                                                     WATER SEDGE

        34 Bract below the lowest spikelet much shorter than the inflorescence (in wet or moist habitats and mostly above 3000 ft., 910 m) . . . . *C. scopulorum* subsp. *bracteosa*
                                                  ROCKY MOUNTAIN SEDGE

20 Individual spikelets typically not more than 1.5 cm long, often in tight clusters that in some species may seem, unless looked at carefully, to be single spikelets; each spikelet usually with pistillate and staminate florets, one type above the other

   35 Spikelets with staminate florets on the upper portion, pistillate florets below (in some populations of *C. cusickii* and perhaps certain other species, individual plants may be strictly pistillate or strictly staminate)

   36 Teeth at the tips of the perigynia at least 1 mm long, flattened and flexible (both margins of the perigynia with a prominent flange, these especially conspicuous when a perigynium is viewed with the concave surface uppermost; scales below individual perigynia as long as, or longer than, the perigynia; introduced into North America, well established on sandy beaches of the Atlantic coast and occasionally encountered in suitable habitats of our region; probably brought to our region with ballast) . . . . *C. arenaria*
                                                     SAND SEDGE (Europe)

   36 Teeth at tip of perigynium not so much as 1 mm long, and plants not in all respects, including habitat, as described in the other choice 36

      37 Scales below individual perigynia abruptly tapered, then tipped with a prominent awn usually at least 1 mm long and sometimes longer than 3 mm; front faces of leaf sheaths with cross-corrugations (in very wet places)

        38 Neither face of the perigynia with more than 3 distinct veins. . . . . *C. vulpinoidea*
                                                     FOX SEDGE

Carex aperta,
Columbia sedge

Carex vulpinoidea,
fox sedge

38 Both faces of the perigynia with at least 5 distinct veins on one side, at least 3 on the other side . . . . . .
. . . . *C. densa*

DENSE SEDGE

37 Scales below individual perigynia usually tapered gradually to a point, sometimes rounded at the tip, but in either case without an awn so much as 1 mm long

  39 Leaf blades more than 5 mm wide, sometimes as wide as 10 mm (front of leaf sheaths with cross-corrugations; in wet habitats) . . . . *C. stipata* subsp. *stipata*

AWL-FRUITED SEDGE

  39 Leaf blades rarely so much as 5 mm wide (certain species under this choice may also have cross-corrugations on the leaf sheaths)

    40 Upper half of the convex side of the perigynium with a low brown ridge along the midline (the ridge originates at the tip; inflorescence relatively loose, most of the individual spikelets easily distinguished; front of leaf sheaths sometimes with cross-corrugations; perigynia to 4 mm long; in wet habitats, especially sphagnum bogs) . . . . *C. cusickii*

CUSICK'S SEDGE

Some populations of *C. cusickii* are strictly staminate or pistillate.

    40 Upper half of the convex side of the perigynium without a brown ridge along the midline

      41 Perigynia widest in the lowest one-fourth of their length

        42 Rim of the mouth of the leaf sheath somewhat thickened; perigynia nearly half as wide as long (S Oreg. to Calif.) . . . . *C. nervina*

SIERRA NERVED SEDGE

        42 Rim of the mouth of the leaf sheath not noticeably thickened; perigynia only about one-third as wide as long (front of leaf sheaths usually with cross-corrugations; not likely to be found below about 4500 ft., 1370 m) . . . . *C. neurophora*

ALPINE NERVED SEDGE

      41 Perigynia widest at or above the lower third

        43 Perigynia widest near the middle

          44 Inflorescence to about 3 cm long, very slender, the spikelets only about 5 mm long, the lower ones widely separated; perigynia longer than the scales below them; beak of perigynia much less than 0.5 mm long (leaves only 1–2 mm wide; spreading by slender rhizomes) . . . .
. . . . *C. disperma*

SOFT-LEAVED SEDGE

          44 Inflorescence to about 1.5 cm long, the spikelets close together; beak of perigynia about 0.5 mm long (young stems upright but later falling down and becoming stolons that take root; in very wet habitats) . . . . *C. chordorrhiza*

CORD-ROOT SEDGE

        43 Perigynia widest below the middle

          45 Edges of the upper half of perigynia without serrations (front of leaf sheaths occasionally with cross-corrugations; S Wash. to Calif.; not likely to be found below about 3000 ft., 910 m)
. . . . *C. jonesii*

JONES' SEDGE

          45 Edges of the upper half of the perigynia with small serrations

            46 Perigynia distinctly longer than the scales below them (inflorescence to about 2.5 cm long, usually so compact that the individual spikelets are not easily distinguished; perigynia strikingly colored: the central portion copper, the edges green) . . . . *C. hoodii*

HOOD'S SEDGE

            46 Perigynia about as long as, or shorter than, the scales below them

              47 Bract below the lowest spikelet typically nearly or fully as long as the inflorescence; base of perigynia tapering gradually to form a stalk that is longer than wide . . . . *C. tumulicola*

FOOTHILL SEDGE

47 Bract below the lowest spikelet typically scarcely if at all longer than this spikelet; base of perigynia tapered abruptly to form a stalk that is no longer than wide (mostly E of the crest of the Cascades but known from Josephine Co., Oreg., and NW Calif.) . . . . ***C. praegracilis***
CLUSTERED FIELD SEDGE

35 Spikelets with pistillate florets on the upper portion, staminate ones below

48 Perigynia with thin, flangelike margins on both edges, especially of the upper half or two-thirds (look carefully, because the flange may be only slightly developed)

49 Bract below the lowest spikelet of an inflorescence rather distinctly leaflike, tapering gradually from near the base (and reaching up to or beyond the top of the inflorescence)

50 Inflorescence dense; flangelike margins of the perigynia extending to the base; most perigynia 4 by 1.5 mm. . . . . ***C. unilateralis***
ONE-SIDED SEDGE

50 Inflorescence rather loose, the spikelets well separated; flangelike margins of the perigynia not extending below the middle third; most perigynia 4 by 1.25 mm (occasional weed). . . . . ***C. projecta*** (E North America)

49 Bract below the lowest spikelet of an inflorescence usually tapering abruptly to its slender, long or short prolongation

51 Bract below the lowest spikelet of at least some inflorescences very slender, sometimes nearly hairlike, and reaching to or beyond the tip of the inflorescence

52 Perigynia usually more than 3 times (sometimes fully 3.75 times) as long as wide (inflorescence compact; Brit. Col. to Oreg.) . . . . ***C. athrostachya***
SLENDER-BEAKED SEDGE

52 Perigynia usually 2–2.75 times as long as wide

53 Spikes to 1 cm long; perigynia commonly 4.5–5 mm long (Brit. Col. to Oreg., also much of E North America) . . . . ***C. scoparia***
POINTED-BROOM SEDGE

53 Spikes to about 8 mm long; perigynia less than 4 mm long . . . . ***C. subfusca***
RUSTY SEDGE

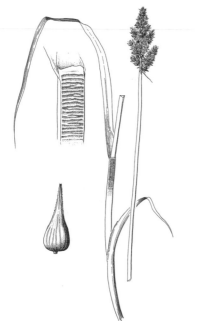

Carex stipata subsp. *stipata,*
awl-fruited sedge

Carex neurophora,
alpine nerved sedge

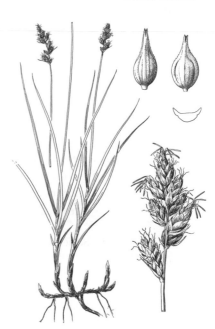

Carex praegracilis,
clustered field sedge

51 Bract originating below the lowest spikelet not reaching even close to the tip of the inflorescence
  54 Leaf ligules usually at least 3 mm long, sometimes as long as 8 mm
    55 Leaf sheath reaching nearly to the tip of the ligule; flangelike margins of the perigynia disappearing about 0.5 mm from the tip (Wash. to Calif.) . . . .*C. fracta*
                                     FRAGILE-SHEATHED SEDGE
    55 Leaf sheath not reaching close to the tip of the ligule; flangelike margins of perigynia not disappearing until about 0.2 mm away from the tip . . . .*C. feta*
                                       GREEN-SHEATHED SEDGE
  54 Leaf ligules not so much as 3 mm long
    56 Perigynia at least 3 times as long as wide
      57 Perigynia usually 4.5–5.5 mm, sometimes as long as 6 mm, the flangelike margins prominent
      . . . . *C. praticola*
                                       MEADOW SEDGE
      57 Perigynia not more than 4 mm long, the flangelike margins very slightly developed
        58 Spikelets about twice as long as wide (S Wash. to Calif. and eastward) . . . .*C. leporinella*
                                        SIERRA HARE SEDGE
        58 Spikelets plump, only about 1.5 times as long as wide (Brit. Col. to Wash., also in E North America) . . . .*C. crawfordii*
                                        CRAWFORD'S SEDGE
    56 Perigynia not much more than 2.5 times as long as wide
      59 Perigynia, on the side facing the axis of the spikelet, with at least 10 closely spaced lengthwise veins
        60 Perigynia not so much as twice as long as wide; perigynia longer than the scales below them (mostly in the Cascades but also known from the Siskiyou Mountains) . . .*C. straminiformis*
                                      MOUNT SHASTA SEDGE
        60 Perigynia about 2.5 times as long as wide; perigynia shorter than the scales below them (Wash. to Calif.) . . . .*C. multicostata*
                                      MANY-VEINED SEDGE
      59 Perigynia, on the side facing away from the axis of the spikelet, with fewer than 10 lengthwise veins
        61 Scales as long and as wide as the perigynia, thus covering the perigynia completely (or perhaps leaving just the tip exposed)
          62 Perigynia usually 3.6–4.8 mm long; flangelike margins of perigynia conspicuous, at least 0.2 mm wide . . . .*C. ovalis* (includes *C. tracyi,* and *C. leporina* of some references)
                                    OVAL-FRUITED SEDGE (Europe)
          62 Perigynia rarely more than 3.3 mm long; flangelike margins of perigynia inconspicuous, less than 0.1 mm wide . . . .*C. integra*
                                      SMOOTH-BEAKED SEDGE
        61 Scales at least slightly shorter and narrower than the perigynia, thus the tips and upper portions of the sides of the perigynia exposed
          63 Scales not more than two-thirds as long as the perigynia (some may be only half as long; rare weed in Brit. Col.) . . . .*C. tribuloides*
                           BLUNT-BROOM SEDGE (E North America)
          63 Scales more than two-thirds as long as the perigynia (usually in rather dry habitats) . . . . . .
          . . . .*C. pachystachya* (includes *C. preslii*)
             In the treatment of *Carex* in *Flora of North America*, *C. preslii* is given the rank of species but is not very clearly separated from *C. pachystachya*.
48 Perigynia without thin, flangelike margins on both edges (but there may be a slight ridge on each edge)
  64 Entire inflorescence only to 15 mm long, so dense that most of the spikelets cannot be distinguished (beaks of perigynia protruding conspicuously beyond the tips of the scales; not likely to be found below about 4000 ft., 1220 m) . . . .*C. illota*
                                      SMALL-HEADED SEDGE

64 Most inflorescences much more than 15 mm long, the majority of the individual spikelets easily distinguished

  65 Perigynia diverging widely from one another as achenes ripen within them, the lower ones sometimes even turning downward (spikelets usually with not more than 15 perigynia)

    66 Edges of slender upper portion (beak) of perigynia with evenly spaced, conspicuous serrations (in wet habitats but not in sphagnum bogs) . . . . *C. interior*
      INLAND SEDGE

    66 Edges of slender upper portion of perigynia either smooth or with irregularly spaced, mostly inconspicuous serrations

      67 Convex portion of perigynia without lengthwise veins (mostly in sphagnum bogs) . . . . *C. echinata* subsp. *echinata* (*C. muricata* of some references)

      67 Convex portion of perigynia with at least a few lengthwise veins (mostly coastal) . . . . *C. echinata* subsp. *phyllomanica* (*C. phyllomanica*, *C. muricata* subsp. *phyllomanica*)

  65 Perigynia at most diverging only slightly away from one another and definitely not turning downward as achenes ripen

    68 Spikelets generally with fewer than 12 perigynia

      69 Perigynia usually 3–3.5 mm long, the beak bent and prominent, more than one-fourth of the total length (mostly in moist habitats in forested areas) . . . . *C. laeviculmis*
        SMOOTH-STEMMED SEDGE

      69 Perigynia not often more than 2.5 mm long, the beak straight, not distinctly set off from the rest of the body and not more than one-fifth of the total length (not likely to be found below about 2500 ft., 760 m) . . . . *C. brunnescens*
        BROWNISH SEDGE

    68 Spikelets commonly with more than 15 perigynia

      70 Beak of perigynia about as long as the wider lower portion; leaf blades to 5 mm wide

        71 Spikelets not often more than 10 mm long (sometimes, however, to 13 mm); scales not covering the beaks of the perigynia . . . . *C. deweyana* subsp. *leptopoda*
          SHORT-TAILED SEDGE

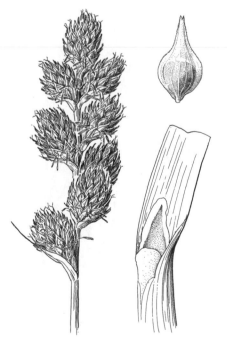

Carex feta,
green-sheathed sedge

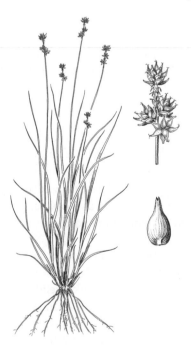

Carex interior,
inland sedge

71 Spikelets commonly 15 mm long; scales often covering the beaks of the perigynia . . . . . .
. . . . *C. bolanderi* subsp. *bolanderi*
BOLANDER'S SEDGE

> The length of the spikelets is the more reliable and more easily dealt with of the choices that distinguish *C. deweyana* subsp. *leptopoda* from *C. bolanderi* subsp. *bolanderi*. Numerous other characters have been proposed to separate them, but none is decisive.

70 Beak of perigynium at most only about half as long as the wider lower portion; leaf blades rarely if ever so much as 5 mm wide

72 Beak of perigynia about half as long as the wider lower portion (plants forming dense tufts) . . . . *C. arcta*
NORTHERN CLUSTERED SEDGE

72 Beak of perigynia much less than half as long as the wider lower portion (rhizomes short, the plants therefore more likely to be tufted than to spread)

73 Perigynia with distinct brownish veins; beak of perigynia often dark or with a dark line near the tip; leaf blades to 2.5 mm wide . . . . *C. praeceptorum*
TEACHERS' SEDGE

73 Perigynia with veins but these not brownish; beak of perigynia not dark or with a dark line near the tip; leaf blades to 4 mm wide (not likely to be found below 3000 ft., 910 m) . . . . *C. canescens*
HOARY SEDGE

19 Stigmas 3 or 4, the achenes 3- or 4-angled

74 Larger leaf blades at least 10 mm wide, sometimes as much as 15 mm (stigmas 3)

75 Pistillate spikelets (these to 15 cm long) conspicuously drooping (garden plant, sometimes escaping)
. . . . *C. pendula*
DROOPING SEDGE (Europe)

75 Pistillate spikelets typically upright (but sometimes nodding to some extent in *C. amplifolia*)

76 Pistillate spikelets to more than 10 cm long; perigynia plump, about 3 mm long, the beak distinct and about 1 mm long, sometimes curved; usually in damp ground in open areas; spreading by rhizomes . . . .
. . . . *C. amplifolia*
AMPLE-LEAVED SEDGE

76 Pistillate spikelets not often more than 5 cm long; perigynia slender, about 5 mm long, tapering to an indistinct beak; usually in damp ground in forested areas; forming tufts
. . . . *C. hendersonii*
HENDERSON'S SEDGE

74 Larger leaf blades seldom more than 8 mm wide

77 Stigmas usually 4, very rarely 3 (achenes usually 4-angled, sometimes 3-angled; leaf blades to 5 mm wide; perigynia hairy, and with a distinct beak and with the lower portion narrowed rather abruptly to a short stalk; usually in forested areas, sometimes where rather dry) . . . . *C. concinnoides*
NORTHWESTERN SEDGE

77 Stigmas 3 (sometimes 4 in *C. scabriuscula*) and not in all other respects as described in the other choice 77

78 Perigynia hairy or bristly (look carefully, because in some species under the other choice 78 and first choice 77, these outgrowths are limited to the upper portion of the perigynia, to the edges, or to the 2 teeth of the beak)

Carex praeceptorum, teachers' sedge

79 Achene tightly filling the space within the perigynium (in several of the sedges under this choice, some inflorescences have only pistillate or only staminate spikelets, or pistillate and staminate plants may be separate; furthermore, certain species may produce short-peduncled pistillate spikelets that easily escape notice because they are hidden by the leaves)

  80 Leaves hairy; perigynia distinctly 3-angled (with 3 flat surfaces; SW Oreg. to Calif.) . . . . *C. gynodynama*
OLNEY'S HAIRY SEDGE

  80 Leaves not hairy; perigynia not 3-angled (they have either 2 flat surfaces or are so plump that the 3 sides would be scarcely noticeable except for the fact that they are separated by ridges)

    81 Perigynia with 2 flat surfaces (but there is a bulge on both surfaces, marking the location of the achene), shiny, purplish black (Josephine and Jackson Cos., Oreg.) . . . . *C. scabriuscula* (*C. gigas*)
CASCADES SEDGE

    81 Perigynia plump, without broad, flat surfaces, not shiny, green, brown, or purple

      82 Perigynia with distinct veins as well as ridges separating the divisions (usually with not more than 6 perigynia on each spikelet)

        83 Beak of perigynia usually at least 1 mm long; plants forming tufts (SW Oreg. to Calif.) . . . . *C. brainerdii*
BRAINERD'S SEDGE

        83 Beak of perigynia much less than 1 mm long; spreading by rhizomes . . . . *C. inops* subsp. *inops* (*C. pensylvanica* of some references)
LONG-STOLONED SEDGE

      82 Perigynia with prominent ridges separating the 3 divisions but without distinct veins

        84 Beak of perigynia usually about 0.5 mm long, much shorter than the plump portion (in areas where the soil is derived from serpentine rock, Josephine and Curry Cos., Oreg., to Calif.) . . . . *C. serpenticola*
SERPENTINE SEDGE

        84 Beak of perigynia usually more than 0.5 mm long, sometimes fully 1 mm and often nearly as long as the plump portion

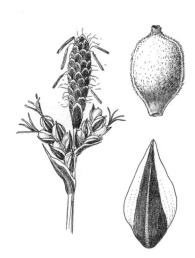

Carex hendersonii,
Henderson's sedge

Carex concinnoides,
northwestern sedge

85 Perigynia not often more than 1.5 mm wide; scales of staminate florets not roughened by bristly hairs along the midrib near the tip; plants commonly at least 20 cm tall; mostly in forests at higher elevations .... *C. rossii*
ROSS' SEDGE

85 Perigynia typically at least 1.7 mm wide; scales of staminate florets roughened by bristly hairs along the midrib near the tip; plants not often more than 10 cm tall; on backshores of beaches, including dunes, where the sand has been stabilized by grass .... *C. brevicaulis*
SHORT-STEMMED SEDGE

79 Achene not tightly filling the space within the perigynium (in other words, there is at least some empty space around it, especially above it)

86 Perigynia densely hairy or bristly almost all over

87 Leaf blades and bracts below the spikelets of the inflorescence folded or rolled up, thus appearing to be only about 1–1.5 mm wide; lower portions of upright stems typically bare of leaf blades; perigynia with a beak about 1 mm long, the 2 prominent teeth forming about half of its length (in very wet habitats, especially bogs, mostly below about 4000 ft., 1220 m) ....
.... *C. lasiocarpa* subsp. *americana*
SLENDER BOG SEDGE

87 Plants not in all respects as described in the other choice 87

88 Beaks of perigynia without 2 prominent teeth (the tip of the beak is usually finely serrated, however)

89 Plants spreading extensively by rhizomes; perigynia about twice as long as wide (Jackson Co., Oreg., to Calif.; also E of the crest of the Cascades) ...... *C. scirpoidea* subsp. *pseudoscirpoidea*
WESTERN SINGLE-SPIKED SEDGE

89 Plants forming clumps, not spreading extensively by rhizomes; perigynia about 3–3.5 times as long as wide (montane, mostly above 5000 ft., 1520 m) ...... *C. scirpoidea* subsp. *stenochlaena*

88 Beaks of perigynia with 2 prominent teeth

90 Perigynia about 3 times as long as wide .... *C. hirta*
HAIRY SEDGE

90 Perigynia (including the beak and teeth) not obviously more than twice as long as wide

91 Lower portion of each stem arising from the creeping rhizome with crowded, well-developed leaves (in the Cascades, mostly on exposed, dry habitats above 4000 ft., 1220 m; N Wash. to Calif.) .... *C. halliana*
HALL'S SEDGE

91 Lower portion of each stem arising from the rhizome without well-developed leaves (only leaf sheaths present); typically in very wet habitats ....
.... *C. pellita* (*C. lanuginosa* of some references, misapplied)
WOOLLY SEDGE

86 Hairs or bristles on perigynia limited to the upper portion, especially the edges and beak

92 Pistillate spikelets essentially sessile; scales below perigynia, especially those in the upper portion of the spikelet, with awns 0.5–1 mm long; teeth of beak of perigynia with very small bristles on their inner surfaces (SW Oreg. to Calif.) .... *C. serratodens*
SAWTOOTH SEDGE

92 Pistillate spikelets with substantial peduncles; scales of perigynia pointed but without awns; teeth of beak of perigynia without bristles on their inner surfaces

93 Pistillate spikelets usually nodding to some extent; perigynia tapering gradually almost to the tip, so there is only an indistinct beak, the upper portion usually conspicuously hairy (SW Oreg. to Calif.) .... *C. mendocinensis* (*C. debiliformis*)
MENDOCINO SEDGE

93 Pistillate spikelets upright; perigynia with a distinct beak more than 0.5 mm long, hairy only along the edges of the beak and upper portion, hairs sometimes few and obscure ..... *C. luzulina*
LUZULA-LIKE SEDGE

78 Perigynia not hairy or bristly (but they may be densely covered with small bumps, these sometimes glandular)

  94 Pistillate florets of the terminal spikelet of the inflorescence above the staminate ones

    95 Perigynia not pressed tightly together and not hidden by the scales accompanying them; tips of scales with awns to more than 2 mm long; spikelets below the terminal one nodding to some extent; plants spreading by rhizomes (usually in very wet habitats) . . . . *C. buxbaumii*
                                                                           BUXBAUM'S SEDGE

    95 Perigynia pressed tightly together; perigynia hidden by the scales accompanying them; tips of scales pointed but without awns; spikelets below the terminal one not nodding; plants forming tufts. . . . . *C. mertensii*
                                                                           MERTENS' SEDGE

  94 Staminate florets of the terminal spikelet of the inflorescence above the pistillate ones, or the terminal spikelet completely staminate

    96 Scales of perigynia prolonged into rough-edged awns more than 3 mm long, sometimes as long as 10 mm (perigynia about 3 times as long as wide, with a short beak; pistillate spikelets nodding to at least some extent; mostly near the coast) . . . . *C. macrochaeta*
                                                           ALASKA LONG-AWNED SEDGE

    96 Scales of perigynia without awns or with awns not more than 1 mm long

      97 Pistillate spikelets (at least the lower ones) drooping

        98 Perigynia with a beak about 1.5 mm long; plants forming tufts (perigynia not pressed tightly together; larger leaf blades to 5 mm wide; occasional weed) . . . . *C. sylvatica*
                                                          WOOD SEDGE (Europe)

        98 Perigynia either without a beak or the beak not more than 0.5 mm long; plants spreading by rhizomes

          99 Perigynia without a beak (but they may have a stalk at the base)

            100 Scales of perigynia 3–4 times as long as wide, much too narrow to hide the perigynia (in sphagnum bogs, especially above 1500 ft., 460 m) . . . . *C. paupercula*
                                                         STUNTED SEDGE

Carex lasiocarpa subsp. *americana*, slender bog sedge

Carex pellita, woolly sedge

Carex stylosa, long-styled sedge

100 Scales of perigynia 2–3 times as long as wide, nearly wide enough to hide the perigynia (mostly near the coast; Alaska to NW Oreg.) . . . . *C. pluriflora*
MANY-FLOWERED SEDGE

99 Perigynia with a beak

101 Beak of perigynia divided into 2 teeth; base of perigynia without a distinct stalk (mostly montane and not common below about 3500 ft., 1070 m) . . . . *C. spectabilis*
SHOWY SEDGE

101 Beak of perigynia not divided into 2 teeth; base of perigynia with a distinct stalk (usually in sphagnum bogs) . . . . *C. limosa*
SHORE SEDGE

97 Pistillate spikelets not drooping

102 Perigynia without beaks (bract below the lowest pistillate spikelet reaching beyond the inflorescence, and usually at least 7 cm long) . . . . *C. livida*
LIVID SEDGE

102 Perigynia with distinct beaks (at least 0.3 mm long)

103 Bracts beneath the pistillate spikelets without distinct sheaths

104 Perigynia with prominent, raised, lengthwise veins (Jackson and Klamath Cos., Oreg., to Calif.)
. . . . *C. whitneyi*
WHITNEY'S SEDGE

104 Perigynia smooth or with inconspicuous veins (Alaska to N Wash., mostly near the coast) . . . .
. . . . *C. stylosa*, p. 383
LONG-STYLED SEDGE

103 Bracts beneath the pistillate spikelets (at least the lowest one) with substantial sheaths

105 None of the bracts below the pistillate spikelets reaching beyond the inflorescence; plants spreading by rhizomes, most leaves on the upright stems rather than basal (Wash. to Calif.) . . . .
. . . . *C. californica*
CALIFORNIA SEDGE

105 Bract below the lowest pistillate spikelet reaching beyond the inflorescence; plants forming dense tufts with many basal leaves

106 Perigynia 2.2–3.3 mm long, the beak straight or only slightly curved; leaf blades not often more than 3 mm wide (often in sphagnum bogs but also in other wet habitats) . . . .
. . . . *C. viridula* subsp. *viridula* (*C. oederi*)
GREEN SEDGE

106 Perigynia 3.7–6.2 mm long, the beak usually conspicuously curved; leaf blades to 5 mm wide
. . . . *C. flava*
YELLOW SEDGE

Cyperus

1 Plants with a single flowering stem and with stolons bearing nearly round tubers at their tips; florets rarely producing mature achenes (leaves to about 8 mm wide; perennial) . . . . *C. esculentus*
YELLOW NUT GRASS

1 Plants typically with at least 2 flowering stems and without stolons (but they may have underground rhizomes); florets commonly producing mature achenes

2 Pistil with 2 stigmas; fruit convex on both sides, its shape thus resembling that of a lens (annual, usually less than 25 cm tall; each branch of the inflorescence with not more than 10 spikelets; leaves not more than 2 mm wide; mostly E of the Cascades but also in Jackson Co., Oreg.; to Calif.) . . . .
. . . . *C. bipartitus* (*C. rivularis*)
SHINING CYPERUS

2 Pistil with 3 stigmas; fruit 3-angled (but the 3 sides may be of different widths)

3 Tips of floret bracts curving downward (annual; plants not often so much as 20 cm tall, usually much smaller; leaves not more than 2.5 mm wide)

  4 Floret bracts with 3 lengthwise veins, the tip pointed but not drawn out into a slender awn . . . .
. . . . *C. acuminatus*
POINTED-BRACT CYPERUS

  4 Floret bracts with at least 5 veins, sometimes as many as 11, the tip drawn out into a slender awn
about 1 mm long . . . . *C. squarrosus* (*C. aristatus*)
AWNED CYPERUS

3 Tips of floret bracts directed toward the tip of the spikelet, not curving downward
  5 Spikelets jointed at each floret bract, readily falling apart when dry (spikelets densely crowded on
branches of the inflorescence; achene with a short but definite beak after the style has separated from
it; bracts 2–3 mm long; one surface of the achene about twice as wide as the other 2 sides; leaf blades
to about 5 mm wide; annual; from warm habitats, including portions of Calif.; introduced into our
area) . . . . *C. odoratus*
FRAGRANT CYPERUS

  5 Spikelets not jointed to the extent that they readily fall apart
    6 Achene with a short but distinct stalk and also with a persistent short beak (about 0.4–0.5 mm long)
after the style has separated from it (perennial; leaf blades to about 10 mm wide; spikelets usually
8–9 mm long, forming dense, nearly round masses on branches of the inflorescence) . . . .
. . . . *C. eragrostis*, pl. 615
TALL CYPERUS

    6 Achene without a stalk and without a persistent short beak
      7 Floret bracts not often more than 1.5 mm long; achenes not more than 1 mm long or so much as
twice as long as wide; annual (leaf blades to about 9 mm wide) . . . . *C. erythrorhizos*
RED-ROOTED CYPERUS

      7 Floret bracts at least 2 mm long; achenes at least 2 mm long; perennial
        8 Floret bracts 3–3.5 mm long, about half as deep as long when viewed from the side, the midrib
prolonged as a stout awn about 0.5 mm long; achenes 3 mm long, thus nearly as long as the
floret bracts; leaf blades to about 4 mm wide . . . . *C. schweinitzii*
SCHWEINITZ' CYPERUS

        8 Floret bracts 3.5–4 mm long, only about one-fourth as deep as long when viewed from the side,
the midrib not prolonged as a stout awn; achenes to about 2 mm long, not more than half as
long as the floret bracts; leaf blades to about 10 mm wide . . . . *C. strigosus*
STRAW-COLORED CYPERUS

Cyperus esculentus,
yellow nut grass

Cyperus strigosus,
straw-colored cyperus

Eleocharis

1 Florets with 2 stigmas (rarely 3); achenes 2-sided, lens-shaped (and at the top with a caplike, conical, or elongated projection that is distinctly demarcated from the rest of the body; in some species under the other choice 1, the projection is also demarcated from the rest of the body)

    2 Plants perennial, spreading by rhizomes and forming extensive mats; projection at top of achene sometimes conical, sometimes elongated; flowering stems usually at least 30 cm tall, sometimes more than 1 m . . . . *E. palustris*, pl. 616
                                       COMMON SPIKE RUSH

            Eleocharis mamillata and *E. macrostachya* are similar and could be encountered in our region. Separating them convincingly from *E. palustris* is difficult to do in a simple key. In some references, both have been placed in synonymy under *E. palustris*. The systematics of this complex is dealt with in detail in *Flora of North America*.

    2 Plants annual, forming separate tufts

        3 Caplike projection less than one-third as wide as the body of the achene; flowering stems to about 15 cm tall . . . . *E. atropurpurea*
                                       PURPLE SPIKE RUSH

        3 Caplike projection at least half as wide as the body of the achene; flowering stems to about 30 cm tall (but sometimes only a few cm tall)

            4 Caplike projection about half as wide as the body of the achene . . . . *E. ovata*
                                         OVATE SPIKE RUSH

            4 Caplike projection usually at least two-thirds as wide as the body of the achene . . . . *E. obtusa*
                                         BLUNT SPIKE RUSH

1 Florets with 3 stigmas; achenes 3-sided or egg-shaped, definitely not 2-sided and lens-shaped

    5 Achene with 6–12 slender, lengthwise ridges other than those that may slightly separate the 3 sides, and with a caplike, conical, or sombrerolike projection that is set off from the rest of the achene by a groove

        6 Perennial, forming dense tufts and also spreading by rhizomes; flowering stems usually to about 15 cm tall but sometimes taller than 50 cm; achene nearly twice as long as wide, with 8–12 lengthwise ridges . . . . *E. acicularis*
                                       NEEDLE SPIKE RUSH

        6 Typically annual, only occasionally perennial, usually forming dense tufts but not often spreading extensively by rhizomes; flowering stems to about 7 cm tall; achene about 1.5 times as long as wide, with 6–10 lengthwise ridges . . . . *E. bella* (*E. acicularis* subsp. *bella*)
                                       PRETTY SPIKE RUSH

    5 Achene without slender lengthwise ridges other than those slightly separating the 3 sides

        7 Achene with a plate-, cap-, or pyramidlike covering set off from the rest of the achene by a shallow but distinct groove

            8 Inflorescences usually 2 to nearly 3 times as long as wide; covering of the achene plate- or pyramidlike, not so high as wide, and usually at least half as wide as the achene; angles of the covering, when viewed from above, so broad as to resemble lobes, the outline of the covering as a whole thus not rigidly triangular (Oreg. to Calif. and eastward) . . . . *E. bolanderi*
                                      BOLANDER'S SPIKE RUSH

            8 Inflorescence usually at least 5 times as long as wide; covering of the achene pyramidlike, sometimes higher than wide, usually much less than half as wide as the achene; angles of the covering, when viewed from above, not so broad as to resemble lobes, the outline of the covering as a whole thus rather rigidly triangular (Oreg. to Calif. and eastward) . . . . *E. parishii*
                                      PARISH'S SPIKE RUSH

        7 Achene with a snoutlike prolongation, the base of which is not set off from the rest of the achene by a shallow but distinct groove

            9 Flowering stems to more than 40 cm tall; inflorescences usually with 10–20 florets; stems often touching down and rooting, the plants thus forming mats . . . . *E. rostellata*
                                      BEAKED SPIKE RUSH

9 Flowering stems rarely more than 30 cm tall; inflorescences usually with fewer than 10 florets; plants forming mats by rhizomes

   10 Flowering stems usually 10–30 cm tall; inflorescence with 3–10 florets; lowest bract of the inflorescence with a floret above it . . . . *E. quinqueflora*
FIVE-FLOWER SPIKE RUSH

   10 Flowering stems usually only 2–6 cm tall; inflorescence with 6–10 florets; lowest bract of the inflorescence without a floret above it . . . . *E. parvula*
SMALL SPIKE RUSH

Eriophorum

1 Perianth bristles usually 6–7 (brownish, 6–8 mm long, with small barbs; SW Oreg. to Calif.) . . . .
. . . . *E. crinigerum*, pl. 618
FRINGED COTTON GRASS

1 Perianth bristles numerous, at least 10 mm long, without barbs

   2 Each inflorescence consisting of a single spikelet (perianth bristles generally 13–15 mm long, usually white, sometimes brownish or reddish) . . . . *E. chamissonis*, pl. 617
CHAMISSO'S COTTON GRASS

   2 Most inflorescences consisting of at least 2–3 spikelets

      3 Inflorescence with a single leaflike bract beneath it (high montane) . . . . *E. gracile*
SLENDER COTTON GRASS

      3 Inflorescence with 2 or more leaflike bracts beneath it

         4 Spikelets nodding, with peduncles to more than 3 cm long; perianth bristles white (montane, mostly above 3000 ft., 910 m) . . . . *E. angustifolium* (*E. polystachion* of some references)
TALL COTTON GRASS

         4 Spikelets mostly upright, with peduncles not more than about 1.5 cm long; perianth bristles brownish (apparently introduced in a few places) . . . . *E. virginicum*
VIRGINIA COTTON GRASS (E North America)

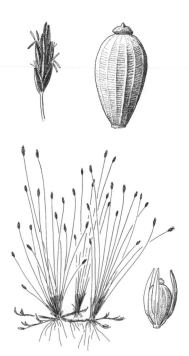

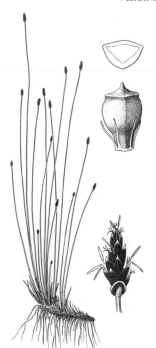

Eleocharis acicularis,
needle spike-rush

Eleocharis bolanderi,
Bolander's spike rush

Scirpus-Schoenoplectus-Bolboschoenus-Isolepis-Trichophorum Complex

In most references, all species in this complex have been placed in a single genus, *Scirpus*. It is not really wrong to do so, although the treatment of the assemblage in *Flora of North America* revives four older generic names applicable to some of the species in our region.

1 Plants submerged up to the leaf tips and inflorescences, which float (spikelet single on each flowering stem; bract originating below each inflorescence much like a continuation of the cylindrical stem) . . . . **Schoenoplectus subterminalis** (*Scirpus subterminalis*)
WATER CLUB RUSH, WATER BULRUSH

1 Plants not in all respects as described in the other choice 1
    2 Each inflorescence consisting of only 1 spikelet (stems nearly cylindrical; lowest or only bract beneath the spikelet drawn out into a slender, somewhat awnlike tip that reaches only slightly beyond the spikelet)
        3 Perennial, often more than 20 cm tall; perianth bristles present, usually 6; most leaves reduced to brownish scales on the lower portion of each stem, but at a slightly higher level there is usually a green blade about 5 mm long . . . . **T. caespitosum** (*Scirpus caespitosus*)
TUFTED CLUB RUSH

        3 Annual, not often more than 20 cm tall; perianth bristles absent; plants usually with at least a few slender leaves, about half as long as the flowering stems, originating from the base (coastal, mostly in wet, saline habitats) . . . . **I. cernua** (*Scirpus cernuus*)
LOW CLUB RUSH

    2 Each inflorescence usually with more than 1 spikelet
        4 Stems cylindrical, not at all 3-angled at any level; leaves without blades
            5 Stems not more than about 20 cm tall, less than 1 mm thick; leaves with blades about 1 mm wide; achenes with lengthwise ribs . . . . **I. setacea** (*Scirpus setaceus*)
BRISTLE-LEAVED CLUB RUSH (Eurasia, Africa, Australia)

            5 Plants commonly more than 50 cm tall (often considerably more than 1 m tall), the larger ones at least 4 mm thick; leaves without blades (they are represented only by sheaths); achenes smooth
                6 Bracts below individual florets usually 3.5–4 mm long and with reddish brown markings . . . . **Schoenoplectus acutus** subsp. **occidentalis** (*Scirpus acutus* subsp. *occidentalis*)
TULE

                6 Bracts below individual florets usually 2.5–3 mm long, without reddish brown markings . . . . **Schoenoplectus tabernaemontani** (*Scirpus tabernaemontani, S. validus*), pl. 619
GREAT BULRUSH
Schoenoplectus acutus subsp. *occidentalis* and *S. tabernaemontani* hybridize.

        4 Stems somewhat to distinctly 3-angled, sometimes sharply so, usually at least on the portion just below the inflorescence, but look also at various levels lower down; leaves with blades
            7 Inflorescence with a single bract, this appearing to be a continuation of the stem and to more than 10 cm long (leaf blades to about 4 mm wide)
                8 Awns of bracts below individual florets at least 0.5 mm long, sometimes as long as 1.5 mm; sides of the stem, between the angles, nearly flat; blade of uppermost leaf usually longer than the sheath . . . . **Schoenoplectus pungens** (*Scirpus pungens*)
COMMON THREE-SQUARE

                8 Awns of bracts below individual florets not more than 0.5 mm long; sides of the stem, between the angles, markedly concave; blade of uppermost leaf usually shorter than the sheath . . . . **Schoenoplectus americanus** (*Scirpus americanus*)
AMERICAN THREE-SQUARE
Schoenoplectus pungens and *S. americanus* hybridize.

            7 Inflorescence usually with at least 2 bracts beneath it, these leaflike and not appearing to be a continuation of the stem

9 Only 1–2 blade-bearing leaves present, these near the base and their blades to only about 5 cm long (probably introduced) . . . . ***Schoenoplectus triqueter*** (*Scirpus triqueter*)
   TRIANGULAR CLUB RUSH (Europe)

9 Leaves on stems conspicuous, with blades much longer than 5 cm

  10 Spikelets, when fully developed, more than 1 cm long (and at least 1.5 times as long as wide)

    11 Perianth bristles as long as, or slightly longer than, the achenes; achenes somewhat 3-angled, with 3 convex sides; stigmas usually 3; leaf blades to about 15 mm wide . . . . ***B. fluviatilis*** (*Scirpus fluviatilis*)
   RIVER BULRUSH

    11 Perianth bristles, if present, not more than about half as long as the achenes; achenes more or less lens-shaped, with 2 convex sides; stigmas usually 2; leaf blades to about 10 mm wide . . . . ***B. maritimus*** **subsp.** ***paludosus*** (*Scirpus maritimus* subsp. *paludosus*), pl. 611
   MARSH BULRUSH

  10 Spikelets not more than 1 cm long (usually less, except in some *Scirpus pallidus*)

    12 Spikelets (usually about 8 mm long) nearly or fully 3 times as long as wide, with distinct peduncles (leaf blades to about 7 mm wide; Willamette Valley and Curry, Josephine, and Jackson Cos., Oreg., to Calif.; widespread in other parts of North America) . . . . ***Scirpus pendulus***
   DELICATE CLUB RUSH

    12 Spikelets not more than twice as long as wide, sessile

      13 Spikelets usually 7–8 mm long, more or less rounded, scarcely if at all longer than wide (leaf blades to about 10 mm wide) . . . . ***Scirpus pallidus***
   PALE BULRUSH

      13 Spikelets usually not more than 6 mm long, distinctly longer than wide

        14 Achenes somewhat lens-shaped, with only 2 edges; perianth bristles usually 5, upright, not curling (leaf blades commonly more than 10 mm wide) . . . . ***Scirpus microcarpus***
   SMALL-FRUITED BULRUSH

        14 Achenes slightly 3-angled, with 3 distinct edges; perianth bristles usually 5, curling to at least some extent (leaf blades usually 5–7 mm wide) . . . . ***Scirpus congdonii***
   CONGDON'S BULRUSH

Schoenoplectus acutus
subsp. *occidentalis,* tule

Scirpus congdonii,
Congdon's bulrush

HYDROCHARITACEAE Waterweed Family

The Hydrocharitaceae consists of submerged aquatics growing in fresh or brackish water. All have sessile leaves, but these differ considerably in form and arrangement. Staminate flowers are usually separate from pistillate flowers; both types, however, have three sepals and three petals, and originate above a pair of separate or united bracts. Pistillate flowers are borne singly on a long stalk; staminate flowers are usually produced in clusters of a few to many. In some populations of *Egeria* and *Elodea*, flowering either does not happen very often or the plants are entirely staminate. *Najas* (see under Najadaceae) is sometimes included in Hydrocharitaceae.

1 Leaves basal, to more than 50 mm long and generally about 5–6 mm wide (staminate flowers produced in clusters of many, becoming detached and floating free) . . . . *Vallisneria americana*
TAPE GRASS (E North America)

1 Leaves opposite or in whorls, rarely more than 30 mm long or 4 mm wide
    2 Leaves rarely more than 15 mm long, mostly opposite or in whorls of 3; petals not often more than 5 mm long . . . . *Elodea*
    2 Leaves commonly 15–20 mm long, mostly in whorls of 3–6 (except on the lower part of the stems, where they are opposite); petals of staminate flowers 8–10 mm long, those of pistillate flowers 6–7 mm long (cultivated in aquaria and garden pools, and occasionally escaping; in some areas, all populations consist of staminate plants) . . . . *Egeria densa* (*Elodea densa*)
BRAZILIAN WATERWEED

Elodea

1 Leaves 6–13 mm long and to 2 mm wide, tapering rather gradually to a pointed tip; petals either absent or less than 1 mm long . . . . *E. nuttallii*
NUTTALL'S WATERWEED

1 Leaves 9–15 mm long and to 3 mm wide, blunt or abruptly tapered to the tip; petals of pistillate flowers about 2.5 mm long, those of staminate flowers about 5 mm long . . . . *E. canadensis*
COMMON WATERWEED

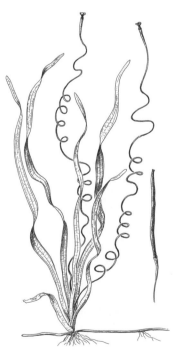

Vallisneria americana,
tape grass

Elodea canadensis,
common waterweed

IRIDACEAE Iris Family

Irises and their relatives are perennials with rather narrow leaves. The flowers have three petals, three sepals, and three stamens, the latter in line with the sepals. The petals and sepals are sometimes similar, sometimes different, and in *Iris* the three branches of the style are two-lobed and resemble petals. The fruit-forming part of the pistil is below the petals and sepals. Flowers arise from between a pair of substantial bracts.

Besides irises, gladioli, crocuses, freesias, and tigridias, this family has given us a plant commonly called montbretia (*Crocosmia* ×*crocosmiiflora*), a hybrid with orange-red flowers. It is rather hardy and sometimes multiplies enthusiastically in places where it has been dumped or planted intentionally.

1 Petals and sepals decidedly different (petals narrower than the sepals); branches of the style (3, in line with the sepals) petal-like and 2-lobed; filaments of stamens separate from one another . . . . ***Iris***
1 Sepals and petals similar; branches of the style neither petal-like nor 2-lobed; filaments of stamens united for some or all of their length
  2 Filaments of stamens fused nearly to their tips; perianth bright yellow, blue, purplish blue, or violet-blue; flowers typically facing upward or outward . . . . ***Sisyrinchium***
  2 Filaments of stamens fused for not more than half their length; perianth reddish purple (rarely white); flowers typically facing outward or slightly nodding . . . . ***Olsynium***

Iris

There is considerable hybridization among the following species, whose ranges overlap: *Iris bracteata, I. chrysophylla, I. douglasiana,* and *I. innominata.* The most distinctive of the hybrids is keyed below as *I.* ×*thompsonii.*

1 Perianth tube usually at least 1.5 cm long (if shorter, then with leaves at least 8 mm wide)
  2 Perianth tube not so much as 2 cm long; most leaves at least 8 mm wide (prevailing color of petals and sepals ranging from cream to lavender, blue, and deep purple; coastal, from Coos Co., Oreg., to Calif.) . . . . *I. douglasiana*, pl. 622
    DOUGLAS' IRIS
  2 Perianth tube usually more than 2 cm long; leaves not so much as 8 mm wide
    3 Perianth tube 2–3 cm long; petals and sepals usually deep yellow with dark lines but sometimes yellow almost throughout, and sometimes lavender or somewhat brownish; Josephine and Curry Cos., Oreg., to Calif.) . . . . *I. innominata*, pl. 623
      GOLDEN IRIS
    3 Perianth tube at least 4 cm long (sometimes more than 6 cm); petals and sepals usually cream-yellow or nearly white, sometimes faintly bluish, commonly with darker lines (Marion and Polk Cos., Oreg., to Calif.) . . . . *I. chrysophylla*, pl. 621
      SLENDER-TUBED IRIS
1 Perianth tube less than 1.5 cm long
  4 Flowering stems to more than 1 m tall; plants usually rooted in mud at the borders of lakes and ponds; leaves to about 2.5 cm wide (corolla mostly yellow or cream-yellow, with brown markings; commonly planted) . . . . *I. pseudacorus*
    YELLOW FLAG (Europe)
  4 Flowering stems rarely more than 50 cm tall; plants not rooted in mud at the borders of lakes and ponds (*I. missouriensis,* however, commonly grows in habitats that are damp much of the year); leaves to about 1.5 cm wide
    5 Flowering stems leafless or with only 1 leaf (most flowering stems with 2 flowers; petals and sepals commonly pale lilac or pale blue with purplish lines but sometimes mostly dark blue; common in damp habitats E of the Cascades but occurring in our region in W Brit. Col., Whidbey Island, Island Co., Wash., and formerly found near Sequim, Clallam Co., Wash.) . . . . *I. missouriensis*
      WESTERN IRIS

5 Flowering stems with at least 2–3 leaves

    6 Leaves pale, whitish green, to about 15 mm wide; flowering stems commonly branching and producing at least 3–4 flowers (petals and sepals white, with purple lines and usually some yellow, occasionally with purple blotches; at moderate elevations along the Clackamas River and Eagle Creek, Clackamas Co., Oreg.) . . . . *I. tenuis*, pl. 625

                CLACKAMAS IRIS

    6 Leaves green or yellowish green (not at all whitish green), not often more than 10 mm wide; flowering stems producing 1–2 (occasionally 3) flowers, otherwise not branching

      7 Leaves 6–10 mm wide, yellowish green on the underside (petals and sepals yellow with maroon or brown lines; perianth tube to 10 mm long; Josephine Co., Oreg., to Calif.) . . . . . . *I. bracteata*, pl. 620

                SISKIYOU IRIS

      7 Leaves not so much as 6 mm wide, the same shade of green on both surfaces

        8 Leaves not often more than 3 mm wide; perianth tube about 10 mm long; petals and sepals less than 4 cm long, mostly blue or purple (Curry Co., Oreg., to Calif.; also cultivated) . . . .

        . . . . *I. ×thompsonii* (believed to be *I. douglasiana × innominata*), pl. 626

                THOMPSON'S IRIS

        8 Leaves 3–5 mm wide; perianth tube about 5 mm long; petals and sepals 5–6 cm long

          9 Petals and sepals usually lavender, blue, or purple, sometimes white, pinkish, or orchid (widespread in W Oreg., also in W Wash. as far N as Thurston and Grays Harbor Cos.) . . . .

          . . . . *I. tenax* var. *tenax*, pl. 624

                TOUGH-LEAVED IRIS

          9 Petals and sepals to a considerable extent yellow (very local in Washington Co., Oreg.) . . . .

          . . . . *I. tenax* var. *gormanii*

             Studies have shown that while *I. tenax* vars. *tenax* and *gormanii* are interfertile, cross-pollination is less successful than pollination of var. *tenax* by itself, and var. *gormanii* by itself.

Olsynium

In many references, the species of *Olsynium* are placed in *Sisyrinchium*, and this is perfectly acceptable.

1 Tube formed by the united portions of the stamen filaments with a nearly spherical dilation about 3 mm wide near the base; flowering stems typically bearing 3 flowers (mostly E of the Cascades but also in Douglas, Jackson, and Josephine Cos., Oreg., and N Calif.) . . . .

    . . . . *O. douglasii* var. *inflatum* (*Sisyrinchium douglasii* var. *inflatum*)

                PURPLE GRASS WIDOWS

1 Tube formed by the united portions of the stamen filaments with only a slight dilation about 1.5 mm wide near the base; flowering stems typically bearing 2 flowers (S Vancouver Island and Gulf Islands, Brit. Col., the San Juan Islands and Island Co., Wash., and in a few places in the Willamette Valley, Oreg.; also E of the crest of the Cascades) . . . . *O. douglasii* var. *douglasii* (*Sisyrinchium douglasii* var. *douglasii*), pl. 627

                DOUGLAS' GRASS WIDOWS

Sisyrinchium

1 Perianth yellow (usually in wet habitats, often around bogs, and sometimes close to ocean shores) . . . .

    . . . . *S. californicum*, pl. 629

                GOLDEN-EYED GRASS

1 Perianth primarily blue, purplish blue, or violet-blue, usually with a yellow center

    2 Outer perianth segments 2–2.5 times as long as wide; underside of perianth segments mostly much lighter than the upper surface, the darker veins therefore very prominent (Oreg., especially S of Lane Co., to Calif.) . . . . *S. bellum*, pl. 628

                BLUE-EYED GRASS

2 Outer perianth segments usually at least 2.7 times (sometimes more than 3 times) as long as wide; underside of perianth segments nearly or fully as dark as the upper surface

   3 Slender tip of each perianth segment not originating in a distinct notch (mature fruits 6.2–9 mm long; coastal, Alaska to Pacific Co., Wash.) . . . . ***S. littorale***
                                        COASTAL BLUE-EYED GRASS

   3 Slender tip of each perianth segment originating in a distinct notch; mature fruits not often more than 7 mm long but sometimes 8 mm long in *S. hitchcockii* (because of extensive intergradation, species and subspecies within the *S. idahoense–S. hitchcockii* complex are difficult to define precisely; this is obvious in the rather inconclusive set of contrasting choices in the rest of the key)

      4 Perianth segments to 20 mm long; column formed by the united filaments of the stamens 6–9 mm long and usually dark purple; yellow center of perianth small, sometimes scarcely noticeable; mature fruit usually 6–7 mm long, sometimes as long as 8 mm (Lane and Douglas Cos., Oreg., to N Calif.) . . . . ***S. hitchcockii***, pl. 630
                                      HITCHCOCK'S BLUE-EYED GRASS

      4 Perianth segments rarely so much as 20 mm long except in some specimens of *S. idahoense* subsp. *macounii*); column formed by united filaments of the stamens not more than 6 mm long, yellow or violet; yellow center of perianth conspicuous; mature fruit usually less than 6 mm long, sometimes as long as 6.5 mm

         5 Perianth segments rarely so much as 15 mm long (widespread, Brit. Col. to Calif., also E to the Rocky Mountains) . . . . ***S. idahoense*** var. ***idahoense***, pl. 630
                                        IDAHO BLUE-EYED GRASS

         5 Perianth segments usually at least 15 mm long

            6 Outer bract of inflorescence at least twice as long as the inner bract (Vancouver Island and Gulf Islands, Brit. Col., and San Juan Islands, Wash.) . . . . ***S. idahoense*** var. ***macounii***
                                      MACOUN'S BLUE-EYED GRASS

            6 Outer bract of inflorescence less than twice as long as the inner bract (Gulf Islands of Brit. Col., and San Juan Islands to Lewis Co., Wash.) . . . . ***S. idahoense*** var. ***segetum***
                                   GRASS-FIELD BLUE-EYED GRASS

JUNCACEAE Rush Family

In general appearance, and in the way their leaf sheaths clasp the stems, rushes are somewhat similar to grasses. The flowers of these plants, however, have definite perianth segments, the three inner ones usually slightly different in size or other characteristics from the three outer ones (see p. 394). There are commonly three or six stamens and a single pistil, the style of which typically branches into three stigmas. The fruit, often with a short, beaklike remnant of the style, may contain just three seeds or many.

1 Leaves not flat and the sheaths usually open; margins of leaf blades without a fringe of hairs; fruit with numerous seeds . . . . ***Juncus***
1 Leaves with flat blades and with sheaths that enclose the stem (the plants therefore closely resembling grasses); margins of leaf blades usually with a fringe of hairs; mature fruit with only 3 seeds . . . . ***Luzula***

Juncus

1 Small, generally rather delicate annuals, less than 5 cm tall, except for *J. bufonius;* largest leaf blades not more than 1 mm wide (for mostly submerged aquatic perennials that have very slender leaf blades, take the second choice 15)

   2 Plants commonly more than 5 cm tall, sometimes more than 30 cm, branching at various levels above the base (often, however, sprawling on the ground); flowers developing along the stems as well as at the tips of the stems (stamens 6; common on drying mud, on damp, disturbed soil, and in gardens) . . . . . .
. . . . ***J. bufonius***, p. 395
                                        TOAD RUSH

        Juncus bufonius is widespread in North America and Eurasia, and several subspecies or varieties have been given names.

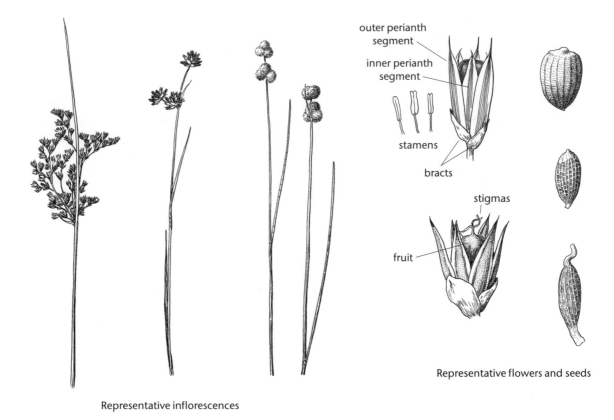

outer perianth
segment

inner perianth
segment

stamens

bracts

stigmas

fruit

Representative flowers and seeds

Representative inflorescences

Juncaceae

2 Plants not often so much as 5 cm tall, not branching above the base; flowers borne singly or in clusters
  at the tips of leafless stems

  3 Flowers 1–2 (rarely 3) at the tips of the stems, the 2 bracts below them of nearly equal size . . . .
    . . . . *J. kelloggii*
                                              KELLOGG'S DWARF RUSH

  3 Flowers borne singly at the tips of the stems; bracts below the flowers decidedly unequal, the smaller
    one (about 0.5 mm long) sometimes absent (both bracts may have fallen or been damaged by the
    time fruits have developed; mostly montane and E of the crest of the Cascades but present in the
    Willamette Valley and SW Oreg.) . . . .*J. hemiendytus*
                                                 DWARF RUSH

1 Plants perennial, commonly more than 15 cm tall if upright; largest leaves usually at least 1 mm wide
  4 Leaves without distinct blades (they are represented by sheaths, and these sometimes have a short,
    slender prolongation); inflorescence at one side of the flowering stem, the bract originating beneath it
    more or less cylindrical, appearing to be a continuation of the stem, and usually extending well beyond
    the inflorescence

    5 Stamens 3

      6 Upper leaf sheaths dark brown, reddish brown, or blackish

        7 Upper leaf sheaths dark reddish brown (chestnut), so glossy as to appear to be varnished; tip of
          the sheath, where the awnlike remnant of the blade originates, symmetrical, the edges not touch-
          ing, the upper margin thick, without a membranous border; inflorescence compact; perianth seg-
          ments 2.5–3 mm long, typically with a green midline area and a brown border . . . .
          . . . .*J. laccatus* (*J. effusus* subsp. *gracilis*)
                                                VARNISHED RUSH

7 Upper leaf sheaths dark brown or blackish, not so glossy as to appear to be varnished; tip of the sheath asymmetrical, the edges overlapping, the upper margin with a membranous border; inflorescence compact or loose; perianth segments 2.5–3.5 mm long, of uniform color (brown or green) .... *J. effusus* **subsp.** *pacificus,* pl. 632
PACIFIC RUSH

6 Upper leaf sheaths not especially dark

8 Stems with a few conspicuous ridges; inflorescence compact, all of the many flowers usually within 2.5 cm of its base .... *J. conglomeratus* (*J. effusus* subsp. *compactus*)
CLUSTERED RUSH (Europe)

8 Stems smooth or with inconspicuous ridges; inflorescence compact or loose

9 Perianth segments 2.5–3.5 mm long, green to pale brown ....*J. effusus* **subsp.** *effusus*
COMMON RUSH (Europe)

9 Perianth segments usually about 2 mm long, not often so much as 2.5 mm, with dark brown stripes

10 Tips of leaf sheaths not tending to roll up, usually asymmetrical, the 2 sides distinctly unequal, the uppermost edges with a membranous margin but not noticeably darkened ....
.... *J. hesperius* (*J. effusus* var. *hesperius,* var. *bruneus*)
WESTERN RUSH

10 Tips of leaf sheaths tending to roll up, symmetrical, the 2 sides essentially equal, the uppermost edges slightly darkened but without a membranous margin ... *J. exiguus* (*J. effusus* var. *exiguus*)
SMALL RUSH

5 Stamens 6 (perianth at least 3.5 mm long; upper portion of fruit not distinctly 3-angled)

11 Bract originating below the inflorescence at least half as long as the stem, sometimes even equaling the stem; stem less than 1.5 mm thick .... *J. filiformis*
THREAD RUSH

11 Bract originating below the inflorescence not so much as half as long as the stem; stem often more than 1.5 mm thick

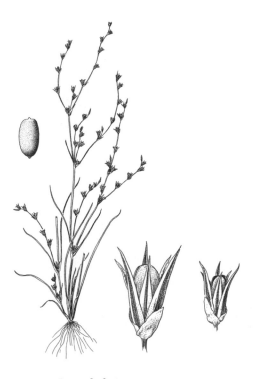

Juncus bufonius,
toad rush

Juncus kelloggii,
Kellogg's dwarf rush

12 Perianth 2.5–3 mm long; plants forming tufts . . . . *J. patens*
SPREADING RUSH

12 Perianth usually at least 4 mm long

   13 Inflorescence dense, globular; restricted to backshores of sandy beaches (perianth segments 5–8 mm long; membranous margins of inner perianth segments about as wide as those of the outer segments; aboveground stems arising singly in rows along underground rhizomes) . . . . . .
. . . . *J. breweri*
SALT RUSH

      Juncus breweri is often misidentified as *J.* "*lesueurii*" (properly *J. lescurii*), which is restricted to a small part of the Calif. coast in the San Francisco Bay region.

   13 Inflorescence usually loose, its general form not at all globular; not growing on backshores of sandy beaches (except where there may be standing water)

     14 Inflorescence usually with not more than 3 flowers, occasionally as many as 5; perianth segments 5–8 mm long; membranous margins of inner perianth segments about as wide as those of the outer segments (montane and high montane, mostly above 5000 ft., 1520 m) . . . .
. . . . *J. drummondii*
DRUMMOND'S RUSH

     14 Inflorescence commonly with numerous flowers but sometimes as few as 6–7; perianth segments usually 3.5–6 mm long; membranous margins of inner perianth segments distinctly wider than those of the outer segments (usually forming large clumps but also spreading by rhizomes; common lowland and montane species, mostly in very wet habitats) . . . .
. . . . *J. arcticus* var. *balticus*
        (includes vars. *montanus* and *vallicola,* difficult to separate from var. *balticus*)
BALTIC RUSH

4 Leaves with blades, these flattened (sometimes folded lengthwise) or cylindrical; bract originating below the inflorescence not appearing to be a continuation of the stem and usually shorter than the inflorescence

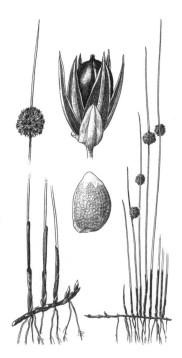 

Juncus breweri,
salt rush

Juncus arcticus var. *balticus,*
Baltic rush

15 Leaf blades folded lengthwise, commonly more than 5 mm wide when spread out (leaf blades incompletely marked off into units by cross-lines, which divide the pithy tissue that forms the core of the blade)

  16 Fruit tapering very gradually from below the middle to the tip; anthers sometimes as much as 1.5 times as long as the filaments but sometimes shorter than the filaments . . . . *J. oxymeris*, pl. 633

        POINTED RUSH

  16 Fruit egg-shaped, tapering rather abruptly to the beak at the tip; anthers not longer than the filaments

    17 Stamens 3 . . . . *J. ensifolius* var. *ensifolius*

        DAGGER-LEAF RUSH

    17 Stamens 6 . . . . *J. ensifolius* var. *montanus* (*J. xiphioides* var. *triandrus*)

        The systematics of the *J. xiphioides*–*J. ensifolius* group has been debated inconclusively by specialists for many years. According to the treatment in *Flora of North America*, *J. xiphioides*, which regularly has 6 stamens and is typically much larger than *J. ensifolius*, occurs only in Calif., Baja Calif., Arizona, Nevada, and New Mexico.

15 Leaf blades not folded lengthwise

  18 Leaf blades marked off into units by complete or incomplete cross-lines (the cross-lines divide the pithy tissue that forms the core of the blade)

    19 Plants submerged in fresh water during winter and spring, and sometimes during other seasons; nodes of the stems rooting and/or producing tufts of new leaves

      20 Mature fruit 5 mm long, decidedly longer than the perianth; seed about 0.75 mm long . . . . *J. supiniformis*

        HAIR-LEAVED RUSH

      20 Mature fruit about 3 mm long, scarcely longer than the perianth; seed about 0.5 mm long . . . . *J. bulbosus* (*J. supinus*)

        BULBOUS RUSH

    19 Plants not normally submerged; nodes of stems not rooting or producing tufts of new leaves

Juncus ensifolius var. *ensifolius*, dagger-leaf rush

Juncus supiniformis, hair-leaved rush

21 Stamens typically 3 (occasionally 6 in some flowers)
  22 Both ends of the seed drawn out into a tail, this at least one-third as long as the main portion
    23 Flower clusters usually with not more than 6 flowers; mature fruit tapering gradually to the tip and much longer than the perianth; seeds not often more than 1 mm long, the tails not more than half the length of the main portion; branches of inflorescence nearly upright
.... *J. brevicaudatus*
SHORT-TAILED RUSH (E North America)
    23 Flower clusters usually with at least 6 flowers, sometimes many; mature fruit usually tapering rather abruptly to a nipplelike tip; seeds 1.3–1.8 mm long, the tails at least two-thirds as long as the main portion; branches of inflorescence tending to spread outward ....*J. canadensis*
CANADA RUSH (E North America)
  22 Seed with only a nipplelike projection at each end
    24 Each inflorescence with a few dense, ball-like clusters, each usually consisting of at least 25 flowers; plants spreading by rhizomes ....*J. bolanderi*, pl. 631
BOLANDER'S RUSH
    24 Inflorescence typically extensively and loosely branched, the flower clusters not ball-like, each usually with fewer than 20 flowers; plants forming tufts
      25 Mature fruit about as long as the perianth ....*J. acuminatus*
SHARP-FRUITED RUSH
      25 Mature fruit about twice as long as the perianth ....*J. diffusissimus*
DIFFUSE RUSH (E United States)
21 Stamens typically 6
  26 Flowers generally borne singly (occasionally in pairs) at the tips and nodes of the inflorescence (fruit about 3 times as long as wide, tapering gradually to the tip and longer than the perianth; known to occur in cranberry bogs, where introduced) ....*J. pelocarpus*
BROWNISH-FRUITED RUSH (E North America)
  26 Flowers in clusters of at least several, sometimes many
    27 Inflorescence generally consisting of a single dense cluster of flowers (filaments of stamens longer than the anthers; perianth segments shiny and brownish black; not often found below about 3000 ft., 910 m) ....*J. mertensianus*
MERTENS' RUSH
    27 Inflorescence consisting of at least several clusters of flowers, the clusters often nearly spherical
      28 Anthers of stamens at least as long as the filaments (sometimes twice as long)
        29 Clusters of flowers few, nearly spherical, sometimes more than 1 cm in diameter, restricted to one group at the top of the stem (coastal, Oreg.) ....*J. nevadensis* subsp. *inventus*
OREGON COAST RUSH
        29 Clusters of flowers numerous, not distinctly spherical or more than 1 cm in diameter, scattered on separate short branches of the inflorescence as well as at the top ....
....*J. nevadensis* subsp. *nevadensis*
SIERRA NEVADA RUSH
      28 Anthers of stamens distinctly shorter than the filaments (usually about one-third to half as long)
        30 All perianth segments similar in tapering gradually to a pointed tip ....*J. acuminatus*
SHARP-FRUITED RUSH
        30 Inner perianth segments about the same width for most of their length and more or less rounded at the tip, the outer ones tapering gradually for most of their length but even then without distinctly pointed tips ....*J. alpinus*
ALPINE RUSH
18 Leaf blades (usually flattened, but sometimes very narrow) not marked off into units by cross-lines

31 Stamens 3

  32 Leaves entirely basal; inflorescence usually with not more than 8 flower clusters, each cluster rounded, with numerous flowers; perianth segments without membranous margins; seeds about 0.3 mm long, smooth (found in bogs where the cranberry is cultivated) . . . . *J. planifolius*
                                            FLAT-LEAVED RUSH (Europe)

  32 Leaves not entirely basal, at least 1–2 along the stems; inflorescence with as many as about 20 flower clusters, each cluster with as many as 12 flowers; perianth segments with membranous margins; seeds about 0.5 mm long, with many lengthwise ribs (probably introduced) . . . . *J. marginatus*
                                       MARGINED RUSH (E North America)

31 Stamens 6

  33 Leaf blades rarely more than 2 mm wide; flowers borne singly at the tips or nodes of the inflorescence (look carefully, because flower-bearing nodes may be close together)

    34 Tips of inner perianth segments blunt but the outer ones with a small beaklike tooth, this usually pointing inward (in salt marshes, S Brit. Col. to N Wash.) . . . . *J. gerardii*
                                   GERARD'S RUSH

    34 Tips of perianth segments pointed, none with a beaklike tooth pointing inward
      35 Fruit divided by partitions into 3 chambers . . . . *J. brachyphyllus*
                                   SHORT-LEAVED RUSH

      35 Fruit not divided into 3 chambers (the partitions are incomplete; common in wet habitats)
      . . . . *J. tenuis*
                                    SLENDER RUSH
          Juncus tenuis is a widespread species with several named but intergrading subspecies or varieties.

  33 Leaf blades at least 2.5 mm wide; flowers a few in each cluster

    36 Mature fruit at least twice as long as wide, decidedly longer than the perianth, the remnant of the style 0.8–1 mm long . . . . *J. covillei* subsp. *covillei*
                                   COVILLE'S RUSH

    36 Mature fruit not so much as twice as long as wide, usually not appreciably longer than the perianth, the style remnant only about 0.5 mm long . . . . *J. articulatus*
                                    JOINTED-LEAVED RUSH

      37 Remnant of the style set typically in a notch or depression at the tip of the mature fruit (seeds about 0.7 mm long, lopsided, broadest near one end; a plant of coastal habitats) . . . . *J. falcatus* subsp. *sitchensis*
                        SICKLE-LEAVED RUSH

      37 Remnant of the style not set in a notch at the tip of the fruit
        38 Body of seed about 3 times as long as wide and with a conspicuous whitish outgrowth at each end, the total length about 1.5 mm (montane and not likely to be found below about 3500 ft. (1070 m) . . . .*J. regelii*
                  REGEL'S RUSH

        38 Body of seed only about twice as long as wide and with only a short outgrowth at each end, the total length about 0.5 mm (Jackson and Josephine Cos., Oreg., to Calif.) . . . . *J. orthophyllus*
                  STRAIGHT-LEAVED RUSH

Juncus acuminatus,
sharp-fruited rush

Luzula

1 Flowers borne singly, in pairs, or in clusters of 3–4 at the tips of ultimate branches of the inflorescence
  2 Flowers borne singly at the tips of branches of the inflorescence; perianth segments drawn out into slender tips, these usually bent outward and downward at least slightly (montane, Wash. to Calif. but not likely to be found below 4000 ft., 1220 m) . . . .***L. divaricata***
                                              SPREADING WOOD RUSH
  2 Flowers almost always borne in pairs or in clusters of 3–4; perianth segments pointed, but not drawn out into slender tips or bent outward and downward
    3 Perianth segments 2.5–3.5 mm long; fruit 2.5–3.5 mm long with a beak to 1 mm long (high montane, S Brit. Col. to S Oreg., possibly Calif.) . . . .***L. hitchcockii***
                                      HITCHCOCK'S WOOD RUSH
    3 Perianth segments not more than 2.5 mm long and often considerably shorter; fruit less than 2.5 mm long, without a distinct beak
      4 Plants, when in flower, commonly at least 30 cm tall, sometimes as tall as 1 m; anthers of the stamens not so much as 1 mm long and typically shorter than the filaments . . . .***L. parviflora***
                                    SMALL-FLOWERED WOOD RUSH
      4 Plants not often more than 30 cm tall; anthers of the stamens sometimes to 1.3 mm long and typically longer than the filaments (montane and high montane, Alaska to Oreg.) . . . .***L. piperi*** (*L. glabrata* of some references)
                                    PIPER'S WOOD RUSH

1 Flowers numerous in a single dense inflorescence at the top of the main stem or in clusters at the tip of each branch of the inflorescence (most of the clusters with more than 4 flowers)
  5 Inflorescence consisting of as many as about 10 clusters of flowers at the top of the main stem (the clusters on such short branches that their individuality may not be obvious except where there are breaks between them) and typically nodding; perianth segments rather abruptly drawn out into slender tips (high montane) . . . .***L. spicata***
                                      SPIKED WOOD RUSH
  5 Inflorescence usually either with obvious branches or the individuality of the flower clusters, even if these are crowded together, readily apparent; perianth segments pointed but not abruptly drawn out into slender tips (in other words, they are tapered very gradually)
    6 Bracts of the pair directly beneath each perianth nearly as long as the perianth (inflorescence freely branched, the flower clusters widely separated; bracts beneath the perianth conspicuously hairy; montane and high montane, Alaska to Wash. and eastward) . . . . . .***L. arcuata* subsp. *unalaschkensis***
                                      UNALASKA WOOD RUSH
    6 Bracts of the pair directly beneath each perianth much shorter than the perianth
      7 Bracts of the pair beneath the perianth conspicuously hairy as well as frayed (mostly in sunny habitats) . . . .***L. comosa*** (*L. multiflora* subsp. *comosa*, *L. subsessilis*), pl. 634
                                      PACIFIC WOOD RUSH
      7 Bracts of the pair beneath the perianth typically frayed but not hairy
        8 Plants spreading by stolons and long rhizomes (a rare weed in Brit. Col., apparently introduced) . . . .***L. campestris***
                                     FIELD WOOD RUSH (Europe)
        8 Plants forming tufts, not spreading by stolons, and only with short rhizomes (mostly in shaded or partly shaded habitats) . . . .***L. multiflora* subsp. *multiflora***
                                      MANY-FLOWERED WOOD RUSH

JUNCAGINACEAE Arrow-Grass Family

Members of the arrow-grass family grow in wet places, including salt marshes and freshwater pools and marshes. The leaves are entirely basal and somewhat succulent but otherwise resemble those of grasses in general appearance and in having sheaths that clasp the stems. In species of *Triglochin*, the flowers are in elongated inflorescences at the tops of unbranched stems that usually rise above the leaves. They have three or six sepals and stamens, and the fruiting part of the pistil is partitioned lengthwise into three or six divisions (these are sometimes considered to be separate pistils). The staminate flowers are characterized by a distinct bract; the pistillate flowers rarely have this structure. In *Lilaea*, each inflorescence consists of flowers that have a pistil and a stamen or only one or the other. At the base of the plant, however, there are pistillate flowers of a different type; these are unusual in that they have a style that grows out to form a beak more than 4 cm long.

1 All flowers in terminal racemes, and all with a pistil and 3 or 6 sepals and stamens; pistil with 3 or 6 stigmas and splitting lengthwise, when ripe, into 3 or 6 divisions .... ***Triglochin***

1 Some flowers (those in a terminal raceme) either with a pistil and a stamen or with only a pistil or a stamen; others (enclosed within the sheaths of the basal leaves) with only a pistil, the style of this becoming a beak to more than 4 cm long (leaves to about 30 cm long, the flowering stems shorter; in freshwater ponds, rarely encountered W of the Cascades) .... ***Lilaea scilloides*** (*L. subulata*)
FLOWERING QUILLWORT

Triglochin

1 Pistil consisting of 3 divisions

    2 Mature or nearly mature fruits much longer than wide, with only indistinct lengthwise ridges; in freshwater marshes .... ***T. palustris***
MARSH ARROW GRASS

    2 Mature or nearly mature fruits about as wide as long, conspicuously 3-ridged lengthwise; in coastal salt marshes (Oreg. to Calif., rare in our region; also SE United States) .... ***T. striata***
THREE-RIBBED ARROW GRASS

1 Pistil consisting of 6 divisions; in coastal salt marshes and saline and/or alkaline freshwater marshes inland)

    3 Ligule at base of leaf blade either not lobed or only slightly 2-lobed; leaf blades noticeably, even if only slightly, flattened; plants usually at least 50 cm tall when flowering (the predominant species in coastal salt marshes) .... ***T. maritima***
SEASIDE ARROW GRASS

Luzula parviflora,
small-flowered wood rush

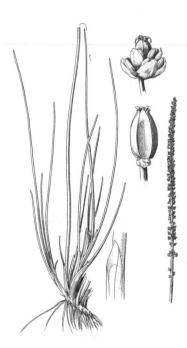

Triglochin maritima,
seaside arrow grass

3 Ligule at base of leaf blade markedly 2-lobed; leaf blades nearly cylindrical; plants not often more than 30 cm tall when flowering . . . . *T. concinna*
SLENDER ARROW GRASS

> There is much intergradation between *T. maritima* and *T. concinna* with respect to one or more of the characters given in the key; furthermore, the characteristics may be assorted differently. Some specialists are satisfied to identify both types as *T. maritima*. When plants conforming to one extreme or the other definitely prevail, it may be advisable, in environmental studies, to note this fact. Both forms, incidentally, produce cyanide and are therefore poisonous to grazing livestock.

LEMNACEAE Duckweed Family

The little duckweeds that float at or near the surface of lakes and ponds do not, at first glance, look like flowering plants. They do not have leaves; what we see are their green stems, which may be flattened, egg-shaped, spherical, or slender and curved. Some species have simple roots, others have none. The plants reproduce by budding, and this explains why they are often attached to one another. When flowers are produced—and this rarely or never happens in some populations—they are extremely small and located in little pockets along the edges of the stems; one or two of the flowers in each pocket consist of a stamen, another is represented by a pistil.

This assemblage is believed to be closely related to the Araceae, which includes calla lilies and skunk cabbages, and in some references it is even placed within that family.

1 Individual plants without roots and without lines resembling veins of a leaf . . . *Wolffia-Wolffiella* complex
1 Individual plants with 1 or more roots and with 1 or more faint or distinct veins that resemble those of leaves
   2 Individual plants with 1 root, 3 veins . . . . *Lemna*
   2 Individual plants with at least several roots and several veins
      3 Individual plants 1–1.5 times as long as wide, with as many as 16 veins, only 1–2 of the roots perforating the scales on the underside . . . . *Spirodela polyrhiza*
COMMON DUCKMEAT
      3 Individual plants 1.5–2 times as long as wide, not often with more than 7 veins, all the roots perforating the scales on the underside . . . . *Landoltia punctata* (*Spirodela punctata*)
DOTTED DUCKMEAT

Lemna

1 Individual plants mostly 6–10 mm long, joined to one another by slender stalks; often submerged below the surface . . . . *L. trisulca*
IVY-LEAVED DUCKWEED
1 Individual plants to about 4 mm long, connected directly to one another; floating or left on mud at the shore when the water level drops
   2 Greatest distance between veins above or near the middle; reddish coloration, if present, less pronounced on the underside than on the upper surface . . . . *L. minor*, pl. 635
COMMON DUCKWEED
   2 Greatest distance between veins usually below the middle (but sometimes near the middle); reddish coloration, if present, more pronounced on the underside than on the upper surface . . . . *L. turionifera*

Wolffia-Wolffiella Complex

1 Individual plants slender, sword-shaped, and slightly curved, mostly 5–9 mm long, 0.5 mm wide, submerged except at the point where several are attached to one another . . . . *Wolffiella gladiata* (*Wolffia floridana*)
SWORD-SHAPED WATERMEAL
1 Individual plants about 1 mm long, egg-shaped, nearly spherical, or somewhat boat-shaped (flattened on the upper surface and convex on the lower surface)

2 Individual plants egg-shaped or nearly spherical, 1–1.5 times as deep as wide, one side just touching the surface of the water, the rest submerged

   3 Individual plants 1–1.3 times as long as wide, 0.4–1.2 mm wide .... ***Wolffia columbiana***
            COLUMBIA WATERMEAL

   3 Individual plants 1.3–2 times as long as wide, 0.3–0.5 mm wide .... ***Wolffia globosa***
            ROUND WATERMEAL

2 Individual plants somewhat boat-shaped, only about 0.3–1 time as deep as wide, the upper surface exposed

   4 Individual plants 1–1.5 times as long as wide (widespread in E United States and tropical America; perhaps introduced into our region) .... ***Wolffia brasiliensis***
            BRAZILIAN WATERMEAL

   4 Individual plants 1.3 to slightly more than 2 times as long as wide ....
   .... ***Wolffia borealis*** (*W. punctata* of some references)
            NORTHERN WATERMEAL

LILIACEAE Lily Family

The lily family consists entirely of perennial plants, but most of those in temperate regions die back at the end of the growing season to underground bulbs, corms, or rhizomes. The flowers usually have three sepals and three petals, but when the distinction between sepals and petals is not clear, they are all called perianth segments, or simply tepals. There are typically six stamens. The pistil is partitioned into three seed-producing chambers, and in most species it dries and cracks apart. There are important departures from the formula. Fleshy fruits are characteristic of certain genera, including *Maianthemum*, one species of which has only four perianth segments and four stamens, and a fruit consisting of two chambers.

Research on relationships within this large assemblage suggests that certain genera represented in our region should be removed from Liliaceae and placed in other families: Alliaceae (*Allium*) or Melanthiaceae (*Trillium, Veratrum, Xerophyllum*).

1 Plants large, sometimes more than 1.5 m tall when flowering; basal leaves numerous and grasslike, to more than 75 cm long, very tough and with rough edges; flowers, with white perianth segments, numerous in a dense raceme at the top of a stout flower stalk, this with crowded bracts that resemble the basal leaves)
   .... ***Xerophyllum tenax***, pl. 685
            BEAR GRASS

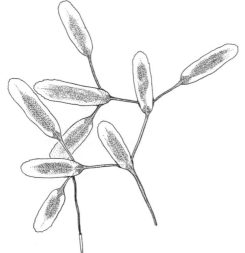

Lemna trisulca,
ivy-leaved duckweed

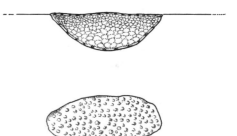

Wolffia borealis,
northern watermeal

1 Plants not as described in the other choice 1
   2 At least some of the leaves in 1 or more whorls on the flowering stem
      3 Plants with a single whorl of 3 leaves, these nearly as wide as long, beneath the single flower; flowers with 3 petals, 3 green sepals . . . . ***Trillium***
      3 Plants with 1 or more whorls of leaves on the flowering stem but these at least several times as long as wide; flowers with 6 similar perianth segments
         4 Anthers attached by their middle portions to the tips of the stamen filaments; perianth segments usually at least 3 cm long; plants usually more than 50 cm tall, sometimes more than 1 m . . . ***Lilium***
         4 Anthers attached by their bases to the tips of the stamen filaments; perianth segments generally less than 3 cm long; plants generally less than 50 cm tall (*F. recurva* and *F. gentneri* are commonly much taller than 50 cm, and their perianth segments are often longer than 3 cm; their flowers are so distinctive, however, that they are not likely to be confused with any species of *Lilium*) . . . ***Fritillaria***
   2 None of the leaves in distinct whorls
      5 At least 2 or more substantial, broad leaves present above the base of the flowering stems
         6 Each flower (this hanging down) appearing to originate on the underside of a leaf axil but its peduncle in fact originating in the axil of the leaf below (fruit fleshy, red) . . . . ***Streptopus***
         6 Flowers at the tips of the stems or in terminal inflorescences
            7 Flowering stems with only 2–3 leaves (these broad); flowers with 4 perianth segments and 4 stamens (fruit fleshy, red) . . . . ***Maianthemum dilatatum***
                                                   FALSE LILY-OF-THE-VALLEY
            7 Flowering stems with more than 3 leaves; flowers with 6 perianth segments and 6 stamens
               8 Stems branching and also spreading at least slightly, the flowers (hanging down) 1–3 at the ends (fruit fleshy, orange) . . . . ***Prosartes***
               8 Stems upright or spreading, not branching, except in the inflorescence; flowers in racemes or panicles
                  9 Stems upright, generally more than 1 m tall; larger leaves usually more than 8 cm wide; fruit dry when mature . . . . ***Veratrum***
                  9 Stems usually spreading, the plants generally less than 75 cm tall; leaves rarely so much as 8 cm wide; fruit fleshy when mature . . . . ***Maianthemum***
     5 Leaves, if proportionately broad (not more than 5 times as long as wide), strictly basal (in most genera under this choice the leaves are many times as long as wide, and the flowering stems have slender, bractlike leaves or lack leaves altogether)
      10 Basal leaves 2 to several, the blades broad, usually not so much as 5 times as long as wide
         11 Petals (3) upright, smaller than the 3 green sepals; stamens 3 (W Oreg.; flowering early, usually by late March) . . . . ***Scoliopus hallii***, pl. 674
                                                 FETID ADDER'S-TONGUE
         11 Perianth segments (6) similar
            12 Leaves 2, mottled (at least when young) in most species; tips of petals curving backward (stems arising from deeply buried corms; fruit dry when mature) . . . . ***Erythronium***
            12 Leaves 2 or more, not mottled; tips of petals not curving backward (flowering stems arising from creeping underground rhizomes; fruit fleshy, bluish) . . . . ***Clintonia***
      10 Basal leaves slender (and sometimes numerous), many times as long as wide (and sometimes withering by the time flowering is well underway)
         13 Pistil with 3 distinct styles
            14 Leaves in 2 rows on opposite sides of the stem . . . . ***Triantha***
            14 Leaves not in 2 rows on opposite sides of the stem
               15 Each perianth segment (white, cream, or greenish) with a prominent gland near the base; perianth segments similar but 3 sometimes shorter than the others; perianth as a whole broadly open or slightly bell-shaped . . . . ***Zigadenus***

15 Perianth segments (purplish green or yellowish green) without a prominent gland near the base; all 6 perianth segments of the same size; perianth as a whole narrowly bell-shaped, longer than wide when fully open (SW Brit. Col. to NW Calif., also SE Brit. Col. to SW Alberta, to Idaho, Montana, and NE Wash.) . . . . *Stenanthium occidentale*
WESTERN STENANTHIUM

13 Pistil with 1 style, this often short and indistinct

  16 Flowers with 3 petals that are distinctly different from the 3 sepals . . . . *Calochortus*

  16 Flowers with 6 similar perianth segments

    17 Flowers usually single (sometimes 2; perianth segments about 1 cm long, white, with greenish or purplish lines; Saddle Mountain, Clatsop Co., Oreg.; widespread outside of our region) . . . . *Lloydia serotina*
ALP LILY

    17 Flowers several to many in each inflorescence

      18 Flowers in an umbel or very crowded raceme

        19 Flowers in a very crowded raceme (thus appearing to be in a dense head) . . . . . . *Dichelostemma*

        19 Flowers in a typical umbel

          20 Flowers with 3 fertile stamens and 3 sterile stamens (lacking anthers) . . . . *Brodiaea*

          20 Flowers with 6 fertile stamens

            21 Perianth segments joined only at the base; plant, if bruised, with the odor of onion . . . . *Allium*

            21 Perianth segments united to the extent that they form a short tube; plant without the odor of onion . . . . *Triteleia*

      18 Flowers scattered on a long raceme or panicle

        22 Leaves in 2 rows on opposite sides of the stem; perianth segments bright yellow (in bogs, Josephine Co., Oreg., to Calif.) . . . . *Narthecium californicum*, pl. 672
BOG ASPHODEL

        22 Leaves not in 2 rows on opposite sides of the stem; flowers not bright yellow

          23 Flowers on a branched inflorescence (most leaves basal, sometimes numerous; tops of inflorescences usually at least 50 cm high; flowers opening in the evening, closing by the next morning; perianth segments white with at least slightly darker midveins). . . . . . . *Chlorogalum*

          23 Flowers on an unbranched raceme

            24 Racemes loose; perianth segments at least 20 mm long, normally blue (rarely white) . . . . *Camassia*

            24 Racemes crowded; perianth segments not more than about 12 mm long, white to purplish . . . . *Hastingsia*

Allium

Allium triquetrum, three-cornered garlic, with drooping white flowers on a sharply three-angled stem to about 40 cm tall, occasionally escapes from gardens or forgivingly forms new colonies in places where garden trash has been dumped.

1 Leaves (usually 2) distinctly divided into a narrow petiole and blade, the blades to more than 5 cm wide, usually not more than 6 times as long as wide (flowers in umbels of about 25–30; perianth white; stamens shorter than the perianth; garden plant, sometimes escaping) . . . . *A. ursinum*
RAMSONS (Europe)

1 Leaves not distinctly divided into petiole and blade, and the blades (sometimes hollow) much more than 6 times as long as wide (in some species under the second choice 2, the leaves wither by the time flowering begins)

2 Leaves hollow, either cylindrical or flattened on one side and with a lengthwise furrow

  3 Leaves flattened on the upper side and with a lengthwise furrow (flowering stems to more than 1 m tall; some or all flowers of the inflorescence usually replaced by bulblets; perianth, when flowers present, about 5 mm long, pink or greenish white; stamens protruding beyond the perianth segments; mostly on vacant land in or near cities and towns) . . . . *A. vineale* **var.** *vineale*

                                                               COW GARLIC (Europe)

  3 Leaves cylindrical (flowers in dense umbels to about 3.5 cm wide; perianth segments 8–12 mm long, pink or violet-pink; stamens shorter than the perianth segments) . . . *A. schoenoprasum* (*A. sibiricum*)

                                                                    CHIVES

               Allium schoenoprasum is widely distributed in N North America, Europe, and Asia. Wild plants occur in montane habitats E of the crest of the Cascades, but any found in our region have almost certainly escaped from gardens.

2 Leaves not hollow, but they may be proportionately thick

  4 Plants growing in wet montane habitats; stem of inflorescence usually at least 50 cm tall; leaves several, flat, to 15 mm wide; perianth segments usually 8–10 mm long, pink; stamens protruding well beyond the perianth segments; in the Cascades and Siskiyou Mountains, Oreg. to Calif., and eastward; not likely to be found below 4000 ft., 1220 m) . . . .*A. validum*

                                                          TALL SWAMP ONION

  4 Plants not conforming in all respects to the description in the other choice 4

    5 Garden plants, mostly robust, occasionally found as weedy escapes, especially in waste places near human habitations, sometimes on backshores of sandy beaches

      6 Stamens, when flowers are produced, protruding well beyond the perianth segments, but at least some flowers replaced by bulblets (leaves rough along the margins and along the veins on the underside; perianth segments 5–7 mm long, blunt at the tip, lilac or purplish) . . . . *A. carinatum*

                                                         ROUGH-LEAVED ONION (Europe)

      6 Stamens, when flowers are produced, not protruding beyond the perianth segments (see second choice 7 for description of *A. nigrum,* whose inflorescences may produce bulblets instead of flowers)

        7 Each stamen with 2 lateral projections just below the anther; inflorescences not producing bulblets in place of some or all flowers; leaves generally less than 2.5 cm wide (inflorescences with more than 100 flowers, these on pedicels to more than 2 cm long; perianth segments about 6 mm long, pinkish or purplish) . . . .*A. sativum*

                                                         GARLIC (Europe)

        7 Stamens without lateral projections below the anthers; inflorescences usually producing bulblets in place of some or all flowers (leaves of large plants usually at least 1.5 cm wide, sometimes more than 5 cm; perianth segments, when flowers are produced, white with a green lengthwise vein) . . . . *A. nigrum*

                                                         BLACK GARLIC (Europe)

    5 Obviously native species, usually common in relatively undisturbed areas

      8 Inflorescences nodding (perianth 4–6 mm long, white or pale pink; stamens about twice as long as the perianth segments; widespread in North America but in our region mostly coastal and on the W slope of the Cascades, and not reaching any farther S than Lane County, Oreg.; often in lightly shaded habitats) . . . . *A. cernuum,* pl. 639

                                                         NODDING ONION

      8 Inflorescences upright

        9 Stigma not distinctly lobed; stamens as long as, or longer than, the perianth segments (flowering stems often more than 40 cm tall; perianth segments generally 6–8 mm long, white to pink, with a darker midvein; fruit with 6 conspicuous protuberances; in areas of serpentine rock, SW Oreg. to Calif.) . . . . *A. sanbornii* **subsp.** *sanbornii*

                                                         SANBORN'S ONION

        9 Stigma distinctly 3-lobed; stamens at least slightly shorter than the perianth segments

10 Leaves (usually 2, at least 4 mm wide) somewhat sickle-shaped (that is, the outline of the broad surfaces curved), still fleshy when the plants are in flower; flowering stem distinctly flattened, with a winglike ridge on both edges

  11 Perianth segments (8–11 mm long, pink) about as wide at the middle as near the base (not likely to be found below about 2500 ft., 760 m; Jackson Co., Oreg., to Calif.) . . . . *A. siskiyouense*
         SISKIYOU ONION

  11 Perianth segments much wider near the base than near the middle

    12 Perianth segments (10–14 mm long, usually rather deep rose-purple but sometimes white) narrowing abruptly at the middle, the narrowness accentuated by inrolling of the edges; ridges on opposite sides of the flowering stem without close-set, rounded teeth (Josephine Co., Oreg., to Calif.) . . . . . .
     . . . . *A. falcifolium*, pl. 640
         SICKLE-LEAVED ONION

    12 Perianth segments (8–11 mm long, rose or rose-purple) tapering rather evenly from near the base to the tip, the edges not inrolled; ridges on opposite sides of the flowering stem (at least above) usually with close-set, rounded teeth (not likely to be found below about 2500 ft., 760 m; Brit. Col. to SW Oreg.) . . . . *A. crenulatum*
         OLYMPIC ONION

10 Leaves not sickle-shaped, often withered by the time the plants are in flower; flowering stem not distinctly flattened and without winglike ridges

  13 Plants generally forming dense colonies, owing to production of bulbs and therefore of additional leaves and inflorescences along the underground stems (leaves usually 2–3, these sometimes to about 8 mm wide; perianth segments usually 11–15 mm long, pale pink or white; pedicels to 3 cm long; known to occur in Yamhill Co., Oreg., where perhaps introduced; otherwise N Calif. southward) . . . .
   . . . . *A. unifolium*, pl. 641
         CLAY ONION, ONE-LEAVED ONION (a misnomer)

  13 Plants not forming dense colonies (even when plants are abundant, they are separate, having originated from seed)

    14 Perianth segments with slender tips, these curving rather sharply backward; outer perianth segments decidedly longer than the inner ones (inner and outer perianth segments with slightly inrolled edges, the edges of the inner ones with small teeth; perianth usually rose-purple, sometimes pink, occasionally white) . . . . *A. acuminatum*, pl. 636
         HOOKER'S ONION

    14 Perianth segments without slender tips that curve sharply backward; outer perianth segments only slightly longer than the inner ones

     15 Upper portion of developing fruit with 6 rather prominent rounded protuberances

      16 Stamens not much more than half as long as the perianth segments; leaves usually withering by the time the plants begin to flower (perianth pink or white, and if pink, changing to white on aging; widespread W of the Cascades, also E of the crest) . . . . *A. amplectens*, pl. 637
         PAPER ONION

      16 Stamens nearly as long as the perianth segments; leaves still green when the plants begin to flower (perianth usually pink, sometimes white; almost entirely E of the crest of the Cascades except in S Brit. Col.) . . . . *A. geyeri* var. *tenerum*
         GEYER'S ONION

Allium validum,
tall swamp onion

15 Upper portion of developing fruit either with 3 pointed protuberances or with only low, indistinct out-growths; bracts beneath flower heads commonly more than 12 mm long

   17 Edges of perianth segments not inrolled and without distinct teeth (they may, however, be slightly wavy); upper portion of developing fruit with 3 pointed protuberances (perianth usually rose; Jackson Co., Oreg., to Baja Calif.) . . . .*A. peninsulare*
PENINSULAR ONION

     The species name of *A. peninsulare* refers to Baja Calif., not to any peninsula in our region.

   17 Edges of perianth segments inrolled, thus appearing narrower than they are, at least the inner ones with small teeth; upper portion of developing fruit without prominent outgrowths (perianth white to deep pink; Douglas Co., Oreg., to Calif.) . . . .*A. bolanderi*, pl. 638
BOLANDER'S ONION

     Two varieties of *A. bolanderi* have been named, mostly on the basis of size of the bulbs and characteristics of the bulb coats. There is overlap in the length and shape of the perianth segments; those of var. *bolanderi* are 7–12 mm long and stated to be proportionately broader than those of var. *mirabile,* which are 9–14 mm long.

Brodiaea

1 Sterile stamens distinctly longer than the fertile stamens; edges of upper quarter of sterile stamens slightly inrolled

   2 Aboveground portion of flowering stem commonly 20–30 cm tall, sometimes even taller; perianth usually pale lilac, at least 25 mm long, sometimes as long as 35 mm; anthers usually at least 8 mm long (Jackson Co., Oreg., to Calif.) . . . .*B. californica* **subsp.** *californica*
CALIFORNIA BRODIAEA

   2 Aboveground portion of flowering stem rarely more than 5 cm tall, often nearly negligible; perianth 15–25 mm long, usually deep blue-violet; anthers 3–4 mm long (coastal, Coos Co., Oreg., to Calif.) . . . .
. . . . *B. terrestris* **subsp.** *terrestris* (*B. coronaria* var. *macropoda*), pl. 644
DWARF BRODIAEA

1 Sterile stamens only slightly shorter to slightly longer than the fertile stamens; edges of sterile stamens either inrolled for nearly their entire length or not at all inrolled (perianth usually about 25 mm long, dark bluish purple or bluish violet)

   3 Perianth tube somewhat rounded at the base, therefore shaped like a long bell; sterile stamens leaning toward the center of the flower, their tips positioned between the fertile stamens (edges of sterile stamens inrolled) . . . . *B. coronaria* **subsp.** *coronaria*, pl. 642
HARVEST BRODIAEA

   3 Perianth tube pointed at the base; sterile stamens leaning away from the fertile stamens

     4 Sterile stamens flat, the tips not bent (Wash. to Calif.) . . . . *B. elegans* **subsp.** *elegans*, pl. 643
ELEGANT BRODIAEA

     4 Sterile stamens with inrolled edges and bent tips (Oreg. to Calif.) . . . .*B. elegans* **subsp.** *hooveri*
HOOVER'S BRODIAEA

Calochortus

1 Petals (usually 3–4 cm long) mostly white or cream but the hairs above the nectar gland at the base dark purple, nearly black, collectively forming a dark spot (plants mostly about 30 cm tall; fruit upright; on serpentine deposits, Douglas and Josephine Cos., Oreg.) . . . .*C. howellii*
HOWELL'S MARIPOSA LILY

1 Plants not in all respects as described in the other choice 1

   2 Maturing fruit upright (flowering stem with 1 or more flowers at the top but otherwise not branched)

     3 Petals at least 3 cm long, purplish, usually with a distinct purple crescent near the base of the outer surface; in dry habitats (Jackson Co., Oreg., to Calif.) . . . .*C. greenei*
GREENE'S MARIPOSA LILY

3 Petals less than 2 cm long, lavender, without a dark purple crescent near the base of the outer surface; in fairly moist habitats (SW Oreg. to Calif.; not likely to be found below 4000 ft., 1220 m) . . . *C. nudus*
NAKED MARIPOSA LILY

2 Maturing fruit hanging downward or at least nodding

4 Inner surface of petals without hairs or at most only sparingly hairy except perhaps near the nectar gland at the base (petals about 2 cm long, lilac; plants low, often somewhat sprawling, the stem usually with 1 flower and 1 or more bulblets near the base; Lane Co., Oreg., to Calif.) . . . . *C. uniflorus*, pl. 646
MEADOW MARIPOSA LILY

4 Entire inner surface of petals densely hairy almost throughout

5 Stems usually with 2 branches, each branch with 1 or more flowers, and with a prominent leaf at the point of branching (petals 12–25 mm long, white to cream, usually tinged with purple or rose)
. . . . *C. tolmiei*, pl. 645
TOLMIE'S MARIPOSA LILY, CAT'S-EAR MARIPOSA LILY

5 Stem not often branching (but it may have more than 1 flower) and without a prominent leaf above the basal ones

6 Upper surface of leaves hairy

7 Hairs surrounding the gland near the base of each petal yellow; reddish lines present below the petal gland (petals mostly white; Douglas Co., Oreg.) . . . . *C. coxii*
COX'S MARIPOSA LILY

7 Hairs surrounding the gland near the base of each petal not yellow (the hairs often with a zone of lime green around them, however); reddish lines not present below the petal gland (petals white to cream; Douglas Co., Oreg.) . . . . *C. umpquaensis*
UMPQUA MARIPOSA LILY

6 Upper surface of leaves not hairy

8 Hairs on upper surface and margins of petals rather thick and stiff; petals white or faintly greenish, sometimes with a purplish, crescent-shaped mark above the basal gland; upper edge of basal gland bordered by warty, fingerlike outgrowths similar to those bordering the lower edge (typically in grassy or lightly forested habitats; Douglas, Jackson, and Klamath Cos., Oreg., to Calif.; not likely to be found below 4500 ft., 1370 m) . . . . *C. elegans* subsp. *nanus*
ELEGANT MARIPOSA LILY

8 Hairs on upper surface and margins of petals slender and flexible; petals mostly pale yellow, sometimes tinged with lavender, and sometimes with a purplish, crescent-shaped mark above the basal gland; upper edge of basal gland bordered by a continuous membrane, thus not like the series of warty, fingerlike outgrowths that border the lower edge (typically on volcanic soils in the Cascades of S Wash. and N and central Oreg., also the Calapooya Mountains, Oreg.; not likely to be found below 3000 ft., 910 m) . . . . *C. subalpinus* (*C. lobbii*)
CASCADE MARIPOSA LILY

Camassia

1 All perianth segments spaced about the same distance apart; perianth segments, as they wither, becoming twisted around the developing fruit; fruits not becoming pressed close to the axis of the inflorescence as they ripen

2 Fruit nearly round, not often more than 1 cm long, shiny green, each seed-producing chamber with 2–5 seeds (perianth segments to about 2 cm long, violet-blue; SW Oreg.) . . . . *C. howellii*, pl. 647
HOWELL'S CAMAS

2 Fruit oval or oblong, 1–2.5 cm long, dull green, each seed-producing chamber with 6–12 seeds

3 Perianth segments creamy white, to 4 cm long; plants sometimes more than 75 cm tall (Douglas Co., Oreg., to Calif.) . . . . *C. leichtlinii* subsp. *leichtlinii*, pl. 648
GREAT WHITE CAMAS

3 Perianth segments violet-blue (rarely white), not often more than 3.5 cm long; plants not often so much as 75 cm tall (Vancouver Island, Brit. Col. to Calif.) . . . . . *C. leichtlinii* subsp. *suksdorfii*, pl. 649
SUKSDORF'S CAMAS, GREAT BLUE CAMAS

1 One perianth segment, usually the one pointing almost directly downward, typically more widely separated than the others; perianth segments withering separately, not becoming twisted around the developing fruit; fruits sometimes tending to be pressed close to the axis of the inflorescence as they ripen . . . . . *C. quamash*
COMMON CAMAS

The range of *C. quamash* subsp. *quamash* begins E of the crest of the Cascades and extends to the Rocky Mountain area. Of the other named subspecies of *C. quamash,* 4 occur in the region W of the Cascades. Because of variability and intergradation, none is especially well defined; the key below will show this.

4 Developing fruits not pressed close to the axis of the inflorescence
  5 Perianth segments light blue-violet; plants usually growing in well-drained prairie soils; bulbs rather shallowly buried (SW Wash.) . . . . *C. quamash* subsp. *azurea*
  5 Perianth segments medium to deep blue violet; plants growing in a variety of habitats, including meadows that are wet much of the year; bulbs rather deeply buried (SW Brit. Col. to NW Oreg.) . . . . .
. . . . *C. quamash* subsp. *maxima*, pl. 650
4 Developing fruits usually pressed close to the axis of the inflorescence
  6 Perianth segments equally spaced, 12–20 mm long; flower pedicels usually 5–10 mm long (SW Oreg. to NW Calif.) . . . . *C. quamash* subsp. *walpolei*
  6 Perianth segments equally spaced or one of them slightly more widely separated than the others, usually more than 20 mm long; flower pedicels 10–25 mm long
    7 Perianth segments medium to deep blue-violet; anthers violet (SW Brit. Col. to NW Oreg.) . . . .
. . . . *C. quamash* subsp. *maxima*, pl. 650
    7 Perianth segments pale blue or blue-violet; anthers bright yellow (strictly limited to SW Oreg.) . . . .
. . . . *C. quamash* subsp. *intermedia*

Chlorogalum

1 Larger leaves not more than about 5 mm wide, the margins not wavy; perianth segments 8–12 cm long, with a yellow-green midvein, the tips only slightly turned back; flowering plants not often more than 60 cm tall (Jackson Co., Oreg., to Calif.) . . . . *C. angustifolium*
NARROW-LEAVED SOAP PLANT

1 Larger leaves generally at least 1 cm wide, sometimes more than 2 cm, the margins wavy; perianth segments commonly 15–20 mm long, occasionally longer, with a dark green or purplish midvein, and tips that are turned back conspicuously; flowering plants usually at least 1 m tall (Coos, Josephine, and Jackson Cos., Oreg., to Calif.) . . . . *C. pomeridianum* var. *pomeridianum*, pl. 651
SOAP PLANT

Clintonia

1 Flowers borne singly; perianth segments white; each flowering stem with 2–3 basal leaves (Alaska to Calif., mostly at low to moderate elevations in the mountains) . . . . *C. uniflora*, pl. 653
WHITE BEAD-LILY, WHITE CLINTONIA

1 Flowers several to many in an umbel-like inflorescence, often with smaller umbels below it; perianth deep pink; flowering stems usually with 4–5 leaves (in redwood forests, Curry Co., Oreg., to Calif.) . . . .
. . . . *C. andrewsiana*, pl. 652
PINK BEAD-LILY, PINK CLINTONIA

Dichelostemma

1 Perianth tube 20–25 mm long, red, the lobes turned back (Curry Co., Oreg., to Calif.) . . . .
. . . . *D. ida-maia* (*Brodiaea ida-maia*), pl. 655
FIRECRACKER FLOWER, IDA MAY'S DICHELOSTEMMA

1 Perianth tube not so much as 15 mm long, not red

  2 Fertile stamens 6, 3 shorter than the other 3 (flowering stems sometimes more than 40 cm tall; Josephine and Jackson Cos., Oreg., to Calif.) . . . .***D. capitatum*** subsp. ***capitatum*** (*Brodiaea pulchella*)
BLUE DICKS

  2 Fertile stamens 3, sterile stamens 3

    3 Inflorescence a crowded raceme, the pedicels coming off at distinctly different levels . . . . ***D. congestum*** (*Brodiaea congesta*), pl. 654
OOKOW

    3 Inflorescence nearly an umbel, all pedicels coming off close to one another (Rogue River valley, Oreg., to Calif.) . . . . ***D. multiflorum*** (*Brodiaea multiflora*)
WILD HYACINTH

Erythronium

The presence or absence of brownish markings on the leaves is helpful in identification of certain species of *Erythronium*, but these markings, even when present on young leaves, disappear by the time fruits have ripened to some extent.

1 Lobes of the stigma not conspicuous, less than 1 mm long

  2 Perianth predominantly pale purple, with dark purple markings (bordered by yellow) at the base (Josephine and Jackson Cos., Oreg., to Calif.) . . . . ***E. hendersonii***, pl. 658
HENDERSON'S FAWN LILY

  2 Perianth mostly white with yellow at the base or yellow with yellowish orange at the base

    3 Bases of inner 3 perianth segments without saclike folds (Josephine Co., Oreg., mostly below 3000 ft., 910 m) . . . . ***E. howellii***
HOWELL'S FAWN LILY

      Except for the absence of saclike folds on the inner perianth segments, *E. howellii* is very similar to *E. citrinum*, second choice 4.

    3 Bases of inner 3 perianth segments with a pair of saclike folds

      4 Leaves green before and during flowering; perianth mostly white with yellow at the base (in the Siskiyou Mountains and Cascades of S Oreg. to Calif., mostly above 3500 ft., 1070 m) . . . . . ***E. klamathense***
KLAMATH FAWN LILY

      4 Leaves mottled with brown before and during flowering; perianth mostly pale yellow but distinctly yellow at the base (Josephine Co., Oreg., to Calif.; mostly below 3500 ft., 1070 m) . . . . ***E. citrinum***, pl. 656
LEMON FAWN LILY

1 Lobes of stigma conspicuous, at least 1.5 mm long

  5 Perianth bright yellow; leaves uniformly green (Brit. Col. to Calif., mostly E of the crest of the Cascades, but occasionally found in the Coast Ranges, Wash. and Oreg.; plants in the Coast Ranges have pale, instead of dark reddish anthers, and have been referred to the var. *pallidum*) . . . . ***E. grandiflorum*** subsp. ***grandiflorum***, pl. 657
YELLOW FAWN LILY

  5 Perianth, when fresh, predominantly white, cream, or light to dark pink

    6 Perianth deep pink (white in extremely rare specimens; leaves, before and during the time of flowering, with conspicuous brownish mottling; coastal, Brit. Col. to Calif.) . . . . ***E. revolutum***, pl. 661
PINK FAWN LILY

    6 Perianth white, cream, or pale pink (leaves usually with brownish markings, except in some *E. elegans*)

      7 Filaments of stamens not becoming noticeably broader at the base than above (the width at the base is not more than 0.5 mm; perianth pure white with yellow or light orange at the base; in the Olympic Mountains, Wash., and in the Cascades of Wash. and Oreg.; not likely to be found below 4000 ft., 1220 m) . . . . ***E. montanum***, pl. 659
AVALANCHE LILY

7 Filaments of stamens distinctly broader (usually more than 0.5 mm) near the base than above

   8 Perianth white to cream, usually with yellow and sometimes also with reddish markings at the base; leaves, before and during the time of flowering, with conspicuous brownish markings (widespread lowland species W of the Cascades, Brit. Col. to S Oreg., possibly Calif.; usually flowering by early April) . . . . ***E. oregonum***, pl. 660

                    OREGON FAWN LILY

> In plants of *E. oregonum* on S Vancouver Island, Gulf Islands, Brit. Col., and San Juan Islands, Wash., the perianth is usually almost completely pure white except for rather prominent reddish markings at the base.

   8 Perianth white to pale pink (sometimes deep pink), yellow at the base; leaves, before and during the time of flowering, uniformly green or with brownish markings, sometimes completely brownish (at higher elevations in the Coast Ranges, Tillamook and Lincoln Cos., Oreg.) . . . . ***E. elegans***

                    ELEGANT FAWN LILY

> A plant somewhat similar to *E. elegans,* found up to about 3000 ft. (910 m) in the Olympic Mountains, Wash., has been named *E. quinaultense.* The lower portions of its perianth segments are mostly white, but the tips are light to dark pink. It is apparently the result of hybridization, *E. montanum* (first choice 7) × *E. revolutum* (first choice 6).

Fritillaria

1 Perianth segments mostly bright orange-red to rather dark, slightly purplish red, the inner faces yellow-spotted (plants sometimes more than 60 cm tall)

   2 Tips of perianth segments usually turned sharply back; nectar glands not more than one-fourth as long as the perianth segments; branches of the style more or less upright, not spreading widely outward (Douglas, Josephine, and Jackson Cos., Oreg., to Calif.) . . . . ***F. recurva***, pl. 665

                    SCARLET FRITILLARY

   2 Tips of perianth segments spreading outward, not turned sharply back; nectar glands about half as long as the perianth segments; branches of the style spreading widely outward (Jackson and Josephine Cos., Oreg.) . . . . ***F. gentneri***, pl. 663

                    GENTNER'S FRITILLARY

1 Perianth segments not bright or dark red

   3 Perianth bright yellow (sometimes faintly tinged with red or with reddish lines), not mottled; plants not often more than 15 cm tall (Rogue River valley, Oreg.; widespread E of the crest of the Cascades) . . . . ***F. pudica***

                    YELLOW BELLS

   3 Perianth mostly greenish brown, brownish purple, grayish, greenish yellow, or pale reddish, often streaked or at least partly mottled or spotted; plants generally at least slightly more than 15 cm tall

      4 Leaves alternate

         5 Nectar gland on each perianth segment not more than about one-third as long as the segment; leaves only 3–4 on each flowering stem; perianth usually grayish or pale purplish, sometimes with greenish or yellow dots; plants not more than 20 cm tall (Curry and Josephine Cos., Oreg., to Calif.) . . . . ***F. glauca***, pl. 664

              SISKIYOU FRITILLARY

Fritillaria camschatcensis, chocolate lily

5 Nectar gland on each perianth segment narrow, not conspicuous, colored much like the rest of the segment but reaching nearly to its tip; leaves generally more than 4, those on the lower part of the stem often crowded; perianth whitish or tinged with pink or purple spots or lines; plants commonly more than 20 cm tall (Curry and Josephine Cos., Oreg., to Calif.) . . . . *F. purdyi*
PURDY'S FRITILLARY

4 At least the lower leaves in whorls

  6 Perianth dark brownish purple, sometimes streaked or dotted with yellow but usually rather uniformly dark (mostly near the coast, sometimes at the edges of tideflats, and at low elevations on the west slope of the Cascades, Alaska to N Wash.) . . . .*F. camschatcensis*
CHOCOLATE LILY

  6 Perianth not uniformly dark brownish purple or as otherwise described in the other choice 6

    7 Leaf blades generally slender, to more than 8 cm long but not often more than 6 mm wide; perianth pale purple with white, yellow, or yellowish green spots (Oreg. to Calif. and also eastward; in our region not likely to be found below 4000 ft., 1220 m) . . . . *F. atropurpurea* (*F. adamantina*)
PURPLE FRITILLARY

    7 Leaf blades not especially slender, the larger ones more than 10 mm wide

      8 Perianth usually almost uniformly greenish yellow to reddish; nectar gland on each perianth segment not more than about one-third as long as the segment (Josephine Co., Oreg., to Calif.) . . . . *F. eastwoodiae*
ALICE EASTWOOD'S FRITILLARY

      8 Perianth commonly greenish brown to brownish purple, with greenish yellow markings but sometimes almost uniformly pale greenish yellow; nectar gland on each perianth segment about one-half to two-thirds as long as the segment (widespread in our region) . . . .*F. affinis* subsp. *affinis* (*F. lanceolata*), pl. 662
MISSION BELLS

Hastingsia

1 Perianth segments 9–12 mm long, white or purplish (stamens decidedly shorter than the perianth segments; in wet fens, especially those in which *Darlingtonia* grows, Josephine Co., Oreg.) . . . . *H. bracteosa* (*Schoenolirion bracteosum*), pl. 667
LARGE-FLOWERED RUSH LILY

        Specimens with distinctly purplish perianths have been named *H. atropurpurea*. There is, however, considerable intergradation between plants with white and purplish perianths, even at a single locality, and it will perhaps be best to give the ones with purplish perianths no more than the status of variety or form.

1 Perianth segments not more than 8 mm long, mostly white or pale yellowish (but the 3 lengthwise veins may be purplish, at least after the flowers have aged)

  2 Anthers protruding well beyond the perianth segments; outer perianth segments not noticeably wider than the inner ones (in dry habitats, especially where there are deposits of serpentine; Curry, Josephine, and Jackson Cos., Oreg., to Calif.) . . . .*H. serpentinicola*
SERPENTINE RUSH LILY

  2 Anthers at most protruding only slightly beyond the perianth segments; outer perianth segments nearly twice as wide as the inner ones (in wet habitats, especially in areas where there is serpentine; Curry, Josephine, and Jackson Cos., Oreg., to Calif.) . . . .*H. alba* (*Schoenolirion album*), pl. 666
WHITE RUSH LILY

        Many specimens do not fit cleanly into either *H. serpentinicola* or *H. alba*. On some plants, for instance, 1 or more stamens of a particular flower may be shorter than the perianth segments, others longer. The proportionate width of the outer perianth segments is also variable. Some botanists would be satisfied to refer all specimens to *H. alba*.

Lilium

1 Flowers, after opening, not hanging directly downward (they may face upward, be directed outward, or nod slightly)

   2 Perianth segments more or less white or tinged with pink or purple, generally becoming darker in age; flowers upright or directed outward

      3 Outer 3 perianth segments 4–7 cm long, dotted with maroon or magenta; anthers 4–8 mm long (Josephine and Jackson Cos., Oreg., to Calif.) . . . . ***L. rubescens***
REDWOOD LILY

      3 Outer 3 perianth segments 6–10 cm long, not dotted with maroon or magenta; anthers usually more than 8 mm long (Oreg. to Calif.; not likely to be found below about 4000 ft., 1220 m) . . . .
. . . . ***L. washingtonianum* subsp. *purpurascens*, pl. 671**
WASHINGTON'S LILY

   2 Perianth segments usually yellow, yellow-orange, reddish orange, or red, sometimes pinkish

      4 Leaves typically with a grayish cast, the margins often wavy; flowers nodding or directed outward; perianth segments usually 3–5 cm long, reddish orange or red, sometimes nearly magenta; in dry habitats (Josephine Co., Oreg., to Calif.) . . . . ***L. bolanderi*, pl. 668**
BOLANDER'S LILY

      4 Leaves clear green, the margins usually not wavy; flowers nodding or directed outward or upward; perianth segments 3–4 cm long, mostly yellowish, yellow-orange, or pinkish; in places that are wet, at least seasonally (Josephine and Jackson Cos., Oreg., to Calif.; not likely to be found below about 4500 ft., 1370 m) . . . . ***L. parvum***
ALPINE LILY

1 Flowers, after opening, hanging downward

   5 Perianth segments mostly deep pinkish red but the lower half of the inner surface yellow or orange and spotted with maroon (coastal, sometimes in sphagnum bogs, Coos Co., Oreg., to Calif.) . . . .
. . . . ***L. occidentale*, pl. 670**
WESTERN LILY

      In areas where *L. occidentale* is found, there may also be *L. columbianum* (first choice 7); hybrids whose perianths show intergrading color patterns are often common.

   5 Perianth segments mostly yellow, yellow-orange, or reddish orange, sometimes at least partly bright red

      6 Perianth almost uniformly yellow except for dark maroon spots (Jackson, Josephine, and Curry Cos., Oreg., to Calif.) . . . . ***L. pardalinum* subsp. *wigginsii***
WIGGINS' LILY

      6 Perianth segments mostly orange, reddish orange, or partly red, spotted with dark maroon

         7 Perianth segments usually 4–5 cm long, rarely more, uniformly orange or reddish orange, except for maroon spots; in dry habitats . . . . ***L. columbianum*, pl. 669**
COLUMBIA LILY
See note under *L. occidentale,* first choice 5.

         7 Perianth segments usually 5–7 cm long, sometimes even longer, decidedly 2-toned, the upper portion red, the lower portion orange; in or around wet places (Jackson, Josephine, and Curry Cos., Oreg., to Calif.) . . . . ***L. pardalinum* subsp. *vollmeri***
VOLLMER'S LILY

Maianthemum

1 Flowering stems with only 2–3 leaves, these heart-shaped and nearly as wide as long; flowers with 4 perianth segments and 4 stamens (fruit red) . . . . ***M. dilatatum***
FALSE LILY-OF-THE VALLEY

1 Flowering stems with at least several leaves, these not heart-shaped, decidedly longer than wide; flowers with 6 perianth segments and 6 stamens

2 Flowers usually about 7–12 in a simple raceme; perianth segments mostly 4–7 mm long; stamens shorter than the perianth segments . . . . ***M. stellatum*** (*Smilacina stellata*)
SMALL FALSE SOLOMON'S SEAL

2 Flowers numerous in a branching panicle; perianth segments about 1.5 mm long; stamens longer than the perianth segments . . . . ***M. racemosum*** (*Smilacina racemosa*)
LARGE FALSE SOLOMON'S SEAL

Prosartes

1 Perianth segments conspicuously narrowed at the base, only about as long as the stamens, the latter therefore clearly visible; lobes of the stigma not so much as 0.5 mm long . . . ***P. hookeri*** (*Disporum hookeri*), pl. 673
FAIRY BELLS

1 Perianth segments not conspicuously narrowed at the base, longer than the stamens, the latter therefore not clearly visible; lobes of stigma 0.5–1.5 mm long . . . . ***P. smithii*** (*Disporum smithii*)
FAIRY LANTERNS

Streptopus

1 Perianth segments opening so widely that the perianth as a whole is saucer-shaped; perianth segments 3–4 mm long; plants usually less than 20 cm tall (in our region, Brit. Col. to N Oreg.) . . . . . . ***S. streptopoides***
SMALL TWISTED-STALK
Specimens in W North America are usually assigned to *S. streptopoides* subsp. *brevipes*.

1 Perianth segments sometimes recurving but the perianth as a whole more or less bell-shaped; perianth segments usually at least 6 mm long; plants commonly more than 20 cm tall
  2 Junction of pedicel and peduncle kinked; flowers usually single; perianth segments 9–15 mm long, white, greenish, or yellowish green . . . . ***S. amplexifolius***, pl. 675
  LARGE TWISTED-STALK

  2 Junction of pedicel and peduncle not kinked; flowers 1–2; perianth segments 6–10 mm long, white, greenish (often spotted with rose) to rose with white tips (not likely to be found below 3000 ft., 910 m) . . . . ***S. lanceolatus*** (*S. roseus*)
  ROSY TWISTED-STALK
  Specimens in W North America are usually assigned to *S. lanceolatus* subsp. *curvipes*.

Maianthemum dilatatum,
false lily-of-the-valley

Maianthemum stellatum,
small false Solomon's seal

Maianthemum racemosum,
large false Solomon's seal

Triantha

The seeds of *Triantha* have a short stalk by which they are attached, and a similar appendage at the free end. The appendage is especially important in segregation of species.

1 Appendage at the free end of the seed as long or longer than the seed itself; seed with a thin but firm coat; inflorescences usually longer than wide, sometimes interrupted (widely distributed across North America but in our region only in W Brit. Col. and SW Oreg.) . . . . **T. glutinosa** (*Tofieldia glutinosa*)
STICKY FALSE ASPHODEL
1 Appendage, if present at the free end of the seed, much shorter than the seed; seed with a spongy coat
  2 Inflorescence typically somewhat elongated, sometimes interrupted; styles of pistil 0.6–1.5 mm long (Alaska to Oreg. but not SW Oreg.) . . . .
. . . . **T. occidentalis** subsp. **brevistyla** (*Tofieldia glutinosa* subsp. *brevistyla*)
SHORT-STYLED FALSE ASPHODEL
  2 Inflorescence typically a compact, round head (occasionally elongated or even interrupted); styles of pistil 1.3–3 mm long (SW Oreg. to N Calif.) . . . .
. . . . **T. occidentalis** subsp. **occidentalis** (*Tofieldia glutinosa* subsp. *occidentalis*)
WESTERN FALSE ASPHODEL

Trillium

1 Flowers with distinct peduncles
  2 Petals usually about 2 cm long, white, with pink or purplish spots (rarely pink with darker spots); leaf blades not often so much as 5 cm long, distinctly longer than wide, dark green, with distinct petioles (SW Oreg. to Calif.) . . . . **T. rivale**, pl. 679
CREEK TRILLIUM
  2 Petals usually 3.5–4.5 cm long, white, without spots, aging to deep pink or rose; leaf blades commonly at least 10 cm long, often nearly as wide as long, sessile, bright green; plants typically robust, to more than 35 cm tall (usually beginning to flower by late March) . . . . **T. ovatum** subsp. **ovatum**, pl. 678
WESTERN TRILLIUM, WESTERN WAKE-ROBIN

> A dwarf form of *T. ovatum* subsp. *ovatum,* to only about 15 cm tall and with petals that already have some pink when the flowers open, has been found at several localities on the W side of Vancouver Island, Brit. Col. In cultivation, it retains its small size. It was named *T. hibbersonii,* then *T. ovatum* var. *hibbersonii,* but it may be best, for the time being at least, to consider it just a diminutive race of *T. ovatum* subsp. *ovatum.*

1 Flowers sessile
  3 Petals maroon or brownish purple (commonly 5–8 cm long and usually at least 5 times as long as wide); flowers with an unpleasant or at least musky odor (coastal, Curry Co., Oreg., to Calif.) . . . .
. . . . **T. kurabayashii** (*T. chloropetalum* var. *angustifolium*), pl. 677
KURABAYASHI'S TRILLIUM
  3 Petals predominantly whitish, yellowish, or pinkish; flowers with at least a slightly sweet odor
    4 Leaf blades with 5 main veins originating at the base, sometimes mottled, sometimes nearly uniformly green; petals commonly at least 4 cm long, 4–5 times as long as wide; fruit, when nearly ripe, still green; plants often more than 30 cm tall (S Willamette Valley, Oreg., to Calif.) . . . . . **T. albidum**, pl. 676
WHITE TRILLIUM
    4 Leaf blades with 3 main veins originating at the base and usually conspicuously mottled; petals commonly 2.5–4 cm long, 5–6 times as long as wide; fruit, when nearly ripe, dark maroon; plants not often more than 25 cm tall (Thurston Co., Wash., to Polk Co., Oreg.) . . . .
. . . . **T. parviflorum** (*T. chloropetalum* of some references)
SMALL-FLOWERED TRILLIUM

> The distinctions between *T. albidum* and *T. parviflorum* are fuzzy; furthermore, the geographic ranges of these plants overlap. Some botanists prefer to identify all trilliums of this general type as *T. albidum.*

Triteleia

1 Perianth, when fresh, predominantly pale to bright yellow, the lobes with dark midveins

    2 Perianth pale yellow (often drying bluish); filament of each stamen with a 2-lobed expansion that is about as long as the anther (Josephine and Jackson Cos., Oreg., to Calif.) . . . . ***T. ixioides*** subsp. ***anilina*** (*Brodiaea scabra* var. *anilina*), pl. 682

                               PRETTY FACE

    2 Perianth bright yellow; filaments of stamens without 2-lobed expansions (Josephine and Jackson Cos., Oreg., to Calif.) . . . . ***T. crocea*** subsp. ***crocea*** (*Brodiaea crocea*)

                                 YELLOW TRITELEIA

1 Perianth predominantly white, pale lilac, blue, or purple

    3 Perianth tube distinctly shorter than the lobes (perianth lobes white to pale lilac, with dark midveins) . . . . ***T. hyacinthina*** (*Brodiaea hyacinthina*), pl. 681

                                HYACINTH TRITELEIA

    3 Perianth tube nearly or fully as long as the lobes

        4 Filaments of stamens flattened for their entire length, much wider than thick (3 of the stamens shorter and originating at a slightly higher level than the other 3; perianth usually at least 2 cm long, white to pale purplish blue; flowering stems to more than 50 cm tall; Brit. Col. to Calif. but W of the crest of the Cascades mostly in the Puget Sound region, Willamette Valley, Oreg., and Siskiyou Mountain region of SW Oreg. and NW Calif.) . . . . ***T. grandiflora*** (*Brodiaea howellii*), pl. 680

                               LARGE-FLOWERED TRITELEIA

        4 Filaments not obviously flattened, only slightly wider at the base than above

            5 Stamens originating at 2 different levels (perianth usually 25–40 mm long, purplish blue; Jackson, Josephine, and Curry Cos., Oreg., to Calif.) . . . . ***T. laxa*** (*Brodiaea laxa*)

                                 ITHURIEL'S SPEAR

            5 All stamens originating at the same level

Triantha glutinosa,
sticky false asphodel

Veratrum insolitum,
Siskiyou false hellebore

6 Filaments of stamens 2–3 mm long, the anthers 3–4 mm long; perianth usually violet-purple, 25–35 mm long, becoming abruptly slender by the midpoint of its length (Curry Co., Oreg., to Calif.) . . . . *T. bridgesii* (*Brodiaea bridgesii*)
BRIDGES' TRITELEIA

6 Filaments of stamens 4–5 mm long, the anthers 1.5–2 mm long; perianth typically salmon with dark purplish veins, 20 mm long, not becoming abruptly slender by the midpoint of its length (Umpqua and Rogue River valleys, Oreg. to Calif.) . . . . *T. hendersonii* (*Brodiaea hendersonii*)
HENDERSON'S TRITELEIA

Veratrum

1 Perianth segments rather distinctly fringed by hairlike outgrowths or slender to broad teeth (but the surfaces of the perianth segments not obviously hairy); stems, fruit-forming portion of the pistils, and ripening fruits densely hairy (Benton and Lane Cos., Oreg., to Calif.) . . . . *V. insolitum*, p. 417
SISKIYOU FALSE HELLEBORE

1 Perianth segments not distinctly fringed by hairlike outgrowths or teeth (if there are hairs, these are like the ones on the surfaces of the perianth segments); fruit-forming portion of the pistils and ripening fruits not densely hairy, but the stems sometimes hairy

  2 Branches of inflorescence, at least the lower ones, drooping; perianth yellow-green to green . . . . *V. viride* subsp. *eschscholtzii*, pl. 684
GREEN FALSE HELLEBORE

  2 Branches of inflorescence not drooping; perianth segments white to greenish

    3 Inflorescence branched for most of its length, the upright terminal portion not conspicuously longer than the branches; perianth segments rounded to pointed at the tip (W Wash. to Calif.) . . . . *V. californicum* subsp. *californicum*, pl. 683
CALIFORNIA FALSE HELLEBORE

    3 Inflorescence branched only in its lower half, the upright terminal portion longer than the branches; perianth segments pointed at the tip (mostly montane and primarily E of the crest of the Cascades) . . . . *V. californicum* subsp. *caudatum*
TAILED FALSE HELLEBORE

Zigadenus

1 Perianth segments usually 8–11 mm long, none of them with a narrow basal portion, the gland on each one somewhat V-shaped; most of the fruit-forming portion of the pistil below the level at which the stamens and perianth segments originate; inflorescences usually with not more than about 15 flowers (primarily montane or high montane in our region; Alaska to the Cascades and Olympic Mountains of Wash. but E of the Cascades in Oreg., and eastward to the Rocky Mountain region) . . . . *Z. elegans* subsp. *elegans*
MOUNTAIN DEATH CAMAS

1 Perianth segments not more than about 7 mm long, at least 3 of them with a narrow basal portion, the gland on each one oval; fruit-forming portion of the pistil above the level at which the stamens and perianth segments originate; inflorescences usually with more than 20 flowers

  2 Pedicels usually at least 2 cm long in the flowering stage, sometimes lengthening to more than 4 cm at the fruiting stage

    3 Perianth segments commonly 10–12 cm long (coastal, Coos Co., Oreg., to Calif.) . . . . *Z. fremontii*
FREMONT'S STAR LILY

    3 Perianth segments not more than 6 mm long (Jackson and Josephine Cos., Oreg., to Calif.) . . . . *Z. micranthus* subsp. *micranthus*
SMALL-FLOWERED STAR LILY

  2 Pedicels not often more than 2 cm long in the flowering stage and not lengthening to much more than 3 cm in the fruiting stage

4 Narrowed basal portion of all 6 perianth segments about the same length; upper leaves without prominent, papery basal sheaths (Brit. Col. to Calif. and Baja Calif., in our region W of the crest of the Cas-
cades) . . . . *Z. venenosus* **subsp.** *venenosus*, pl. 686
MEADOW DEATH CAMAS

4 Narrow basal portion of 3 perianth segments much shorter than that of the other 3; upper leaves with
prominent, papery basal sheaths clasping the stems (almost entirely E of the crest of the Cascades, Brit.
Col. to Oreg. and eastward) . . . . *Z. venenosus* **subsp.** *gramineus*
GRASS-LEAVED DEATH CAMAS

NAJADACEAE Water-Nymph Family

The few species of *Najas*, sometimes placed in the Hydrocharitaceae, are found in fresh and brackish water.
They have very slender, flexible stems, and their opposite leaves, not more than about 3 cm long, are less than
1 mm wide except at their somewhat sheathing bases. Many of the pairs of leaves have a second pair directly
above them, and such clusters of four leaves could, at first glance, be mistaken for whorls. The flowers, borne in
the axils of the leaves near the tips of the branches, are not often noticed and have no petals or sepals. Staminate
flowers consist essentially of a single stamen, this surrounded by a somewhat flask-shaped bract; pistillate
flowers consist of a pistil within which a single seed develops, and the fruit matures as an achene. The coating
of the achene exhibits a networklike pattern, generally not visible except at rather high magnification.

Because of their general appearance and flexible stems and leaves, both species of *Najas* in our region could
be confused with *Zannichellia palustris* (see under Zannichelliaceae). In *Zannichellia*, however, there is no tendency for two pairs of leaves to develop close together.

Najas

1 Surface of fruit shiny, the networklike pattern on the surface usually not visible with a hand lens; anthers
usually consisting of 4 chambers (widespread across North America; in our region, Brit. Col. to Calif.) . . . .
. . . . *N. flexilis*
SLENDER WATER NYMPH

1 Surface of fruit dull, the networklike pattern on the surface visible with a hand lens; anthers usually consisting of a single chamber (often in brackish water; widespread across North America; in our region
apparently only in W Wash.) . . . . *N. guadalupensis* **subsp.** *guadalupensis*
COMMON WATER NYMPH

ORCHIDACEAE Orchid Family

The orchid family, with more than 15,000 species, all perennial, is one of the largest assemblages of flowering
plants. The species of our region, unlike most of those in tropical habitats, are rooted in soil rather than in bark
or in moss growing on trees. The flowers of orchids are markedly irregular because the lowermost petal, called
the lip, is very different from the other two. It is often greatly enlarged and saclike, or has a prominent spur originating on its underside. The sepals, however, are usually somewhat similar. Among our genera, all except *Cypripedium* have only one functional stamen. The filaments of one or two other stamens persist, however, and are
joined to the style of the pistil. The fruit-forming part of the pistil is partitioned lengthwise into three divisions,
each of which produces numerous very small seeds.

Like many other plants, orchids have obligatory symbiotic relationships, called mycorrhizae, with fungi that
penetrate their roots. Some species, including those in two genera (*Corallorhiza* and *Cephalanthera*) of our
region, have little if any chlorophyll and depend entirely on nutrients supplied to them by their fungal associates.

1 Vegetative portions of plant mostly white, reddish, brownish red, purplish, or yellowish, definitely not
green; leaves reduced to scalelike structures
    2 Plant, as a whole, mostly reddish, brownish red, purplish, or yellowish . . . . *Corallorhiza*
    2 Plant entirely white or cream, except for yellow on the lowermost petal of the flowers . . . .
. . . . *Cephalanthera austiniae*, pl. 688
PHANTOM ORCHID

1 At least the stem of the plant, and also the leaf or leaves, if present, distinctly green (in certain species, the leaves, present from fall or winter to spring, wither before flowering begins)

    3 Plant to 15 cm tall, with a broad-bladed leaf at the base and a single flower, the lip petal, which is somewhat slipper-shaped, with a conspicuous pouch that is continued as a somewhat flattened projection ending in 2 small nipplelike outgrowths; sepals and upper 2 petals purplish pink, the lip whitish or yellowish, with purplish spots (usually beginning to flower in late April) . . . . *Calypso bulbosa* subsp. *occidentalis*, pl. 687

        CALYPSO, FAIRY SLIPPER

    3 Plant not in all respects as described in the other choice 3

      4 Lip petal enlarged to form a conspicuous, deep pouch at least 1 cm long; lower 2 sepals, beneath the lip petal, partly to completely united . . . . *Cypripedium*

      4 Lip petal not enlarged to form a deep pouch so much as 1 cm long; lower 2 sepals not united

        5 Base of the lip petal with a long, slender spur (in some species, leaves absent at the time of flowering)

          6 Sepals with 3 veins; flowering stem with prominent green leaves well above those at the base (except in *P. orbiculata*, which has only basal leaves) . . . . *Platanthera*

          6 Sepals with only 1 vein; prominent leaves (1–3) strictly basal, well developed in winter and spring but withered by the time flowers appear . . . . *Piperia*

        5 Base of the lip petal without a long, slender spur (it may, however, have a small pouch)

          7 Leaves at least several in a compact basal rosette, usually dark green and with a network of white veins . . . . *Goodyera oblongifolia* (*G. decipiens*)

            RATTLESNAKE PLANTAIN

          7 Leaves either only 2 (in which case they are either basal or nearly opposite not far below the inflorescence) or more than 2 and scattered along the flowering stem

            8 Leaves more than 2, scattered along the flowering stem

              9 Flowers faintly yellowish or cream, spirally arranged in a dense, leafless inflorescence . . . . *Spiranthes*

              9 Flowers mostly greenish, brownish, or purplish, scattered along a loose, leafy inflorescence . . . . *Epipactis*

            8 Both leaves either basal or nearly opposite not far below the inflorescence

              10 Both leaves nearly opposite, not far below the inflorescence . . . . *Listera*

              10 Both leaves basal (leaf blades to about 12 cm long, 2–3 times as long as wide; flowers whitish or yellowish green; sepals about 6 mm long; petals slightly shorter than the sepals, the 2 upper ones slender, the lip petal about half as wide as long; in wet habitats, including bogs, Brit. Col. to Wash., but rare in our region) . . . . *Liparis loeselii*

                LOESEL'S WIDE-LIP ORCHID

Corallorhiza

1 Sepals (with a single vein) not more than about 6 mm long; plant as a whole pale yellow or yellowish green (montane) . . . . *C. trifida*

    YELLOW CORALROOT

1 Sepals commonly more than 6 mm long, sometimes more than 10 mm

    2 Sepals and petals with prominent lengthwise streaks of reddish brown or purple; lip petal without a small lobe on both sides near the base . . . . *C. striata* var. *striata*, pl. 690

        STRIPED CORALROOT

    2 Sepals and petals without lengthwise streaks of reddish brown or purple; lip petal with a small lobe on both sides near the base

      3 Plant as a whole reddish; petals deep pink to reddish, without dark dots, but the base of the lip petal with a pair of raised ridges that are usually reddish purple; underside of the perianth tube with a spur to 3 mm long near the top (mostly above about 3000 ft., 910 m, only occasionally lower) . . . . *C. mertensiana*

        MERTENS' CORALROOT

3 Plant as a whole usually reddish brown or purplish, but yellowish in some populations; lip petal typically white with reddish brown dots, the other petals pinkish with similar dots; underside of perianth tube with a low bump near the top but without a distinct spur .... ***C. maculata***, pl. 689

SPOTTED CORALROOT

Subspecific or varietal names have been proposed for forms that are yellowish, lack spots on the lip petal, or otherwise deviate from the typical appearance of *C. maculata*.

Cypripedium

1 Leaves only 2, nearly as broad as long, more or less opposite not far below the inflorescence (lip petal yellow-green below, purplish above; Josephine Co., Oreg., to Calif.; also E of the Cascades) .... ***C. fasciculatum***

CLUSTERED LADY'S SLIPPER

1 Leaves several, much longer than wide, alternate

2 Lip petal yellow, commonly with purple dots around the edge (known from Josephine and Lake Cos., Oreg., otherwise E of the Cascades; mostly montane) .... ***C. parviflorum*** (*C. calceolus* subsp. *parviflorum*)

YELLOW LADY'S SLIPPER

2 Lip petal white or pale pink

3 Inflorescence with only 1–3 flowers; uppermost sepal and both upper petals more than 3 cm long and usually green or brownish purple; lip petal white, tinged or streaked with purple (in the Cascades and mostly montane) .... ***C. montanum***

MOUNTAIN LADY'S SLIPPER

3 Inflorescence usually with more than 3 flowers, sometimes as many as about 10; uppermost sepal and upper petals about 1.5 cm long, greenish or yellowish; lip petal white or pale pink, sometimes with darker streaks (in wet habitats, including fens in which *Darlingtonia* grows, Douglas Co., Oreg., to Calif.) .... ***C. californicum***, pl. 691

CALIFORNIA LADY'S SLIPPER

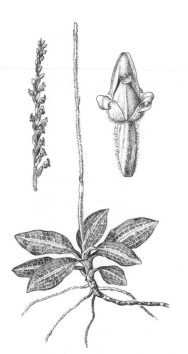

Goodyera oblongifolia,
rattlesnake plantain

Corallorhiza trifida,
yellow coralroot

Cypripedium montanum,
mountain lady's slipper

Epipactis

1 Lip petal about 15 mm long, 3-lobed, the lower half of the middle lobe somewhat bowl-shaped, the upper half tonguelike, often curving downward; sepals usually purplish green, with darker veins; upper petals usually similar to the sepals but more intensely purplish; lip petal greenish to yellowish, with lengthwise purplish lines (usually near springs or along the margins of lakes and streams) . . . . *E. gigantea*, pl. 692
GIANT HELLEBORINE

1 Lip petal about 10 mm long, not 3-lobed, but the upper half tonguelike; sepals usually greenish tinged with purple; upper petals similar to the sepals but the lip petal generally lighter, with considerable dark purple (occasional weed, often abundant where established) . . . . *E. helleborine*, pl. 693
HELLEBORINE (Europe)

Listera

1 Lip petal not divided into 2 lobes (it is either rounded or very slightly notched at the tip) . . . . *L. caurina*
WESTERN TWAYBLADE

1 Lip petal divided into 2 lobes
    2 Lobes of lip petal slender, several times as long as wide, narrowing gradually to the tip; leaf blades slightly heart-shaped . . . . *L. cordata*
HEART-LEAVED TWAYBLADE

    2 Lobes of lip petal broad, about as wide as long, rounded at the tip; leaf blades not heart-shaped (mostly montane and not likely to be found below about 2500 ft., 760 m) . . . . *L. convallarioides*
BROAD-LIPPED TWAYBLADE

Piperia

1 Spur of lip petal not more than 6 mm long
    2 Petals and sepals distinctly greenish; spur of lip petal to 5.5 mm long; inflorescence not obviously 1-sided (common) . . . . *P. unalascensis* (*Habenaria unalascensis*), pl. 695
SHORT-SPURRED REIN ORCHID

    2 Petals and sepals white except for green midveins; spur of lip petal to 4 mm long; inflorescence at least slightly 1-sided (widespread, Alaska to Calif., but rare) . . . . *P. candida*
WHITE-FLOWERED PIPERIA

1 Spur of lip petal at least 6 mm long, sometimes more than 10 mm
    3 Petals and sepals greenish . . . . *P. elongata* (*Habenaria elegans* var. *elata*)
TALL REIN ORCHID

    3 Petals and sepals white except for green midveins
        4 Spur of lip petal typically directed downward (abundant in the Puget Trough region of Brit. Col. and Wash.; also along the coast, Brit. Col. to Calif.) . . . . *P. elegans* subsp. *elegans* (*Habenaria greenei*), pl. 694
ELEGANT REIN ORCHID

        4 Spur of lip petal typically directed horizontally and to the right as one views the face of the flower . . .
. . . . *P. transversa*
HORIZONTAL-SPUR REIN ORCHID, SUKSDORF'S REIN ORCHID

Platanthera

All species of *Platanthera* found in our region, except *P. orbiculata*, are restricted to bogs or other very wet places; *P. orbiculata* occurs in coniferous forests as well as in wet habitats.

1 Leaves, typically only 2, basal
    2 Blades of leaves (after these have fully developed) nearly flat on the ground and usually not so much as twice as long as wide (the width usually at least 5 cm); spur of lip petal 15–25 mm long (in coniferous forests, Brit. Col. to N Wash., but extending to Oreg. E of the crest of the Cascades) . . . .
. . . . *P. orbiculata* (*Habenaria orbiculata*)
ROUND-LEAVED REIN ORCHID

2 Blades of leaves not flat on the ground and usually about twice as long as wide (the width rarely so much as 3 cm); spur of lip petal only about 1 mm long (plants not often more than 15 cm tall; mostly in bogs near the coast, Alaska to Wash., but rarely reported S of 50° N) ....
.... *P. chorisiana* (*Habenaria chorisiana*)
SMALL BOG ORCHID

1 At least some leaves scattered along the stems
   3 Petals and sepals greenish or yellowish; lip petal not widening abruptly after the first quarter of its length
      4 Spur of lip petal about as long as the petal; inflorescence loose, most of the flowers widely separated (SW Oreg. to Calif., also E of the crest of the Cascades) ....*P. sparsiflora* (*Habenaria sparsiflora*)
FEW-FLOWERED BOG ORCHID

      4 Spur of lip petal not more than about two-thirds as long as the petal; inflorescence rather compact, at least some of the flowers usually touching ....
.... *P. stricta* (*Habenaria saccata, H. hyperborea* var. *viridiflora*)
SLENDER BOG ORCHID

   3 Petals and sepals white or cream; lip petal widening rather abruptly after the first quarter of its length
....*P. dilatata* (*Habenaria dilatata*)
WHITE-FLOWERED BOG ORCHID
      Three generally recognized varieties of *P. dilatata* represented in our region are keyed below.

      5 Spur of lip petal much shorter than the petal, usually swelling appreciably toward the tip ....
....*P. dilatata* var. *albiflora*

      5 Spur of lip petal as long or longer than the petal
         6 Spur about as long as the lip petal ....*P. dilatata* var. *dilatata*
         6 Spur about 1.5 times as long as the lip petal ....*P. dilatata* var. *leucostachys*

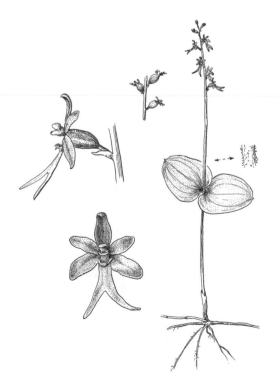

Listera cordata,
heart-leaved twayblade

Platanthera dilatata var.
leucostachys

Spiranthes

1 Perianth white or cream; lip petal rounded at the tip, which is hairy on the upper surface; in meadows and fields whose soil is wet in winter and spring but that usually dries out in summer (in lowland areas, typically flowering in July) . . . . *S. romanzoffiana*, pl. 696
HOODED LADY'S TRESSES

1 Perianth typically yellowish but sometimes cream; lip petal usually somewhat pointed at the tip, which is not hairy on the upper surface; mostly in bogs and marshes that are wet throughout the year (in our region much less often seen than *S. romanzoffiana*) . . . . *S. porrifolia*
WESTERN LADY'S TRESSES

POACEAE Grass Family

The grass family is represented in our region by numerous species, many of them introduced from other areas, especially Europe and Asia. Some grasses were brought intentionally as crop or forage plants, or because they were needed for erosion control. Seeds of others, however, arrived on the hair of animals, on clothing, or with hay, ballast, and mattress filling. The result of all the introductions is that the grass flora of western North America is very different from what it was before the first explorers and colonists arrived. In certain areas, once-prevalent native species have become scarce while alien species have become abundant. But the decline of native species is not due entirely to the success of introduced grasses. The modification of habitats by humans and the aggressive spread of other alien plants has brought about nearly complete destruction or replacement of the natural flora of some areas.

A special set of terms is used for describing grasses. Each major unit of an inflorescence is called a spikelet. This typically consists of two bracts called glumes, one originating slightly above the other, and one or more florets, so called because they are rather different from flowers of other monocotyledonous plants. Each floret usually has a pistil and three stamens, these parts associated with two bracts. The lower of these, called the lemma, is almost invariably well developed; the upper one, called the palea, may be greatly reduced or even absent. Between the pistil and the lemma there are often two, sometimes three, extremely small structures called lodicules; they are believed to correspond to perianth segments. The pistil develops into a one-seeded, dry fruit, here called a grain, although it is closely comparable to what is called an achene in some other flowering plants. In the keys here, lodicules are never referred to, and the palea is brought in only when absolutely necessary. <figure G>

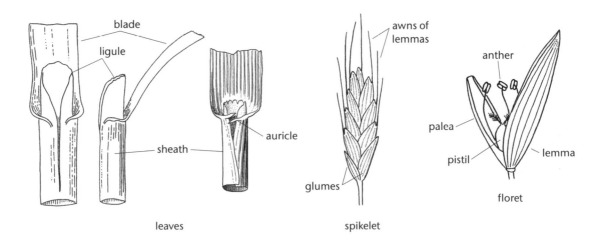

leaves   spikelet

Poaceae

It should be noted that some spikelets lack glumes or that some florets of a spikelet have only stamens or are completely sterile, lacking stamens as well as a pistil. After some experience in using the keys, you will find that the deviations from the usual structure are helpful in identifying certain grasses.

Among the vegetative features used in identifying grasses, the more important ones are the habit of growth, the characteristics of the leaf blade, leaf sheath, and associated structures, and whether the plant is annual or perennial. Especially useful are the ligule, a collar- or fringelike outgrowth from the base of the blade, and the auricles, small outgrowths that sometimes are present on both sides of the top of the sheath.

1 Plants commonly more than 2 m tall, at least when flowering (sometimes more than 3 m tall)
  2 Leaves with blades to 40 cm long, 2–4 cm wide, more or less evenly spaced along upright stems and separating from the stems during the winter; inflorescences to about 35 cm long, 20 cm wide (generally restricted to wet habitats such as lake margins, sloughs, marshes; almost cosmopolitan and one of the most widely distributed vascular plants) . . . . ***Phragmites australis***
  COMMON REED
  2 Leaves with blades sometimes more than 5 cm wide at the base, mostly basal on numerous crowded stems, forming dense masses, persisting; inflorescences plumelike, to more than 1 m long, 15 cm wide
    3 Leaf sheaths densely hairy; leaf blades dark green, not curling near the tips; inflorescences usually violet or purplish when young; plants to 7 m tall when flowering (escaping from cultivation in a few areas and needing control) . . . . ***Cortaderia jubata***
    PURPLE PAMPAS GRASS (W South America)
    3 Leaf sheaths at most only slightly hairy; leaf blades pale, typically with a slightly bluish tinge, curling near the tips; inflorescences whitish or slightly pinkish when young; plants to 4 cm tall when flowering (a serious nuisance in some parts of Calif. and other SW states; occasionally escaping from cultivation in our region) . . . . ***Cortaderia selloana***
    PAMPAS GRASS (E South America)
1 Plants not so much as 2 m tall and not conforming to all the criteria in couplets 2 and 3
  4 All or most spikelets specialized as small, purplish bulblets that serve to reproduce the plant vegetatively (the bulblets have neither stamens nor a pistil) . . . . ***Poa bulbosa*** subsp. ***vivipara***, pl. 705
  BULBOUS BLUEGRASS
  4 Spikelets not specialized as bulblets that serve to reproduce the plant vegetatively
    5 Spikelets (1 or more) completely enclosed within a painfully sharp-spined bur (this is produced by the tight union of short, sterile branches—of the 2 florets in each spikelet, only the upper one is fertile; most likely to be found on sandy shores of rivers, especially E of the crest of the Cascades) . . . .
    . . . . ***Cenchrus longispinus***
    SANDBUR (E United States)
    5 Spikelets not completely enclosed within a sharp-spined bur
      6 Inflorescence (this to about 3 cm long) mostly enclosed by an enlarged leaf sheath (annual) . . . .
      . . . . ***Sporobolus vaginiflorus*** subsp. ***vaginiflorus*** (*S. neglectus*), p. 426
      POVERTY GRASS (E United States)
      6 Inflorescence not enclosed by an enlarged leaf sheath
        7 Awn originating near the base of the lemma of each floret divided by hair-fringed joint, the upper portion extending well beyond the tip of the lemma and ending in a slender, club-shaped thickening (most likely to be found on sandy shores or sandbars of rivers) . . . . . ***Corynephorus canescens***, p. 426
        GRAY HAIR-GRASS
        7 Awn (if present) of lemma not divided by a hair-fringed joint and not ending in a club-shaped thickening
          8 Each spikelet consisting of a single floret, the glumes and lemma very slender and the lemma appearing to have 3 widely diverging awns more than 2.5 cm long (these are in fact branches of a single awn) . . . . ***Aristida oligantha***
          THREE-AWN

8 Spikelets, if with a single floret, not with a lemma whose awn is divided into 3 widely diverging branches
  9 Inflorescence with 2 or more branches originating at the tip of the flowering stem and sometimes with 1–2 sets of branches just below the tip; spikelets arranged on one side of each branch (except in *Paspalum distichum*, in which there are usually just 2 nearly upright branches originating at the tip)
    10 All branches of the inflorescence originating from the tip of the flowering stem
      11 Inflorescence with several branches originating at the tip; most spikelets with 1 floret and 2 glumes; nodes and leaf sheaths not conspicuously hairy .... ***Cynodon dactylon* var. *dactylon***
                                                 BERMUDA GRASS (Eurasia)
      11 Inflorescence with only 2 branches originating at the tip; most spikelets with 2 florets (the lower one represented only by a lemma) but sometimes with only 1 glume (the upper one); ligules membranous .... ***Paspalum distichum***
                                               JOINT GRASS, KNOTGRASS
    10 Some branches of the inflorescence originating below those at the tip of the flowering stem
      12 Rachis of branches of the inflorescence neither flattened nor 3-angled; each spikelet sessile, with several florets; plants not rooting at the nodes .... ***Eleusine indica***
                                             GOOSE GRASS (S Eurasia)
      12 Rachis of branches of the inflorescence flattened and 3-angled; spikelets on short stalks arising from the rachis in pairs (one spikelet has a distinct pedicel, the other is nearly sessile), both spikelets appearing to consist of 1 floret but each in fact with a reduced sterile floret below the fertile one; upper glume much longer than the lower glume, which is sometimes scarcely evident; plants spreading by rooting at the nodes .... ***Digitaria***
  9 Inflorescence not as described in the other choice 9 (if there are branches, these do not originate only at the tip and 1–2 levels below the tip)
    13 Each spikelet accompanied by 1 or more stiff, roughened bristles that originate just below it from the axis of the inflorescence (the bristles are vestigial branches and may be about as long as the spikelets or even longer; inflorescence dense, cylindrical; spikelets with 2 florets but the lower floret either lacking a pistil or lacking stamens and a pistil; lemma of the upper floret finely cross-wrinkled) .... ***Setaria***

Sporobolus vaginiflorus subsp. *vaginiflorus*, poverty grass

Corynephorus canescens, gray hair-grass

13 Spikelets not accompanied by roughened bristles that originate below them

    14 Inflorescence dense and nearly cylindrical but also noticeably lopsided, each short branch bearing 2 dissimilar spikelets; the upper spikelet of each pair with 2–3 fertile florets, the lower one flat, somewhat fanlike, and completely sterile, consisting only of 2 glumes and several lemmas, all similar in appearance . . . . ***Cynosurus***

    14 Inflorescence and spikelets not as described in the other choice 14

        15 Spikelets single or in pairs or trios at each node of the main axis of the inflorescence (they are also sessile or with pedicels not so much as 1.5 mm long; in *Hordeum* the fertile spikelet at each node is flanked on both sides by a staminate or completely sterile spikelet represented mostly by awns)

            16 Spikelets 2–3 at each node of the inflorescence (in *Hordeum* the 2 lateral spikelets of each trio are on short pedicels and reduced to the point that they are represented mostly by awns, but stamens may be present; the fertile spikelet sometimes also has a perceptible pedicel)

                17 With 2 or more similar and fertile spikelets at each node . . . . ***Elymus-Leymus-Taeniatherum* complex**

                17 Inflorescence with 3 spikelets at each node, the middle one sessile (or with a short pedicel) and with stamens and a pistil, the lateral ones definitely with pedicels and either strictly staminate or sterile and represented mostly by awns . . . . ***Hordeum***

        16 Spikelets single at each node of the inflorescence

            18 Spikelets with their narrow edges facing the axis of the inflorescence . . . . ***Lolium***

            18 Spikelets with their broad surfaces facing the axis of the inflorescence

                19 Rhizomes well developed, the plants therefore spreading vegetatively . . . . ***Elymus repens*** (*Agropyron repens*, *Elytrigia repens*)
QUACK GRASS (Eurasia)

                19 Rhizomes absent (plants annual) or poorly developed (perennial, the plants growing like bunchgrasses)

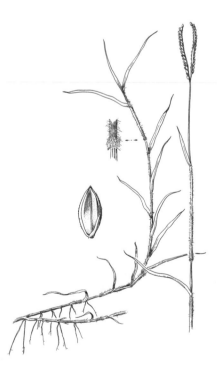

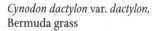

Cynodon dactylon var. *dactylon*,
Bermuda grass

Paspalum distichum,
joint grass, knotgrass

20 Lemmas with bristlelike teeth along the margins and on the awns (when these are present) .... ***Triticum aestivum***
WHEAT (Eurasia)

20 Lemmas without bristlelike teeth along the margins or on the awns (when these are present)

   21 Glumes tapering rather abruptly to blunt tips . . . . ***Thinopyrum***

   21 Glumes tapering gradually to sharp tips . . . . ***Elymus trachycaulus*** (*Agropyron caninum*)
BEARDED WHEATGRASS

15 Spikelets not single or in pairs or trios at each node of the main axis of the inflorescence (in other words, the spikelets are attached to branches of the inflorescence)

  22 Plants usually 75 cm to 1.5 m tall, spreading by rhizomes to form dense colonies; leaf blades to nearly 2 cm wide; spikelets on the branches of the inflorescence in pairs, the pair at the tip consisting of 2 staminate, stalked spikelets, the other pairs consisting of a stalked staminate spikelet and a sessile pistillate spikelet . . . . ***Sorghum halepense***
JOHNSON GRASS (Mediterranean region)

  22 Plants not in all respects as described in the other choice 22

    23 Inflorescence cylindrical and so dense that the branches or the pedicels of spikelets attached to the axis are mostly or completely obscure

> The distinction between the two choices 23 is not exact, but it is helpful. Here there are only a few, easily characterized species, so if you take this first choice you will soon know if it is correct.

    24 Each spikelet with at least 2 florets (most have 2, some may have 3–4) . . . . ***Koeleria macrantha*** (*K. cristata*)
JUNE GRASS

    24 Each spikelet with only 1 floret

     25 Both glumes of each spikelet with a row of stout, bristlelike hairs on the keel as well as with short hairs over much of their surfaces (both glumes also prolonged as awns about 1.5 mm long) . . . . ***Phleum pratense***
TIMOTHY (Eurasia)

> *Phleum alpinum*, alpine timothy, is a montane to high-montane species native to our region. Its inflorescences are nearly 1 cm wide but only about 2–3 times as long as wide; those of *P. pratense* are much less than 1 cm wide and about 10 times as long as wide.

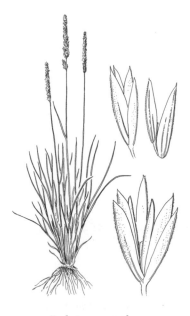

Sorghum halepense,
Johnson grass

Koeleria macrantha,
June grass

25 Glumes without a row of stout, bristlelike hairs on the keel (but hairs or short, stout bristles may be scattered over much of the surfaces of the glumes)

  26 Neither the glumes nor the lemmas with distinct awns

    27 Plants perennial, forming large clumps on backshores of sandy beaches and spreading by rhizomes, the flowering stems sometimes more than 1 m tall; inflorescence to more than 25 cm long, without a leaf at its base; leaves and stems light green (introduced for stabilizing sand dunes and now widespread along the Pacific coast) . . . . *Ammophila arenaria* **subsp.** *arenaria*, pl. 697
EUROPEAN BEACH GRASS (Europe)

    27 Plants annual, not often more than 40 cm tall; inflorescence not often more than 5 cm long, with a leaf at its base, the sheath broadened in such a way as to partly enfold the lower part of the inflorescence; leaves and stems typically dark purplish or blackish rather than green (uncommon weed, usually in habitats that are damp) . . . . *Crypsis alopecuroides* (*Heleochloa alopecuroides*)
FOXTAIL (Europe)

  26 At least the lemmas with awns

    28 Glumes and lemmas (the latter with awns) about the same length (awns of lemmas originating near or below the middle of the back, sometimes sharply bent) . . . . *Alopecurus*

    28 Lemmas shorter than the glumes (do not include awns in measurement)

      29 Lemmas and glumes with awns (the awns of the glumes, arising between 2 lobes at the tip, very long, extending far beyond the awns of the lemmas; glumes roughened by short, bristlelike hairs) . . . .*Polypogon monspeliensis*, pl. 707
RABBIT-FOOT GRASS, ANNUAL BEARD GRASS (Europe)

      29 Lemmas with awns but the glumes (very unequal) merely tapered to sharp points (stalk of each spikelet with an appreciable thickening just below the glumes) . . . .
      . . . . *Gastridium phleoides* (*G. ventricosum* of some references)
NIT GRASS (Europe)

23 Inflorescence not so dense that the branches or the pedicels of spikelets attached directly to the main axis are not easily visible

  30 Spikelets without glumes (perennial to more than 1 m tall, spreading by rhizomes; leaf blades 6–10 mm wide; inflorescence open; lemmas about 2.5 times as long as wide, with numerous short bristles; in marshy habitats) . . . . *Leersia oryzoides*, p. 430
RICE CUT-GRASS

Phleum pratense,
timothy

Gastridium phleoides,
nit grass

30 Each spikelet usually with 2 glumes but sometimes with only 1

  31 Spikelets borne on one side of branches of the inflorescence, the branches therefore appearing lop-sided

    32 Spikelets in dense clusters, not in distinct rows

      33 Most spikelets with at least 3 florets; lemmas and lower glumes tipped with short awns (extremely common weed) . . . .***Dactylis glomerata***, pl. 702
           ORCHARD GRASS (Eurasia)

      33 Spikelets usually with 2 florets, the lower one sterile or strictly staminate; lemma of lower floret bristly and with an awn (except in *E. colona*), and accompanied by a much smaller, membranous palea; lemma of upper floret not bristly, with or without an awn, the palea of about equal length . . . . ***Echinochloa***

    32 Spikelets in 2 distinct rows

      34 Each spikelet with 2 florets but the lower one usually sterile, consisting only of a lemma (spikelets usually with a single glume, the upper one) . . . . ***Paspalum dilatatum***
           DALLIS GRASS (tropical America)

      34 Each spikelet with a single floret

        35 Ligules to about 1 cm long, tapering gradually from the base to the tip; glumes nearly equal, about 3 mm long, nearly flat, with winglike structures on both sides; in freshwater marshes and wet meadows, and at the edges of ponds and ditches . . . . ***Beckmannia syzigachne***
           SLOUGH GRASS

        35 Ligules consisting of a fringe of hairs, these less than 3 mm long; glumes unequal, the lower one at least 4 mm long, the upper one at least 6 mm long, both rather slender and more or less boat-shaped (usually with hairs on the keel); in salt marshes . . . . ***Spartina***

  31 Spikelets not borne on only one side of branches of the inflorescence (but in *Pleuropogon refractus*, first choice 57, the long spikelets, with 7–13 florets, are borne singly and are widely spaced, and may all be directed away from one side of the axis of the inflorescence)

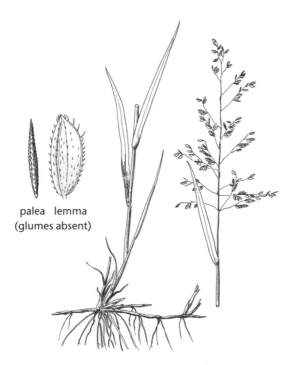

palea lemma
(glumes absent)

Leersia oryzoides,
rice cut-grass

Polypogon interruptus,
ditch beard grass

36 Each spikelet almost always with only 1 floret (in the *Panicum-Dichanthelium* complex, first choice 37, there are 2 florets, but the lower one, with a lemma similar to the large, conspicuously ribbed upper glume, is either completely sterile or has only stamens)

  37 Glumes unequal, sometimes strikingly so, the larger upper one similar to the lower lemma in size, texture, and in being conspicuously ribbed lengthwise; upper lemma hardened, not ribbed lengthwise, its edges partly wrapped around the similarly hardened palea, these 2 components of the floret tightly enclosing the grain as it matures; spikelets shed as a whole when mature, the glumes falling with the lemmas and paleas (lower portion of the ligule of a leaf consisting of a membrane, the upper portion consisting of a fringe of separate hairs) . . . . ***Panicum-Dichanthelium* complex**

  37 Spikelets not as described in the other choice 37

    38 Awn of the lemma usually at least 2 cm long, spirally twisted for nearly its entire length and also bent twice (lemma becoming hard and tightly enclosing the grain) . . . . ***Achnatherum***

    38 Awn, if present on the lemma, not so much as 1 cm long and not spirally twisted for nearly its entire length (in *Calamagrostis*, however, the awn may be bent)

      39 Lemmas with conspicuous long hairs at the base . . . . ***Calamagrostis***

      39 Lemmas without such long hairs at the base

        40 Glumes much longer than the body of the lemma they enclose (glumes and lemma with long awns; perennial, growing along ditches and streams) . . . . ***Polypogon interruptus***

DITCH BEARD GRASS (South America)

        40 Glumes from much shorter to only slightly longer than the lemma they enclose

          41 Each floret on a short stalk, this prolonged behind the palea as a stiff bristle (lemma usually with a short awn at the tip; leaf blades to 1.5 cm wide; plants to more than 1.5 m tall) . . . . ***Cinna latifolia***

WOODREED

          41 Floret without a stalk and without a stiff bristle behind the palea

Cinna latifolia,
woodreed

Holcus lanatus,
velvet grass

42 Glumes (exclusive of the awn, if this is present) longer than the lemma; awn, if present on the glumes, arising on the back below the tip; palea usually negligible or lacking . . . . *Agrostis-Apera* **complex**

42 Glumes, whether with or without an awn, shorter than the lemma (include the awn in the comparison); awn, if present on the glumes, a prolongation of the tip, not arising on the back below the tip; palea well developed, nearly as long as the lemma (or the body of the lemma, if this is prolonged into an awn) . . . .*Muhlenbergia*

36 Each spikelet with at least 2 florets, as suggested by the number of similar lemmas (but the lower floret may lack a pistil; when there are 3 florets, the lower 2 may lack pistils; when there are several florets, some of the upper ones may lack pistils or be completely sterile)

43 Glumes usually at least 2 cm long . . . .*Avena*

43 Glumes not so much as 1.5 cm long

44 Nearly all spikelets with only 2 florets

45 Lemma of the upper floret, after this has ripened, with a hooklike awn originating just below the tip; lemma of the lower floret without an awn . . . . *Holcus lanatus,* p. 431
VELVET GRASS (Europe)

45 Neither of the lemmas with a hooklike awn, but the lemma of at least 1 floret may have a rather sharply bent awn originating on the back

46 Lemma of the lower (staminate) floret with a long, twisted, bent awn originating near the middle of the back, the upper floret with a short awn originating near the tip . . . .
. . . . *Arrhenatherum elatius* subsp. *bulbosus*
TALL OAT GRASS (Europe)

46 Either the lemmas of both florets with long awns, or only the lemma of the upper floret with a long, bent awn

47 Only the lemma of the upper floret with a long, bent awn

48 Perennial, generally at least 40 cm tall, spreading by rhizomes; nodes with downward-pointing hairs; awns originating near the tips of the lemmas . . . . *Holcus mollis*
CREEPING VELVET GRASS (Europe)

48 Annual, rarely more than 30 cm tall; nodes without downward-pointing hairs; awns originating below the middle of the lemmas . . . . . . *Aira caryophyllea* subsp. *capillaris*
(*A. elegans, A. elegantissima*)
EUROPEAN SILVER HAIR-GRASS (Europe)

47 Lemma of both florets with long, bent awns

49 Stalk of the upper floret not prolonged beyond the base of the lemma (annuals, generally less than 30 cm tall) . . . . *Aira*

49 Stalk of the upper floret prolonged for at least a short distance beyond the base of the lemma, and also with conspicuous hairs

50 Tips of the lemmas split into 2 slender lobes; awns originating well above the middle of the lemmas . . . . *Trisetum*

50 Tips of the lemmas acutely pointed, not split into 2 lobes; awns originating at or below the middle of the lemmas . . . .*Deschampsia*

Arrhenatherum elatius
subsp. *bulbosus,*
tall oat grass

44 Most spikelets with 3 or more florets (but 1 or more of them may lack a pistil)

  51 Most spikelets with 3 florets (but some of these may lack a pistil and/or stamens)

    52 Lemmas of all florets without awns

      53 Two lower florets without stamens and often much reduced in other respects . . . . ***Phalaris***

      53 Two lower florets with stamens . . . . ***Hierochloe***

                  Hierochloe alpina, a northern and mostly montane species not occurring in our region, has awned lemmas.

    52 Lemmas of at least some florets with conspicuous awns (glumes decidedly unequal)

      54 Awn of the lemma of the lowest floret, unlike those of the other 2 florets, originating at the tip and not bent . . . . ***Ventenata dubia*** (Eurasia)

      54 Awn of the lemma of the lowest floret, like that of the second floret, originating on the back and bent (lemma of the fertile uppermost floret without an awn) . . . . ***Anthoxanthum***

  51 Most spikelets with more than 3 florets (some upper ones may lack pistils or be represented only by empty lemmas that successively fit tightly inside one another)

    55 Upper 2–4 florets nonreproductive, consisting of empty lemmas that successively fit tightly inside one another; glumes somewhat papery in texture (lemmas of fertile florets—there are at least 2 of these—sometimes with an awn, sometimes without; stems sometimes with bulblike bases) . . . . ***Melica***

    55 Upper 2–4 florets, if nonreproductive, not empty and successively fitting tightly inside one another; glumes not papery (but they may be mostly membranous)

      56 All or most lemmas with conspicuous awns (more than just short, abruptly narrowed tips)

        57 Awns of lemmas, when present, attached to a triangular, membranous tooth between 2 similar teeth at the tip (in lemmas that do not have an awn, the tip is generally divided, sometimes rather asymmetrically, into 3 teeth; ribs of glumes and lemmas nearly parallel, not converging; glumes almost entirely membranous; in damp or wet habitats) . . . . ***Pleuropogon refractus***
                                                   SEMAPHORE GRASS

        57 Awns of lemmas not attached to a membranous tooth between 2 similar teeth, and the florets in other respects not conforming to the description in the other choice 57

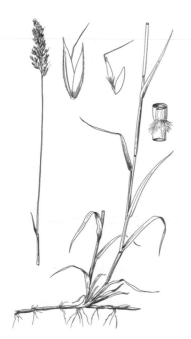

Holcus mollis,
creeping velvet grass

Pleuropogon refractus,
nodding semaphore grass

58 Awns of lemmas twisted near the base; glumes reaching to or beyond the lemmas (lemmas hairy along the margins and often also on the back) . . . . ***Danthonia***

58 Awns of lemmas not twisted near the base

  59 Lemmas either gradually narrowing to form prominent awns or the awns originating on the backs of the lemmas well below the tip

    60 Spikelets nearly sessile; glumes hardened and with at least 5 lengthwise ribs (lemmas also hardened); leaf sheaths without auricles . . . . ***Brachypodium***

    60 Spikelets usually with obvious pedicels; glumes not hardened and with not more than 3 lengthwise ribs; leaf sheaths often with well-developed auricles . . . . ***Festuca-Vulpia*** complex

  59 Awns of lemmas usually originating in a notch (often very shallow) between 2 lobes or teeth at the tip, or from the tip itself, in which case this is typically blunt, not gradually tapering into an awn as in the genera under the other choice 59

    61 Lemmas with 5–9 ribs, these usually rather faint; awns of lemmas usually much more than 1 mm long; glumes (at least the upper one), with more than 1 rib . . . . ***Bromus***

    61 Lemmas with 3 ribs; awns of lemmas only about 0.5–1 mm long but originating in a distinct notch; both glumes with a single prominent rib on the midline (this like a keel, and roughened by short, spinelike outgrowths pointing upward) . . . . ***Leptochloa***

56 Lemmas without awns (but they may be abruptly narrowed to pointed tips)

  62 Spikelets conspicuously flattened (and usually hanging down or at least nodding); glumes and lemmas similar, broadly boat-shaped, not much longer than wide

    63 Lemmas not abruptly narrowed to pointed tips . . . . ***Briza***

    63 Lemmas abruptly narrowed to pointed tips . . . . ***Bromus briziformis***

                                RATTLESNAKE BROME

  62 Spikelets not conspicuously flattened; glumes and lemmas not as described in the other choice 62

    64 All inflorescences on each plant either pistillate or staminate

      65 Plants forming large, continuous colonies, not separate tufts, the leaves alternating on opposite sides of the stems; stems not hollow; growing in salt marshes . . . . ***Distichlis spicata***

                                  SEASHORE SALT GRASS

      65 Plants forming dense tufts (the tufts generally well separated, even when joined by underground rhizomes), the leaves not alternating on opposite sides of the stems; stems hollow; growing on backshores of sandy beaches . . . . ***Poa confinis***, pl. 706, or *P. macrantha* (see p. 460)

    64 Most functional florets on each plant with stamens and a pistil (in any case, the plants are not strictly pistillate or staminate)

      66 Bases of lemmas usually with cobwebby hairs; lengthwise ribs (usually 5) of lemmas converging at the tip . . . . ***Poa***

      66 Bases of lemmas without cobwebby hairs; ribs of lemmas not converging at the tip

        67 Lemmas with 7 lengthwise ribs (most spikelets with at least 5 florets; leaf sheaths closed; ligules prominent; plants of lake margins and other wet places) . . . . ***Glyceria***

        67 Lemmas usually with not more than 5 lengthwise ribs

          68 Lemmas with 3 lengthwise ribs . . . . ***Eragrostis***

          68 Lemmas typically with 5 lengthwise ribs . . . . ***Puccinellia-Torreyochloa*** complex

Achnatherum

1 At least the lowest segment of the awn of the lemma hairy, some of the hairs 0.5–1 mm long (plants often more than 80 cm tall, sometimes more than 1 m)

  2 All 3 segments of the awn hairy (high montane) . . . ***A. occidentale*** subsp. ***occidentale*** (*Stipa occidentalis*)

                                  WESTERN NEEDLEGRASS

  2 Only the lowest segment of the awn markedly hairy

3 Hairs at the tip of the lemma about as long as those at the base (mostly E of the crest of the Cascades but also known from various localities W of the crest) . . . .
. . . . *A. occidentale* subsp. *californicum* (*Stipa occidentalis* var. *californica*)
CALIFORNIA NEEDLEGRASS

3 Hairs at the tip of the lemma longer than those at the base (mostly E of the crest of the Cascades) . . . .
. . . . *A. occidentale* subsp. *pubescens*
HAIRY WESTERN NEEDLEGRASS

1 Lowest segment of the awn of the lemma bristly, otherwise roughened or with only very short hairs
4 Palea about half as long as the lemma; plants often more than 80 cm tall, sometimes more than 1.5 m (mostly montane W of the crest of the Cascades but sometimes at lower elevations E of the crest) . . . . .
. . . . *A. nelsonii* subsp. *dorei*
COLUMBIA NEEDLEGRASS

4 Palea at least three-fourths as long as the lemma; plants not often more than 80 cm tall
5 Awn originating between a pair of short, rounded, and slightly thickened lobes about 0.1 mm long (mostly E of the crest of the Cascades but also found in the Columbia River Gorge, and in W Brit. Col., Wash., including the Olympic Mountains, and Oreg., S to Calif.) . . . .
. . . . *A. lemmonii* subsp. *lemmonii* (*Stipa lemmonii*)
LEMMON'S NEEDLEGRASS

5 Awn originating between a pair of membranous lobes, these to nearly 1 mm long (known to occur in montane habitats in at least Lane and Klamath Cos., Oreg.; in general, however, limited to the region E of the crest of the Cascades) . . . . *A. lettermanii*
LETTERMAN'S NEEDLEGRASS

Agrostis-Apera Complex
1 Lemmas with awns
2 Awns of lemmas originating well below the middle, usually sharply bent and also twisted (on rocks, Columbia River Gorge) . . . . *Agrostis howellii*
HOWELL'S BENT GRASS

2 Awns of lemmas originating near the middle or above the middle

Distichlis spicata,
seashore salt grass

Achnatherum lemmonii
subsp. *lemmonii*,
Lemmon's needlegrass

3 Awns of lemmas originating close to the tip (annual)

 4 Palea about half as long as the lemma ....*Agrostis capillaris* (*A. tenuis* of some references)
                       COLONIAL BENT GRASS

 4 Palea nearly as long as the lemma

  5 Inflorescence rather compact, the branches generally more or less upright, shorter than the spikelets
  .... *Apera interrupta*
                       INTERRUPTED BENT GRASS

  5 Inflorescence open, the branches mostly directed outward, at least many of them longer than the
  spikelets .... *Apera spica-venti*
                       SILKY BENT GRASS

3 Awns of lemmas originating near or only slightly above the middle

 6 Inflorescence compact, the branches and their spikelets usually held close to the main axis

  7 Palea prominent, more than half as long as the lemma ....*Agrostis viridis* (*A. semiverticillata*)
                     WATER BENT GRASS (Europe)

  7 Palea small, not so much as one-third as long as the lemma

   8 Lemmas not more than 2 mm long; awns fully 3 times as long as the lemmas ....
   .... *Agrostis microphylla*
                     SMALL-LEAVED BENT GRASS

   8 Lemmas slightly more than 2 mm long; awns not much more than twice as long as the lemmas

    9 Anthers 0.7–1.8 mm long .... *Agrostis pallens* (*A. diegoensis*)
                     DUNE BENT GRASS

    9 Anthers 0.3–0.6 mm long ....*Agrostis exarata* (*A. ampla, A. longiligula*)
                     SPIKE BENT GRASS

 6 Inflorescence loose, the primary branches diverging widely from the main axis

  10 Palea prominent, more than half as long as the lemma

   11 Branches of the inflorescence not bearing spikelets to their bases (mostly montane and high montane) .... *Agrostis humilis* (*A. thurberiana*)
                     ALPINE BENT GRASS

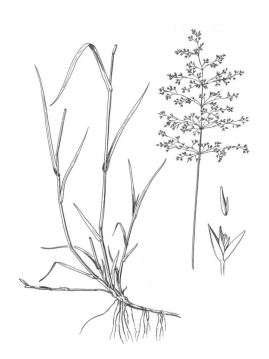

Agrostis capillaris,
colonial bent grass

Agrostis stolonifera,
creeping bent grass

11 Branches of the inflorescence bearing spikelets to their bases (spreading by stolons) . . . .
. . . . *Agrostis stolonifera* (*A. alba* of some references, *A. palustris*)
CREEPING BENT GRASS

A weedy European grass, *A. gigantea,* called redtop, is very similar to *A. stolonifera* but spreads by underground rhizomes rather than by aboveground stolons.

10 Palea, if present, not so much as half as long as the lemma
12 Palea absent (Alaska to Wash.; mostly high montane in our region) . . . .
. . . . *Agrostis mertensii* (*A. borealis*)
MERTENS' BENT GRASS

12 Palea usually present, but sometimes very small and difficult to distinguish
13 Inflorescence loose, the primary branches diverging widely from the main axis and not bearing spikelets close to their bases (mostly low to high montane) . . . . *Agrostis scabra*
ROUGH BENT GRASS

Agrostis scabra is here considered to include the low-growing, high-montane *A. geminata* of some references.

13 Inflorescence fairly compact to very compact, the branches bearing spikelets close to their bases
14 Anthers 0.7–1.8 mm long . . . . *Agrostis pallens*
DUNE BENT GRASS

14 Anthers 0.3–0.6 mm long . . . . *Agrostis exarata* (*A. ampla, A. longiligula*)
SPIKE BENT GRASS

1 Lemmas without awns
15 Hairs originating just below the base of the lemma 1–2 mm long (NW Oreg. to Calif.) . . . *Agrostis hallii*
HALL'S BENT GRASS

15 Hairs, if present below the base of the lemma, not so much as 1 mm long
16 Stalk of the floret usually prolonged behind the palea as a bristlelike structure (this may be very small and sometimes absent, so look carefully at several spikelets)
17 Bristlelike prolongation of the stalk of the floret 0.5–1 mm long; anthers 0.8–1.5 mm long (Alaska to Oreg., from the lowlands to midmontane habitats but not at high elevations) . . . .
. . . . *Agrostis aequivalvis*, p. 438
ALASKA BENT GRASS

17 Bristlelike prolongation of the stalk of the floret, when present, less than 0.5 mm long (high montane, Alaska to Calif.) . . . . *Agrostis humilis* (*A. thurberiana*)
ALPINE BENT GRASS

16 Stalk of the floret not prolonged as a bristlelike structure
18 Palea rather prominent, about half as long as the lemma
19 Branches of the inflorescence not bearing spikelets to their bases . . . .
. . . . *Agrostis capillaris* (*A. tenuis* Sibthorp, not Vasey)
COLONIAL BENT GRASS

19 Branches of the inflorescence bearing spikelets to their bases . . . .
. . . . *Agrostis stolonifera* (*A. alba* of some references, *A. palustris*)
CREEPING BENT GRASS

See note concerning *A. gigantea* after the second choice 11.

18 Palea inconspicuous (not more than one-fourth as long as the lemma) or absent altogether
20 Inflorescence narrow, rather congested, the primary branches sometimes bearing spikelets at their bases
21 Leaf blades commonly more than 2 mm wide, sometimes as wide as 8 mm; primary branches of the inflorescence often bearing spikelets at their bases (mostly in very dry sandy and rocky habitats) . . . . *Agrostis pallens* (*A. diegoensis*)
DUNE BENT GRASS

21 Leaf blades to 2 mm wide; primary branches of the inflorescence only occasionally bearing spikelets at their bases . . . . *Agrostis variabilis*
MOUNTAIN BENT GRASS

20 Inflorescence broad, branching freely, the primary branches not bearing spikelets at their bases

  22 Plants rarely so much as 40 cm tall; inflorescence not often more than 10 cm long; leaf blades not more than 2 mm wide; palea not so much as one-fifth as long as the lemma (in dry habitats)
. . . . *Agrostis idahoensis*
IDAHO BENT GRASS

  22 Plants commonly more than 40 cm tall; inflorescence usually 10–30 cm long; leaf blades 2–4 mm wide; palea one-fifth to one-fourth as long as the lemma . . . . *Agrostis oregonensis*
OREGON BENT GRASS

Aira

1 Only the lemma of the upper floret with a long, bent awn . . . .
. . . . *A. caryophyllea* subsp. *capillaris* (*A. elegans, A. elegantissima*)
ELEGANT EUROPEAN HAIR-GRASS

1 Lemma of both florets with long, bent awns

  2 Inflorescence loose and about as wide as long; glumes rarely so much as 3 mm long . . . .
. . . . *A. caryophyllea* subsp. *caryophyllea*
SILVER EUROPEAN HAIR-GRASS (Europe)

  2 Inflorescence narrow and rather compact, several times as long as wide; glumes usually at least 3 mm long . . . . *A. praecox*
LITTLE HAIR-GRASS (Europe)

Alopecurus

1 Awns of lemmas straight, originating near the middle of the back and rarely projecting so much as 1.5 mm beyond the glumes . . . . *A. aequalis*
SHORT-AWN FOXTAIL

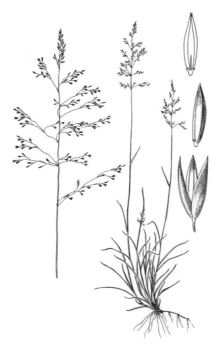

Agrostis aequivalvis,
Alaska bent grass

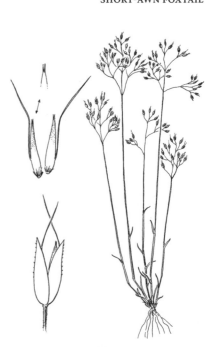

Aira caryophyllea subsp. *caryophyllea,*
silver European hair-grass

1 Awns of lemmas rather sharply bent, originating well below the middle of the back and usually projecting at least 1.5 mm beyond the glumes

    2 Glumes usually less than 3 mm long (but sometimes to 3.5 mm in *A. geniculatus*)

        3 Perennial; anthers at least 1.2 mm long (typically in very wet habitats, often in shallow water) . . . . *A. geniculatus*

           WATER FOXTAIL

        3 Annual; anthers less than 1 mm long (in damp habitats but not often in standing water) . . . . *A. carolinianus*

           CAROLINA MEADOW FOXTAIL (central and E United States)

    2 Glumes at least 3.5 mm long

        4 Anthers more than 2 mm long (usually 2.5–3.5 mm); ligules typically squared-off at the tip, the edge of the tip usually tearing so that it appears bristly or hairy; perennial to more than 50 cm tall . . . . *A. pratensis*

           MEADOW FOXTAIL (Eurasia)

        4 Anthers not so much as 1.5 mm long; ligules typically narrowing to a pointed tip, the edge not often tearing; annual to about 30 cm tall (usually in damp habitats, such as drying vernal pools; in our region mostly in SW Oreg.) . . . . *A. saccatus*

           PACIFIC MEADOW FOXTAIL

Anthoxanthum

1 Annual, usually not so much as 30 cm tall; leaf blades 1–2 mm wide . . . .*A. aristatum* subsp. *aristatum*

           VERNAL GRASS (Eurasia)

1 Perennial, commonly at least 40 cm tall; leaf blades usually 3–7 mm wide . . . . *A. odoratum*, pl. 698

           SWEET VERNAL GRASS (Europe)

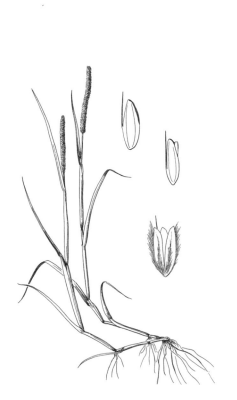

Alopecurus aequalis,
short-awn foxtail

Alopecurus pratensis,
meadow foxtail

Avena

1 Tips of lemmas divided into 2 slender lobes 2–6 mm long . . . .***A. barbata***
SLENDER WILD OAT (Europe)

1 Tips of lemmas divided into 2 slender lobes less than 1 mm long

   2 Awns of the upper and lower florets of a spikelet about the same length, both at least 2.5 cm long . . . . .
. . . .***A. fatua***
WILD OAT (Europe)

   2 Awn of the upper floret at least 1.5 cm long, the awn of the lower floret, if present at all, much shorter
. . . .***A. sativa***
CULTIVATED OAT (Europe)

Brachypodium

1 Perennial, commonly more than 50 cm tall; inflorescences usually with more than 5 spikelets; margins and backs of glumes and lemmas conspicuously hairy, the hairs flexible . . . .***B. sylvaticum***
TALL FALSE BROME (Europe)

1 Annual, not often more than about 30 cm tall; inflorescences with not more than 5 spikelets; margins of glumes and lemmas with stiff hairs, the backs somewhat roughened but not hairy . . . .***B. distachyon***
SHORT FALSE BROME (Europe)

Briza

1 Spikelets usually at least 10 mm long, sometimes more than 15 mm . . . .***B. maxima***, pl. 699
BIG QUAKING GRASS (Europe)

1 Spikelets not more than about 3 mm long . . . .***B. minor***
LITTLE QUAKING GRASS (Europe)

Bromus

1 Plants perennial (on larger plants there will be remnants of leaves of preceding years)

   2 Spikelets conspicuously flattened (the width, at the level of the tips of the glumes, usually at least 3 times the thickness); backs of lemmas typically with a distinct keel

Avena fatua,
wild oat

Brachypodium distachyon,
short false brome

3 Inflorescence rather compact, most of the branches shorter than the spikelets (coastal, Lane Co., Oreg., to Calif.) . . . . *B. maritimus* (*B. carinatus* var. *maritimus*)
COASTAL BROME

3 Inflorescence loose, at least the lower branches considerably longer than the spikelets

    4 Plants not often more than 1 m tall; branches of the inflorescence, before dividing, rarely more than 5 cm long; leaf blades usually less than 10 mm wide; ligules generally not more than 4 mm long . . . . *B. carinatus*
CALIFORNIA BROME

    4 Plants commonly more than 1 m tall; inflorescences very loose (and drooping), some of the branches, before dividing, more than 7 cm long; leaf blades often more than 10 mm wide, sometimes as wide as 15 mm; ligules generally at least 4 mm long, sometimes as long as 8 mm (primarily coastal) . . . . *B. sitchensis*
SITKA BROME

2 Spikelets not conspicuously flattened (the width, at the level of the tips of the glumes, not much more than twice the thickness); backs of lemmas usually rounded rather than with a distinct keel

  5 Plants spreading by creeping rhizomes; lemmas either merely sharp-pointed or with distinct awns to 2 mm long, occasionally longer . . . . *B. inermis*
SMOOTH BROME, HUNGARIAN BROME (Eurasia)

  5 Plants not spreading by rhizomes; awns of lemmas usually more than 2 mm long

    6 Inflorescence compact, the short branches upright

      7 Leaf blades less than 3 mm wide, the edges typically inrolled; awns of lemmas 5–6 mm long . . . . *B. erectus*
UPRIGHT BROME (Europe)

      7 Larger leaf blades usually at least 6 mm wide, flat; awns of lemmas 2–4 mm long (generally montane at moderate to higher elevations, and in our region mostly limited to SW Oreg.) . . . . *B. suksdorfii*
SUKSDORF'S BROME

    6 Inflorescence loose, the branches spreading outward or drooping

      8 Backs of lemmas hairy on their lower two-thirds or three-quarters but not above

        9 Ligules not more than 1.5 mm long; awns of lemmas usually 2–4 mm long (mostly E of the crest of the Cascades) . . . . *B. ciliatus*
FRINGED BROME

        9 Ligules at least 2 mm long, usually 3–4 mm; awns of lemmas usually 5–10 mm long but occasionally shorter . . . . *B. vulgaris*
COMMON BROME

      8 Backs of lemmas hairy throughout

      10 Stems distinctly hairy almost throughout; branches of inflorescences directed outward but not obviously drooping; ligules 1–2 mm long, not hairy (but they may have irregular margins) . . . . *B. orcuttianus*
ORCUTT'S BROME

      10 Stems not hairy except at the nodes; branches of the inflorescences generally drooping at least slightly; ligules 2–5 mm long, distinctly hairy (along the coast, Alaska to Oreg.; also in the Puget Trough, Brit. Col. and Wash., and in the Willamette Valley, Oreg.) . . . . *B. pacificus*, p.442
PACIFIC BROME

Bromus carinatus,
California brome

1 Plants annual (without remnants of leaves of preceding years)

  11 Lemmas ending in a sharp tip, this not long enough to qualify as an awn (lemmas broad and somewhat inflated, fitting together rather tightly) . . . . ***B. briziformis***

                                                                  RATTLESNAKE BROME (Europe)

  11 Tips of lemmas with an awn, this originating between 2 slender teeth or between 2 lobes or broad teeth

    12 Awns of lemmas originating between 2 slender teeth that are several times as long as they are wide at their bases

      13 Spikelets less than 2.5 cm long; upper glumes less than 13 mm long . . . . ***B. tectorum***

                                               CHEATGRASS, DOWNY BROME (Eurasia, N Africa)

      13 Spikelets more than 3 cm long; upper glumes more than 15 mm long

        14 Inflorescence very dense, the branches rarely as long as the glumes . . . . ***B. madritensis*** subsp. ***rubens*** (*B. rubens*), pl. 700

                                               FOXTAIL CHESS (Europe, N Africa)

      14 Inflorescence rather loose, most of the branches longer than the glumes

        15 Lower glume usually at least 15 mm long; upper glume usually at least 20 mm long; lemmas 22–30 mm long . . . . ***B. diandrus*** (*B. rigidus*)

                                               RIPGUT BROME (Europe, N Africa)

        15 Lower glume rarely more than 10 mm long; upper glume rarely more than 15 mm long; lemmas rarely more than 20 mm long . . . . ***B. sterilis***

                                               POVERTY BROME (Eurasia)

    12 Awns of lemmas originating between 2 rounded lobes or between 2 teeth that are scarcely if at all longer than they are wide at their bases

Bromus pacificus,
Pacific brome

Bromus briziformis,
rattlesnake brome

16 Inflorescence compact, the branches not appreciably longer than the spikelets

   17 Lemmas thin and papery, with prominent ribs; anthers not so much as 1 mm long . . . .

   . . . . *B. hordeaceus* subsp. *hordeaceus* (*B. mollis*)

                                        SOFT BROME (Eurasia)

   17 Lemmas not especially thin or papery, the ribs not prominent; anthers usually 1.5–2 mm long . . . .

   . . . . *B. racemosus*

                                        SMOOTH BROME

16 Inflorescence rather loose, at least some of the branches longer than the spikelets

   18 Edges of lemmas inrolled for their full length and tightly clasping the grain when this is well developed

   . . . . *B. secalinus*

                                 RYE BROME (Eurasia, Africa)

   18 Edges of lemmas inrolled only in the lower two-thirds and not tightly clasping the grain when this is

      well developed . . . . *B. japonicus* (*B. commutatus*)

                                   JAPANESE BROME (Eurasia)

Calamagrostis

1 Awns of lemmas sharply bent and reaching at least 1.5 mm beyond the tips of the lower glumes

   2 Awns of lemmas reaching 7–11 mm beyond the tips of the lower glumes; tips of ligules sharply pointed (rocky areas in the Columbia River Gorge, Clark and Klickitat Cos., Wash., and Multnomah and Hood River Cos., Oreg.) . . . . *C. howellii*

                                   HOWELL'S REED GRASS

   2 Awns of lemmas reaching not more than 6 mm beyond the tips of the lower glumes; tips of ligules blunt, squared-off, or ragged but not sharply pointed

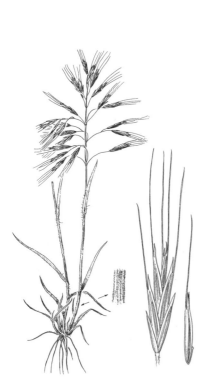

Bromus tectorum,
cheatgrass

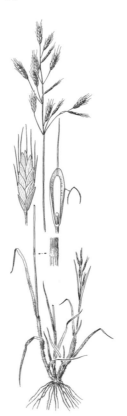

Bromus japonicus,
Japanese brome

3 Awns of lemmas reaching 3–6 mm (usually 4–5 mm) beyond the tips of the lower glumes; glumes rough along the keel, but not elsewhere; collar of leaf sheath usually not hairy (montane in the Olympic Mountains, Wash., and Cascades, Brit. Col. to Oreg.) . . . .*C. sesquiflora*

TUFTED PINE-GRASS

3 Awns of lemmas reaching only 1.5–2 mm beyond the tips of the lower glumes; glumes rough over much of their surface; collar of leaf sheath usually hairy (montane in the Olympic Mountains, Wash., and Cascades, Brit. Col. to Calif. and eastward) . . . .*C. purpurascens*

PURPLE REED GRASS

1 Awns of lemmas (whether straight or bent) not reaching more than 1 mm beyond the lower glumes

4 Hairs at the bases of the lemmas about half as long as the lemmas

5 Awns originating near the base of the lemmas and sharply bent; leaf blades mostly 2–6 mm wide . . .
. . . . *C. koelerioides*

DENSE REED GRASS

5 Awns originating near the middle of the lemmas and either straight or just slightly curved; leaf blades mostly 6–12 mm wide . . . .*C. nutkaensis*

NOOTKA REED GRASS

4 Hairs at the bases of the lemmas at least three-fourths as long as the lemmas

6 Inflorescences loose, the branches spreading widely; glumes keeled nearly to the base

7 Glumes typically 3–4 mm long, not obviously rough all over, the keels only slightly bristly (mostly coastal) . . . .*C. canadensis* subsp. *canadensis*

BLUE-JOINT REED GRASS

7 Glumes typically 4–6 mm long, obviously rough all over, especially on the very bristly keels (mostly montane and E of the Cascades) . . . .*C. canadensis* subsp. *langsdorffii*

LANGSDORFF'S BLUE-JOINT REED GRASS

Because of intergradation, some specimens do not fit perfectly into either *C. canadensis* subsp. *canadensis* or subsp. *langsdorffii*.

6 Inflorescences rather congested, the branches not spreading widely; glumes rounded rather than keeled in the lower quarter

Calamagrostis purpurascens,
purple reed grass

Calamagrostis stricta subsp.
inexpansa, narrow-spike

Danthonia unispicata,
one-spike oat grass

8 Leaf blades usually rough on both surfaces; ligules usually 3–6 mm long, often split above . . . . ***C. stricta* subsp. *inexpansa*** (*C. crassiglumis*)
NARROW-SPIKE REED GRASS

8 Leaf blades usually rough only on the upper surface or on neither surface; ligules not often more than 3 mm long, usually not split above . . . . ***C. stricta* subsp. *stricta*** (*C. neglecta*)
SLIM-STEM REED GRASS

Calamagrostis stricta subspp. *inexpansa* and *stricta* are obviously not sharply distinct; subsp. *inexpansa,* however, is the only one likely to be found in coastal areas.

Cynosurus

1 Inflorescence less than 1 cm wide; awns of lemmas of fertile florets less than 1 mm long; glumes and lemmas of sterile spikelets close together, usually touching; ligules of leaf sheaths not so much as 2 mm long; perennial . . . . *C. cristatus*
CRESTED DOGTAIL (Europe)

1 Inflorescence usually more than 1 cm wide; awns of lemmas of fertile florets 3–10 mm long; glumes and lemmas of sterile spikelets distinctly separated, their tips drawn out into long, bristlelike awns; ligules of leaf sheaths at least 2 mm long, sometimes more than 7 mm; annual . . . . *C. echinatus*, pl. 701
DOGTAIL (Europe)

Danthonia

1 Lemmas without awns (the tip has 3 teeth, the one in the middle smaller than the other 2; in our region most likely to be found in grassy coastal habitats) . . . . *D. decumbens* (*Sieglingia decumbens*)
HEATH GRASS (Europe)

1 Lemmas with awns

2 Inflorescence almost always consisting of a single spikelet at the top of the stem (occasionally there is a second spikelet below it, and a very few plants may have a third spikelet; lemmas smooth on the back but with prominent hairs along their margins; leaf sheaths hairy, the hairs at the collar 3–4 mm long) . . . . *D. unispicata*
ONE-SPIKE OAT GRASS

Deschampsia caespitosa,
tufted hair-grass

Digitaria sanguinalis,
crabgrass

2 Inflorescence consisting of 2 to several spikelets

    3 Lemmas hairy on the back as well as along the margins . . . . ***D. spicata***

                    POVERTY OAT GRASS

    3 Lemmas smooth on the back but with prominent hairs on the margins

        4 Branches of the inflorescence spreading; teeth bordering the awn of the lemma drawn out into awnlike structures to about 4–5 mm long . . . . ***D. californica***

                    CALIFORNIA OAT GRASS

        4 Branches of the inflorescence usually upright, the inflorescences rather compact; teeth bordering the awn of the lemma generally only 1–2 mm long, acutely pointed . . . . ***D. intermedia***

                    TIMBER OAT GRASS

Deschampsia

1 Annual, with only a few leaves (leaf blades rarely so much as 1.5 mm wide; glumes usually 6–8 mm long) . . . . ***D. danthonioides***

                    ANNUAL HAIR-GRASS

1 Tufted perennial, with many leaves

    2 Leaf blades 3–6 mm wide, flat; ligules usually blunt or squared-off; spikelets purplish (montane and high montane, in our region not often found below about 5000 ft., 1520 m) . . . . ***D. atropurpurea*** (*Vahlodea atropurpurea* of some more recent references)

                    MOUNTAIN HAIR-GRASS

    2 Leaf blades not often more than 3 mm wide, typically folded or with the margins inrolled; ligules usually pointed

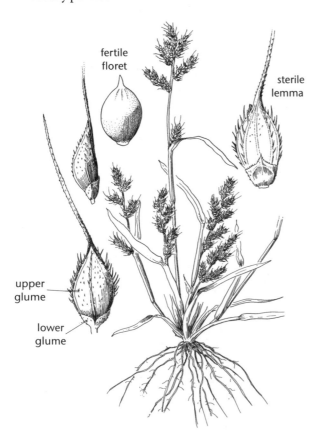

Echinochloa crus-galli,
barnyard grass

Elymus alaskanus subsp. *latiglumis,*
Alaskan wild rye

3 Inflorescence slender, less than 2 cm wide, the branches usually nearly upright and pressed to the main axis (awns of lemmas originating close to the middle; leaf blades usually 1–1.5 mm wide) . . . . ***D. elongata***
SLENDER HAIR-GRASS

3 Inflorescence either more than 8 cm wide, open, and with the branches spreading, or congested and only about 2 cm wide; leaf blades usually 1.5– 4 mm wide

4 Inflorescence more than 8 cm wide, open, the branches spreading; awns of lemmas originating close to the base (in varied habitats, including edges of coastal salt marshes) . . . . ***D. caespitosa,*** p. 445
TUFTED HAIR-GRASS

4 Inflorescence about 2–2.5 cm wide, congested, the branches angled upward; awns of lemmas originating a little below the middle (mostly in coastal marshes and on riverbanks close to the coast) . . . . ***D. holciformis*** (often treated as *D. caespitosa* subsp. *holciformis*)
CALIFORNIA HAIR-GRASS

Digitaria

1 Leaf sheaths usually with long hairs; upper glume about half to two-thirds as long as the lemma of the fertile floret; lower glume considerably longer than wide, pointed at the tip . . . . ***D. sanguinalis,*** p. 445
CRABGRASS (Europe)

1 Leaf sheaths without hairs, or at least without long hairs; upper glume nearly or fully as long as the lemma of the fertile floret; lower glume about as long as wide, blunt at the tip . . . . ***D. ischaemum***
SMOOTH CRABGRASS (Europe)

Echinochloa

1 Primary branches of the inflorescence not much more than 2 cm long and without secondary branches; lemma of the lower floret of each spikelet not drawn out into a distinct awn (widespread in S United States; only occasionally found in our region) . . . . ***E. colona***
AWNLESS BARNYARD GRASS (tropics)

1 Primary branches of the inflorescence commonly more than 2 cm long, sometimes with secondary branches; lemma of the lower floret of each spikelet typically drawn out into an awn

2 Lemma of lower floret typically with an awn at least 2 cm long; lemma of upper floret without an awn but with a somewhat membranous tip to which the hairs at the margins of the upper part of the lemma do not extend . . . . ***E. crus-galli***
BARNYARD GRASS (Eurasia)

2 Lemma of lower floret not more than 1 cm long, usually much shorter; lemma of upper floret drawn out into a short awn, the hairs at the margins of the upper part of the lemma extending to the drawn-out portion (believed to be native to W North America) . . . . ***E. muricata*** subsp. ***macrostachya***
AMERICAN BARNYARD GRASS

Elymus-Leymus-Taeniatherum **Complex**

1 All or most nodes of the inflorescence with a single spikelet (nodes with 2 spikelets are generally only on the upper part of the inflorescence)

2 Plants forming tufts, not spreading by rhizomes; anthers 1–2 mm long . . . . ***E. alaskanus*** **subsp.** ***latiglumis*** (*Agropyron caninum* var. *latiglume*)
ALASKAN WILD RYE

2 Plants spreading extensively by rhizomes; anthers 4–7 mm long . . . . ***E. repens*** (*Agropyron repens, Elytrigia repens*), p. 448
QUACK GRASS (Eurasia)

1 Most nodes of the inflorescence with at least 2 spikelets

3 Awns of lemmas at least 3 cm long, the inflorescence thus very bristly; each glume divided for much or all of its length into 2 or more bristles that resemble the awns of the lemmas (and sometimes accompanied by additional glumes of spikelets that have not developed)

4 Annual; each glume divided for its full length into 2 long bristles resembling the awns of the lemmas (thus there may appear to be 4 glumes) .... *T. caput-medusae*
MEDUSA'S HEAD (Europe)

4 Perennial; each glume divided for all or part of its length into 2 or more bristles

  5 Each glume divided for part of its length into 3 or more bristles that resemble the awns of the lemmas; auricles of leaf sheaths 0.5–1.5 mm long (in our region only in SW Oreg. but widespread E of the Cascades; also in Calif.) .... *E. multisetus* (*Sitanion jubatum*)
BIG SQUIRRELTAIL

  5 Each glume divided for all or part of its length into 2 (occasionally 3) long bristles that resemble the awns of the lemmas; auricles of leaf sheaths poorly developed ......*E. elymoides* (*Sitanion hystrix*)
SQUIRRELTAIL

> There are named subspecies of *E. elymoides,* but these vary widely and intergrade, making it difficult for anyone who is not an expert to separate them with a high degree of confidence. Furthermore, some specimens of *E. elymoides* resemble some of *E. multisetus,* but the extent to which the auricles are developed will be helpful in separating the species.

3 Awns, if present on the lemmas, sometimes conspicuous but not often so much as 2 cm long; glumes not divided into long bristles (each glume has a short awn at the tip)

  6 Plants limited to coastal sand dunes and sandy areas around bays and salt marshes, spreading vegetatively by rhizomes; leaf blades to 1.5 cm wide; lemmas 12–20 mm long, without awns .... *L. mollis* subsp. *mollis,* pl. 704
DUNE GRASS

  6 Plants not limited to coastal sand dunes and sandy areas around bays and salt marshes, but often found in coastal regions; leaves not often more than 1 cm wide; lemmas not often more than 12 mm long

    7 Inflorescence rather flexible; lemmas mostly 7–10 mm long, hairy along the margins, with awns (Alaska to NW Oreg.) .... *E. hirsutus*
BRISTLY WILD RYE

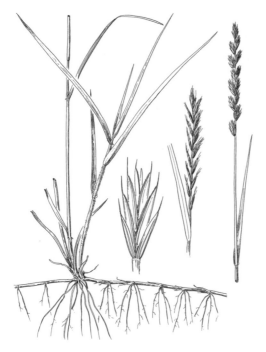

Elymus repens,
quack grass

Taeniatherum caput-medusae,
medusa's head

7 Inflorescence stiff; lemmas mostly 10–12 mm long, not hairy along the margins, with or without awns
  8 Lemmas with a sharp tip, but if an awn is present, this is not so much as 5 mm long . . . .
  . . . . *E. glaucus* subsp. *virescens*
  8 Lemmas with awns at least 1 cm long
    9 Leaf blades and sheaths hairy . . . . *E. glaucus* var. *jepsonii*
    9 Leaf blades and sheaths not hairy (but they may be rough to the touch); widespread . . . .
    . . . . *E. glaucus* subsp. *glaucus*
    BLUE WILD RYE

Eragrostis
All species of *Eragrostis* in this key except *E. curvula* are annuals.

1 Small craterlike glands present in at least one of the following places: along the keels of the lemmas, on the stems below the nodes, on the branches of the inflorescence, along the margins of the leaves (in *E. minor* the pedicels are sometimes encircled by glandular rings)
  2 Spikelets to 2 cm long, with at least 10 florets, sometimes more than 30; lemmas 2–2.8 mm long, typically with craterlike glands along the keels; anthers usually yellow . . . . *E. cilianensis*, p. 450
  STINK GRASS (Eurasia)
  2 Spikelets rarely so much as 1 cm long and rarely with more than 15 florets; lemmas rarely with craterlike glands (but there may be glands elsewhere, and the pedicels of the spikelets are sometimes encircled by glandular rings; known to occur in SW Brit. Col.; also E of the Cascades, Brit. Col. to Oreg.) . . . .
  . . . . *E. minor*
  LITTLE LOVEGRASS (Europe)
1 Craterlike glands not present
  3 Stems typically touching down and taking root, the plants thus forming mats (mostly in moist habitats, including borders of lakes and rivers) . . . . *E. hypnoides*
  CREEPING LOVEGRASS
  3 Stems not touching down and rooting

Elymus hirsutus,
bristly wild rye

Elymus glaucus subsp. *glaucus*,
blue wild rye

4 Plants perennial, forming dense clumps; leaf blades tapering to very slender, curving tips (introduced mainly for erosion control) . . . . *E. curvula*
WEEPING LOVEGRASS (S Africa)

4 Plants annual, not forming especially dense clumps; leaf blades not tapering to very slender, curving tips

  5 Spikelets tending to be kept close to the branches of the inflorescence; grains without a lengthwise groove on one side (S Canada to Argentina) . . . .*E. pectinacea* subsp. *pectinacea*
TUFTED LOVEGRASS

  5 Spikelets diverging, not tending to be kept close to the branches of the inflorescence; grains with a distinct lengthwise groove on one side (widespread in W North America and Central and South America) . . . .*E. mexicana* subsp. *virescens*
MEXICAN LOVEGRASS

Festuca-Vulpia Complex

1 Small annuals, usually withered by midsummer

  2 Lower glume not more than 2.5 mm long, less than half as long as the upper glume . . . . *V. myuros*
FOXTAIL FESCUE, RATTAIL FESCUE (Europe)

  2 Lower glume usually at least 3 mm long and at least half as long as the upper glume

    3 Awns of lemmas usually shorter than the lemmas; spikelets usually with 7–12 florets . . . .
. . . . *V. octoflora* subsp. *octoflora*
EIGHT-FLOWERED FESCUE

    3 Awns of lemmas at least as long as the lemmas; spikelets usually with fewer than 7 florets

      4 All branches of the inflorescence upright; leaf sheaths not hairy; lemmas roughened but not hairy
. . . . *V. bromoides*
SIX-WEEKS FESCUE (Europe)

      4 Lower branches of the inflorescence drooping; leaf sheaths sometimes hairy; lemmas sometimes hairy but not roughened . . . . *V. microstachys*
SMALL FESCUE

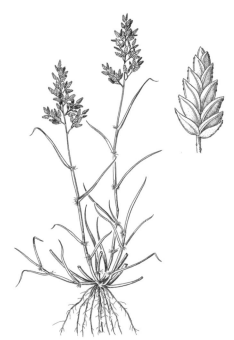

Eragrostis cilianensis,
stink grass

Vulpia myuros,
foxtail fescue

1 Perennials, usually forming substantial clumps, and with persistent leaves
    5 Leaf sheaths with prominent slender auricles (the 2 species under this choice are probably most logically placed in *Lolium,* and in this book they are keyed under that genus as well as here)
        6 Auricles with hairy margins; awns of lemmas usually 0.5–1.5 mm long ....
....***Lolium arundinaceum*** (*F. arundinacea*), p. 455
TALL FESCUE (Europe)
        6 Auricles without hairy margins; awns of lemmas barely evident or absent ....
....***Lolium pratense*** (*F. pratense*), p. 455
MEADOW FESCUE, PERENNIAL RYEGRASS (Europe)
    5 Leaf sheaths without prominent auricles
        7 Either the ligules or the collars of the leaf sheaths (sometimes both) with long, soft hairs
            8 Awns, when present on the lemmas, less than 5 mm long ....***F. californica***
CALIFORNIA FESCUE
            8 Awns of the lemmas usually at least 10 mm long ....***F. subuliflora***
CRINKLE-AWN FESCUE
        7 Neither the ligules nor the collars of the leaf sheaths with long, soft hairs
            9 Leaf blades flat and flexible, usually at least 4 mm wide, sometimes as wide as 10 mm; ligules typically at least as high in the center as at the sides ....***F. subulata***
BEARDED FESCUE
            9 Leaf blades usually conspicuously folded or inrolled, but even if flat (as often the case in *F. viridula*) rarely so much as 4 mm wide when flattened; ligules typically at least slightly higher on the sides than in the center
                10 Awns nearly or fully as long as the lemmas (sometimes longer) ....***F. occidentalis***
WESTERN FESCUE
                10 Awns shorter than the lemmas
                    11 Plants spreading to a considerable extent by rhizomes; leaves green (leaf sheaths typically reddish, with hairs directed downward, and commonly splitting apart into fibers)
                        12 Awns of lemmas about half as long as the lemmas; plants commonly more than 60 cm tall (widespread, and the prevailing subspecies in inland habitats but sometimes coastal) ....
....***F. rubra*** subsp. ***rubra***
RED FESCUE
                        12 Awns of lemmas about one-third as long as the lemmas; plants rarely more than 60 cm tall (on backshores of sandy beaches and in sandy habitats around bays and salt marshes) ......
....***F. rubra*** subsp. *littoralis*
BEACH FESCUE

Because of intergradation, native specimens cannot always, on the basis of just a few characters, be confidently assigned to either *F. rubra* subsp. *rubra* or subsp. *littoralis*. Furthermore, Chewings' fescue (*F. rubra* subsp. *commutata*) and imported cultivars of various other subspecies and varieties are widely used as lawn and pasture grasses. These sometimes become naturalized, at least temporarily, and may hybridize with native plants.

                  11 Plants forming dense clumps, not spreading by rhizomes; leaves gray-green (characteristic of prairie habitats and rocky or gravelly slopes)
                    13 Awns less than one-fourth as long as the lemmas and sometimes lacking; leaf blades flat or only loosely folded (montane and high montane, sometimes in rockslides) ....***F. viridula***
MOUNTAIN BUNCHGRASS
                    13 Awns usually at least one-fourth as long as the lemmas; leaf blades rather tightly folded or inrolled
                        14 Awns about half as long as the lemmas and noticeably bristly ....***F. trachyphylla***
HARD FESCUE (Europe)
                        14 Awns not half as long as the lemmas and not noticeably bristly

15 Spikelets usually with 4–5 florets; awns of lemmas usually less than 2.5 mm long; flowering plants generally less than 40 cm tall (mostly montane and high montane) ....
.... ***F. saximontana*** (*F. ovina* vars. *purpusiana, rydbergii,* and *saximontana*)
ROCKY MOUNTAIN FESCUE

15 Spikelets usually with 5–7 florets; awns of lemmas usually at least 2.5 mm long, sometimes as long as 6 mm; plants often more than 50 cm tall

  16 Inflorescences 7–11 cm long; leaves, when sliced crosswise into thin sections near the middle of their length and examined at a magnification of at least 50×, folded in such a way that they are nearly as wide as deep, and the hairs along the ridges facing the cavity are conspicuous (mostly E of the crest of the Cascades) ....***F. idahoensis*** subsp. ***idahoensis***
IDAHO FESCUE

  16 Inflorescences 9.5–16 cm long; leaves, when sliced crosswise into thin sections near the middle of their length and examined at a magnification of at least 50×, folded in such a way that they are only about two-thirds as wide as deep, and the hairs along the ridges facing the cavity are very short and inconspicuous (W of the Cascades, including SE Vancouver Island, Brit. Col.) ....
....***F. idahoensis*** subsp. ***roemeri***
ROEMER'S FESCUE

    In some references, *F. idahoensis* subspp. *idahoensis* and *roemeri* are given the rank of species.

Glyceria

1 Spikelets not more than about 7 mm long
  2 Leaf sheaths smooth when rubbed upward or downward ....*G. grandis*
AMERICAN MANNA GRASS

  2 Leaf sheaths usually perceptibly rough to the touch when rubbed upward or downward
    3 Spikelets usually with at least 7–9 florets (sometimes more than 9 in *G. canadensis*)
      4 Ribs of lemmas only slightly raised, not conspicuous; paleas commonly partly exposed, without a notch at the tip ....*G. canadensis*
RATTLESNAKE GRASS (E North America)

      4 Ribs of lemmas prominently raised; paleas usually hidden by the lemmas and with a notch at the tip ....*G. maxima*
GIANT MANNA GRASS (Eurasia)

    3 Spikelets typically with 5–7 florets
      5 Ligules typically deeply open in front, those of the lower leaves 3–6 mm long; lemmas sometimes more than 2 mm long ....*G. elata*
TALL MANNA GRASS

    Glyceria elata and *G. striata* are so similar that some references treat *G. elata* as a synonym of *G. striata*.

Festuca idahoensis subspp. *idahoensis,* Idaho fescue, left (scale bar, 0.5 mm), and *roemeri,* Roemer's fescue, right (scale bar, 0.7 mm); cross sections of leaf blades

5 Ligules typically not open in front or with only a slight cleft, those of the lower leaves usually 1–3 mm long; lemmas not more than 2 mm long . . . . *G. striata*

FOWL MANNA GRASS

1 Spikelets more than 10 mm long

6 Spikelets usually more than 20 mm long (and with at least 10 florets); grains about 3 mm long . . . . *G. fluitans*

FLOAT GRASS (E North America, also Eurasia)

6 Spikelets not so much as 20 mm long; grains not more than 2 mm long

7 Tips of paleas divided into 2 slender, sharp teeth (still mostly restricted to Brit. Col.) . . . . *G. declinata*

WAXY MANNA GRASS (Europe)

7 Tips of paleas not divided into 2 slender, sharp teeth

8 Ribs of lemmas slightly roughened by short, stiff hairs, but the spaces between the ribs not roughened . . . . *G. borealis*

NORTHERN MANNA GRASS

8 Ribs of lemmas conspicuously roughened by short, stiff hairs, and the spaces between the ribs similarly roughened

9 Membranous tips of lemmas typically rounded . . . . *G. leptostachya*

SOFT MANNA GRASS

9 Membranous tips of lemmas typically toothed, the teeth in line with the veins . . . . *G. occidentalis*

WESTERN MANNA GRASS

Hierochloe

1 Lemmas with blunt, sometimes notched tips; most leaf blades at least 5 mm wide . . . . *H. occidentalis*

WESTERN VANILLA GRASS, SWEET GRASS

1 Lemmas with pointed tips; leaf blades not often more than 5 mm wide . . . . *H. hirta* var. *arctica* (*H. odorata* of some references)

COMMON SWEET GRASS

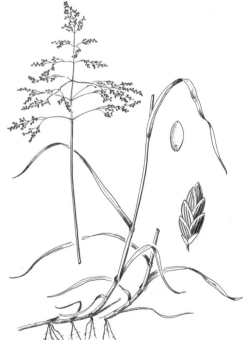

Glyceria elata,
tall manna grass

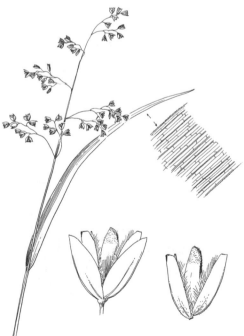

Hierochloe occidentalis,
western vanilla grass

Hordeum

1 Most leaves with well-developed auricles, these usually at least 1.5 mm long

    2 Leaf blades usually at least 5 mm wide, sometimes as wide as 15 mm; awns of lemmas usually more than 8 cm long . . . . *H. vulgare*

        BARLEY (Europe)

    2 Leaf blades not often more than 5 mm wide; awns of lemmas to 5 cm long

        3 Fertile spikelet with a stalk nearly as long as the stalks of the sterile spikelets . . . . *H. murinum* subsp. *leporinum*, pl. 703

            HARE BARLEY (Europe)

        3 Fertile spikelet with a perceptible stalk but this much shorter than the stalks of the sterile spikelets . . . . *H. murinum* subsp. *murinum* (Europe)

1 Leaves either without auricles or with auricles less than 1 mm long

    4 Glumes at least 2.5 cm long, sometimes more than 6 cm . . . . *H. jubatum*

        FOXTAIL BARLEY

    4 Glumes not so much as 2 cm long

        5 Perennial, usually at least 40 cm tall; leaf blades usually at least 4 mm wide . . . . . . *H. brachyantherum*

            MEADOW BARLEY

        5 Annual, rarely so much as 40 cm tall; leaf blades rarely more than 4 mm wide

            6 Awns of lemmas of fertile spikelets not more than 12 mm long . . . . *H. depressum*

               LOW BARLEY

            6 Awns of lemmas of fertile spikelets usually at least 2 cm long (sometimes much longer) . . . . *H. marinum* subsp. *gussoneanum* (*H. geniculatum*)

          MEDITERRANEAN BARLEY (Europe)

Hordeum marinum subsp. *gussoneanum*,
Mediterranean barley

Leptochloa fusca subsp. *fascicularis*,
sprangletop

Leptochloa

1 Blades of upper leaves reaching beyond the inflorescences; inflorescences usually partly enclosed within the leaf sheaths; lemmas 4–5 times as long as wide, with long awns (occasional weed) . . . . ***L. fusca* subsp. *fascicularis* (*L. fascicularis*)**
SPRANGLETOP (E United States)

1 Blades of upper leaves not reaching beyond the inflorescences; inflorescences usually free of the leaf sheaths; lemmas about 3 times as long as wide, without awns (they may, however, have a short point at the tip) . . . . ***L. fusca* subsp. *uninervia* (*L. uninervia*)**
MEXICAN SPRANGLETOP (S United States to Argentina)

Lolium

The first two species in this key have only relatively recently been transferred to *Lolium* from *Festuca*. Because some will expect to find them in *Festuca*, they are keyed under that genus as well as here.

1 Spikelets situated on branches of the inflorescence, and with 2 glumes; leaf sheaths with prominent auricles

    2 Auricles of the leaf sheaths with hairs along their margins; at least some branches of the upper half of an inflorescence bearing more than 1 spikelet . . . . ***L. arundinaceum* (*Festuca arundinacea*)**
TALL FESCUE (Europe)

    2 Auricles of the leaf sheaths without hairs along their margins; branches of the upper half of an inflorescence rarely bearing more than 1 spikelet . . . . ***L. pratense* (*Festuca pratensis*)**
MEADOW FESCUE (Europe)

1 Spikelets sessile on the inflorescence, most or all with 1 glume, corresponding to the upper one of other grasses (the uppermost spikelet of the inflorescence, and sometimes a few below it, may have a lower glume as well as an upper glume); leaf sheaths without auricles

Lolium arundinaceum,
tall fescue

Lolium pratense,
meadow fescue

3 Glumes at least as long as the spikelets; annual . . . . *L. temulentum*
DARNEL (Mediterranean region)

3 Glumes shorter than the spikelets; perennial

    4 Lemmas without awns or only with short awns; leaf blades rarely so much as 4 mm wide . . . *L. perenne*
PERENNIAL RYEGRASS (Europe)

    4 Most lemmas, especially the upper ones of the spikelet, with awns that may be longer than the lemmas themselves; leaf blades at least 4 mm wide, sometimes more than 10 mm . . . . *L. multiflorum*
ITALIAN RYEGRASS (Europe)

Melica

1 Lemmas with awns (these originating between 2 lobes at the tip); stems without bulblike thickenings at the base

    2 Awns of lemmas rarely more than 4 mm long . . . . *M. harfordii*
HARFORD'S MELICA

    2 Awns of lemmas usually 4–7 mm long, sometimes as long as 10 mm . . . . *M. smithii*
SMITH'S MELICA

1 Lemmas without awns (but they are pointed at the tip); stems with bulblike thickenings at the base

    3 Lemmas conspicuously hairy, especially near the base . . . . *M. subulata*
ONIONGRASS

    3 Lemmas not obviously hairy (but they may be roughened by very short, stiff hairs) . . . . *M. geyeri*
GEYER'S ONIONGRASS

Muhlenbergia

1 Bases of the lemmas not conspicuously long-hairy; individual florets not more than 3 mm long, the lemmas and glumes without prominent awns; leaf blades not so much as 2 mm wide

    2 Inflorescences widely open, many of the primary branches more than 2 cm long, the spikelets widely separated on secondary branches . . . . *M. uniflora*
SCATTERED-FLOWER MUHLENBERGIA (E North America)

Lolium temulentum,
darnel

Melica subulata,
oniongrass

    2 Inflorescences not widely open, the primary branches not more than 1 cm long, the spikelets close together

        3 Plants perennial, with rhizomes from which upright stems originate; stems usually at least 1 mm thick, roughened by small bumps, not often branching; inflorescences to about 15 cm long, 15 mm thick (mostly E of the Cascades) . . . . ***M. richardsonis***

                    RICHARDSON'S MUHLENBERGIA

        3 Plants typically annual (occasionally perennial), without rhizomes, but the stems sometimes touching down and rooting at the nodes; stems not more than 1 mm thick, not roughened by small bumps, sometimes branching; inflorescences to about 6 cm long, less than 5 mm thick (mostly E of the crest of the Cascades but also in the mountains of SW Oreg., to Calif.; montane, especially around springs, and not likely to be found below about 4000 ft., 1220 m) . . . . ***M. filiformis***

                    THREAD-STEM MUHLENBERGIA

1 Bases of the lemmas conspicuously long-hairy; individual florets usually more than 3 mm long, sometimes more than 10 mm, due to the presence of long awns on the lemmas or glumes (caution: not all lemmas or glumes may have well-developed awns; look at more than a single inflorescence or, better still, at more than a single plant); leaf blades usually at least 2 mm wide

    4 Hairs on the bases of the lemmas as long as, or longer than, the lemmas (excluding the sometimes very long awns; inflorescence very crowded, most of the successive branches touching; in wet habitats; widespread in W North America but in our region reported only from SW Oreg.) . . . . ***M. andina***

                    FOXTAIL MUHLENBERGIA

    4 Hairs on the bases of the lemmas much shorter than the lemmas

        5 Glumes, partly because of their long awns (more than 2 mm), considerably longer than the lemmas, even when these have distinct awns (in wet habitats; widespread in North America but known from only a few localities in our region) . . . . ***M. glomerata***

                    SPIKE MUHLENBERGIA

        5 Glumes, even when distinctly awned, not obviously longer than the lemmas

            6 Upper and lower glumes of nearly equal length (rare in our region but otherwise widespread in North America; in spite of the species name, not found in Mexico) . . . . ***M. mexicana***, p. 458

                    BROADLEAF MUHLENBERGIA

            6 Upper and lower glumes, including their awns, decidedly unequal (the lower one only about two-thirds as long as the upper one; rarely encountered in our region but widespread in E North America) . . . . ***M. frondosa***

                    WIRE-STEM MUHLENBERGIA

Panicum-Dichanthelium Complex

1 Glumes and the lemma of the sterile lower floret distinctly hairy (the hairs are short, however); perennial

    2 Most spikelets about 3 mm long . . . . ***D. oligosanthes*** subsp. ***scribnerianum***

                    SCRIBNER'S WITCHGRASS

    2 Spikelets rarely more than 2 mm long (most common in wet habitats) . . . . ***D. acuminatum*** subsp. ***fasciculatum***

                    WESTERN WITCHGRASS

1 Glumes and the lemma of the sterile lower floret not hairy; annual

    3 Spikelets nearly sessile, the pedicels only about 1 mm long (widespread in E North America but in our region known only in W Oreg., where probably introduced) . . . . ***P. rigidulum*** subsp. ***rigidulum***

                    REDTOP PANICUM

    3 Spikelets on pedicels at least 2 mm long

        4 Most spikelets 4–5 mm long . . . . ***P. miliaceum***, p. 458

                    BROOMCORN MILLET (Europe)

        4 Most spikelets 2.5–3 mm long

5 Lower glume about half as long as the spikelet; leaf sheaths conspicuously hairy . . . .
. . . . *P. capillare* **subsp.** *capillare*
COMMON WITCHGRASS

5 Lower glume not more than about one-fourth the length of the spikelet; leaf sheaths not obviously
hairy . . . . *P. dichotomiflorum* **subsp.** *dichotomiflorum*
SPREADING WITCHGRASS (central and E North America)

Phalaris

1 Inflorescence accompanied and partly enclosed by a broad, boat-shaped bract; each fertile spikelet surrounded by several smaller sterile spikelets, these usually somewhat club- or spatula-shaped and falling
with the fertile spikelet (annual) . . . . *P. paradoxa*
PARADOX CANARY GRASS (S Europe)

1 Inflorescence not partly enclosed by a broad, boat-shaped bract; fertile spikelets not surrounded by smaller
sterile spikelets

  2 Plants perennial (most specimens will have remnants of leaves of the preceding year's growth); spreading by rhizomes, thus forming dense stands, especially in wet habitats

    3 Inflorescence conspicuously branched; leaf blades usually 7–17 mm wide; most spikelets with
2 sterile lemmas; glumes usually 4.5–5 mm long . . . . *P. arundinacea*
REED CANARY GRASS

    3 Inflorescence cylindrical, the spikelets so crowded that branches are not readily apparent; leaf blades
usually 3–8 mm wide; most spikelets with only 1 sterile lemma; glumes usually about 6 mm long . . . .
. . . . *P. aquatica*
HARDING GRASS (S Europe)

  2 Plants annual; not spreading by rhizomes (inflorescence very compact, about 2 to several times as long
as wide)

    4 Larger inflorescences about twice as long as wide; glumes 7–10 mm long (when fresh, with a conspic-
uous green streak along the midline) . . . . *P. canariensis*
CANARY GRASS (S Europe)

Muhlenbergia mexicana,
broadleaf muhlenbergia

Panicum miliaceum,
broomcorn millet

4 Larger inflorescences usually at least 3 times as long as wide; glumes 4–6 mm long

  5 Larger inflorescences generally at least 5 cm long, sometimes as long as 10 cm, typically about 5 times as long as wide (Curry Co., Oreg., to Calif.) . . . . **P. angusta**
                                                    NARROW-HEAD CANARY GRASS

  5 Larger inflorescences to 5 cm long, typically about 3 times as long as wide

    6 Each spikelet with 2 sterile florets below the fertile floret; fertile lemmas usually 3.5–4 mm long

    . . . . **P. caroliniana**
                                         CAROLINA CANARY GRASS (E United States)

    6 Each spikelet with only 1 sterile floret below the fertile floret; fertile lemmas usually about 3 mm long . . . . **P. minor**
                        MEDITERRANEAN CANARY GRASS (Mediterranean region)

Poa

1 All or most spikelets specialized as small, purplish bulblets that serve to reproduce the plant vegetatively (the bulblets have neither stamens nor a pistil) . . . . **P. bulbosa** subsp. **vivipara**, pl. 705
                                  BULBOUS BLUEGRASS (Europe)

                          Poa pratensis and *P. laxiflora*, choice 16, are also known to produce bulblets but do this only rarely.

1 Spikelets not specialized as small, purplish bulblets

  2 Plants annual (if a large specimen has no remnants of old stems and leaves of the previous year's growth, the grass is probably an annual)

    3 Upper glume tapering gradually from the base, therefore not obviously widest near the middle; in moist habitats in prairies and open woods . . . . **P. howellii**
                                         HOWELL'S BLUEGRASS

    3 Upper glume decidedly widest near the middle

      4 Anthers 0.5–1 mm long, distinctly longer than wide before cracking open (very common weed) . . .
      . . . . **P. annua**
                             ANNUAL BLUEGRASS (Europe)

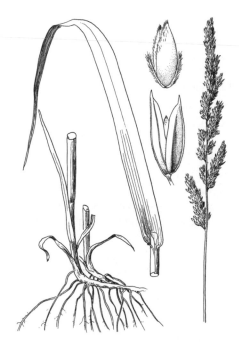

Phalaris arundinacea,
reed canary grass

Poa annua,
annual bluegrass

4 Anthers not more than 0.5 mm long, nearly round before cracking open (rarely encountered weed in our region) . . . . *P. infirma*
WEAK BLUEGRASS (Mediterranean region)

2 Plants perennial (large specimens usually with remnants of stems and leaves of the previous year's growth)

  5 All florets on a particular plant functionally either with a pistil or stamens, not both (if some plants have both, and others in the same population have only a pistil, take the other choice 5)

    6 All plants (in our region) functionally pistillate, producing seed without benefit of pollination (some florets may have stamens, but these are abnormally small and soon wither; in inland habitats, mostly montane and high montane)

      7 Inflorescences generally rather loose, with 2–5 spreading and often nodding branches at each node; glumes essentially equal; lemmas usually sharp-tipped . . . . *P. wheeleri*
WHEELER'S BLUEGRASS

      7 Inflorescences generally compact, with only 1–2 nearly upright branches at each node; glumes decidedly unequal; lemmas pointed but not sharp-tipped

        8 Inflorescences generally with more than 20 spikelets; lemmas not hairy (but they may be slightly roughened) . . . . *P. cusickii* subsp. *epilis*
HAIRLESS CUSICK'S BLUEGRASS

        8 Inflorescences generally with fewer than 20 spikelets; lemmas (at least of lower florets of some spikelets) decidedly hairy at the base and along the keel . . . . *P. cusickii* subsp. *purpurascens*
HAIRY CUSICK'S BLUEGRASS

    6 Plants typically either pistillate or staminate, but both types usually present in the same population (in *P. macrantha* some pistillate florets may have reduced stamens)

      9 Plants of high-montane habitats, usually less than 20 cm tall when flowering; lemmas without hairs (SW Oreg. to Calif.) . . . . *P. pringlei*
PRINGLE'S BLUEGRASS

      9 Plants of montane habitats or backshores of sandy beaches at the coast, generally more than 20 cm tall; lemmas usually with a tuft of hairs at the base (but not always in *P. chambersii*)

        10 Plants of montane habitats in the Cascades and Calapooya Mountains, Lane Co., Oreg.; leaf blades 2–5 mm wide (lemmas with 5–7 ribs, the lower portion of the keel and other ribs sometimes hairy) . . . . *P. chambersii*
CHAMBERS' BLUEGRASS

        10 Plants restricted to backshores of sandy beaches; leaf blades to about 3 mm wide

          11 Lemmas less than 4.5 mm long, weakly 5-ribbed, the keel roughened but not hairy; upper glume not more than 4 mm long; plants usually less than 30 cm tall . . . . *P. confinis*, pl. 706
BEACH BLUEGRASS

          11 Lemmas much longer than 4.5 mm, conspicuously 7- to 11-ribbed, the lower portions of the keel and other ribs hairy; upper glume usually 7–8 mm long; plants often more than 30 cm tall . . . . *P. macrantha*
LARGE-FLOWERED BEACH BLUEGRASS

  5 All florets on a particular plant normally with stamens and a pistil (except *P. suksdorfii*, second choice 21, in which the florets of some plants are strictly pistillate)

    12 Stems conspicuously flattened, thus 2-edged . . . . *P. compressa*
CANADIAN BLUEGRASS (Europe)

    12 Stems nearly or quite cylindrical, not at all 2-edged

      13 Lemmas with a tuft of long hairs at the base (these hairs, often somewhat cobwebby, are much longer than any that may be on the backs or edges of the lemmas)

        14 Lemmas usually at least 3 mm long (lemmas hairy close to the edges)

          15 Lemmas 4.5–5 mm long; spikelets usually with only 2 florets (Brit. Col. to NW Oreg.) . . . . *P. marcida*
WEAK BLUEGRASS

15 Lemmas usually 3.5–4 mm long

    16 Spikelets usually with 3–5 florets (widely cultivated in lawns and pastures) . . . .
. . . . *P. pratensis* subsp. *pratensis*

BLUEGRASS, KENTUCKY BLUEGRASS (Eurasia)

    16 Spikelets usually with 2–4 florets . . . . *P. laxiflora*

See note about P. pratensis and P. laxiflora under P. bulbosa subsp. vivipara, first choice 1.

14 Lemmas not often more than 3 mm long

  17 Ligules usually at least 3 mm long, tapering to an acute tip

    18 Ligules usually 3–7 mm long; lemmas not hairy close to the edges . . . . *P. trivialis*

ROUGH BLUEGRASS (Europe)

    18 Ligules usually 3–5 mm long; lemmas hairy close to the edges . . . . *P. palustris*

FOWL BLUEGRASS (Europe)

  17 Ligules (at least of lower leaves on the flowering stems) not more than 1 mm long, nearly squared-off at the tip

    19 Flowering stems, when fully developed, with as many as 5 nodes, the uppermost one generally located well above the middle; upper glume to 3.5 mm long; lower glume rather broad, not awl-like . . . . *P. nemoralis*

WOODS BLUEGRASS (Europe)

    19 Flowering stems, when fully developed, usually with not more than 3 nodes, the uppermost one generally at or below the middle; upper glume rarely more than 3 mm long; lower glume slender, awl-like (mostly montane; native) . . . . *P. interior*, p. 462

INTERIOR BLUEGRASS

Some authorities consider P. nemoralis and P. interior to be subspecies of P. nemoralis.
It is true that the distinctions given here are variable and intergrading, but the 2 grasses
appear not to mingle.

13 Lemmas without a tuft of long hairs at the base (but there may be short hairs on the lower halves of the backs of the lemmas)

  20 Backs of lemmas without hairs (if the plant has stamens and a pistil and the anthers are 1.5–3 mm long, and if it is obviously taller than *P. suksdorfii*, consider the possibility that it is *P. secunda* subsp. *juncifolia*, first choice 24, whose lemma ribs are sometimes hairless)

    21 All florets on a particular plant typically with a pistil and stamens; plants rarely more than 10 cm tall; anthers only about 0.5 mm long (high montane) . . . . *P. lettermanii*

LETTERMAN'S BLUEGRASS

    21 All florets on a particular plant either with a pistil and stamens or with only a pistil (as a rule, both types of plants occur together); plants to about 20 cm tall but often much shorter; anthers at least 1 mm long (high montane, Wash.) . . . . *P. suksdorfii*

SUKSDORF'S BLUEGRASS

  20 Backs of lemmas typically with short hairs on their lower halves (the hairs may, however, be limited to the ribs)

    22 Inflorescence compact, 2–6 cm long, the main branches scarcely longer than the spikelets; spikelets oval in outline, distinctly flattened; plants not often so much as 30 cm tall (coastal bluffs, S Wash. to Calif.) . . . . *P. unilateralis* (*P. pachypholis*)

OCEAN-BLUFF BLUEGRASS

    22 Inflorescence compact or loosely branched, to about 10 cm long; spikelets usually at least twice as long as wide, not distinctly flattened; plants usually more than 30 cm tall, sometimes more than 80 cm (mostly in inland, often montane habitats)

      23 Lower halves of lemmas obviously hairy on the ribs and sometimes between the ribs (ligules usually more than 2 mm long, sometimes as long as 3.5 mm) . . . .
. . . . *P. secunda* subsp. *secunda* (*P. gracillima*, *P. sandbergii*)

ONE-SIDED BLUEGRASS

      23 Lower halves of lemmas hairy only on the ribs

24 Keels of lemmas becoming much less prominent in the lower half, sometimes scarcely recognizable; leaf blades rarely more than 1.5 mm wide; ligules not more than 2 mm long . . . . *P. secunda* subsp. *juncifolia*
NEVADA BLUEGRASS

24 Keels of lemmas prominent for their entire length; leaf blades 1.5–4 mm wide; ligules typically 2–3.5 mm long . . . . *P. stenantha* subsp. *stenantha*
NARROW-FLOWERED BLUEGRASS

Puccinellia-Torreyochloa Complex

1 Blades of larger leaves commonly at least 5 mm wide, sometimes more than 10 mm; ligules at least 3 mm long, sometimes more than 7 mm; in wet freshwater habitats but not in coastal salt marshes . . . . *T. pallida* subsp. *pauciflora*
FEW-FLOWERED ALKALI GRASS

1 Blades of larger leaves rarely more than 4 mm wide; ligules rarely more than 3 mm long; usually in coastal salt marshes or inland saline or alkaline habitats

  2 Anthers about 2 mm long (lemmas 3–5 mm long; branches of inflorescence usually smooth; rarely encountered in our region and only where introduced) . . . . *P. maritima*
GOOSE GRASS (E North America, Europe)

  2 Anthers decidedly less than 2 mm long

    3 Branches of inflorescence smooth

      4 Margins of the lemmas, near the tips, usually slightly roughened; ligules usually more than 2 mm long; plants commonly at least 30 cm tall, sometimes more than 50 cm . . . . *P. nutkaensis*
NOOTKA ALKALI GRASS

      4 Margins of the lemmas, near the tips, smooth; ligules 1–2 mm long; plants not often more than 25 cm tall . . . . *P. pumila*
SALT-MARSH ALKALI GRASS

    3 Branches of inflorescence roughened

Poa interior,
interior bluegrass

Poa stenantha subsp. *stenantha,*
narrow-flowered bluegrass

5 Lemmas rarely so much as 2 mm long; lower branches of the inflorescence usually drooping (rarely encountered in our region) . . . . *P. distans*
EURASIAN ALKALI GRASS (Eurasia)

5 Lemmas usually more than 2 mm long; lower branches of inflorescence usually not drooping
 6 Upper glume usually 3–3.5 mm long; lemmas usually 3.5–4.2 mm long . . . . *P. lucida*
  TIDELAND ALKALI GRASS

 6 Upper glume less than 3 mm long; lemmas rarely more than 3.2 mm long . . . . *P. nuttalliana*
  NUTTALL'S ALKALI GRASS

Setaria

1 Long bristles beneath each spikelet with barbs pointing toward the bases of the bristles . . . . *S. verticillata*
 FOXTAIL MILLET (Europe)

1 Long bristles beneath each spikelet with barbs pointing toward the tips of the bristles
 2 Each spikelet with at least 4 bristles, sometimes as many as 12, beneath it . . . .
  . . . . *S. pumila* subsp. *pumila* (*S. lutescens, S. glauca,* both misapplied), p. 464
  YELLOW FOXTAIL (Europe)

 2 Each spikelet with not more than 3 bristles beneath it (occasionally 4, rarely 5–6 in *S. faberi*)
  3 Upper surface of leaf blades soft-hairy . . . . *S. faberi*
   FABER'S FOXTAIL, CHINESE FOXTAIL (Eurasia)

  3 Upper surface of leaf blades smooth or slightly rough to the touch, not soft-hairy
   4 Spikelets 1.8–2.2 mm long; lemma and palea of the upper (fertile) floret of a spikelet becoming tightly enclosed by the lemma of the lower floret and the upper glume, and usually falling with them . . . . *S. viridis* var. *viridis*
    GREEN FOXTAIL (Europe)

   4 Spikelets 2.5–3 mm long; lemma and palea of the upper (fertile) floret becoming only loosely enclosed by the lemma of the lower floret and upper glume, usually falling separately . . . . . . *S. italica*
    ITALIAN FOXTAIL MILLET (Eurasia)

Torreyochloa pallida
subsp. *pauciflora,*
few-flowered alkali grass

Puccinellia lucida,
tideland alkali grass

Spartina

1 Margins of leaf blades very rough to the touch

   2 Rhizomes, when present, to 10 mm thick but short, the flowering stems therefore crowded; upper glumes with a single vein at the midrib (mostly in coastal salt marshes) . . . .*S. densiflora*
                              DENSE-FLOWERED CORDGRASS (South America)

   2 Rhizomes not often more than 5 mm thick, spreading widely, the flowering stems scattered along them; upper glumes with 2 veins on one side of the midrib (mostly in and around coastal salt marshes)
   . . . . *S. patens*
                  SALT-MEADOW CORDGRASS (Atlantic North and Central America)

1 Margins of leaf blades at most only slightly rough to the touch

   3 Inflorescences commonly with more than 12 branches, sometimes as many as 25; glumes typically without hairs along the margins or on the outer surface (in coastal salt marshes) . . . .*S. alterniflora*
                       SALT-WATER CORDGRASS (E North America)

   3 Inflorescence rarely with more than 12 branches; glumes typically with hairs along the margins and on the outer surface

      4 Ligules, including the hairs above the membranous base, 2–3 mm long; anthers of stamens normal, splitting open and releasing pollen at maturity (in coastal salt marshes) . . . .*S. anglica*
                       ENGLISH CORDGRASS (Europe)

      4 Ligules, including the hairs above the membranous base, 1–1.8 mm long; stamens abnormal, not plump, and not splitting open at maturity (in coastal salt marshes; introduced) . . . . . .*S. ×townsendii*
        (a sterile hybrid, *S. alterniflora*, first choice 3, from E North America, × *S. maritima*, from Europe)
                       TOWNSEND'S CORDGRASS

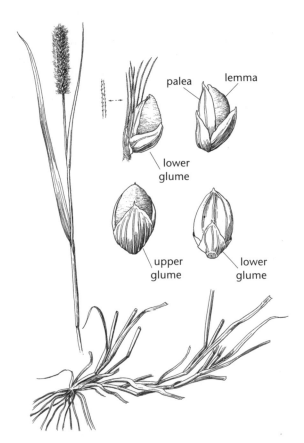

Setaria pumila subsp. *pumila*,
yellow foxtail

Spartina alterniflora,
salt-water cordgrass

Thinopyrum

1 Margins of leaf blades inrolled but not noticeably thickened or hardened, the upper surface roughened and conspicuously hairy; plants forming tufts, not spreading by rhizomes .... *T. ponticum* (*Elymus elongatus* var. *ponticus*)
TALL WHEATGRASS (Eurasia)

1 Margins of leaf blades not inrolled but noticeably thickened and hardened, the upper surface usually hairy but not roughened; plants spreading by rhizomes .... *T. intermedium* (*Agropyron intermedium*, *Elytrigia intermedia*)
INTERMEDIATE WHEATGRASS (Eurasia)

Trisetum

1 Inflorescences dense, the separate branches not readily distinguished (mostly montane and high montane) .... *T. spicatum*
SPIKE TRISETUM

1 Inflorescences not especially dense, the separate branches easily distinguished
    2 Inflorescences very open, many of the branches drooping; lower glume usually 3–4 mm long, upper glume usually 5–6 mm long .... *T. cernuum*
DROOPING TRISETUM
    2 Inflorescences compact, the branches mostly angled upward; lower glume rarely more than 2 mm long, the upper glume rarely more than 4 mm long .... *T. canescens*
TALL TRISETUM

Trisetum canescens,
tall trisetum

PONTEDERIACEAE Pickerelweed Family

Heteranthera dubia (*Zosterella dubia*), called water star grass, is the only representative of the Pontederiaceae in our region. It is a weak-stemmed plant that grows in shallow water of ponds, ditches, and sluggish streams. The leaves, 7–15 cm long but not more than 5 mm wide, are nearly translucent and do not have a distinct midrib, but they do have a pair of prominent stipules at their bases. The flowers, originating singly in the axils of rolled-up bracts, open at the surface of the water. The perianth, consisting of a slender tube and six lobes about 5 mm long, is pale yellow. There are three stamens and a pistil that becomes a many-seeded fruit. You can take your pick of genus name for this plant; at the moment, neither *Heteranthera* nor *Zosterella* seems to be definitely right or wrong.

Heteranthera dubia,
water star grass

POTAMOGETONACEAE Pondweed Family

The pondweed family consists entirely of aquatic plants and is represented in our area by two genera. In both, the leaves, whose blades vary greatly in size and shape among the numerous species, are accompanied by structures that are interpreted to be stipules. These stipules may be closed in such a way that they ensheathe the stems. In some species all leaves are submerged; in others there are floating leaves as well as submerged leaves, and the two types are usually distinctly different. The small flowers, borne in terminal inflorescences raised above the water level, typically have four stamens, each one arising from a structure that resembles a sepal but that may be part of the stamen. There are also usually four pistils, which ripen into one-seeded fruits.

1 Sheaths of stipules of submerged leaves united for a least half their length with the petioles of the leaves (all leaves submerged, not more than about 1 mm wide) .... *Stuckenia*
1 Sheaths of stipules of submerged leaves not united for more than a quarter of their length to the petioles of the leaves (in most of the species the sheaths are not at all united to the petioles; leaves sometimes of 2 types, submerged and floating) .... *Potamogeton*

Potamogeton

This key is based almost entirely on vegetative features. Nevertheless, the several species of *Potamogeton* that are characterized by floating leaves usually do not have these early in the growing season. Furthermore, in species with floating leaves, by the time these have developed, the submerged leaves may have begun to deteriorate. Even if the material available is not fully satisfactory, try both choices in any couplet that seems to be a stumbling block. It is likely that succeeding couplets will show which choice was the better one.

1 Leaves (all submerged, rather stiff, and generally 3–4 mm wide, with at least 20 lengthwise veins) arranged in 2 distinct rows on opposite sides of the stem; sheaths of stipules united for at least one-quarter of their length to the petioles (usually in lakes) .... *P. robbinsii*
                           ROBBINS' PONDWEED
1 Leaves not stiff and not arranged in 2 distinct rows on opposite sides of the stem; sheaths of stipules either free of the petioles or not attached for so much as a quarter of their length to the petioles
 2 Leaf blades (mostly 4–6 cm long, to about 1 cm wide) with conspicuously wavy ("crisped") and toothed margins (all leaves submerged; plants often forming dense growths) .... *P. crispus*
                  CURLY-LEAVED PONDWEED (Europe)
     In *P. alpinus*, first choice 16, the leaf blades are slightly wavy but not distinctly toothed.
 2 Leaf blades (at least the submerged ones) not toothed and usually not wavy-margined
  3 All leaves submerged
   4 Stems with winglike ridges (leaves to about 20 cm long, 5 mm wide) .... *P. zosteriformis*
                  EELGRASS PONDWEED
   4 Stems without winglike ridges
    5 Leaves notched at the base, clasping the stem, and commonly more than 1 cm wide (sometimes more than 2 cm), about 4–7 times as long as wide
     6 Stipules usually persisting, whitish; leaf blades usually at least 10 cm long, often more than 2 cm wide .... *P. praelongus*
                 WHITE-STEMMED PONDWEED
     6 Stipules soon disintegrating into fibers; leaf blades rarely so much as 10 cm long or 2 cm wide
      .... *P. richardsonii*
                 RICHARDSON'S PONDWEED
    5 Leaves not notched at the base, not clasping the stem, rarely if ever more than 5 mm wide, many times as long as wide
     7 Stem nodes without a pair of nearly round glands

8 Stipules not forming a tube around the stem (often shed early) ································· ···***P. pusillus* subsp. *tenuissimus*** (*P. berchtoldii*)
COASTAL SMALL PONDWEED

See the second choice 7, which may also lead you to *P. pusillus* subsp. *tenuissimus*.

8 Stipules forming a tube around the stem, sometimes becoming reduced to the fibrous veins ········ ···***P. foliosus***
LEAFY PONDWEED

In our region, the prevailing subspecies of *P. foliosus* is *foliosus,* typically with an inflorescence that is continuous rather than interrupted, as it is in the rarer subsp. *fibrillosus.* Furthermore, the stipules of subsp. *foliosus* tend to disappear completely, whereas those of subsp. *fibrillosus,* although shredding and reduced to the fiberlike stipular veins, usually persist.

7 At least some stem nodes with a pair of nearly round glands, these yellow, yellow-green, or golden
9 Leaves usually with 5 or 7 veins, sometimes 9 (leaves to about 3 mm wide, 6–7 cm long; stipules conspicuously fibrous, often whitish; mostly E of the crest of the Cascades) ·················***P. friesii***
FRIES' PONDWEED

9 Leaves usually with not more than 3 veins (occasionally 5 in *P. pusillus*)
10 Leaf blades bluntly rounded at the tip, 1–3.5 mm wide, to 8 cm long, with 3 veins (known from relatively few localities in W North America) ·····································***P. obtusifolius***
BLUNT-LEAVED PONDWEED

10 Leaf blades usually pointed at the tip, rarely more than 2 mm wide, to 6 cm long, with 1 or 3 veins (rarely 5)
11 Stipules, for most of their length, forming a tube around the stem, usually persisting ··········· ···***P. pusillus* subsp. *pusillus*,** p. 468
SMALL PONDWEED

11 Stipules not forming a tube around the stem, usually shed early ···························· ···***P. pusillus* subsp. *tenuissimus*** (*P. berchtoldii*)
COASTAL SMALL PONDWEED

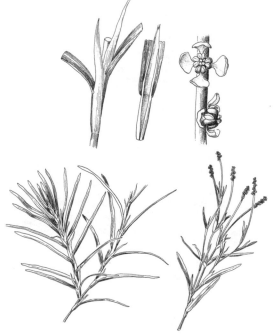

Potamogeton robbinsii,
Robbins' pondweed

Potamogeton richardsonii,
Richardson's pondweed

3 Plants usually with some floating leaves, these generally at least 1 cm wide (depending on the species, the submerged leaves may be very slender or to about 5 cm wide; the floating leaves are usually, but not always, distinctly different from the submerged leaves)

12 Submerged leaves over 10 cm long but not more than 2 mm wide (floating leaves to about 10 cm long by 5 cm wide, usually notched at the base) ....*P. natans*, pl. 708
FLOATING PONDWEED

> *Potamogeton oakesianus,* widespread in E North America, has been found in Brit. Col. The petioles of its floating leaves, just before they meet the blade, lack the short, distinctly lighter green zone that is characteristic of *P. natans;* furthermore, the blades are not notched at the base.

12 Submerged leaves either more than 2 mm wide or less than 10 cm long

  13 Submerged leaves somewhat sickle-shaped, to 5 cm wide, folded lengthwise, and with at least 25 lengthwise veins .... *P. amplifolius*
LARGE-LEAVED PONDWEED

  13 Submerged leaves not sickle-shaped, usually not more than 2 cm wide, not folded lengthwise, and with fewer than 25 lengthwise veins

    14 Stipules generally more than 3 cm long, sometimes as long as 8–9 cm, conspicuous

      15 Petioles of submerged leaves rarely so much as 2 cm long; petioles of floating leaves usually shorter than the blades ....*P. illinoensis*
ILLINOIS PONDWEED

      15 Petioles of submerged leaves usually at least 2 cm long (these leaves are sometimes sessile); petioles of floating leaves usually longer than the blades .... *P. nodosus*
LONG-LEAVED PONDWEED

    14 Stipules usually less than 3 cm long, slender and inconspicuous

Potamogeton pusillus subsp.
pusillus, small pondweed

Potamogeton amplifolius,
large-leaved pondweed

16 Floating leaves similar to the submerged leaves; plants often tinged with red .... *P. alpinus*
NORTHERN PONDWEED

16 Floating leaves very different from the submerged leaves (blades of floating leaves, exclusive of the winged petiole, mostly 3–6 cm long, slightly more than twice as long as wide)

   17 Submerged leaves 10–20 cm long, 3–10 mm wide .... *P. epihydrus*
RIBBONLEAF PONDWEED

   17 Submerged leaves less than 10 cm long but as wide as 10 mm .... *P. gramineus*
GRASS-LEAVED PONDWEED

Stuckenia

1 Tips of leaves tapering very gradually to a slender, sharply pointed tip; style bearing the stigma distinct, persisting on the fruit as a short beak (widespread) .... *S. pectinata*
FENNEL-LEAVED PONDWEED

1 Tips of leaves tapering rather abruptly to the tip, which may be pointed or nearly blunt; style bearing the stigma barely evident, the fruit therefore without a beak (montane and mostly E of the crest of the Cascades except in SW Oreg. and NW Calif.) .... *S. filiformis* subsp. *alpina*
THREADLEAF PONDWEED

RUPPIACEAE Ditch-Grass Family

Ditch grasses (*Ruppia*) are sometimes joined with pondweeds in the Potamogetonaceae. Their leaves, however, are not more than 1 mm wide and have comparatively broad, sheathing bases. The flowers, in loose inflorescences, have four pistils, as in pondweeds, but only two stamens, and these lack sepal-like appendages. In coastal regions, ditch grasses typically grow in brackish water of streams that enter bays and salt marshes; inland, they are more likely to be found in water that is slightly saline, alkaline, or sulfurous. The classification of ditch grasses will not settle down. The plants themselves vary a great deal, and published interpretations of distinctions between species are equally diverse.

Ruppia

1 Peduncles of inflorescences to 30 cm long, with as many as about 30 coils when fruits are maturing; leaves blunt at the tip .... *R. cirrhosa* (*R. occidentalis*)
COILED DITCH GRASS

1 Peduncles of inflorescences not more than 3 cm long, either not coiled or with only 1–4 coils when fruits are maturing; leaves pointed at the tip .... *R. maritima*
DITCH GRASS

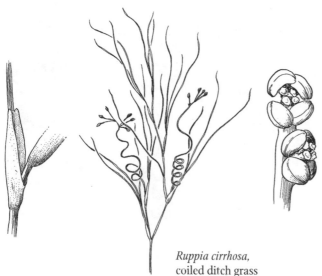

Ruppia cirrhosa,
coiled ditch grass

SCHEUCHZERIACEAE Scheuchzeria Family

The Scheuchzeriaceae has a single species, *Scheuchzeria palustris,* a plant whose slender, nearly cylindrical leaves, to about 40 cm long, look like those of some rushes (*Juncus*). There is, however, a prominent collarlike ligule, similar to that of grasses, at the base of the blade. The inflorescences are racemelike; each one may have as many as about ten flowers, these borne on pedicels arising in the axils of prominent bracts and increasing in length as the fruits ripen. The six perianth segments, approximately 3 mm long, are widest above the middle and greenish white; there are six stamens and a pistil that consists of 3 (sometimes 6) divisions, these united only at the base. *Scheuchzeria,* widespread in northern parts of North America, Europe, and Asia, is typically found at the edges of lakes and ponds, and also in sphagnum bogs. The subspecies in North America is *americana.*

SMILACACEAE Greenbrier Family

In North America the greenbrier family is represented by a single genus, *Smilax.* Both species in our region are perennials with tendril-bearing, climbing stems. The leaf blades are broad, more or less triangular or heart-shaped, and commonly at least 5 cm long; the major veins are interconnected by networks of smaller veins. Staminate and pistillate flowers are separate; both types have six greenish perianth segments. The round fruits, about 6 mm in diameter, are fleshy.

Smilax

1 Stems herbaceous throughout, dying down in winter, without prickles; perianth of staminate and pistillate flowers, when open, about 3 mm wide, the segments about as wide as long (Josephine Co., Oreg., to NW Calif.; rare) . . . . ***S. jamesii***
JAMES' GREENBRIER

1 Stems partly perennial, the woody lower portions usually with slender prickles; perianth of staminate flowers, when open, 5–6 mm wide, that of pistillate flowers 3–3.5 mm wide, the segments of both types much longer than wide (Josephine and Curry Cos., Oreg., to NW Calif.) . . . . ***S. californica,*** pl. 709
CALIFORNIA GREENBRIER

Scheuchzeria palustris
subsp. *americana*

Sparganium eurycarpum,
broad-fruited bur reed

SPARGANIACEAE Bur-Reed Family

Bur reeds, belonging to the genus *Sparganium,* are believed to be rather closely related to cattails (*Typha,* Typhaceae) and are sometimes placed in the same family. The leaves are submerged to a greater extent than those of cattails and are sometimes completely under water or partly floating. On the inflorescences, raised above the surface of the water, the globular clusters of staminate flowers, with three to five stamens, are located above the larger clusters of pistillate flowers, each of which has a single pistil whose lower portion develops into an eventually dry, somewhat achenelike fruit. This usually has only one seed, sometimes two, rarely more. The perianth of both types of flowers consists of three to six somewhat membranous, scalelike structures.

Sparganium

1 Styles in all or most pistillate flowers with 2 stigmas (1–2 mm long; they are also generally evident on the beaklike styles that remain attached to the fruits); leaves and inflorescences upright, raised above the surface of the water (inflorescences branched, each branch usually with several staminate heads above 1–2 pistillate heads) . . . .*S. eurycarpum* (*S. erectum* subsp. *stoloniferum, S. greenei*)
BROAD-FRUITED BUR REED

1 Pistillate flowers with only 1 stigma; leaves and inflorescences either floating or upright and raised above the surface of the water

  2 Leaves, at least on their lower portions, folded and thickened along the midline to the extent that they have a distinct keel; inflorescences upright and raised above the surface of the water; leaves sometimes upright and raised above the surface of the water, sometimes floating; inflorescences occasionally with more than 4 staminate heads . . . .*S. emersum* (*S. simplex* subsp. *simplex*)
SIMPLE-STEMMED BUR REED

  2 Leaves flat, without a keel, even on their lower portions; inflorescences and leaves floating; inflorescences with not more than 4 staminate heads

    3 Inflorescences usually branched (reported from Brit. Col. and scattered localities in central Canada; widespread in NE United States and adjacent portions of Canada) . . . .*S. fluctuans*
FLOATING BUR REED

    3 Inflorescences not branched (a peduncle supporting a pistillate head does not count as a branch)

      4 Inflorescences usually with 2–4 staminate heads (rarely only 1), these typically so close to one another that there may seem to be just 1 head . . . .*S. angustifolium* (*S. simplex* subsp. *multipedunculatum*)
NARROW-LEAVED BUR REED

      4 Inflorescences usually with only 1 staminate head (occasionally 2)

        5 Beaklike style persisting on the fruit usually more than 0.5 mm long (sometimes about 1.5 mm long); leaves green (Alaska to Calif. and eastward across much of N North America) . . . .*S. natans* (*S. minimum*)
SWIMMING BUR REED

        5 Beaklike style persisting on fruit not more than 0.5 mm long (sometimes scarcely or not at all evident); leaves usually somewhat yellowish (a N species, Alaska to Brit. Col. and across Canada; not likely to be found in our region) . . . .*S. hyperboreum*
FAR-NORTHERN BUR REED

Sparganium emersum,
simple-stemmed bur reed

TYPHACEAE Cattail Family

All cattails are generally placed in a single genus, *Typha*. Their pithy, upright aerial stems arise from creeping rhizomes rooted in mud of swamps, ditches, ponds, and lakes, and their leaves, for the most part exposed, resemble those of grasses. The flowers are so small and so tightly packed in a terminal inflorescence that they are individually inconspicuous. The perianth consists of bristlelike structures. Staminate flowers, intermixed with slender hairs, may have as many as seven stamens and are above the pistillate flowers, which produce one-seeded dry fruits (achenes).

Typha

1 Inflorescence not interrupted by a gap between the staminate and pistillate portions; pistillate portion usually at least 25 mm thick after achenes have developed; leaves usually 10–25 mm wide . . . . *T. latifolia*, pl. 710
BROADLEAF CATTAIL

1 Inflorescence interrupted by a gap of about 1–3 cm (sometimes more) between the staminate and pistillate portions; pistillate portion usually not more than 18 mm thick after achenes have developed; leaves commonly about 5 mm wide (much less common in our region than *T. latifolia*) . . . . *T. angustifolia*
SLENDER-LEAVED CATTAIL

> Hybrids of *T. latifolia* and *T. angustifolia,* which are more or less intermediate but whose inflorescences usually have the pronounced gap typical of *T. angustifolia,* have been named *T.* ×*glauca.*

ZANNICHELLIACEAE Horned-Pondweed Family

Horned pondweed, *Zannichellia palustris,* is a nearly cosmopolitan plant found in ponds and sluggish streams. It resembles some species of *Najas* (Najadaceae) in having slender stems, narrow, opposite leaves, and tiny flowers borne in the axils of the leaves. Certain species of *Ruppia* (Ruppiaceae) and slender-leaved potamogetons (Potamogetonaceae) could also be confused with it, but their leaves are mostly or completely alternate, and their flowers are produced in terminal inflorescences. In *Zannichellia* there is usually a staminate flower, with a single stamen, in the same axil as a pistillate flower with three or more pistils, these located above a nearly cup-shaped bract.

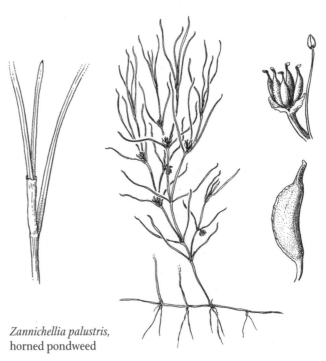

Zannichellia palustris,
horned pondweed

ZOSTERACEAE Eelgrass Family

Eelgrasses (*Zostera*) and surfgrasses (*Phyllospadix*) are marine plants that are usually exposed only at low tide. Their narrow, alternate leaves arise in two rows on branches of creeping rhizomes. The flowers, which lack petals and sepals, are concentrated in somewhat boat-shaped structures that develop on the leaves. They are either staminate or pistillate; staminate flowers have a single anther, and each pistillate flower produces a one-seeded fruit.

1 Pistillate and staminate flowers present in the same inflorescence; plants mostly rooted in sand and mud in bays but occasionally found in pockets of sediment on quiet rocky shores .... *Zostera*
1 Pistillate and staminate inflorescences on separate plants; on rocky shores where there is moderate to strong wave action .... *Phyllospadix*

Phyllospadix

1 Leaves typically 1.5–2 mm wide and about half as thick as wide; flowering stems usually at least 30 cm long
.... *P. torreyi*
TORREY'S SURFGRASS
1 Leaves mostly 2–4 mm wide, thin; flowering stems not often more than 20 cm long
  2 Leaves usually with 5–7 veins and with marginal serrations that can be felt by stroking a leaf toward its base .... *P. serrulatus*
SERRATED SURFGRASS
  2 Leaves usually with 3 veins and without marginal serrations that can be felt by stroking a leaf toward its base .... *P. scouleri*
SCOULER'S SURFGRASS

Zostera

1 Leaves commonly 8–10 mm wide (but varying from about 4 to 12 mm) and to more than 1 m long; leaf sheaths closed, forming complete tubes; in low intertidal to shallow subtidal habitats .... *Z. marina*
EELGRASS
1 Leaves mostly 1.5–2 mm wide and to about 30 cm long; leaf sheaths not closed but the free edges overlapping; generally at middle to lower levels of the intertidal region .... *Z. japonica* (*Z. nana* of some references)
DWARF EELGRASS (Asia)

Phyllospadix scouleri,
Scouler's surfgrass

Illustrations of Plant Structure

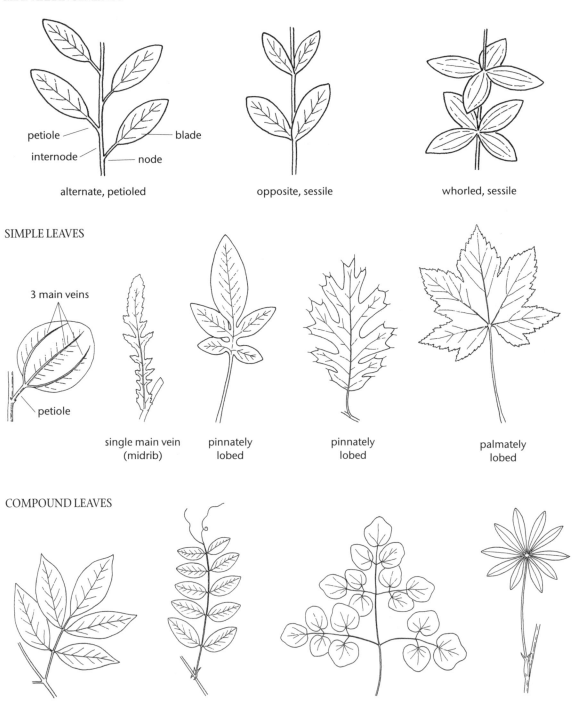

LEAF ARRANGEMENTS

petiole — blade
internode — node

alternate, petioled

opposite, sessile

whorled, sessile

SIMPLE LEAVES

3 main veins

petiole

single main vein
(midrib)

pinnately
lobed

pinnately
lobed

palmately
lobed

COMPOUND LEAVES

once-pinnately
compound

once-pinnately
compound

twice-pinnately
compound

palmately
compound

FLOWER STRUCTURE

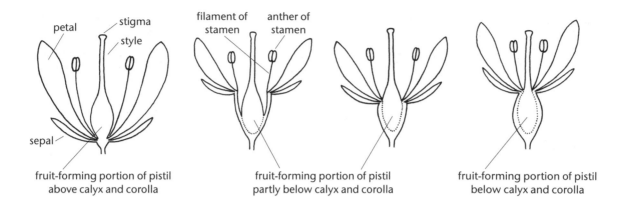

petal
stigma
style
filament of stamen
anther of stamen
sepal
fruit-forming portion of pistil above calyx and corolla
fruit-forming portion of pistil partly below calyx and corolla
fruit-forming portion of pistil below calyx and corolla

FLOWERS WITH REGULAR COROLLA OR PERIANTH

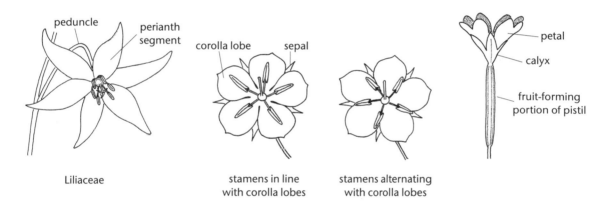

peduncle
perianth segment
corolla lobe
sepal
petal
calyx
fruit-forming portion of pistil

Liliaceae

stamens in line with corolla lobes

stamens alternating with corolla lobes

FLOWERS WITH IRREGULAR COROLLA

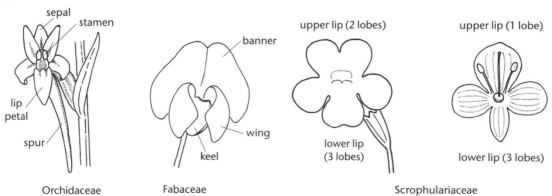

sepal
stamen
lip petal
spur
banner
wing
keel
upper lip (2 lobes)
lower lip (3 lobes)
upper lip (1 lobe)
lower lip (3 lobes)

Orchidaceae

Fabaceae

Scrophulariaceae

INFLORESCENCES

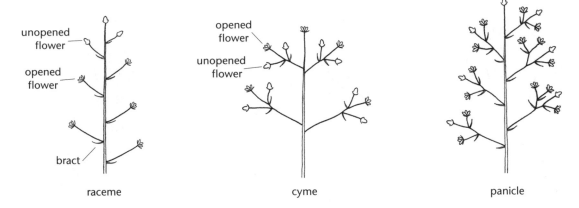

raceme   cyme   panicle

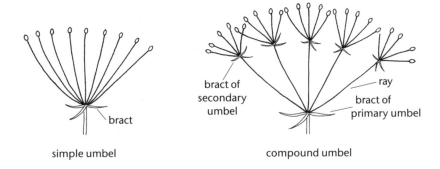

simple umbel   compound umbel

Glossary

achene dry, usually hard, one-seeded fruit that does not split open; achenes are especially characteristic of the sunflower family (Asteraceae) but are also found in some other families

acorn hard, one-seeded nut whose base is enclosed by a scaly cup

alternate referring to leaves or branches that originate singly at the nodes rather than in pairs or whorls

annual plant that produces flowers and fruits in its first year, then dies

anther sac or sacs in which a stamen produces pollen

awn bristle, the term commonly applied to prominent bristles on glumes, lemmas, and paleas of grasses, and to those on similar structures of the florets of sedges

axil upper surface of the junction between a leaf (or bract) and a stem, where a branch, flower, or inflorescence may originate

banner uppermost petal (usually broad) of flowers of the pea family (Fabaceae); sometimes applied to a similar petal in other irregular flowers

basal leaves leaves that originate at the base of a plant; they often form a compact cluster and may be the only substantial leaves on the plant

biennial plant that does not produce flowers and fruit until the second year, then dies

bipinnate referring to leaves that are divided twice in a pinnate manner

bract modified, usually much reduced, leaf below a flower or an inflorescence

branchlet small, usually young, branch of a tree or shrub; also often used for the branch of an inflorescence

bur dry fruit covered with prickles, scales, or hooks

calyx collective term for the sepals of a flower, whether these are separate or united

calyx cup, calyx tube cup or tube formed by union of the sepals

calyx lobes free portions of sepals that are united for part of their length

capsule fruit that consists of more than one chamber and that cracks open when dry

catkin condensed inflorescence of flowers that lack petals; typical of willows, birches, alders, and some other trees and shrubs

chlorophyll green pigment that enables plants to absorb the light energy needed for synthesis of organic compounds

composite head in the sunflower family (Asteraceae), an aggregation of several to many sessile flowers attached to a disk-shaped, conical, or concave receptacle; the receptacle is usually surrounded by bracts called phyllaries

compound leaf leaf with two or more completely separate leaflets, as in a rose, clover, or pea

corolla collective term for the petals of a flower, whether these are separate or united

corolla lobes free portions of petals that are united for part of their length

corymb more or less flat-topped inflorescence in which the pedicels of the outer flowers, which generally open first, are longer than those of flowers closer to the center

crown persistent base of a perennial herbaceous plant; also applied to the top of a tree

cyme flat-topped or convex inflorescence in which the central or uppermost flowers open first, and the outermost or lowermost flowers open last

deciduous falling after its functions have been performed; most often applied to leaves that drop off, and to trees and shrubs that lose their leaves in the fall

dichotomous referring to stems that branch into two equal or nearly equal divisions

disk flowers in the sunflower family (Asteraceae), flowers that have tubular corollas, as distinct from ray flowers, in which the corollas are flattened—some members of the family have a central mass or cluster of disk flowers surrounded by ray flowers; in others all flowers are of the disk-flower or ray-flower type

endemic restricted to a limited geographic area (Jackson Co., Oreg.; Olympic Mountains, Wash.; etc.), especially when this involves a specific environment, such as soil derived from serpentine rock

evergreen retaining leaves from one year to the next (as opposed to deciduous)

filament slender stalk of a stamen; also applicable to any threadlike structure

floret a small, much-modified flower, especially of a grass or sedge

flower head in the sunflower family (Asteraceae) and some other families, a dense aggregation of several to many flowers

fruit ripened, seed-containing structure into which a pistil of a flower develops; in some plants, such as apples and pears, the fruit consists partly of a pistil, partly of fleshy tissue that envelops the pistil—some so-called fruits, such as blackberries, are in fact aggregates of separate fruits

glandular referring to a hair, bump, or pit that secretes a sticky substance

glumes in the grass family (Poaceae), the two bracts below each spikelet

grain in the grass family (Poaceae), the one-seeded fruit produced by a floret; it is essentially an achene

head an especially compact inflorescence; in this book the term is used primarily in connection with inflorescences of some grasses (*see also* flower head)

herb a plant that does not have woody stems, at least above ground

indusium in ferns, a fold or shieldlike structure that covers a sorus, at least when the sporangia are young

inflorescence cluster (or several clusters) of flowers

inrolled applied to leaves or leaflets in which the margins are rolled upward and inward

internode portion of a stem between two nodes; *see* node

involucre in the sunflower family (Asteraceae), one or more circles of phyllaries (bracts) that partly enclose the flower head; in some other families, a circle of bracts below a cluster of flowers

irregular applied to a corolla or calyx in which the petals or sepals (or corolla lobes and calyx lobes) are of unequal size and shape, as the petals are in a sweet pea; also applied to entire flowers in which the corolla is irregular

keel in the pea family (Fabaceae), the structure formed by the union of the two lower petals (the keel partly encloses the pistil); in other cases, a ridge, such as is formed when a bract or the glume of a grass is folded, or when the midrib of a bract is pronounced; also, in grasses, the prominent rib extending along the midline of a glume or lemma

leaf generally the main food-producing structure of a plant, usually composed of a stalk (petiole) and expanded portion (blade)

leaf axil upper side of the junction between a stem and a leaf, where a branch, flower, or inflorescence may originate

leaf blade flattened, expanded portion of a leaf

leaflet each division of a compound leaf

leaf sheath base of a leaf blade or a broad petiole that is wrapped around the stem; the character of leaf sheaths is especially important in identification of grasses and sedges

lemma larger of the two bracts that enclose the pistil and stamens of a grass flower; *see also* palea

ligule in the grass and arrow-grass families (Poaceae and Juncaginaceae), a collarlike outgrowth that originates at the base of the leaf blade and partly encircles the stem

lip upper or lower portion of an irregular, united corolla, as in the mint and snapdragon families (Lamiaceae and Scrophulariaceae)

lobe one of the deeply separated divisions of a leaf, such as that of a maple; the separations are not so deep as to make the leaf compound (*see also* calyx lobes, corolla lobes)

needle narrow, stiff leaf such as is characteristic of pines, firs, yews, and their relatives

nerves *see* ribs

node joint of a stem where one or more leaves are attached and where a branch, flower, or inflorescence may originate; in the grass family (Poaceae), the place where spikelets attach to the rachis of the inflorescence

nutlet small, dry, one-seeded fruit, or comparable structure into which a fruit separates early in its development, as is typical of the borage family (Boraginaceae)

opposite referring to leaves or branches that originate in pairs or whorls at the nodes

palea smaller of the two bracts that enclose the pistil and stamens of a grass flower; *see also* lemma

palmate divided in such a way as to resemble a hand, with fingers spread; used in describing the way lobes or principal veins of some leaves are arranged

palmately compound referring to compound leaves in which the leaflets are arranged in a palmate pattern, as in a lupine

panicle corymb, cyme, or raceme type of inflorescence in which the pedicels branch, thus a compound corymb, cyme, or raceme

pappus in the sunflower family (Asteraceae), modified sepals, appearing as scalelike, bristlelike, hairlike, or plumose structures at the top of the achene

parasitic drawing nourishment from another plant, as mistletoes and dodders do

pedicel the stalk of each individual flower of an inflorescence; in the grass family (Poaceae), the stalk of a spikelet

peduncle the stalk of a flower that is borne singly, or the stalk of an inflorescence that consists of several to many flowers

perennial applied to plants that live indefinitely, as opposed to those that live only 1–2 years

perianth complex formed by the corolla and calyx; the term is especially useful in connection with flowers in which the divisions of the corolla and calyx are similar, as they are in rushes and some members of the lily family (Liliaceae)

perianth segments divisions of a corolla or calyx

perianth tube tube formed by the union of the lower portions of the petals and sepals

perigynium in sedges (*Carex*), a more or less flask-shaped bract that encloses the pistil of each floret, and subsequently the achene derived from the pistil

petals the divisions of a corolla when these are separate to the base; *see also* corolla lobes

petiole the stalk of a leaf

phyllaries in the sunflower family (Asteraceae), the bracts that surround the receptacle of a flower head

pinnate referring to compound or lobed leaves in which either the leaflets or lobes are arranged on both sides of the rachis, as in a pea or rose

pistil portion of a flower in which a seed or seeds are eventually formed; a flower may have more than one pistil

pistillate referring to flowers that have one or more pistils but no stamens; also applied to plants that produce only pistillate flowers

pollen microscopic reproductive structures produced by stamens of flowering plants and by certain short-lived conelike structures of gymnosperms; each pollen grain is at first a one-celled spore—before it is released, however, the nucleus of the cell divides, initiating the formation of a microscopic male plant, but development is not complete until the pollen grain reaches the stigma of a flower or the scale of a cone that is destined to produce seeds

prickle hard, sharp-pointed outgrowth of the epidermis of a stem; the so-called thorns of roses and blackberries are prickles (*see also* spine, thorn)

prostrate applied to stems that lie on the soil

raceme inflorescence in which the flowers are borne all along the peduncle, on short pedicels of more or less equal length

rachis main axis of a compound or nearly compound leaf; in the grass and sedge families (Poaceae and Cyperaceae), the main axis of a spikelet

ray in the sunflower family (Asteraceae), the flattened corolla of a ray flower; in the parsley family (Apiaceae), the primary branches of a compound inflorescence

ray flowers in the sunflower family (Asteraceae), the marginal flowers, with flattened corollas, that surround the disk flowers in the central portion of a flower head—the distinction between ray flowers and disk flowers is clearly seen in daisies, asters, and sunflowers; some members of the family (such as thistles) lack ray flowers, and in others (such as dandelions) all flowers are of the ray-flower type

receptacle portion of a flower peduncle or pedicel on which the flower parts are mounted; in the sunflower family (Asteraceae), several to many sessile flowers are attached to each receptacle

regular flower flower that has perfect or nearly perfect radial symmetry, as in a lily, poppy, wild rose, or morning glory

rhizome horizontal underground stem from which leaves or other stems arise

ribs thickened lengthwise veins (sometimes called nerves) on a glume or lemma of a grass

rosette cluster of crowded basal leaves that form a compact circle or circles

saprophyte plant that subsists on decaying organic matter, usually with the aid of fungi that penetrate its roots; saprophytes, due to the apparent absence of chlorophyll, are not green

sepals the divisions of a calyx when these are separate to the base; *see also* calyx lobes

sessile attached directly to a stem or some other structure; the term is generally applied to leaves that lack petioles and to flowers that lack pedicels

shrub perennial plant whose stems are woody but that usually does not have a distinct trunk and is not often more than 10 ft. (3 m) tall. Some large shrubs may have the form of a small tree, so the distinction between the two categories is not absolute

sorus in ferns, a cluster of sporangia; *see also* sporangium

spikelet in grasses, each unit of an inflorescence, consisting of a pair of glumes and one to several florets; in sedges, a similar group of florets, but without glumes

spine needlelike projection from an areole (a small pit or small raised area) on the stem or fruit of a cactus (in some cacti, the areoles also give rise to leaves, but these are usually small, cylindrical, fleshy, and short-lived); the term is also used for firm, sharp-pointed projections of a leaf, bract, or fruit, but these, derived from the epidermis, are essentially prickles

sporangium in ferns, fern relatives, and lower plants, a structure within which spores are formed

spur hollow, saclike or tubular extension of a petal or sepal, as in a larkspur, columbine, or violet

stamen pollen-producing part of a flower, usually consisting of an anther and filament; most flowers have at least two stamens, and some have many

staminate referring to flowers that have stamens but no pistils; also applied to plants whose flowers have only stamens

sterile referring to modified stamens that do not produce pollen, and to flowers that do not function in reproduction; also applied to a fern leaf (or to a major division of a fern leaf) that does not bear sporangia

stigma sticky tip of a pistil, which traps pollen

stipules paired appendages at the base of a leaf petiole; these may be so large as to resemble leaves, and they may also be mistaken for leaflets of a pinnately compound leaf

stomate microscopic pore on the surface of a leaf or herbaceous stem; stomates permit escape of water vapor and the exchange of oxygen and carbon dioxide

stone seed that is tightly enclosed by a hardened inner layer of the wall of the fruit, especially characteristic of some members of the rose family (Rosaceae), such as cherries, plums, apricots, peaches, blackberries, and raspberries

style usually slender upper portion of a pistil, at the tip of which the stigma is located; in many plants, the pistil has more than one style

succulent referring to leaves and stems that are thick and juicy

tendril slender, twining structure, usually part of a leaf, by which a climbing plant, such as a pea or grape, clings to its support

ternate, ternately referring to compound leaves and other structures with three primary divisions that may then be divided again in the same way

thorn short, usually leafless side stem that is sharply pointed at the tip; *see also* prickle, spine

trichotomous referring to stems that branch into three equal or nearly equal divisions

tripinnate referring to a structure, usually a leaf, that is divided (lobed or compound) three times in a pinnate manner

two-lipped referring to flowers in which the corolla, consisting of united petals, and often also the calyx, have distinctly different upper and lower portions, as in a snapdragon or mint

umbel nearly flat-topped inflorescence in which the pedicels of the flowers originate at the top of the peduncle; in compound umbels, such as are typical of many species of the carrot family (Apiaceae), the primary stalks originating at the top of the peduncle are called rays, and the secondary divisions are called pedicels

urn-shaped referring to a corolla or calyx that is more or less cup-shaped but also noticeably constricted near the opening

vegetative referring to a part of a plant that is not concerned with reproduction

vein in a leaf or petal, a branching structure consisting of tissues that distribute water and nutrients; in the case of petals, the term is often applied to colored lines

vernal referring to spring; the term is commonly used in connection with ponds that become filled with water in winter or spring, then dry out in summer

whorl type of leaf or branch arrangement in which three or more originate at a single node

wing thin expansion of a dry fruit, such as that of a maple; also applied to the two side petals of flowers of the pea family (Fabaceae)

Abbreviations

Brit. Col.	British Columbia
Calif.	California
Co.	County (plural, Cos.)
cm	centimeter (about $2/5$ inch)
E	east, eastern
f.	form, or forma
ft.	feet (measurement used only in connection with elevation)
km	kilometer (about $3/5$ mile)
m	meter (about 39 inches)
mm	millimeter (0.1 cm)
µm	micrometer (one-thousandth of a millimeter), used in connection with structures such as spores of ferns, which can be measured accurately only when examined with high magnification
N	north, northern
Oreg.	Oregon
p.	page
pl.	color plate (plural, pls.)
S	south, southern
sp.	species (plural, spp.)
subsp.	subspecies (plural, subspp.)
var.	variety (plural, vars.)
W	west, western
Wash.	Washington
×	multiplication sign, indicating hybridity

Index